HANS CHRISTIAN ANDERSEN

HANS CHRISTIAN
ANDERSEN
EUROPEAN WITNESS

PAUL BINDING

YALE UNIVERSITY PRESS
NEW HAVEN AND LONDON

For information about this and other Yale University Press publications, please contact:
U.S. Office: sales.press@yale.edu   www.yalebooks.com
Europe Office: sales@yaleup.co.uk   www.yalebooks.co.uk

Set in Minion Pro by IDSUK (DataConnection) Ltd
Printed in Great Britain by TJ International Ltd, Padstow, Cornwall

Library of Congress Cataloging-in-Publication Data

Binding, Paul.
   Hans Christian Andersen : European Witness / Paul Binding.
      pages cm
   Includes bibliographical references and index.
   ISBN 978-0-300-16923-2 (hardback)
   1. Andersen, H. C. (Hans Christian), 1805-1875. 2. Authors, Danish–19th century–
Biography. I. Title.
   PT8119.B526 2014
   839.8'136—dc23
   [B]
                                                                            2013050567
A catalogue record for this book is available from the British Library.

10 9 8 7 6 5 4 3 2 1

FOR STEIN INVERSEN
A TRUE FRIEND

Contents

Acknowledgements

At Syddansk Universitet (SDU, University of South Denmark) in Odense I must thank Professor (now emeritus) Johan de Mylius, Andersen expert and critic, for the generous time he has spent talking to me in the most stimulating and informative way. He also invited me to give two lectures of my own choosing at the Hans Christian Andersen Centre there, one on *The Improvisatore*, the other on 'The Ice Maiden'; these contributed substantially to the chapters in this book. Also in Odense I profited greatly from the knowledge and friendliness of the Director of the Hans Christian Andersen Museum, Ejnar Stig Askgaard. At SDU the Professor of American Literature, Jan Nordby Gretlund took a personal interest in my work, and kindly drove me to see places on Fyn and Langeland with Andersen connections; these enriched my appreciation immeasurably.

The Cultural Attaché at the Royal Danish Embassy in London, Lone Britt Christensen has been tirelessly helpful to me over the years, with introductions and practical suggestions. Through her I met Annette Bach of the Danish Arts Council who took an interest in my work, leading to handsome grants of inestimable help to me. I must also give heartfelt thanks to Dr Jakob Stougaard-Nielsen, Senior Lecturer in Scandinavian Literature at UCL School of European Language, Culture and Society for checking my Danish quotations and material.

At Yale University Press I must first thank its Managing Director, Robert Baldock, who commissioned this book, playing a most creative part in its whole evolution. To Managing Editor Candida Brazil, Assistant Editor Tami Halliday, both at Yale, and to my painstaking copy-editor and proofreader, Beth Humphreys and Loulou Brown I owe inexpressibly much. Also to Jane Horton whose index is a model of thoughtfulness and sensitivity to my text.

I also must include in my gratitude my friend and neighbour in Shropshire, Carol Wright, for unflagging assistance with the original typescript, especially over superscript numbering. And also of course my agent Christopher

Sinclair-Stevenson who has always understood my hopes and intentions in addition to my actual published work.

In *Hans Christian Andersen: European Witness* I have made my own translations of all quotations from its subject's imaginative work. For his non-fiction I have relied on the best obtainable translations of others (impossible to find a satisfactory one in the case of *A Poet's Bazaar*). I therefore owe a particular debt to Eric Lane of Dedalus for making accessible to me, at some trouble to himself, the text of W. Glyn Jones's new revised translation of *My Fairy-Tale Life*.

I want also to acknowledge the help of the London Library and of the Royal Literary Fund; Eileen Gunn at the latter has been responsible for the easing of my working life. This last has benefited enormously too by my regular dealings with the *Times Literary Supplement* and the *Independent*, dealings which also assist a writer's sense of identity. In this context too I must mention Christopher MacLehose, great friend to European literature and a helpful mentor to myself.

Introductory:
Europe, Denmark, the World

Europe and Denmark – Andersen's work is born of the relationship between the two, and his own relation to both. If, during important years of his life, Andersen had to look outside Denmark for the degree of appreciation he felt his due, if his creative mind was constantly sharpened by travel, by encounters with European writers, his own art owed quite inestimably to Danish tradition, to Danish artists and pundits of the Golden Age, and to the Danish language itself, its characteristic rhythms and idioms. Conversely, while much of the appeal of his writings (and of his own personality), both at home and abroad, depended on his Danish provenance – a freshness, an intelligence comparatively free of dogmatic or political alignments, the factions and commercialism of elsewhere – it is also the case that they were admired, even loved, because they articulated the tensions and hopes, the trials and satisfactions, of a whole continent undergoing re-formation.

On 26 January 1852 the newspaper *Fædrelandet* (The Fatherland)[1] published Hans Christian Andersen's prose-piece 'Om Aartusinder' ('Thousands of Years to Come') envisaging the remote future and linking two continents. Two days later – on 28 January – the oldest Danish newspaper *Berlingske Tidende* (Berling's Times)[2] featured 'Svanereden' ('The Swan's Nest') dealing with Denmark itself, its distinguished past, its present difficulties, its survival in increasingly uncertain times.

The last few years had been peculiarly testing ones for Denmark. Between 1848 and 1850 the country – from 1849 a Constitutional and not, as it had been since 1660, an Absolute Monarchy – was engulfed by Treårskrigen,[3] the Three Years War with Prussia over the disputed duchies of Schleswig and Holstein. In 1850 Andersen, whose feelings about his native country had often been at best equivocal, at worst actively resentful, wrote a patriotic song: 'I Danmark er jeg født, der har jeg hjemme', ('In Denmark was I born, there I have [my] home').[4]

The Danish victories of 1850 brought about a resolution of the conflict, and this was endorsed two years later by the London Protocol of August 1852 which decreed the unity of Denmark a 'European necessity and standing principle'.[5] But the settlement did not prove durable, and not the least interesting aspect of Andersen's two newspaper pieces is their underlying unease.[6]

The opening sentence of 'Thousands of Years to Come'[7] introduces hordes of young Americans regularly travelling over the Atlantic to Europe, through the air on wings of steam. An airship is crowded with passengers living up to their favourite book, *Europa set i otte Dage* (Europe seen in eight days). Thanks to the electromagnetic wire beneath the sea they have all telegraphed their hotel reservations in advance. The first country they see below them is Ireland, but they go on sleeping until above England, their first stop: Shakespeare's land to the more cultured, the land of politics or machines to the others. This first day of their European tour takes in Scotland as well as England, after which they proceed via the Channel Tunnel to France, which gave the world Charlemagne, Molière, Napoleon. By this unspecified date, observes Andersen, many illustrious French men and women whose names we do not know will have been born in 'Europe's Crater', Paris. And thence to Spain which still corresponds to the old images, with beautiful dark-eyed women and ballad-singers extolling El Cid.

Next they travel through the air to Italy, and here we readers are in for a grim surprise. The Eternal City of Rome no longer exists; only one wall of St Peter's stands, and the authenticity of that is in doubt. The Campagna – the countryside round Rome so esteemed by nineteenth-century painters – has become a desert. Many readers would have recalled the rich evocations of Italy in Andersen's first novel, *Improvisatoren* (*The Improvisatore*, 1835), actually narrated by an Italian, a performing artist whose personality and early circumstances mirror his creator's. But sadly the fate of Italy is, we soon learn, not unique; the future has treated the tourists' next stops, Greece and Turkey, subjects of Andersen's best-received travelogue, *En Digters Bazar* (*A Poet's Bazaar*, 1842), no more kindly. As it is something to boast about back home, these Americans stay in a luxury hotel on top of Mount Olympus. In similar spirit they relax for a few hours by the Bosporus, on the site of great Byzantium, idly watching poor fishermen repair nets or listening to stories of long-ago harems, a far cry from the great bustling metropolis and palimpsest of successive civilisations honoured in Andersen's travel book. Then the young Americans re-board their airship to fly north-west along the length of the Danube. The large cities once flourishing on its banks are now in ruins, but with enough monuments of former greatness to warrant a respectful visit.

The remaining two days of the Americans' excursion are given to Germany (not a nation state in 1852) and Norden (Scandinavia). Germany was once criss-crossed with railways and canals, Andersen reminds us, but is so no longer. The famous names the tourists think of here are Luther, Mozart and Goethe, nobody of any later date, though Andersen concedes that many renowned Germans will have been born in the long interim period. The Americans revere Scandinavia because of Linnaeus, the great Swedish naturalist, and H.C. Ørsted,[8] the eminent Danish writer and scientist and discoverer of the electromagnetism that made the telegraph wire possible. Norway is allocated no representative figure but honoured as 'de gamle Heltes og de unge Nordmænds Land,' ('the old eternal heroes' and the young Norwegians' country'), surely a covert plea for the independence it still did not enjoy. Iceland, flown over on the way home, disappointingly lacks its famed geysers and active volcanoes, but its great cliffs stand in tempestuous seas 'som Sagas evige Stentavle,' 'as evige stone memorial to the sagas.'[9] And so back to the United States with a happy feeling of accomplishment.

By the time 'Thousands of Years to Come' came out between hard covers, an actual airship had taken off, on 24 September 1852, designed and flown by Henri Gifford (1825–58). Filled with hydrogen, it used a steam engine to drive its propeller, so Andersen's phrase 'wings of steam' is not inapt. Ever since the Montgolfiers in 1783, steerable balloons (or airships) were desiderata for the progress-minded. Alfred Tennyson's great poem, *Locksley Hall* (1842)[10] presents both inspiring and alarming images of their likely forms and uses.

> For I dipt into the future, far as human eye could see,
> Saw the Vision of the world, and all the wonder that would be;
> Saw the heavens fill with commerce, argosies of magic sails,
> Pilots of the purple twilight, dropping down with costly bales.

But commerce, Tennyson realised, invariably means competition, and all too frequently that means warfare.

> Heard the heavens fill with shouting, and there rain' d a ghastly dew,
> From the nations' airy navies grappling in the central blue.'

But in the end our young visionary sees how 'the battle-flags were furl'd/In the Parliament of man, the Federation of the world.'

> Yet I doubt not thro' the ages one increasing purpose runs,
> And the thoughts of men are widen' d with the process of the suns.

Unlike Tennyson's, Andersen's airships are associated exclusively with peaceful activity: with tourism, so fast-growing in the mid-nineteenth century and so much more accessible to ordinary men and women than at any previous period, the author himself being one of its most enterprising proselytisers. His understanding of the growing new phenomenon was totally consonant with his lively interest in technical advance generally. That year of 1852 he was fascinated by the laying of the telegraph line connecting Helsingør (Elsinore) with Hamburg, via Copenhagen and Fredericia (to be opened in February 1854). In a letter of 3 June 1853 to his friend, the writer, Carsten Hauch (1790–1872)[11] occasioned by his delight in the latter's new novel, *Robert Fulton* about the inventor of the steamship, he would declare, 'I feel and see God's infinite love also in every new insight which he allows us into the laws and powers of nature, and the elevated power he thereby grants mankind.' Through technology, 'people are drawn closer to each other; ideas may be exchanged more easily, more and more we become one people, one nation of spirit.' Had he appreciated when younger the magnificent capabilities of science, 'I would probably have taken an avenue in life other than the one I now follow, or rather I would have attained knowledge within such fields that my authorship would have blossomed quite differently than is now the case.' In all this he is surely at one with that last-quoted couplet from *Locksley Hall* with its sure belief that behind evolving history 'one increasing purpose' existed, by implication benevolent.

But benevolence cannot have characterised a good deal of what mankind (or at any rate, European mankind) has been up to in the centuries leading to 'Thousands of Years to Come', to judge from its cameos: Rome and Danubian cities destroyed, the main edifice of Catholic Christendom reduced to a single, probably fake wall, the Campagna and all Greece laid waste, Constantinople an impoverished wreck, Germany depredated by the removal of railway lines and canals, and seemingly lacking in great men. In what direction was Andersen's mind moving?

As a young man Andersen had not been a fortnight in Italy before noting in his diary – on 2 October 1833[12] – that this was the country of the imagination as France was that of reason, and Germany and Denmark of the heart. But any ideal of Italian unification[13] had become harder to believe in after Austria's defeat of Sardinia–Piedmont and of Lombardy–Venetia in 1849, while the Republic of Rome had lasted a mere six months of the same year. The French interventionist restoration of Pope Pius IX in Rome, and the consequent mounting anti-clerical feeling among Italians (Cavour's legislation in Piedmont–Sardinia) must clearly have aroused doubts in the Andersen of 1852 that the Church could survive as a power beyond his own century, though in both his private and his creative writings he had treated Catholic practice and practitioners with real warmth.

Perhaps there was another reason for presenting the desolations of Italy. On his visit of 1833/34 the abundant ruins of classical civilisation had made a tremendous impression on Andersen, nowhere more so than the cities of

Herculaneum and Pompeii destroyed by the eruptions of Vesuvius. He evoked them both memorably in *The Improvisatore* and singled out Pompeii for the Twelfth Evening in *Billedbog uden Billeder* (*Picture-Book Without Pictures*, 1839–40).[14] The deserted, once-buried streets and houses provided lasting images of the harsh truth that *Respice finem!* ('Remember the end!') applies not only to human beings but to what they have made and left behind, their monuments, their homes, their workplaces, a truth in need of emphasis in an age so triumphantly sure of its material achievements as his own.

As astonishing as the absence of Italy on the Americans' itinerary is the unimportance of Germany and Austria to them. Andersen had enjoyed creative friendships with Ludwig Tieck, Adelbert von Chamisso, Felix Mendelssohn and Robert Schumann, among others. He had been the beneficiary of a large, appreciative German readership, which indeed put him on the international literary map. But how after the carnage of the First Dano-Prussian War could Andersen look on the German lands with equanimity? Some of his most cordial and cherished relationships had suffered the gravest knocks already. Yes, he paid visits of reconciliation and renewal to Germany in 1851, and, after a strained interval and a fraught exchange of letters, returned to his beloved Weimar in May 1852, to restore his friendship with its Hereditary Grand Duke and his wife. But he could never forget the realignment of priorities that the war had enforced. Moreover what had occasioned these hostilities was very far from over and done with. Schleswig and Holstein, economically vital to Denmark's strength, might now be obliged by international agreement to acknowledge no other head of state than the Danish monarch, but Schleswig still retained significant ethnic Germans, while in Holstein these formed a clamorous, discontented majority. Pan-Germanism continued its rise, and Prussia its determination to be dominant both within the German Confederation and outside it.

The future, by inference, would seem to lie with Britain (England and Scotland) and France. Andersen's own lionised visit to Britain – during which he met Dickens and was much moved by his friendliness – had taken place only six years earlier, in 1847; London Society had positively fallen over itself to invite and entertain him, while Shakespeare and Scott had long been fixed stars in his literary firmament. He could even have felt that Dickens, in *David Copperfield* (1848), owed a creative debt to his own *Improvisatore*. Britain and France had supported Denmark, without intervening on its behalf, in the Schleswig-Holstein war, and both powers were now moving towards taking Turkey's part against Russia. The tumultuous events of the last few years in France which Andersen had followed very attentively – the 1848 Revolution, the founding of the Second Republic with the election of Louis-Napoleon as president, and then, in 1851, the *coup d'état* leading to his 1852 proclamation of the Second Empire – were as impressive, as undeniable, as those leading

French writers, intellectuals and artists Andersen had respectfully encountered. Small wonder then that he could hail, even in a short and basically non-polemical piece like this, Paris as 'Europe's crater'.

The reference in it to Scandinavia if brief is entirely honorific, but, apart from saluting Ørsted, he makes no specification of Denmark. This absence was made good by 'The Swan's Nest', of just two days later.

> Mellem Østersøen og Nordhavet ligger en gammel Svanerede, og den kaldes Danmark; i den er født og fødes Svaner, hvis Navne aldrig skulle døe. [15]
>
> Between the Baltic Sea and the North Sea lies an old swan's nest and it is called Denmark; in it have been and will be born swans whose names shall never die.

Andersen's placing of his country geographically on the map of Europe makes a brilliant beginning for his reflection on its identity and destiny. Denmark's situation, where the Skaggerak and the Kattegat connect the North Sea with the Baltic, accounts for its inhabitants' most substantial achievements – their extensive voyaging, their colonies, their wide mercantile endeavours – and also for their vulnerability. Andersen's own early life was spent in the shadowed consequence of that vulnerability: the pre-emptive attacks by Britain in 1801 and 1807; the virtually obligatory alliance with Napoleon's France; the subsequent humiliations after 1813 dealt them by the victorious powers, entailing a long period of bankruptcy that lasted until 1830. But the by no means inconsiderable compensation for this last was the country's ability, suspended as it was from certain external pressures, to realise its immense social, artistic and intellectual potential as never before – and this despite a still archaic governmental system and political censorship.

Not only is Andersen's opening to his piece topographically exact, it is a beautiful, unforgettable literary conceit – of his sea-girt homeland, consisting of one sizeable peninsula (Jutland) and over four hundred named islands, as a swan's nest. Swans, together with storks, were the birds of greatest imaginative importance to the writer from childhood onwards. One of his earlier stories closest to actual folk tale was 'De vilde Svaner' ('The Wild Swans', 1838)[16] based on a Danish story collected by his older compatriot, Matthias Winther, while in arguably his most famous story of all, 'Den grimme Ælling' ('The Ugly Duckling', 1844), he celebrated his artistically gifted self – and by extension the selves of all sensitive others – in the form of a newly fledged swan once considered an unsatisfactory, unappealing duck. Now, in 1852, he makes the swans stand for the Danes themselves, collectively and individually, though Andersen is most concerned with those emanations from the nest which have made the greatest impression on the wider world.

In earlier periods, he reminds us, the nest released fierce menacing birds whose strength, scope and stamina for undertaking enormous distances terrified whole swathes of Europe, and who ventured considerably beyond that continent: the Vikings. The aggressive qualities of the Vikings and of the religion that animated them troubled Andersen as much as, if not more than, their creativity and ambition impressed him. Since the Viking age, however, Danes have distinguished themselves more by intellectual and imaginative daring than by brute force, and Andersen provides us with four examples, only one of whom he actually names, and that only after paying him poetic, metaphoric homage. This first bird, he tells us, flapped its wing and behold, the mists concealing the heavens dispersed so they were more clearly visible from Earth: 'det var Svanen Tycho Brahe', 'that was the swan Tycho Brahe.'[17] Tycho Brahe (1546–1601) refined astronomic instruments to an unprecedented accuracy and clarity. He identified comets as celestial bodies, not terrestrial as previously thought, and, through the studies he carried out at his great observatories on the Danish island of Hven, established the Tychonic System, a cosmology which, though incorrectly setting the sun and moon in motion round the earth (which Brahe saw as a constant centre 'at rest'), correctly identified the other five known planets as in rotation round the sun.

But have there been no swans nearer to us in time than Brahe? Of course! There was one who touched a golden harp with his wings and set the stark mountains of Norway glowing anew with light while in the forests beneath the Northern gods and heroes and heroines walked again. This was a reference, perfectly obvious to his readers, to Adam Oehlenschläger (1779–1850)[18] with his *Nordiske Digte* (Northern Poems, 1807) and *Nordens Guder* (Gods of the North, 1819). Another swan beat a cliff so strenuously with its wings that the beautiful marble within was revealed: unmistakably sculptor Bertel Thorvaldsen (1770–1844).[19] Finally there was a swan responsible for linking countries so words could travel between them at the speed of light: H.C. Ørsted (1777–1851).

What unites these Danish swans? They were all leading figures of that period *c.*1800–1850 to be christened in 1890 by the Danish philosopher Valdemar Vedel,[20] *Guldalderen*, 'The Golden Age'. This term quickly passed into intellectual currency, outside as well as inside Denmark. Heirs to, if not actual followers of, the European Enlightenment, its leaders as well as their admirers shared a belief in disinterested activity for the general good and the individual's enhancement. Though all of them won both national and international recognition, and held highly responsible positions, their prime concerns were the furtherance of knowledge and the development of (artistic) forms which nevertheless respected the work of their predecessors. They did not spare themselves; they saw their work *sub specie aeternitatis*, and in truth eternity itself greatly preoccupied them, its definition in astronomical, mathematical, philosophic and theological terms. Yet personally they were warm-hearted men who believed in assisting others, in bringing out their talents. To use appropriately Kantian terminology – and Ørsted's university dissertation was on Kant,[21] while Oehlenschläger brought into Danish literature the ideas of the eminent Kantian, Johann Gottlieb Fichte[22] with his Universal Mind or Ur-Ich – they pursued 'the true, the good and the beautiful', the expressed goals of the scholar-protagonist in Andersen's powerful, gravely alarming tale, 'Skyggen' ('The Shadow' 1846/1847).

Bertel Thorvaldsen, Adam Oehlenschläger, Hans Christian Ørsted, these giants in their fields, were all friends, and in the deepest sense colleagues or co-workers, and to any study of Hans Christian Andersen they are vital. They make many appearances as themselves in Andersen's work too, Thorvaldsen and Ørsted being central to more than one tale.[23] When Andersen wrote 'The Swan's Nest', he did so as one regretfully appreciating that the lives of all three men had come to an end: Thorvaldsen, with whose humble beginnings his own had something in common, had died eight years earlier; he had been dining with Oehlenschläger and Andersen on the last day of his life, before going to the Royal Theatre where he suffered a fatal aneurysm. The death of Oehlenschläger, whom the young Andersen had set out to emulate, rival and even overtake, had occurred just two years previously, and only the year before he had lost Ørsted, to whom he owed an immeasurable amount – not least the notion of the airship with which we opened. For the scientist, who gave the world electromagnetism, aluminium and the 'thought experiment' (Gedankenexperiment)[24] was also a distinguished man-of-letters, and in 1836 produced a series of semi-humorous poems called what else but Luftskibet (The Airship)? . . .[25]

After Oehlenschläger died on 20 January 1850, three newspapers[26] published Andersen's verse tribute, 'Farvel, Du største Skjald i Norden' ('Farewell, you greatest poet in Scandinavia'). As for Ørsted, Andersen was with him all the day he was dying (though he missed the actual moment of death by taking a short break to see his friends, the Collins). By the time he was writing their elegy as swans who had sung their last, Andersen must surely have felt that the epoch they had helped to create and had endowed with their own character and ideas, that still untitled Golden Age, was itself turning into the past. His own art, while still in progress and addressing the future, (he was, after all, not yet fifty) was so bound up with its main figures and prevailing ethos that it also would, sooner or later, stand as a monument of this unequalled period of Danish achievement. And it is true to say – though this study hopes seriously to redress this imbalance in his reputation – that almost all Andersen's now most famous or best-loved stories are from before the year with which Vedel seals his period, with 'The Shadow' as a dark climactic masterpiece. Posterity has not accorded the same honours to 'Dynd-Kongens Datter' (The Marsh King's Daughter' 1858), 'Vinden fortæller om Valdemar Daae og hans Døtre' ('The Wind tells [the story] of Valdemar Daae and his Daughters' 1859) or 'En Historie fra Klitterne' ('A Story from the Dunes' 1859) as it has to, say, 'Sneedronningen' ('The Snow Queen', 1844) or even 'The Shadow' itself, though Andersen knew full well that artistically and intellectually they were as good as anything he had written before, with adventurous features all their own. And even during his lifetime, there were those – to his intense irritation – who persisted in thinking of him in terms of his earlier achievements. And while 'Iisjomfruen' ('The Ice Maiden', 1861) has, rightly, earned admiration – partly as a result of Stravinsky's ballet *Le Baiser de la fée* (The Fairy's Kiss, 1928) – even that indisputable masterpiece does not hold the firm place in the canon to which its complexity and artistry entitle it. Perhaps then the mutedly valedictory tone of 'The Swan's Nest' had something personally prophetic about it.

But in fact Andersen decided to end the piece optimistically, or at least in exhortatory mode:

> Aarhundreder vil endnu gaa hen, Svaner flyve fra Reden, ses og høres rundt i Verden, før den Tid kommer, at der i Aand og Sandhed skal kunne siges, 'Det er den sidste Svane, den sidste Sang fra Svanereden.'[27]

> Centuries will yet go by, the swans will fly from the nest, be seen and be heard around the world, before that time comes when in spirit and truth it could be said: 'That is the last swan, the last song from the swan's nest.'

The more that was known (and read) about Andersen's personal history – that journey from an impoverished section of the proletariat to inclusion, and later eminence, within his nation's vigorous, productive intelligentsia and upper class, paralleling Denmark's own ascent from the disaster of the Napoleonic Wars – the more it was felt to reflect the forward movement of Europe itself. This movement was indisputably towards a wider prosperity and a higher standard of living than history had ever witnessed anywhere. But who dared predict what crises lay head? And were there not signs, which Andersen, like every major writer, not only sensed but embodied in art that, for this sizeable and uniquely favoured section of humanity, conflicts of potentially catastrophic dimensions were probable, not to say inevitable? In making such signs artistically palpable Andersen proved his deep universality for he repeatedly transcended his Europeanness. Continually he lighted on constant, basic human, not to say animal, characteristics to be discovered in every continent, at every period, and he realised, and often named, these in unforgettable metaphors that are now the the property of the whole reading and listening world.

PART 1

FROM *SKYGGEBILLEDER* (*SHADOW PICTURES*) TO 'SKYGGEN' ('THE SHADOW')

CHAPTER 1

William Christian Walter

1

Hans Christian Andersen was born in Odense on the island of Fyn on 2 April 1805, his parents having married exactly two months previously.[1] His mother, Anne Marie Andersdatter (1773 or 1775–1833) was herself illegitimate. The identity of her father is still unknown. Her mother, twice married, twice widowed, bore three children out of wedlock, thereby earning herself a spell in the city's gaol, the notorious Odense Tugthus, popularly known as O.T. This grim place provided Andersen's second novel with its most haunting symbol and its curious, unforgettable title, and makes an appearance in Andersen's autobiography, *Mit Livs Eventyr* (*My Fairy-Tale Life*, 1855) without the real family connection being explained.[2] Anne Marie had a bastard child of her own, Karen Marie (22 September 1799–18 November 1846), by Daniel Rosenvinge, a potter with a bad reputation who fathered another daughter on another woman that same year. In all his copious writings about his life Andersen never once mentions his half-sister, speaking of himself persistently and insistently as an only child.[3] But of course he must have known Karen Marie, who spent her childhood with their maternal grandmother before being put out to work. She makes surreptitious appearances in his *oeuvre*, most memorably as the baleful Sidsel in *O.T.* whom the hero is mistakenly, to his horror, led to believe is his sister. He is heartily relieved when it is proved that she is not. By contrast Andersen, when he exchanged Odense for Copenhagen, was fearful that his 'mother's daughter' would turn up in his life, and when she actually did, confided her existence to his guardian who never disclosed it.

Andersen's father, Hans Andersen (1782–1816),[4] was a shoemaker, and the son of a shoemaker, Anders Hansen. By the time Andersen knew him, his grandfather was committed to the Gråbrødre hospital, a lunatic asylum where he occupied himself with his wood carving, at which he was very accomplished, creating strange figures – men with beasts' heads and beasts with wings; these he packed in a basket and carried out into the country, where he was every-where warmly received by the peasant women on whom he bestowed them. The town children, however, did not treat the elderly man, with his habit of wearing self-made paper hats, at all kindly, taunting him when he walked out in the streets, and Andersen, who was afraid of him anyway, recalls hiding from one of these callous displays; he was after all close kin to the man whom they were mocking. Anders (Træs) Hansen died in 1827, mentally deranged and with no money, at 72. His wife, Anne Cathrine Nommensdatter (1785–1822) tended the asylum garden, and would bring flowers round to Andersen's home every Sunday evening, instilling in him the deep love for them which is such a characteristic of his work. (His mother's rooftop garden – a chest filled with soil – which he was feelingly to evoke in his work, also encouraged this.) Anne Cathrine, seemingly a serene woman, was devoted to her grandson and he to her. He always wrote about her warmly, though his ascription to her in his autobiography of an elevated family lineage has proved to have no foundation whatever. She was in fact the daughter of a military drummer, and she knew poverty intimately before and beyond her marriage as well as inside it. But she provided him with a model for the wise older women in his stories who prevail in all circumstances, as his maternal grandmother, with her rackety life and insalubrious connections, and whom he saw far less of, certainly could not have done.

Unlike Andersen's mother, a virtual illiterate, Hans Andersen was a great reader[5] whom his son loved to present as an intellectual manqué. Certainly he knew, and was attached to, Shakespeare, the fables of La Fontaine,[6] the *Arabian Nights* and Holberg,[7] and introduced young Hans Christian to them; all of ines-timable influence on his mind and art. Once – *My Fairy-Tale Life* tells us – Hans Andersen, after measuring a grammar school youth for his boots and seeing his books and hearing him talk of the learning he had recently acquired, was moved to exclaim, ' "That's the way I ought to have gone, too." ' Lack of money had made this impossible, and Hans Andersen found no real fulfilment in his work. He was a freethinker, in politics a radical, often greatly alarming Anne Marie with his heterodox views, particularly when they bordered on the (to her) blasphemous. As when he declared, after pondering on his readings in the Bible: 'Christ was a man like us, but an unusual man!' and once later (worrying his small son as well) 'There is no other Devil than that which we have in our hearts', views with which his son would concur throughout his life. His father then was, as far as we can see, a lively, restless and dissatisfied man, with a youthful reputation for womanising and a chronic hankering after adventure, an attribute Andersen would bestow on his hero's father in the third and greatest of his novels, *Kun en Spillemand (Only a Fiddler*, 1837).

In 1812 Hans Andersen,[8] an admirer of Napoleon, accepted a cash offer from a local farmer's son, Gregers Hansen, to take his conscripted place in the Danish army and fight for the French. When he returned in 1814 – from no further than Holstein, and without seeing combat – he was a broken man. He talked repeatedly of Napoleon and his campaign in the delirium of his final illness, the last stages of tuberculosis; he even hallucinated that he was in command of the French army. When he died on 26 April 1816, Hans Christian and his mother remembered how in his winter-long sickness he had identified the form of a maiden in the patterns of the iced-up windows, saying she had come to fetch him. Now, observed Anne Marie, she had. Consequently the figure of Iisjomfruen (The Ice Maiden) became a major property of Hans Christian's mind, inspiring one of his finest achievements. Hans Andersen was buried in a pauper's grave, and left his wife and son in penury.

Hans Christian's education had begun in 1810 at Fedder Carsten's small school for mostly Jewish boys in Odense,[9] with one outstanding girl, the vivacious original for the little artiste (initially believed to be Jewish) in *The Improvisatore,* and for the more sustained character of Naomi (daughter of a Jewish mother) in *Only a Fiddler.* Throughout his life, both personally and in his writings, Andersen was decidedly philo-Semitic, and two distinguished Danish Jewish families were especially dear to him in his last years. Now, with his father dead and his mother obliged to go out washing clothes, and with no family connections of any means or standing, indeed signally lacking in these, Andersen was put to work in a cloth mill and in a tobacco factory, before being sent to a charity school. In the first of these places his fellow employees, after hearing him sing, tore his clothes off to find out whether he was a boy or girl. The gender ambivalences and transpositions in his fiction doubtless owe much to this humiliation, which must have struck at difficulties in gender identity he was already experiencing as well as making him fearful of the cruelties a group of males can perpetrate. He held back from the company of other boys, preferring to play on his own, for example with the marionette theatre his father had constructed for him.

Anne Marie made a second marriage in 1818,[10] to a man considerably younger than herself, Niels Jørgensen Gundersø (or Gundersen), who was to die in 1822. He too was a shoemaker. In her son's opinion he was far more similar to her in character and way of life than her first husband had been. But the couple were no better off economically. Their cramped living quarters presented obvious difficulties for both themselves and the woman's adolescent son. Professor Johan de Mylius is surely right in his supposition that Andersen's mother's sexual activities with her new partner, as well as being something of an embarrassment to her, had a deleterious psychic effect on her son, and galvanised him into moving away from Odense altogether.

After Gundersø's death Anne Marie[11] found economically supportive employment even as a washerwoman ever harder to find, and slipped further into poverty and alcohol dependence until she too had to be installed in the Gråbrødre Hospital/Asylum, on the second floor called Doctors Boder, where, in fact, her first husband's grandmother had spent her own last institutionalised years. She was to die in 1833 in her fifties, and the church records registered her death as 'Delirium Tremens', a state she had known for some years.

Andersen maintained, indeed actually wrote in his notes for it, that his moving story ' "Hun duede ikke' " (' "She Was No Good" ', 1855) was inspired by an old woman of his mother's acquaintance whom she had always defended from neighbours' censoriousness.[12] But his mother is surely not only the charitable friend here, but the doomed washerwoman herself. ' "Hun har drukket sig ihjel!" ' (' "She has drunk herself to death!" ') is the magistrate's verdict on her. Her son goes to her pauper's grave, with, by his side, her friend who has planted a little rose bush on it:

'Min søde Moder!' sagde han, og Taarerne strømmede, 'er det sandt: hun duede ikke!'

'Jo, hun duede!' sagde den gamle Pige og saa op imod Himlen. 'Jeg ved det fra mange Aar og fra den sidste Nat. Jeg siger dig, hun duede! og Vor Herre i Himmeriges Rige siger det med, lad Verden kun sige: hun duede ikke!'[13]

'My dear mother!' he said, and the tears streamed, 'Is it true she was no good!'

'Yes, of course she was good!' said the old woman and looked up to heaven, 'I have known that for many years and from the [her] last night. I tell you, she was good! And Our Father in Heaven will say the same; just let the world say she was no good!"

Of course Anne Marie could well have had a friend who went the same terrible way she herself was to go; alcoholism was then far from uncommon in Odense, along with relentless poverty, unemployment, promiscuity, disease, crime both petty and serious, and mental degeneration often caused by too much hardship as well as by venereal disease. All of these were to be found among Hans Christian's own blood relations, their friends and associates. Odense was Denmark's second city, but half its 6,000-strong population was made up of workers forced to put up with whatever scratch jobs came their way. In the last year of his life, 1875, Andersen would make Odense the subject of an eponymous lyric poem:

Du kjære gamle Fødeby,
Er altid i min Tanke.[14]

You dear old birthplace
Are always in my thought.

Certainly Andersen took pride in later improvements to it. In 1855 he could write: 'In my earliest childhood, Odense itself was quite a different town from what it is now that it has beaten Copenhagen with its street lighting and running water and I don't know what else! In those days I think it was a hundred years behind the times; a whole lot of customs and traditions were still observed there, which had long since disappeared from the capital.'[15] He cites the procession of the guilds (the shoemakers' ranked as the lowest), with a harlequin in motley at its head, the wreath-bedecked ox led through the streets on the first Monday in Lent ridden by a boy dressed as an angel, the groups of spinning women in the asylum with their fund of tales, to which Andersen as a child contributed. Many townsfolk of Odense, including Anne Marie herself, saw a far less strict demarcation line between this world and the next, the realm populated by spirits, the souls of the dead, both recent and long-gone, and God himself, than the educated classes could countenance. Indeed for the present writer to label them 'superstitions and rituals' does them less than justice; they were expressions of a widely acknowledged folk belief-system which, however full of illogical improbabilities, served its psycho-social purpose. To an imaginative, impressionable child they must have added up to an inspirited universe of literally endless (eternal) dimensions. While Andersen, as soon as he embarked on serious education, shed the supra-natural knowledge he had been proffered, he knew of its reality in the minds of ordinary people, and this reality asserts itself repeatedly in his writings, even though they are also informed by the rationalist, undogmatic deist belief which was his virtually all of his life.

   If life was often stark and attended by the fears which invariably compound the problems of poverty, there were regular alleviations, notably for young Andersen the Odense Theatre,[16] already a substantial playhouse with its own experienced director, but regularly hosting visiting companies. Annually Det kongelige Teater (the Royal Theatre), Copenhagen sent performers, who provided for the boy an ever more eagerly anticipated window on to a richer, more exhilarating world.

   Andersen saw his first Holberg play – in a German musical adaptation – when he was only seven. He delighted in the performances of Giuseppe Casorti's[17] troupe (season 1814–1815), which presented masked figures of the *commedia dell'arte*, mime artists, tightrope walkers and other acrobats; all these stalk his creative work. He watched professional actors from Copenhagen perform a tragedy by Oehlenschläger and an operetta by Grétry, and viewed them as 'earthly divinities', alongside whom he was privileged to stand on stage as a supernumerary; he would participate in productions in this way when actually resident in the capital. But he not only wanted to appear *on* the boards, he wanted to write songs to be sung *from* them, and, even more than this, he wanted to create actable plays. He compiled a list of twenty-five possible titles for dramatic works.

Odense had its small quota of better-off, better-educated families who took an interest in this unusual boy who so early displayed astonishing powers of invention, an ability to act and recite, and a remarkable lack of shyness about performing: among them Madame Bunkeflod, a pastor's wife, who lived opposite his home, and the printer Herr Iversen.[18] Two factors above all must have determined him to leave Odense to try his luck in Copenhagen: his mother Anne Marie's remarriage in 1818 and his own Confirmation at St Knud's Church, a year later.

Andersen's Confirmation on 18 April 1819 endorsed his own opinion of himself because he knew he had greatly impressed those preparing him for this rite of passage, having insisted that they instructed him alongside the more educated children rather than the ordinary town boys and girls. He left Odense on 4 September not only leaving behind him well-wishers in a higher station than his own but also holding a letter of introduction from one of them, the printer Iversen, to the ballet school in Copenhagen. After an adventurous journey by land and by sea (a choppy crossing from Fyn to Sjælland), he arrived in Copenhagen on 6 September 1819,[19] one day after the outbreak in the city of Denmark's last pogrom. Its visible aftermath – chaos everywhere, with many soldiers trying to clear up the damage – made so strong an impact on him that he would recreate it in *Only a Fiddler*, with the Jewish girl Naomi exposed to personal danger, giving us vivid, convincing scenes hideously prophetic of what would occur all over Europe just under 120 years hence.

Andersen's first three years in Copenhagen abounded in disappointments and disillusionments, though what is most remarkable about them in hindsight is his constant and resolute self-belief, and what would seem an all but total lack of homesickness. Andersen knew he belonged not to Anne Marie's Odense but to the world of culture and the arts, that he had a temperamental affinity with those who not only comprised but formed it, and possessed both the free-floating enthusiasm necessary for serving it and gifts and insights entirely his own – whether the arts were dance, drama, vaudeville, poems, long fiction or short stories. All his life Andersen would express himself in many different art forms, enjoying the challenge of each and giving to it something highly original, indeed uniquely his. He even developed an art he made curiously his own: paper-cuts, which complement the dramatis personae of his stories superbly. Andersen's pursuit of people who could be of assistance to him in his artistic endeavours was unremitting. When still an obvious adolescent, he never passed by an opportunity to put himself in the path of cultural personages, even celebrities, even members of the nobility or the royal family. In truth he proactively sought them out.

Of course, some of his attempts to interest people ended in insulting dismissal, sometimes in the ridiculing laughter he most feared. But however hurt such treatment might make him feel, he was not daunted, or only momentarily, and his eye and ear for who was important and who, among the important, would be responsive to him and also trustworthy, were preternaturally acute. Andersen had next to no money, and lived in sordid lodgings. For a time he was housed in a street frequented by prostitutes, and when he looked up a close relation, his aunt Christiane (his mother's half-sister), it turned out she actually ran a brothel.[20] It would be extremely unlikely for the sensitive, intelligent and very observant youth that Andersen was not to be profoundly disquieted by exposures of the urban underbelly, and the early story 'Tællelyset' ('The Tallow Candle'), discovered as recently as December 2012, suggests, as we shall see, that this was strongly the case. 'I was in the midst of the mysteries of Copenhagen,' he was to write in his autobiography, 'but did not understand enough to interpret them.'[21]

What principally occupied his time and energies was proving to himself and others that he was possessed of outstanding and flexible artistic capabilities. Just under a fortnight after his arrival in Copenhagen he secured an interview with the well-known musician Giuseppe Siboni (1780–1839),[22] now head of the Royal Choir School. Present at this meeting were Denmark's pre-eminent composer C.E.F. Weyse[23] (1774–1842) and the distinguished writer Jens Baggesen[24] (1764–1826). Siboni was so impressed that he offered him singing lessons, Weyse embarked on a campaign to collect funds for the boy, and kept in constant touch; he was later to collaborate on an opera with him. Nothing – even in Andersen's own writings – can do justice to the extraordinary nature of this episode: readers must concentrate their minds on it, and envisage an obscure youth with a strong regional way of speaking and no education somehow conveying to three highly sophisticated men, who met candidates for their interest virtually every day, the magnitude of his talents and ambitions.

Siboni discontinued the lessons a year later (in June 1820) when the boy's voice broke. This crucial and upsetting episode made Andersen feel that he had returned to the beginning of his Copenhagen life and should perhaps go back to Odense. But that would be too shameful! The voice-breaking is commemorated in his last novel, *Lykke-Peer* (*Lucky Peer*, 1870) which constitutes an invaluable, if perhaps sanitised, gloss on Andersen's entry into the artistic world – and commands the reader's sympathy more memorably than any autobiography.

Andersen wrote three autobiographies.[25] The earliest, *Levnedsbogen* (*The Book of Life/The Biography*, 1832–33) was written for private consumption (principally for Louise, the daughter of his chief patron, Jonas Collin), ends in mid-sentence (!) and was not discovered until 1926. The second *Das Märchen meines Lebens ohne Dichtung* (*The Fairy-Tale of My Life without Poetry*, 1846) was written (in Danish) at the behest of his German publisher Carl Lorck (in fact a Dane), who wanted it to coincide with the collected edition of Andersen's stories he was bringing out and so published it in a German version, hence the title. The third, *Mit Livs Eventyr* (*My Fairy-Tale Life*, 1855) is an enormously expanded and updated progeny of this memoir, but published in the language in which Andersen wrote it – i.e. Danish – and hence, so far as the reading world has been concerned, is the only Andersen autobiography. The book was later revised and amplified. It is the life story of a famous man written for a public wanting to hear how that fame came about, and to have it vindicated by salient memories and reflections. Essential as it is to anyone curious about Andersen, and containing illuminating delights, particularly in its magical (though not always accurate) earlier chapters, it inevitably, through its very nature, largely lacks rawness. As is only to be expected, diaries and letters give us his state of mind and heart in the way these studied recollections cannot do. And often we may find that the (sometimes necessary) transpositions of key episodes of his life come across in their true significance more strongly in his creative work – not least in his three early novels – than in the more official version where for tactical reasons he often could not say what he really thought of a person or action. Though sometimes – especially concerning the Danish literary establishment as he encountered it in his twenties – and as it encountered him – he is quite surprisingly candid.

Andersen's first years in Copenhagen coincided with lively, ground-breaking ones for Danish literature. In 1820 B.S. Ingemann (1789–1862),[26] to whom he was to send poems that very year and soon to become friendly with, brought out *Eventyr og Fortællinger* (*Fairy Tales and Narratives*), which stands behind Andersen's own collection of fifteen odd years later. Ingemann went on to produce a Scott-influenced (by *Marmion* etc.) narrative poem, *Valdemar den Store og hans Mænd* (*Valdemar the Great and His Men*, 1824) and Scott-influenced historical novels *Valdemar Seir* (1826) and *Erik Menveds Barndom* (*The Childhood of [King] Erik Menved*, 1828). Andersen also sent poems to N.F.S. Grundtvig (1783–1872)[27] ecclesiastic, reviver of interest in Norse legend and lore, founder of Danish folk schools (that template for the rest of the world) and principal architect of Denmark's burgeoning welfare democracy. And he introduced himself to the writer, Just Mathias Thiele (1795–1874)[28] successively secretary, councillor and president of the Royal Academy of the Arts, who showed him much kindness, and to H.C. Ørsted who lent him books.

Ørsted had made his ground-breaking discovery of electromagnetism only the year before, in July 1820.

These were also the years when Europe's leading novelist, Walter Scott, was being translated into Danish, by Knud Lyne Rahbek (1760–1830)[29] – from 1820 on. Rahbek was a writer himself, and a lively figure in the cultural world, whose home 'Bakkehuset' would be a focal point for those interested in the arts, and where open days were held to which young Hans Christian Andersen would eventually find his way.

But it was the theatre that principally generated a magnetic attraction for Andersen, and by this – for Kierkegaard was right when he declared 'In Denmark there is but one city and one theatre'[30] – is meant Det kongelige Teater (The Royal Theatre), on Kongens Nytorv in Copenhagen. In March 1821, after a walk-on debut there, he paid a call on its managing director, the court official Jonas Collin. Without Jonas Collin (1776–1861),[31] and the trust and friendship he extended, without his family of which the writer became an established, de facto member, Andersen's history – and his *oeuvre* – would be completely unimaginable. In 1822, Andersen, a mere seventeen years of age after all, produced two dramatic works and offered them to the Royal Theatre, *Røverne i Vissenberg i Fyn* (*The Robbers of Vissenberg in Fyn*)[32] – the very title of this verse-drama suggests Schiller's *Die Räuber*[33] – and *Alfsol* (*Elf-Sun*),[34] a tragedy in three acts, with Ingemann and Oehlenschläger as detectable presences. The actual writing – done at great speed – was full of grammatical errors and spelling mistakes, and the result would have been impossible to stage. But, and especially *Alfsol* (the name of a princess who kills herself, though loved by two men), the plays were accomplished enough to make the Royal Theatre management, headed by Collin, appreciate that no ordinarily precocious youth had written them. So they took a decision and then summoned him: [35] 'Rahbek spoke on their behalf . . . they had found so many "nuggets" in [*Alfsol*] that they cherished a hope that through serious study and by going to school and learning everything necessary from the start I might perhaps one day be able to write plays for the Danish theatre which were worthy of being performed. In order that I might be able to live and acquire the necessary education, Collin had spoken on my behalf to King Frederik the Sixth who had graciously granted me a sum from the state finances' – *ad usus publicos* – 'that was sufficient to live on for some years. In addition, he said that the Grammar School Board had agreed I should have free tuition at Slagelse [Latin] Grammar School, to which they said, an energetic new headmaster had recently been appointed' – Simon Meisling (1787–1856).[36] Andersen was to go to Slagelse forthwith. And Jonas Collin became Andersen's official guardian, the most important single event to befall him after his birth.

1822 was a watershed year for Andersen in another respect. At his own expense he had a volume published called *Ungdoms-Forsøg* (*Youthful Attempts*)[37] containing three recent works, a verse prologue, then *Alfsol* and a story, 'Gjenfærdet ved Palnatokes Grav' ('The Apparition at Palnatoke's Grave'). In this last the heroine's mother – mad Stine of Broby who attempted to have her drowned as a baby – was clearly inspired by the character of Madge Wildfire in Scott's *The Heart of Midlothian* (1818), out that year in Danish. Andersen paid Scott further homage in the pseudonym under which he chose to publish his book: Villiam Christian Walter. At his own confession Villiam was after William Shakespeare, Christian was his own name and what his mother and her friends called him, and Walter a tribute to Scott. For though Scott did not make official in Britain until 1827 what in fact was common knowledge there, his authorship of the Waverley novels, in Denmark all of his books were published under his name. The whole enterprise is further proof of Andersen's phenomenal tenacity of purpose and belief in himself. The volume did not sell, even on a second try in 1827 by the bookseller in question, with a new title page. But it had a tangible existence, and for a seventeen-year-old that in itself would act as proof that ambitions could be realised.

There was no doubt that Andersen needed to be educated further, though he was always to be an indifferent speller and uncertain of grammatical rules. How, without the rigid and closely monitored programme of the next six years, could he have participated in the cultural world of his choice and mixed with contemporaries, his peers in intelligence, with compatible and stimulating interests? This served at least to mitigate his consuming self-absorption. Yet a good case could be made for calling his schooling at Slagelse – later he trans-ferred to Helsingør, with Meisling still his headmaster – the unhappiest period (1822–27) of Andersen's entire life, containing the greatest number of public and private humiliations and the fewest opportunities for respite from them. Undoubtedly this was how he later looked on it.

A tall, clever youth of seventeen (and with an entire published book containing work in three genres to show for himself), he was forced to join a class of eleven-year-olds unflatteringly amazed by his size, his gawkiness, his social origins and his ignorance. Nor was catching up an easy process; indeed he had to endure being kept down a year. To compound his misery he was expressly forbidden to pursue his writings, these being considered – understandably, one reluctantly concedes – a harmful distraction from hard, necessary cerebral labours frequently so uncongenial and strength-sapping.

'*Monday 19 September 1825* My God! My God! Thy will be done; just reward me for my effort this year, nothing more. (God only knows what fate has in store for me when this page is turned!) Unlucky me! Did miserably in Latin. You won't be advanced into the fourth form! Out of school! To become an artisan or corpse is your fate! God, God, are you really near? But all the same

'Praised be Thy name!' – I did better in Latin grammar, maybe a 'good', also a 'good' in German . . . Oh God, the man who earns his bread in the sweat of his brow is happier than the one who labours in the so-called higher spheres. He knows no better, for food and sustenance are his only concerns. . . . Whereas the other man must struggle against a sea of difficulties and hindrances, is maligned and picked to pieces. Gifted with a greater sensitivity, his heart is crushed.[38]

And so on and on, many times over. Andersen started his lifelong practice of diary-keeping, of taking blank pages into his confidence, at Slagelse, and the portrait he involuntarily gives of himself is of somebody with an enormous aptitude for suffering, easily cast down, not to say wounded, as the short quotation above makes clear, to the point of ontological despair; small setbacks, unwanted or unanticipated occurrences, less than sympathetic or complimentary remarks, and the puzzling behaviour of persons he judged fundamentally hostile to him could all bring him to this point. This portrait is reinforced by his letters of these years, particularly those written to Jonas Collin at the latter's request telling him how he was finding school; these often ran to many pages. Suffering is inseparable from his art; indeed the sense of helplessness that overcomes well-disposed, unusual and gifted individuals when confined in situations to which they are fundamentally unsuited provides the engine for many of his most memorable works: *The Improvisatore*, 'The Little Mermaid' and 'The Ugly Duckling'.

Understanding of suffering was enforced by his headmaster's decision to give the top class a holiday to watch the execution of three persons at Skælskør.[39] The case had caused a sensation in the locality. A rich farmer's daughter had persuaded her lover to murder her father, who had opposed their union, and the farm servant, his sights on marrying his employer's widow, had helped them: 'It made a terrible and unforgettable impression on me to see the condemned being driven up, the deathly pale girl leaning her head on her powerfully built lover's breast. Behind them sat the farm servant, pale and with wispy black hair; he had a squint and nodded to a few acquaintances who shouted goodbye to him. On the scaffold, where they stood at the side of their coffins, they sang a hymn together.' After the moment of the deaths, 'I saw a poor sick creature, whose superstitious parents, in order to cure him from a stroke, made him drink a bowl of the blood of the executed criminals. . . .' How could a youth of Andersen's sensibility ever forget so dreadful a scene?

Slagelse/Helsingør established a pattern we can discern right through to Andersen's last years. But quite objective witnesses at the time, and all biographers ever since, have agreed that Simon Meisling entertained a deep antagonism towards his remarkable charge. Despite several happier interludes and reconciliations, this was an intolerably crass man, despotic, even bullying, touchily vain about his own accomplishments (markedly limited ones as a writer), sneeringly dismissive of those of younger others, and caught in a difficult marriage to a woman who half-propositioned the timid, hypersensitive Andersen (at least, so he thought). Meisling himself undoubtedly deteriorated psychologically during the years Andersen was under his authority, drinking too much, letting himself go in appearance so that his clothes were dishevelled and even malodorous. Andersen would have his revenge on both the Meislings in due course. In *The Improvisatore*, for example, Meisling becomes the ludicrously named headmaster, Habbas Dahdah (with his delusions about his own poetic judgement and inability to perceive the greatness of Dante), while his wife turns into the pathetic predatory Santa who so scares the somewhat over-innocent narrator. The picture of Herr and Fru Knepus in *Only a Fiddler* is only marginally less disparaging. Andersen regularly complained about Meisling to Jonas Collin – and to others of the Copenhagen literati with whom he was on good terms – and in April 1827 his guardian at last took him out of the school, to have him tutored in Copenhagen, a way of life – and learning – that suited him infinitely better.

But before he left his jurisdiction Andersen had gone against the firm injunctions of his sponsors and had produced both a story (unknown until 2012) and a poem which gave him a taste of early public notice.

2

'The Tallow Candle' was discovered in October 2012[40] in the National Archives of Fyn in one of four cases containing a total of 1,000 documents relating to the distinguished clerical Plum family. The historian Esben Brage took in the signature and the telltale dedication, and two months later it had been authenticated by some leading Andersen experts, while others remain unconvinced, even dubious. It was then released to a fascinated world, arousing immediate attention in, for example, Britain, Germany and Japan. Handwriting, not easy to read, points to its dating from the 1820s, that is, during Andersen's time at the Slagelse school, to the Latin compositional exercises of which it bears a formal resemblance. The dedicatee is Andersen's old friend from Odense who believed in him and lived near his home, Madame Bunkeflod, the pastor's wife, with whom he had kept in touch and whom he doubtless wanted to impress. Though widely hailed as a fairy tale it is not exactly this, though in its personification of an inanimate object it bears a recognisable kinship to those that Andersen would so famously write about later. Rather, it is better described as a short, concentrated prose allegory, a sustained reflection on a limited subject of a kind that was fashionable as a schoolboy/student's exercise. That having been said, it is an original, revealing and affecting work, though it has to be admitted that we would look at it differently if we knew the author to be other than Andersen.

The Tallow Candle emerges into the world perfect in form, shining white, promising to everyone who sees it a bright future which it will itself illuminate, this being the purpose for which it was made. The candle's mother was a sheep (tallow comes from sheep), its father a great smelting-pot (the detailing of its pedigree being highly characteristic of the Andersen we now know with his love of personalising the non-personal). While the candle owes its physical body to its mother, it is from its father that it has received 'Lysten til den flammende Ild',[41] 'the desire for the flaming fire', which must eventually pass through it (via the wick) so that it can shine out. Fulfilment of its spiritual patrimony is what the candle expects Life to offer it, though first there comes the question 'finde den Plads, hvor det selv passede bedst' 'to find the place where it fitted in best'.

This task proves not just difficult but impossible. The great world, with all its varieties, 'brød sig kun om sig selv og slet ikke om Tællelyset', 'cared only about itself and not at all about the Tallow Candle'. Worse, it actually misuses the candle with 'de sorte Fingre', 'dirty fingers', which leave ever-bigger 'Pletter', 'stains/blemishes' on 'den reene Uskyldsfarve', 'the clean colour of purity'. Inside its purity remains, but 'de falske Venner', 'the false friends' don't appreciate this. Instead they cast the candle aside 'som en unyttig Tingest', 'as a useless thing'. Indeed its dirty exterior positively repels them and drives them away.

The candle comes extremely close to sharing the general contemptuous evaluation of itself, and feels 'uendelig ulyksalig', 'infinitely unhappy' (under-lining Andersen's own). It even wonders whether it might not be sullying its own surroundings. It sees no point in its existence past, present or future. One line at this juncture is most telling – and mysterious too. 'Det saae sig forstødt af det Gode og det opdagede nu, at det kun havde været et Redskab til at fremme det slette.' 'It saw itself repudiated by the good and it now realised that it had only been an instrument to further the wicked.' What, we ask, can *really* have been happening to this candle? Who are these wicked people, and for what purposes and in what ways did they use it to further their aims? It is as if we have abruptly stepped outside the metaphor into a terrible real-life land-scape the chief components of which are not going to be supplied. The more the Tallow Candle broods on its situation the greater 'dets Mismod', 'its dejec-tion', its sense of the futility of its very being; it looks out on existence as through a grubby veil.

'Men da traf det en lille Flamme, et Fyrtøi; det kjendte Lyset bedre, end Tællelyset kjendte sig selv.' 'But then it met a little flame, a Tinder Box; it knew the candle better than the Tallow Candle knew itself.' What it knows is that the candle is clean and pure within, and therefore capable of achieving that very illumination for which it had been designed. And for its part the candle understands that the Tinder Box's benign knowledge of itself is not without foundation, and therefore allows the ignition to take place until a flame shines out – in a poetic phrase – 'som Formælingens Glædesfakkel' 'like marriage's jubilation torch'. Moreover this is a marriage with – in a decidedly curious image – issue: all those drops of tallow that trickle copiously down the candle's body are progeny both physical and spiritual, and they satisfactorily hide all the horrible stains it acquired in bad times. Now 'true friends' appear, replacing the false ones. The Tallow Candle has at last 'dets rette Plads i Livet' 'its right place in life', and its light will give happiness to itself and 'dets Medskabninger' 'its fellow creatures' for a long while.

What does this Tinder Box (the eponymous central object of the first fairy-story in Andersen's first collection) mean? It's hard not to think of it, in its specificity, as standing for Jonas Collin (and his colleagues), who perceived the goodness (the likeability behind the sometimes unfortunate exterior), as well as the creative gifts of the still young Andersen, rather than for some more generalised force of goodwill. Biographically this identification fits the facts of the (rough) date of the piece's composition. What is more difficult to come to terms with – and perhaps the parable's most fascinating feature – is its repeated and unflinching emphasis on outer dirtiness, inflicted by the world-at-large, and concealing the innocence within, and even disguising or traducing it to the point of destroying the protagonist's confidence in its own preservation. One might well have expected this story by an ambitious youthful artist to embody doubts, his own and other people's, about his talents (which, interestingly, he ascribes solely to his father's contribution to his selfhood). But no, it is his inner virtue (innocence) around which the painful misgivings cluster. Will, the writer wonders fearfully, the world, which has done him the damage in the first place, look at him and believe him to be as corrupt as (apparently) he seems? Who can possibly tell how inwardly pure – how capable of pure creations – he still is? This brief work contains no fewer than fifteen terms connoting filth and its besmirching of the pristine, while even to a pre-Freudian age the candle must have suggested the phallus. The phallus appears here as an instrument that invites – and can thus promote – uncleanliness, even if in its structure and proper usage it is consonant with a beneficent scheme of things. . . . Still, the piece ends affirmatively. It is clear that Andersen, even at this early age, believes in the artist, the light-giver, as a benefactor, someone whose work does *good*, irradiating people and their surroundings, and in so doing satisfying the artist/provider himself too.

Another piece written when still a schoolboy under a writing interdict is the three-stanza-long poem 'Det døende Barn'[42] ('The Dying Child', 1826, published 1827). At a time when in every European country deaths of infants occurred regularly in almost all families, understandably inspiring quantities of verse, often all too predictable in style and ideas, the youthful Andersen trusted to the dictates of his individualistic mind, and produced, within parameters of metre and rhyme expertly handled, a piece so imaginatively fresh as to reach the heart. Many a poem dealt with a child's death from the grieving mother's point of view. Andersen's does something quite different. For he becomes the *child*, aware of what is momentously happening to him, and anxious only that his mother, the one other being in this world known to him, be not too distressed:

> 'Moder, jeg er træt, nu vil jeg sove,
> Lad mig ved dit Hjerte slumre ind;
> Græd dog ej, det må du først mig love,
> Thi din Tåre brænder på min Kind.'

> 'Mother, I am tired, now I will sleep,
> Let me doze off close to your heart,
> Don't cry, that you must promise me first,
> For your tears burn on my cheek.'

The perspective proffered is a strange, shocking one, that of an inarticulate being whose sense of reality is more acute than that of the older, articulate person, and whose instinctual courage extends to altruistic empathy. Unsurprisingly 'The Dying Child' made a strong immediate impression on readers who were obviously completely unfamiliar with the author's name, and it was translated into German for simultaneous publication in 1827. It is our first example of Andersen's astonishing ability to position himself as interpreter of the wordless, as messenger from that unnameable region linking the living and the dead, to a society, indeed a world (unlike that into which he had been born) increasingly uncertain of the relation between the two.

The poem did not please the envious Meisling, who saw its very appearance in print as an affront to his regimen.

> Trembling all over I gave him the poem; he read it, laughed and said it was nothing but a lot of sentimental nonsense, and then gave vent to his anger in a stream of cruel words.... Day by day my situation became increasingly unhappy; I suffered such mental anguish that I was in danger of completely breaking down unless a change soon took place.[43]

3

When growing up in Odense, Andersen had held back from other children, almost never playing games with other boys, or even wanting to, preferring to occupy himself with his toy theatre. In Copenhagen, once he had become surer of himself with some of his precocious literary hopes realised, his disposition proved rather a sociable one. Even in these trying Slagelse years, he struck up many mutually communicative and rewarding friendships with other young men in the last stages of their education or starting out on their careers. He had been able to go off from time to time when free to the distinguished Academy in Sorø and there made two friends who wrote poetry, had more adventurous temperaments than his own, and a frank interest in sexual matters: Fritz Petit and Carl Bagger.[44] These companions crop up regularly in his diaries and letters, and will find their way into his creative work. Andersen's writings are emphatically not those of a recluse, of somebody who failed to connect with his contemporaries. Such connections were not free of difficulties, some of them painful, but of whom would that not be true?

The focus of his yearning, his need, to connect was the family of Jonas Collin whom Andersen would later address as 'Father' Collin, just as his household was the 'Home of Homes'. Jonas Collin was the very pattern of a Golden Age intellectual, with his early absorption of Rousseau and Kant, his translation into Danish of Fichte, his belief in education as both a remedial and a harmonising social force. And appropriately he was one of that age's most active and respected key figures, carrying the most universally applicable philanthropic ideals of Absolute Monarchy into the public domain and seeing to their practical realisation, a friend of Oehlenschläger and Ørsted, financial manager of the Royal Theatre and chief secretary of *ad usus publicos*. Unflagging on behalf of every project or cause he espoused, dutiful, resourceful, he also – as his shrewd, kindly face suggests – was capable of unusual sympathy. His treatment of Andersen combines an imaginative understanding of his adopted son's problems with the ability to view him and his sometimes precarious dealings with others with a sensible objectivity. But – though Andersen was perhaps slow fully to admit this to himself – the younger man could find the older's pedagogic attitude to himself and his work irksome, restrictive. It was, of course, immensely to Andersen's advantage to have Jonas Collin and his family as socially accepted stand-ins for kinsfolk, and the effusion he lavished on both surely springs from his determination that his all but unbelievable good fortune after so many hardships should continue, should never weaken. But there were natural, indeed virtually automatic assumptions of superiority in the Collin family that someone so gifted and original as Andersen would inevitably find frustrating and worse, oppressive.

Jonas Collin's offspring were Ingeborg (1804–77), who married Adolph Drewsen, Gottlieb (1806–85), Edvard (1808–86),[45] Louise (1813–98) who married J.W. Lind, and Theodor (1815–1902). The last became a doctor, indeed was physician to the Royal Theatre itself, but him apart, the men of the family – not just Jonas Collin's sons and sons-in-law but his grandsons, with three of whom Andersen enjoyed close, if sometimes fraught, friendship – were involved, and at high levels, with the law, administration, banking, finance and business. Standing on the firmest economic and social foundations, principled, worldly, conscious of their own status, comfortable, united (indeed, like many close families, they had evolved a host of private expressions, catchphrases and rituals), the Collins provided Andersen with a security he was in desperate need of, and which he never ceased to cherish; he was proud of them, proud to be one of them. . . . But did he really belong? After the passage of many years, perhaps yes – so much shared, so many intimate matters mutually known. Yet the gulf between them and himself was for too long too palpable for complete acceptance. Cultured and in the social swim, therefore knowing almost everybody who was anybody in Copenhagen, including in the arts and media, the Collins were ultimately committed to *Weltanschauungen* and activities very different from Andersen's own. Even at their most generously disposed, it is debatable whether they appreciated their protégé's works as so many, many others did, or even understood what it was about his writings that had earned such esteem. Later when they travelled abroad, members of the family were surprised to find how famous and how highly regarded Andersen was. Did he truly deserve all this éclat?

Though both Ingeborg and Gottlieb were nearer him in age, it was on the second Collin son, Edvard, that Andersen's attentions – and his affections – soon focused. At first he was the most stand-offish of the siblings; he didn't much take to the odd-looking youth his father brought to the house. Andersen realised this and resolved to win his regard. But an improvement in his appearance and manners brought about by Slagelse caused the second Collin son to thaw in attitude and behaviour towards him. Also, because Andersen had had to make up for lost time educationally, the two of them emerged into the adult world side by side. Initially Edvard was asked to help Andersen with his Latin prose and to check his spelling and grammar, the last a service he continued to perform throughout their lives, for he became his friend's scrupulous agent, negotiating with publishers and supervising the presentation of his manuscripts. But he was also supposed to assist Andersen to find his place in educated society, a duty he discharged not always with good grace or warm feelings, probably because his father didn't give him much choice in the matter. The pair enjoyed much real quasi-fraternal companionship, and Andersen's letters to Edvard about his travels, about distinctive features of places, could only have been written to someone he judged essentially sympathetic to him and quickly responsive to his words. And their friendship, despite its not inconsiderable setbacks especially during the first six years or so, was to endure strongly; indeed, in a late letter Edvard calls himself Andersen's 'oldest and constant friend', Andersen became devoted to Henriette (Jette), Edvard's wife – a case could be made for her being his greatest confidante in the later decades of his life – and – with certain reservations and hiatuses – to his son, Jonas, his companion in major later travels. Andersen's relationship with Edvard Collin is, in truth, the single most significant one in his life, and a prime animating presence in his *oeuvre*.

Andersen's fond admiration cannot have been at all easy for Edvard to accept. Edvard represented for this highly talented, eccentric outsider the very pattern of an intelligent insider (and of a privileged section of the inside at that): personable, assured, dependable, well-informed, good-looking in a well set-up, stolid way, intelligent and articulate (Edvard qualified early as a lawyer) and worldly-wise. And basically conventional. The qualifying adverb of course covers those times when Edvard forfeited upper-class decorum and yielded to mood or to the sincerity of his own immediate responses, sometimes showing tenderness to this arriviste who so eagerly declared himself his 'brother', some-times displaying genuine amusement at his ready fund of anecdotes and quips, but at other times unable to curb an exasperation that crossed the border into downright unkindness. Hundreds of letters between them survive, covering many situations and states of mind, and then there is the book Edvard Collin published seven years after Andersen's death, *H.C. Andersen og det Collinske Huus* (*H.C. Andersen and the Collin family,* 1882), which contains both tributes and strictures. For all Edvard's belief in dignified straightforwardness, complexity is the essence of their lifelong association.

4

In October 1828 Andersen succeeded in passing the *examen artium*, the second rite of passage after Confirmation for educated Danish youth, though his academic interests did not stop there; in 1830 he went on to submit a dissertation for a university prize (which, for all its merits, he didn't win) on humankind's development – through religion and mythology – from original monotheism to polytheism and then, after perceiving unity in diver-sity, back to a more sophisticated monotheism.[46] Unlike all the others sitting the *examen artium* Andersen was a mere three weeks away from seeing in print chapters of a book on which he had been working, in the fashionable *Kjøbenhavns flyvende Post* (Copenhagen's Flying Post), edited by J.L. Heiberg[47] (1791–1860), also powerful in the theatre and a constant figure in Andersen's world as long as he lived: *Fodreise fra Holmens Canal til Østpynten af Amager i Aarene 1828 og 1829 (Journey on Foot from Holmen's Canal to the East Point of Amager 1828 to 1829).*[48] Andersen approached the publishers C.A. Reitzel, but they could not agree on terms, and so he self-published the work in January 1829. It attracted some attention, and rightly; here clearly was a young writer of phenomenal prolificacy of invention.

It is basically a squib, as its very title slyly proclaims: the sonorously announced route is in plain fact a perfectly unremarkable one, familiar to every one of his readers, from Copenhagen city centre, past the Stock Exchange and, after a choice of bridges, over to the island borough of Amager, where Andersen himself had gone to be tutored for his *examen*. (Today you would take the Langebro bridge after proceeding down H.C. Andersens Boulevard.) And the titular naming of the two calendar years is a further joke, suggesting as it does a substantial length of time, when what we have is the account of a single nocturnal walk on New Year's Eve, beginning in one year, 1828 and finishing – an apparent waiving of normal rules of time and space – in the next. The persona is that of an innocent abroad, precociously learned, light-hearted, merry to the point of intoxication as befits this night of festivities, with a ready profusion of words and images, from his wide reading, from life, from the poetically inclined author's own head. From time to time, indeed, he breaks out into verse. He can no more resist his own imagination, he tells us in the first of the fourteen chapters – the last is a *Tristram Shandy*-like sequence of punctuation points (indicating that 1829 is as yet terra incognita) – than ordinary people can stifle the promptings of the flesh, a truth about his own character he was not yet ready to face. He is accosted by myste-rious female creatures, by a talking cat, by Prince Zerbino, eponymous hero of the 1799 *Märchendrama* (fairy-tale play) of the great German Romantic, Ludwig Tieck (1773–1853),[49] by a Tom Thumb version of Louis XIV emanating from the Planet Sirius, and by St Peter himself. He is transported into the Copenhagen of three centuries ahead, a foretaste of that interest in peering into the future which led him to write 'Thousands of Years to Come'. But at age twenty-four Andersen is principally interested in what the theatre might be like in this remote age: wouldn't it have a kaleidoscope of monster proportions and quite amazing stage-shifting devices? Denmark in 2129 still reveres its great literary sons: Holberg of course, and Jens Baggesen who had died two years previously, but also members of its living 'Golden Age' pantheon, Ingemann, Ørsted, Thorvaldsen, Oehlenschläger. We have the definite feeling (not unintentionally given us) that Andersen would like to find himself in this fine company. Mocking his own already much-mocked vanity, he admits to searching this library of the far future for his own *Journey on Foot*, alas, to no avail.

The playful allusions, some bedded in small humorous incidents, to literary characters from Washington Irving's to Walter Scott's are surely too prolix to affect readers now as they must have done at the time, when they showed just what a bright young spark had produced these pages. But there is one important source yoking these varieties, and accounting for both the buttonholing, deceptively jocular manner and the phantasmagorical matter: E.T.A. Hoffmann (1776–1822).[50] Not only do we actually encounter *Kater Murr*, the autobiographically disposed cat after whom Hoffmann named his last unfinished novel (two volumes 1819 and 1821), we have a whole chapter narrated by nothing less than an actual *edition* of Hoffmann's best-known completed novel, *Die Elixiere des Teufels* (*The Devil's Elixirs*, 1815–16). (This is a complex study of dual nature, featuring a monk born of evil stock who therefore cannot stop himself committing evil deeds, and his double, a half-brother whom he believes himself to have killed. Traces of it persist in Andersen's 'The Shadow'.) Mention is made of the *Serapionsbrüder* (Serapion Brothers), that group of Hoffman's friends who provided a framing device for his tales, among whom was the novelist and poet Adelbert von Chamisso (1781–1838) in two years' time to become a good friend of Andersen's (and an important literary influence). More intrinsically *Journey on Foot* relates to two particular Hoffmann works, one referred to in its course, *Der Goldne Topf* (*The Golden Pot*, 1814, revised 1819), a novella generally thought to be the writer's most perfect production, and a short story, 'Die Abenteuer der Silvester-Abend' ('The Adventures of St Silvester's Night' – i.e. New Year's Eve, 1816).

The Golden Pot takes us to the respectable quarters of a vividly rendered Dresden, where we meet eminent burghers such as the Konrektor and Registrator plus a distinguished, less conventional Archivist. And it shows us – through the bemused adventures of a clumsy, susceptible student Anselmus – how behind this prosaic world another one exists, of competing spirits both malevolent and beneficent: the Archivist (he is also a salamander!) proves an effective go-between. *Journey on Foot* makes a comparable demonstration, and through a similar intelligence, of Copenhagen and its adjunct, Amager. Who would have thought such fantastic beings lurked behind such mundane façades? However, its relationship to 'The Adventures of New Year's Eve' is not only more obvious (the concurrence of the all-important time of year) but more biographically interesting because we can see in it pointers to later imaginative work of Andersen's own. In it one character lacks a shadow, another has no reflection. The man without a shadow is none other than the by now celebrated Peter Schlemihl, the misfortune-plagued hero of Adelbert von Chamisso's popular novel, *Peter Schlemihls wundersame Geschichte* (*Peter Schlemihl's Wonderful Story*, 1814),[51] which Hoffmann admired enormously, and to which he wished to pay the highest form of writer's homage, honouring its hero as an autonomous being. Chamisso's friendship and his sincere regard for Andersen's writings (he was to translate some of his best poems to date into German) would in the near future become of immense value to Andersen, and, like Hoffmann earlier, he would put Peter Schlemihl (unnamed but unmistakable) into a story of his own. Both the shadow and the reflection – and the parodies and truths they present about the self – are to stalk Andersen's *oeuvre*. In *Journey on Foot* we have the first evidence of this obsession.

Johan de Mylius[52] observes that this work of a Fyn-born literary newcomer is the first-ever Copenhagen novel, and in its atmospheric and detailed portrayal of a multi-faceted yet inescapably singular city we can see the young Andersen imaginatively at one with Scott's feeling for Edinburgh (or Hugo's and Balzac's for Paris), and anticipating those of Dickens for London and Dostoevsky for St Petersburg. But de Mylius qualifies his remark by saying: 'if, that is, you think of it as a novel'. From the perspective of this study I do not; the novel, a form which Andersen was soon enthusiastically and with great distinction to embrace, deals with characters subordinate to the physical laws of space and time, indeed it is in this very subordination and in the tensions consequent on it that a large portion of its inestimable value resides. Better, then, to think of *Journey on Foot* as a fantasia on literary and personal themes.

If Andersen debuted as a printed writer of fiction in January 1829, April of the same year saw, remarkably, his debut as a playwright. Under the aegis of J.L. Heiberg, *Kjærlighed paa Nicolai Taarn (Love on [St] Nicholas's Tower)*[53] was performed at the Royal Theatre. The delight in parodying what was then acceptable and applauded, an irreverence playing over just about everything and everybody, were characteristics of Andersen at the outset of his literary career, and perhaps survive more strongly in his later, famous works than their public – outside Denmark – realises. They survive in the half-mocking addresses to readers that begin and conclude so many of his tales, often inversions of current sentimental clichés. *Love on St Nicholas's Tower* guys the dilemmas of romantic dramas, and poses an ingenious resolution of them. Will Ellen, daughter of the watchman of that Copenhagen tower featured in *Journey on Foot*, marry her tailor suitor after the only-to-be-expected vicissitudes? Why not let the audience decide? This deliberate twist, though it may suggest to us modernist or postmodernist defiance of convention, is perfectly conso-nant with the vernacular art of vaudeville of which Heiberg and Andersen were devotees, and proof of a lively newcomer's eagerness to make his mark on a sizeable public with genial snook-cocking at tradition.

Andersen's love for the stage, expressed in his earliest years in Odense, never left him. He went to the theatre whenever and wherever he could. In Copenhagen he declared it to be the chief subject of conversation among city-dwellers, and he was keen to provide them with further material. It will give us a wider view of our subject if we briefly look ahead at Andersen's contribution here. Altogether he wrote twenty-one works for the stage, an achievement largely overlooked by non-Scandinavians. One of them, *Liden Kirsten* (*Little Kirsten*, 1846), the libretto for a composer of world reputation, J.P.E. Hartmann (1805–1900), was greeted in review after review as the first real Nordic opera, and to date has had more performances than any other Danish contribution to the genre. Lucky Peer, eponymous hero of Andersen's last novel, will have as his crowning success the production of a great opera based on that Arabian Nights story of such particular interest to the Danes, *Aladdin*. Frederick J. Marker in his *Hans Christian Andersen and the Romantic Theatre* (1971) draws our attention to an article by critic Erik Bøgh in *Folkets Avis* (*The People's Newspaper*) on 29 April 1864 on the subject of Andersen's plays:

> '[Although Andersen] has never succeeded in forming a work for the stage according to the accepted rules of the art, he is a far greater poet [i.e. for the theatre] than someone possessing the most complete talent for dramatic construction, and when he leaves his limitless realm in the world of the fairy-tale to visit the narrow stage with the slanting floor, upon which each step must be measured, he should be considered as a guest who brings rich gifts from another land, where art makes other demands.'[54]

After *Love on St Nicholas's Tower* Andersen worked on a libretto *Bruden fra Lammermoor*, based on Scott's novel *The Bride of Lammermoor* (1819), for music by Ivar Bredal (1800–64) and performance in May 1832. This would so impress Denmark's senior composer, C.E.F. Weyse (1774–1842) with whom, as we have already noted, he was early on terms of friendship, that he commissioned from him a second Scott libretto, this one based on a novel at that time a great favourite with readers, though now finding few admirers, *Kenilworth* (1821), a somewhat a-historical tribute to the glories of Elizabethan England, full of shameless anachronisms: *Festen paa Kenilworth* (*The Feast at Kenilworth*, 1836).[55]

If William Shakespeare, his own self and Walter Scott were the trio he honoured in the nom de plume of his first published book, Andersen would proclaim another trinity – though there is one overlap – as the writers who most deeply influenced him: Scott, Hoffmann and Heine. As regards Shakespeare we do well to recall a conversation in an English novel of the previous decade, Jane Austen's *Mansfield Park* (1814), between Henry Crawford and Edmund Bertram. Henry says: ' "But Shakespeare one gets acquainted with without knowing how. . . . His thoughts and beauties are so spread abroad that one touches them everywhere, one is intimate with him by instinct. – No man of any brain can open at a good part of one of his plays, without falling into the flow of meaning immediately." ' Edmund agrees: ' "No doubt, one is familiar with Shakespeare. . . . From one's earliest years. His celebrated passages are quoted by everybody; they are in half the books we open, and we all talk Shakespeare, use his similes, and describe with his descriptions . . .'[56]

One of youthful Andersen's most generous and considerate benefactors in Copenhagen, Commodore Peter Frederik Wulff (1774–1842),[57] was the Danish translator of Shakespeare. Wulff had Andersen to stay with himself and his large family for Christmas 1825, and gave him three volumes of the plays as a Christmas present. This good fortune made Andersen compare himself to Aladdin. That comparison is significant because the Chinese boy of the Arabian tales had become synonymous in Denmark, thanks to Oehlenschläger's universally loved poetic drama (1805), with (eventual) good fortune.

Andersen's enthusiasm for Scott and Hoffmann hardly made him unusual; all over Europe it was almost de rigueur to revere them. '[The Heart of Midlothian] was popular to the point of mania', writes John Sutherland in The Life of Walter Scott (1995);[58] 'Lady Louisa Stuart reported being "in a house where everybody is tearing [It] out of each other's hands, and talking of nothing else". ' The Bride of Lammermoor – the second of Scott's 'Tales of My Landlord' – would soon inspire an opera far more widely known than the Andersen/Bredal collaboration, indeed one of the best-loved of all operas, Gaetano Donizetti's Lucia di Lammermoor (1835), with the librettist Salvatore Cammarano making significant departures from the original.[59] 'In the garden you can see where Jeanie Deans (in The Heart of Midlothian) spoke with the queen,' wrote Andersen on 14 July 1847 after a visit to Hampton Court, while in May 1849 he was reading Scott's great novel again.[60] On 12 and 13 August 1847 on his Scottish trip his thoughts travelled back to Scott and The Bride of Lammermoor: 'In Scotland I'm called the "Danish Walter Scott". . . . Sunny day. Sailed by steamer over to Kirkcaldy; passed a small island where the lighthouse was. We walked out to a ruin, Ravenscraig – at first Hambro said it was Ravenswood [setting of The Bride of Lammermoor], but one of the fishermen's wives said there was no shifting sand there. . . . We walked through a garden to the ruin, where there were dark prison cells. It lay by a jutting cliff; the tide was out; a small oak grove close by and thick ivy growing up the cliff, as if it were a tombstone. I wrote a poem about Scotland's Romeo and Juliet (Lucy and Edgar, heroine and hero of this novel).'[61] And on returning from Britain he wrote his novel with the closest kinship to Scott, De to Baronesser (The Two Baronesses, 1848) whose heroine deliberately emulates the heroine of The Heart of Midlothian.

Technically Andersen was undoubtedly impressed by Hoffmann's predilection for insetting one story into another or providing a frame for a sequence of narratives as in the German master's Serapion novels. Thematically he was drawn to Hoffmann's unflagging obsession with metamorphosis, ranging from metempsychosis to such wild destinies as the imprisonment of a person in a bottle (the fate of student Anselmus in *The Golden Pot* before he is removed to Atlantis). Neither 'Lykkens Kalosker' ('The Galoshes of Fortune', 1838),[62] with its transpositions of characters in time and place or *Picture-Book Without Pictures*, 1839–55, with its cameos of happenings and epiphanies in past eras and distant places – to name only two of his works – could have been written without long-standing inner engagement with Hoffmann. And when we come to the stories of toys – for example, that most moving creation, 'Den stand-haftige Tinsoldat' ('The Steadfast Tin Soldier', 1838) we have to turn to Hoffmann again, to *Nussknacker und Mausekönig* (*Nutcracker and Mouse King*, 1819!).[63] But Andersen the novelist, so soon to emerge – 'I want to be the top Danish novelist',[64] he would declare, with warranted confidence – owes immeasurably more to Scott than to Hoffmann, and we can feel the interests the Wizard of the North early aroused in him throughout the corpus he produced. With hindsight it seems fitting that Andersen's life as a prose writer started with a frank derivation from *The Heart of Midlothian*. It is therefore worthwhile recalling this masterpiece now in some detail as we shall be encountering its influence as we proceed through Andersen's *oeuvre*, and at some of the most important ports of call.

5

A clue to Andersen's perennial fascination with the novel lies in its title, an only half-ironic sobriquet for the Tolbooth, Edinburgh's 'ancient prison, which, as is well known to all men, rears its front in the very middle of the High Street'.[65] (Andersen's first novel of Danish life, *O.T.* which visits his own native city, will also be called after its penitentiary.) Set in 1736, Scott's novel gives us a girl of eighteen, Effie Deans, imprisoned in the Tolbooth, condemned to death for an infanticide she never perpetrated: her baby survived the confusions in which it vanished. But bastard children were, with disturbing frequency, being killed by mothers and their accomplices all over Scotland: the hanging of Effie Deans would be a necessary warning.

The book's central character is Effie's half-sister, Jeanie, determined to deliver her from this cruel fate. She could in truth have saved her at the trial by swearing that Effie had informed her of her pregnancy, and thus had faced up to her condition. However, pious Jeanie will not tell a lie under oath. Consequently the death sentence is passed.

But Jeanie has learned that royalty can grant reprieves in such cases as Effie's. She therefore undertakes a long, gruelling journey down to London to plead on her behalf. Thanks to Scotland's de facto regent, the Duke of Argyle, she is successful in her mission. He skilfully engineers a meeting between Jeanie and Queen Caroline, who is moved to promise to intercede on Effie's behalf with her husband, King George II. The confrontation of the two women constitutes the climax of the novel. The freed Effie must marry her rogue-Englishman seducer for whom she has, throughout her tribulations, preserved her fondness and achieve, in a further irony, a position in grand society. Jeanie must also marry, and have a family with, her fiancé, a cleric-schoolmaster, gentle, virtuous Reuben Butler. Nor is the Duke of Argyle's role as dispensing *deus ex machina* over; he installs key characters, including the sisters' redoubtable ex-Covenanter father, on his model estate on Roseneath, a 'Highland Arcadia', testifying to Scott's Tory/Hanoverian conviction that only strong but benign government from the top could unify so faction-ridden yet energetic a country as Scotland, which had broken out twice in a half-century into bloody rebellion. Yet Scott's respectful acknowledgement of the hidden currents of human behaviour persists to the novel's end with the unexpected appearance of Effie's wild son by her seducer, the Whistler. He unwittingly kills his own father, but escapes justice by going overseas to North America.

Evidence that *The Heart of Midlothian* entered the creative chambers of Andersen's mind is found in the survival of major elements from it in his fiction, starting with his first novel, and in one of his supreme fairy tales, 'The Snow Queen'. Andersen, now learning the ropes of a refined, cultured section of society with access to the Court itself, must in his heart have welcomed Scott's generous social inclusiveness, from members of the mob storming the Tolbooth, criminals and rejects among them, through the very respectable individuals around whom the central emotional situation revolves and thence upwards to some of the grandest in the precariously united kingdom. There is in Scott a democracy of *emotion*. Whether the person is a fervid Bible-saturated 'cow-feeder' (small dairy-farmer) like David Deans or a sorry criminal turned informer like Ratcliffe, or a sexy flirt like Effie herself or a half-educated, prurient bore like her landlord, Mr Saddletree, Scott will make each express the world of their minds in recognisable, particularised words and speech rhythms. Further, Scott is interested in both people affected by mass sentiment (the Edinburgh mob's vengeance against Porteous) and singly (David Deans's reflections on his errant daughter; Jeanie understanding what she must say on oath because of being 'educated in deep and devout reverence for the name and attributes of the Deity').[66] (In *The Improvisatore* Andersen will show us both the Roman Carnival turned giddy through its Lords of Misrule, and the girl Flaminia attesting to a convent life's superiority to that of the sinful world.) Scott honours the dutiful, the worthy citizens (Jeanie and her husband Reuben) and accords them the dignity they deserve, but he also can empathise with, and give impassioned language to, the unworthy, the lawless, the half-witted, even the mad.

In the stew of promiscuity and crime that we – and Effie and her class-traitor of a young seducer, George – find in Edinburgh, Andersen must have recognised many of his own circumstance-enforced dealings and involuntary encounters in both Odense and Copenhagen. The mad Stine in 'The Apparition at Palnatoke's Grave' marks his first recognition of such galvanic, disturbing figures in Scott as Madge Wildfire and her terrifying mother Meg Murdockson (whose child-killing actions inspired the incident in Andersen's piece of juvenilia, and who comes to a horrifying end). There can be no possible rational discourse with Madge Wildfire, though there may be disquieting psychic parallels between her and ourselves. In Andersen's *oeuvre* she will be there behind Sidsel in *O.T.*, and in the Robber Girl and her dangerous mother in 'The Snow Queen'.

Again, faced with constant enforced admission, to himself and to others, of his own lowly origins, Andersen must have relished the centrality both to Scott's narrative and its moral burden of an uneducated, socially insignificant character. Unremarkable outwardly, unremarkable in intelligence, Jeanie Deans yet has the qualities to serve her principles for which 'heroic' is the only suitable word. In what other novel of the period does a heroine, quite alone, and on behalf of another woman, assume, with total success, the traditional male role of the quester, braving any dangers in the way? (We have to wait for Andersen's own 'The Snow Queen' (1845) for the young hero's venturesome part to be occupied by a girl, the fearless Gerda.) And when Andersen read the outbursts of feeling-charged speech that Scott gives to his Lowland Scots, then he surely recalled comparable women in Odense, and their sisters elsewhere:

In seeming contrast to so much feeling for the vernacular, the illiterate and the semi-literate alike, we have Scott's Tory endorsement, already mentioned, of the power wielded by the Duke of Argyle. This may well have appealed to Andersen too. In his own life, as it was now shaping, what did a poor, rootless boy from an indigenous, largely uneducated section of society need more than some *deus ex machina* to secure his removal from it? And who fulfilled this role more than Jonas Collin who secured for him approval and money from royalty itself? *Ad usus publicos* was an arm of the Court.

Behind Scott's judicial persona of the novelist as historian lies an appreciation of another dimension, however: the numinous, the fruit of Scott's deep knowledge of folklore, both at first hand and acquired through research. Thus his characters do not live only in the here-and-now, but in a more timeless realm which a rich inheritance of songs and stories can make accessible. Of the many instances of this in *The Heart of Midlothian* we have the deathbed of poor Madge Wildfire to which Jeanie is a witness:

But the spirit of melody, which must originally have so strongly possessed this unfortunate young woman, seemed, at every interval of ease, to triumph over her pain and weakness. And it was remarkable, that there could always be traced in her songs something appropriate, though perhaps only obliquely or collaterally so, to her present situation . . .:

Proud Maisie is in the wood,
    Walking so early;
Sweet Robin sits on the bush,
    Singing so rarely.

'Tell me, thou bonny bird,
    When shall I marry me?' –
'When six braw gentlemen
    Kirkward shall carry ye.'[67]

As for the third person of the second trinity, Heinrich Heine (1797–1856),[68] Andersen's introduction to his work was, according to Andersen's own memoirs, yet another major event of this *annus mirabilis*, 1829. It took place in June and through a new young friend of his, intimate with the German language, Orla Lehmann (1810–70),[69] later leader of the Liberal Party and Minister of the Interior. Orla, whose 'sparkling vivacity and eloquence' combined with his 'sensitivity and profound feelings' greatly appealed to Andersen, lived in Valby, in the countryside near the royal castle of Frederiksborg.[70] 'One day I went out to visit Lehmann. . . . And he jubilantly declaimed a verse by Heine as he came to greet me: "Thalatta, Thalatta, Du ewiges Meer." ("Thalatta, Thalatta, you eternal sea.")[71] And now we read Heine together; the afternoon and the evening passed, and the night moved on. I had to stay there until the next morning, but I had got to know a poet who sang as though from my very soul, plucking the most vibrant strings in it.' Certainly the poems he included in his publication of the next January *Digte*[72] (*Poems*, 1830) lyrical, personal, ballad-like, bring Heine to mind, though for us the volume's most interesting item is the prose fairy tale, 'Dødningen, Et fynsk Folkeeventyr' ('The Ghost, A Fyn Folk Tale'), later to be worked into 'Reisekammeraten' ('The Travelling Companion', 1835), one of the finest, the most impassionedly written, of the earlier fairy tales. These poems brought him a certain amount of kudos, and when he toured Jutland in the summer – partly to collect material for a Scott-like historical novel never completed on King Christian II's dwarf[73] – he met responsive audiences who thought of him as an up-and-coming poet. Andersen wrote to Edvard Collin about girl admirers in a disarmingly boastful way that didn't, unfortunately, disarm the recipient.

The development of the relationship between Andersen and the second Collin son is something that must now engage our attention.

6

'The one really important thing I have to talk to you about I have left till last,'[74] Edvard wrote from Copenhagen on 13 July 1830 (Andersen was at that time back in Fyn). 'I was speaking about you to a person in the town who holds you in friendship and respect but who firmly maintained you were, to an unforgivable degree, an egoist and so conceited' ('i en utilgivelig Grad Egoist og saa indbildsk') 'that if one said about a poem of yours that Oehlenschläger could not have written it better, you would think: "That's what I think too, but mine would be the more original poem."' 'Of course,' continued Edvard, 'as your friend, I defended you as you have the right to expect of me. But just because I am your friend, I should point out what's correct in this adverse judgement of you.' And he proceeded to do so with a quote from a recent conversation on this very matter with his own father. The two of them, Edvard told Andersen, were of one mind here, with the father expressing himself in a more robust ('drøjere') fashion. So often Andersen's remarks really annoyed people, Jonas Collin had said. For instance, he himself had remarked that the budding young author would surely want to write a novel like Ingemann's, and got the reply, 'No, God knows, I don't want to do that at all.' If this, Edvard went on, were truly Andersen's opinion (which he hoped it wasn't), then he wouldn't want to embark on so thankless a task as the improvement of a person who thought so ludicrously highly of himself. But whatever his private opinions, it was unwise to ignore those of others, and of these Edvard had a friend's duty to inform him.

Andersen wrote back to Edvard from Odense the very day he got this letter (14 July). A good part of its contents had greatly distressed him. Who *was* this person who viewed him so unfavourably? He might proclaim friendship and respect, but he didn't at all sound as if he wished him well. ('Den Person . . . har ikke ment mig det Godt.') But what clearly upset Andersen most was that *Jonas* Collin was less than wholly pleased with him, something Edvard must himself have calculated on, judging by the way, at once casual and emphatic, in which he referred to his own father. Andersen protests that nobody could be more mindful of his own shortcomings than himself, but of one thing he is convinced: he has literary gifts which, with God's help, he can realise. It's only natural, pleads poor Andersen, to want to take one's place among the good writers of the day, but he well knows that he will always stand way below Oehlenschläger (never would he think himself more original than he) and Ingemann. The letter is not without effusive appeals to its recipient's emotions: 'De er min eneste, sande Ven.' ('You are my only true friend'), he tells Edvard, and the final sentences are a plea for an immediate and, by implication, reassuring reply. He sends greetings to everybody and remains 'Deres altid hengivne Ven', 'Your always devoted friend'.

If Andersen really believed that Edvard was now going to write back a letter exonerating him and completely restoring their easier relations, he made a severe misjudgement. Edvard begins his reply (on 22 July) by telling Andersen, ominously enough, that although he had received his letter In the morning, he'd deferred writing till evening so much had he to say. And say it at length he does, very much the rising young jurist assessing a case and making telling point after telling point.

Most definitely he will not disclose Andersen's critic. That would be a breach of etiquette, and merely satisfy Andersen's curiosity and offended vanity, as well possibly as his wish for revenge. He does concede these are normal enough human responses, but at once takes this back by opining that in Andersen's case curiosity and vanity would triumph over any professional-style reticence. So what was to be done in the face of so many negative verdicts? 'Remember,' Edvard enjoins him, 'the two alternatives I set down in my last letter. Either you actually *are* conceited (which means you are beyond change, except perhaps at the very source of your nature) or you are not, in which case we can address your varying faults.' The tone of the last letter did, he admits, suggest awareness of his deficiencies ('De anatomerer Deres Egoisme' 'You anatomise your egotism') so they can cast aside the first of these alternatives and attend to the second.

At this point we may well wonder how anybody, even the beholden, needy Andersen, could read through a letter of such pompous, self-righteous conde-scension without tearing it up and resolving to have nothing further to do with its sender. Not that Edvard had yet shot his bolt. Having established his generalities, he was now ready to give devastating particulars: Andersen's behaviour at the Bangs', for instance, about which they'd had a long conversa-tion the morning after, proof of his inability to comport himself within a family context and see himself through other eyes. 'Maaske De ikke rigtigt forstaar mig?','Perhaps you don't properly understand me?' When in company Edvard finds the connection ('Forholdet') between them – but he does not deny there is one – 'en Nedværdigelse', 'a degradation', which term could hardly be more wounding, especially to someone as socially and psychologically insecure as Andersen. When Edvard told one of those mysterious 'other people' with whom he discussed his friend that Andersen had enjoyed himself at the Bangs', the reply was yes, because at Hoffmansgave (the Bangs' Copenhagen house), he was able to read all his poems out loud. This habit of Andersen's had got seri-ously on Edvard's nerves. Andersen in his autobiography relates (rebuking himself, not his friend) how at one family gathering Edvard had said to him: 'If you recite a single piece of yours this evening, I shall get up and leave.'

But his epistolary lecture ends with sentences that Andersen, with his fervent, ever-hopeful reading of their relationship, would have been unable to resist:

'Har De kun en eneste sand Ven foruden mig, som ej generer sig for at sige Dem sin Overbevisning, da spørg ham, og De skal se, De faar samme Svar.'

'If you have only one true friend apart from myself, who is not shy to tell you his conviction, then ask him, and you will see, You'll get the same answer.'

It is doubtful whether Andersen followed this advice; instead he sent Edvard a letter full of further apologies for having unwittingly upset people (he was truly sorry about what happened at the Bangs', but perhaps they could forget that episode now?). Edvard had of course been absolutely right not to divulge the name of his uncomplimentary critic, it would have done harm not good. The effusiveness of the whole reply, with the lavish signing-off professions of eternal friendship, would have confirmed anybody's – and particularly Edvard's – view of the author's egotism, but its general drift seems to have been judged more satisfactory than otherwise.

This exchange represents, if in extreme form, the tensions informing the two men's entire – deep and long-lasting – relationship. Behind the manly, legalistic phraseology of Edvard's letters lie real anger and resentment, and we should take *his* feelings on board to arrive at any adequate picture of their relationship. Posterity has ironically rendered the pair as unequal as at the start of their lives, but in reverse proportion. This too can entail injustice. Edvard Collin – a young man of only twenty-two after all – had feelings of his own, and, as the articulacy of his letters demonstrates, a not inconsiderable intelligence and personality.

The most significant words in the last-quoted letter are surely 'Far', 'Father' and "en Nedværdigelse", 'a degradation'. There must have been times when Andersen seemed an invader of a space Edvard had the birthright to think of as private, indeed his very own, and when his father's exigent protégé appeared something of a cuckoo in the nest, and so aroused jealousy. Did he realise just how extremely out of the ordinary, how inapplicable to mundane yardsticks of judgement, this 'connection' wished on him truly was? Probably at first he did not. Yes, he knew Andersen's ambitions were literary, but then (as now) so were those of a good many young men in their twenties, and Golden Age Denmark was kindly disposed to them. But clearly Edvard thought it both ludicrous and objectionable of Andersen to fancy himself the equal, let alone the superior of, such luminaries as Oehlenschläger and Ingemann, both personal friends of his father and therefore members of his own social set.

Even without his high evaluation of himself, Andersen was in other respects hardly a regular fellow, and this most likely was another source of embarrassment to Edvard, one virtually impossible to put into words without being more overtly offensive that he wished. For in addition to those shortcomings in education and bearing which marked him out from Edvard's peer-group companions, well brought up scions of the *haute bourgeoisie* – such as his Odense inability to pronounce the letter 'd' properly – he was gushing in manner, or, as some would term it, effeminate. Certainly he had none of the usual dignified masculine reticence about testifying to his physical or emotional condition, or about attracting attention to himself in public, or bombarding those he met (often, like the Müller brothers, as a result of knowing Edvard himself) with intimate confessions or professions of affection. Even within the Romantic Age, to which the late 1820s/early 1830s essentially belong, and which permitted, even encouraged, a certain emotionalism between young men, Andersen defied the norms. And Edvard's feeling of an exasperating personal encumbrance was only increased when he and his friends turned their attentions, as was obviously inevitable, to the opposite sex, to the rituals of courtship within their own society.

The opposite sex was in Andersen's mind too. Shortly after that last reply to Edvard, he went down to Fåborg,[75] a little port on Fyn's south coast, and called on the town's richest family, the mercantile Voigts, hoping to see a former study-mate of his, Christian, to whom he had grown warmly attached. Christian Voigt was not at home, but his sister Riborg was, and, given her friendly manner and her brown-eyed charm, Andersen found himself strongly attracted to her. Later he told his love in letters, and later still the two met in Copenhagen. There seems never to have been any question of reciprocation: she had a long-standing engagement to a local forester, as Andersen well knew. In his memoir Andersen would confess, 'She was my only thought, but there was disappoint-ment in store for me; she loved someone else and she married him.' 'Not until many years later did I feel and admit that this, too, was the best thing that could happen, both for me and for her.'[76] These are disingenuous words, and the last sentence an exaggeration of the time involved. But certainly for months the delusion acquired its own reality, principally, one assumes, because he didn't or wouldn't recognise that this was what it was, and his ready vociferousness on the subject to friends both mature and young only furthered it. His feelings for Riborg Voigt inspired the poems of his January 1831 collection *Phantasier og Skizzer* (*Fantasies and Sketches*);[77] now subject as well as style could bring the idolised Heine to mind. The first line of 'Bøgetræet' ('The Beechtree') 'Hist står et Bøgetræ paa Højen ene' ('Yonder stands a beech-tree on the height, alone') an analogue of the poet's isolated emotional position, echoed Heine's 'Ein Fichtenbaum steht einsam/Im Norden auf kahler Höh' ('A fir-tree stands soli-tary/In the North on the barren height') in his *Buch der Lieder* (1827). Other poems, no less Heine-like, bespoke the unrequited lover: 'Taaren' ('The Tear'), 'Mit Hjerte er en Himmel graa' ('My heart is a grey sky'), 'Digteren og Amor' ('The Poet and Cupid'), 'Jeg min Kjærlighed maa Dølge' ('I my love must conceal') and, wistfully, 'Kjærlighed' ('Love'): 'Se Solen blusser saa elskovsrød' ('See the sun blushes so passion-red').

Concerned older friends, such as the poet and novelist B.S. Ingemann and H.C. Ørsted, could not fail to notice from his behaviour and his literary productions alike how unhappy this unusual young writer was. But can we really attribute his misery during these months to disappointment over Riborg? Can it even be legitimately considered an affair of the heart at all? And Andersen's saying so persistently how good frustration in love is for any developing poet/writer decidedly diminishes any sense we might have of emotional anguish on his part. The greater truth is, surely, that while Andersen had brought out three books in less than two years and had had a play staged, no small achievement, he had not received the wide glowing appreciation either as a person or as a writer he felt he merited. On the contrary, he was only too often derided, even criticised as under-educated – despite all he had been put through! – with *Journey on Foot* pronounced full of grammatical errors, and the poems bogged down in risibly reiterated adjectives, and superficial, facile and self-indulgent into the bargain. In December 1830 the writer Henrik Hertz (1798–1870)[78] published (anonymously) his witty *Gjengangerbreve* (*Letters from a Ghost*) in which he ridiculed Andersen for the formlessness of his productions. In *My Fairy-Tale Life*, Andersen told his readers: 'I was too sensitive and unforgivably patient. Everyone knew this, and so a small number of people became almost cruel. The bonds of dependence and gratitude were often thoughtfully or unconsciously put to a hard test. Everyone lectured me, and almost everyone said that I was being spoiled by praise so that *they* at least would tell me the truth. Thus I constantly heard of nothing but my own faults, of weaknesses both imagined and real. . . . And at this time I was often so lonely as to be in danger of giving up and perishing because of a lack of confidence in myself and my abilities.'[79]

CHAPTER 2

Germany 1831 and After

1

Andersen could not continue in this state of chronic melancholy; it was injurious to his health. So 'Father Collin' 'believed it would be a good thing for me to go away on a short trip abroad, even if only for a few weeks so that I could move among strangers, tear myself away from my usual surroundings and receive some new impressions. By virtue of hard work and careful living I had managed to save up a small sum of money, and with this I would be able to spend a couple of weeks visiting Northern Germany.'[1] And Ingemann and Ørsted provided him with introductions to Tieck in Dresden and Chamisso in Berlin respectively.

In the autobiography he wrote at his German publisher, Carl Lorck's request – its very title *Das Märchen meines Lebens ohne Dichtung* (*The Fairy Tale of My Life without Poetry*, 1846) evoking Goethe's monumental *Dichtung und Wahrheit*, (*Poetry and Truth*, 1811–33) – Andersen speaks of Germany as 'my second father-land',[2] dating his feeling of kinship to this summer of 1831 when Tieck and Chamisso, both men familiar with his work before meeting him, greeted him as a fellow writer. They, of course, unlike their distinguished Danish friends, had not been witness to his jerky progress from under-educated gaffe-prone neophyte to ambitious (yet still gaffe-prone) fledgling member of Denmark's literati. This was a huge advantage as far as Andersen was concerned. Tieck gave him 'the kiss of consecration'; Chamisso and he 'understood each other from the very beginning'.[3]

The travelogue was an established, indeed positively fashionable genre at this time, and in deciding to write one about his German journey Andersen was bidding to be taken seriously as a prose-writer. The great Danish precedent here was *Labyrinten* (*The Labyrinth*, 1792–93), an account by Jens Baggesen of his European *Helsereise* (journey for health). Baggesen interested Andersen because like himself he had come from a poor background, and had been precocious in youth, only to be entangled later in difficulties with the Danish literary Establishment. (We have seen how in *Journey on Foot* Andersen expected Denmark to be still honouring Baggesen in the year 2129.) 'Everything [in Germany],' he tells us in *My Fairy-Tale Life*, 'surprised me and filled my thoughts. There were still no railways here. A broad, sandy road led across the Lüneburg Heath, which looked just as I imagined after reading about it in Baggesen's much admired *The Labyrinth*.'[4]

But of course a far more potent mentor was his virtual contemporary, Heine whose *Die Harzreise (The Harz Journey)* written in 1824, had been published to real acclaim in 1826, and formed the first instalment of his best-selling *Reisebilder* (*Travel-Pictures* 1826–31).[5] Andersen's title echoes Heine's: *Skyggebilder af en Reise til Harzen, det sachsiske Schweitz etc i Sommeren 1831* (*Shadow Pictures from a Journey to the Harz Mountains, Saxon Switzerland etc in the Summer of 1831*) announcing both the territory common to the two books and their similarities in form, a succession of connected cameos, though Andersen has a novel and personal take on this. Like Heine's his book interpolates verses in the prose.

Andersen made a judicious choice in starting his literary career proper with this work. He started writing up his journey shortly after he got back to Copenhagen, and three months later, in September 1831, *Shadow Pictures* was published. It is a work of real freshness, liveliness and acuity of observation, and if readers straight away thought of Heine as its exemplar, the word 'Skygge' ('Shadow') in the title promises a certain (achieved) originality of approach. They could not have known that it was in itself a portent of one of the great masterpieces of Andersen's middle years, the genesis of which can, in a double sense, actually be traced back to these travels of 1831.

Andersen left Copenhagen for Lübeck on 16 May 1831. According to his diary[6] he woke up that morning to anxiety about a possible storm, and heard a swallow chirping outside his window as though to tell him something. He records that he was later seen off at the quayside by a group of friends, one of whom he calls simply 'Christian' – presumably Christian Voigt,[7] brother of Riborg, who had got married not three weeks before, on 27 April. None of these details appears in the published book, however, any more than does the appalling toothache then plaguing him, as it would do throughout the tour.

Instead he opens with the tyro's problem of how best to write his travelogue, confessing that vanity is the besetting sin of all young writers, so desperate to stand out from the others that they are tempted into self-defeating displays of originality. Before departure he had planned 'a travel drama with overture, prologue and interludes. . . . On the steamship I was bound to come across passengers whom I could hastily turn into instruments. I would make my heart play a minor solo part for the harp.'[8]

Yet as soon as his travels actually begin, he abandons his scheme. The impact of what he is seeing, its newness, its own intrinsic interest, is too strong for so artificial a construct. Instead his mind turns to a popular family entertainment of the day, the positioning of objects or persons between some source of light (such as a lamp) and a larger white surface (such as a wall), so that a play of shadows ensues. Paralleling this, his readers will have the white pages of the book before them, and he, its author, will provide the images, 'but we must bear in mind they are only shadow pictures of reality'.[9]

After a little burst into verse à la Heine, Andersen abruptly and effectively switches to the actual moment of leaving Copenhagen: not merely the true start of his travels but of his entire published *oeuvre*, for it sounds the quintessential Andersen note in its infectiously kinaesthetic sentences:

> But now the steamer, Prindsesse Wilhelmine is departing for Lübeck.
> The coast is already moving! Will it gain a lead over us so that we do not run away from it? No, it is us. The black column of smoke rises from the chimney. The wheels cleave the surface of the water, drawing a long furrow after us in the water.[10]

He was, however, being disingenuous in his proposal of personal abdication from his work. We find veiled and not-so-veiled references to Riborg and his disappointment in love throughout *Shadow Pictures*. In St Blasius's Cathedral, Brunswick, Andersen witnesses a wedding ceremony, and sees in the bride's eyes both joy and sadness. Is she not looking round for somebody? Couldn't that somebody be himself? Near Meissen at night, the young writer catches sight of a young couple kissing: 'This was something I would not have minded doing myself!'[11] he admits. A number of significant Danish readers would have spotted the references immediately. Andersen consoled himself with words from none other than Heine himself: 'Es ist eine alte Geschichte, doch bleibt sie immer neu' ('It is an old story, but remains eternally new'), from one of *Buch der Lieder*'s already best-known songs, 'Ein Jüngling liebt ein Mädchen' ('A young man loves a girl'); it continues 'und wem sie just passieret,/Dem bricht das Herz entzwei' ('and for him to whom it has just happened/it breaks his heart in two').[12]

Andersen is here using quotation to endorse the Heine-like persona he has assumed. He was not actually to meet the poet in person for another two years, and then it was in Paris, to which Heine had moved in April 1831, temporarily and mistakenly judging its July Revolution of 1830 as a victory for Enlightenment. Andersen had personally taken an interest in the July Revolution, was to hear more about the event and its aftermath when he himself visited the city two years hence, and made it play an interesting part in both his second novel *O.T.*, and his third, *Only a Fiddler*. If, however, he is pleased to give hints of matters of the heart linking him to Heine, he most decidedly does not allude in his book to a much longer-lasting, undoubtedly more acute, emotional pain suffered during the course of his German travels.

When he reached Hamburg, he found the courage to write Edvard Collin a letter (dispatched 19 May 1831), as to his greatest friend, to the person he felt closest to in the world, confiding in him the great unhappiness (as an unrequited lover) he was still enduring. In point of fact Edvard, so in the thick of Copenhagen social life, would certainly have already known of Andersen's feelings for Riborg Voigt. 'Of all people, you are the one that I in every respect regard as my true friend. Always be that for me, dear Collin. . . . Say "Du" to me. I could never ask you this in person, it has to be done now, while I'm away!'[13] Real brothers, of course, would automatically use 'Du', the intimate or informal second person singular in Danish, but friends usually had to make a decision to do so, and then initiate the correspondingly new phase of their relationship with the little ceremonial known as 'drikke Dus', 'to drink Dus'.

Andersen must surely, in his habitual hypersensitive way, have worried all German journey long about how Edvard would receive his letter, both bold and honest – and yet, it must be admitted, also a little wheedling, a little too consonant with those gushing apologies of the previous chapter. He would not know the response until 12 June, after he'd arrived in Berlin, and his more morbid fears would then be unforgettably confirmed. Heine's last line about his 'Jüngling', 'it breaks his heart in two', would, in this case, not have been in the least inapt.

Andersen spent three nights in Hamburg,[14] and then went on to Braunschweig (Brunswick) for four more. From Brunswick he travelled to Goslar (25 May),[15] starting-point for his walking tour of the already celebrated, indeed popular Harz Mountains, covering much of the same ground that Heine had done for his own *Harzreise*. Then, after overnight stops in Harzgerode and Eisleben, on to Leipzig. Here he stayed three days before moving forward to Dresden on 2 June where he met Tieck and the distinguished Norwegian painter and art teacher, Johan Christian Dahl (1788–1857),[16] famous for his renderings of mountains. He used Dresden as the base for exploring Saxon Switzerland, so did not depart from the city to head northwards until 10 June. By the 11th he was in Berlin, where he took up the introduction to Chamisso. On 16 June he began the journey back to Hamburg where he passed a further two days. At Lübeck a cholera outbreak detained him for three nights, so that he did not arrive back home in Copenhagen until 24 June.

Andersen's travels took him through member states of the Deutscher Bund (German Confederation)[17] which had come into being in 1815. Denmark was itself a signatory of this union because of Holstein, which nevertheless remained under the Danish crown, just as Hanover remained under the British. (After crossing the Elbe by ferry, Andersen wrote with childlike pride: 'We disembarked and now stood on English soil in the kingdom of Hanover.')[10] Lubeck and Hamburg were Free Cities, the latter looking determinedly westwards, as Andersen's picture of its vigour and social variety indicates. The Grand Duchy of Mecklenburg-Schwerin to the port's east and south was, by contrast, solidly traditionalist.

Andersen then proceeded through the Duchy of Brunswick, and the Kingdoms of Prussia and Saxony. Both these last had undergone major alterations to their territories since 1815. Prussia's huge expansion greatly increased its political status within the Bund, with territory well beyond the Rhine (in consequence a truly 'German river' now), and the absorption of a sizeable portion of Saxony, including the important city of Leipzig. This last was by way of a reward. Saxony, alone of the Bund members, had supported Napoleon, with Saxons fighting alongside French until the disastrous Battle of Leipzig in 1813, during which many deserted; loss of life was considerable on both sides.

'It was a strange sensation,' wrote Andersen, 'as I rolled over the vast Leipzig Plain where every village is so remarkable in military history. This was where the great *Napoleon* had been. This was where the great commander had thought and felt. The corn waved luxuriantly across the immense battlefield yet Nature is the great healer of all wounds! All it takes is a spring to decorate the oldest ruin with flowers and foliage. A new road was being built. I saw human bones and bullets which had been found while the road was being dug. An old groom with a wooden leg sat underneath a tree. He had undoubtedly seen a bit more here than the waving corn in front of him; heard a deeper sound than the birds twittering above him. With his small pipe, he rested and ruminated about days gone by.'[19]

And there follows perhaps the most impressive of the book's poems, which does not yield to brief quotation, a recapturing by this old soldier of grim experiences thirteen years before. Possibly Andersen was remembering here Heine's 'Die Grenadiere' ('The Grenadiers')[20] in his *Buch der Lieder* (1827), but we cannot forget Andersen's own provenance too; how Denmark had been savagely punished by the Allies economically and politically for its alliance with France, how his own father, Hans Andersen, had returned from going to fight for Napoleon a wrecked man to die young. 'Mein Kaiser, Mein Kaiser gefangen!' ('My Emperor, my Emperor taken prisoner!') bemoans Heine's soldier in the aftermath of the Battle of Leipzig. Andersen's disabled survivor has heard a French soldier uttering similar last words.

Dresden, unlike Leipzig, stayed Saxon, and was the capital of the reduced kingdom, a city as active culturally as it was beautiful architecturally. Andersen saw it as a living monument to Peace itself. He must have recalled the evocation of the city in Hoffmann's *The Golden Pot*,[21] though ironically, as he also must have known, Hoffmann himself had experienced Dresden in the grip of armed conflict, and, personally brave, had watched the combat: between soldiers at close range.

'Directly in front of Anselmus the golden yellow waves of the beautiful River Elbe rippled and murmured, while beyond it the magnificent city of Dresden stretched its gleaming spires boldly and proudly into the translucent expanse of the sky which hung over the flowery meadows and fresh green forests, and the jagged peaks half-hidden by twilight announced the far land of Bohemia.'[22]

In Saxon Switzerland Andersen, to his pleasure, actually crossed over into that 'far land' of Bohemia, ruled by Austria–Hungary, which, Prussia excepted, was the greatest power within the Deutscher Bund. Here 'everything around me had an entirely new character; a strange, peculiar mark!'[23] This was on account of the patent Catholicism of the rural communities, with their pictures of Christ or the Madonna over the doors of 'neat, red-painted houses' which delighted rather than shocked him for all his Danish Protestantism, their ubiquitous talent for music ('almost every peasant plays the violin or the flute'), and children delightfully uninhibited in their behaviour. He was to relish similar evidences of Catholicism's appeal to the senses in Italy, as his first epistolary impressions of the country and later his depictions in *The Improvisatore* of Italian mores, both Roman and provincial, abundantly testify. This corner of Bohemia was the southernmost point of his whole journey, and Andersen realised, a little ruefully, 'I, after having been here, would constantly return to the Nordic countries.'[24]

Certainly Andersen did not find the same gratification of his senses in Prussia, least of all in Berlin, its capital. 'Potsdam really gives a pretty good foretaste of Berlin; only Berlin has hardly a green plant outside its gates except for what was put there by order. But then, this is also how the city was founded and is nowadays.'[25]

As for the city itself: 'I cannot help telling you that I did not like Berlin at all! It is set out in order to startle. When you come from the mountains . . . then all this grandeur seems too trite by comparison . . . if I may put it like this: Everything seems so artificial! I just cannot consider form as having top priority.'[26] But we now know another powerful reason why he was not happy in his stay in Berlin, and this we shall examine in due course.

In truth Andersen's negative reaction to Prussian achievement continued after he had left the capital: 'Spandau greeted us with its tall, old walls; practically all its inhabitants, at least those we saw, wore a military uniform; Prussia is truly a country of soldiers where Berlin is the big military barracks.'[27] These words of his must have haunted him with their prescient accuracy during the dreadful Three Years War.

2

Though he gives gentle hints that this visit to Germany might be of a restora-
tive nature to his spirits, and so in that sense, a Baggesen-like *Helsereise* of his
own, Andersen presents himself as someone travelling out of sheer interest,
eager to get the most out of any place he visits, boyishly excited at being abroad
for the first time ever. Moreover his mind contains a reasonable store of information about German writers past and present; indeed *Shadow Pictures* opens
with a quotation in German from Matthias Claudius,[28] poet, 'father of German
popular journalism', and a great friend to Denmark generally, through having
worked in Copenhagen. Only when he reaches first Leipzig, with all its book-
shops and publishers, and then Dresden, home to Tieck and his circle, do we
realise the special intensity of this young man's relationship to literature. But
everywhere he seizes on legend or pieces of folklore with evident pleasure, he
has open and grateful recourse to easily available guides, and relishes mountain
walks and views, the more so when enjoying them in company. When in
Sächsische Schweiz (Saxon Switzerland) he is delighted to visit the zigzag
ravine which inspired the librettist of Weber's *Der Freischütz*,[29] already a
favourite of his, to create its haunting Wolf's Glen scene. In other words
Andersen comes before us frankly and happily as a tourist and a young man on
holiday, even if under the rather bland surface graver feelings and speculations
are active.

Andersen's diary for October 1825 (when at the Latin School at Slagelse)
shows him to have been at twenty an appreciative reader of Tobias Smollett
(1721–71):[30] of *Humphry Clinker* (1771) and *Sir Launcelot Greaves* (1762) to
both of which, however, he still prefers *Roderick Random* (1748) 'a far better
work'. It is easy to see why Andersen, the schoolboy who in years and literary
discernment was not a schoolboy, rated Smollett's first novel above its successors. Its fast pace and picaresque structure, which includes its eponymous hero
living in disguise but eventually marrying the young woman whose beauty had
struck him earlier, left their mark on Andersen's own first novel, *The
Improvisatore*. But the Andersen of *Shadow Pictures* is surely closer to the two
later books by Smollett. Sir Launcelot's instructive sojourns with the insane
might well have come to his mind as he wrote his sincere and affecting account
of the mental patients in Saxon Switzerland's asylum, Sonnenstein. Yet *The
Expedition of Humphry Clinker* is the more discernible ancestor. Smollett's
mellow, basically kindly masterpiece presents travel with its spontaneous
contact with human varieties as a desirable and even a morally instructive end
in itself. Admittedly, Smollett's representative or alter ego in this epistolary
novel, Matthew Bramble,[31] is – like Jens Baggesen in *The Labyrinth* – ostensibly
making his journey, from Wales, through England, up into Scotland, and back

again, for the sake of his health. But, given his general cantankerous valetudi-
narianism, we do not take his problems very seriously. The book celebrates the
constant self-renewal and sense of proportion that travelling brings us, its
unflagging reminders that other people (if only in their own eyes) are as important as oneself, a point perfectly demonstrated by the author's use of letters by
markedly different persons. *Shadow Pictures* – and Andersen's writing often
has something of the excitement, freshness, and lively exaggeration of a good
letter – is a similar celebration.

> We were twenty passengers who left Hamburg together and now our numbers
> had dwindled to six. We now sat next to each other in the large 'Postkutsche'.
> Somehow we formed the six of hearts as there were three hearts on either
> side. The one heart, that is to say, with bodily case and appurtenances, was a
> young student from Hamburg, full of wit and ideas. He found that just now
> we formed a small circle of family members and that therefore we ought to
> know each member closely. We were not asked about our names but which
> country we came from and were given names of some outstanding person,
> man or woman, living there. Because I was Danish, I was given the name of
> Thorvaldsen. The person sitting next to me, a young Englishman, was given
> the name of Shakespeare.[32]

This casual-seeming evocation tells us so much. Andersen has fallen in
easily with the other passengers. In his autobiographies he calls himself 'shy' at
this stage of his life, but in these ordinary enough circumstances he doesn't
seem to be. He clearly was more relaxed when he did not feel he was being
constantly judged, as he too often was in Denmark. The great Danish sculptor
Thorvaldsen, then resident in Rome, and as yet unmet by Andersen, is clearly
sufficiently famous for the motley group to bestow his name on a fellow
national. They all seem without suspicion of one another, amiably and inclusively inquisitive. The war against Napoleon that had torn the continent a
decade and a half earlier, and in which Denmark and Prussia had taken opposite sides, has not, it would seem, resulted in any general bitterness or xeno-
phobia. Is tourism then, as so pleasantly evidenced here, to be a (or even *the*)
major constituent of Europe's economic and social future, a principal means to
a greater harmony? In his major work 'The Ice Maiden' of 1862, Andersen, still
the indefatigable tourist and interested in tourism as such, was much taken
with this possibility; the cultural clashes this entails are at the heart of the story.
And in *Shadow Pictures* he sees the psychic, if not spiritual side of the growing
phenomenon: 'To be a traveller is surely the happiest lot, which is why we all
travel. Everything in the whole universe travels! . . . We are all on a journey.
Even the dead in their quiet graves move with the earth around the sun.'[33]

Tourists welcome the sense of being temporarily delivered from the limitations of their normal conditioned lives and thus enabled, however fleetingly, to glimpse themselves as components of a greater whole. At Blankenburg Andersen meets six theology students whom he joins for a long, demanding walk to the Rosstrappe, 'the wildest, most romantic point in the entire Harz Mountains'.[34] Then their ways diverge:

> When I was halfway down the mountain, they waved their hats and handkerchiefs as a token of farewell. Receiving their 'live well' was strange because it was bound to be the last one from them in this life. Because how were we all to be gathered once again in this world? It is an interesting thought: You meet, get to know people, and then you part forever.[35]

Andersen also responded to individuals, observing or sensing their particularities even within a temporarily homogeneous group. Another traveller in that Hamburg-Brunswick carriage is a girls' school headmistress, with sadness in her eyes even when she is smiling. Her 'Now I'm home!'[36] on arrival in Lüneberg is virtually her first voluntary statement. The other passengers take advantage of the scheduled break in the journey to escort her to her house nearby, but, after they have returned to the coach, Andersen looks back and notices the woman peeking out at them all.

> When the driver blew his horn for us to enter the coach again, I saw light in her room: A shadow moved over the curtain. It was she who glanced at us through the window. Now her journey had come to an end. Perhaps she had been looking forward to it for several years. Perhaps it might stand as one of the brightest moments in her monotonous life. From now on she will probably look back many times with joy on her trip. There is something very touching about such a woman's secluded life. Who knows what pain she harbours in her heart? There are emotions and thoughts which we often do not confide to even our dearest friends. Tomorrow she may begin teaching again, hearing the children in *les verbes réguliers*. '*Aimer, amant, aimé*.' What a lot of memories such a regular verb can contain.[37]

Andersen in no way appropriates this woman; he grants her autonomy, mysterious to him but interesting in its own right. Throughout he does not portray himself as some kind of seer, more as a typical enough young man, pleased at the sight of pretty girls (even though he has conjugated the verb 'to love' to its sad conclusion), glad to take part in adventurous expeditions whether up a mountain or down a mine, but, recalling Smollett's travellers here, just as keen to find comfortable accommodation or a good meal to stoke him up for further sightseeing. On arrival in the old town of Goslar, Andersen gives readers a piece of worldly, anti-romantic, common-sense advice (and common sense was a quality he was never to despise):

> Although you are nothing less than a hero by nature when you write a travelogue, you always become the hero on your own journey. Yet what is a hero without food and drink? When you are on a journey and want to savour nature and the world, you also have to satisfy the body with a solid meal, which is a more important ingredient of enjoyment than you believe. An Englishman once said that it was worth the trouble to travel in order to work up an appetite, and then satisfy it. This was how I felt and followed my intuition and when I had filled my mouth with food, I decided to go for a stroll and look at the sights of Goslar.[38]

Goslar had evoked an even more anti-romantic response in Heine, who came to the town from Göttingen to its south-west, where he was a student (with an already chequered academic history) at the university:

> The name Goslar has such a gladsome ring to it and stirs so many memories of the Emperor that I was expecting an imposing and stately city. But that's how it goes when you glimpse the famous up close! What I found was a one-horse town, a dank, run-down dump with narrow, labyrinthine, winding streets, the pavement as shoddy as that of the Berlin Hexameter, down the middle of which runs a small stream, probably the Gose.[39]

Goslar is the convergence-point for Heine's and Andersen's journeys, as it was, and remains to this day, the centre from which to explore the Harz Mountains, the fault-block range rising steeply from a plain on the south side of the town, with its highest point, the Brocken, celebrated in legend and lore, and 3,744 feet (1,141 metres) high, lying to its south-east. It is at this point that readers would be making the – on the whole solicited – comparison between Andersen and the still young German poet. In fact Andersen had already slyly but directly referred to Heine. For the first stage of his journey out of Hamburg he was placed in a side coach with two of its citizens as companions, one of them Jewish:

> 'Let's be merry,' was the first thing [the Jewish citizen] said almost before he had seated himself. . . . Thus we rolled out of the old city of Hamburg.
>   I mentioned the poet, Heine.
>   'Heine,' he said, 'Heine is certainly a great poet and his brother an important man on the Stock Exchange. Only I find his poems too short, which I don't like. You get a rap over the nose and that's the end of the poem.'

'Yes,' said the other man from Hamburg. 'He's always so ready to give a rap on the nose! He wrote that the Romans and the Italians are so handsome and have regular features and that we Germans have "Kartoffel-Gesichter." Do our faces look like potatoes?' He showed me a face, which honestly resembled a potato. 'I would not,' he added, 'travel with such a person because all of a sudden he could write a whole book about you.'[40]

Both young writers (not so anti-romantic here) are overwhelmed by the wild beauty of the mist-beset Brocken. Both delight in the Brocken Book, in which hikers sleeping over in mountain accommodation had to write down their responses to the scenery. The hearts of both men go out admiringly to miners after descending into the depths where they work. (Andersen contrasts the lives of sailors and miners; sheer space makes the first, for all its dangers, preferable.) The gorge of the Ilse elicits comparable ecstatic homage from the two, both stirred by the tragic legend behind the river. But – 'Beautiful?' quizzes Andersen. 'Not even the artist with his vivid colours can depict nature in its grandeur. How then would it be possible for a poet to do so with words? If tones could become corporeal, then tones could be painted with ink and the pen. Then it would be possible to conjure up the spiritual; that which moves the heart when the physical eye sees a new and wondrous piece of nature.'[41]

We can only wonder what effect the following passage of Heine would have had on Andersen, when looking to the earlier travelogue as exemplary:

It is only through such a deeply contemplative life, through such an immediate rapport between man and his surroundings, that the German fairy tale could come into being, for its uniqueness consists in the fact that not only animals and plants, but also seemingly altogether lifeless things have the capacity to speak and act. For only such contemplative, harmless folk, cloistered away in their forest cottages, in that secret, cosy corner of these low mountains, could fathom the inner life of such things.[42]

Heine might have been describing the stories about tin soldiers, ornamental shepherdesses and chimney-sweeps, tops and balls to which Andersen would before long give creative attention though he could also be referring to the proto-types of these to be found in Hoffmann (e.g. in *Nutcracker and Mouse King*).[43]

But the strength of Andersen's art would also lie (as would Heine's own) in his refusal to ignore pain and frustration even while presenting the beauties of sentient lives and their capacity for mutual tenderness. In Saxon Switzerland he visited Sonnenstein, a progressive sanatorium for the mentally ill:

'Here imagination, this life's best cherub that conjures up an Eden in the desert sand, lifting us on its strong arms above the deepest abyss, over the tallest mountain and into God's glorious heaven, is an awful Chimera whose Medusa head paralyses every common sense, breathing a magical circle around the unfortunate victim, who is thus lost to the world.'[44] And he proceeds to give us vignettes of such empathic poignancy – of the naked man who believes himself a king and swats at flies as troublesome subjects, of the woman who knows herself to have been celebrated by both Tasso and Heine – that we cannot doubt that the writer will go on to works in which the imaginative presentation of diverse and autonomous beings is paramount.

Intellectually and spiritually, nothing in Andersen's German travels of 1831 had a stronger or more lasting effect on his development than his warm reception in Dresden by Ludwig Tieck. The older and the young man must somehow have acknowledged, inwardly and to each other, that in important areas of experience, temperament, ability and outlook, they were kinsmen.

Like Andersen, Tieck had been a prodigy. A rope-maker's son whose first ambition was to go on the stage, he had produced by the time he was twenty-three no fewer than three novels, one a horror story, one (in three volumes) epistolary with a sensationalist plot, and one, *Peter Leberecht*[45] (1795), cast as the eponymous hero's autobiography and including unwitting incest. His prolixity of invention and execution was astonishing, yet his very ease and speed of writing were – as with the young Andersen – a liability as well as an enviable asset. He developed early a great interest in the medieval and Renaissance past, and, under the name of his own character, Peter Lebericht, issued three volumes of *Volksmärchen* (*Folk Tales*, 1797).[46] He also produced *Märchendramen*, harvesting for the stage from the same rich field of ballad and legend; one of these – *Prince Zerbino* – Andersen actually refers to in *Shadow Pictures* as he had already done in *Journey on Foot*. Among later stories of Tieck is a version of *Die Schöne Melusine* (*The Beautiful Melusine*), which had passed into German literature from medieval France, the story of the mermaid who married the Count of Poitiers on condition that he never looked for her on Saturdays. He broke his vow, and so discovered her half-fish identity, thus driving her back into the sea. Obviously Andersen remembered this tale – together with *Undine* (1811) by Friedrich de la Motte Fouqué (1777–1843), friend of both Tieck and Chamisso and of Hoffmann (who composed music for an opera based on it) – when he wrote *The Little Mermaid*.

A work with equal interest for us in tracing Andersen's career is another Tieck novel, *Franz Sternbalds Wanderungen* (*Franz Sternbald's Wanderings*, 1798).[47] Originally planned with his intimate friend, Wilhelm Heinrich Wackenroder (1773–98), art critic and novelist, whose posthumous writings Tieck edited, it was deliberately published as an unfinished work. What Tieck gives us concerns a young painter, Franz Sternbald of lowly origin, who, after studying with Albrecht Dürer, embarks on a journey of discovery, not least as to his identity, for he learns that the poor couple he had believed to be his parents are in fact only his adoptive ones. He journeys through Italy, a country that would become personally dear to Tieck himself, and whose art will have enormous repercussions on his protagonist's own. Franz falls in love with a girl, Marie, whom he sees but once, but who inspires in him something far stronger than the feelings occasioned by the other women he has encountered; and he enjoys the travelling companionship of a dashing and adventurous young man (Florestan). The resemblances that Andersen's first novel, *The Improvisatore* will bear to this story of Tieck's are remarkable, both in actual situations and in its overriding theme of spiritual growth.

The Tieck who befriended Andersen during his visit to Germany was dramaturg for the Dresden Theatre, and involved in Shakespeare studies, strengthened by his visit to England in 1818, and aided by his daughter Dorothea with whom he would give public readings. So here are two further reasons for Andersen's fellow feeling for the older writer: first, admiration for Shakespeare, his own having been stimulated by his friendship with Commodore Wulff and enhanced by rapt reading of the most 'Shakespearean' of all novelists, Walter Scott,[48] and second, a taste (and, matching it, an extraordinary ability) for reading aloud. He will make his first self-representative, Antonio in *The Improvisatore,* a young master of verbal improvisation on stage. Tieck – in addition to being a kindly and hospitable man, who spared no pains in editing after their deaths the works of writers he had admired: not only Wackenrode but Novalis[49] and Heinrich von Kleist[50] – represented precisely the world-view of those German thinkers and writers to whom the central figures of Denmark's Golden Age – Oehlenschläger, Ørsted, Jonas Collin himself – looked up to: Fichte, Schelling, the Schlegel brothers. Even the then ongoing great verse translations of Shakespeare into German with which Tieck was connected (1825–33) had been initiated by August von Schlegel (1767–1845).[51]

There are two particularly charming tributes to Tieck in *Shadow Pictures*, the first occurring before Andersen's account of their meeting but surely – simply because of the subject of Elves, associated with one of the German writer's most famous stories, *Die Elfen* (1812) – reflecting his admiration for the older man's work, while strikingly anticipating subsequent productions of Andersen's own, notably 'Tommelise' ('Thumbelina', 1835):

The long grass straw that was hanging over the broad road covered in dust was the loveliest macadamized road for the tiny elves. Such a tiny, smiling face peeped out from every leaf. The pine trees resembled the most perfect towers of Babel with myriads of elves from the lowest, broad branches to the very top. The whole atmosphere was filled with those marvelous beings, and all were transparent and swift as light. Four or five flower spirits rode on a white butterfly they had driven out of its sleep while others built castles from the strong fragrance and the fine moonbeam.[52]

The second is the actual farewell the two bid each other:

Tieck greeted me in his study and looked me so cordially into my face with his big, wise eyes; I tried to be strong, as I felt the sadness, which was creeping up on me, return more intensely. He seemed to like me, praising the many things he was familiar with of my authorship. Since I had not brought along my own guestbook, he wrote down the following lines on a loose sheet of paper for me as a token of friendship:

'Please remember me also when you are far away. Please move happily and inspired along the pathway of poetry, which you have pursued with such grace and courage. Do not lose heart when sober criticism annoys you. Please remember me to my treasured friend, Ingemann, and all acquaintances. Please return soon to Germany, invigorated, healthy and enriched by the Muses.

Dresden, 10 June 1831.

Your true friend,
Ludwig Tieck.'[53]

3

In Berlin (11–16 June) Andersen's personal/emotional and creative/literary lives converged. He received his anxiously awaited letter from Edvard Collin and he made friends with the distinguished poet, novelist and natural scientist, Adelbert (sometimes 'Adalbert') von Chamisso (1781–1838). Chamisso and Andersen took to each other at once, and possibly Andersen soon appreciated that the best-known book of his new German friend would one day provide the key to how best to fictionalise the misery inflicted on him by his closest Danish one.

Chamisso was born into the French nobility, his parents then fleeing from the Revolution to Prussia. When they chose to return to their native country, their son remained behind, serving in the Prussian army for some years, before devoting himself to literature – in French at first, though it was in German that he achieved his successes – and to science. His novella, *Peter Schlemihls wundersame Geschichte* (*Peter Schlemihl's Wonderful Story*, written 1813, published 1814) was a tremendous success from the first, and has since enjoyed much the same long life as a proverbial crystallisation of existential truth as such Andersen stories as 'The Emperor's New Clothes' or 'The Ugly Duckling'. A work of consummate artistry, indeed perfect in its way, with every sentence contributing to the whole, and of flawless intellectual design, it nevertheless preserves the mystery at its core, building up to an unexpected, logical and thought-provoking conclusion. Chamisso was also a poet – his admiration for Andersen's poetry led him to translate a selection from it – and in this year of 1831 his most enduring poem sequence, *Frauenliebe und – Leben* (*A Woman's Love and Life*) was published. Known to the world now through Robert Schumann's miraculously lovely settings (1840),[54] it impresses us today by doing justice to both the masculine and the feminine standpoints in an emotional relationship. From 1815 to 1818 Chamisso made a round-the-world voyage as a scientist, particularly as a botanist (he was a friend and associate of Alexander Humboldt) and subsequently – 1834–35 – was to write up his diaries and notes from this enterprise. We can imagine how in conversation his accounts of his travels must have fascinated Andersen, who would become so ardent and serious a traveller himself.

But sullying the time in Berlin was the arrival of Edvard Collin's answer to Andersen's beseeching request. It was negative, and, in the light of such letters between them as those we have examined in the last chapter, we could speculate indefinitely as to whether Andersen ever really expected it to be otherwise. What, asked Collin, would be the point of this change in form of address? What good would it do the two of them, what difference would it make to how they stood with one another?

But the matter didn't end there, any more than, in that earlier exchange of letters we looked at, Edvard had been prepared to let Andersen get away without hearing further and uncompromising details of his own reactions to him.

What I am trying to explain are my feelings on the question of saying 'Du' to each other, and this is something I would like to make clear to you. . . . I remember, just one time when, having drunk Dus with a young man at his pressing, I later, after careful consideration, went on addressing him as 'De', and however sad I was at insulting this person I never afterwards regretted it. Why did I do it? It was someone I had known a long time and liked a lot. There was something certain inside me which I cannot explain that made me do it. There are many trivial things [of] which people have what I think is an innate dislike; I knew a woman who disliked wrapping-paper so much that she was sick whenever she saw it – how does one explain such things? But when someone whom I respect and like and have known a long time, asks me to say 'Du', then this nasty and inexplicable feeling surfaces within me. . . . Let us speak no more about it. I hope we shall both forget this mutual exchange. When you come back I shall be in Jutland, so we shall not see each other till the winter. There could never be any question of my being angry at your request. I do not misunderstand you, and I hope you will not misunderstand me either.[55]

Certainly Andersen never did forget 'this mutual exchange', whatever Edvard Collin might 'hope'. On the contrary, it is no exaggeration to state that Andersen never got over this refusal, the very wording of which would memorably surface in that most intensely felt, and uncompromisingly revelatory of his stories, 'The Shadow', arguably the single most impressive artefact for which this German visit was emotionally and artistically responsible. Of course to Edvard himself, Andersen sent back a warm, understanding, characteristically self-abasing letter, intended both to vindicate himself and to inspire remorse in its recipient: 'Yes, indeed I love you as a brother, thank you for every line! – No, I do not misunderstand you, I am unable even to become sad, for you open your heart in so honest a way to me. If only I had your character, your whole personality!'[56] There can surely be no mistaking the sincerity of this last exclamation, whether one accepts Jens Andersen's attribution of crafty disingenuousness to the writer or not. This was a *cri de coeur* that was to resound inside Andersen and his writing for the rest of his life. We shall hear its echo in both *The Improvisatore* and *O.T.* For we cannot doubt he would profoundly have liked to have resembled Edvard Collin, handsome, masculine in a traditional mould, and so at home in the society into which he had been born that he did not need to look beyond it, if indeed he ever did so.

In one sense the rebuff was, as Edvard himself predicted, not greatly to alter either man's life externally. They remained close for the rest of their long lives – albeit with varying shifts in that closeness, and with a caesura at the time of the wedding of Edvard and Jette, later so especially dear a friend. . . . But back in 1831 Andersen felt utterly devastated, his very social identity, achieved with such difficulty, cruelly struck at. For this is surely the real point. Didn't social class lie behind Edvard Collin's denial of him, and therefore the whole ontological question of where fate had elected to place him in the world? Andersen may indeed have felt himself, at twenty-six, after only a few years of familiarity, a member of the Collin family, and therefore Edvard's true brother. But whatever their affection and regard for him, this letter received in Berlin proved conclusively that the feeling was not reciprocal. And the exclusion was articulated by the family member – 'Father' Collin excepted – most important to him. Beyond doubt Andersen carried the wound of Edvard's coolly polite but absolutely unambiguous letter of rejection for the rest of his life, referring to it repeatedly in letters and in conversation. And Edvard for his part remained steadfast in his use of the formal 'De' to Andersen, to the end of his friend's days.

If Edvard's denial makes no kind of appearance in his 1831 travelogue, it can be no coincidence whatever that, fifteen years later, when he at last felt able to make it central to an imaginative story, Andersen turned to the greatest literary achievement of the man who, by contrast, had irradiated his Berlin visit, and given him both personal and intellectual admiration: Chamisso's novella about the loss of a shadow, *Peter Schlemihl's Wonderful Story*.

Here a young man is persuaded by a man in grey to part with his shadow in exchange for Fortunatus's Purse. But he finds he cannot live with the consequences of this unhappy bargain. How 'The Shadow' reworks Chamisso's story (acknowledging in an unmistakable phrase that this is what he is doing) will be deferred till we reach this masterpiece in the course of our journey through Andersen's *oeuvre*. Now we can only note that the story will rebuke not just Edvard (with whom by now he was on largely excellent terms) but Andersen himself for acceding to the whole hierarchical social caste system, with its destructive effects on individuals and their mutual dealings. But its galvanic tensions – of shifting class relations, of irreversible changes in public manners and private relationships – are also those of its time of composition, 'the eve' of the 1848 revolutions which convulsed France, Germany and Italy, and which were to bring about the transformation of Andersen and Edvard's own Denmark, still almost two decades away.

4

And what overall impression has Andersen formed of the mainland continent he has visited for the first time? He tries to tell us: 'We are moving in strides towards a new and better era. Yet Europe needs to fight. But first of all, the wild lava must seethe from the mountain before it can carry the rich vines of peace and prosperity. A *sensible* independence coupled with natural enlightenment will then spread its gentle summer breeze over the nations. Then the new Gimle will rise behind the fighting Ragnarkr (Ragnarök). Our time is also interesting! It is wonderful to see how nature and minds are in strong ferment. We are all working towards the common goal.'[57]

This interesting passage surely means more than it actually says (or more than its young writer is yet adequately able to articulate). Why does Europe *need* to fight? What is this 'wild lava'? The humbled and discontented Saxons? The suffering Poles squeezed between Prussia and Russia, and referred to in the text? The latent problems of the Double Duchy, Schleswig-Holstein? The view of progress here is, as we have already seen, one that Andersen will never altogether relinquish. But Ragnarök[58] with Gimle[59] arising afterwards . . .? Nordic mythology was becoming increasingly central to Dano-Scandinavian thinking, thanks eminently to N.F.S. Grundtvig,[60] author of major books on Nordic mythology (1801 and 1809) and in key respects a social progressive, and of course to Oehlenschläger himself. Indeed we can see the reference to Gimle as a kind of homage to these two writers, for later Andersen was – as we shall see in his 'Det nye Aahundredes Musa' ('The New Century's Muse'

1861) – to become decidedly equivocal about the uses ancient myth could be put to. But now, here, he evokes Ragnarök, the appalling preordained darkness of the gods, when (to quote Snorri Sturluson) 'brothers will kill brothers for the sake of greed, and neither father nor son will be spared in the killings and the collapse of kinship'[61] – and the wolf will swallow the sun. But after such blood-shedding chaos will come Gimle. Snorri again:

> At the southern reaches of heaven's end is a hall, the most beautiful of them all and brighter than the sun. It is called Gimle. It will remain standing when both heaven and earth are gone, and good and righteous men will inhabit that place through all ages.[62]

Hindsight can indeed tragically locate Ragnarök in mid-twentieth-century Europe. It can also find something of the ideals of Gimle in the welfare-based social democracies that the Scandinavian countries began to build up in the nineteenth century and which would flourish in the twentieth.

'Please return soon to Germany, invigorated, healthy and enriched by the Muses,' Tieck had implored him. And yet despite this good advice from someone whose opinion he now greatly valued, Andersen did not move, to quote from the letter again, 'happily and inspired', nor always with 'grace and courage', in the two years following the successful publication of *Shadow Pictures* (19 September 1831). The Home of Homes was still the centre of his personal life; Edvard and he, the former's letter of rejection notwithstanding, went about together as comrades, more so than ever, it would appear. But in fact this increase in inclusion created further problems for Andersen. His feelings of friendship for Louise Collin,[63] pretty, kind, appreciative, intelligent, turned into something stronger, hard actually to name as 'love' though it may have seemed to be this to Andersen himself, and certainly did to her watchful elder sister, Ingeborg Drewsen. Andersen wrote to Louise copiously (letters which were intercepted and read by other family members), and for her he composed that first (never completed) memoir, *The Book of Life/The Biography*. This was not a development that was at all welcomed within the Home of Homes. In the words of Ejnar Stig Askgaard: 'Edvard Collin was *appalled* at the very idea that Andersen could marry his *sister!*'[64] and he bestirred himself to see that he did not. Ejnar considers social class as *the* main factor in Andersen's never marrying at all. (By the time he was rich and famous, the women he was most drawn to – the great singer, Jenny Lind, for example – were significantly younger and looked for husbands nearer their own age. Besides, he was more and more incurably a bachelor in habits and outlook. But of course in that bachelorhood profound sexual unease surely also played a determining role.)

Louise Collin became engaged to W. Lind, an auditor, early in 1833, though the two did not marry until 1840. Andersen – who was to honour Louise in his first two novels, in the second of which (*O.T.*) he called her by her real first name – subsequently fell into deepest depression.

He had not been unproductive. If *Shadow Pictures* had no immediate successor to win over the Copenhagen literati, he still had no cause to be rueful, let alone apologetic. He wrote his libretto for *The Bride of Lammermoor* (first performance 13 May 1832)[65] and a singspiel *Ravnen* (*The Raven,*[66] first performance 29 October 1832) with a score by J.P.E. Hartmann, (1805–1900)[67] marking *his* opera-debut. This work greatly impressed a future distinguished friend of Andersen's who would also set verses by him to music: Robert Schumann, who praised it in his highly influential *Neue Zeitschrift für Musik*. And in December Andersen published a beautiful poem-sequence: *Aarets tolv Maaneder, tegnet med Blæk og Pen (The Year's Twelve Months, drawn with ink and pen).*[68] Partly as a consequence of this publication he became the recipient of more funding from *ad usus publicos*.

A further shadow over his existence was the serious deterioration of his mother. In December 1831 he made arrangements that she be provided by the almshouse with food rather than cash which he knew she would only spend on drink. She protested at this but was forced to accept his terms. He visited Odense in the summer of the following year. 17 July 1832 was the last time he ever saw the woman who had given him birth and whose image he never forgot. Anne Marie was to die while he was away on the long European journey he judged (for the second time) needful if he were to put his palpable miseries into an acceptable perspective. 'I was a child until I was beyond youth', he wrote at this time, 'I've never really experienced what youth was. I feel a desperate need and desire to tear myself away from whims and habits, and as a sensible person enjoy life; there is so much I want to forget, to learn something better.'[69]

He left Copenhagen on 22 April 1833 and did not return until 3 August 1834.[70] In Paris, where he stayed over three months, he met Heine for the first time and also Victor Hugo. On 15 August he embarked on a journey to Switzerland where he stayed for three weeks, in Le Lôcle in the Jura, with the family of Jules Houret, watchmaker and brother of a Copenhagen friend. His sojourn there is of enormous importance for the student of Andersen's works, because it awoke a feeling for and interest in Switzerland that, many years hence, would inform one of his most profound creations, 'The Ice Maiden' (1861). He entered Italy via the Simplon Pass on 19 September. He would recall the approach to the wild pass in an important passage of *O.T.* In his diary he exhibits a wholly genuine, indeed very personal, response to Alpine grandeur which is nevertheless very much that of contemporary Romanticism:

The weather turned bad; the valley was hidden by clouds and the mountain-tops as well. You could only see the middle section of the slopes where we were driving. Waterfall after waterfall; then we came to the first gallery, a hollowed-out place in the rock through which the road runs, with only a deep, dark abyss on one side filled with fir trees that had grown to a monstrous height and stuck up like flimsy sticks out of the wall of the cliff. The conductor told us that he had this winter seen a bear walking right across the road and growling a little.[71]

It was 18 October when he arrived in Rome, and he stayed there until 12 February 1834, when he departed for Naples. When he left, he had learned if not 'something better' than anything Denmark had taught him, then how, through expansion of himself and his mental horizons, to review his past while maintaining attentiveness to people and places around him. Sven Hakon Rossel's '*Do You Know The Land, Where the Lemon Trees Bloom?*' *Hans Christian Andersen and Italy* (2009)[72] is indispensable for its account of the awakening that Italy was for Andersen, as for so many Nordic artists. Chief among these stands Bertel Thorvaldsen, and fittingly it was in Rome that the great Danish sculptor (at the time still resident there) and the great Danish writer entered on their deep reciprocal friendship. Just as Thorvaldsen[73] used annually to celebrate 8 March as his 'Roman birthday', the date of his arrival in 1797, Andersen, one sometimes feels, would have been justified in doing likewise. In Rome friendships among fellow artists flourished, including one with the sharp-tongued, sensuous, even lubricious Henrik Hertz[74] whom Andersen forgave for his unkind printed humour at his expense, and got to like, and another with a not altogether dissimilar character, and quite possibly the single most gifted student of Dresden's Norwegian painter/teacher, Johan Christian Dahl. This was Thomas Fearnley[75] (1802–42) also Norwegian, though with an English (Yorkshire) paternal grandfather. Fearnley's lifestyle and his landscape paintings, at once romantic and scrupulous, and often part-done *en plein air*, greatly impressed him. (Still, Andersen couldn't help observing that these Scandinavians with whom he associated were not quite as interested in one another's well-being as they liked to make out. But they could at important times be bulwarks against loneliness or self-doubt, and even positively supportive.) Among its many merits Rossel's book conveys in detail Andersen's now ever-expanding knowledge and understanding of the visual arts. One has the feeling that, though always latent, these needed Italy and the presence there of articulate practitioners to be brought out, becoming a major component of his intellectual personality. . . . News from, and contact by letter with, Denmark and the Collin family could bring shade to the Italian sunshine, at times distressingly engulfing, but ultimately dispersible.

But for this study the most important fact about Rome is that we owe to the city the novel *The Improvisatore* (to be published in April 1835), which was to change Andersen's fortunes, and indeed the very nature of the corpus under examination. It is an interactive affair we are now confronting: Italy imposed on Andersen its unique allure and complexity, and in return Andersen was stimulated first to stretch his capabilities and then to impose a cohesion on them as he had never managed to do before.

CHAPTER 3

The Improvisatore

1

On 27 December 1833 Andersen wrote in his diary:

> People are saying here there was a complete eclipse of the moon last
> night. Suddenly everything turned dark, and the moon looked like a big
> mushroom. – Went for a stroll with Hertz to S. Pietro in Vincoli and saw the
> statue of Moses. There was almost no one in the church, but lovely music.
> Was up at S. Maria in Aracoeli. Portraits of nuns and monks were hanging
> between each pillar. The Christ Child was displayed in cloth-of-gold.
> It's taken around to the sick, and soldiers shoulder their arms in honour
> of it. – On the stairs people were selling pictures of it; I bought one for four
> *baiocci*. Was in the church of S. Maria degli Angeli – it is a veritable picture
> gallery. Began this evening on my novel *The Improvisatore*. Today, and I was
> comparing Italy with back home, Hertz said: 'God only knows how it will go
> for us when we get back home. There, it is much too different, indeed.'[1]

This entry tells us more about the novel begun that day than perhaps even
its writer at the time appreciated. The total eclipse of the moon – which
apparently he himself did not witness – must have recalled recent news
that had turned everything temporarily dark: on Monday 16 December he got
a letter from Jonas Collin telling him his mother had died. 'My first reaction
was,' he'd noted, 'Thanks be to God! Now there is an end to her sufferings,
which I haven't been able to allay. But even so I cannot get used to the thought
that I am so utterly alone without a single person who must love me because of
the bond of blood.'[2] Both his mother, divided between two characters, and the
de facto father who informed him of her death will appear in the book now
under way.

Andersen writes up his diary in Rome very much as he'd done in Germany, as a tireless, intellectually curious sightseer always glad of instructors, especially if they were also practising artists. Of the Roman buildings mentioned above, S. Pietro in Vincoli displays the chains that allegedly shackled the founder of the Church himself, St Peter, perhaps in Jerusalem, perhaps in Rome. But most visitors, like Hertz and Andersen here, go there to see Michelangelo's great horned statue of Moses. Into its bearded face the sculptor incorporated a likeness of himself – just as Andersen put himself quite unmistakably into his novel's protagonist/narrator, an Italian though he be. The third church cited, S. Maria degli Angeli was actually designed by Michelangelo. But it is S. Maria in Aracoeli which has the decisive role to play in the novel. Before its image of the Christ Child the hero, aged nine, will give public testimony to his faith. His entrancing performance is eclipsed by that of only one other child, a little girl who will grow up in confused circumstances and become the famous singer Annunziata, and the hero's first love. Of this great church, on the site of which the Emperor Octavian/Augustus supposedly had a prognostic vision of the Virgin and her son, Georgina Masson, architectural historian of Rome, writes:

> The Aracoeli is perhaps the most typically Roman of all Roman churches. Rising above the ruins of a temple dedicated to a pagan mother-goddess and now consecrated to the Madonna – a transformation which is far from rare in Italy – its interior provides a perfect illustration of the continuity of Roman life, with its magnificent columns that once graced classical temples and palaces. . . . Simply to walk round the church is like turning the pages of a history of Rome. . . . Before leaving the Aracoeli we must pay our respects to the 'Santo Bambino', that curious little figure said to have been carved out of the wood of one of the olive trees of the Garden of Gethsemane, which is so revered and loved by the Roman populace. Except at Christmas, he stands in a glass case above the altar of a small chapel of the sacristy when he is not out bringing comfort to the sick and dying in the hospitals of Rome.[3]

The Improvisatore begins and ends with a blessed child.

But the most interesting item in the diary entry is Andersen's name for his novel. This shows that the figure of an improvisatore (an Italian improvising performance-artist) was part of its very inception. Here again the diary entry for 16 December is illuminating. Andersen also heard that day from J.L. Heiberg who, always equivocal and sometimes dismissive about Andersen's work, expressed misgivings about the two singspiels submitted to him. To him, thought Andersen, 'I am just an improvisatore'.[4] Not for the first time in public or private history the recipient of an adverse judgement converted a disparaging term into an honorific one. Andersen knew from Goethe's *Italian Journey* and Madame de Staël's novel *Corinne* (1807) that improvisatori were not to be despised, were inventive, lively entertainers worthy of the name 'artist'. If this was what he was thought to be, then he would celebrate his identity by writing as though a member of this fraternity. Paradoxically *The Improvisatore* could scarcely be less of a work of improvisation. On the contrary, it is outstanding in its original and meticulously executed design, which in itself is meaningful.

In truth nothing in Andersen's previous productions – even the most touching of the poems or the most imaginative of the *Shadow Pictures* – prepares us for *The Improvisatore*. In addition to its structural beauty, this is a first-person narrative frankly and singlemindedly concerned with the narrator's successive stages of development. It takes us through the gamut of psychological states: security and severance, grief and solace, fear and trust, despair and happiness, rejection and fulfilment, identifying with each but seeing them as contributing to a larger whole. The author, through the medium of Antonio, has attempted, and at a time of personal crisis, nothing less than an operation on his own life. Prolonged separation from a Danish milieu (the Collins and their circle), to which he was at once too close and vulnerably ambivalent, must have assisted inestimably. As did the sheer force, both sensuous and intellectually stimulating, of Italy's impact on him. He was far from alone among artists of northern provenance; all those he consorted with on a virtually daily basis would have felt similarly re-educated. With hindsight we can see that, only by recasting himself as an Italian, by allowing his sojourn in Rome and Naples and his journeys through the Italian peninsula to penetrate and be absorbed into his psyche, could Andersen have arrived at that level of understanding – of himself, of other people and their motivation, and the physical world in which they have their being – so essential for the creation of serious literature. The willed indulgence in emotions supposedly suitable for a poet, the over-ardent local-colourism, the slightly arch facetiousness and taste for whimsicalities that can mar poems and whole passages of *Journey on Foot* and *Shadow Pictures* have all gone. Now in his novel he can discover – and concentrate on – what had so far eluded him: satisfactory correlatives in people and predicaments for difficult truths of existence to which he had already faced up.

The Improvisatore presents itself as its central figure's autobiography. Antonio informs us in the very opening paragraph of his birthplace's precise location: Rome, the corner of Piazza Barberini and Via Felice, in full sight of one of Bernini's masterworks, the famous Triton Fountain. And in its last pages he relates what occurred on a specified, recent date, 6 March 1834: his return to the Blue Grotto of Capri with the woman now his wife and the mother of his daughter, whom he had first encountered there, living in poverty. *The*

Improvisatore covers therefore three decades of experience, and if it ends with Antonio happy in marriage and fatherhood, this return to Capri is evoked so that we may appreciate – as the narrator himself does – that we should take nothing for granted. Nature holds sway over life and administers death. Human beings are emphatically *not* in control of their destinies, even though, for the most part, they have it in them to make the best of their natural attributes and gifts. The dangerous waters can always rise and inundate the grotto, as the final paragraphs warn us. But this stark truth has already been brought home by the many tragedies, unanticipated, distressing and sometimes violent, in the novel's course, beginning with the cruel death, in Antonio's childhood, of his widowed mother, killed by a cart pulled by runaway horses during the Flower Festival at Genzano. Yet the recovery of the past through artful narrative can soothe, if not heal, experiential sorrows. Like Wordsworth's *The Prelude* (1805 and 1850), *The Improvisatore* is the history of the 'growth' of a 'mind', one shaped by external events and persons but also by its own reception of these; Antonio's narrative establishes points of reference, associations, concordances, as motifs to reassert themselves, in one form or another, later on.

Antonio strives for complete honesty with his readers about his personal make-up. He records criticisms of himself made by others, and supplies (usually) qualified agreement; here Andersen is answering all those admonishing voices back in Copenhagen. He admits to vulnerability to particular temptations, starting with vanity from his earliest years, and to limitations of capability; he confesses to errors made. Yet he is also concerned to demonstrate the fluidity of personality as he describes his own constant adaptation to the movement of time and to the unheralded varieties of situations this inevitably brings. He addresses us in a voice which takes mutability as a given. So while it rises to those occasions which dramatically manifest this truth – the bewildering moments after his mother's death, his first excursion to Capri, his last sight of his once beloved Annunziata – it never relinquishes its hard-earned maturity, its sense of happenstance or of the unsought exigencies of place, each with its own complexity of connections. In these two last respects Andersen surely learned from Scott's *The Heart of Midlothian*, with the reverses faced by the Deans family and Reuben Butler, and the apparent coincidences that disrupt Jeanie's journey from Edinburgh to London, all testifying to a universal truth: that even while venturing into the new, one encounters the past, and often in its most recalcitrant and troubling shapes. As he sought analogues for his own almost thirty-year-long journey, Andersen found himself gaining in a self-confidence that (as diary entries admit) had become bruised by too much anxiety to conciliate the Collins, Edvard above all. He was becoming ever more his own man, an assurance intimately bound up with his sense of himself as *artist*. Regular association in Rome's Scandinavian circle with others similarly dedicated fostered this, and in particular his growing friendship with Thorvaldsen whose phenomenal mind was able to do justice to Andersen's own, to an extent that so far only Ørsted had managed.

Andersen's belief in his novel as purveyor of truth is evidenced in the *sui generis* construction referred to in its subtitle 'Roman i To Deele' ('Novel in Two Parts'): two mutually reflecting entities, presenting incidents and encounters both complementing and inverting each other. Its strict adherence to this patterning – like a two-movement symphony wrought from intimately related thematic material – renders the literary terms most often favoured for it – *Bildungsroman, Künstlerroman* – less than satisfactory. Yes, of course, its subject matter parallels that of Goethe's *Wilhelm Meister* (1795–96 and 1821–29), Antonio undergoing both the apprenticeship and the necessary wanderings chronicled in that mighty sequence. But it is on Antonio's authority that we rely for their presentation. He it is, the final evolved individual, who selects for us what to him appears really important in his history; he it is who determines what should be emphasised or explained, who assesses the quality of particular experiences, becoming more personally confidential when the subject matter requires this. And here we arrive at a second paradox. While, as stated above, the art of *The Improvisatore* is severely and knowingly under authorial control so that there are no superfluous episodes or characters, these more intimately revelatory passages do in literal fact recall the medium at the novel's symbolic centre and honoured in its title: the improvisatore's. And they make Antonio's own triumphs in it both credible and imaginatively engaging. Also, with our minds still on *Wilhelm Meister*, it doesn't seem frivolously obvious to point out that while Goethe's is a work of monumental proportions, *The Improvisatore*, though certainly a novel and not a novella, is, by most nineteenth-century standards rather short, the length – to move ahead to Dickens who, as we shall examine, was surely influenced by it – of the more concentrated *Hard Times* and *A Tale of Two Cities* rather than, say, of its nearer relation, *David Copperfield*. Andersen's knowledge right from the start of what his book was called shows he thought of it as an organic whole unified by the profession named in the title and vividly described in the second chapter.

One moon-bright evening, Antonio and his mother have made their way homewards from a visit to the Trastevere quarter of Rome and come to the square of the Trevi Fountain. Street-vendors are still offering their goods; noisy conversation is in spate. Then a country fellow arrives with a guitar improvising a song in celebration of his surroundings. He is, little Antonio is told, an improvisatore, and such is the man's impact on the child – whose own disposition has already been revealed to us through his splendid performance in S. Maria in Aracoeli – that he then and there emulates him, singing inspirationally of the wares in the grocer's shop opposite.

It is not hard to understand the fascination, stoked by his readings of Goethe and Madame de Staël, felt by Andersen – the wunderkind in Odense so given to recitation, so incurable an addict of vaudeville and theatre – for the phenomenon of the improvisatori (sometimes spelt improvvisatori). With medieval and Renaissance ancestry and increasingly popular in the later years of the eighteenth century, they enjoyed a heyday in the first three decades of the nineteenth, appealing hugely to the Romantic imagination so enamoured of spontaneity and folk art, and peaking around 1840.[5] Antonio, at the applauded height of his own improvisational powers, is specifically likened to the most famous virtuoso of them all, Tommaso Sgricci (1789–1836) whose gifts impressed Percy Bysshe Shelley, Lord Byron and Madame de Staël herself, not least for the libertarian sentiments he expressed. To the Andersen who had applauded France's July Revolution this would have been a point greatly in his favour.

Frequently improvisatori performed in a street or marketplace with a ready-made audience of passers-by and shoppers. But they also gave demonstrations at private salons, or (usually after having built up a reasonable public reputa-tion) in proper theatres, as Sgricci himself did, or, in the novel's second part, Antonio, in the renowned San Carlo, Naples, playing to a packed, clamouring, rapturous house. The usual procedure followed is conveyed accurately enough by Antonio in the chapter on his own Neapolitan debut. Members of the audi-ence would write on slips of paper words or phrases they wanted the artist to use as starting-point for his improvisations. As a rule – as in San Carlo in the novel – these would be vetted by a representative of the police force to ensure that nothing too seditious or inflammatory was being requested (especially in view of Sgricci's known radicalism). The improvisatore himself would then make his choice. Antonio, for instance, is stumped by the invitation to speak on 'il cavalier servente' (he hasn't yet enjoyed a love-life) and 'Capri' (which he has not visited), but 'Fata morgana' appeals to him, almost instantly arousing from mental depths long-dormant ideas and images.[6] Once he has embarked on the improvisation, he (like his peers in the art) simply cannot stop the flow of verbal pictures, anecdotes, associations and rhetorical exclamations, speaking not so much ad-lib as under the possession of his chosen (but ramified) topic. In Antonio's case the audience is ecstatic, and he in turn is moved by both its response and by his own ability to have brought this about.

It was a brilliantly appropriate art form in which to make Antonio excel, in the first place because it was peculiar to Italy and therefore related to traditions and practices – emotive and inclusive Catholic ceremonial, rococo architec-ture, bel canto opera – which had already struck Andersen as representing a pronouncedly different outlook on life from that dominant in Protestant Northern Europe, one characterised by Mediterranean expansiveness not

Danish reticence and concomitant horror of the exhibitionistic. (We recall: 'I was comparing Italy with back home, Hertz said: "God only knows how it will go for us when we get back home. There, it is much too different, indeed." ')[7] But, for all its encouragement by some ambitious hostesses, this improvisation was emphatically demotic, a quality Andersen would later attribute to The New Century's Muse (who, he says, inherited it from her father). It therefore awoke in Andersen memories of the conversations, lore and improvised stories of a less convention-bound and guarded section of his own Danish people: Odense's variegated, superstitious, promiscuous working class. More importantly, it served as a metaphor for his own boundless-seeming creativity so prone to overwhelm himself and overpower others.

Andersen never really resolved (as how could he?) the questions raised by the lavishness of his own talents, as we shall see when we come to the ambiguities of 'The Ugly Duckling'. Is everybody *au fond* an improvisatore (or a beautiful swan), if in need of some external force to draw out what's already present but occluded? Or is the artist an exceptional being, operating under different laws from everybody else, capable of producing, and for the enrichment of others, perspectives, colour combinations, sounds, unions of words, even hypotheses and ideas that ordinary people could never have arrived at on their own? And it has to be admitted that in the case of Antonio, while we see and believe in the enthusiasm accorded his performances, and can enjoy the flights of fancy responsible for these, we do not end up knowing just how remarkable an artist he is. (As remarkable as his creator or merely an interesting brother of the Italian countryman who improvised by the Trevi Fountain?) The sharp-tongued Francesca reminds Antonio that there is a world of difference between a successful evening and serious, consistent creativity. Members of the Collin family (Ingeborg, Edvard, Louise) had repeatedly reminded Andersen likewise, and perhaps he faced these doubts deliberately implanted in him too often and too disconcertingly for him to make any reasonably objective assessment of his own gifts.

The doubts spill out into Andersen's presentation of Antonio's experiences outside performance art. He is accused – particularly by the friend most important to him, Bernardo – of being so different from other young men that he scarcely knows what the genus is like. His abilities, his values, his aspirations, even his temptations are not theirs; they are more exalted, more spiritual. Often this does seem to be the case, but not always; Antonio enjoys company, travel, the jollities of festival and street-life, and increasingly the sight of a pretty girl, all pleasurable mainstays of normal young males. And yet . . . he himself knows in his heart that he does stand apart from them, that deep within but indestructible are psychic regions they could not, and would not care to, enter. So the novel is informed by hesitancy over any pronouncement of exceptionalism, a hesitancy we shall encounter in subsequent work; it is equally there in *O.T.* and in Andersen's last novel, *Lucky Peer*. However, our doubts on this matter do not detract from this novel's impact. Rather we realise its ambivalences come from genuine, honestly admitted irresolution.

2

Part One of the novel takes us through the vicissitudes of Antonio's early life until that moment when his youth comes dramatically to an end. Its first two chapters constitute a wonderful fusion of the exterior and the interior, of a child's responsive, often uncomprehending yet ever-enlarging view of the land- and cityscapes all about him and his incorporation of them into his sense of self. In Part Two, Antonio forsakes Rome and its environs for another region, another Italy, another life. And yet what he has learned in his first years never ceases to be of the greatest assistance to him. With Wordsworth in *The Prelude* Antonio could truly say 'Fair seed-time had my soul, and I grew up/Foster'd alike by beauty and by fear,'[9] the beauty lying initially not so much in the splendours of Rome itself as in the affection given him by his widowed mother, a seamstress (there is a conspicuous absence of interest in his paternity) and by her lodger, a young Dane known as Federigo.

Federigo has a young girl as model, the warm-hearted Mariuccia, a great help to Antonio at a key juncture in his life. But as a child he is repelled by her, as indeed he is, he confesses, by all the girls and women he meets. This obvious antipathy on his part gives rise to a general idea that he has a priestly vocation, and while Antonio explicitly exempts his mother from his aversions, the reader questions whether she might not be a principal cause of them. She does not stay in the novel long, a fact revealing in itself. Andersen then transfers her maternal virtues to the countrywoman who takes his narrator in after her sudden death. Many women calling themselves seamstresses had in bleak reality less respectable-sounding occupations, and what exactly *was* an easy-going young Danish artist doing living in this small artisan apartment (though he and Antonio's mother, we are told, actually sleep in separate rooms)? One thinks of the trouble the cramped quarters of his mother and her second husband had brought Andersen as a youth. For much of the novel's first part, and indeed in important pages afterwards, Antonio recoils from the female sex, especially when members of it approach him with overt sensuality (conspicuously Santa, so transparently and unkindly based on Headmaster Meisling's propositioning wife). Perhaps Andersen is remembering here that image of his earlier self as a tallow candle dirtied by worldly experience integral to the fairy tale written in his schooldays. An important measure of Antonio's education in *The Improvisatore* does indeed relate to effective relationships with women – with Annunziata (whom he has met, at the age of nine, as the wondrously accomplished little girl in S. Maria in Aracoeli), with Flaminia destined to be a nun, with the girl in Amalfi as drawn to him as he to her, and, to conclude, with Lara/Maria with whom the novel rewards him. But we may well feel in this last case that she is not substantial enough a figure to elicit belief as an autonomous, and therefore lovable, human being, deriving as she does a little too palpably from Marie in Tieck's *Franz Sternbald's Wanderings*.[9]

If Antonio endows his whole native neighbourhood – beyond which his mother rarely strays – with the warm intimacy of her own person, he also learns fear here, every bit as durable a lesson: through the neighbourhood church with the metal crucifix on its door, through the convent with its secret colonnaded garden, and through what leads off this, a gallery crammed with skulls and skeletons among which the little boy is told he will one day, like every other mortal, take his place. Here too is his detested Uncle Peppo, of the two withered legs, who sits on the Spanish Steps begging passers-by and molesting rival supplicants. Federigo also takes Antonio on expeditions outside the city gates, unforgettably to the solemn subterranean labyrinth of the Catacombs, where they become, to their alarm, temporarily entrapped. Afterwards the proximity of another (spiritual) domain, challenging all comfortable conventions, is conveyed in the scenes in Genzano before Antonio's mother is killed. An old wise-woman, Fulvia virtually wills into physical exist-ence a terrifying contest on the legend-hallowed lake of Nemi: an eagle swoops down on to a fish, the two creatures struggle fiercely, then both disappear into the waters where they perish. Both the old woman and the alarming scene will recur in Part Two of the novel, having been assimilated into that inner world of images and subconscious intimations which plays so determining a role in Antonio's as in all our life stories.

After the death of his mother the pattern of Antonio's life is irrevocably broken, and nothing shows the radically interior preoccupations of this novel more vividly than the very first sentence of Chapter IV: 'Hvad skulde der nu egenlig gjøres ved mig, det var Spørgsmaalet....'[10] 'What should really now be done with me, that was the question...' Such a question would be entirely in place in *Jane Eyre* or *David Copperfield*, both of which this novel, thirteen years their senior, frequently brings to mind. What follows takes us to the lowest point in Antonio's life, informed not only by his grief but by desolation, helplessness. To share the sordid, dishonest lifestyle of Uncle Peppo would be terrible, though the account of the beggars' mores contributes to the novel's overall meaning: the true artist – an Antonio, a Bertel Thorvaldsen, a Hans Christian Andersen – will always turn out to have had a particular empirical as well as imaginative relation to the unfortunate, the disinherited. He is not limited to the bland, prosperous society of the Collins' circle, and his knowledge of the world's human varieties is – for all his apparent innocence – far greater than theirs.

Antonio is happily delivered out of the mendicant life, but his time with the humble of this earth has not come to an end. Mariuccia arranges for him to go to the Campagna, to her parents; he must honour them as his mother and father. It is possible surely to link Mariuccia, from whose easy femininity Antonio has recoiled but who proves a sterling character, with Andersen's sister Karen Marie, and so to see this episode as a righting of the emotional/social wrongs he had done her in his heart. Andersen always declared Domenica to be a portrait of his own mother (with, though this he did *not* say, her character defects removed), and Domenica was, after all, Mariuccia's flesh-and-blood mother as well as his hero's adoptive one.

Before he leaves for the Campagna, Antonio has an extraordinary vision of the Roman past, of representative figures haunting the Capitoline Hill and the Colosseum, gladiators, soldiers, tormentors of beasts and unfortunate humans. Nothing in *The Improvisatore* is there by accident; these scenes, evidence of Andersen's basic meliorism, of those values to be purveyed later in 'The New Century's Muse' are given us as a warning. What was fine in the past must be respected, but it must never obscure its darker aspect. The artist's duty is primarily to serve the present, to make way for a brighter future. This tenet is, if you like, a complete and essential antidote to the prevalent Romantic tendency to worship all that lay furthest from what they regarded as the mounting worldliness of their age.

We can find something of the same fidelity to realities of existence in the two chapters concerned with Antonio's rural life with Domenica and her husband, Benedetto. Painter after painter had honoured the Campagna on canvas, and even in his reflective, ambiguous poem of 1855, 'Two in the Campagna', Robert Browning was moved to apostrophise:

The champaign with its endless fleece
    Of feathery grasses everywhere!
Silence and passion, joy and peace,
    An everlasting wash of air –
Rome's ghost since her decease.

Such life there, through such lengths of hours,
    Such miracles performed in play,
Such primal naked forms of flowers,
    Such letting nature have her way
While Heaven looks from its towers.[11]

'Letting nature have her way ...' It is a ruthless, uncaring way according to Andersen/Antonio who, passing through these 'champaigns', burned up by unremitting sun and crowded with thistles, looked out at a harsh landscape imposing on people equally harsh means of eking out a livelihood. Andersen had little to no extended experience of country living, he had never depended on the weather or worried about what it did to natural resources or how it affected sheep and buffalo; his would always be essentially an urban life. Nonetheless, he looked at the Campagna not with a tourist's or an amateur painter's eyes but with a realist's, and saw the difficulties existence there would entail and their effect on a burgeoning sensibility such as Antonio's. In the two months of high summer the boy feels, in the isolated peasants' house, as though aboard a ship wrecked on the world's sea. He and his foster-parents are the scorching heat's captives, able to carry out tasks only at night, when they fervently pray for rain. Not until November do these circumstances change. And in these altered conditions an accident brings to the remote croft a stranger, clearly from a noble family, who is soon entranced by young Antonio's abilities – to read and understand what he has read, to draw, and to make improvisations. This man, the Eccellenza, goes on to summon the unusual youngster to Rome, to the Palazzo Borghese to meet his family, which includes a daughter Francesca and the man who becomes her husband, Fabiani (*sic*). So struck are they by Antonio that it is agreed with Domenica that they should adopt him and pay for his education at a leading (Jesuit) school.

The concurrence of Antonio's and Andersen's lives will be obvious to all, and who among Denmark's cultured class reading of a stuck-up, self-inflated school principal jealous of his more gifted pupils, holding preposterous intellectual views, and mockingly named Habbas Dahdah, could have failed to spot Dr Simon Meisling? Or to identify Eccellenza with Father Collin and the Palazzo with the Home of Homes, and Francesca and Fabiani with Ingeborg and Adolph Drewsen, hospitable, virtuous but (truer of Ingeborg than her husband) censorious too? Yet we are persuaded – through a wealth of convincing details about church and city life – that these individuals are Italians, with behind them a more ceremonious, tradition-steeped culture than the Danish. This is evidenced above all in the treatment of the daughter born to Francesca and Fabiani, Flaminia, dedicated from the cradle as a Bride of Christ. Antonio, who gets to know her well and becomes fond of her, initially resents this imposition of a destiny on her, but comes not only to accept it, but to feel its moral beauty, its intrinsic rightness for this particular girl.

The emotional dynamics of the novel derive from Antonio's relationship with Bernardo, a Senator's nephew and thus a privileged pupil at Habbas Dahdah's elitist school, and with the girl Bernardo falls for, the singer Annunziata, supposedly Jewish and an acquaintance from Antonio's childhood: she had been that wondrously accomplished little girl of obscure provenance in S. Maria in Aracoeli whose art surpassed his own. Bernardo is a galvanising, commanding presence in Part One, and a palpable absence in Part Two; glimpses of him fail to lead to direct confrontation until the very last chapter of all. The dashing young man, with his aura of conscious Byronism, his jubilant flirtatiousness, his high-class impertinence, his cavalier social manner as befits one who knows he is of high rank and arresting appearance, does not, it must be admitted, in the slightest suggest the solid, respectable, industrious Edvard Collin, as we have come post-humously to know him. But Antonio's attitudes to Bernardo – his open admira-tion, his anxiousness to stand in his good esteem, his insistence that they are profoundly, eternally, uniquely friends (and as members of the same academy-school they, unlike their prototypes, use 'Du' to each other quite naturally, from the start) – are unmistakably those of Andersen to Edvard. Were we in any doubt on this matter we have only to turn to his letters to his friend, and to diary entries, extracts from which have already been quoted. In such passages as the following, significant to plot development, we can hear echoes not only of Andersen himself but of Edvard's responses to him:

> 'Vi ere meget forskjellige, Bernardo!' sagde jeg, 'og dog hænger mit Hjerte forunderligt ved Dig, tidt ønsker jeg, at vi altid kunde være sammen.'
> 'Det vilde være daarligt for Venskabet,' svarede han, '. . . . Venskab er som Kjærlighed, det bliver stærkest ved Skilsmissen . . .'[12]
> 'We are extremely different, Bernardo,' I said, 'and yet my heart clings strangely to you, at times I wish we could be always together.'
> 'That would be bad for [our] friendship,' he answered '. . . Friendship is like love, it becomes strongest with separation.'

With yet greater exasperation Bernardo rebuffs his friend's imploring confes-sions of feeling:

> 'Og hvad din Hengivenhed angaaer, den Du altid omtaler, saa forstaaer jeg det ikke; vi give hinanden Haanden, vi ere Venner, fornuftige Venner, men dine Begreber ere overspændte, mig maa Du tage, som jeg er.'[13]
> 'And as regards your devotion which you are always talking about, I don't really understand it; we give each other the hand, we are friends, sensible friends, but your notions are overstretched, you must take me as I am.'

It was surely in just this spirit that Edvard wrote his never-forgotten, never-forgiven letter of June 1831 refusing the intimate second person that here Bernardo actually employs.

Yet Andersen, I feel, conflates Edvard with two companions of his Italian residence: Henrik Hertz and the Norwegian painter Thomas Fearnley, who by
both precept and example endeavoured to make their friend less sexually diffi-
dent. In the following passage Bernardo has noted that his bashful, virginal
friend looks with decided interest at the opposite sex:

> 'Du begynder jo alt at blive et Menneske,' sagde Bernardo, 'et Menneske, som
> vi Andre, og har dog endnu kun nippet til Bægeret. . . . Du er jo ogsaa af disse
> aandelige Amphibier, man ikke veed, om de egenlig høre Legem- eller
> Drømmeverdenen til.'[14]
>
>   'You're beginning to become a man,' said Bernardo, 'a man like us others,
> and yet have only just now sipped from the cup. . . . You are also one of these
> spiritual amphibians, one doesn't know whether they belong to the body or
> the dream world.'

Bernardo and Antonio fall in love with the same woman, Annunziata,
which, in his Byronic superiority, causes the more sophisticated of the pair
some amusement:

> 'Jeg kunde have Lyst at see, hvor rødt dit Blod er, Antonio; men jeg er et
> fornuftigt Menneske, Du er min Ven, min oprigtige Ven! Vi ville ikke slaaes,
> selv om vi mødtes paa samme Elskovs Eventyr.'[15]
>
>   'I have a longing to see how red your blood is, Antonio; but I am a reasonable
> man, you are my friend, my sincere friend! We will not fight, even if we are
> bound on the same love adventure.'

   Antonio's blood, however, is red enough for him to take on Bernardo in a
duel, during which the pistol given him for the purpose by the young Byronist
himself goes off, wounding his adversary (fatally, it is mistakenly and briefly
thought). The visually compelling snappiness of this scene – learned, one
suspects, from similar climactic scenes in Scott – is sufficient to make it acceptable. More acceptable still, because animated by strong currents in the author's
own emotional personality, is Antonio's horrified supposition that he has killed
his greatest friend. And with this duel Antonio's virginity can be said to end.
Despite his understandable reputation for belonging more to the spirit than to
the flesh, he proves his manhood in the very testing-ground traditional for the
young male – for the sake of love, self-defence and honour. As a consequence
he is forced to flee Rome – and in doing so finds himself in lonely marsh
country, as pertinent symbolically as it is challenging physically. Marsh is an
in-between realm where water and earth meet in uneasy, often treacherous
union, where fugitives can disappear for ever. It is also a second womb, but safe

rebirth, even once the waters have broken, cannot be guaranteed. Andersen declared himself 'a swamp-plant', and, from now on in his *oeuvre*, marshes will persistently recur. The haunting rendering here of the Pontine Marshes marks their first appearance.

Antonio's successful struggle to get out of them opens Part Two *of the novel*. Once he has the marshland behind him, and can take the road again thanks to the help of social outcasts in the form of a robber band, Antonio can begin Part Two *of his life*. Temporarily in forced exile from Rome, he has been provided with a new passport for frontier guards. And so, accompanied by his old friend, the Danish painter, Federigo, his mother's former lodger, he bids goodbye to his native part of Italy, the Papal States, in favour of the very different Kingdom of the Two Sicilies. Here he makes his way to its capital, Naples, then the Italian peninsula's largest city and indeed the third largest in Europe.[16]

To what extent can Antonio, adventurous as he now appears, still be thought a 'swamp-plant', an amphibian? Even in the novel's second part there is agreement that he is not like other men, and the episodes connecting Antonio to the blind girl, and to the beautiful Maria whom she grows into, never sufficiently escape from the Tieck-inspired romantic glow cast over them to become serious scenes of man–woman love.

As an improvisatore Antonio's only peer, we are told, is the great Tommaso Sgricci himself. It is hard to believe that Andersen and his more sophisticated readers (such as members of the artistic circles he frequented in Rome) did not know Sgricci's sensational reputation.

In the words of Byron, his most famous admirer, he was 'a celebrated Sodomite'.[17] Great fame and influential patrons protected him from getting into trouble for his most flagrant antics – cruising the streets of Florence at night flamboyant in gait and attire – but the Italians were generally easy-going about erotic matters, unlike Europeans further north. Were Antonio's ecstatically received improvisations – like those of Sgricci himself – charged with androgynous exuberance, expressive of the artist's release of all his frustration at his uncertain socio-sexual identity? (For it is clear from those exchanges with Bernardo that, when not giving lively rein to his inspirations, Antonio is aloof, even asexual in manner.) Yet to offset this one has to say that, at the height of his fame as an improvisatore, Antonio is both more attracted by and attractive to women than when in Rome as a protégé of Eccellenza and his family. Only too tragically late does he learn that Annunziata was in love with himself and not Bernardo, whom she proceeded to take as second best. The later Antonio would have not been so imperceptive about women's feelings.

And one cannot but feel that Antonio is more confident of his masculinity after separation from his overweening, arrogant friend, and that his creator, knowing this to be so, simply dared not risk writing confrontation scenes for fear of diminishing this quality. When at last the old friends do meet again, in the concluding chapter – in Milan, by Napoleon's triumphal arch, the Porta Sempione, with Bernardo heading for Switzerland and Antonio turning in the opposite geographical direction, towards marriage and life on a small country property, and with neither mentioning the woman they both loved – we sense that no subsequent rapprochement is psychologically necessary to either man, that rapprochement indeed may well never occur.

Bernardo, once a Papal Rider, belongs essentially to Rome, wherever his destiny finally delivers him, while Antonio is permanently changed by experience of the very different Naples. When we turn to the first *Eventyr* (fairy-tale) we shall find a successful analogue for this.

3

Entering Naples, Antonio is delighted by the hugger-mugger of its street life: the card game played by two scantily clad men crouching by a brazier, the barrel-organs, the hurdy-gurdies, all the singing and shouting and rushing round, and a contest for the crowd's attention between a monk and a puppet -theatre inside which Punchinello jumps about. He defines his reaction thus: 'Jeg følte mig henflyttet i en ganske anden Verden; et sydligere Liv end det, jeg havde kjendt. . . .'[18] 'I felt myself transported to a truly other world; a more southern life than that I had known. . . .' The woman in the same conveyance as he – the sensually inclined Santa – is delighted to be back here. 'Signora klappede i Hænderne for sit lystige Neapel; Rom var en Grav mod hendes leende By.'[19] 'The Signora clapped her hands at her merry Naples; Rome was a grave compared with her laughing city.'

Rome is of course not a grave, neither has Antonio presented his birthplace as one, but we can tell from this quotation that he feels the Signora's observation to contain a defensible truth. Rome centres round the Church and those administering it, and this we have felt in both the working-class scenes which open the novel and those dealing with the Jesuit School and the Palazzo Borghese. Assuming his hero to be Andersen's exact contemporary – we can back this up with the 1834 date supplied in the concluding chapter – then from the age of nine, the year in which he first encountered the girl Annunziata in S. Maria in Aracoeli (1814), Antonio would have grown up at the epicentre of the Papal States, handed back to actual Papal control after the Congress of Vienna's dismemberment of Napoleonic Italy. Rome was a highly conservative, not to say reactionary, society. (To this we might add that, very different as Denmark was from the Papal States, Andersen may well have seen and intended a – not derogatory – parallel between the Eccellenza's closeness to Vatican hierarchy and Jonas Collin's to his own country's Absolute Monarchy.) After the defeat of

Napoleon Naples became the capital of the Kingdom of the Two Sicilies under Ferdinand I (formerly Ferdinand IV of Naples and III of Sicily). Rigid border control – accurately depicted in the novel – meant that Naples scarcely did any trade with the Papal States, relying on exports to other European powers including Britain. The historian David Gilmour (in *The Pursuit of Italy*, 2011) feels that its indubitable later shortcomings have obscured some more positive features of the Kingdom in general and of Naples in particular:

> Naples in fact enjoyed a number of industrial 'firsts'. It possessed the largest shipyards in Italy, it launched the first peninsular steamboat (1818) and it enjoyed the largest merchant marine in the Mediterranean; it also built the first iron suspension bridge in Italy, constructed the first Italian railways [by contrast the Papal States vetoed the railway] and was among the first Italian cities to use gas for street lighting.[20]

Andersen arrived in Naples on 16 February and didn't return to Rome until 20 March, when he came back for the Easter he evokes so vividly in his novel. The more southern city's palpable erotic appeal (greater than Rome's) he registered extremely quickly. Within three days (by 19 February) he was recording:

> In the dusk of the evening I was surrounded by a bunch of pimps who wished to recommend to me a *bella donna*. I've noticed that the climate is affecting my blood – I felt a raging passion, but resisted. – God only knows what Hertz [who had accompanied him] was up to when I got home! The room was locked, and when I knocked on the door he came out and, speaking to me outside the door, apologized for the fact that I couldn't come in.[21]

Andersen makes many entries to the effect that he is sexually aroused to the brink of capitulation, then finally succeeds in self-mastery. A man accosts him and asks whether he wants a *ragazza* or a *ragazzo*; it is interesting that he troubles to note this down. But even bearing in mind Naples's reputation for homosexual pleasures, Andersen's interests appear to have focused on the other sex. He makes Antonio emerge from the city's pervasive sensuality better able to relate to women than before, more frankly, more personally.

Andersen's own rapt reception of the celebrated Malibran in the title role of Bellini's *Norma* at the Teatro San Carlo (23 February 1834) convinced him of the vitality of the city's cultural life. And, in truth, that great Spanish diva, Maria Felicita Malibran (1808–36)[22] was the direct inspiration for Annunziata, who is, after Antonio himself, even allowing for some melodrama in her eruptions into the narrative, the novel's greatest triumph in characterisation. It contains nothing more moving than the sight (and sound) of her seven/eight years later in a flyblown little theatre in Venice. She is now singing a supporting, not a lead, role and is uncertain in her tonal register. A member of the audience actually compares her as she was in her prime, so different to her present emaciated condition, with Malibran. Antonio seeks her out, and comes to learn of her previous love for him. This situation of a man who once adored a singer seeing her, after years of separation, on stage in an Italian opera house (in this instance La Scala, Milan) will recur in a fine later story inspired by Andersen's friendship with an even greater opera singer, Jenny Lind: 'Under piletræet' ('Under the Willow-tree,' 1853).[23] But there the diva is an acclaimed success about to marry another man, and Knud the hero realises the hopelessness of his emotions and with a heavy heart sets off home to Denmark.

From the very day of their arrival in Naples Andersen and his Antonio are fascinated by Vesuvius, and its magnificent and menacing domination of the city. Andersen's first diary entry from Naples contains this:

> While I was sitting in my room at dusk, waiting for the others . . . I heard all of a sudden a strange sound in the air, like when several doors are slammed all at once, but with a supernatural power. I pricked up my ears; right away the sound came again. It's Vesuvius erupting, I thought and ran over to the square. It wasn't spewing any column of fire, but one side of the mountain was a river of fire flowing downward, and the crater was burning like a bonfire.[24]

An hour or so later Andersen is given a night-time rooftop view of 'Vesuvius, which was overflowing with red lava'.

Antonio on *his* first day in Naples also gazes from his bedroom's balcony through the darkness at the mountain. Watching it, even from this safe distance, is, he at once knows, a spiritual as well as a sensory experience, begging the unanswerable questions of why such an agent of death-dealing destruction exists in a world made by an allegedly benevolent Deity and why this agent appears so tremendous, even ennobling, as to render such doubts redundant: 'Min Sjæl var greben ved det store Skuespil, Gudsstemmen, som talte fra Vulkanen, som fra den still, tause Nathimmel.'[25] 'My soul was held by the great spectacle, the voice of God which issued from the volcano, as from the still, silent night-sky.'

Such instinctual reverence demands an expedition to the volcano itself, and to the two famed cities destroyed by its violent eruptions, Herculaneum and Pompeii. So Antonio undertakes one with his companions and thus brings about his history's supreme moment of self-understanding. The impact of the once-buried cities has been strong enough – so lively a culture, such low expectation on the part of their inhabitants that their priorities and their everyday business, their pleasures and their civic and domestic achievements would not extend indefinitely into an unmapped future, and that instead a few instants of activity on Nature's part would put a stop to it all for ever. Antonio, unlike his companions, does not concern himself overmuch with the letters of Tacitus and Pliny or with Bayardi's ten folio volumes on the 'Antique Monuments of Herculaneum'. Instead he prefers to brood on *Respice finem* 'Remember the end!' The party leaves the ascent of Vesuvius until evening, when, in the moonlight, the glowing lava would show to best advantage. In, for me, the most powerful and persuasive prose Andersen had yet composed, Antonio tells of the transforming effect of the volcano on his receptive if inadequately prepared personality. He feels naked terror, for the savage force before him is real, unstoppable, life-threatening, and dangerous, no mere opportunity for aesthetic sensation. But he also cries out to the huge, fierce, active crater:

'Mægtige Gud, din Apostel vil jeg være! i Verdensstormen vil jeg synge dit Navn, din Kraft og Herlighed. . . . Digter er jeg; forleen mig Kraft, bevar min Sjæl reen, som din Naturens Præst bør eie den.'[26]

'Almighty God, I will be your Apostle. In the world's storm I will sing your name, your power and glory. . . . I am a poet; give me power, keep my soul pure, as your Nature's priest ought to have it.'

And it is as a result of these exalted moments on the mountain top that the young man gives the most impassioned – and impassioning – improvisation of his life so far, to private friends but of such quality that his next move must obviously be a public performance. This takes place at the Teatro San Carlo itself, and solicits rapture from the audience. It is perhaps the single most discomfiting feature of Andersen both as man and writer – and of his principal character surrogates – that acclaim was so vital to their well-being, so indispensable to identity. Certainly here the applauded Antonio feels he has attained a veritable apotheosis of his own essential self:

Næste Morgen var jeg for Federigo et nyfødt Menneske, jeg kunde udtale min Glæde, det kunde jeg ei Aftenen forud; Livet rundt om tiltalte mig mere, jeg følte mig ældre, syntes at være mere modnet ved den Opmuntringsdug, der var faldet paa mit Livstræ.[27]

Next morning I stood before Federigo a newborn man, I could express my happiness which I could not do before that evening; the life all round appealed to me more, I felt myself older, seemed to be more mature through the encouragement which had fallen on the tree of my life.

Antonio's experience of Vesuvius has one further, equally significant sequel. A stream of erupted lava flows into one of the outlying urban districts of Naples, and he decides to take a boat to the resonantly named Torre del Annunziata to be out of its molten wake. But even on the far side of the shore there is danger, and a statue of the Madonna is caught by the ensuing fire. A woman rushes to rescue the image, a foolish, potentially lethal act from which she is rescued by the sudden action of a dashing young man – Bernardo himself. But Antonio, even in these extreme circumstances, cannot bear to confront him. He turns and finds himself face to face with members of his adoptive Roman family, Fabiani and Francesca. This omnium-gatherum of characters, executed with a painterly chiaroscuro, has a dramatic vividness once again reminiscent of Scott. These people, all emotionally important to Antonio, have entered his life, not as a result of his conscious exertions, but by their chance placement on his route through time. Likewise the eruption of Vesuvius is an act of Nature not suscep-tible to human orders. The fiery light it sheds on persons and surroundings illuminates the alarming truth that we all are at the mercy of the non-human. This is the ultimate lesson *The Improvisatore*, right up to its last scene in the Blue Grotto, has to teach us, and it uses Italian geography – as well as Italian dramatis personae – to bring it convincingly home.[28]

If the nineteenth century's greatest writer of Danish prose was in Naples in 1834, so was the nineteenth century's greatest Italian poet, Giacomo Leopardi (1798–1837). After racking emotional unhappiness, with unrequited love its major component, he moved to Naples on 2 October 1833, to make his home with his friend, Antonio Ranieri who would stay with him until his death just under four years later. In provenance Leopardi could not present a bigger contrast to Andersen: he came from a well-to-do, aristocratic, ultramontane Catholic family in Recanati, in the Marche region of the Papal States. But in other respects – disconcerting precocity, abiding restlessness, essential solitude of spirit, unflagging angst and ceaseless creativity (in the Italian's case exer-cising itself on philosophic prose as well as on the far better-known poetry) – the similarities between the two are remarkable.

Vesuvius, and the Roman cities its effluence had buried and extinguished, fascinated the poet as much as they did the novelist. In 1836, obliged to leave central Naples because of an outbreak of cholera, Leopardi and Ranieri, together with Ranieri's sister, took a villa at the base of the volcano between Torre del Greco and the Torre del Annunziata of Andersen's novel. From his awed contemplation of the mountainside Leopardi wrote one of his most profound meditative poems: 'La Ginestra o Il Fiore del Deserto', 'Broom or the Flower of the Desert', broom being, as the poem makes clear, able to flourish in conditions which defy other plants, despite itself being vulnerable.

Qui su l'arida schiena
Del formidabil monte
Sterminator Vesevo,
La qual null' altro allegra arbor nè fiore,
Tuoi cespi solitari intorno spargi,
Odorata ginestra,
Contenta dei deserti . . .

Here on the dry flank
Of the terrifying mountain,
Vesuvius the destroyer,
Which no other tree or flower brightens,
You spread your solitary thickets,
Scented broom,
At home in the deserts. . . (translation Jonathan Galassi)[29]

Like Andersen, Leopardi is moved to think how entire societies, deceived into believing themselves permanent, could in mere instants be wiped out. Though himself inclined to the progressive ideals later espoused by the architects and champions of Il Risorgimento – the title indeed of another of his major poems – the writer feels they cannot, should not constitute the basis of any faith. Don't they ignore the destructive power within Nature conditioning our existence? Nor should religion recite the beauties and benevolence of God's creation. 'in cura/All' amante natura' 'in the care/Of loving Nature' is a regrettable, unwise sentiment, because founded on a many-times proven untruth. Rather Nature is 'la dura nutrice', 'the hard-hearted nurse' which can turn on those in its charge, 'Annichilare in tutto', 'to destroy everything'. Perhaps however the spectacle and the knowledge of this power could bring people together more closely, more lovingly, for mutual protection's sake. We pause in our thoughts and . . .

Caggiono i regni intanto,
Passan genti e linguaggi; ella nol vede:
E l'uom d'eternità s'arroga il vanto.

Meanwhile kingdoms fall,
Languages and peoples die; she doesn't see.
Yet man takes it upon himself to praise eternity.[30]

Better for oneself, for a whole people (for a nation like emerging Italy) to take as its rallying symbol a plant like the beautiful broom growing on the slopes of

Vesuvius, its only aim limited self-accommodation, its very being sweetness. The poem concludes,

Ma più saggia, ma tanto
Meno inferma dell' uom, quanto le frali
Tue stirpi non credesti
O dal fato o da te fatte immortali.

No, far wiser and less fallible
Than man is, you did not presume
That either fate or you had made
Your fragile kind immortal.[31]

Andersen was always, passionately to cherish a belief in immortality. But in truth the attitude to existence permeating the end of this stupendous Italian poem and that informing the end of the novel (in Capri's Blue Grotto) are the same: an anti-heroic stoicism which is itself a form of heroism.

The Improvisatore came out 9 April 1835 to plaudits. On 8 May there appeared a booklet of four stories by the same author, *Eventyr, fortalte for Børn* (*Fairy Tales told for Children*). These were 'Fyrtøiet' ('The Tinder-Box'), 'Lille Claus og store Claus' ('Little Claus and Big Claus'), 'Prinsessen paa Ærten' ('The Princess on the Pea') and 'Den lille Idas Blomster' ('Little Ida's Flowers'). And on 16 December a second booklet of fairy tales (three in all) was published: 'Tommelise' ('Thumbelina'), 'Den uartige Dreng' ('The Naughty Boy'),[32] 'Reisekammeraten' ('The Travelling Companion'). Ørsted, Andersen recorded, in a judgement that has rightly gone down in literary history, 'says that if *The Improvisatore* will make me famous, my fairy tales will make me immortal, for they are the most perfect of all that I have written'. He did not at the time agree, and neither did many critics. But posterity has sided with Ørsted. All the same *The Improvisatore* deserves a much firmer place in literary history than it now occupies. It is a truly *European* novel, in which a sensibility nurtured in one culture identifies with that begotten and reared in another, and is stimulated by the differences between them to appreciate and then to demonstrate the profundities of kinship.

Even while waiting for the publication of his first novel and his first fairy-tale booklet, Andersen was hard at work on another novel, *O.T.* (1836). This was duly received with interest as a novel about Denmark and recognisable people there, in distinction to its predecessor with its Italian settings and characters. So, jumping strict chronology, we shall deal with Andersen's second novel in the next chapter.

CHAPTER 4

O.T.

1

The eponymous initials *O.T.* stand for the novel's protagonist, Otto Thostrup, and also for Odense Tugthus, Odense Gaol. Here, surprisingly, this son of the landed gentry was born and passed his first years. His memories of the grim institution are dim, patchy, and camouflaged by his subsequent life on his grandfather's Jutland estate as his heir. Yet, because branded on the upper part of his body, like some mark of Cain, the two letters of the alphabet and the only partially assimilated history behind them are always with him. Not until two chapters from the novel's end does Otto fully understand how he comes to carry them. (Andersen surely again learned here from Scott who in *The Heart of Midlothian* postpones until the same distance from the end the all-important fact that the son of Effie and her seducer/husband is still alive, living as a young criminal.) But that his past contains a dark secret haunts Otto continually, distancing him from even his close friends. He will not undress in front of them lest they see the telltale initials. At fairs or public shows he dreads bumping into the mountebank, Tydske (German) Heinrich, former inmate of the Tugthus, who blackmails him with threats of disclosure. With Heinrich is a hideous, coarse, gypsy-like girl, Sidsel, also once an inmate. When the juggler tells him she is Otto's own missing sister, his sense that both his present identity and any desirable bright future are under threat becomes almost unbearable.

As a student in Copenhagen Otto has as best friend young Baron Vilhelm, with whose family he before long becomes intimate. He frequents their Copenhagen house and visits their estate on Fyn. His first happy stay here is the highlight of the novel's First Part, for hitherto his life has been lonely, clouded by black moods when the past obtrudes too strongly. Otto is drawn first to Vilhelm's older sharp-witted sister, Sophie, so like her brother in looks, but in the end it is the quieter younger sister Louise, pious and practical, who wins his heart – and, we assume, his hand. Vilhelm and Otto – both their serious conversations and their badinage are lively and convincing – have tastes, values, even important traits in common. Sanguine Vilhelm attributes Otto's melancholia and mood swings to the differences between his own beloved Fyn and Otto's Jutland. He delights in hearing his friend talk about the wild west Jutland coast: the fishermen doubling as wreckers; the gypsies roaming the heaths; the relentless winds and the North Sea. ' "Derovre maa jo ethvert poetisk Gemyt blive en Byron! . . . Paa mine Forældres Gods have vi uden Idyller; hele Fynen er en Have.'[1] 'Over there every poetic soul must become a Byron! . . . On my parents' estate we have only idylls; all Fyn is a garden.'

Vilhelm doesn't know that Otto's traumatic, emotionally conditioning first years were in fact spent in this very 'garden', in Odense, in its Tugthus, in British terms something between a prison and a workhouse. Hans Christian Andersen knew this institution personally and early, as we have seen: his grandmother, Anne Sørensdatter was sent there for having three children out of wedlock. She suffered a week's incarceration on a bread-and-water diet. After her release she married a fellow ex-inmate, and, as friends of O.T.'s doorkeeper, the pair would often go along and hold or attend parties inside the establishment, taking little Christian with them. The embarrassed small boy was asked to perform for the merrymakers, but so alarmed was he by many of the occupants that, uncharacteristically, he declined. Shaming recollection of such visits accounts for the lurid colours in which the author paints Tydske Heinrich and his mates, emanations from his own reluctant memories as well as representatives of an identifiable social underclass. Thus it is only too easy to see why *The Heart of Midlothian,* with the many derelicts and criminals in its cast, appealed so much to Andersen. O.T. may have been no Tolbooth, and its treatment of its occupants comparatively humane, even easy-going. Yet some of its more wayward inmates would have borne similarities to such outcasts of society as Scott's crafty Ratcliffe; how could they not have done?

We hear about Otto before we meet him. Andersen opens *O.T.* with a vivid rendering of that great occasion in Danish student life: celebration at having passed the *Examen artium.* The time of this one is specified: October 1829. As in *The Improvisatore,* and as again in *Only a Fiddler* and 'The Ice-Maiden' (to mention just two other cases), the dating is most important, making a vital contribution to the overall meaning; perhaps Andersen has never been given sufficient credit for this meticulous aspect of his art. Otto is not present at the party, even though he is a first-class student, because he took exception to the mathematics paper, handing in, as protest, a blank sheet of paper and thus botching his results. Here, one might say, is Byronism in action, cocking a snook at conventional measurements of intellect. The young host remarks of Otto:

'Ja, han er vistnok en flink Fyr, men han seer saa storagtig ud. Han har noget i sit Væsen, som slet ikke behager mig.'[2]

'Yes, he is a good fellow, but he seems so haughty. He's got something in his nature which doesn't at all please me.'

Vilhelm comes straight away to his friend's defence, though with a qualification:

'Thostrup er bestemt en herlig Fyr! Vi have gjort en Tour sammen med Dampskibet fra Helsingøer til Kjøbenhavn.... Jeg synes just godt om ham, paa Stoltheden nær, og den maa man vænne ham af med.'[3]

'Thostrup is definitely a splendid fellow! We have made a journey together by steamboat from Helsingør to Copenhagen.... I like him very much, except for his pride, and one must break him of that.'

And certainly by the end of the novel Otto – largely thanks to Vilhelm and his family – displays less of this undesirable quality. (Maybe this is a covert suggestion on Andersen's part, intended for Edvard Collin, that Otto had learned profitably from all the criticism.) It is in Vilhelm's company that we first encounter him, a few weeks later (now November): two young men ensconced in comfortable Copenhagen quarters smoking pipes, reading classical authors, exchanging personal anecdotes. Andersen warned Edvard in letters that he would appear in the new novel; indeed it was actually to be called *The Two Students*.[4] But if Andersen and Edvard Collin could truthfully have been contained within this simple designation, their relationship would not have incurred the painful difficulties we have noted, and *O.T.* would lack its considerable nervous narrative impetus and its most memorable scenes – Sidsel's detention in the manor house for theft, Otto's final set-to with Tydske Heinrich at Odense Fair – which undoubtedly derive from the psychologically effective distinction in provenance between the two real-life friends, and from Andersen's own bitter, gnawing awareness of it.

'What would I be like if I had actually been born into the happy, prosperous, well-connected Collin family?' Andersen is asking himself in this book, and answering, 'No, I couldn't be the person (the artist) I am without having seen sorrow first-hand at a young age, or without encountering the miseries of proletarian life where poverty undermines character and moral codes, where uncertainty about the future is detrimental to both physical and psychological health, and where constantly having to look up to other people results in permanent self-deprecation and tension.' All this is true, however, of Otto, paradoxically, because unlike his creator he is also, by blood and inheritance, a member of Denmark's upper class (in point of fact of a higher stratum than the Collins' *haute bourgeoisie*; he hails from the landed gentry). Though wish-fulfilment may indeed have played a part here in Andersen's choice of Otto's background, it is also – in terms of the novel's purpose – a fictive necessity. 'How best to realise oneself?' 'What existence most satisfies the spirit?' are *O.T.*'s dominant concerns. For this reason it was essential that his two young heirs could do what they wanted with their lives – fall in love, look after their property and/or travel extensively. They are under no imperatives for qualifications or money (although in reality all the Collins and their kin joined the higher professions, and Andersen had a hard financial struggle during the 1830s to maintain himself as a writer).

But ultimately such freedom has its limitations, and these too the novel will address. Further, Andersen will show us tremor-causing fault lines beneath the agreeable, assiduously cultivated and protected terrain that the privileged occupy, and even brings home – to readers and possibly to the characters themselves – what they only too consistently fail to notice.

Andersen had also warned Edvard Collin that the character based on him would possess not only his virtues but his flaws (for he *did* have them, he half-jokingly observed). But hindsight makes us appreciate that Andersen deliberately portioned out key attributes of himself and his dearest friend between his two central figures. In *O.T.* it is Edvard's stand-in, Vilhelm, not Andersen's stand-in Otto, who is the dedicated practitioner of the arts, as violinist, pianist and composer; he finds the other's musical tastes superficial. And it is Vilhelm, with a ready eye for pretty girls, who is prepared to defy caste when it comes to love and the opposite sex. In contrast Otto, for all his embrace of French revolutionary ideals, is displeased, perturbed, when faced with his friend's feelings for humbly born Eva (not knowing that she is in truth his own blood sister); Andersen even manipulates him (though this may be little more than a plot device) into speaking sternly against close association with members of the lower classes (just as Antonio warned Bernardo against association with a lowly Jewish girl in *The Improvisatore*). It will be Vilhelm not Otto, however, who favours strong (even capital) punishment when the humbly born transgress, and who admires England for its practice of hanging thieves. When his cousin Joachim informs him of the outbreak of revolution in July 1830 in Paris, Vilhelm is moved, sympathetic. Yet his natural tendency seems to be a lightly worn, moderately inclusive conservatism; however, the concluding chapter doesn't permit us to accept this as definitive. It is for a Switzerland transforming itself, after serious birth pangs, into Europe's most successful and efficient republic that we last hear him expressing enthusiasm.

Otto is cut from rougher, more sombre-hued cloth than his friend, just as Jutland's west coast, its wild heaths and dunes, differs from eastern Fyn. Even when his history is uncovered and his mother, the detainee in the Tugthus, is shown to have been demonstrably guiltless, he has in his family background (and therefore in his genetic inheritance? – this likelihood is never overtly posed) such socially obstreperous qualities as passionate prejudice and pig-headed resentment (his grandfather), moral recklessness (his father), and a morbid capacity for surrender to adversity (his mother). The figures we shall encounter again and again in Andersen's fairy tales will embody just such attributes, and make us appreciate how aware the writer was of his own deep asocial urges springing from the confusions of heredity and a fraught boyhood which at times – as he admitted to his confidante Henriette Wulff – seemed more a domain of dark dream than a once-lived reality.

Unsurprisingly then, fears of his earlier years overtaking him can turn Otto violent. The first and gravest instance of this occurs when, after a swim, Vilhelm jokingly removes Otto's clothing. Dreading lest his worst secret be quite liter-ally exposed (by his naked torso), Otto swims far out, away from his friends, and nearly drowns as a consequence. When Vilhelm rescues him, all he can say is, with trembling lips, '*Jeg hader Dem!*'[5] 'I hate you!' and even proposes they fight a duel. (They do not.)

'Jeg hader *Dem!*' Otto uses the formal second person to Vilhelm, even at this moment of heightened emotion. *O.T.* constitutes a veritable history of the forms of personal address as used by two close friends outwardly both firm members of the Danish Establishment. And in no respect is Andersen's redis-tribution between these two more striking than here. Provocative, also. While at work on his novel, Andersen wrote Edvard a letter he never sent, addressing him in that proscribed second person singular, and paying fulsome tribute to their relationship. But even in the letter he *did* send Edvard, giving him advance notice of his imminent fictional appearance, Andersen alludes pointedly to the hurtful refusal of 1831, implying that it will feature in the book. Edvard cannot therefore have been wholly surprised by *O.T.*, and remarks in his correspond-ence suggest he was far from delighted by it. Nevertheless his never-forgotten, never-forgiven snub to Andersen not merely fails to occur, it undergoes a highly complex and significant metamorphosis. If 'The Shadow' is the most sophisticated and disturbing artistic consequence of this major trauma of Andersen's youthful life, *O.T.* is its fullest treatment. For the novel form – as received from Scott and currently practised by Hugo, Stendhal, Balzac – gave him scope to represent the ebb and flow of a friendship over a swathe of time and in a variety of testing situations, as a short story never could. *O.T.* is in fact an indicator of continent-wide shifts in class that would expand as the century progressed. This novel is therefore to be read alongside such later classic treat-ments of friendship versus social mores as Turgenev's *Fathers and Sons* (1859)[6] and Dickens's *Great Expectations* (1860)[7] – and can be seen as a forerunner of these masterpieces.

As we have seen, in his seminal letter of refusal Edvard spoke of having, despite himself, acceded to the use of 'Du' at various social gatherings of his peer group, and of then regretting his weakness in doing so – so much that he would subsequently revoke it. We have noted that *O.T.* begins with Vilhelm at just such an occasion where 'Drikke Dus' is the order and high spot of the evening:

> Glassene hævede sig, den unge Baron loe, klinkede og raabte til dem rundtom: 'Du, Du!' men der laa dog noget tvungent i hele Maaden, som dog intet af de unge Gemytter lagde Mærke til, mindre gjorde sig Tanke over, at hans plud- selige Trædentilbage, medens den første Dusdrikken fandt Sted, maaskee ene og alene var for at undgaae den. Men snart igjen var han En af de meest overgivne . . . . [8]
> The glasses were raised, the young baron laughed, clinked and called out to the assembly 'Du, Du!' but there was something forced in his whole manner, which however none of the young blades noticed, let alone gave thought to, so that his sudden withdrawal, while the first Du-drinking took place, was possibly solely to avoid it. But soon he was again one of the most high-spirited . . . .

But Vilhelm's ambivalence about 'Dusdrikke' persists, and he leaves the party early. When, a short while later, we first hear him engaged in intimate talk with Otto, the two are using 'De' to each other; this sounds and feels natural enough. Then on Christmas Eve the two friends are walking together through the city along the snow-covered Langelinie, with the Swedish shore so close that indi- vidual houses can be seen across the Sound. A beautiful girl passes by, the sister (as they believe her to be) of a working-class boy, Jonas whom Vilhelm has thoughtfully befriended earlier, to help him develop his musical gifts. Otto notices the keenness of Vilhelm's glances at her and advises him to be careful; Vilhelm protests that he is virtuous in his dealings with girls, unlike so many in their circle. At that very moment some members of this circle show up, greeting Vilhelm heartily – and informally. Otto is flabbergasted: 'Er De Dus med alle disse?' he inquires, sharply. 'Are you [De, formal usage] on Du terms with all these?' Vilhelm defends himself by referring to the particular social occasion which made this unavoidable. 'Jeg giver ellers ikke gjerne mit Du uden til mine Nærmeste.' 'I do not like otherwise to use Du except to my closest relatives.' But at the time how could he have refused? 'Hvorfor ikke det?' 'Why ever not?' counters Otto, now sounding far more like Edvard Collin than his creator, 'det vilde aldrig have generet mig.' 'That would never have bothered me!' And the two continue – for the time being – with the formal pronoun, though with this exchange Vilhelm has gained fresh insight into Otto's unpredictable, difficult character.[9]

When Vilhelm sees Otto off as he returns to Jutland after his happy stay on the Fyn estate, he says warmly, 'Altid blive vi Venner! trofaste Venner!'[10] 'Always we will stay friends! Steadfast friends!' Otto then feels he should thank Vilhelm for this by some act of affirmation. So he writes him a letter: 'Vilhelm, vi sige herefter Du til hinanden, det er meer fortroligt.'[11] 'Vilhelm, from now on we'll say Du to each other, it is more intimate.' But no sooner has he dispatched this declaration, than he is filled with regret.

Just as this letter – a firm, manly proposal – could hardly be more different from Andersen's imploring one to Edvard, so Vilhelm's reply will be emotional worlds away from the latter's reply:

'Min fortræffelige Otto! Vi have alle drukket Otto Thostrups Skaal, jeg hævede Glasset og drak *Din*. Venskabsdissonansen *De* er opløst i et harmonisk *Du*, og selv har Du angivet Accorden. Alle tale om Dig hjemme . . . .'[12]

'My excellent Otto, We have all drunk Otto Thostrup's health, I raised the glass and drank yours (thine). The friendship's dissonance De is dissolved in the harmonious Du, and you have yourself given assent. Everybody is talking about you at home . . . .

And the letter is signed '*Din* Ven og Broder', 'Your (thy) friend and brother'.[13] But this does not turn out to be the satisfactory end of the matter we might expect. Otto's regrets at his proposal of Du do not diminish but are stoked by the surfacing of unhappy elements from his hidden past. An unexpected glimpse of Tydske Heinrich ('mit Livs onde Engel,'[14] 'my life's evil angel'), ominously concludes the novel's First Part. Back in Copenhagen, after his squire-grandfather's death, Otto begins to feel more acutely than ever the dissimilarity between his and Vilhelm's lot in life. Consequently he avoids using 'Du' to him by means of ingenious circumlocutions. Vilhelm of course notices these, and there follows the conversation which, of all the novel's cunning transpositions, is surely the most audacious, and the nearest to a retaliation to Edvard:

'Vær oprigtig Otto!' sagde Vilhelm, da denne en Dag besøgte ham. 'De kan ikke komme ud af det med at sige Du til mig. Nu, saa lad være! derfor ere vi lige gode Venner. Det er jo dog kun en Form! Skjøndt De maae indrømme mig, at i Grunden ere De heri en stor Nar.'

Otto udviklede, hvilken sælsom Uvillie han havde følt, hvilken piinlig Følelse der havde betaget ham og gjort ham det umuligt.

'Der har De nu gaaet og spillet Martyr!' sagde Vilhelm leende. 'Kunde De ikke strax have sagt, hvorledes De havde det? '[15]

'Be honest, Otto,' said Vilhelm, when he one day visited him, 'You can't get on with saying Du to me. So let it be. We're still the same good friends. It's after all only a form. Though you must admit to me, that in this respect you are truly a great idiot.'

Otto explained what strange aversion he had felt, what painful feeling had taken hold of him and made it [use of Du] impossible for him.

'There you've gone and played the martyr,' said Vilhelm laughing. 'Could you not have told me at once how you felt about it?

Vilhelm is then moved to speak sympathetically of Otto's earlier 'Ulykke', 'misfortune/unluckiness' in early life, resulting in wild deeds when living 'i Vildskap', 'in the wilderness'. But now surely his friend should be thinking of the future, of 'Glædens Land', 'Land of Happiness', which is every youth's rightful place. Thus the question of which second person they employ is relegated to an entirely secondary place.[16]

And so the friends intensify their friendship even while maintaining formal address, with Vilhelm blithely and sensibly accepting Otto's de facto refusal. Tempting as it is to read all this as a compensatory rewrite of an agonising episode which still had ongoing repercussions, we must also acknowledge a brave self-awareness on Andersen's part, a realistic appreciation of the phenomenon so obsessively preoccupying him. Friendship, according to the prevailing Romantic tenets, was a masculine ideal, and if it demanded a fullness of both verbal and physical expression spurned by later male codes, it was nonetheless masculinity that it celebrated. Andersen knew that, neither by nature nor by upbringing, was he capable of this kind of bonding; of what, in his fiction, Otto and Vilhelm (it would seem) succeed in forging. He feared that Edvard would think him 'womanish', yet his pleas on behalf of their friendship would only confirm him in such a view. In the novel Andersen tries to redress this tendency of his, showing his protagonist acting towards his friend in a manner he would surely approve. We can see an earnest of his hopes that he could achieve this himself in a moving exchange between the two young men before they depart for a couple of years' travel on the Continent – a venture Andersen of course longed to undertake with Edvard, but never did. Vilhelm congratulates Otto for his restrained behaviour on learning of his sister Sophie's engagement to their strongly conservative middle-aged neighbour, the Kammerjunker:

'Min kjære, trofaste Otto,' sagde Vilhelm og lagde Haanden om hans Skulder.'
'De var ret munter og nydelig i Aften! Bliv altid saaledes ved!'[17]

'My dear, steadfast Otto,' said Vilhelm and laid a hand on his shoulder, 'you were really cheerful and nice this evening. Always stay that way!'

With heartfelt gratitude expressed in such a manner, what does it matter that the formal 'De' is employed, or that the adjectives of commendation belong to the manly tradition of self-control?

Yet we cannot quite leave it there, cannot avoid taking from this scene a sadness that dignified convention (however vital for oiling the wheels of social intercourse) can triumph over the natural inclinations of the heart, and that Society/the Establishment expects and encourages this. Nor is the friendship under review without significant puzzling equivocations.

First there is the extraordinary Valentine's Day ball. Vilhelm dresses up in women's clothes. He flings his arms round Otto, lays his cheek against his, sits on his knee, and compliments him on the beauty of his eyes. His doing so inflames Otto's blood, we are told, though this turns out to be because of his resemblance when cross-dressed to Sophie, the sister to whom at this time Otto is most attracted. Such an antic may sound very unlike the sturdy conventional Edvard Collin, until we recall Andersen's diary entry for Saturday 31 October 1840, telling how his friends saw him off on the boat: 'Edvard Collin was the last one out there. I said goodbye; he pressed a kiss onto my mouth. Oh, it was as if my heart would burst!'[18] And we shall see that transvestism has an important part to play in *Only a Fiddler*.

When he falls in love with Eva, Vilhelm comments on her striking resemblance (at this stage inexplicable) to his best friend, again singling out the eyes for praise. Had she accepted his ardent class-defying proposal of marriage, he thus would, without knowing it, have become Otto's brother-in-law. The same relation would obviously have ensued had Sophie reciprocated Otto's feelings, aroused not least because *she* looked so like *her* brother. Instead the book closes with Otto about to marry Vilhelm's younger sister, Louise. So these two friends will be brothers-in-law after all. And perhaps what first *really* endeared Louise to Otto was her refusal to believe that the criminal, repulsive Sidsel could be Otto's sister, and her deduction that Eva, so dear to her from the first, was in truth precisely this.

Apart from Otto's grandfather's Catholic Swiss housekeeper, Rosalie (one of Andersen's tenderest tributes to a woman virtually of the servant class), the novel's portraits of women lack depth, though Sophie (Ingeborg Drewsen, née Collin) is drawn with a firm if light hand. But neither Louise nor Eva have enough individuality; indeed the fearsome Sidsel has infinitely more galvanic vitality.

Andersen was undoubtedly hampered in these pages by his knowledge that in reality his social provenance was an obstacle to courtship of those young women who most appealed to him. In Sidsel and her routing there can be little doubt that Andersen is offloading his worries about his half-sister, Karen Marie, though *O.T.* was begun almost seven years before it became necessary for him to inform the Collins of her existence; she was living in Copenhagen to which she had moved as long before as November 1822![19] Andersen had for years been haunted by the notion that she would turn up somewhere as a maid – for example, at Slagelse School, working for the Meislings – and so bring shame to him. (There are those who think she too was involved in prostitution for a while.) Then in February 1842 she actually called on him and asked for help – she was living unmarried with a man-friend in poor circumstances – and Andersen admitted in his diary that this visit from her was like his novel *O.T.* coming to life to vex him.[20] When he informed Edvard about it, his friend was adamant that he have nothing to do with her and her partner, and that he should deny them any further money. (Karen Marie died, in a squalid part of Copenhagen, on 18 March 1846.)

The two years in Europe, which Andersen and Edvard Collin never spent together, contribute inestimably to the fused development of Otto and Vilhelm. Just as our first proper picture of July Revolution Paris comes from Vilhelm, so it is from him we hear about the European tour. Of his letter to his sister Louise describing the friends' travels, we are told 'hver Linie aandede Livslyst og Glæde',[21] 'every line breathed joy in life and happiness.' ('Livslyst/ Livsglæde' as a characteristic of Continental rather than Nordic life will be reaffirmed by Osvald in Ibsen's great play *Gengangere* (*Ghosts*, 1881).[22] While Vilhelm admits he has been changed by travel and is able to appreciate the luxuriance of Italian landscape and women, it's clear that Switzerland has inspired him more intensely – its dramatic scenery, the huge engineering feat of the Simplon Pass ordered by Napoleon. Italy, on the other hand, is what overwhelms the Byronic Otto, who scribbles in the letter's margin, 'Italien er et Paradiis! her er Himlen tre Gange saa høi, som hjemme'. 'Italy is a paradise! Here the sky is three times as high as at home.' Vilhelm playfully refutes this: 'Det er Vrøvl, hvad han skriver om den italienske Himmel. Vor, der hjemme, er lige saa god.'[23] 'That's rubbish what he writes about the Italian sky. Ours, at home, is just as good.'

Travel matures Vilhelm physically, casting a shadow of sadness over his otherwise open and life-loving face, and on his return he has to face bitter loss: Eva, his loved one's death. By contrast Otto, now moustached, appears more handsome than before (and this in a character who represents a writer continually plagued by a sense of his own ugliness). Otto's sombreness of expression has given way to a wise, thoughtful look – and, when talking to Louise, he smiles.

That the courses of *The Two Students* of the book's original title are intended to form a meaningful pattern becomes clear from an authorial observation in the text on his fictive methods:

Vor Fortælling er intet Phantasiebillede, men Virkeligheden vi leve i, Blod af vort Blod og Kjød af vort Kjød. Vi skulle see vore Dage, vor Tids Mennesker. Dog er det ikke blot Hverdagslivet, ikke blot en Dvælen ved Overfladens Mosarter; det hele Træ, fra Rødderne til de duftende Blade, ville vi beskue. Den tunge Jord skal trykke Roden, Hverdagslivets Mos og Bark binde sig om stammen, de stærke Grene brede sig ud med Blad og Blomst, medens Poesiens Sol skinner ind mellem dem og viser Farver, Duft og qviddrende Fugle. . . . Vi maae søge vort Forbillede i Naturen. Ofte kan det synes, som var her en Stillestaaen, men den finder ikke Sted. Ligesaa i vor Fortælling; medens vore Characterer ved gjensidig Tale træde frem for Øiet, finder der, som med de enkelte Grene paa Træet, en usynlig Forvikling Sted. Grenen, som høit skyder ud som vilde den adskille sig fra Moderstammen, stræber just frem for at danne Kronen, give Træet Heelhed. De fra det fælleds Midtpunkt divergerende Linier skulle just skabe Harmonien.[24]

Our story is not a fantasy-creation but the reality we live in, blood of our blood and flesh of our flesh. We shall see our days, our contemporaries. However it is not simply everyday life, not simply a lingering on the moss of the surface; the whole tree, from the roots to the fragrant leaves, we will contemplate. The heavy earth shall press the root, the moss and bark of everyday life bind themselves on the trunk, the strong branches spread themselves out with leaf and flower, while the sun of poetry shines in among them and shows the colours, fragrance and chirping birds. . . . We must seek our model in nature. Often it can seem as though there is a standstill, but that does not take place. Likewise in our story; while our characters in reciprocal talk step forward before our eyes, there arises, as with the individual branches on the tree, an unseen complication. The branch, which shoots high up as though it wants to separate itself from the mother-trunk, merely exerts itself to form the crown, to make the tree a whole. The lines diverging from the common midpoint shall merely give rise to harmony.

And the concluding pictures of the two young men's relative positions seem sufficiently surprising as to demand scrutiny, a probing for ambiguity. Otto, confessedly happy to be back in Denmark, will devote himself to running his Jutland estate, making it productive, with Louise at his side. (He will lead the life, in other words, that the Duke of Argyle provided for Jeanie Deans's family at Roseneath.) Vilhelm, his beloved Eva gone, will, in contrast, resume travelling, so unlike the Denmark-bound Edvard Collin. Otto, for all his unhappy childhood, youthful anxiety states and dubious connections, will (it would appear) become a stalwart, though probably innovative contributor to Danish society, Vilhelm, of the contented manner and way of life, will seek further learning experience, both from the mountains and from human encounters. Is Andersen saying that it is necessary for someone (Otto earlier, Vilhelm only now; himself throughout his growing-up, Edvard so far never) to suffer loss, neglect, discomfort, worry and sorrow in order to become a rounded human being who can give satisfactorily to his society?

Perhaps, but even so the disquieting nature of the novel's last pages, above all of its final paragraph, remains unaccounted for.

> Otto lukkede sine Øine, hans Hænder foldede sig. 'Louise elsker mig. Jeg er saa lykkelig, at jeg frygter for, at der snart maa møde mig en stor Sorg, saaledes pleier det jo altid at skee. Var dog tydske Heinrich død! Først naar han er borte, kan jeg blive fuldkommen rolig, fuldkommen lykkelig.'[25]

> Otto closed his eyes, folded his hands. 'Louise loves me. I am so happy that I am frightened that soon a great sorrow must meet me, such as has been always apt to happen. If only German Heinrich were dead! Only when he's disappeared can I become perfectly at peace, perfectly happy.'

By the time we come to this, the immediately preceding page has informed us of news that has most definitely *not* come Otto's way: that German Heinrich actually *is* dead, the casualty of a shipwreck. His last moments were not merely dreadful but distinguished by atavistic bravery. He died attempting to rescue Sidsel, who was, we are now at last informed, his own daughter. With the pair there also tragically perished Eva's young foster-brother, little Jonas, the talented, poverty-blighted boy-musician, a beautiful and memorable creation, whom Vilhelm had befriended years before. The end of these three persons, marginal to their society but important to each other, and to the whole design of the book, are evoked with great feeling; indeed, no passage of the novel is more compelling than this. So when we read of Otto's sentiments, we protest indignantly, ignorant though he is of what has just happened. It surely goes without saying that nobody should know happiness *only* when someone has vanished, when another's life is extinguished. And what can we honestly think of a protagonist for whom this would seem to be the case?

To understand this undoubtedly deliberate ambivalence further, we should turn to the political sympathies of the main characters, and to the novelist's detectable attitude to them. Here must lie the key to this most disquieting passage.

2

The street uprisings in Paris of 27–29 July 1830 – 'les trois journées de juillet' or simply 'les trois glorieuses' – came about in protest against Charles X's refusal to accept the liberals' electoral victory of 13 July. To counter it, the king, following the advice of his ultra-royalist Prime Minister, Jules de Polignac, issued the Four Ordinances reaffirming the authority he had enjoyed since 1824 and curbing press freedom. The intensity of Parisians' response to the Ordinances roused a group of powerful *Notables* into forcing Charles's abdication in favour of his cousin, Louis Philippe of the House of Orléans. Louis Philippe was judged to span divergent sections of French society; his (royal) father had been known for his revolutionary sympathies while he himself had in his youth allegedly been a member of a Jacobin society. Many – like Andersen's admired Heine (to start with) – viewed the July Revolution as a welcome surge of revolutionary spirit into Europe's most sophisticated and intellectually adventurous society, corrupted for a decade by a materialistic, retrogressive regime. For Otto Thostrup (see *O. T.* First Part, Chapter 18), newly returned to the wilds of traditionalist Jutland, 'les trois glorieuses' seemed like a re-enactment of Schiller's *William Tell*.

Otto learns of the above events only fragmentarily to begin with, through German-language newspapers, which are all he can obtain; what he reads greatly excites him. But the reaction of the two people closest to him in his rural existence, Rosalie and the old village preacher, is one of horror at yet more bloodshed on the Continent. It is while Otto awaits further information about France that Andersen brings us up to date on his whole intellectual and spiritual history. Easily moved by 'Alt Stort og Skjønt',[26] 'Everything great and beautiful', he has hitherto kept himself apart from politics, with which, out in his backwater, his grandfather had been so obsessed. But, growing up at the time he did, he had always been fascinated by Napoleon, taking him as his hero. His name and deeds amounted to 'et stort Verdens-Eventyr',[27] 'a World-Adventure', from – and these are specifically cited in the text – his campaigns in Egypt (1798) and Europe (Austerlitz, 1805 to Friedland, 1807) through to the burning of Moscow (1812) and his return from disaster to reimpose himself: a career born of superhuman self-confidence and played out on as great a segment of the globe as Alexander the Great had commandeered. Who, Andersen asks his readers, remembering his own self, hasn't written a play in childhood? Otto did, his only subject being Napoleon's life, an undertaking so important to him that he came near to dealing a servant's child a fatal injury because he played with the paper on which he was writing it. Otto's interest in France continued after 1815. That country was still, more than any other, the disseminating centre of liberating ideals. He is therefore infinitely curious about this latest upturn in French political life, but only knows the details of it from that letter of Vilhelm's joyfully addressing him as Du. So thematically a triumph of the democratic spirit in France is inextricably linked with the democratic spirit of the second person singular.

Vilhelm's enthusiastic letter, the information in which comes from the eyewitness account of his Paris-based officer cousin, Joachim, declares that if the 1789 French Revolution was a 'Blodfrugt', 'Bloodfruit', these 'glimrende Julidage' 'brilliant July days' are a 'Passionsblomst' 'Passion-fruit'.[28] After its magnificent emergence will follow tranquillity. This second Revolution will do the necessary business of getting rid of an arrogant despot but will leave only peace in its wake.

> Denne var selve Virkeligheden, i hvilken han levede. Hans Hjerte var opfyldt af Beundring for Frankerige, der havde kjæmpet Frihedens hellige Kamp, med Sværdets Ord udtalt Tidsalderens Banstraale over Oplysningens og Forædlingens Fjender.[29]
>
> This was the reality in which he lived. His heart was filled with admiration for France, which had fought Freedom's holy fight, had with the word of the Sword spoken the anathema of the age on enemies of the Enlightenment and Progress.

Otto later meets Joachim, at Vilhelm's Copenhagen residence, aflame with fashionable revolutionary zeal and wanting to support his fellow officers, the Democratic Reds, in Warsaw in their (ultimately inept) struggle against Russia's violation of the 1815 treaty. Joachim's presentation of the achievements of 'les trois glorieuses' is at once accurate and exhilarating, alarming and exemplary: the bullets, the barricades (that most obvious reminder of 1789) which were so frequently ad hoc constructions from trees cut down in the boulevards, the hand-to-hand, sometimes lethal street-fighting. Andersen supplements the account with a footnote quotation from Victor Hugo:

> Ceux qui pieusement sont morts pour la patrie
> Ont droit qu'à leur cercueil la foule vienne et prie . . .
> La voix d'un people entier les berce en leur tombeau.[30]

> Those who have piously died for their country
> Have the right that at their coffin the crowd come and pray . . .
> The voice of an entire people cradles them in their tomb.

Joachim gives his listeners pretty well all the salient features of the July Revolution: Charles X's intransigence, his doctrinaire hostility to the Charter thus inspiring protesters to chant 'Vive la Charte!', his sympathies for a back-ward-looking Church, the diversionary nature of the Algerian expedition (of such far-reaching consequences for his country), his increased dependence on the unpopular arch-reactionary Polignac. If the career of Napoleon was a 'Verdens-Eventyr', then this revolution is surely a 'Verdensbegivenhed' a 'world-event'. All these details show Andersen's own engaged inwardness with Paris

1830 and its aftermath, and he well conveys their impact on Otto. Author and readers of course know that by the time of writing (1835/36) the France that had emerged was a great disappointment to liberal hopes. All along the *Notables*, who instated Louis Philippe for fear anarchy would break out, had intended that their chosen monarch preserve the status quo and safeguard the interests of the well-off. And this is exactly what the Citizen King, who morphed into the Bourgeois King, did.

This disappointment, however, is still in the future. Earlier in 1830, Victor Hugo had effected another revolution which came to seem to his admirers a foretaste of the summer's political one: his Romantic drama *Hernani*[31] defied Classicism's constraining Unities, and so provoked a furore in the audience which the author's enthusiastic, extravagantly dressed claque of supporters met head-on. Otto listens enviously to Joachim's descriptions of Parisian theatre and artistic achievements, and thinks: Surely Copenhagen has the capacity to become a 'Paris of the North' – with the works of Thorvaldsen gracing a Danish Pantheon? Vilhelm and Otto vow to go to Paris, and do so two years later, after spending autumn in the Rhineland.

Presumably both young men enjoyed their time in this city, yet, as we have seen, it is Vilhelm, grieving for his Eva, who announces: 'Til Paris vil jeg!'[32] 'To Paris I'll go!' In sending his fictional counterpart to Paris, Andersen was probably signalling something important to Edvard Collin which he hoped others would pick up on. Edvard severely underrated Paris's importance, had disparaged any glowing accounts of the city Andersen had given him. For all the political shortcomings of Louis Philippe's France, it harboured a bold, vigorous artistic community unsurpassable anywhere – Hugo, Gautier, Balzac, Lamartine, de Vigny, de Musset – all men whom Andersen had either met on his first visit to Paris and/or was to see more extensively on his second, his stay there of two months in 1843. So is Andersen saying that Vilhelm/Edvard could still benefit from a centre of so many sharp intellects? Or is he, more slyly – for we have evidence of how up-to-date he was about French affairs – implying that a fundamentally conservative young man such as Edvard/Vilhelm hadn't much to fear from the capital of the Bourgeois King?

But if he is admonishing Vilhelm/Edvard, he is surely yet harder on himself. Otto has betrayed those feelings of social justice that drew him to the July Revolution as thoroughly as any French citizen initially enamoured of its values. He not only has no feeling for the social outcasts he knows, he still cannot forgive them for being what they are, still wishes for their suppression (which, in bleak reality, includes the death of the charming, talented, innocent boy Jonas). Similarly he cannot handle the matey warmth of 'Du'. Such frank egotism is implicitly the consequence of having Napoleon for hero. On one line of vision the Corsican was the powerful embodiment at home and abroad (creator of the

Code Napoléon) of what the Revolution had stood for, but on another, obviously, he was its betrayer, its self-appointed antagonist (*pace* Beethoven's cancellation of the dedication of his Third Symphony, the *Eroica* to Napoleon), its historical and literal declarer of its death (in 1799). But whichever of these contrasting readings one accorded him, he represented the possibilities, the triumphs and the disasters of the human will, or better, remembering his own concept of Destiny, the *supra-human* will, as completely as any figure in the history (even that of the often cited Classical age) stretching out behind him.

Otto Thostrup is nowhere more representative of his generation than in his Napoleon-worship, and the way that it can blight an over-impressionable sensibility. Take a near fictional contemporary of his, the protagonist of a novel actually subtitled 'A Chronicle of 1830' and dedicated by its author in English (because it's a quotation from Shakespeare's *Henry V)* 'To the Happy Few', those with spirit enough to rise above the unimaginative conventions. He is Julien Sorel in Stendhal's *Le rouge et le noir* (published 13 November 1830). In fact the July Revolution makes no appearance in this chronicle of the year in which it was the key event, and the publishers, on this account, printed a note explaining that the book was in preparation *before* these 'great events', and had been mostly written in 1827. (This last was untrue; part of this great novel had in fact been written in 1830 itself, and coincided with the storm over Hugo's *Hernani*, a work its author much admired.)

> For years now Julien had never let an hour of his life pass without telling himself that Bonaparte, an obscure lieutenant without fortune, had made himself master of the globe with his sword. This thought consoled him for his sufferings, which he believed to be great, and increased any pleasure which came his way.
>
> The building of the church [was]. . . a sudden flash of illumination for him. He was struck by an idea which drove him almost crazy for several weeks, and finally took hold of him with the overwhelming force characteristic of the very first idea a passionate individual believes he has thought of himself.
>
> When Bonaparte first made a name for himself, France was afraid of being invaded; military prowess was necessary and in fashion. Nowadays you find priests of forty earning a hundred thousand francs, in other words three times as much as the famous generals in Napoleon's army. They need people to back them up. Look at that justice of the peace, such a level-headed and honest man up till now, dishonouring himself at his age for fear of displeasing a young curate of thirty! The answer is to be a priest![33]

We readers cannot – any more than his creator — *empathise* with Julien Sorel in his terrible ambition, his career of exploiting others' weaknesses and faults, and thereby augmenting his own to the monstrous degree of becoming a murderer. Stendhal's prose is too unflaggingly analytical for this, its exposure of the deceptions of self and other people, brought about by rampant egotism, too thorough. Nor, for all his unfortunate beginnings (psychological, rather than economic) do we even *sympathise;* Julien brings too much misery in his wake, his hopes are too spiritually deficient, this being emphasised by his frankly cynical attitude to the religion he professedly serves. But we can come troublingly close *to* him, we are permitted a disquieting level of intimacy with the workings of his mind and senses and are invited to look to ourselves for parallels. Andersen's approach to Otto Thostrup is not dissimilar. Like Julien, Otto importantly embodies constituents of our own make-up, and situations of archetypal intensity exhibit this. The same is true of the protagonists of the *Eventyr* (*Fairy-tales*), to which we now turn. They too represent key aspects of ourselves, and predicaments of psychic metaphorical resonance reveal this often troubling truth. We do not seek to become these persons; sometimes they may even distress or repel us way beyond any wish to identify with them. But because of the vivid reality bestowed on them by their creator, we see them as we ourselves could be seen in glimpses of truth, ineluctable representatives of humankind itself.

By the time the *third* of Andersen's novels, *Only a Fiddler* appeared (22 November 1837), there had been a *third* booklet of fairy-tales (7 April 1837). The two this contained (there were only the two stories) crowned the achievements of the previous booklets, and are among the most famous fairy-tales of all time: 'Den lille Havfrue' ('The Little Mermaid') and 'Keiserens nye Klæder' ('The Emperor's New Clothes').

CHAPTER 5

Eventyr, Fortalte for Børn (Fairy-Tales Told for Children)

1

'Der kom en Soldat marcherende henad Landeveien: een, to! een to!'[1] 'There came a soldier marching along the road: one, two! one, two!' This is how 'Fyrtøiet', 'The Tinder-Box', *first* story of the *first* booklet, opens: no literary preamble, no fuss of any kind, instead buttonholing directness. In *The Improvisatore* Andersen lost no time in letting his hero point out his birthplace to us; from this moment forth we could tell that the evolution of his life was his subject. Likewise here; this rhythmically brisk, onomatopoeic first sentence sets the story's central figure advancing towards us inexorably. No escaping him will be possible!

We have met such a soldier before in fairy-tales, in the Brothers Grimm's 'The Blue Light'[2] for instance – and in ordinary life even more frequently: a young man needed by king and country when fighting's to be done, and then, when it's all over, cast aside, dismissed. We know nothing about this particular one's provenance, and the kind of person he is we have to deduce as we go along for we are clearly not going to be informed. There is not the invitation to identify with the protagonist Andersen offered us in his first novel. Rather we are being asked to put ourselves *alongside* him, to watch what he does, to listen to what he says, and every now and again we will be permitted to know what he is feeling. But as in the fairy-tale 'The Tinder Box' purports to be, it cannot allow introspection any more than analysis. Things (persons, animals, objects, events) rise up or occur, to be faced and dealt with. And if our soldier is unable to stand back and search his soul for the moral desirability of his next action, then neither can we who accompany him. Later perhaps, when the story is completed and a pattern has emerged, we may be able to do so, but it will be too late – by then we are looking back at a rapid succession of faits accomplis.

So we have no time even for surprise when, in the soldier's company, we are accosted by a hideous, flattering old witch, nor for caution about meeting her amazing request. When she refuses to divulge why she wants an object enormously troublesome to fetch, the soldier simply dispatches her by cutting off her head. We ourselves might not have done this, but this young man did, so why not wait a moment and find out what followed this spontaneous and brutal act of his? To repeat: we are *not* being asked to *become* or even approve of him. We are being asked merely to accept him – but in the knowledge that we are following an ordinary enough human being: no conventional hero but no villain either. We also know that we ourselves are a bewildering mixture of qualities, and cannot be sure how we would behave in the soldier's position (any more than he himself could have done before things started happening to him). This is part of the exhilaration of 'The Tinder Box' with its no-nonsense style. Unsurprisingly, it shocked many a *bien pensant* critic – and still can. Should children (the nominal readership, after all) be given stories seemingly so dismissive, or excluding of, moral debate? Is this story not in truth amoral?

So discerning a contemporary critic as Maria Tatar (2008) is worried by its protagonist: 'Brutal, greedy and impetuous, he is not much of a role model for children listening to the story. Indeed stories about soldiers returning from war were generally intended for adult audiences rather than for children, although Andersen adds enough magic and whimsy to make the tale attractive to young and old.'[3] It would certainly be hard to reject these adjectives for many of the soldier's actions – starting with severing the old witch's head – but are they not reductive when applied to the whole person himself? 'The Tinder Box' is – the apparent ethical flouting notwithstanding – a story rich in humanity. This, I believe, is what made Ørsted see Andersen's fairy tales as greater than his novels because they are ultimately more inclusive in their sympathies and knowledge of how men and women tick. In *The Improvisatore* and *O.T.* the writer's power of understanding is principally exercised on the 'special case' of himself. Here, happily, it is quite otherwise.

So – yes, the soldier has all the regrettable attributes Tatar accords him, and certainly isn't shown as experiencing any kind of shame (even allowing for the folktale-like exterior method of characterisation). But he possesses other admirable, far from unimportant qualities. And these lead to behaviour on his part far more within the moral reach of normal imperfect mortals than any valiant deeds of spotless heroes and heroines. When well-off, the soldier remembers what it feels like to have no money and therefore gives generously to the poor. When he's getting married, he thinks of his good friends the dogs who have been of such invaluable assistance. So he invites them to partake of his great wedding feast.

Andersen's request to his audience for fellow feeling towards his focal characters – not only the soldier of 'The Tinder Box' but the ruthlessly crafty Little Claus, and the vain, foolish Emperor and his ministers – is compounded by our carefully stimulated sense that they have, involuntarily, wandered into situations familiar enough to all of us from tradition and literature, but requiring from the given individual a first-hand response. How will the soldier handle an object (the eponymous Tinder Box) with properties which probably even he himself, and certainly we readers, can liken to those of Aladdin's lamp in the *Arabian Nights*? (Interestingly, now we have 'The Tallow Candle', these only become apparent to the soldier, because, needing a *candle*, he recollects seeing the stump of one in the tinder-box retrieved at the witch's behest.) ' "Hvad for noget!" sagde Soldaten, "det var jo et moersomt Fyrtøi, kan jeg saaledes faae, hvad jeg vil have!" '⁴ ' "Whatever's this!" said the soldier, "it's certainly a fun tinder-box if I can get in this way what I want." ' (Nothing is harder to do justice to than the instantaneous-sounding colloquialisms of Andersen's demotic dialogue.) Wouldn't we too be likely to run through money suddenly and largely effortlessly acquired yet mind bitterly returning to penurious quarters – especially when our smart, newly made friends then drop us? 'selv børste sine Støvler og sye paa dem med en Stoppenaal, og ingen af hans Venner kom til ham, for der var sae mange Trapper at gaa op ad.'⁵ 'he brushed his boots himself and mended them with a darning-needle, and none of his friends came [to see] him because there were so many stairs to go up'. This is a light but pointed touch characteristic of the Andersen of the fairy tales but absent from the novels. And yet it is both socially and psychologically acute, more what we might expect to find in a novel-of-manners than in a fantasy. We understand that the soldier is being shunned by his new friends because he no longer has money to spend on them, but see that he prefers to tell himself that they don't come to visit him because of the steepness of the stairs up to his attic room.

In every case the carefully arranged meeting between literary/folkloric precedent and human spontaneity depends for success on the lively, liberty-taking use of the vernacular in both direct and indirect speech. Choice of phrase reveals the speaker's mindset, and 'The Tinder-Box' is, on one level, an enactment of a mindset. When at last in the company of the beautiful princess (asleep on the back of his messenger dog): 'Soldaten kunne slet ikke lade være, han maatte kysse hende, for det var en rigtig Soldat.'⁶ 'The soldier couldn't in the least help it, he had to kiss her because this was a real soldier.' Or when – an all-too-common fate in fairy tales! – he is imprisoned for his audacity in wooing a king's daughter – 'Uh, hvor der var mørkt og kjedeligt, og saa sagde de til ham: "imorgen skal Du hænges!" Det var ikke morsomt at høre . . .'⁷ 'Oh, how dark and miserable it was, and then they said to him: Tomorrow you will be hanged. That wasn't fun to hear . . .' Someone who can express himself in this sort of way is surely bound to win through!

The patent presence of the story of Aladdin behind 'The Tinder-Box' would only have increased its galvanic appeal for Danish readers. We have noted that as a young man, transported into a social milieu hugely different from his own and on the threshold of having his precocious ambitions partly realised, Andersen specifically compared himself to Aladdin. He even jotted this down in his diary for 19 December 1825 when staying with his benefactor, Shakespeare translator Commodore Wulff and his family, in their Amalienborg Palace apartment: 'Oh. What hasn't God done for me! It is going for me as it did for Aladdin. . . . .'[8] He would continue to make this comparison throughout his life, for example when in 1868 the city of Odense was illuminated to honour him, while his last novel, *Lucky Peer* climaxes on the performance of the hero's very own Aladdin opera. The story had become familiar throughout Western Europe through the French orientalist, Antoine Galland (1646–1745) who included it, in a somewhat reworked version of a Syrian storyteller's tale, in the 1712 volume of his *Thousand and One Nights*. The prime (and psychically appealing) ingredients of the tale are all conspicuously here in this first *Eventyr*: the hero's initial poverty; the demand that he descend into dangerous subterranean regions to fetch something a person with magic powers desperately wants; his refusal to hand this over when back above ground; his chance discovery of the object's extraordinary powers; his subsequent use of it to benefit himself and to win the hand of the princess with whom he will live happily ever afterwards in marriage.

But for Danes it was Adam Oehlenschläger's long, romantic verse-drama of 1805, from which indeed the young Andersen proceeded to quote in his December 1825 diary after the exclamation included above, which gave the Eastern story its wide imaginative currency. After the defeat of Denmark in 1813, this became a totemic work for the nation, representing the Danes' essential character as they saw it, their hopes and their inevitable splendid recovery. As a people they were resourceful like Aladdin during indigence (national bankruptcy) and obscurity (low international standing), and by building up a strong, lively society with its emphasis on both peaceful (educational and artistic) activity and practical commerce, they would take up their rightful and exemplary place in the European world.

By extension – especially when one contrasts the tale with his previous literary productions – Andersen was doing something not at all dissimilar in writing 'The Tinder-Box' and the *Eventyr* that directly follow. The tale emanates a gauntlet-throwing sense of release – shown indeed by Andersen's masterly decision to use it as the opening of his first fairy-tale book. He was abandoning the anxiety accompanying the (admittedly successful) upward progress of Antonio the Improvisatore. He could stop forcing himself to adapt to – or show himself as familiar with – persons for whom learning, *politesse*, familial security and privileges had come with their birth. To present himself as the intimate of Otto or Vilhelm (as he was doing contemporaneously with these first tales), of young men educated according to class expectations and moving unapolo-getically in Denmark's best society, must often have been a painful process, inducing yet further self-doubt. But in these *Eventyr* he could instead pay attention to a considerably larger world – made up of (often literally unnamed) ordinary folk such as he had known in childhood, and from some of whom he had heard stories he could now put to use. He was free at last to give unimpor-tant individuals the literary benefit of his own private and phenomenal abilities to observe and to listen.

In 'The Tinder-Box', for instance, the condemned soldier sees out of his cell window a cobbler's boy running to join the crowd that is in fact gathering to watch his own imminent execution. The boy is still wearing his leather working-apron and his slippers. In his haste one slipper flies off, to land just below the cell's iron bars through which the soldier can address him. If the boy can run back fast to the soldier's former rooms and bring him the tinder-box he left behind there, he will have earned himself a whole shilling. This appeals so hugely to the cobbler's boy that he complies. Thus the resolution of the plot is effected by a character with no relationship whatsoever to the soldier yet without whom he could not have survived. But we don't see the boy merely as an agent of deliverance, as some young *deus ex machina*. Andersen renders him as an autonomous, thoroughly convincing human being. How true to life it is that, keen though the boy is to see the ghastly public show, he can pause on his way because of his missing slipper and turn out to be even keener on getting an extra shilling! Andersen the novelist would have included such a boy only because he contributed to the scheme of the whole, and thus make him carry thematic baggage – like Eva's penniless musical brother in *O.T.* Here, however, we can see him unconsciously typifying human behaviour and, equally uncon-sciously, altering the life of another person by his accidental presence at the right time, by the happenstance of contiguity.

The soldier attempts no reconciliation with his future in-laws who after all arranged his hanging (and here Andersen probably recollected his own horri-fied witness of an execution near Slagelse when a pupil there). So he lets his faithful dogs seize the royal couple as indeed they have already seized the courtiers, hurling them into the air so that, almost certainly, they are smashed to smithereens. This is wholly consistent with the emotional mood of the story, and doubtless with the *Weltanschauung* of its central character. To ascribe forgiveness here to the soldier would be committing a literary untruth. Andersen, who personally believed in compassion and abhorred vindictive-ness and punishment, is purposefully *not* creating a role model, just as initially he withheld from his soldier those sympathetic aspects of his condition that the Grimms ascribed to theirs; he continues intellectually faithful to what he has set up. But maybe it is a little disingenuous to leave it at that. The *Eventyr* takes Andersen back down into the Odense world, of Tugthus, penury and superstition. As a result its driving forces are championship of the unfortunate, and rejection of those in arbitrary power. The effecting of that championship, that rejection may well involve ruthlessness, even brutality of action that many a *bien pensant* may prefer not to contemplate.

The same is true also of the succeeding story, 'Little Claus and Big Claus', based on a Danish peasant tale and therefore even more audacious in its bypassing of polite society with its often Pharisaic decrees of what was morally suitable for the young and what subversive. That somewhat grovelling tone in which Antonio speaks of, and to, Eccellenza in *The Improvisatore* – honouring him for being so kind and helpful to someone as lowly as himself – belongs to another discourse entirely. This tale regards parity as a desideratum and fair dealing among people as a moral obligation.

Big Claus and Little Claus live in the same town in a farming district. The adjectives prefixed to their identical first names indicate the most obvious difference between them: economic status. Big Claus has four horses, Little Claus only one. Inwardly they are very different men, however, and if measured by attributes the adjectives should rightly be reversed. Little Claus is cheerful, clever, and resourceful, Big Claus sullen, stupid and crassly imitative. He takes pains only when he wishes to catch up with another's (apparent) good fortune. In shape this story is of that chain-sequence type, which Andersen was to use with yet greater dexterity in two well-received later productions: 'Klods-Hans' ('Clumsy Hans', 1855)[9] and 'Hvad Fatter gør, det er altid det Rigtige' ('What Father Does is Always Right', 1861).[10] Anglophones will also think of such accumulative riddle songs as 'The House that Jack Built' or 'There was an Old Woman who Swallowed a Fly', which build on themselves until a final stroke which exposes the precariousness and the absurdity of the whole construct.

Little Claus ploughs for Big Claus all week long, lending him for the job the one horse he himself possesses. But on Sunday Big Claus lets Little Claus use his four as well as his own. Little Claus gets over-excited as he drives these five horses along, calling out 'Hyp, alle mine Heste!' 'Gee-up all my horses!' so much irritating Big Claus, who, of course, knows four of these beasts to be his own, that one morning he strikes Little Claus's single horse dead. Little Claus has his animal skinned and the horsehide dried out, and then goes into town to sell it. The weather turns bad, but propitious for Claus's fortunes; it enables him to use the (financially quite worthless) skin to his advantage, making it squeak and pretending that a troll lives inside it capable of magic feats. He employs this trick on a farmer's wife whom he has witnessed, unseen by her, entertaining the local church deacon to a fine dinner in her husband's absence and then, on hearing the latter return, hastily hiding both guest and the meal. This gives cunning Little Claus his opportunity, and he emerges from his visit to the farmhouse the richer by a whole bushel of money, having persuaded the gullible husband to buy his 'magic' horsehide. Jackie Wullschlager shrewdly observes: 'Andersen sanitizes the sexual innuendo of the traditional version [the original Danish folk tale] by giving the farmer an irrational dislike of deacons, though the cuckold is clear to adult readers.'[11] One might add that this antipathy of the farmer's is presented very much tongue-in-cheek (like the soldier's friends' aversion to the steep stairs) as readers are not expected to take it as the whole truth. And there is also a significant social component to the wife's hospitality; she aspires to more sophisticated company than her husband can provide. Readers of D.H. Lawrence's *Sons and Lovers* (1911) will remember Mrs Morel's delight in entertaining the refined young neighbourhood minister while her rough-spoken miner husband is out and how infuriated the latter is by this when he comes home. Andersen anticipates such a scene here; adultery (of the flesh anyway) need not be involved.

Little Claus's success with his horsehide leads the absurdly brainless and competitive Big Claus to kill all his own horses and try to flog *their* hides – obviously to no avail. And so the multiplication of episodes continues, Little Claus ingeniously bettering himself each time, Big Claus both copying and trying to outdo him, until the fool lets himself be tied up in a sack with a big stone, and dropped in the river.

Place is an important consideration in Andersen's *Eventyr* and also in their relative successes as literary artefacts. Topography was integral to *The Improvisatore* and *O.T.*, and has an even more vital role in *Only a Fiddler*; it is therefore a major constituent of Andersen's grasp of reality. *The Improvisatore* continuously relates Antonio's inner growth to his external experience of Italian cities and landscapes – from the hustle of Rome's poorer quarter to the extraordinary natural phenomena of the volcano Vesuvius and Capri's Blue Grotto. In *O.T.* we see the differentiating personal characteristics of Otto and Vilhelm as to a good measure deriving from the surroundings of their younger years: harsh, wild coastal Jutland in Otto's case, the benevolent, fruitfully farmed countryside of Fyn in that of Vilhelm, with Copenhagen itself as a sophisticated melting-pot which also contains prohibitive class divisions.

When it came to the fairy-tale, however, imposing as it did far tighter literary economy, Andersen appreciated that such specificities presented grave problems since they would inevitably demand fuller descriptions than the story itself could stand. Too many details about a place – which in a novel would only endorse its authenticity – could well detract from, or undermine, the non-realistic elements intrinsic to a fairy-tale and its meaning. On the whole the stories we know best from the Brothers Grimm, or even from the Danish Matthias Winther, unfold in a generalised landscape with components familiar to their audience but without fidelity to any definable geographical actuality; indeed they do not recognise the need for this. A large forest can give way in no time to a huge city where we will see only what serves the working-out of the situation: a palace, say, or unnamed streets from which amorphous mobs appear, or a public square. In certain respects their scenery resembles those syncretic 'World Landscapes' of sixteenth-century Flemish painters such as Patenier,[12] through which key figures – from the Bible or later Christian lore – could move without being marked by norms of region or period.

Andersen was concerned from his very first fairy story on with the inward significance of the happenings he is relating, and inwardness often – as in the longer fiction – meant his visualising (and in some amplitude) the circumstances of his people and his events. Hence he faces in this new genre a problem which, time and again throughout his career as fairy-tale writer, he will find difficult to solve. Go one way, and the positioning in time and space interferes with, or even renders impossible, any dramatic, imaginatively challenging external acting-out of the psyche. Go the other, and we are suspended from the physical world in a state of literary or folkloric metaphor. Sometimes Andersen had to rely, as any traditional storyteller did, on 'World Landscapes', on juxtapositions that no atlas or chronological chart would have found likely or even possible. But in my opinion when he did this, he invariably detracted from the success of the work-in-question as a convincing totality. The first two published stories, however, provide excellent examples of productive ways of tackling the question.

'The Tinder-Box' concentrates with painterly precision on a single figure, who comes marching towards us in that spell-binding first sentence. Such concentration means the actual milieus visited in his company are of importance *only* as regards *him*. Beyond his response to them there's no need to concern ourselves. Anyway, the narrative voice is such that, enthralled, we import into the story of the soldier fragments of our own experiences, as is intended. The address to the psyche is such that it doesn't matter a jot who the king and queen are or who they rule over, and it works primarily through the vernacular language of the presentation – further extending to the speech of the soldier and those he deals with. We have entered a vast commonalty of persons and life histories, as we have also in the tale of Big and Little Claus. But this pair have their being in a recognisable context: a rural community with small-holder farmers and men obliged to work for them, with markets, church deacons, inns and cattle drovers. If the peasant-crowded canvases of Brueghel come to mind, so does the Danish country scene before (or at a significant spatial distance from) the encroachment of industrialisation. By rigid artistic selection Andersen has set his far-fetched farce in a world we can legitimately think of as an adjunct of our own.

'The Princess on a Pea' is a little *jeu* based on a tale that Andersen claimed he heard as a child. Delightfully mocking the claims of the ruling class and their lackeys to refinements of sensibility, and even of physical sensation in excess of ordinary folk's, it has justly become proverbial. But it scarcely needs any setting, though the wet weather bringing the princess to her future father-in-law's castle is vividly caught in colloquial language not usually applied to royalty. And the nice detail of the class-proving pea being put on display in the Royal Museum (Copenhagen) belongs to the younger Andersen of the humorous *Journey on Foot*. The fourth tale of the first collection, 'Little Ida's Flowers' – unlike the others, entirely Andersen's invention – is basically a cameo of domestic life of a kind Andersen will provide repeatedly in his *oeuvre*. By his own admission, it was inspired by conversation with the small daughter of his friend (and benefactor) Counsellor Just Mathias Thiele whose importance in Copenhagen's cultural life we have already noted. It creates with accumulated strokes just such an *haute bourgeois* home as the Counsellor's must have been, so plausibly that we can easily accept its fanciful extension into a place where fading flowers can be restored to life and even hold a ball. Though perhaps the least interesting story of the first two collections and not free from archness, it is a complete success in its handling of milieu.

But in a greatly superior production, indeed at its best the most moving of the seven stories of the first two collections, 'The Travelling Companion', Andersen's obvious equivocation about the physical actualities of his story is vitiating, though not fatally. Taken from an established tale with extensive kin – that section known as the Grateful Dead in folklorist Stith Thomson's generous-sized Category E, 'The Dead' – one, moreover, Andersen had written a version of before in his *Youthful Attempts*, 'Dødningen',[13] 'The Ghost' – it conducts us in its first part to country we feel both the author and ourselves know well. We can even call it rural Denmark if we want to: the old church, the churchyard with the crosses placed on the recent graves, the fields and woods through which Johannes begins his journey, the little church on the hill where he takes refuge for the night and sees two bad men violating a coffin. Even the next part, the intermediary stage of Johannes's journey – with the mysterious stranger insisting on accompanying him – seems totally of a piece with the reality Andersen has established, springing, as in 'The Tinder-Box', from his empathic relation to his central figure, the bereaved youth, who is no piece of self-presentation from the novels but an individual with representative attributes. But Johannes then proceeds to pass through great forests and high mountains (not just unknown to, but apparently undreamt of, by him) and thence to a magnificent city with a hundred towers shining like silver. Disappointedly we acknowledge we are being asked into a world as impossible for the humdrum hero to visit, let alone to inhabit later as a married man, as it would be for ourselves. We feel that Johannes's movement into this world – where a distressed king grieves for his daughter's innocent hanged suitors, and the princess herself, under the domination of a troll, flies nightly to visit her master on his throne of horses' skeletons – is beyond observed (observable) life and into mental artifice. Therefore what now befalls him doesn't quicken our feelings or minds as his earlier plight did; it has been too patently grafted on. If he had stuck with the credible locality of the beginning sections, Andersen would probably have produced a far more integrated work with a more satisfying overall effect. But he was, of course, following here the prescribed course of a well-known story with its own exigent demands.

2

'The Tinder-Box' and 'Big Claus and Little Claus' are very masculine tales, and indeed *deal* with men, not flinching from the predatory and acquisitive aspects of malehood. Hitherto, it has to be admitted, those glimpses of girls and women in *Shadow Pictures* apart, Andersen's prose writings have not been distinguished by sensitive portrayal of women. (In this he did himself far less than justice, since responsive friendships with women were always a strong feature of his life.) Annunziata in *The Improvisatore* affects us more as an artist than as a woman; her undying feelings for Antonio do not ring true, and too clearly originate in the author's own narcissistic wish-fulfilment. Sophie, Louise and Eva in *O.T.* are ciphers. The feminine in the Eventyr enters with 'Little Ida's Flowers', and Ida's relationship to the student who frequents her father's house is gently, feelingly done. With his scissors ever ready to make amazing paper cut-outs, often caricaturing people and situations, and his propensity for telling fanciful stories, this young man is clearly a self-portrait. As such he sheds light both on the author's relaxed attitude towards children, which includes entering into and stimulating their make-believe, and his sometimes uneasy relations with the important persons with whom he chose to associate. In this story the Counsellor (Thiele himself?) finds his visitor not a little irritating and thinks he is telling his small daughter distracting nonsense! The man is later mocked in the form of a wax doll with a pompous, broad-brimmed hat and a sour expression. Yet surely there is something a little too deliberately sweet in the delineation of Ida herself, and one reader at least heaves a sigh of decided relief when two noisy Norwegian boys appear at the end of the story, firing their bows-and-arrows over the grave Ida has made for her deceased flowers!

But the story which comes first in the second collection, 'Thumbelina'[14] shows real poetic empathy for the feminine. In its inventiveness and its skill in uniting the visible/tangible and the feeling worlds it is the most remarkable of the stories to date. And significantly the landscape of this sustained fantasy has a solid consistency, is true to an easily identifiable natural domain.

'Thumbelina' is in essence a picture of the helplessness of the female, innately tender and giving, and therefore exploitable, in the face of those conventions the world has devised and maintained to preserve an inflexible order. Often these conventions wear the disguise of kindliness and even respect. But, serving a male design, they set at naught the sensitivities, let alone the particularities, of the individual and take ruthless advantage of inferior physical strength and societal position. Though everybody wishes her well, and for the most part treats her decently, Thumbelina is not permitted to make any decisions about her life, not even who she should fall in love with, love being considered an expendable irrelevance in her case. Escape is her only option – and as it mercifully happens, she is able, quite literally, to fly away.

The conceit chosen by Andersen to embody his feminist parable is one of extraordinary brilliance, because it can operate simultaneously on several levels: Thumbelina is a diminutive creature, no taller than a human thumb; her size is the major factor in her appeal, in her vulnerability, in her intimate relationship to the natural world. The rendering of this last is transformative for the story's audience. In living beings we disdain to notice, in places we are too custom-bound to scrutinise, we now see that both joy and terror lurk. Interestingly, Andersen's mediumistic power to reveal these, to compel us to examine, often in very close and surprising detail, our physical contexts in ways our normal senses do not equip us to explore, is displayed more often than not when he attends to – or even takes up – a female identity. In Jungian terms he has to follow his own anima to gain these insights. Ida of the flowers was his first, somewhat clumsily employed conductress here, but 'Thumbelina' is the real inaugurator. 'The Little Mermaid' and 'The Snow Queen' (through the character of Gerda, in direct contrast to her male playmate, Kay) are the most celebrated vindications of this imaginative process.

Thumbelina arrives in our own world in a most curious way. A childless (barren?) woman longs for a child and consults a witch who sells her for twelve *skillings* a grain of barley to plant in a flowerpot. Almost at once a tulip-like flower springs up, and its red-and-yellow petals part to reveal a tiny girl. She has thus come into the world without the preliminary of sexual intercourse and by an exertion-free fusion of male and female sex organs. This in itself, I believe, offers a comment on bourgeois society's increasing aversion to calling a spade a spade where the procedures of procreation were concerned, a feature that swelled to grotesque and dishonest proportions as 'Victorianism' gained a hold all over Europe. (But Thumbelina's 'birth' may well conceal certain psychological revulsions of Andersen's own, revealing his own recoil from overt sexual behaviour; 'The Tallow Candle' would seem to indicate that these date from early years.) Her prettiness is Thumbelina's most striking attribute, though in truth she is as resourceful and enterprising in her own (inevitably more circumscribed) way as the soldier of 'The Tinder-Box' – and, unlike him, kind-hearted, and unselfish by both instinct and principle. Andersen's account of Thumbelina's early life has a magnetic charm which endears us to the little girl while initially preventing us (though we do not recognise this) from viewing her as anything more than a delightful animated object, an unusual toy or doll. Her adoptive mother gives Thumbelina a walnut shell as cradle, and, for her daytime amusement, places on a tabletop a plate filled with water so she can row a tulip-petal raft on it, using two white horsehairs as oars. The pleasantness of this little spectacle is enhanced by the girl's singing. This singing alone could well have told observers of an inner, creative nature behind her so fetching exterior. But none of them draws this conclusion.

The woman who had so long wanted a child and her helper, the witch, soon both disappear – and completely – from the story. It is not unusual in a folk tale to take leave of instrumental characters after they have served their purpose, but 'Thumbelina', like 'Little Ida's Flowers' is not an imaginative variant of any folk tale, or in the least like one. It is an original creation of the author's own, so we can assume that his dropping of the adoptive mother has a meaning, and it is surely an uncomfortable one. Once Thumbelina has ceased being a charming novelty, she ceases to concern even her surrogate parent, and instead has to make her way in the world unprotected and alone, except for her own virtuous nature. Thus, Andersen is implying, are girls beyond number cast out into the marriage market of society's higher ranks, and, in its lower echelons, they are pressed into the ignominies of going into service etc., with all its concomitant hardships and problems. Even a firm morality can't always come to the rescue here.

A toad insists that Thumbelina marries her ugly son. She takes no notice of her distressed reluctance, but instead isolates her on a water-lily leaf. Fishes rescue Thumbelina by nibbling at the plant's stalks, and a butterfly – we think of Psyche[15] and the soul's ability to gain Plato's sphere of absolutes – then draws the leaf and Thumbelina downstream, aided by a ribbon provided by the little girl herself. But a beetle comes along and breaks up the journey, deciding that he is the one whom Thumbelina should marry. Even in her misery the tiny being is concerned for the poor butterfly who cannot release itself from the ribbon. The beetle's female relations so cruelly deride Thumbelina that they put him off his bride, and she flees alone into countryside experiencing the first grip of winter. A field mouse befriends Thumbelina and lets her stay in her snug underground home, but all the time that she is being so hospitable, she is conniving at marrying the diminutive girl to her fine, tunnel-digging neighbour, the mole. His proud pomposity suggested to readers in the know that here was yet another vengeful portrait of Andersen's old headmaster, Simon Meisling!

And now occurs an episode which, in hindsight, seems quintessential Andersen but which is hard to parallel in his previous work. Visiting the mole in his underground quarters Thumbelina comes across the body of a swallow, presumably dead from the cold. Unlike her churlish host she feels sad at this sight, remembering all the sweet songs she has heard swallows sing. So she kisses its closed eyes and later spreads a coverlet of hay over it and moves it to a securer place. When next morning she looks in, she hears a heartbeat and sees that the bird is still alive. This beautifully realised incident has all-important consequences. All winter long Thumbelina looks after the swallow until it is sufficiently restored to health to fly off. However, as it's now summer, it stays in Denmark. But in autumn – the time when Thumbelina, despite her protests, must marry the insufferable mole – it prepares to go with its own kind on the migration to southern lands. Seeing Thumbelina by chance, and hearing from her about her imminent fate, it offers, out of affectionate gratitude, to take her on its long flight. She accepts, and at the journey's end will discover a little man of her own sort, whom she falls in love with and marries.

The notion of Thumbelina being pestered by members of different species from her own succeeds brilliantly as a metaphor for society's all-but-arbitrary yoking of girls and women to males they neither know well nor care for. The eventual finding of the right mate for the heroine – in the fecundity of a southern climate – is less artistically sure than her earlier dilemma; it even has a certain perfunctoriness. Perhaps, considering the miseries Thumbelina has already endured, so flagrantly happy an ending (though there is well-communicated sadness in her inevitable farewell to her redeeming swallow) is simply not consonant with the tone of the rest. Once again conventional fairy-tale apparatus has been applied, even if idiosyncratically handled, and the meeting between the two midgets is too *voulu*. This will not be the last time we are less than comfortable with the conclusion to which a tale is brought. The intensity of Andersen's imagination, admitting as it does rich ambiguities of feeling and moral attitude, means that ending a story was often truly problematic for him. Two of his greatest achievements, 'The Little Mermaid' and 'The Snow Queen', as well as famous but less critically admired stories like 'The Red Shoes', fail at the end to do total justice to the complexities so elaborately and disturbingly established. In this respect the novels do far better. The last pages of *The Improvisatore* are maybe too much of a deliberate tableau, a final curtain beyond which we can't see a believable present or future. But those of both *O.T.* and, as we shall be seeing, *Only a Fiddler* are superb, unexpected, original and thought-provoking extensions of the novelist's art.

It is the use of the swallow that lifts 'Thumbelina' to its high level of literary distinction. For a start the bird is made real to us by its correspondence to ornithological fact. Though this one does not remember how it got into the mole's quarters after tearing its wing on a rose bush, swallows are in fact capable of going underground for nesting purposes: constructions as deep as 17 metres (55 feet) underground have been recorded. Their song with its 'rolling trill' is pleasing to hear, and it's not surprising that Thumbelina so greatly liked listening to it. And the birds stay in northern temperate lands (UK, Denmark) from May to September/October when they gather in large flocks to begin their immense southward journeys, usually to Africa, their likely destination in this story. Thumbelina would seem to be taken across the Alps, over and past Italy with its vines and lemon groves, to some Roman outpost in the Maghreb. Andersen had a particular feeling for swallows – it will be important to 'The Ice-Maiden' that these birds think of the often recalcitrant Little Rudy as one of themselves and speak of 'Vi og I', 'We and You' – and he ends this early story touchingly and individualistically, with Thumbelina's swallow returning to Denmark and telling himself, the writer, 'Manden ... som kan fortælle Eventyr',[16] 'the man ... who can tell fairy-tales', how the tiny girl is faring, a narrative device which Selma Lagerlöf remembered in her classic *Nils Holgerssons underbara resa genom Sverige* (*Nils Holgersson's Wonderful Journey through Sweden*, 1906–07[17] where the author in person, wanting to write her children's travelogue, meets the midget Nils who has been riding the length of Sweden on a gander's back. (Nor will this be the only instance where Nils's rich and fascinating story reminds us of Andersen.) The swallow's part in the story has clear Christian significance, this adjective – whatever the shifting dogmatic heterodoxies of Andersen himself – being absolutely the appropriate one. For, focusing on the person of Jesus himself, on his sayings and deeds as a magnetic human being, Andersen's whole vision of life is indelibly Christian; as much as that of, say, the Strindberg of *Påsk* (*Easter*, 1901), for all its author's previous spiritual excursions, or even as that of the Gerard Manley Hopkins of such poems as 'Hurrahing in the Harvest' or 'Pied Beauty'.

Thumbelina on the first day of her encounter with the swallow thinks it dead, but this does not mean that she cannot feel sorrow at its fate or reverence for its very being; therefore like those who tended to Jesus, she makes its repose a fittingly dignified one. Though the bird has not literally died, in effect he has. So Thumbelina is repeating Jesus' restoration of Lazarus, and has enabled the swallow's return from death by the kiss she instinctively gave. It has come back to life through her care altruistically, gratuitously given. Thumbelina expects no reward from her actions whatsoever, administration of kindness being satisfying in itself. But reward *does* come her way. At a time of great depression, and when, looking at the autumnal harvest all round her, she is thinking of the swallow, she sees it there high in the air above her – and it, recalling all she has done, chirps with joy on spying *her*. Thus the bird is an agent of a wholly new life for her, just as the Gospel of Jesus Christ can be for us. We can even see Thumbelina as kin to the Marys who cared for Jesus after the deposition from the Cross. But of her new life, and what it would entail, we have no real sense. Thumbelina has been removed to a country of idealised fable rather than earthly geography, unlike the Denmark where the swallow-receiving storyteller lives, and where her earlier adventures occurred, which was rendered in convincing detail.

3

The Gospel that so permeates 'Thumbelina' also permeates 'The Travelling Companion'. The (already adumbrated) central occurrence is again a resurrection brought about by means of another's (a stranger's) instinctual unselfishness. The difference here is that a man really *has* died, but has not been left in the peace appropriate for the dead. Through our hero's offices he is enabled to achieve this condition, but not before – like the swallow repaying Thumbelina – he has brought happiness to his deliverer.

The first part of the tale, set in a rural community we can well envisage as that of Fyn, is handled with all a novelist's sureness. The dying father tells Johannes how good a son he has been; 'Vorherre',[18] 'Our Lord', will always look after him. This gives the youth comfort in his desolation. Falling asleep by his dead parent's bed, Johannes dreams that the man is alive and well again, also that the sun and moon are bowing down before him (as in the dream of the biblical Joseph) and that a beautiful girl wearing a crown is his bride. A week later his father is duly buried, and Johannes, taking his inheritance of 50 *rigsdaler* and two silver shillings, sets out to make his way in the world, with no destination indicated. Though his grief is great, he is filled with a sense of life's essential goodness, confirmed by birds, flowers, sunshine, and even 'Kirke-Nissen', 'the little goblin' perched on the tower of the old church in which he used to worship with his father.

On he proceeds, soon entering completely unfamiliar countryside. He attends a service at an unknown church and even tidies up some of the church-yard's more unkempt graves; he sees an old beggar outside the lychgate, and gives him those two silver shillings of his patrimony. The fine weather changes to storm, and that night Johannes has to take shelter, and does so inside a little church on top of a hill. In the middle of the night he wakes up to notice a dead body inside an open coffin, and two obviously villainous men ('slemme Folk') beside it. He even sees these thugs take hold of the body and prepare to chuck it outside the church door. Johannes, being of good conscience, is not at all frightened by the sight of the corpse, and is bold enough to remonstrate with this pair. Their excuse is that the dead man owes them money which they can't now get back, and so he should lie outside the church door like a dog. Johannes then hands them the rest of his inheritance insisting they promise to leave the deceased alone. Then, like Thumbelina with the swallow, Johannes positions his corpse in the coffin in the correct, dignified attitude. This is the body that will rise up to help him as his Travelling Companion,

In this capacity he assists Johannes to the hand in marriage of a beautiful princess tragically under a troll's evil spell. Every suitor of hers has to guess what she is thinking of, and every suitor has failed to do so and been hanged, much to her father's sorrow. But the Travelling Companion, with the magic help of swan's wings which he attaches to his own person, follows the princess on her nightly flight to the troll, learns from their talk the object for the next day's conundrum and so enables Johannes to give the right answer. Eventually the man succeeds in cutting the troll's head off and when the princess sees it, she has to agree to marry Johannes. But she is still bewitched, and it is not until his Travelling Companion gives Johannes drops to put in her bath-tub that she is released from the enchantment. Then the couple fall properly in love. Johannes begs his friend of the journey to stay for the festivities. But he says he cannot do this, and reveals his identity. He was the dead man whom the two rogues wanted to harm in the church; he wanted to repay Johannes for his good deed, and now it is time for him to return to the peace of death.

There is a strong, indeed inescapable, scriptural antecedent for this story: the Book of Tobit in the Apocrypha.[19]

Tobit, a resident of Nineveh, has buried according to protocol a man he found murdered on the city streets. But during his vigil over the buried man, he was blinded by bird droppings (causing an obfuscating whiteness), leaving him depressed and unable to work as normal. His young son, Tobias, together with his dog, makes a journey from Nineveh to Media to retrieve money owed to his father and now needed. On the way Tobias is joined by a stranger who says he is a kinsman of Tobit's called Azariah and that he will protect him from any dangers. In fact this man is the angel Raphael in disguise. He comes to Tobias's rescue when a great fish, Asmodeus, attacks him as he washes himself in the river Tigris. When the fish has been killed, he tells Tobias to burn the entrails. This will be useful for the courtship he advises Tobias to conduct with his beautiful cousin, Sarah. She is plagued by devils, and the stench from the burnt offal will drive them away. This works. Now in love the young couple marry, and it is Azariah who takes the money back to old Tobit. Later he cures him of blindness, and then reveals his angelic identity. Tobit lives to a great age, but in the end Tobias gives him that same solemn burial that he, long ago, had given the known man in the Nineveh street.

When we review the two stories side by side we see interesting things in common: first, Johannes and Tobias are both only sons of loving and virtuous men. They return their fathers' feelings for them and try to live up to their moral codes. We can note that, before he dies, Johannes's father looks at him 'med alvorlige, milde Øine',[20] 'with serious, gentle eyes', also that in the dream he has shortly afterwards, asleep against the hard posts of his father's last bed, 'han saae sin Fader frisk og sund igjen og hørte ham lee',[21] 'he saw his father lively and healthy again and heard him laugh'. Johannes vows to be good, on the day of his burial, largely, it would seem, because this will ensure his eventual going to Heaven and being reunited there with his father. What a lot of things the two will have to tell each other!

Again, burial (the actual act of it, as a religious imperative) is of key importance to both histories. In Andersen's tale the burials of both his father and the unknown man are seen to dutifully by Johannes himself, the first as an act of love, the second of the compassion that is love's twin. He watches till the last corner of his father's coffin has been covered by earth; in the case of the stranger he arranges the body back inside the coffin according to prescribed rite, with the hands folded over his breast, so that the proper Christian burial can be carried out by the parish priest. In the Book of Tobit it is Tobit's determination that the dead stranger he finds will receive the burial appropriate to a religious Jew that is the seminal action of the whole work.

In both histories a specific sum of money is a plot determinant. In both too the fiscal value of this sum, actually quantified in Andersen, means less than the moral value of using it well, not to say altruistically. Johannes inherits from his father 50 *rigsdaler* and a couple of silver shillings, but parts with this quite happily to the two villains to make them entrust the dead man to his own care. As he says, he will get on all right without the money, he is healthy and strong, and Our Lord will always help him. With Tobias the very getting of the money has only been possible through the angel Raphael, yet, as we have noted, he is not treated as a faithful servant but as a real friend. The Book of Tobit belongs to the genre of Jewish 'wisdom stories', and to this category many a traditional story (like those Andersen consciously drew on here) also belongs. That virtue will be rewarded as it should be, even if tribulations are gone through first, is the 'wisdom' here, and we have to admit that the heroes of both do pretty well for themselves. Tobias inherits amply from both his father and his father-in-law, and Johannes becomes a king's son-in-law and then king himself. For in both histories the hero's good fortune (in both the spiritual and the worldly sense of the term) derives from his having delivered a beautiful young girl from a curse.

This, perhaps more than any other correspondence, suggests that Andersen had the Book of Tobit in mind during composition. In both works an honourable, cheerful young man woos a girl all of whose previous lovers have been killed. Tobias, while encouraged to be hopeful, and possessed of the potent fish innards, is afraid he will meet their fate, Johannes who, of course, also relies on supernatural help without realising it, is far more cheerful, sure that the Lord will see him through. The help is provided by the supernatural companion's arcane knowledge of the natural world: Raphael's of the fish, and its inner properties, while Andersen's character knows how to avail himself of a swan's wings. Evil has to be overcome with more than mere human wit or strength. In the Apocrypha there is a strong suggestion that Asmodeus possesses the girl so that she herself becomes responsible for the deaths of her grooms. Certainly her maids believe this is so. 'Dost thou not know, said they, that thou hast strangled thine husbands?' A psychoanalytical interpretation would be that she kills the young men before they are able to penetrate her. Virtuous Tobias aided by the angel divests her of her terror, hence their peaceful sleeping together. Johannes's princess is also under the dominion of an evil spirit, the troll, but in this case he has control of her whole life, her whole personality. It is her father who grieves at the death of so many fine young males. When, after Johannes's submersion of her in the bath-tub with the drops, she becomes a free human being again, she must remain as profoundly beholden to her groom/husband as Sara is to Tobias. Appropriate passages from the Book of Tobit have been used as celebratory readings in wedding ceremonies; Andersen's story is no less traditionalist in its celebrations, even though these are leavened with light-hearted, not to say undignified humour. And before either story comes to an end we have witnessed the respect-worthy elders enjoying the company of their grandchildren; Tobias and Sara provide Tobit with six grandsons while Johannes and the princess have children whom her king-father dandles on his knee and allows to play with his sceptre.

Inevitably the mind moves also to the story of the Road to Emmaus, Mark 16, verses 12 and 13, and Luke 24 verses 13–32 (where the road is actually given a name). In Luke's far fuller version the companion, hearing the two travellers whom he has joined talking about Jesus's crucifixion and the absence of his body in the tomb, actually speaks about how these events fulfil the old prophecies. Even so, it isn't until the evening when they see him break bread at supper that the men realise his identity. The eponymous Travelling Companion is also a man from the realm of death, and Johannes, who, after all, in positioning him in his coffin, had had the most intimate contact with his body, has never once suspected, let alone recognised who he was, and would never have known had the other not made his revelation. If readers do find themselves reminded of this Gospel episode, it only substantiates the story's all-encompassing tribute to the moral beauty of (non-doctrinaire) Christian faith.

4

Thumbelina, resisting the field mouse's insistent and very nearly successful plan for her to become the mole's wife, anticipates the first famous heroine of Andersen's admirer, Henrik Ibsen, Nora in *Et Dukkehjem* (*A Doll's House*, 1879).[22] Thumbelina, realising the cost to selfhood of the marriage arranged for her, takes off on the swallow's back for North Africa. And Nora – finally appreciating the deathly suffocation of a life where her husband thinks of her as a twittering lark and a rummaging squirrel while denying her the freedom proper to these wild creatures – abandons home and family, slamming the door on them for liberty every bit as venturesome and uncharted as the Andersen heroine's. In his next fairy story, also with a female protagonist, 'The Little Mermaid' – the first of the two fairy tales in the third collection – Andersen points to a later Ibsen work, that most disquieting presentation of the invaded, disturbed female psyche, *Fruen fra havet* (*The Lady from the Sea*, 1888). Not only does its title echo Andersen, not only is one of its most sympathetic characters, and a Dane at that, Ballested, at work on a painting entitled *The Dying Mermaid*, but the heroine, Ellida, apostrophises the sea in ecstatic terms which bring the richly worked descriptions of 'The Little Mermaid' immediately to mind. Here Ellida is telling her husband, Wangel, about the effect on her of the mysterious seaman who desired her, The Stranger:

> ELLIDA: We spoke mostly about the sea.
> WANGEL: Ah! About the sea?
> ELLIDA: About the storms and calms. About dark nights at sea. And about the glitter of the sea on sunny days. But mostly we talked about whales and dolphins, and about the seals that lie out in the rocks in the warmth of the sun. And we talked about the gulls and the eagles and all the other sea-birds. And you know ... Isn't it strange? ... when we talked about such things I used to feel that he was somehow of the same kith and kin as these sea-creatures.
> WANGEL: And you ...?
> ELLIDA: I too almost felt as though I were one of them.[23]

The sea had been greatly exercising Ibsen's mind before he set to work on this play; he had stayed in Denmark, in the summer of 1887, in the little town of Sæby on Jutland's east coast, and had also visited Skagen, and in his preparatory notes for the play jotted down:

> The sea's power of attraction. The longing for the sea. People akin to the sea. Bound by the sea. Dependent on the sea. Must return to it. One fish species

forms a basic link in the evolutionary series. Do rudiments of it still remain in the human mind?[24]

And, earlier, more amply:

Has human evolution taken the wrong path? Why have we come to belong to the dry land? Why not the air? Why not the sea? The longing to have wings. Curious dreams that one can fly and that one does fly without feeling any astonishment – how to explain all this?[25]

The ambition of the eponymous Little Mermaid is, of course, to *leave* the sea – for life on land, for love of a landsman (the handsome prince), for the immortality denied sea creatures but attainable through love of a human being. For most readers of the story, however, the most dazzling aspect of this virtuosic work is its sumptuous rendering of the underwater world, its glories and satisfactions which content the majority of its denizens, even those like the Mermaid's five sisters who have glimpsed existence in the air and on earth. In fact one of the most curious features of this deeply ambivalent tale is the author's attempt to make sympathetic to us his heroine's single-minded intention of spurning what he has succeeded in evoking in mesmerising detail and with lyrical exuberance – stemming from his own fascinated knowledge of the multifarious life forms the ocean nourishes. Ibsen – and nowhere more overtly than in *The Lady from the Sea* – was very much a *post*-Darwin writer. And while his idea of evolution having taken a (not irreversible) wrong turning might not have met with Darwin's intellectual concurrence, the notion of developed species preserving instinctual memories of earlier modes of existence would surely have done so. Andersen, who was writing his first fairy tales many years before *The Origin of Species* (1859), the impact of which he would follow with keenest interest,[26] was nonetheless familiar with the theory of some great pool (and in the literal aquatic sense) out of which all life might have emerged, consequently linking all later disparate living beings. In addition, Andersen and Ibsen were both interested in folklore as a preservation of atavistic relationships between our present developed selves and more primitive forms, some aeons-earlier *participation mystique*. There are nowhere better to look to for these than the numerous legends of mer-folk, selkies and seal maidens on which both writers drew.

But in the half-century that divides these two great Nordic works, a difference in conscious attitude of the most immense importance has evolved towards such states of being as these legends convey. Andersen feels the gravitational pull of the underwater realms with his ever-fertile imagination – its corals, its amber, its teeming fishes, its wealth of plant-life, even its hideous tangles of polyps – but his heart and mind are convinced that human/ terrestrial life is superior to anything down there because it recognises moral codes founded on altruism (even if it regularly and incessantly and barbarously betrays them). Ibsen, on the other hand, was writing at a time when bourgeois/ commercial values had triumphed all over Europe, and it was allegedly moral codes that were invoked as a way of keeping the money-based status quo functioning. It was wrong, according to these, to want to realise your own full identity; better that submission to societal authority which Nora and Ellida refuse to countenance. Therefore Ibsen looked to the depths of the sea – as later in *Lille Eyolf* (*Little Eyolf*, 1894)[27] he was to look at lonely mountain wastes – as harbouring and, if respectfully attended to, promoting a morality far deeper and more satisfying than that of the conventionally organised community. True, he also acknowledged the impracticability of this, and both these magnificent later plays end with some reconciliation with the norm. Ellida does not go off with the Stranger; she will put her yearnings for the sea into context and become the loving wife of a man who, she knows, unselfishly loves her. But audiences and readers have never been completely convinced by this. Today we are obviously far closer to Ibsen's world and mindset than to the prevalent *Weltanschauungen* of the late 1830s/1840s of Andersen's tales. We can feel therefore at one with Ibsen in his notes for further desiderata reuniting us with the elements:

> We should take possession of the sea. Build our towns floating on the sea. Move them to the south or to the north according to the season. Learn to harness wind and weather. Something marvellous like that will come. And we – will not be there to enjoy it! Will not experience it.[28]

Andersen, who loved the sea and swam in it as regularly and vigorously as his hero Otto Thostrup, might well have responded with ready fantasy to such exhortations as these, but as criticisms of our own civilisation they would have had scant appeal. We can find no traces of such thinking in 'The Little Mermaid', and we do well to reflect on the reactions of the mermaid siblings to the terrestrial.

Each celebrates her fifteenth birthday by swimming up from the ocean bed to the surface. Taken together, their different experiences constitute a picture of what distinguishes the quasi-human from the truly human. The eldest sister sees city lights twinkling like stars, and hears music, notably church bells, from the same direction. The second sister is impressed by the beauty of the sky over the sea, and of a flock of wild swans moving towards the setting sun. The third sister – the most daring of the mermaids – actually swims up the mouth of a river (as many mermaids of legend supposedly do), delighting in the vineyards, castles, manors on its banks, in birdsong and in the liveliness of human children playing in the water. The quiet fourth sister stays out in the open sea, admiring dolphins and, from a distance, ships. The fifth sister, who positions herself near icebergs, also sees ships, watches how they avoid these natural perils which to her are merely beautiful, yet all but founder in storms nevertheless. These mermaids' responses are therefore aesthetic, a quality accentuated by the beautiful singing they give vent to in chorus; none seems capable of any degree of sympathy with what she is witnessing. The fifth sister reminds us of those many mermaids of sailors' tales and shanties who positively welcome the fierce weather (indeed may be in league with the spirits that cause it) as an opportunity for drawing humans to themselves and claiming them – as lovers, as partners in their own elemental domain remote from earthly connections. The folklorist Katharine Briggs notes that Scandinavian mermaids tend to be sweeter and more seductive than those of the Celtic regions of the British Isles, who are almost always intent on destruction for their own personal purposes.[29]

The youngest sister is quite different, and in that difference lies the key to her utterly dissimilar destiny which will remove her from the element of the sea altogether. None of the other mermaid princesses has looked forward to her fifteenth birthday with the same ardour. The very words in which she expresses her impatient longing are significant: 'jeg veed, at jeg ret vil komme til at holde af den Verden deroven for og af Menneskene, som bygge og boe deroppe.'[30] 'I know that I will come to be really fond of the world above and of the human beings who make their homes up there.' Such a prospect has been no part of the expectations of any other merfolk. And the literal rendering of 'bygge og boe' – 'build and dwell' – suggest an anticipatory admiration for all the constructive work which humans, unlike sea-folk, regularly undertake. Her life down in the ocean, essentially aesthetic or kinaesthetic like her sisters', has been deficient in a quality that she knows intuitively to be of inestimable importance to her and which, young though she is, she can even go some way towards articulating: delight in a life extraneous to her own, delight so strong that she could well devote all her being to it. And the strength of this difference – so deep that it appears innate – she will demonstrate on her very first visit to the over-world.

It is evening and she swims up to a tall, three-masted ship on board which a party – with music and fireworks – is in progress, in honour of an extremely handsome young prince who has turned sixteen. Her immediate attraction to him is superficially consonant with the ways of her own species. But when a storm breaks and the wrathful waves turn the ship over, snapping the mast in two, and she watches the prince disappear into the ocean depths, her reactions are not at all those of the usual mermaid, particularly not those of her immediate sister, the fifth. True, for a moment she does experience a positive stab of happiness that death is about to deliver him to her father's kingdom, where he can become hers. But then another emotion overcomes her: this prince is too good and too young to die. He deserves life. She swims after him, finds him more dead than alive, supports him by holding his head above the water, kisses him (as Thumbelina did the swallow), and finally brings him to land. Land is a beautiful bay with lemon- and orange-trees by the shore, and nearby a kind of temple. Eventually a girl emerges from this and sees the stranded young man; she runs away to fetch help. Soon he is restored enough to be smiling at his fellow human beings but he has no smile for his true rescuer, now observing the scene from a distance, because he has no idea of her existence. Full of sorrow at this, the Little Mermaid returns to her oceanic home, and the most demanding part of her Eventyr is now set in train.

She is utterly unable (and, for that matter, unwilling) to forget the handsome prince whose resurrection she effected. She finds out where he lives and even ventures up the little channel leading to his palace, admiringly to watch him, up on a marble balcony. The more she sees of human beings, the more she likes them, and the less the non-human world pleases her. Her wise old grandmother makes her appreciate a deeper reason for her comparative evaluation. Human beings have souls, are therefore immortal, with an existence beyond the disintegration of their bodies. Their spirits will ascend to the stars after death. The Little Mermaid had not, to this point, understood her own lot. While, unlike those in the world above, she can count on a good three hundred years of corporeal life, when she dies she will become nothing more than foam on the sea's surface, quickly to disperse. From this moment on, her yearning to see and to get to know her prince and her thirst for immortality intertwine, and many readers – following her arduous, self-torturing, half-successful quest to abandon her mermaid identity for a human one – have felt that a greater distinction should have been made between the two. Isn't the first a love for an individual separate from one's self? Isn't the second a burning concern for the preservation of that self? Nor has the procedure by which the Little Mermaid, of her own choice, enters terrestrial life and comes heartbreakingly close to attaining her goals, elicited from twentieth- and twenty-first-century readers the wide sympathetic admiration that made her so iconic a figure to those of the nineteenth century. We draw back in repulsion as we watch her obediently following the witch's instructions painfully to sacrifice both her bodily being and her selfhood, and are not even convinced of the moral validity of her reasons for doing so.

In order to endear herself to her prince, or any human, she first has to get rid of her mermaid's fish-tail, an agonising business. The splitting of the tail into two legs resembles a sharp knife passing through her whole body, and this cruel sensation will affect all subsequent movement of her newly achieved feet.

Once in human shape she can never return to being a mermaid, and so is self-banished from everything familiar and dear from childhood. Nor, even after having put herself through such an ordeal, is she assured of either a relationship with a human man or her immortality. The second is absolutely consequent on the first; she has to win the love of a mortal – in her case, the handsome prince from the three-master – win it so unstintingly that he forsakes all others and marries her. Then, and then only, can she acquire an immortal soul such as every other human possesses. But to make the winning of the man an even more gruelling business she has to be deprived of speech. The Little Mermaid assents to this; the witch cuts out her tongue. Not only is she mute, she cannot sing, so she has lost that accomplishment in which she surpassed even her melodic sisters.

If we wish to come to terms with this sequence of mutilation and self-abasement – or, more accurately, to see it as Andersen's earlier readers would have done – we must turn to one of the masterpieces of German Romanticism (a case could be made for its being *the* German Romantic Novelle par excellence) on which it is, to an important degree, a resourceful and sharply pointed take.

Friedrich Freiherr de la Motte Fouqué (1777–1843), friend and literary associate of both Tieck and Chamisso, came from a Prussian military family, served in the army but resigned his commission in 1803 to devote himself to literature. It was a wise decision: he proved a fluent, productive writer and soon enjoyed an enormous enthusiastic readership, his tales meeting contemporary tastes with their generalised romantic medievalism, their easily assimilated eroticism and the kind of narrative compulsion not incommensurate with folk *Märchen* (fairy-tales). Only *Undine* (1811)[31] has survived today, and even that is far better known among scholars than ordinary readers, not least for the works it inspired: an opera by E.T.A. Hoffmann (1816) and another by Albert Lortzing (1845). Its Never-Never-Land setting where it is virtually impossible to make out what social systems or even what physical laws pertain, the unabashed extravagance of its central events and the absence of that common-sense logic linking them that we find in the folk tale proper are not congenial to the serious modern sensibility, to say nothing of the work's constant titillation of both the sex- and death-appetites, especially in its great climactic scene, so irresistible to its contemporary readers. But in fact the author's literary control and inventiveness, and the unflagging interest provided by the eponymous heroine, make *Undine* a lively work with intrinsic merits. Andersen knew it well, and that it was in his mind while writing 'The Little Mermaid', his letter to B.S. Ingemann of 11 February 1837 admits. But he disagrees, he tells his old friend, with one of the novella's key premises and heralds his own intentional departure from it. His story-in-progress then – which he claims will be better even than 'Thumbelina' – can legitimately be seen as standing in recognisable relation to Fouqué's. So hugely popular was *Undine* that Andersen would surely have expected all readers of 'The Little Mermaid' to see its presence behind his own work, and to take his offering as a kind of challenge, ideological as well as imaginative, to the assumptions and ethics of the earlier bestseller. If we read 'The Little Mermaid' with this in mind – for the correspondences are numerous and specific, and the breakaways wholehearted and significant – then some of the antagonism that many of us today feel towards what for over a century was one of Andersen's most revered and deeply loved works may be tempered.

Undine is a lively, mischievous, beautiful girl who lives as the daughter of a pious fisherman and his wife in their home on a lonely lakeside promontory. At its back is a vast forest full of threats from both natural and supernatural denizens. To the old couple Undine is a replacement for their dear daughter who disappeared as a small child into the lake, especially as she arose from it on that same sad day, long golden hair and costly clothes dripping water. Though the pair love Undine, they are irked by her wilful naughtiness, which they have never been able to control. One day a knight, Sir Huldbrand of Ringstetten comes riding through the forest, and the old couple offer him hospitality. He no sooner sees Undine than he is smitten by her beauty, but when, in a childish pet, she runs from her home and he follows her into a forest glen on the other side of a misty stream (in point of fact of her own fashioning), then he is overcome by passion for her. This grows in intensity all during his stay with the fisherman, Undine being delightfully demonstrative to him, though he is disconcerted by her behaviour to her parents. She obviously enjoys a special affinity with water (with the forest's main brook; with the lake), which apparently can obey her moods. The knight tells her of his own past – his involvement with a duke's daughter, the lovely, haughty Bertalda, a name it vexes Undine to hear. But now he has feelings only for Undine, and lives in her home as her fiancé; when a priest calls, he gets him to marry the two of them. 'Both before and during the ceremony, Undine had shown herself gentle and quiet; but it now seemed as if all the wayward humours which rioted within her, burst forth all the more boldly and unrestrainedly. She teased her bridegroom and her foster-parents, and even the holy man whom she had so lately reverenced. . . . At length the priest said in a serious and kind tone: "My fair young maiden, no one indeed can look at you without delight; but remember so to attune your soul betimes, that it may ever harmonize with that of your wedded husband." This admonition Undine greets with mockery: ' "Soul!" said Undine, laughing, "that sounds pretty enough, and may be a very edifying and useful caution for most people. But when one hasn't a soul at all, I beg you, what is there to attune then? And that is my case." '[32] But here Undine is mistaken; the marriage ceremony to Huldbrand has bestowed a soul on her, one just like any other mortal woman's.

Her realisation that she possesses this priceless entity brings about, mercifully, a cessation of teasing and an onset of a quiet period, and she explains to
Huldbrand her true identity: ' "You must know, my loved one, that there are
beings in the elements which almost appear like mortals, and which rarely
allow themselves to become visible to your race." '[33] The rich litany that now
follows makes *Undine* as principal progenitor of 'The Little Mermaid' only too
palpable. ' "Those, however, who dwell there are very fair and lovely to behold,
and for the most part are more beautiful than human beings. Many a fisherman
has been so fortunate as to surprise some tender mermaid as she rose above the
waters and sang. He would tell afar of her beauty, and such wonderful beings
have been given the name of Undines. You, however, are now actually beholding
an Undine. . . . Our condition would be far superior to that of other human
beings – for human beings we call ourselves, being similar to them in form and
culture – but there is one evil peculiar to us. We and our like in the other
elements, vanish into dust and pass away, body and spirit, so that not a vestige
of us remains behind; and when you mortals hereafter awake to a purer life, we
remain with the sand and the sparks and the wind and the waves. Hence we
also have no souls; the element [water] moves us, and is often obedient to us
while we live, though it scatters us to dust when we die. . . .'[34] But now Undine
can be assured she will survive her own body, and with this knowledge (*pace*
the later Andersen) a moral advance takes place. She begins to care for others
as much as, if not more than, for herself. She offers to release Huldbrand from
his marriage vows now he knows her provenance, but, more in love with her
than ever, he clasps her tightly to him, and invokes the Greek Pygmalion who
gave life and devotion to the statue, Galatea. With Undine as his wife, he returns
at last to the capital city from which he had come, but not before the troubling
manifestation of Undine's uncle, Kuhleborn, mighty water spirit who will not
renounce his kinship with the girl even though she is now mortal. A modus
vivendi, no more, can be established between them; thanks to him, Huldbrand
and Undine will not be able to enjoy the married life of a normal couple.

In fact for readers today – not in thrall to that fashionable inspiriting of
woods and waters which the original proffered – the most interesting, the most
psychologically resonant section of the novella now begins. Married bliss doesn't
prove limitless; Bertalda comes back into Huldbrand's life, and while a friendship springs up between the three of them, husband, wife, and his former love,
inevitably this cannot sustain itself. Huldbrand, wearying of Undine's childishness, is drawn back to Bertalda who, though she has not lost her haughtiness,
her capacity for unkindness, appeals to the more worldly, conventional side of
him. But Bertalda now interests readers for a reason they have been gently led
to suspect: she is no duke's child, but the very daughter of the old fisherman and
his wife who vanished into the lake on the day that Undine later arose from it.

The ensuing love triangle becomes a perfectly workable and absorbing metaphor for a man's (a society's) difficulties in accommodating him(it)self to the double properties of woman, to her inestimable, intimate gifts and her equally indispensable social capabilities – these not being as conveniently divisible or experientially separable as some might have hoped. It is in his handling of this, with its abundance of quickly succeeding incidents, that Fouqué's gifts as a novelist are most in evidence, and it's only right at this stage to say that they are beyond anything that Andersen could have achieved. Nothing in any of his fiction – whether novels or stories – approximates to *Undine*'s rendering of Huldbrand's universal problem, and it is just possible that Andersen understood this perfectly himself, which would account for the skilful evasion of any properly comparable scenes in his own story.

Though Undine is extremely hurt by Huldbrand's betrayal, she is also solicitous of him because she knows that her uncle, Kuhleborn will come to her defence in alarming, destructive ways that she cannot prevent. Huldbrand picks a quarrel with his wife when the three of them are voyaging down the Danube, and his awareness of Kuhleborn's venting his anger on the waters arouses his wrath so much that he hurls her jewels into the river and bids her return to her own magical race. In doing this he thus dissolves his marriage to her. 'She vanished over the side of the vessel. Whether she plunged into the stream, or flowed away with it, they knew not: her disappearance was like both and neither. Soon, however, she was completely lost sight of in the Danube; only a few little waves kept whispering, as if sobbing, round the boat, and they almost seemed to be saying: "Oh woe, woe! Oh remain true! Oh woe!" '[35]

But true to her Huldbrand and Bertalda do not intend to be. They marry, though the wedding feast is a joyless one; a shadow lies over it. Undine was much loved and is much missed. And for all her now tested moral sensibility she is unable to undo the laws of nature which brought her into being. She stealthily enters Huldbrand's quarters as he prepares for the night and there, deliberately and literally, kisses him to death, though not without dark consent on his part.[36]

Of course a triangle – one can even call it a love triangle – survives into (is indeed central to) Andersen's reworking of *Undine*, though there could hardly be a bigger contrast in how it comes about. We have seen that the Little Mermaid, in love with the handsome prince from the moment she first saw him, was the means of his rescue from death, and at a cost to her immediate selfish happiness, for by sea conventions he would have been hers had she permitted him to die and descend to the ocean depths. However, as the prince himself sees it, his restoration, after being deposited by the mermaid on dry land, was solely due to the girl from the nearby temple; hers is the image he keeps in his mind with gratitude. So when the Little Mermaid (mermaid no more now) joins his entourage and becomes the most beautiful and sympathetic to him of all his young female attendants, she doesn't replace the other girl in his thoughts, so firm is he in his conviction that it is to the latter alone that he is indebted. He senses the ex-mermaid's unusual unselfishness, she grows inexpressibly dear to him, and indeed – to some more cynical readers a sure proof of the male's capacity to have his cake and eat it – delights in taking her into his arms and kissing her brow. But never does the idea of making her his wife occur to him – and, of course, by the cruel interdict imposed on her, she is herself mute; no verbal communication between them is possible, merely looks of longing on one side, and of uncommitted appreciation on the other. What makes the Little Mermaid's position so ironically painful is that the prince is pleased to tell her that, in a mysterious way, she herself resembles the girl of his deliverance for whom he is searching – some implanting of the mermaid's image had obviously taken place, beneath that of his human rescuer. He also tells her that if he ever had to choose a bride, he would favour one like herself: 'mit stumme Hittebarn med de talende Øine', 'my speechless foundling with the speaking eyes.'[37] The mermaid, convinced that the girl he longs for is consigned to temple life, dreams of an existence of silent devotion to her loved one, thanked but never the object of his passion, let alone his wife – staying by his side every day and devoting herself wholeheartedly to his well-being.

But the girl of the temple turns out – by an unkind stroke of fate – to be none other than the princess his parents have in mind for him. The prince cannot get over his extraordinary good fortune, and with an insensitivity of which he is quite unaware he tells the mermaid: ' "Du vil glæde dig ved min Lykke, thi du holder meest af mig blandt dem Alle!" '[38] You will rejoice at my luck for you love me the most among them all.' And then follow the two infinitely sad sentences which point up the differences between *Undine* and 'The Little Mermaid' more succinctly perhaps than any others: 'Og den lille Havfrue kyssede hans Haand, og hun syntes alt at føle sit Hjerte briste. Hans Bryllups Morgen vilde jo give hende Døden og forvandle hende til Skum paa Søen.'[39] 'And the Little Mermaid kissed his hand, and it seemed to her that her heart was breaking. His wedding-day would mean her death and change her into foam on the seawater.'

Yet – unlike either Bertalda or Undine herself – jealousy, let alone revenge, is totally alien to her nature, and she cannot be tempted to externalise her unhappiness (even her very human feeling of being hard-done-by) as vengeful action. Her sisters rise up from the waters and tell her that, though she has forfeited for ever her chance of becoming truly human, the possessor of a soul, she can undo the black magic of the witch and return to mermaid form again. All she has to do is, before sundown, to kill the prince who has in effect played with her feelings, made use of her. After this deed she can rejoin her own kin again and resume her life, which, after all, has the best part of three centuries still to run. And they hand her a knife, so that she can administer to him what Undine administered to Huldbrand with her deathly embrace and kiss.

The Little Mermaid would appear momentarily tempted to carry out this terrible plan. Had she not been shown as (briefly) tempted, then she would not achieve that courageous self-sacrifice which is the ultimate goal of Andersen's story. She enters the prince's sleeping quarters, following Undine's last movements, she kisses his brow (again emulating her German literary predecessor) and gazes on him as he whispers lovingly the name of his bride. The mermaid's sense of loss could therefore not be more complete, and yet it is at this point that, her hand trembling on the knife, she casts the weapon away. And with that gesture she casts away her own continued existence. Not only has she failed to become human by winning the love of the prince, she has failed to preserve her mermaid identity by refusing to kill him. Now turning to foam is all she can expect.

Andersen's story logically, and, in accordance with the laws of tragedy it has carefully set up, should surely end here. The anti-*Undine* has been written, has come to its required end. Whereas Undine sought pleasure and (if incidentally) position for herself in her dealings with the knight, the Mermaid cared only for the prince's spiritual well-being – and, as she has witnessed his joy at union with the princess from the temple, she is prepared to accept the grim literal workings-out of the conditions she at her own risk agreed to. (They are exceedingly unfair ones, it must be protested, since the deprivation of speech inflicted on her renders her a wholly shackled contestant. A few words of explanation would have made the prince understand at the least whom he had to thank for still being alive.) Her recoil from killing – even for her own advantage – is further evidence of her all but instinctual Christianity which is at the heart of Andersen's tale.

For this is really a miniature *roman à thèse*. It shows that certain individuals rise above the stifling mores of the societies into which they are born, guided by aspirations for an existence fuller than any they have personally – or even vicariously – glimpsed. This existence – to be led in an ampler yet more dangerous world, the very entrance into which demands courage – is inextricable from the willingness to give up one's own security, even one's life, for the sake of others. Love for another is a necessary concomitant of this superior system, and the Mermaid in her feelings for the prince experiences it. But even here she cannot put self and its gratification first. Her final sparing of the prince's life – against the encouragement of the pagan society below the sea – is the culmination of her naturally felt but arduously lived out Christianity, to which, in a non-dogmatic fashion, Andersen felt himself committed. The

Mermaid is a Christ-analogue, and just as Jesus could not let Barabbas die, so the Mermaid faces her own Gethsemane after she has chucked the knife back into the sea.

However, her creator has now brought her to the point of the very annihilation against which, even as a theoretical possibility, he was in lifelong polemical protest. In Andersen's view, belief in immortality was essential not only to a more complete and satisfactory individual life but to moral health. In *Undine* the heroine possessed it because of the sacramental marriage to Huldbrand which could not be undone. Andersen felt that so immeasurably important a matter as the retention of an immortal soul could not be accounted for so lightly. In the letter to B.S. Ingemann already referred to he declares his refusal to let 'the Mermaid's acquisition of an immortal soul depend on an alien creature, on the love of a human being. I'm sure that would be wrong! It would depend rather a lot on chance, wouldn't it? I won't accept that sort of thing in this world. I have permitted my mermaid to follow a more natural, a more divine path.'[40]

This 'more natural, more divine path' might seem to approximate to the Catholic concept of grace. Grace now elevates the dissolving mermaid, native of the element of water, into the ethereal realm. She joins the Daughters of the Air who, although – like mermaids – born without immortal souls, can win souls for themselves through kindly deeds, though this may take three hundred years to achieve. This ending has satisfied few, myself included, and is ethically inimical to twenty-first-century taste. It makes us switch from the ideas of grace and divine love, temporarily prompted by the Mermaid's expiry, to the crudest (and most perfunctory) form of salvation by works, one compounded by the almost Christmas-cracker precept, tacked on to the very end of the tale, that loving, well-behaved children can aid the Daughters of the Air to gain immortality, whereas naughty or morose ones can prevent it.

Has then comparing Andersen's famous tale with *Undine* significantly lightened some of the graver charges made against it by those who disapprove of the sado-masochistic endurances of the Mermaid in the interests of love and eternity? To an important degree I think, yes. There is palpable tenderness in the rendering of the Mermaid's intense but helpless devotion to the prince and of his bemused response to her unalloyed sweetness. And unselfishness cannot exist *in vacuo*: it can only be seen in all its admirable strength when faced with danger and both physical and emotional pain. And to those repelled by the story's insistence on the degradation of the female as a necessary constituent of the test-and-quest imposed, one feels obliged to reply that not only here but throughout Andersen's *oeuvre* altruism belongs not just to the feminine but to the female: Little Ida, Thumbelina, the quietly but magnificently determined Gerda in 'The Snow Queen'. All the same there is, I believe, a real cause for dissatisfaction with the story, and it relates, if somewhat tangentially, to the argument levelled against it by exasperated feminist critics.

Unlike Undine, and unlike the three heroines cited above, we see the Mermaid almost wholly in terms of her eagerness for surrender, self-abasement. Though she is shown in her childhood as possessed of a great deal of natural curiosity, this quality is never adequately developed. She has no real personality distinct from her swooning acts of self-abnegation. Our hearts of course go out to those who sacrifice comfort, health, safety, life because in their integrity of being they have bestowed emotions and thoughts on persons and causes which seem to them worthy of every support, even if that means dying in the process. We can all supply moving instances of such priorities, such behaviour, and feel inspired by them. But sacrifice for its own sake is quite another matter, and not an appealing one, since it devalues the importance of life itself. Andersen began 'The Little Mermaid' on Fyn, on the day after the marriage of Edvard Collin from which he was (virtually) encouraged to stay away. Like 'Thumbelina' – to which, differing from Andersen himself, I believe the story to be ultimately inferior – this is a work governed by the wounded 'anima', by Andersen's own feminine self, unwell, unhealthy, self-punishing.

It is impossible to imagine our globally disseminated Western culture without 'The Emperor's New Clothes', as current in our conversation, writings and thoughts as the best-known Aesop Fables ('The Dog in the Manger', 'The Fox and the Grapes')[41] or the parables of Jesus ('The Wise and Foolish Virgins', 'The Prodigal Son'). Merely to mention the title is to set in motion a whole immediately understood line of inquiry. Yet this tale was not of Andersen's own invention, though the changes he made to the Spanish original – 'De lo que acontesció a un rey con los burladores que hicieron el paño', 'What Happened to a King with the Rogues Who Wove the Cloth' (which he read in German) – exhibit supremely both his own acuity of moral and literary judgement, and his imaginative originality.

The Spanish story comes from a collection of fifty-one framed stories, *El Conde Lucanor* (*Count Lucanor*, 1328), sometimes known as *El Libro de Patronio* (*Patronio's Book*) and *El Libro de los ejemplos* (*The Book of Exemplary Stories*). This is the work of Infante Don Juan Manuel (1282–1349).[42] This nephew of King Alfonso X, courtier and military man involved in turbulent political events, was also a distinguished orientalist, learned in Arab, Jewish and Hispanic folklore, from which he took many of his tales. Interestingly, his book is written in the vernacular – in a conversational form of the Romance/Castilian language which his royal uncle had devoted himself to developing. Sometimes cited, despite its courtly provenance and standpoint, as the first example of European demotic prose fiction, and with a notably large social canvas, *El Conde Lucanor* is outstanding for exactly those qualities which made (and still make) Andersen's *Eventyr* so remarkable; directness of voice, eschewal of all literary devices in the interests of pulling its audience right into the story, admittance into this of many different ranks and types of people, all rendered articulate. Annette Madsen's essay, '*Count Lucanor* by Don Juan Manuel as Inspiration for Hans Christian Andersen and Other European Writers' (1999)[43] is invaluable in its demonstration of just how closely Andersen's story follows Don Juan Manuel's, even – though she makes no overt critical comment here – the famous change to its ending made by the author at the eleventh hour, holding up scheduled March publication until April. Paradoxically, though, appreciation of this closeness only makes clearer the independent-mindedness of Andersen's tale, and its significance for its own times. Madsen says that Don Juan's 'motive was to give knowledge to the laymen, and to teach young noblemen how to defend their high rank in the society into which they were born'. Andersen's story would seem to propose the precise reverse: that high rank, while not objected to as such, should be accorded only to the virtuous, and more particularly, the honest.

Though does it quite say this?

In the Arab-derived Spanish story three rogues (Andersen reduces them to two) weave invisible cloth into invisible fine clothes and gull the royal court into believing that only persons of legitimate birth can see the splendid results of their labours. This is a matter of life-and-death importance, for Arab culture accepted only a legitimate son as a monarch. Consequently the deceived king risks losing his throne if he admits that he cannot see his own attire. His courtiers and their hangers-on are similarly afraid of compromising themselves and so losing their positions. Only a stable-boy has the guts to say out loud that the king is naked, being himself quite outside the official social order. After he has spoken the king has no alternative but to admit that he has been fooled –and in front of his subjects at that!

There is no question of anybody's illegitimacy in Andersen's story. His Emperor – who, as the opening sentence tells us, virtually lives for elegant new clothes, spending all available money on them – hears that the garments made by the two new weavers are not just beautiful but have special properties, and these greatly attract him. The clothes are invisible to anyone 'som ikke duede i sit Embede, eller ogsaa var utilladelig dum',[44] 'who was not fit for his [official] post or else was disgracefully stupid'. Andersen's Denmark may still have been an Absolute Monarchy, but it was also an emerging meritocracy. It found the idea of anybody holding any position, even an inherited royal one, for which he was unfitted abhorrent– and obviously nobody anywhere wants to be revealed as stupid. The Emperor thinks that by wearing these unusual new clothes he can learn who in his country should not hold the posts they do, and who is genuinely intelligent rather than simply purporting to be so. Considering the social transformations taking place throughout Europe in the 1830s – the July Revolution and the Citizen King's ascendancy in France; the passing of the 1832 Reform Bill in Britain; the accession of Queen Victoria in the very year of the story – Andersen's Emperor seems essentially modern in his concerns, especially when we compare him with his Spanish original. He is less interested in his own power, in his own sway over his subjects, than in having trustworthy, capable officials and a society where the intelligent and the unintelligent do not get confused. It does not occur to him that he himself might fail either one of these tests. It is the eminently understandable inability of the two successive ministers to tell him the truth – that they see no cloth, that the weavers, before their eyes, are busy working at *nothing* – that leads to his self-doubt. For indubitably when it comes to it, he also sees nothing. Yet though he admits this to himself, he has been sufficiently hoodwinked and is insufficiently inwardly confident not to take the weavers' implicit interpretation of his failure as true – as opposed to the more obvious (and correct) one. What more terrible than to be unfitted for so exalted an office as his own, except the possibility – especially for an Emperor – of being stupid?

Until the rogue weavers arrive, life in the Emperor's capital city has gone on 'fornøieligt',[45] 'pleasantly/delightfully'. Perhaps this important fact has not been stressed enough by critics. The destructive element comes wholly from *outside* the Empire; moreover its representatives are unabashedly wicked men, intending the Emperor nothing but harm. The lavish materials bought for them they stash away for themselves and their profit, they are utterly pitiless in their demands for ever more money, and they have most carefully prepared the whole plot. Without their horrible enterprise there is no reason to suppose that life would not have continued in the Empire as delightfully as before. And yet ... were not the seeds of its capitulation to trickery not already germinating when its ruler cared more about his appearance than about defence or culture? Is it not an indictment of its culture that ministers can't come back from their errands and report the plain truth? Or that two patent rascals could have such a devastating social impact? But perhaps the most disturbing point about the Empire's moral health is that ordinary people go along en masse with the whole charade rather than trust the evidence of their own senses. As they watch their naked Emperor walk along in the grand procession, under a canopy and with chamberlains holding on to a train that of course simply isn't there, they not only fail to admit their monarch's true physical condition, they excitedly vie with one another in delivering absurd, gushing compliments about the Emperor's magnificent garments.

And there Andersen originally left the story. With a vast vivid tableau of human cravenness in the face of its duped ruler and his cowardly retinue! Then on 25 March 1837 he wrote to Edvard Collin saying that he wanted to add something to the tale, that sentence which is perhaps now its best known feature, and which he thought essential to his satiric purpose. ' "Men han har jo ikke noget paa!" sagde et lille Barn.'[46] ' "But he hasn't got anything on!" said a little child.' And his father – and soon all those all around – find themselves unable to deny the truth of what the boy has said.

We now think of the child among the disciples whose innocence Jesus admired and held up to them, we think of Jesus himself among the elders of the Temple, we recall 'Out of the mouths of babes and sucklings', we remember the Wordsworth of 'Anecdote for Fathers' or 'We Are Seven'.[47] What adult society dare not say, the uninhibited, uncorrupted child cannot stop himself from uttering aloud.

And yet the frightening truth remains that until that solitary child spoke up, a vast crowd of human beings fell in with officialdom's timorous ineptitude and stupidity (for obviously, thanks to the weavers, everybody has proved himself to be exactly those things he was most afraid of being) – and even compounded it. Perhaps in truth the two endings are not really so very different after all: the initially planned one – of the Emperor going on his way to vocal cries of admiration – is essentially the same as the subsequent one only without its (ambiguous) ray of light (the child's statement of *fact*) breaking into the darkness. When we turn, as in the following chapter we will, to his third novel, *Only a Fiddler* we shall find an Andersen profoundly exercised by social order and class shifts, and for all his sympathies for the unfortunate everywhere, and his loathing of subservience, see that he is far from unqualifiedly hopeful about the Danish, indeed the European, mid-century ahead.

It is tempting to say that perhaps the most humane detail of this story comes at the very end. By now the Emperor knows that what the child has said corresponds to reality, that he has been made an idiot of and is now out there in front of his subjects stark naked. Yet he becomes 'stoltere',[48] 'prouder' than ever before, and continues with his dignified walk at the head of his procession. And isn't that somehow sympathetic behaviour? This essentially modern man stays truer to his own self as he has come to perceive it (and as others have desired it) than did his fictional medieval Spanish forebear. This begets a reluctant admiration.

CHAPTER 6

Kun en Spillemand
(Only a Fiddler) and 'Den Standhaftige Tinsoldat' ('The Steadfast Tin Soldier')

1

The writing of *Only a Fiddler* in the summer of 1836 went well, Andersen telling his friend Henriette Hanck as early as May that he intended to be 'the top novelist in Denmark' with this new work presenting 'the poetic traits of our age'.[1] The time seemed propitious. *O. T.* had appeared on 21 April, to sell out by early June. And during this summer a French critic, Xavier Marmier interviewed Andersen for a 'biography' (published as 'Une vie de poète' in the influential *Revue de Paris* in October 1837). Andersen had now also behind him well-received fairy stories, a handful of which, vindicating Ørsted, are vigorously alive in our own century. A certain satisfaction with what he had accomplished must account for his third novel's extraordinary structural and stylistic confidence, as well as its scope. To disturb feelings of self-vindication there was only his de facto exclusion from Edvard Collin and Henriette (Jette) Thybjerg's wedding on 10 August. But disturb them this surely did. *Only a Fiddler* is permeated by self-doubt, and doubts about the goodwill and integrity of others. Intellectually it jousts with ideas of life's justice (divine or natural), and how these apply to the self one has been given. Though more richly peopled than either *The Improvisatore* or *O. T.*, Andersen's third novel presents loneliness and failures in communication, social, artistic and sexual, as ineluctable facts of existence in a way neither of those novels was able to do.

Andersen's ambition for and subsequent high estimation of this novel have proved justified; *Only a Fiddler* – published 22 November 1837 – turned out in terms of critical reception and sales alike, to be his most successful production to date. Its two dedicatees, B.S. Ingemann and the poet Carsten

Hauch (1790–1872)[2] had already predicted this, even to the specifics of the enthusiastic reception in Germany (1838) which would mark Andersen's European breakthrough. Yet this is a profoundly tragic novel, both in the conclusions to which both its male and its female protagonists move, and in the scenes through which they pass, as through some Purgatory definable in both topographical and chronological terms. Its German readers – to go no further – were right to greet it as a work which gave them piercing insights into their times, bound into a narrative, which, while complicated, itself amounts to an artistic trajectory metaphorical of these. Posterity, particularly outside Denmark, has been less than fair – despite the sensitive assessments of biographer Jens Andersen and others[3] – to *Only a Fiddler*, an achievement of the very first rank, and a most original one, a milestone in the history of the novel-form.

2

Andersen calls his central character Christian, the name he himself was known by as a child, and places his boyhood in his own Fyn. Christian, like Andersen himself, feels himself an artist early, in his case a musician with the potential to become a great violinist. Yet, as the book's title tells us, he ends up '*Kun* en Spillemand', '*Only* a Fiddler', the sad, ironic, yet in worldly terms wholly apposite words that end the work. Can it be read then as a *Künstlerroman* – or even, considering Christian's lack of success, as a kind of anti-*Künstlerroman*? It has indeed been taken as this, as we shall see. But, as Andersen's words to Henriette Hanck suggest, artists and their attainments are seen in the context of the times, the evolution of societies as then detectable. Also, and as important, all personal and public histories are viewed against a background of *natural* history, as is made engagingly clear from the start.

Where *O.T.'s* first chapter plunged us into the social specificities of Copenhagen student life among the well-to-do, *Only a Fiddler's* beautiful opening cadences proclaim the novel's preoccupation with the laws governing birth, growth and maturation, and, just as intractably, sickness, decay and death; this will include the termination of lives that have not yet run their full course. How to come to terms with these laws? What *Weltanschauung* can accommodate them?

Naar Sneen smelter, naar Skovene blive grønne, da komme Storkene tilbage fra deres lange Reise. I det fjerne Africa have de været, drukket af Nilens Vande, hvilet paa Pyramiderne.[4]

When the snow melts, when the woods become green, then the Storks come back from their long journey. They have been in furthest Africa, drunk of the Nile's water, rested on the Pyramids.

This paragraph and its three successors constitute a declaration of the inescap-able correspondence between the ways of birds and the ways of humans. Both individually and collectively storks possess instinctual knowledge that enables them not only to traverse vast distances in their seasonal journeys but to arrive at precisely identifiable, predetermined sites:

> Hver enkelt kjender den Havbugt, han maa søge, kjender Skovens Bøining og den hvide Skorsteen paa Herregaardens takkede Gavl, hvor Reden venter.[5]
>
> Every single one knows the bay he must look for, knows the bend of the wood and the white chimney on the manor farm's crow-stepped gable, where the nest waits.

Emulating the stork's exactitude, the author now positions us alongside particular persons in a particular place, a country road leading inland from Svendborg,[6] a port on Fyn's southern coast. All three of them are watching a pair of storks repair the old rooftop nest to which they have returned for the spring: they comprise an army sergeant, a tailor and the tailor's small son, our hero Christian. Storks, we are reminded, have many inborn virtues to make them inspirational for us: fidelity (they usually mate for life), kindness to their young (most pairs have only one offspring), and careful attention to their education so that all are prepared for the arduous annual journeys. Proverbially storks bring pleasure and good luck wherever they settle.

Each of the three here – but little Christian most of all – relates thematically to the birds. The sergeant, who yields to none in his high regard for them, is delighted that the farmhouse's Jewish owner is once again receiving this pair on his roof. But he also encourages his friend, the tailor, to admire, even to iden-tify with and emulate, storks' ability to undertake hazardous travel. For Christian's father has behind him a young manhood as itinerant journeyman in Austria and Italy. His thirst for adventure (emphatically not shared by his wife, Christian's mother) has not yet been slaked, and the sergeant knows this, knows therefore that, like Andersen's own father, the man feels seriously under-stretched.

Storks thus combine an intense capacity for local devotion with a biological need for change effected by high-risk migration. To varying degrees so do the principal characters of the novel; it is in the *imbalance* of the combination that their tribulations and ultimate frustrations will reside. *Only a Fiddler,* like the birds, covers enormous geographical distances – Copenhagen, the Øresund, Sweden, Germany, Vienna, Italy, France – and cultural ones, for we meet char-acters of Jewish, Norwegian and Polish provenance as well as Danes from Fyn and Copenhagen. And, because the storks' flights are strictly seasonal, and therefore measurable in temporal terms, this novel is also one of passage through a particular period of history, with dates as important to it (and its overall meaning) as places: 1813, when the battle in which the tailor takes part is fought in Holstein; 1819, when the principal (Jewish) female protagonist experiences Copenhagen's last pogrom; 1833, and the empty jubilations in Paris to commemorate its July Revolution.

Throughout the novel, individuals' awareness of the turns their lives are taking is prompted by the sight of a stork (or storks).

The tailor, about to join the 10,000-strong Danish auxiliary corps who will march off to swell the French ranks, looks up and observes: 'Der flyve Storkene! Men iaar flyver jeg med.'[7] 'There fly the storks. But I now fly with them!' Later on Christian, fatherless, and feeling that his mother, stepfather and godfather are all lost to him, finds a solitary stork and thinks he recognises him as one deprived a short while back of his partner and young. 'Den hoppede rundt om Christian, syntes slet ikke ængstlig og saae paa ham med sine kloge Øine.'[8] 'He hopped around Christian, did not seem at all anxious and looked at him with his wise eyes.' Those wise eyes remind Christian of his father's admiration for the birds, and his wish to travel under their wings, and accordingly he too sets out on a journey with irrevocable consequences.

To return to the novel's opening pages. The recruiting sergeant, an expert on storks, adds to his encomium an account of a manoeuvre of theirs which he personally had witnessed in Kværndrup, not far from Svendborg.

Here, in their usual place, the storks had assembled in their hundreds before starting their southbound autumn migration. Suddenly all clacked their beaks together as though having reached a communal decision. Next a majority of the birds bore down on ten or so of the flock, and killed them. They had, deduced the sergeant, judged these birds insufficiently strong for the long, exhausting flight ahead. How to regard this grim behaviour (unverified, one must add here, by ornithology)? As Nature looking after its own, sparing less robust birds the hardships for which they are ill-equipped, and preventing others from being endangered by their inabilities? Or as a dramatic instance of the cruelty inherent in the very survival process, the innocent but weaker going to the wall, and the strong abetting, even instigating this elimination?

This passage has enormous resonance. We absorb this stark piece of information (for it is offered us as this) before we start to follow the fortunes of any of the characters, and we hold it in our mind as we go on to do so.

Christian, as he grows up, is not only creatively moved by sightings of stork, he will be repeatedly likened to one. In the middle age into which he just about manages to survive as an unsuccessful, unfulfilled but always kind and honourable man, a single lame stork becomes his last true companion. Christian has discovered the bird in his chimney; a leg injury has incapacitated him for the autumn journey south. For a whole year, relates Andersen, Christian's three greatest friends are his bible, his fiddle and his stork. Man and bird sustain each other, the former's consistent care restoring the latter's strength.

But in the course of things autumn comes round again in the form of a glorious September; Christian feels (albeit reluctantly) that he should now release the stork to escape Denmark's cold as is the practice of his kind. But first he ties a red ribbon round the bird's leg so that he will recognise him on his return. Less than one day after he has let him go, he finds his dear year-long companion dead alongside several other storks, all deemed unsuitable by the others for the southward flight and therefore slaughtered. Grieving, Christian gives his bird a fitting burial. 'Nu er jeg igjen alene! Du kommer ikke til mig med Vaaren! død! Alt skal døe! Alt skulle vi miste!'⁹ 'Now am I again alone! You won't come back to me with the spring! Dead! Everything has to die! Everything we have to lose!' He tries to console himself, but does not succeed. During the ensuing winter he turns poorly, and when spring arrives it is clear he will not recover. Nature, one could say, has jettisoned the fiddler, as it had the bird he loved, regarding even his merits as expendable.

And with it the arc of Christian's trajectory is in literary terms completed. For all his wanderings he is back in Fyn again; his hopes and ambitions have come to nothing. Andersen, himself now as successful as for so many years he had intended to be, had striven to be, can no longer keep at bay his previous sufferings, or the difficult questions about selfhood, circumstances and chance that his life story so far surely raises. With fortitude he imaginatively faces the (to him frightening) possibility that he might never have arrived at success at all. Why should he have done? What unnameable elements in existence and in his personality had been responsible for his doing so, rather than sinking into depression and obscurity? This question he can feelingly pose, through metaphor, through the stories of imagined others, but he cannot answer it to either his own, or his readers', satisfaction.

Before we examine Christian's life journey in some detail, we should look briefly at that of his father. Not only does Christian owe his existence to him (though there is room for a sliver of doubt here), but the pattern of the older man's career has imprinted itself on his own. In *Only a Fiddler* Andersen created powerful situations as correlatives of those he had experienced himself, but which – except partially in the never-published, never-completed autobiography he wrote for Louise Collin – he had not cared to externalise. For all the discrepancies between their stories, his own father, Hans Andersen, stands behind Christian's father's.

The tailor's experience of war epitomises important aspects of Denmark's situation in the second and third decades of the nineteenth century. Goaded by his own restlessness, the recruiting sergeant's flattering incitement and the sight of a stork flying off, the tailor accepts, as Hans Andersen did, cash from a farmer, to take his place in a regiment. The reforms of 1788[10] had placed the onus of military service substantially on to the farming community, and however widely welcomed by the Danish people in general, there were always individuals like the young farmer in Fyn here glad to get out of it by paying someone to take his place. The tailor may have been infected by the war fever induced by Denmark's virtually inescapable support of Napoleon's France, but we cannot doubt that what is really driving him is a longing to get away from a domesticity that stifles him. Though he is fond of Christian who has been severely ill, with his total recovery far from certain, the call to arms has a greater appeal for him than the boy's welfare.

This, extremely bloody, phase of the European struggle against Napoleon is known as the War of the Sixth Coalition (Austria, Prussia, Russia, Britain, Portugal, Spain, Sweden and certain German states). Andersen chooses to give us the moves of the Dano-Norwegian military against this force in the chivalric language with which the tailor would justify his enlistment: 'Krigens Gud, Tidsalderen kaldte ham *Napoleon,* kæmpede alene med alle Landenes Riddere. Det var en stor Tournering, det var det sidste Ridderspil, han gav, og derfor kæmpede han alene ;'[11] 'The God of War, the age called him *Napoleon,* struggled alone against the knights of all countries. It was a huge tournament, it was the last knights' contest he waged, and therefore he struggled alone.' Reality, not least for Napoleon's Danish supporters, was distressingly different. The Battle of Bornhøved,[12] in which the tailor took part (fought on Holstein heathland near the German village now called Bornhöft on 7 December 1813) was a decisive loss for Denmark. Danish and Norwegian infantry and cavalry led by Prince Frederik of Hesse encountered Swedish cavalry forces with devastating results; almost 200 out of 2,500 Danes were killed. Christian's father is reported dead, but what actually happens is that, more ignominiously, he is taken prisoner by Cossacks, forced to go to Russia, and after captivity and an arduous journey – about both of which he is less than truthful – returns, via Memel (Klaipeda), Königsberg (Kaliningrad), and Helsingør, to Fyn. Here he makes his way to the house of the very farmer whose brother paid him to join up, only to get a disagreeable surprise. This man has married Maria, his wife, Christian's mother, and, to avoid unpleasant embarrassment all round, pays him to disappear a second time.

At least this is what he himself relates when Christian meets him, in Odense, some four years later, to hear firstly, of the man's great affection for him, and secondly, in virtually the same breath, that their ways will never cross again. The next day the tailor sets off on his travels once more.

But we, though not Christian, do hear of him again, some three years later, and learn of whereabouts, if anything, stranger than a Russian prison camp. We are in

Rome, among a circle of visiting aristocrats and artists, some of them members of the German *Kneipsbund* or fellowship known as the Nazarenes;[13] a monk, in tune with their tastes, calls collecting donations for his convent. This monk is the tailor. Denmark, he admits, is still very dear to him, but he is prevented from contact with his countrymen by the religious order he now serves.

The tailor is therefore a stork only in his propensity for arduous travel, his ability to exchange one living-place for another. Of the stork's devotion to nest, to partner and to progeny he knows nothing. In cultural terms he articulates the vaingloriousness of those who overrated Denmark's military capabilities in its alliance with France, the inability of the more obdurate among the defeated to adapt responsibly to changed fortunes, and the subsequent fashionable retreat into a retrograde religiosity.

Christian is likened to his father at several key points, on the whole not commendably, for he shares both the older man's aversion to dulling regimen and his wanderlust. But he has a far greater sense of responsibility, and then there are his artistic aspirations, which it is a principal business of the novel to explore, even to assess. But as an individual and as a representative type, he is always to be considered in conjunction with another person, a member of the opposite sex. In this *Only a Fiddler* differs from all Andersen's previous fiction.

We have already noted that the farmhouse to which the storks returned had a Jewish owner. It stands next to the home of the tailor and Christian, and contains the old Jewish man himself, his devoted factotum, Joel and his grand-daughter, Naomi. Naomi is a few years younger than Christian, forward for her age, beautiful, strong-willed, her personality suggested to Andersen by memories of that lively little girl he'd known at his largely Jewish infants' school in Odense.[14] The tailor's house lacks a garden, but the farmhouse has a large, well-stocked, luxuriant one into which Christian finds his way through a chink in the stone wall. In this paradise – the Eden parallel is too overt to be unintended; in Naomi we see 'den asiatiske Slægt',[15] 'the Asiatic lineage' of Eve herself – the two children establish a connection. The girl leads the boy into a little garden-house containing a single window of dark red glass which makes everything beyond appear on fire. Looking at the stork's nest through this prism Christian cannot avoid crying out: 'Det brænder!'[16] 'It's burning!' Naomi laughs at his error, and suggests they should play at currency exchange, with different-coloured leaves and his eyes as a pledge. Christian's mother, Maria, angry at this game, thwacks her young son, and next morning blocks up the entrance into the garden. But in truth her son's eyes will be pledged to Naomi for the rest of his life.

That same night Christian wakes up to see out of his bedroom window that fiery landscape he had looked on from the garden-house window. But now the

Jew's property really *is* burning. Of the house's three occupants Naomi's grandfather perishes in the calamity, and Joel, his devoted factotum, a Jewish pedlar, has to attend to the interment of his charred body in the traditional Jewish burial ground, the Bet Achaim, some distance away. But Naomi is rescued, with great bravery, by Christian's Norwegian godfather and taken by Christian's parents into their house. The casualties of the fire are not all human. 'Storken, den stakkels Stork!' raabte de Alle.'[17] 'The stork! The poor stork!' cried everybody.' Attempts are made to rescue the mother bird and her young ones, but to no avail; they all burn to death. When the father stork returns confused, and searches in distress, for his lost family, he arouses the strong sympathies of the tailor and son, and thus enlists readers on their side when they might be tempted to make other less favourable judgements on them.

Naomi settles down with Christian's parents easily enough. Andersen observes, with ruthless common sense, that children operate on a different timescale from adults, and are therefore much more adaptable. Christian and the little girl play together, and soon their principal game is weddings, with neighbourhood children joining in. Christian and Naomi as the bridal pair embrace and kiss, Naomi giving her groom a locket. But this enthralling amusement is interrupted. An old-fashioned coach draws up outside the tailor's house, and out steps an aristocratic old lady claiming Naomi as a member of her family and forthwith removing her. Maria – whose characteristic dealings with her son are generally far from tender – tells Christian to stop weeping over his playmate's departure, and dispatches him to his Norwegian godfather. This man, vital to the novel as a whole, indeed central to it despite the comparative brevity of his actual appearances, lives in nearby Svendborg, at a tangent to its community. It is on the boy's visit to him that selfsame day that music claims him as her own, no less irrevocably than the grand old lady had claimed Naomi, and, we might add, with hardly happier consequences. Christian pauses outside the Norwegian's house, leans his head against the door and hears from within the wild strains of his violin. Once he is indoors his godfather offers him his first lesson in the instrument.

The family situations of Christian and Naomi as they grow up are alike in having serious irregularities, indeed deficiencies. But one major factor, unknown to both parties for some years, links them: Christian's godfather and Naomi's blood father and rescuer are one and the same, a man with a history of murderous violence back in Norway and of amorous and artistic exploits and smuggling affiliations in Denmark. The relationship of genetic inheritance to personal evolution, the difficulty of how to weigh this against the pressures of sheer experience (including such blows to the individual as severance and loss) are as strongly integral to *Only a Fiddler* as to *O.T.* And this Norwegian musician is the pivotal figure on both sides of the debate, a disturbing, haunting creation.

We could, I think, read key incidents and their imaginative fallout in the novel with the supposition that Christian's Norwegian godfather is also his biological father. The only textual evidence for this comes when Maria is remonstrating with her husband, the tailor, about his longing to be away as a soldier, and reminds him that Christian is his: 'og Drengen er Din egen, det veed jeg med en frelst Samvittighed',[18] 'and the boy is your own, that I tell you with a clear conscience.' But, bearing in mind the fuller picture of her that the novel presents, we might well wonder why she finds it necessary to assure him. If she is not being truthful here, then it will not be the only time; she lies later about not intending to remarry. Most probably Andersen imaginatively toyed with the possibility of his hero being the Norwegian's son, went some way to meet this, and then decided not to follow the paternity through, primarily because of thematically important connections between Christian and his attributed father.

But were Christian fathered by the Norwegian, whose own career of musician (and violinist at that) he does after all pursue, then he and Naomi would be (half) brother and sister: the male and the female, the fair and the dark, halves of a single, but forcibly severed, whole. And this is indeed how they appear to us readers when we stand back and contemplate the novel as an entity. We find the same ambiguity in Emily Brontë's *Wuthering Heights* where authorial hints have us see Cathy and Heathcliff as brother and sister in blood (through Mr Earnshaw) as well as experientially (through the intimacies of their shared early childhood). Yet they are also compelled towards each other sexually, as Christian is to Naomi. The two are, at every level, one.[19]

Andersen likens Christian's godfather to an already famous (though considerably younger) Norwegian musician, Ole Bull, 'Nordens Amphion', 'Amphion of the North'.[20] Andersen's cultural antennae here were, as usual, acute. Bergen-born Ole Bull (1810–80), a child prodigy who never lost his powers and knew huge success from his youth onwards – in 1837 he gave almost 300 enthusiastically received recitals in England alone – connects creatively with early to mid-nineteenth-century Scandinavia's appreciation of its own great folk inheritance, both inspired and still nurtured by its mighty mountain- and seascapes. Ole Bull's famous pieces for virtuoso violin – such as 'Sæterjentens Søndag' ('Herdgirl's Sunday', 1872) – anticipate, in mood and in characteristic musical intervals, the compositions of Bull's younger kinsman, Edvard Grieg (1843–1907).[21] Like Grieg's compositions, his convey the movements of untrammelled Nature: Christian himself responds to this feature of his godfather's playing. Andersen would himself meet Bull in Copenhagen one year after *Only a Fiddler* had come out, in November 1838. He would write to him: 'Thanks for the lyric strains of your violin – if they could be rendered in words, we should have a wonderful cycle of poems.'[22]

Bull enjoyed a reputation as a womaniser, and a gambler (Andersen greatly disapproved of the latter), and his surrogate in the novel is a conspicuously reckless individual with lawless associates who ends his life most terribly. He ascribes his musicianship to Nøkken, the white-bearded Nix[23] who sits in the moonlight on Norwegian waterfalls casting spells on listeners through his fiddle-playing. Ever afterwards – his being Christian's *god*father thus has a bitterly ironic significance – the man has lived by a proudly pagan code, in opposition to Christianity. We have inside us, he pronounces, a wild beast; what is important for us is to know its comparative strength. There may well be those for whom it is best not merely to acknowledge the beast but to give it its forceful head.

'Det Hele kommer an paa Skik og Brug, og hvo siger os, om vi just følge den bedste, fordi vi gjør, som de Fleste gjøre? Hvo veed, om ikke Dyret indeni os har større Ret end Mennesket, som følger sin Skolelov? Er det ikke Sandhet?'[24]

'The whole thing depends on custom and usage, and who is to tell us whether we only follow the best because we do as the majority does? Who knows whether the beast within us has not greater right than the man who follows his school rules? Isn't that the truth?'

This is Nietzsche *avant la lettre*, but Christian, while he does indeed bravely strike out for himself, does not live up to this version of vitalist doctrine, nor does he wish to, finding his needed guidance in the Bible and, in his premature last years, in the consolations of Pietism. His godfather, well before delivering his anti-moral credo, has already played a far from exemplary role in Christian's life.

In addition to teaching him the fiddle, he takes him on an expedition to islands now connected by bridge to Svendborg: Thorseng (today's Tåsinge) and Thurø. And here an extraordinary episode, seminal to Christian's whole development, occurs: an evening's accidental and terrifying imprisonment in a bell tower when the hour of sunset is being struck. The boy has to avoid the swings of the huge metal bell if he is not to be crushed to death. Eventually the Norwegian rescues him (as years before he had rescued Naomi from the fire), but harm, not physical but psychological, has already been done. Christian suffers a nervous crisis, bringing on regular fits and occasioning visits to a nearby holy well. All this elicits no sympathy whatever from the tough Norwegian, and scant responsible interest from his named father, the tailor.

Parents, godfather and teacher, the community – all consistently fail to give Christian any congenial background, any belief in life as worthwhile, let alone propose a good part for himself to play in it. We have already dealt with the shortcomings of his father; we can now turn to Maria, his mother, who cuts an even less admirable figure. She married the tailor as a second-best, and when news comes that he has been killed in battle, has no problem at all in becoming the wife of her first choice, the farmer, now a widower. Unlike the majority of mothers, as Andersen himself points out, she considers her one child ugly and unappealing, and as for his musicianship, she has no interest whatever in it. She rates the success of her second marriage as greatly more important than her relationship to Christian, to the point of brazenly and humiliatingly siding against him in any disputes. This is particularly hurtful when it involves the crass, bullying Niels, the farmer's own son. With insensitive unkindness Maria gets rid of the fiddle Christian loves, and this indeed is the turning-point for him. For Christian his instrument is a guarantee of the beauty and interesting-ness of existence beyond the merely humdrum. He pines grievously once the fiddle has gone.

His decision to leave his home coincides with the arrest of his Norwegian godfather for the killing of a girl in Norway. The death of the Jew's daughter, Naomi's mother, is also laid at the musician's door (as, we later discover, it well might be). In the whole novel, indeed in all Andersen's oeuvre, there is no scene more shocking than Christian's discovery of his godfather's post-arrest suicide. This is preceded by the man's invasion, in some rationally inexplicable extra-sensory fashion, of the boy's dream as he sleeps, self-exiled from his home, in a neighbouring dark wood. The godfather appears in Christian's unconscious in a curiously sinister guise which suggests that already the boy, on the threshold of puberty, is damaged too much to enter the phases of youth and maturation with the resilience of health. The dream's Norwegian male pulls Christian on to his knee and confides in him a hideous history of perverted virtue; how he, once virtuous, yielded to the devil of sensuality, drank of his milk, and became an erect monstrous creature – swollen cocks are actually cited – whose appe-tites and deeds are murderous. When Christian wakes up, it is to find his godfather hanging lifeless from a nearby tree, a trauma of the first magnitude.

From the point of profession and education Christian tries first to adapt himself to life as a trainee sailor. Yet, for all the avuncular kindness of his educator, the sea captain, Peter Wik, one of Andersen's warmest portraits of an adult male – as a fiddler himself, he admires the boy's violin-playing – our hero turns out no more temperamentally suited to life at sea than to his stepfather's farm. Equally he cannot, at any satisfying level, cope with the schooling subse-quently willed on him as a preferable alternative: in Odense under the direc-tion of the Knepus husband and wife unkindly based, once again, on the Meislings (though, as already stated, they come off a bit better than they did as the Headmaster and Santa in *The Improvisatore*).

The Meislings, however, are surely not the only targets in *Only a Fiddler* of Andersen's retrospective bitterness. If Hans Andersen, with his love for the

Arabian Nights, his devotion to Napoleon, and his strong vein of fecklessness, stands behind the tailor, then, as we saw in Chapter 1, we have Andersen's own word that Maria is a portrait of Anne Marie. It is, to say the least, a highly equivocal one. It is clear that the author, together with Christian, disapproves of her unsympathetic remarriage, and Andersen's resentful repulsion at their sexual relationship pervades the novel's portraiture of the pair, and points back to hostility he felt towards his mother and stepfather in his Odense boyhood. The conflagration (in point of fact the book's second) destroying Maria's farmer-husband's property owes its vividness, one feels, to its emanation from psychic depths, its flames expressing a long-nurtured revenge on what had served an obviously gifted boy considerably less than mercifully. He does, however, spare his mother from death by fire, and awards her a more conventionally maternal middle age, spent in her son's company, a kind of atonement for his harsh judgement of her earlier.

Emotionally Christian preserves the image of Naomi from his childhood, and never relinquishes, through all that happens to him and all that he sees of her (and despite the presence in his life of a far more sympathetic woman, Luzie), his intense conviction that the two of them belong inextricably to one other. He may end up a lamed stork, but his youthful defiance of social convention and her hostility show a trust in the validity of his own feelings that calls for nothing but admiration. Chapter XVI, ending this tripartite novel's first section, is galvanic in its propulsion of Christian towards the girl who enlivened his early childhood; his subsequent sense of betrayal by her and his dejection at this will create its own momentum.

Christian is on board Peter Wik's ship in its Copenhagen dock. It is summer. The sea captain has taken him into the city to see a ballet at the theatre, and the youth has been overwhelmed by the self-contained world of loveliness and emotional expression, his exhilaration at the show compounded by his sight of Naomi in the audience, seated in smart company in the front row of the stalls. After this experience he likes, in his spare evenings, to retire to his cabin and play airs from the ballet on his fiddle. But on this particular evening he stays out on deck, leaning against the mast, and hears, coming from a grand house near the quay, lively, irresistible music; a ball must be in progress. He makes a decision not susceptible to rational analysis. He climbs up the mast to view the event from above, and looks down on a vista of young guests, festal arrangements, pictures on the ballroom wall, glittering lights and mirrors. And then into this bright throng comes a beautiful dark girl – Naomi herself. So Christian swings himself down one of the mast-ropes and enters the ballroom through its open French windows, to the amazement and consternation of all there. The whole scene has a dramatic fusion of the interior (Christian's rush of renewed attraction for his old playmate) and the exterior (Copenhagen high society in full swing), and points to later similar fusions in novelists of the subsequent two decades – in English, the Brontës, Dickens (*Great Expectations* with Pip and Estella), the early Meredith. 'Naomi!' Christian stammers out to the girl advancing towards him. 'Hun blev rød som Blod. "Smudsige Dreng!" udbrød hun og rev sig løs.'[25] 'She turned red as blood. "Dirty boy!" she burst out and tore herself away.' A servant escorts Christian out of the grand house, and, humiliated and grieving, he returns to his ship. 'Et saadant Øieblik giver Livs Erfaring.'[26] 'One such moment yields the experience of a lifetime.' How many other novelists of Andersen's time would have insisted on this truth and made us appreciate it so intensely?

But this summer docking of the ship in Copenhagen offers Christian another window into the troubled relations between the sexes from which the young are usually shielded: his encounters with the woman Steffen-Karreet. Again it is hard to parallel this epiphany among his fiction-writing contemporaries. One of the few in whose work we could find comparable subject matter is the Swedish novelist Fredrika Bremer (1801–65)[27] whom Andersen met in Sweden in June 1837, and to whom he actually showed the very pages of *Only a Fiddler* in which this haunting character appears. Bremer was enormously impressed, as one might expect from the Christian-feminist author of the applauded *Grannarne* (*Neighbours*, 1837) and *Hemmet* (*The Home*, 1839). (Sadly Andersen could not return this compliment; much as he liked and respected the author, her novels left him cold.)

When we first meet Steffen-Karreet,[28] we are as bemused as Christian himself, though obviously suspicion breaks through; Andersen handles our introduction to her and the girls in her company with great literary dexterity. Captain Peter Wik has gone ashore in Copenhagen for personal reasons, and two of his crew have permission to go on land themselves. Christian begs them to take him along with them, and though one of the sailors protests it wouldn't really do to take a boy to Steffen-Karreet's, join them he does. They make for a quarter of the city where women sit in the windows of tall houses greeting passers-by in a, to Christian, curiously friendly manner, and a pale, ill young woman cowers on a street corner. But the house that is the object of their expedition is brightly lit and full of people, casually attired men together with women dressed up as for evening celebrations. Steffen-Karreet is the centre of attraction; she throws her arms about the sailors and kisses them so affectionately that Christian thinks she must be a relation of theirs. To him she is all sweet friendliness, giving him a glass of punch, and thus making him think that in her he might well find a patron for his music. The sailors forbid him to tell their captain where they have taken him to that evening, but fired by his favourable impressions of her, the youth decides to call on Steffen-Karreet himself the following Sunday, when he has leave to go into the city to attend a church service. How different the deserted street and shuttered house appear in the morning light! Steffen-Karreet comes into the hall in negligée and fur-trimmed boots, and thinks Christian must have brought her a message from Søren (one of the two sailors), which he has not. But she is friendly enough for him to confide in her his hopes of being a great musician and the unhappy frustration of these so far. The lady laughs, gives him more punch, and says she is afraid she can be of no help to him as a budding fiddler; she could have done more for him had he been a girl.

By now the reader realises that Steffen-Karreet is the madame of a brothel, that the girls glimpsed the other night were prostitutes and the sailors their clients. Jens Andersen in his biography, so commendably admiring of *Only a Fiddler*, is surely right in relating these visually strongly realised scenes to the author's experience, so soon after his arrival in Copenhagen in 1819, of the menage (brothel) run by his mother's sister, Christiane. She too remarked that she could have helped him had he been a girl! What is remarkable about these pages is Andersen's rendering of his innocent boy-hero's warm, proto-erotic response to Steffen-Karreet. Conventional moral censoriousness is suspended in favour of a frank inclusiveness about human conduct.

But an even more disturbing scene centring on this woman, and one which especially struck Fredrika Bremer, is yet to come. A severe winter follows the above adventures; the ship is marooned in the ice of the Øresund, and on this frozen Sound between Denmark and Sweden Christian comes into enthralling new contact with Naomi and her adoptive father, the Count, entailing further humbling of himself, further dints to his already battered self-confidence. It is in a depressed state of mind therefore that one night he falls asleep in his cabin to dream of Steffen-Karreet, whom he has kept, during this interval of time, in fond inward regard. He now sees himself with her 'i en deilig, blomstrende Have, hvor Alt var Musik og Glæde. Hun gave ham en Violin af Sølv, og da Buen gled over Strængene, klang den høit over de tusinde andre Instrumenter; han vaagnede op ved den stærke Klang og fandt Trøst og Glæde i sin Drøm',[29] 'in a lovely, blossoming garden, where everything was music and joy. She gave him a violin of silver, and then the bow glided over the strings, rang out high above the thousand other instruments; he woke up at this loud sound and found comfort and joy in his dream'.

And when he awakes, it is to hear Steffen-Karreet's voice addressing not himself in some beautiful garden of music but on board the ship and in distressed private colloquy with the sailor, Søren. As in the earlier case of the Norwegian's suicide, Christian first apprehends human disaster through the medium of a dream, from which he emerges to confront the bitter culmination of the plight featured in it. It is as if his artistic gifts, to which both his godfather and poor Steffen-Karreet are linked, have enabled him to arrive at their apotheosis: a soul who surrendered his sensitivity to savage sensual appetite (the Norwegian), a soul who opted too soon for happiness and has now forfeited it (the madame). Christian now hears her – once a young girl with an unusual capacity for 'Livslyst', 'Joy in Life', and now a despairing whore about to turn twenty-eight – begging Søren to marry her. She will serve him like a slave if he does, she declares! What, and introduce you to my old father and mother, jeers the sailor quite unmoved . . . . And then Christian ceases to see and hear her, though her words have cut into his heart. 'Et Drømmebillede slukkedes, og han saae Skyggesiden af en Virkelighed.'[30] 'A dream picture was extinguished, and he looked at the shadow side of reality.' It may well be that in cold factual terms Christian never actually witnessed this meeting at all, that Steffen-Karreet's apotheosis was followed by a psychic glimpse into the slough her life had become. But a few days later the ice enclosing the ship has to be hacked away, and in the course of this operation, a woman's body is discovered: Steffen-Karreet, wearing necklace and earrings, with her hands folded as if in prayer.

'Christian haabede ikke mere paa sine Drømme. I Verden var ingen Feer, som i Eventyret.'[31]
    'Christian did not trust any more in his dreams. In the world there were no fairies as in the fairy-tale.'

But we who can place *Only a Fiddler* alongside some of the most famous fairy stories of all time, and from the same pen, can think differently. We know that only if we put trust in the unconscious life can we approach truth; essentially the dreams of flesh-and-blood people and the fairy-tales they compose when awake are one and the same. Perhaps if Christian's circumstances had been more propitious, he too could have entered the ranks of those who have attended to the depths of self, created art and thus spiritually enriched others. But they were not.

That a sympathetic milieu is required for genius/talent to be brought to fruition was long an article of faith for Andersen. But what happens if that milieu is unresponsive, uncaring, permeated by inadequate or mistaken values? How easy for the talent to die of undernourishment! In the following key passage in the novel Andersen draws his analogy from sculpture which, since his sojourn in Rome and his friendship with Thorvaldsen, had come to interest him greatly:

Omgivelse hedder den usynlige Haand, som omformer Grundstoffet i dets Udvikling.

Medens Billedhuggeren former det bløde Leer, fatte vi ikke strax, hvilket Værk der vil skabes. Det kræver Tid og Arbeide før Gipsafstøbningen frem-staaer og efter denne ved Meiselens Slag Marmoret lever op! hvormeget vanskeligere da at slutte sig fra Mennesket som Barn, til dets Udvikling og Skjæbne som Mand. Vi see her den fattige Dreng i Svendborg; Instinctet i ham og Indvirkningen udenfra peger som Magnetnaalen kun i to Retninger, hinanden aldeles modsatte. Han maa enten blive en sjelden Kunstner eller et usselt, forvirret Væsen. Omgivningens Blomsterstøv indvirker allerede med Duft og Farve.[32]

Environment is what the invisible hand is called which converts the basic material in its development.

While the sculptor is moulding the soft clay, we do not immediately under-stand what work will be created. It demands time and labour before the plaster cast is ready and after this with a blow from the chisel the marble comes to life! How much harder then to deduce from the human being as a child his development and fate as a man! We see here the poor boy in Svendborg; the instinct in him and the influence from outside point like the magnetic needle only in two directions, totally opposite to one another. He must either become an exceptional artist or a poor, miserable wretch. The pollen of the environment is already influencing him with its scent and colour.

Andersen's black-and-white binary divisions here did not at all impress *Only the Fiddler*'s most famous critic and antagonist. Søren Kierkegaard (1813–55) made the novel the subject of his own first published book, *Af en endnu Levendes Papirer* (*From the Papers of One Still Living*, 1838),[33] a minatory ad hominem attack, and the first public convergence of the paths of the two greatest Danish writers of their time. Kierkegaard thought that Christian 'was bound to be a "poor wretch" because he was one. . . .'[34] not least in Kierkegaard's view, because, apart from his response to his Norwegian violinist godfather, 'nothing has occurred which discloses even a moderate aptitude for music'.[35] He continued: 'The expression itself' ['poor wretch'] 'seems to us very descrip-tive. . . . One of the things that usually characterize the genius and give him his ascendancy over the world is pride, which usually becomes stronger in adver-sity and is therefore also often able to hold the individual's head erect. With Christian, however, all is vanity. What matters to him is drawing attention to himself, being admired; yes, if he can enjoy it for but a moment, he is content even with applause that he at heart nevertheless knows conceals mockery.'[36]

This (a far from wholly accurate summary of Christian's progress as first would-be, then practising musician) was, of course, as Kierkegaard presum-ably knew, the disparaging view of Andersen himself as man and writer still current in Copenhagen at this time. Both Jonas and Edvard Collin had warned him about it many, many times. I believe that, despite the confidence and fluency of its composition, Andersen was tormented all through the writing of this novel by questions about his own relative strengths and shortcomings, and troubled by how badly things might have turned out for him – given both his temperament and the grim conditions for its early development – had he not been as abundantly, as spectacularly gifted as he was. Or if he had had the same gifts, and not had the good fortune of meeting perceptive people who recognised them, his benefactors in the Danish cultural world. If, above all, there had been no Jonas Collin for him! Captain Wik, however kindly, is no substitute for the director of that royal fund for the assistance of artists and intellecuals in financial need, *ad usus publicos* in Christian's life, as the Eccellenza was Antonio's in *The Improvisatore*. The ease of composition during the summer of 1836 may well relate, paradoxically, to Anderson's being taken over by just these unsettling preoccupations. And this brought about an important difference between this novel and its predecessors. Whereas when writing *O.T.* Andersen had worked to a carefully thought out plan, when engaged with *Only a Fiddler* he did not, he confessed, always know where he was heading. He had almost too much he wanted to review, to express, to reveal.

To us now, in contrast to how he appeared to Kierkegaard, Andersen showed courageous honesty in facing up to deficiencies of his earlier self and allotting these to Christian. He shows how awareness of what was missing from his home and background inevitably turned that young man into an incorrigible daydreamer, longing for applause, recognition, fame just as it had changed Andersen himself. He is demanding that we realise that not all daydreamers can have the success he was already enjoying himself, and is pleading for empathic charity on their behalf. Nevertheless it has to be granted that if his immersion in Christian's predicament accounts for the comparatively on-the-hoof method of composition, it also explains the book's failure in proportion, its less than complete hold on the demands of narrative and character alike. Though both more profound and wider-ranging in interest than either *The Improvisatore* or *O.T.*, it is more flawed, these flaws at times dissipating its emotional power. This may worry some readers more than others; for this critic the novel's strengths enormously outweigh its structural weaknesses.

Needless to say, for Kierkegaard, who only begrudgingly acknowledged these strengths' existence, they did not. In particular he was determined to ram home the (to him completely vitiating) inequalities of interest in the third and last part. 'Yet [Andersen] has reserved another chapter of [Christian's] life for the third volume, and the few pages dealing with this are almost the only ones in the whole volume [i.e. Part Three] that actually have to do with the novel. The rest, containing almost nothing but bits and pieces of Andersen's reminiscences smuggled into Naomi's diary, could best be published separately. . . .'[37] Superficially this objection has validity; in the third part we abandon Christian for much too long, so that, regrettably, some measure of intensity in our relation to him is lost. Yet most certainly its various components could *not* have been published separately. They are irreplaceable in their contribution to the whole design, as well as having definite affecting qualities of their own. It was impertinent of Kierkegaard to have written as though he knew better than its author the true identity and intention of this work. Have we not already heard that Andersen intended the book as a presentation of the 'poetic traits *of our age*'? (The last phrase cannot be emphasised enough.) In its third section Andersen makes his purpose plain enough, and in narratological terms. In Chapter VI, after describing the death of Christian's mother, Maria, Andersen addresses his readers:

> Vi ville ei see den Jammer og Nød, men ile bort derfra, langt bort, fremad i Tiden! et dristigt Spring ville vi gjøre i Naomis og Christians Historie, ikke for at forbigaae enkelte Punkter, men for at samle disse og beskue dem fra et bedre Standpunkt.[38]

> We will not look at this sorrow and distress, but hasten away from it, far away, forwards in Time! One bold jump will we make in Naomi's and Christian's history, not to pass over individual points, but to assemble these and contemplate them from a better standpoint.

This compares interestingly with an earlier authorial declaration in *O.T.*:

> Ikke Skridt for Skridt vi følge Hovedpersonerne i vor Fortælling; men kun gjengive de fremtrædende Livsmomenter, disse være smaae eller store; vi gribe dem, naar de kunne bidrage til at gjøre det hele Malerie mere beskueligt.[39]

> Not step by step do we follow the chief characters in our story; but only present the prominent moments in their lives, whether they are small or great; we catch them, when they can contribute to making the whole picture easier to contemplate.

Such announcements make it clear that neither novel is, in its author's mind, a true *Künstler/Bildungsroman,* which is clearly how Kierkegaard read *Only a Fiddler*. In both quotations the analogy is from landscape painting, but Andersen's canvas takes in time also, and the movement of both individuals and communities through it; historically identifiable time at that. His novel therefore aims to be a picture of people, events, places and changes in political and societal atmosphere, constituting a unified whole that can impart its own singular truth. Both Andersen's tone and thought here are strikingly similar to

Stendhal's in, for instance, his opening to Chapter 27, Part One of *Le Rouge et le noir*:

> The reader will obligingly allow us to give very few clear and precise facts about this period in Julien's life. Not that they are lacking; far from it; but what he lives through in the seminary is perhaps too black for the moderate tones we have sought to preserve in these pages. One's contemporaries who undergo certain ordeals cannot recall them without experiencing a horror which paralyses any other pleasure, even that of reading a story.
>
> Julien had little success with his attempts at hypocrisy in the matter of gesture; he fell into bouts of repugnance and even of total demoralization. He wasn't succeeding, and in a lousy career, what's more. The least little bit of outside help would have sufficed to restore his morale – the difficulty to be overcome was not that great – but he was alone like a frail craft abandoned in the middle of the ocean.[40]

These sentences make clear Stendhal's comprehensive knowledge of his subject, a historian's as regards Julien's circumstances, actions, movements, a confessor's with respect to his intimate life. Both positions necessitate thoughtful, principled detachment. For all his celebrated declaration in the same novel of the writer being 'a mirror on the roadway' positioned in a travelling coach, Stendhal is highly selective in what he presents; nothing must impede overall harmony. Likewise Andersen in his second and third novels, but more particularly and effectively in *Only a Fiddler*.

We have again evoked Stendhal as *the* great novelist mindful of his art to emerge from the early 1830s, and whose interests notably coincide with Andersen's own. The jump that Andersen asks us to make moves us (it can easily be worked out) from Denmark 1821 to Paris 1833. The years' advance towards the future, as inevitable as storks' flights, while full of misadventures and calamities, impacts on all the persons of the book. But it is Naomi, Christian's foil, and both his desired complement and his active antagonist, who – to a greater extent than he, whose energy has been too sapped by experience – is our conductor into the world of the times (including in fact Stendhal's France). Her history is a representative – and a cautionary – one.

3

When the imperious lady descended on Christian's home to take Naomi away with her, readers were led to assume that the girl was transported to security. For all her early childhood with a Jewish grandfather, she would later emerge, thanks to this new grandmother, as an indelible member of the Danish aristocracy/upper classes, with all their attitudes and assumptions. The ironic truth is that her new circumstances in a grand manor are shot through with deceptions and unspoken secrets. These will bring about in Naomi an instability of personal identity and a sense of the precariousness of the social order. Her own impulsive, wilful temperament derives, she comes to understand, from her parents whom she can never admit to when out in Society.

The sight of a picture, which her 'grandmother' has kept hidden from others, showing a young woman, very beautiful and obviously Jewish, rouses Naomi into eliciting the true history she has so far been denied. Yes, she is told, the woman in the portrait is her mother, daughter of the Jew who lived near Svendborg, but the old lady's son, the Count, Frits, is not, as she has been supposing all this time, her biological father. Her mother was employed as *gouvernante* in this manorial establishment, and Frits, then a susceptible young man, fell in love with her. The young Jewish woman had to return to Svendborg. Though the two lovers kept up a correspondence, this did not ensure fidelity. Naomi's mother grew intimate with the Norwegian violinist and became pregnant by him. She confessed all this to Frits in letters, to which he was unresponsive, and so she killed herself. This sensational story is corroborated by the Count, while later Christian himself – whom Naomi meets again, and hears play the violin – fills her in about her *real* father, his own godfather and erstwhile teacher, and the dreadful way in which he died.

Naomi thus has to come to terms with being in blood neither a member of the family to whom society has assigned her nor even Danish. Her Norwegian and Jewish antecedents may explain her increasingly defiant feeling of not belonging, while the manner in which she has been brought up has unfortunately encouraged in her the hauteur of the over-privileged, the expectation that deference and accommodation of her tastes are her due. And there are psychological complications too. She sincerely loves the Count, and he her, but as time passes, his pleasure in the beautiful young woman everyone believes to be his daughter cannot be purely paternal. Christian's own connection with her actual father, his youthful devotion to the older man's art, and the now long-past episode of his breakdown after being trapped in the bell tower, have repercussions for her too. They make the youth more interesting to her than before. She tries to goad him into striking out for a freer, more ambitious life than that he enjoys, but does not succeed. Her contempt for him after this failure is swelled by resentment – for he carries in his person so much of her own past, and her blood relations', and she wants these to be vindicated through him, not passively surrendered to.

Naomi is also the child of two suicides. When she learns that her mother took her own life, she is impressed. 'Jeg hørte, at min Moder var smuk! Jeg hørte, at hun havde Forstand, og at hun havde Mod til at døe, da man krænkede hende for dybt.'[41] 'I heard that my mother was beautiful! I heard that she had a good mind, and that she had the courage to die, when they hurt her too deeply.' The recklessness of her subsequent conduct, her contempt for caution and custom, bear out her sincerity here, yet this is offset by a desire and an ability to look after her own interests, and when we take our leave of her it is of a woman occupying affluent and titled social eminence.

But her path to this position is a troubled one, and by no means all the dangers are of her own making. She arrives in Copenhagen from the country-side of Fyn on 4 September 1819, to find the city in chaos; the pogrom, the fallout from which Andersen himself witnessed, is in full vicious progress. The army is uncertain how to deal with the violence, the populus is aflame with both excitement and panic, and a crew of young thugs assaults the very carriage in which Naomi is travelling, and with insults and threats they identify her as Jewish. She behaves with great composure, and is rescued from outrages on her person by Peter Wik, Christian's former sea captain whom she had met earlier. The evil events of this day have a lasting effect on the two central figures of the novel – obviously on Naomi herself who, having seen the bloodlust which lies only too near the surface of so-called civilised life, never quite trusts it again and ever afterwards seeks more aggressive, confrontational approaches to people and situations, but also on Christian. The artist in him responds to the upheaval of the pogrom and to Naomi as its victim, as he cannot do to the more ordinary girls (represented by Luzie) who enter his life:

> Uvilkaarligt stillede han sig tæt ved Naomi, stirrede paa hende, til hans Blod blev Ild; han følte en Trang, et vildt Instinct til at trykke sine Læber til hendes. I Beskuelsen inddrak han Kjærelighedens stærke Gift.[42]
>
> Involuntarily he placed himself close to Naomi, gazed at her until his blood became fire; he felt a desire, a wild instinct to press his lips against hers. In contemplation he drank in love's strong poison.

But though he may feel that his soul and body alike are possessed by Naomi, he cannot win her; he is essentially too gentle for her. Whereas *she* has been stirred into bold activity by her difficulties, *he* has been rendered significantly passive by his. Even here his desire does not result in overt expression. Her sexuality, on the other hand, cannot submit to such repression. When, six months later (February), a circus troupe arrives in Copenhagen, so great is the impression one of its star performers, the Polish rider, Ladislaus, makes on her that she takes equestrian lessons from him. He makes her long for a life where instinct dictates its course, and soon she is surpassing all the Pole's pupils in agility, daring and skill. Ladislaus looks like the Apollo of the Belvedere come to life, has the bronzed complexion of Napoleon himself, and the dark, bright eyes of an Arab. Naomi is determined not to resist him. The year 1820, says Andersen, was a bad one for Denmark generally, with a serious leak in its already wonky finances, a leak in party loyalties in the face of this, and a leak in Danish girls' hearts because of Ladislaus. Then – with an extraordinary light ness of touch, showing how he was in total control of his fictional material – Andersen moves us on a fortnight, to the deck of the ship on which Ladislaus and the other circus artistes are sailing away from Denmark. The troupe has gained one extra member since their performances in Copenhagen, a Danish boy of no more than eighteen travelling under the name of Mr Christian. He is one of the two players in the astonishing scene that follows, presented in one short, attention-calling paragraph:

> Den danske Knøs trykkede et Kys paa Ladislaus's Læber. 'Din!' sagde han, 'Din alene!'[43]
>
> The Danish lad pressed a kiss against Ladislaus's lips. 'Yours!' he said, 'only yours!'

No, this is not an instance of homosexual love, though it is impossible to believe that either the author or any imaginative reader was unaware of its homoerotic appeal, particularly in view of the description of Ladislaus's many charms. The lad is, of course, Naomi, travelling with Ladislaus in disguise, and using for the purpose the passport earlier faked for Christian in the hope that he would do the venturesome thing and leave Denmark. (This last is perhaps the episode that comes nearest to the kind of plot-device, inherited from Henry Fielding, that first Scott then Dickens also made use of, though, as in the best of their cases, it has enough symbolic resonance to be – just about – acceptable.) The scene is there principally as a way of accentuating Naomi's readiness – thanks both to her dissatisfaction with her upbringing and to her genetic make-up – to jettison conventional morality, even to violate it. We remember, however, that curious ball sequence in *O.T.* where Vilhelm, dressed as a girl, seats himself on Otto's knee, and is physically demonstrative to him, thereby rousing his blood, allegedly through his resemblance to his sister, Sophie. Cross-dressing has obvious appeal to the androgynous, to the amphibious of Bernardo's retort to Antonio. If the tenderness that a conventional male exterior often shields was saluted in *O.T.*'s Vilhelm, the stand-in for Edvard Collin, Naomi has a boy-like energy that enables her, like some young hero of historical romance, to accomplish the demands of her strong will. This tableau on board ship – which to any uninformed onlooker would have comprised two males – is also there as a reminder of possibilities in human behaviour that decorum and strong taboos encourage us to ignore. We should beware, however, of seeing these gender transpositions in too personal a light.

They fascinated the age altogether, especially its vanguard spokespeople, the second Romantic generation, and owe something surely to its reverence for Shakespeare, with female–male crossovers at the centre of such popular works as *As You Like It* (1600) and *Twelfth Night* (1601).

And no writer put *As You Like It* to more prominent or elaborate literary use than Théophile Gautier (1811–72) in his sensational novel *Mademoiselle de Maupin*, where it provides a climax to the complicated gender interchanges already developed. The second volume of this novel came out in France in the same year as Andersen was writing *Only a Fiddler*, the first having appeared the year before (1835). But the contract for it had been signed in September 1833[44] so it is possible that Andersen may have known about the novel – perhaps from Victor Hugo whom he called on the previous month – during his first stay in Paris. It is worthwhile briefly considering this amazing, revolutionising work, since Naomi's rule-flaunting behaviour is prefigured in it, so to speak, and a substantial portion of *Only a Fiddler*'s third part takes us, with Naomi, to the Paris of 1833, and gives us its cultural climate, its moral tone.

Gautier, almost as precocious as Andersen himself, had been an enthusiastic member of the audience for Hugo's ground-breaking *Hernani* in February 1830 and before long, this poet, journalist, critic and short-story writer was one of those labelled 'les Jeunes-France'. His now classic epistolary novel derives from the real history of La Maupin/Julie d'Aubigny (1670–1707), who, educated as a royal page in all the traditional male pursuits such as swordsmanship and hunting, went on to have love affairs and scandalous liaisons with both sexes. In Gautier's complex novel (complex not least in its artistic design, mirroring its theme of disguises, their assumption and their discarding) a young, bored aristocrat, Chevalier d'Albert, is bowled over by a handsome young man, Théodore de Sévannes. In his letters to his friend Silvio, up to now swaggeringly frank in their attitudes to women and sex, d'Albert has to make the following difficult confession:

'You have commiserated with me for not being in love with anyone. Now take pity on me that I am, and especially that it is with this One. . . . I no longer know who I am or who others are. I'm uncertain whether I am man or woman, I have a horror of myself, I have peculiar, inexplicable urges and at times it seems as if I am losing my mind; the feeling that I exist has left me for ever. For a long time now I have not been able to believe what has happened to me. I have listened to my self, observed my self with great attention. I have tried to unravel the confused tangle in my soul. Finally, through all its veils, I have uncovered the awful truth. . . . Silvio, I am in love with. . . . Oh, no, I shall never be able to say it. . . . I am in love with a man.'[45]

And so he is, though Théodore is *not* a man but Mademoiselle de Maupin *en travestie*. The implications of the passage therefore deliberately exceed its (literally false) statements; the unthinkable can be said, and because it *has* been said, can be realised too.

Whatever his attitude towards Naomi's resourcefulness in her leaving Denmark in the company of Ladislaus, it is exceedingly doubtful that Andersen saw her as a desirable or even appealing figurehead for European civilisation as it makes for the future. He is unquestionably fascinated by the life of theatrical disguises and pretences the pair lead in Vienna, the subject of the first two chapters of Part Three. He is also clearly of the opinion that in so living they act out a struggle against oppressive conventionalism and reactionary politics representative of the period following the downfall of Napoleon. But fascination, percipience about contemporary mood, even sympathy for the defiant are not at all the same thing as approval. It would be hard to read the last part of *Only a Fiddler* as evincing this for Naomi, especially when taken in juxtaposition with Christian.

Ladislaus, sexual athlete, Byronic breaker of hearts, though he may be, proves not just callous and exploitative but downright cruel, even giving Naomi the lash to show his authority. She therefore has to leave him and Vienna: no easy undertaking, in or out of transgender disguise, for, as even she understands, she is compelled as well as appalled by her Polish rider. And during her fraught escape, which he attempts to thwart, she encounters her Danish aristocrat foster-father, the Count. When he reclaims her and rebukes her for her wild conduct, she remonstrates that her birth (the secret behind which, obviously, he knows better than anybody) was its cause; that and the treatment of her it led to. 'Min Tilværelse er en Ungdomssynd, og som Frøet er, bliver Frugten!'[46] 'My existence is a youthful sin, and as the seed is, so develops the fruit.' The Count turns out, perhaps because of his non-filial feeling for her, to be forgiving and generous, and takes her with him to Italy, proclaimed as the true country of the Fata Morgana, though whether, in the light of Naomi's subsequent febrile life, we should take this as praise is unclear.

It has to be admitted here (again) that – especially true of the chapters prior to the narrative leap in time – Kierkegaard's objections to Part Three are not wholly groundless. Naomi's movements from Austria to Rome to Paris do have too much of the quality of extracts from a travelogue of the author's own, since some of the treatment of places is perfunctory, as are such episodes as Naomi's meeting with the Austrian writer, Franz Grillparzer (1791–1872), there, one suspects, solely because Andersen himself met the man whom he liked and admired in 1834.[47] But the seeming superficiality of these pages, in contrast to the depth-plumbing of so many of the novel's sequences, must surely also be intentional, mimetic of the superficiality, the surrender to the artifice and pleasures of the moment pursued by Europe's peripatetic upper echelons. One of these, the young son of a French aristocrat, the Marquis Rebard, a charming-mannered libertine and socialite and friend of the Count's, is drawn to Naomi, and in his company she frequents the highest circles Rome has to offer, where famous artists such as Canova (who was to die the following year) grace parties, and Naomi herself is a star of entertainments like the fashionable *tableaux vivants* where she plays Galatea and the Sphinx.

Very different is Christian's life in Copenhagen: failure to find a proper patron for his music and therefore to have the break he needed as an artist; drudgery in giving ill-paid music lessons to blasé upper-class children, penury at home with his mother who has moved from Fyn to the capital because she mistakenly believes him to be at last successful. Kierkegaard was right to object that these become dwarfed by all the accounts of Naomi's brilliant triumphs. The imbalance here was surely *not* intentional, and has to be honestly regis-tered as somewhat impairing this great work.

However while the imbalance regrettably persists, the rest of the book, following the twelve-year leap, offers, through Naomi, a mediumistic rendering of the temperature of the times. This is ushered in by the concluding paragraph of Chapter VI:

Vi ere in Paris. Den trefarvede Fane vaier paa Vendome-Søilen; udenfor Boutikerne hænge allerede Caricaturbilleder af Folkets selvvalgte Borgerkonge, den kloge, verdensprøvede Louis Philippe. Det er i Begyndelsen af Aaret 1833.[48]

We are in Paris. The tricoloured flag waves on top of the column of the Vendôme; outside the shops already hang caricatures of the people's self-appointed Bourgeois King, the clever, world-experienced Louis Philippe. It is the beginning of the year 1833.

This signals what is to preoccupy us for the strongest sections of Part Three, though, behind the vivid scenes set in Paris of restlessness, hectic activity and the ennui of the over-privileged, the quieter later Danish ones – the bachelor Christian back on Fyn, his lame stork companion, his newfound religion – make their telling and contrasting cultural and moral points. These French chapters can be read also as an extended gloss on the treatment of July Revolution France in *O.T.* – the slide into venality, conspicuous consumption and cynical social policies that the so-called new broom of Louis Philippe, the Bourgeois King entailed, with its depressing, giveaway mantra 'enrichissez-vous!' 'enrich yourselves!'

Naomi has developed into a stout if handsome lady, after twelve years of marriage to the Marquis Rebard and has been at the centre of Parisian social life, with an entrée into every smart, culturally significant salon. She is a regular theatregoer, there at the successful opening night at the Opéra of Meyerbeer's *Robert le diable* (November, 1831),[49] which presented, to a generally godless society, the very ruins of the Catholic religion; she thrills to the ballet of *La Tentation de Saint Antoine* (*The Temptation of St Anthony*),[50] understanding only too well the struggle it depicts between sensuality and spiritual grace, and to Rossini's *William Tell* and *Le Comte d'Ory*;[51] she reads Victor Hugo and meets Alexandre Dumas[52] at a theatre soirée. An intelligent woman who, though her life is also an idle one, has sharpened her mind in Parisian fashion, she is politically aware, astutely seeing just what a betrayal of its (declared) founding ideals the July Monarchy is. Nor is this all she is honestly aware of. Married to a faithless husband, a selfish sybarite, and at times uneasy about the values she has accepted as a result of living with him, she can yet exclaim: ' "Jeg vil ei pine mig selv! jeg vil nyde Duften af dette falske Liv!" '[53] 'I will not torment myself! I will enjoy the perfume of this false life.' But she has difficulty in sleeping, she can't relax, and daytime too often weighs heavily on her; she feels irresistible waves of homesickness for Scandinavia (for her biological father's Norway as well as her own Denmark); she is unhappy and unfulfilled, and knows it.

She knows, too, that for all the country's intellectual and artistic liveliness, her condition mirrors France's own in its hollowness, its disenchantment. All comes to a head, both for her and the French nation she has embraced, with the splendiferous celebrations of the third anniversary of the July Revolution that brought Louis Philippe to the throne. These are elaborately and expensively staged so that 27–29 July 1833 can appear as memorable to citizens, and to the outside world too, as 'les trois glorieuses' of 1830. Their high point is the unveiling of a statue of Napoleon on top of the column of the Vendôme, a solemn event much looked forward to. But Naomi is prescient enough to know that the three-day festivities will only illustrate the true failure of the Bourgeois King to impress his people, to meet their deeper needs. Their disillusion is not confined to the cartoons everywhere, the mocking rhymes; the whole mood in the city is palpably sour, heavy with suppressed violence. Certainly when the statue is actually unveiled in front of Louis Philippe and his sons, it is greeted with cries of 'Vive le roi' (though there are dissenting voices delivering revolutionary oaths) and 'Vive la Mémoire de Napoléon'. But Naomi who – like Otto, like Hans Andersen, like his son in the days of his first German journey – has held Napoleon in the highest esteem, appreciates that here around her is no society like his empire at its greatest, let alone like that of the Revolution itself, but instead, a spoilt, self-pampering, glutted one, its ruling classes able to put up with, or even carry on, any amount of corrupt activity provided the exterior is kept attractive and intact, and the costly pleasures continue.

Naomi herself presently illustrates this prevailing *Weltanschauung*. In the crowd watching the unveiling stands a figure from her unrespectable past, an ill, emaciated Ladislaus. To her dismay he sees her and mimes the writing of a letter. Later that evening her husband shows her a letter he has just received, from her Polish rider, detailing their entire sordid bygone liaison. The Marquis takes a sophisticated attitude to the whole thing. With this proof of his wife's past in his hands, he can continue his own numerous affairs with impunity, and she can do nothing. But as a sop to her he vows that they will spend summer next year in her Denmark!

When that season comes round, Christian, now living in Fyn not far from Naomi's foster-father's estate, hears of her imminent return there, and something of his old romantic yearnings for her possesses him. But by now he is exhausted by his compound failures to achieve what he once desired, and by the death of his beloved stork. Andersen is as true here to the Danish history of these years as he has been to the French. Christian has joined a Pietist group, perhaps quixotically because, like his creator, and to the dismay of some old friends, he has long been sympathetic to Catholic practitioners too. But it is the life of devotion outside the State Church and the Danish establishments that appeals. Maybe here at last he can find the peace he has sought all his life. Possibly he does, towards his untimely end. His last ironic hope is that he will see Naomi before the moment of death. He does not. His coffin is carried to the churchyard just as the Marquis and his wife are making their way to the great hall that is the Count's family home. Peasants of the locality take off their hats to this grand pair as they pass, but no such ceremony is needed for the poor man they are about to bury; he was '*Kun en Spillemand*', '*Only a Fiddler*'![54]

On one level the meaning of *Only a Fiddler* is clear enough: a sorrowful but virtuous life sustained by the comparatively solid Danish values (Christian's) is preferable to one spent chasing after excitement, physical, emotional and cultural (Naomi's), in a culture that has lost its moral focus in exchange for wealth and luxury, and was spreading from France to infiltrate the rest of Europe. But on other levels there is multiple opacity: the role of Nature's laws, of genetics and environment in determining the course of a life; the connection between pathology and art, between ambition and worldly success, and between both of these and those artistic self-realisations with true significance for others. Who can really say where Christian went wrong, or whether it would have been possible for the stronger, higher-spirited Naomi to go right? Perhaps Andersen took on too much thematically, and his large-scale novel suffers too many periodic distortions and contractions as a consequence. But we cannot regret these imperfections; its intelligence, its frankness of confrontation and its emotional power are too strong.

4

The figure who gives his name to 'Den standhaftige Tinsoldat' ('The Steadfast Tin Soldier') is at once kinsman to Christian and his stork, and their antithesis. An entirely original story, published on 2 October 1838, 'The Steadfast Tin Soldier' could well have its roots in Andersen's third novel as he had come to reflect on it. June of that year saw its triumphant German publication; in the autumn it came out in Sweden and Holland. If we pity Christian even as we follow his representative journey, for the Tin Soldier we feel above all else respect. This is how the character himself would have it, of course; it is consonant with the code he so unflinchingly lives up to. Pity he would despise, and it is alien to his make-up. Though his emotional position, his unswerving regard for the ballerina who cannot return his interest in her, has universal resonance, he is perhaps more role model for than representative of ourselves, since – as his singular appearance might suggest – he is a morally outstanding character.

Our Tin Soldier is the last to be made of a set of twenty-five, given, to his enormous delight, to a small boy as a birthday present. All the soldiers were fashioned out of the one tin spoon, but when it came to the twenty-fifth, there was not quite enough tin left. Therefore he had to be satisfied with only one leg. He was naturally 'lidt forskjellig' 'a little different' from all his fellows: 'dog stod han ligesaa fast paa sit ene, som de andre paa deres to, og det er just ham, som bliver mærkværdig',[55] 'yet he stood every bit as steady on his one [leg] as the others on their two, and it was precisely he who became remarkable.' Like the (for many months) one-legged stork who became Christian's dearest companion, like indeed Christian himself, particularly after the incident inside the bell, the soldier is put through sufferings as the others are not. In compensation he earns himself a story. His adventures and how, throughout them, he proves the worth of his character could not have been attached to any of the twenty-four two-legged soldiers. We can even say their very wholeness would have disqualified them.

He reveals his unusual quotient of determination first of all in his unfailing adherence to soldierly comportment despite his deficiency: he holds himself as stiffly, as firmly, as any of the others. Yet (like Christian again) he also differs from them in the strength of his feelings, and in his ability to go against the conventional. Just as Christian dared physically to break into the strongholds of the upper class out of devotion to Naomi (or his ideal of her), the Tin Soldier defies norms of behaviour in his commitment to the ballerina (or, again, his ideal of her). He refuses to keep his eyes to himself when ordered to, instead fastening his gaze on the object of his desire, a female figure made out of paper but dressed in tulle, and positioned outside the toy castle on the same nursery table as himself. To him she too appears to be one-legged; it is this that initially draws him to her. In point of fact she is simply poised with one leg lifted so high that it eludes his vision, standing where he does. Thus the elective affinity he imagines between himself and her is founded on a mistake, more, on both an *illusion* and a *delusion*. The similarity here between his position and Christian's needs no stressing. He wants the ballerina to become his wife despite the obvious difference in status between them given her connection to the castle, so splendid with its lake (a mirror) on which swans are swimming.

After the household has gone to bed, the toys come to life, playing their own rather than their owners' games. Andersen has treated such frolicking of man-made objects when independent of their makers before, in 'Little Ida's Flowers', but the obvious ancestor of this engagingly rendered scene is Hoffmann's *Nussknacker und Mausekönig* (*Nutcracker and Mouse King* 1819).[56] Among the Christmas presents we find inside Hoffmann's Biedermeier nursery there are indeed toy soldiers –the boy Fritz has a 'new squadron of hussars very smartly dressed in red-and-gold uniforms, carrying silver weapons' – and also 'a magnificent castle [with] gilded towers and a great many windows as bright as mirrors' through which little dancing figures can be glimpsed. And Andersen even includes in *his* nursery a nutcracker (who turns somersaults), as if in acknowledgement of his tale's distinguished forebear. In the ruckus that follows the withdrawal of human beings two toys, however, are non-participants, remaining true to their daytime selves and keeping quite still: the one-legged soldier and the apparently one-legged ballerina.

When the clock strikes twelve, the lid of a little snuffbox flies open and the black troll who resides inside it comes out, a being who wields authority over the toys. ' "Tinsoldat!" sagde Trolden, "vil du holde dine Øine hos dig selv!". Men Tinsoldaten lod, som han ikke hørte det.'[57] ' "Tin Soldier!" said the Troll, "will you keep your eyes to yourself!" But the Tin Soldier pretended that he had not heard him.' This is the defining moment of our protagonist's steadfastness, though it should be noted that his steadfastness is to *himself*, to the inclinations of his own nature, and not to the loved one. If he feels like feasting his eyes on the ballerina rather than keeping them fixed straight ahead of him like any other soldier on parade, then he will. If he fancies a female toy of higher station than himself, then he will allow himself to do so, whatever the dictates of authority or etiquette. However, he suffers the consequences.

Andersen leaves open the question of the troll's responsibility for the next morning's disaster. The Tin Soldier is moved to the windowsill, and a gust of wind (or is it the troll himself, the very spirit of evil so palpably at large in our world?) blows the window open, and he falls down at formidable speed, head-first from the fourth storey, to land on his cap, his rifle getting caught between the cobbles of the pavement below. The little boy who owns him and a servant-girl immediately go down to look for him, and nearly step on him, but they do not spot him. Had he been less bound to his soldierly code the Tin Soldier could have called out and alerted them to his whereabouts, but he doesn't; there are grave disadvantages to being so uncompromisingly steadfast.

And now we witness these. The rain comes sheeting down, and when it eases up, two street ragamuffins spy the soldier and set him in a little boat they quickly extemporise out of newspaper, to sail off 'ned ad Rendestenen',[58] 'down the gutter', which in a nineteenth-century city would carry all manner of stinking refuse with it. The Tin Soldier is borne along ever faster flowing waters (swollen beyond normal levels as Andersen, always attentive to practical details, points out because of the recent downpour), until he passes under a long plank into a dark and patently cloacal region. No household, whatever the prettiness of its nursery and the plenitude of its luxury goods (toy castles and diminutive dolls dressed in tulle) is exempt from waste it must dispose of by means of drains and sewers. We will venture to these concealed conduits, rather more explicitly presented, and also with rats as denizens, in the fine late story 'Dryaden' (The Dryad', 1868) which points up the contrast between Paris's elegance and ostentation (a Grand Exposition) and the fact that it cannot escape its own effluence. But the urban currents here are alarming enough, presented with that vivid kinaesthesia of which Andersen had now *sui generis* stylistic mastery. The soldier continues to maintain the unperturbed behaviour and physical composure proper to his calling as he envisions it, while – proof of that stubbornness implicitly inseparable from his idiosyncratic or 'different' constitution – attaching his thoughts to the ballerina and the compatibility of the two of them. He doesn't know where he will end up, but thinks that if the little lady were with him now in the boat, it could be twice as dark for all he would mind! The roar of the water indicates the entry of the gutter into the canal, and though he hears its appalling noise (like an enormous waterfall to human ears), he literally does not bat an eyelid, even as the boat spins round and round, and the paper of its hull disintegrates. Death, he realises, is imminent, yet his mind doesn't stray from that one-legged ballerina whom he will never see again.

Along comes a fish and swallows up the tin soldier. But even inside its stomach (even darker and more cramped than the underside of the gutter-plank) the Tin Soldier preserves his dutiful sense of self. The rifle stays firm on his shoulder as he stretches himself out, and the fish carrying him flails about violently in the water.

Andersen now introduces a caesura of stillness and non-specificity into his narrative, so that we do not know what further reactions to his lot, if any, the Tin Soldier had or how much time has gone by. We have been passed through a state of blank unawareness, and so it is as much of a surprise to us readers as to the protagonist to find light pouring down on us (after such intense darkness), and to hear a voice exclaiming 'Tinsoldat!' (after such silence). Considering the obsession with immortality that informed 'The Little Mermaid' we must take this strange and delicately crafted passage as proceeding from Andersen's obsessive speculations about what the moment of entering another mode of existence than the earthly would be like, what it would offer, how the 'person' one has been would receive it and respond. . . . While the soldier has been oblivious of his surroundings, and, even more importantly, of his very own self, the fish in which he was imprisoned has been caught, taken to the market, bought and then – irony of ironies – brought into the kitchen of the selfsame house where he once formed part of the nursery's toy regiment. On cutting open the fish, the servant-girl who searched for him after his four-storey fall sees him and pulls him out with two fingers. Triumphantly she has him returned to his former quarters, so all about him is familiarity, the persons (the children of the nursery), the objects, his fellow toys, above all

'den nydelige lille Dandserinde; hun holdt sig endnu paa det ene Been og havde det andet høit i Veiret, hun var ogsaa standhaftig; det rørte Tinsoldaten, han var færdig ved at græde Tin, men det passede sig ikke. Han saae paa hende og hun saae paa ham, men de sagde ikke noget.'[59]

'the charming little ballerina; she was still standing on one leg and had the other high in the air, she also was steadfast; this moved the Tin Soldier, he was ready to weep tin, but that would not have been proper. He looked at her and she looked at him, but they didn't say anything.'

No paragraph in all Andersen's fairy-tales is more affecting or richer in subtleties than this, even without what so terribly follows it. The Tin Soldier who has been attracted to the ballerina so intensely and constantly, realises that she herself has that very virtue which he has upheld ceaselessly and uncomplainingly through such a succession of terrible circumstances: steadfastness. And for the first time ever he wishes to yield to actual expression of emotion yet is stayed by that implacable code which binds him. But, significantly, for the first time in their shared if non-communicating existence she returns his gaze; she actually acknowledges him, and, by inference, his love of her. In this Vita Nuova, this parodic afterlife, will some kind of union between the two become a possibility? Are they at last to overcome the limitations of their physical integuments, and merge their souls? Are we to take it that the Tin Soldier in saluting the ballerina's perseverance has at last realised that she stands on one leg by design, to serve her vocation, just as keeping his rifle upright serves his? Or does he still believe that she is the same kind as himself? But these questions cannot be answered, because union of such a kind is to be cruelly denied them.

'Det var bestemt Trolden i Daasen, der var Skyld deri.'[60] 'It was certainly the Troll in the box who was guilty of it.' How else, except by the omnipresence of evil, to explain what happens next: the gratuitous seizing of the tin soldier and the tossing of him into the stove by one of the boys in the nursery (presumably not the boy whose birthday present the toy army was, but we cannot be completely certain of this). The soldier feels the terrible ('forfærdelig') heat, 'men om det var af den virkelige Ild, eller af Kjærlighed, det vidste han ikke,'[61] 'but whether it was from the actual fire or from love, he didn't know'. At any rate he keeps steadfast, looking back through the inferno at the ballerina while she, for her part, looks back at him, a kind of consummation through the eyes, those traditional mirrors of the soul. But we have not yet arrived at quite the end of this soldier's tale. A door opens through which the wind blows – this time not specifically attributed to the troll in the box, though he could well be assumed to be the agent here too – and the beautiful paper girl is blown into the stove next to the melting soldier and bursts into flames lasting a few seconds only. The next day when the servant-girl is clearing out the ashes from the stove she finds the soldier reduced to a little tin heart, while all that is left of the ballerina is her spangle, burnt coal-black.

One can interpret this story in three ways, socio-political, religious, and psychological, but these readings overlap, and their overlaps show 'The Steadfast Tin Soldier' as an intensely moving and affective paradigm of the concerns, more, the angst of its times, *Only a Fiddler* reduced to its essence.

Taking the first way, we have to start with the matter of the ownership of the toys. The boy for whom the twenty-five tin soldiers are a birthday present claps his hands at the sight of them, and he certainly cares enough about our one-legged hero to go looking for him after his fall from the windowsill. But after failing to recover him, he would seem quite to forget him; there is no mention of him in the description of the soldier's return to the nursery nor do we know that the boy reacted in any way to his dreadful demise (assuming he was not responsible). In this way he reminds us of Thumbelina's mother who, once her adopted daughter's antics have ceased to delight her, plays no further part in the little girl's story. The boy lives in a household utterly crammed with luxury goods; there will be something else very soon that will occupy his attention. He therefore stands for the arbitrary placing of the rich and well-born above all others, and for their habitual comparative lack of concern for those beneath them, who may also, quite literally, belong to them.

Among the goodies in the boy's house is a snuffbox, a hallmark of upper-class living, its only use being its ability to provide the privileged with gratuitous pleasure. It can be no accident that it is inside this object that the evil troll dwells. We thus see here a household that implodes from within, thanks to his malefactions, bringing death to its most virtuous, most exceptional inhabitant, and destroying for ever his chance of reciprocated love. It is noticeable that the only human being shown as carrying out altruistic deeds and caring for the

Steadfast Tin Soldier *as himself* is the servant-girl who made her way from the fourth floor to seek him and who was so delighted at his reappearance that she showed him to everybody and restored him to his old companions. She it is who later found him, melted down and all heart.

More disconcertingly for us today, we should have to supplement this observation by appreciating that the real mischief done to the soldier is the work of two street urchins. They, and they alone, set him on the boat (which they have so hastily constructed for their amusement) and sped him down the gutter to danger. Outside the walls of this comfortable prosperous house with its spoiled children and servants awaits an underclass with no refinement of feeling, only coarse humour and roughness.

The religious reading would concentrate on the soldier's strong adherence to his code, to an ethical system if you like, and his forbearance because of his belief in this through appalling situations and bitterest disappointment. It would emphasise that an interesting ambiguity enters here, for this code is actually shown as insufficient – either for the soldier himself or for us following his history under the author's guidance. In certain circumstances it may be a very effective guide, encouraging a certain stoical selflessness. But it omits the life of the heart. Our soldier, however, does *not* exclude this but, on the other hand, does allow the code to inhibit him from spontaneous expression of his feelings. Yet when we look back over his story we see that in truth it is to love, not to regimental duty, that he stays steadfast, love for the ballerina that fills his mind even in the midst of the worst perils, and love which he carries with him even into death. In the purgatorial fire he keeps his eyes on his loved one; this is exemplary behaviour for those who think that God is Love. The reward of the soldier's devotion to Love is his ultimate reduction to a heart, the one essential and durable part of his being.

Psychologically we can see in this soldier impaired from the outset a symbol of how Andersen only too frequently saw himself and how he believed others saw him – and how perhaps they often did. In one sense, he is a more manly, a more successful individual than Christian in *Only a Fiddler* can ever be. Behind the ballerina we can see the figures of Riborg Voigt, Louise Collin and Sophie Ørsted whose love Andersen longed for (or believed himself to long for) but who did not respond to him with either the spontaneity of reaction or the kind of admiration inseparable from sexual attraction that he coveted. Where would he have located his own defects here? What would he have cited as his own 'one' leg? His lack of conventional masculine affect? That natural fastidiousness that had kept him apart from other boys when young, just as the soldier himself does not join in the nocturnal fun-and-games of all the other toys? That knowledge which he, with familial access to the proletariat's less respectable sections, had gained early and which made nice, well-connected girls, human ballerinas in front of *haute bourgeoisie* castles, out of his reach – just as he was permanently below theirs? All of these, perhaps. What Andersen is asking for in this story, in recompense, is recognition of his capacity for devotion (something his lifelong relationship with the Collins more than abundantly bears out) – and recognition too of the sheer strength of will his artistic aims and their execution required.

The age as it progressed was to admire him for exactly this. Andersen became, as he was ever more widely read, for all his abnormalities and eccentricities, the model of a steadfast individual to be relied on for his writings and his appearances alike. The public did not see him as a wounded stork incapable of making the great flight expected of others, or as a poor fiddler. And this not least because in these very stories he expressed what people wanted, what they *thought* they wanted, and what they knew they did not want. They wanted comfort, prosperity and social justice but were frightened of the ragamuffins outside their doors who inevitably could not be let in. They wanted order in society, in the international community, in religion, yet were hampered by an inability to define these areas. They wanted to replace the obsolescent but were afraid of what might take its place. They believed in the individual less wholeheartedly than the Romantic generation had done, but were nevertheless reluctant to submerge him or her in a societal morass; they still placed a high evaluation on such personal achievements as staying true to oneself in the face of all threats and dangers. They believed in love, yes, they esteemed love and its demands on lovers very much, but again, could they let it break up the social orders, as Byron or Lamartine would have had it do?

On 10 February 1955, the eve of his Golden Wedding anniversary, and the twenty-second anniversary of his departure from Hitler's Germany, Thomas Mann wrote to Agnes E. Meyer,[62] writer, journalist, translator and favourite confidante, expressing his ambiguous feelings about two forthcoming occasions: going back to Germany to honour Schiller 150 years after the poet's death and his own eightieth birthday on 6 June: 'I mean to endure with a military stoicism whatever it is that people intend to do with me for 6 June. I have always liked Andersen's fairy-tale of the Steadfast Tin Soldier. Fundamentally it is the symbol of my life.' There have been almost as many interpretations of Mann's tribute as of the story he admired. But looking at the date of the letter the great writer must have been thinking of steadfastness to humane dealings, person with person, peoples with peoples, so appallingly and repeatedly flouted in the decades through which he had just lived, that he himself always maintained by simply keeping on working.

Andersen was as steadfast a man, in his application to his writing, in his trust in his imagination and the meaning for others of the works it produced.

Steadfast too in his determination to travel, and to look into the heart of the places he visited. On 31 October 1840 he started out on a year-long journey which took him as far afield as Turkey. He would describe this in his finest travelogue *En Digters Bazar* (*A Poet's Bazaar*, published 30 April 1842). Andersen was always to say that the accomplishment of this journey was responsible for what are even today his most admired achievements, those fairy stories he wrote after he had returned from these adventurous travels to Denmark.

CHAPTER 7

En Digters Bazar (A Poet's Bazaar)

1

Many of his readers, Andersen acknowledges, will never have seen a railway, and may therefore share the widespread view that it does away with the poetry of travelling ('Reise-Poesi').[1] He strongly disagrees. Being cooped up in a stuffy, crowded diligence, the only alternative, what poetry is there in *that*? Sitting in a railway carriage is a richer experience by far, providing the magical illusion that railings, fields, trees, buildings, people are all flying past the window. You can even find, by the time you've taken a mere pinch of snuff, that you have exchanged one province of a country for another.

Andersen himself, he confesses, felt somewhat apprehensive before boarding his first ever train – in Germany, at Magdeburg, at 7 a.m. on 10 November 1840 to arrive in Leipzig, 110 kilometres away, some three hours later.[2] And he was not put at ease by the starting whistle which sounded like a pig having its throat slit. But soon he was enjoying himself, positively liking the motion, something between a sledge gliding over snowfields and horses at full gallop, and it made him aware as never before of the fact that all of us live after all on a *moving* globe. The signalmen with their flags standing beside the line, the long stops at many stations with food served to passengers through the train windows – he found such things exhilarating. Above all he rejoiced in the railway because it was so patently a triumph of human inventiveness and will, and a peaceful and useful one at that:

'Oh what a great achievement of the spirit is this production! One feels oneself really powerful, like a sorcerer of the olden times. We attach our magic horse to the wagon, and space vanishes.'[3] Mephistopheles carrying Faust through the air on his cloak couldn't do better than the railway train, yet the engineers responsible for it have made no compact with the devil. Quite the opposite: the railway springs from humanity's rational powers and beneficent creativity. 'I remember only a few times in my life that I have felt myself as overcome as here, as if with my whole mind I beheld God face to face.'[4] Andersen could only compare this feeling with that he'd known as a child when alone in a solemn old church, or, at a later stage of life, when walking in a forest as sunlight broke through. 'In the realm of poetry (Poesi) feeling and imagination are not the only things that prevail, they have a brother, who is just as potent, he is called the intellect, he proclaims the eternal truth, and in that dwells greatness and poetry.'[5]

For all that he has been describing his personal reaction to a personal experience – in tones that bring to mind Rousseau, the Wordsworth of 'Tintern Abbey' or *The Prelude*, and the Coleridge of the great Conversation Poems – these last words are clearly not intended as a subjective statement but as a missionary, objective one. Poetry, Andersen is insisting, not for the first or last time, does not belong only to private dream or the intimate moment. It is also discoverable out in the great accessible public world, in works that come from sustained, reasoned endeavour and hard labour, and in circumstances as prosaic as a three-hour journey from one big thriving German city to another.

Yet such tributes to modernity are offset by the extraordinary last third of this book: Andersen's account of his travels by boat from Constantinople into the Black Sea and then slowly up the Danube. Here he is recounting his confrontation with people living lives infinitely more primitive, more distant from the nerve centres of civilisation and in many cases more sequestered, than any he has come across before – even in Jutland, even in the remoter parts of Italy. He understood that Germany – to be precise, Prussia and the Kingdom of Saxony – was building dazzling railways and sustaining a fine orchestra like the Leipzig Gewandhaus because its expanding economy gave it corresponding authority in the world. In contrast, the indigent villagers whom Andersen observed during his Danubian travels owed their miserable conditions to the countries to which they nominally belonged being hemmed in, for all their wild mountains and apparently limitless plains, by powers against which they were helpless on their own: the Ottoman and Russian Empires, and the monarchies of Austria (Hapsburg) and Hungary, which would become the Austro-Hungarian Empire in 1867.

But despite its recording a tour which included, on the one hand, his encounters with Mendelssohn on terms of personal friendship and, on the other, a visit to a river-port in which nearly all the children ran around stark naked, the travelogue possesses artistic unity. (Which is not to say that parts of it are not superior to others, more time-transcending.) This paradox derives from the very title of the book, *En Digters Bazar, A Poet's Bazaar*, 'Digter' (like the German 'Dichter') a loftier yet more encompassing designation than the English 'poet'. Andersen as the ever-curious, responsive, probing witness is what links the diversity of material. But – another paradox – Andersen, never loath to write about himself, does not make his personality or his private feelings during these travels the predominant interest.[6] On the contrary. Throughout he sticks scrupulously to his itinerary, about which he is factually (and accurately) informative, and which he approached with knowledge garnered from history and current affairs. (For example, he surveys Wallachia and its Danubian situation with a good working knowledge of post-classical history, of the Emperor Trajan's Dacia campaigns and its legacy.) In comparison the earlier *Shadow Pictures* seems a trifle callow, the author too obviously anxious to make himself interesting and engaging. Coy references to past love-trouble or attempts to charm with disingenuous little tyro flourishes such as disarm us there would be unthinkable in *A Poet's Bazaar*.

The principal reason for the difference between the two travelogues must be, of course, the change in Andersen's literary reputation in the intervening years, which gave him a firmer place in his society, and consequently a firmer authorial identity. True, he is moved every now and again to tell us how he met during his travels people (some distinguished, some obscure) who knew his name as that of a leading Danish writer, the author of the novel *Only a Fiddler* still enjoying real success in Germany, but one only has to compare the book with the relevant pages of his autobiography to realise how much self-discipline, born of a strong overall purpose, Andersen exercised here. That purpose is to reveal the diversity of life even on the globe's most developed continent, and the diversity of attitude and mores of which humanity is capable.

Periodically, however, the 'Digter' does take a step forward as literary 'maker', for instance to fashion a fairy tale out of his new surroundings – like 'Metalsvinet' ('The Bronze Pig')[7] in Florence – or to express his responses to works of art as only a practising artist can. But, as in the passage which opened this chapter, he is also concerned to testify to the significance to one of his calling of creations unique to the contemporary world, and indicative of its future. He even tells us how he explained the principles of steam (efficiently, and with practical illustrations) to a worried woman traveller. In addition the 'Digter' has, for related reasons, to be concerned also with the chronic, and dangerous imbalances within the Europe he is exploring, and within the Asiatic power closest to it, Turkey, and to realise that the poetic observer can simultaneously empathise and stand at a critical distance.

2

Andersen took his leave of Copenhagen on 31 October 1840. He tells us in his Diary:

I left Copenhagen at 2 o'clock. It was a difficult departure. Yesterday evening my friends held a going-away party for me at Ferrini's, which was attended by Oehlenschläger, Privy Councillor H.C. Ørsted, Collin, Titular Councillor Lund and many of my younger friends. Oehlenschläger and Hillerup composed the songs. I didn't get much sleep during the night. Today I said goodbye to the Collins. They accompanied me out to the ship, *Christian the Eighth*. There was a strong wind with heavy seas driving in off the Baltic. Edvard Collin was the last one out there. I said goodbye; he pressed a kiss onto my mouth. Oh, it was as if my heart would burst.'[8]

Edvard was behaving to him as Vilhelm might have done to Otto in *O.T.* – as a committed friend, capable of expressing the unique feelings between them. Such a momentous episode as this would have affected Andersen as he embarked on his ambitious enterprise, strengthening his self-confidence with the results just adumbrated. (And Edvard and he corresponded during Andersen's months of absence with no repetition of the experiences of *Shadow Pictures*.)

First major stop was Hamburg on 6 November, where Andersen visited radical novelist and dramatist Karl Gutzkov (1811–78)[9] of the Junges Deutschland group, though he does not deal with him in this book, and attended a concert by Liszt[10] which does fulsomely find its way into it. Liszt, Andersen pronounced, was the true modern Orpheus who cast a spell over his audience before he so much as sat down to play. But when he did, a palpable change came over his face; his soul showed through. Liszt's music by its sheer adventurousness united Europeans as much as railway systems or the Bourse, and for his part Andersen heard his music as an overture to his own travels; it would reverberate in his head even as he looked on Vesuvius and Etna, the mountains of Greece or the Asiatic coast.

Then he went via Braunschweig to Magdeburg, and thence, as already mentioned, by train to Leipzig. He does not tell us at this point – saving it for the last chapter of the entire book – about his encounter with Leipzig's most eminent citizen, another composer enjoying Continent-wide reputation, Felix Mendelssohn-Bartholdy (1809–47). On 11 November Andersen went to the Leipzig Gewandhaus to hear Mendelssohn in rehearsal of Beethoven's Seventh Symphony and then introduced himself. (The composer had already read *Only a Fiddler* with pleasure and admiration.) A greater artistic contrast could not be found than that between Liszt and Mendelssohn: the one largely eschewing the classical symphonic form for the dramatic tone-poem, chromatic in his harmonies, flamboyantly Romantic in attitudes while also eminently Roman Catholic; the other devoted to the German classical tradition, reappraising Bach and editing Schubert's hitherto unperformed 'Great' C Major Symphony, writing concertos, symphonies, quartets and trios that carried on the German line of achievement while contributing indelibly to it, and, despite his Jewish provenance, devoutly Protestant. Yet Andersen appreciated both composers, and it could be argued that *A Poet's Bazaar* partakes of the art of both. After all, each is the dedicatee of a major section of the work.

Thence to Nürnberg (Nuremberg) where the city's great past absorbed him; he felt in all but physical contact with the mathematician and astronomer, Regiomontanus,[11] cobbler-genius Hans Sachs ('I am a poet myself' he reminds readers),[12] painter and engraver Albrecht Dürer.[13] But he also hails the city as resembling an old man who has retained the vigour and active mind of his youth. And why? Because Nuremberg was the first German city to enter the railway age, building tracks connecting it to Fürth.[14]

From 17 November to 1 December Andersen was in Munich. He shields us in the travelogue from the irritations and feelings of hurtful let-down inspired in him by his fellow Danes there, who find their way into petulant paragraphs of *My Fairy-Tale Life*. Instead he shows how the Bavarian capital impressed him as the disseminating centre it had now become for theatre and the visual arts. He met Peter von Cornelius,[15] leading mural painter and associate of the Nazarenes, who, though from Düsseldorf, was responsible more than any single other person for putting the Bavarian capital on the artistic map. And he called on Cornelius's protégé (who exceeded him in fame), Wilhelm Kaulbach (later von Kaulbach) (1805–74).[16] After only a few minutes he felt the man was a real friend – rightly, for this friendship lasted the rest of their coeval lives. Kaulbach had grown up in great poverty like Andersen himself, and had been as precocious as he, following his mentor Cornelius to Munich when not yet twenty. To Andersen he still looked young, with a pale, innocent face behind which past sufferings could surely be discerned. So forcefully did Kaulbach's paintings strike him that all other work he had seen in young artists' ateliers seemed insignificant in comparison. The travelogue describes in enthusiastic detail two canvases Kaulbach had just completed, both on historical subjects: *The Battle of the Huns* (1837) and *The Destruction of Rome* (1838). (Andersen praises them in his autobiography also.) Turning to these large-scale works after most paintings, thought Andersen, was like reading *The Divine Comedy* or Goethe's *Faust* after some common-or-garden novel. Posterity would revere them as it does Michelangelo's *Last Judgement* in the Sistine Chapel. Yet in his own art Andersen was never tempted to strive, like Kaulbach, for the huge, the panoramic, the grandly historical or eschatological, and was never guilty of the overreach of these contemporaneous artists who, for all their gifts and plentiful ideas, were most definitely *not* Dante or Michelangelo. Andersen's own ambitious visions – of the rifts between peoples and how to breach these – he was able to express in an intimate, conversational, often casual manner, which has enabled their grateful reception by successive generations, while so many deliberate attempts at mighty masterpieces have become fixed in the aspic of their own times.

Kaulbach was a devout Protestant, and in time he would provide for Andersen's popular fairy story of religious intent, 'Engelen' ('The Angel', 1843),[17] an illustration which would sell in the millions. The angel of the story's title turns out to have been in this world a poor boy ill from birth, whose eyes in his last sickness were always on a wild flower in a nearby earthenware pot, even at the moment when God called him to Himself. Now as angel he has the honour of leading another child departing this world into the flower-loving presence of God. Here is a work of Andersen's that, in contrast to the travelogue in hand, is tethered to the times. So distant is this tale from twenty-first-century tastes that it is hard not to convict it – and with it Kaulbach's pictorial homage – of senti-mental religiosity; hard too to stifle amazement that the same mind which saluted rational thinking and its fruits could be responsible for it. Yet we have to remember that early poem 'The Dying Child' and its author's strong, never-ceasing preoccupation with the experience of death, and with the important truth that the mentally underdeveloped and inarticulate undergo spiritual experiences, awakenings, no less importantly than the educated. Moreover this was an age when child mortality was still high; few families were unaffected.

On 2 December Andersen left Munich for Rome – via Innsbruck, Bolzano, Verona, Mantua, Bologna, Florence (a two-night stopover here), Perugia, Assisi, Foligno, Terni, Civita Castellena and Nepi to Rome. As he neared Mantua, Andersen saw a procession of baggage wagons all laden with ammu-nition and followed by the Austrian cavalry. For Mantua[18] was one of the key Quadrilatero fortress towns of Austrian-occupied Lombardy–Venetia, and Andersen sensed in the town the tension of the whole region. People spoke only of war, the expected war, Andersen records, of France against Germany (by which he specifically meant Austria, within the German Confederation). One woman tells him she expects dreadful times very soon. Andersen says that on hearing this he turned serious, as well he might, understanding the helpless-ness of everybody, including himself, in the face of events still to occur yet inevitable. He has a Turk's acceptance of Providence, he believes, but cannot prevent himself from worrying, above all for his friends back in Denmark. This thought in turn brings about a wave of homesickness, and his surroundings cease for a while to be Mantua and become his own Danish countryside: little lakes surrounded by beech trees, paths winding between wild roses and bracken, a castle in the distance and a stork with its nest on its roof, a clover field and prehistoric tumuli overgrown with brambles and blackthorn – and always, beyond the meadows, the sea. Few lines in A Poet's Bazaar, even those lyrically evoking the wooded Danubian banks, are more beautiful than these, an encomium to Denmark in the form of a reverie. They remind us of the evocations of Fyn in both *O.T.* (Vilhelm's estate) and *Only a Fiddler* (Christian's early and last homes). Their emotional strength also suggests what has been intimated throughout this book and which we will continue to attend to: Andersen's deep disquiet about how things would go in a continent which had been at open war with itself only a quarter of a century before and was still palpably prepared for further conflict. And, as already cited, he was unsure of the success of eventual Italian unification.

Andersen stayed in Rome from 19 December 1840 to 24 February 1841.[19] 'Rome is truly the only city in which a stranger without family or acquaintances can settle down and be at home.'[20] For the solitary person or the troubled spirit, he continues, there will always be something to stimulate and arouse the interest. One should live in Rome for a whole year, or at least from the early autumn vine harvest in its environs to February's riotous Carnival in the heart of the city. This last, which he had memorably celebrated in *The Improvisatore*, he experienced again in 1841 with equal relish, especially its last day, the feast of misrule, with its grotesque masquerading figures, men dressed as bears or *en travestie*, its Harlequins and Columbines, its travelling booths and hurdy-gurdies. We might, we feel, be about to meet his Bernardo again. But then the entire Roman sequence in *A Poet's Bazaar* is full of reminders of his first novel and does not, truth to tell, constitute any measurable advance on it; on the whole the work of fiction, because concerned with its central character's feeling life, brings the culture of street, piazza and church alive more vividly; here Andersen ruefully admits that his accounts cannot really improve on Goethe. Even so we again visit the Capuchin cloister, with its stacked grisly relics of the long-dead, attend services at the Church of the Aracoeli – though *this* time register disgust at its sickly cult of children, among whom were once *The Improvisatore*'s Antonio and Annunziata – 'Father forgive them for they know not what they do!'[21] is Andersen's reaction now to its protracted ceremonial involving a baby Jesus waxwork; nor was he as entranced as he had hoped by the blessing of the donkeys just over a week later, with the mean cruelty of street-boys jabbing with pins an animal carrying an old lady.[22]

Andersen in real life found his second stay in Rome decidedly anticlimactic after his first when he had discovered a stronger creative self because of the therapeutic nature of absence from Copenhagen and, it has to be admitted, from the Collins. This time also there was news from Denmark more discouraging, dampening to the spirits, than anything else: his play *Maurerpigen* (*The Moorish Girl*)[23] had not done well, his friend, the actress Johanne Heiberg, had refused to act the title role, and thus it had failed to generate the money he was hoping for, to facilitate the long journey still ahead of him. Worse, Johanne's husband had just brought out a poem in which he had – again – mocked Andersen. Heiberg had wittily declared that *The Moorish Girl*, like *The Mulatto* of earlier in the year (February) was suitable viewing primarily for an audience in Hell. Unsurprisingly, Andersen brooded unhappily over the gratuitous slight. (In fact it turned out to be less of one than he had been led to believe; Heiberg's lines were written in jest, though he must have known that its target wouldn't much enjoy it.)[24]

December 1840 also saw the Danish publication of a fuller edition (thirty rather than twenty stories) of *Billedbog uden Billeder* (*Picture-Book Without Pictures*, 1839).[25] This holds an interesting place in Andersen's *oeuvre*, especially when taken into consideration with *A Poet's Bazaar*.

3

A poor lad, a painter, is at first unable to reconcile himself to his new urban surroundings and feels lonely in his attic room in a house in a narrow street. He has a large skylight, but even so finds the lack of woods and fields to look out on to be as oppressive as his present lack of congenial friends. Then he opens his window to behold a well-known face looking in – the moon's – and feels so refreshed that he asks him (for the moon is masculine in Danish, as in other Nordic languages) to visit him every night. The moon promises to do this, and each time he will present the youth with short descriptions (for he is never able to stay long in one place) of interesting things seen.[26] There are (in this second edition of 1840) thirty such 'evenings', a thirty-first and a thirty-second being added for the 1844 reprint. These moon-views, says the painter-lad who gives us the compilation, have not been chosen at random but should be taken in the order given. (Much the same procedure will apply to the stories told to Gerda by the flowers in 'The Snow Queen'.) Their range in place suggests that Andersen had decided on travel as essential to his creative mind quite a while before he planned the expedition to Constantinople and back.

In prose-poems remarkable for their linguistic compression, their delicate allusiveness, we are given 'what the moon saw' (in point of fact the usual English title for the sequence) in many parts of our world, past and present, the shafts of his light piercing the perceived so that their behaviour, their mostly solitary movements, reveal how emotions deep within animate them. We begin by the Ganges,[27] with a girl on its banks trying to find out whether her betrothed is alive or not, and, as she prays that he might be safe, not heeding a deadly speckled snake in the nearby grass. From here we move on to, among other places, Germany (a stable there converted into a theatre where a chandelier drips melting tallow down on to the audience),[28] Uppsala, Sweden (which Andersen had visited in 1837), Pompeii, Lüneberg Heath, and Venice (all places familiar to readers of the Andersen corpus to date). The new 1840 sequence ends with the moon shining down on a young merchant from Fezzan (a desert region of south-west Libya), whose camel fell by the wayside, as he was journeying away from his lovely new wife. Away, but where to? While the young wife at home prays for her husband's safety, her merchant-husband is approached by a band of men from the African interior, one of them leading a lion on a string. So what will happen now? The moon does not see, but we appreciate that he has brought us thematically back to our first 'evening' with him, that scene by the Ganges: the woman is desperate for the survival of the man she loves, but there can be no guarantee of this. The whole world over, men, and particularly young men, are exposed – or choose to expose them-selves – to danger, and may even forget the objects of their love in their predic-ament. The women have recourse only to a private world of supplication.[29]

The three most impressive 'evenings' are the Fifth, the Ninth and the Sixteenth. The Fifth[30] takes us to Paris during the height of 'les trois glorieuses' and therefore can be read as yet a further gloss on those sections of *O.T.* and *Only a Fiddler* inspired by the 1830 July Revolution and its aftermath. A half-grown boy from the working class, fighting on behalf of the insurrectionists, is mortally wounded by soldiers with bayonets. His still bleeding body is taken into Charles X's palace and actually laid on his throne, where he agonisingly breathes his last, thus fulfilling a prophecy spoken to his mother at his birth: 'He will die on the throne of France.' The Ninth 'evening'[31] evokes Greenland for us, that Danish possession which had survived as a (huge) outpost of its once great empire. Andersen, drawing on travellers' tales, makes us look at it in two contrasting seasons – first it is winter, when the Northern Lights burn fiercely bright in the dark sky – while presenting us with both the land's animal denizens – polar bear, whale, seal, walrus – and its indigenous humans with their magical dances, ancient religion and traditional legal code. (Andersen surely remembered this imaginary excursion of his to the Arctic North when he wrote 'The Snow Queen'.) Then we change to summer; glaciers are melting and the night is brief but beautiful. We see a Greenlander who is dying. His wife is already sewing his fur shroud, and asking him where he would like to be buried. His whispered reply is unequivocal. In the sea, he says, now summer's here, there will be thousands of seals at play on it, the walruses will be amenable too, and the hunting safe. Death becomes, it would seem, to those nearing it, not fearsome but palatable, even appealing.

The Sixteenth Evening[32] informed by Andersen's grateful memories of Caserti in Odense, derives from the Italian folk theatre's trio of Harlequin, Columbine and Pulcinella, the last an antecedent of English Punch.[33] (We shall detect their influence again in Andersen's later Italian-set story, 'The Shadow'.) Externally Pulcinella is ugly and misshapen with a hump on his back and on his breast, but inwardly he is brilliant and deep in his feelings, with a well-stocked mind and a ready sensitivity. The theatre is the only world in which someone looking as he does can flourish, and even there, despite his longings to be heroic, he is obliged to cut a comic figure, and make people laugh. Most heartily of all they laugh when Columbine, speaking the truth, says that he, this grotesque creature, is seriously in love with her.

A few days ago, the moon now tells us, Columbine died. Her husband Harlequin is grief-stricken, and is unable to perform on the day of her funeral. The theatre director, anxious not to disappoint his audience, commands Pulcinella (who also is grief-stricken) to be extra energetic and amusing that night. He obliges; his public is thrilled, demands an encore. But the moon saw him only last night, looking disconsolate and hideous, sitting beside Columbine's grave, the flowers on which have already withered. And most likely, he observes, the theatregoers whose favourite he is would, irrespective of his strong, true emotions, have cried as usual: 'Bravo, Pulcinella, bravo, bravissimo!'

This tender, visually compelling 'evening' is obviously a correlative for how Andersen only too frequently saw his own predicament and, at his saddest, his whole life's destiny: to be entertaining, even admired, while his emotional life was ignored, discounted, even ridiculed. The piece's brevity adds greatly to its power, its ineffable sadness.

All the same, admiration for the art of Picture-Book Without Pictures has to be qualified by reservation about its dominant subject matter, and in honesty tempered by this. It skates perilously over the thin ice of both the precious and the mawkish, as even these best 'evenings' surely suggest. A Poet's Bazaar, on the other hand, is admirably free of those self-conscious exhibitions of sensitivity that got Andersen labelled (by himself as well as by others) amphibious, androgynous, a marsh-plant, feminine, a stalk on which male and female flowers grew. This travelogue is his most masculine book, in the sense that, throughout its course, as throughout the actual journeys, the writer moves not as someone seeking consolation or attention, but as someone secure in his being and intent on what lies beyond his own self.

4

In Rome Andersen spent much time with members of the colony of Scandinavian painters, particularly his fellow Danes Constantin Hansen (1804–80)[34] and his own portraitist (his likeness was agreed to be one of the finest), Albert Küchler (1803–86)[35] who, Nazarene-influenced, would, like Christian's father in Only a Fiddler, end up a monk, attached to a Franciscan order. Hansen's famous painting of 1837 Et Selskab af danske Kunstere i Rom (A Company of Danish Artists in Rome) is perhaps the locus classicus for the prevalent mood among these Northern Europeans seeking some kind of release in the South, and we shall pause to remember it again when we consider 'The Shadow'. The artists here are lounging about in the welcome coolness indoors, in an apartment with a balcony opening on to a prospect of the city. One artist – the neoclassicist architect, Michael Gottlieb Bindesbøll (1800–56)[36] – lolls on the floor, another, Ditlev Conrad Blunck (1798–1853),[37] major celebrant of Rome's Scandinavian colony, props himself against the entrance to the balcony, his shadow prominent against the folded windows. However genuinely they may relish its atmosphere, these men are clearly strangers in this environment, behaving neither quite like their Danish selves nor like native citizens. And perhaps on his second visit to Rome Andersen was more aware than earlier of these discrepancies in his compatriots.

After a trip to Tivoli to see the fountains and the cataracts of the river Aniene by torchlight, and his already noted second experience of the giddying Carnival, Andersen left Rome on 25 February 1841.

From 28 February to 15 March he was in Naples.[38] Some of Andersen's account of the city in this travelogue – its lively street life conducted with complete disregard for the refined conventions of further north – again points forward to 'The Shadow' with its vivid opening evocation of the city, as well as back to his first visit and his first novel. He was moved also to remember the singer Malibran whom he had honoured as Annunziata in *The Improvisatore*, and to reverence anew Vesuvius, Pompeii and Herculaneum. On 15 March, his destination Athens,[39] he boarded the 'Leonidas'; he changed steamships in Malta where he arrived on 17 March.

His crossing took him past the coast of Morea and the islands of the Cyclades on the way to Piraeus (he was briefly quarantined here). He arrived in Athens on 24 March. The scruffiness of so many of its streets and the unkempt surroundings of its most famous sights had a strong impact; he walked regularly up to the Acropolis, overawed by the view from it and accordingly shocked at the condition of the Parthenon, which had been subjected to much hostile attack and disregard. Yet there was still majesty in its columns. . . . On 6 April he watched the celebrations of Greek independence, and on the 14th attended an evening party held by the king, Otto, at his palace. Greece's independence from the Ottoman Empire dated from the London Protocol of 1830, which had followed years of bitter fighting among different Greek liberty-seeking factions. The king, Andersen's host, whom the European Great Powers (Britain, Russia and France) had put on the Greek throne, belonged to the Bavarian house of Wittelsbach. Andersen, pointing out that the sovereign was Roman Catholic, his Queen Lutheran and his subjects Orthodox, observed that it was not happiness to reign in Greece. But he might well have added here what he did not perhaps realise, that this ruler was autocratically inclined and held authority without constitution or representative parliament. These would be forced on him in 1843; his whole reign lasted only until 1862.)

Andersen left Athens on 20 April with some reluctance, since the city had appealed to him: he had received much hospitality, and had been stimulated by the landscape beyond it, even to writing a story of divided friends set in the countryside near Delphi and Mount Parnassus, 'Venskabspakten' ('Friendship's Pact').[40] Steamships bore him first to Syra; then, after a change of vessel, to Smyrna. But before he had the satisfaction of at last arriving in Asia, he endured, on 22 April, an appalling storm. Everything on the ship rattled, the sea beat savagely against the hull, there was panic among passengers, who started to pray agitatedly, and Andersen himself felt they might well all perish. His thoughts went out to his friends in Denmark, and his principal prayer, so he proclaims, was that he should be allowed to work out in another world what he had failed to achieve in this one – further proof of Andersen's remarkably staunch and literal (almost childlike) belief in a life after this one.[41] However, even bearing in mind the considerable body of fine work already examined in this study, it could truly be said that his most astonishingly *sui generis* creations still lay before him, that he was, if you like, saved from this storm for 'The Snow Queen', 'The Shadow' and 'The Ice Maiden'.

As in *Shadow Pictures*, Andersen conveys kinaesthetically the movement of his ship – here, through the Dardanelles and the Sea of Marmara, to arrive in Constantinople on 25 April. Constantinople[42] was still the capital of an empire in control of (if now with important concessions) an enormous swathe of south-eastern Europe, including regions that Andersen was eagerly planning to visit. But since 1839, *Tanzimât*,[43] or the reorganisation of the Ottoman Empire, had been underway under Sultan Abdülmecid with European-educated advisers. Its aim was reform, to ensure pluralism among its subjects. Bulgaria and Serbia – from 1829 a recognised suzerainty with its own hereditary monarchy and, after 1835, its own constitution – were among its outstanding recipients. And inside Turkey itself, the army and bureaucracy were restructured, Muslims and non-Muslims officially pronounced equal before the law, and, a little later, homosexuality was decriminalised (this, at a time when European countries, including Britain and Denmark, were moving to the reverse position). But Andersen in Constantinople and its environs could not but be engaged by the city's Byzantine inheritance and by its practising Muslim population. Besides, as one who through his father and from early childhood had revered *The Thousand and One Nights*, and been so patently and proudly influenced by it, he felt in this great meeting place of civilisations that he was nearer than at any point in his life to the culture that had produced it.

Splendid though his book's many tributes to Greek and Byzantine/Ottoman glories are – his daily visits to the Acropolis in Athens, his tour of Constantinople's Seraglio with its view of the shining snow-peaks of the Asian mountains – its genius, soon to be apparent in every paragraph, is not, I think, to be found in these painterly tableaux but far more in its more incidental episodes, often seemingly humdrum but in truth chosen because the writer, instinctively but also as a conscious artist, believed them revelatory of hidden truths.

On the Piraeus-bound boat from Malta, on which Andersen believes himself to be the only passenger from Northern Europe, two young cabin boys, 'lively as squirrels', routinely kill the chickens, but before the killing make a humorous little speech to each bird, then exclaim 'Voilà!' and draw the knife across its throat. Very probably, you might think, Andersen has a naturally more respectful and tender attitude to the creature-world than others on this crossing, but happily he turns out not to be alone in this respect.

A gull flutters down to the deck, clearly exhausted, both unwilling and unable to fly away. Among those looking at this new arrival is a Roman Catholic priest who suggests that they should eat it promptly, roasted; it would be so good. Andersen is horrified at the proposal. 'Our little winged pilgrim shall not be eaten!' he exclaims indignantly. Then, to his delight, he finds support from one of the ship's lieutenants. This man picks the bird up, places it high on the quarterdeck sail, and proceeds to give it breadcrumbs and water for a day and a half. When eventually it flies off, it gives a twitter that Andersen interprets as thanks for the kind treatment.[44]

Later Andersen goes to watch whirling dervishes in Scutari, in the company of another traveller whom he has become friendly with, a man from Tripoli. The dancing begins, and the two dervishes are joined by an elderly man of quite horrific appearance, a hermit from Medina. He throws off his cloak and stands before them all wearing only a red woollen blouse which he then proceeds to tear with his own hands, one of which is withered. Looking at him more closely, Andersen realises the man's lips have been cut off, and his mouth is still bleeding. His eyes roll about, the veins on his forehead swell up, and around him the dance gets wilder and wilder, accompanied by strange, obscene-sounding noises. 'Don't laugh!' Andersen's companion bids him, 'or we might be murdered!' 'Laugh?' protests Andersen, amazed. Rather he wants to weep – and leave at once.[45]

5

Andersen was advised that travelling through the Danubian countries could be hazardous because of all the recent unrest. His intention, after crossing the Black Sea to the (now Romanian) port of Küstendje/Constanţa,[46] was to take an Austrian steamboat up the Danube, and pass through Wallachia, Bulgaria, Serbia and Hungary to Pesth (Budapest) and thence to Vienna. A boat did this trip every ten days. But news had come of upheaval in Rumelia, the largely Christian area of the Ottoman southern Balkans which included the northern Thracian plain. These disturbances would surely have a severe knock-on effect on the entire region. Christian families in Sofia had protested against their Turkish rulers with their punitive tax collectors, and had earned for themselves cruel reprisals: Turks forcing their way into churches and abusing women, maybe slaughtering as many as two thousand. Worryingly the Austrian post, which travelled via Belgrade, had not yet made its expected arrival in Constantinople; it was possible the envoys had been murdered. Officials warned Andersen and the two Frenchmen and one Englishman who were proposing to make this trip – the Englishman was the geologist and explorer William Ainsworth, brother of the popular novelist Harrison Ainsworth (1805–82) – that they were taking a considerable, inadvisable risk if they went ahead. The Bulgarians, in their state of unrest, were scarcely likely to respect the Austrian flag under which the boat would be making its way. Yet Andersen and the three others decided to make their planned journey nonetheless.

He was not of the courageous, Andersen admits freely, but he did not want to return to Denmark by the same route he had followed coming out, and besides he very much wanted to see the Danube and these eastern European territories. Not to do so would be to violate something within him, and it is greatly to his credit that he realised this; what he was to see opened up another dimension to his view of life, and both intensified and broadened his art.

Accordingly he left Constantinople for Constanța on 5 May, likening the Bosporus up which he sailed to a large, well-stocked picture gallery, each new prospect replacing in beauty the preceding one, all rich, gentle greens and fertile too, and especially lovely, he thought, on the Asiatic side. Before the Black Sea actually presented itself, the scenery turned wilder, bolder, hillier, and then rocky islands heralded the great tract of water ahead. These were once, said legend, floating rocks determined to crush passing vessels; Jason and the Argonauts,[47] who now came into Andersen's and his companions' minds, had managed to elude them, but then they had the morally dubious magical aid of Medea, whom Jason married and then forsook and who proceeded to take her fierce revenge. They also thought of the great Ovid[48] exiled on the shores of the Pontus Euxinus, the 'Hospitable Sea', as it was called in propitiation. Andersen thought it seemed like the northern seas he was accustomed to – the Baltic was presumably what he had in mind – but during the nocturnal crossing thick fog assailed them. The Black Sea had, Andersen recalled, only recently taken its toll of many up-to-date, internationally owned ships, and the captain of the one he was aboard, for reasons of safety, steered eight miles further north of Constanța than usual.

They landed at this ancient port through heavy surf, and now the most adventurous and inspiriting section of Andersen's long journey – and of *A Poet's Bazaar* – could begin. It was in fact in Constanţa (Tomis) that Ovid lived along the Scythians, not in other putative places put forward by other passengers, and coming to it now was another writer of universal appeal, who realised that what myth and legend fantastically related had its own inexorable truth, who saw that transformation (metamorphosis) was a fact of both natural and psychological life, and who embodied this truth in unforgettable literary art.

It had been in 1809, Andersen reminds us,[49] that Constanţa was destroyed by the Russians, but it might as well have been only a few weeks ago, judging by the desolate look of the place: so many tumbledown houses with caved-in roofs, pillars or columns lying on their sides, the minaret of the one mosque constructed from planks, shavings and dung burned because of dearth of firewood, men raggedly dressed wearing slippers on their feet, a ubiquitous quietness, the sea on one side and an immense, deserted-seeming plain lacking in cattle on the others. In understandably low spirits Andersen made his way down to the shore and there he saw a dead stork. Storks, he says – though he scarce has need to – have always been his favourite birds, frequenting his novels and tales. The sight of this one in so faraway and abandoned a spot makes an instant and powerful impression. (He records it feelingly in both diaries and autobiography.) He imagines it coming across the sea to the land it was making for, and then falling dead forthwith. (The Danube estuary is, of course, one of the world's great places for migrating birds.)

To readers of the travelogue, having taken in the tidings of trouble that Andersen had heard in Constantinople, the stork inevitably constitutes a strong image for the rejected traveller, who expects (indeed has a right to expect) shelter, safety, fulfilment, only to find the denial of life accorded so many in these long war-beset regions, all those human migrants – Roma, Jews, Wallachian nomads, refugee members of ethnic/linguistic minorities unpopular one side of a border or the other – who have with difficulty come so far – in desperate hope – and then no further. The image gains in resonance when Andersen recounts how he went down to the beach that same evening – to collect stones and shells with his new English friend, William Ainsworth – and saw that next to the dead bird was a dead dog, a large poodle, a casualty off some boat. A story could well be written about this pair, Andersen comments, the creature of the air and the creature of land united in premature death, the first redolent of free spaces, the second of civilisation and breeding for urban living, both felled by fate in a foreign land.

In between the two paragraphs about the stork Andersen relates an anecdote told him by the landlord of the inn in which they are staying. Somehow it strikes us readers also as disturbingly apposite for the tumultuous territories ahead of him and his fellow passengers as they journey away from the Black

Sea and up the Danube. In the harsh winter, in which the sea froze for several miles out from the land, wild dogs and wolves (related species) would coincide, often with bloody combats between the two. Sometimes a she-wolf found herself inescapably in the midst of wild dogs and so she suckled their young with the kind of tenderness she would show cubs of her own kind. But when the pups were a few days old, she would drag them down to the river and watch how they drank. If they lapped the water, then she knew them to be dogs, not wolves, offspring of her most dangerous enemy. So she would tear them to bits. What a telling picture of countless members of subject peoples in the Balkans, protected one moment, ripped apart the next.

In order to board the steamer that would take the party up the Danube as far as Orşova,[50] they had to travel by land across the Wallachian plain[51] to the river-port of Czerna-Woda (today's Cernavodă, the name a Romanian form of the former Bulgarian one, itself of possible Thracian origin). The landscape they passed through for the whole of the day was monotonous, dismal, appeared boundless and was so flat that it gave a dramatic significance to whatever objects stood out in it: a large eagle sitting still until they came within fifty paces of him, herds of cattle resembling advancing bands of warriors, and their herdsmen (armed with axes) who didn't seem so dissimilar with their long, wiry hair and their sheepskin clothes turned woolly side out. This country contained evidence of Trajan's attempts to connect Dacia to the Black Sea by means of a canal. Andersen, that German train-ride so recent an experience, noted down that a railway would serve this purpose better, and indeed the Turks proceed to build and open one nineteen years later, in 1860.

Czerna-Woda[52] turned out every bit as dilapidated and ramshackle as Constanţa, and as poor – most of the small children wore no clothing at all! – but here was waiting their boat, and its name was *Argo* which delighted him, because wasn't he about to undertake a voyage possibly rivalling that of the classical hero and his mates in distance and dangers, even if it were by river rather than sea? The captain, Marco Dobroslavich, was a jovial Dalmatian who treated his Italian crew roughly, at times harshly, but they seemed well able to stand up for themselves, and Andersen and the other foreigners found him friendly and excellent company.

On his right hand Andersen would see the continuing Wallachian plains. Wallachia was one of the two Danubian principalities later to become Romania. At present administered by Imperial Russia according to treaty, it was still ultimately under the Ottomans, Orthodox but with a Romance (Latin) language (then still written in Cyrillic script), an uneasy concatenation. On his left Andersen would look out at Bulgaria, the potential source of trouble, Ottoman-held and with a Muslim population and a recalcitrant Orthodox Christian one too, Slavs speaking a South Slavonic language also written in Cyrillic.

On his first full day on the river, 8 May, Andersen views Wallachia as more like a tract of sea than land – no gardens, no trees. Bulgaria, in contrast, seems all cultivation and fecundity. Hedges are luxuriant, wild roses bloom everywhere, the minarets are white in the sunshine, splendid jet-black horses are driven down to the river to be ferried across, little naked boys run about on the shore shouting out to the *Argo*. But when late in the day a Wallachian town appears, today's Giurgiu, the church tower glitters like silver, marsh birds fly out of the rushes, and a crowd of people gather by a fortress recently destroyed by the Russians, demanding to hear news from the ship of happenings in Constantinople, and of the uprisings elsewhere.

Reminders of all the disruptions are not far to seek. They hear of, but do not actually witness, fugitives from Bulgaria making their way across the Danube to the Wallachian shore. At Rustzuk[53] (today's Ruse), a sizeable river-port, two men jump into the river from opposite ends of the bridge; one reaches friendly folk who help him up on to the shore, the other is repelled by stones being chucked at him. After he cries out – in French – that he is about to be killed, the crew of the *Argo* come to the rescue of the second man, and take him aboard. This is enough, however, to draw the attention of soldiers, and soon a small boat is drawing up alongside the steamboat, delivering one of the river-port's three local pashas. A posse of officers accompany this official, and in order to ensure his security attach themselves, one to each wrist, one to each elbow, and one to each shoulder! How the author of 'The Emperor's New Clothes' smiles to himself.

There are inevitably occasions of beauty to offset these eruptions: a rainbow spans the Wallachian plain and the Bulgarian cliffs, and the river's waves rise as if to meet it, the Balkan mountains to the south, topped in snow, are lit up by the setting sun, and a Turk on board the ship kneels down and murmurs his evening prayer.

And now Bulgaria on the left-hand side of the *Argo* is exchanged for Serbia,[54] a small river flowing into the Danube dividing the two. Serbia stood in a different relationship to the Ottoman Sublime Porte, indeed to any great power, than Bulgaria or Wallachia. It enjoyed autonomy, had – since 1835 – its own constitution, and hereditary monarchy and was in train towards the full independence it received in 1867. In his pages – without perhaps knowing too much about the often brutal autocracy he commanded – Andersen salutes Prince Miloš Obrenović (1780–1860), 'the true Serbian', for serving the rich folk culture of his country by collecting many treasures of its priceless balladry and epic poetry, so often recited to musical accompaniment of fiddle and bagpipe, and for holding his regular assemblies with deputations from the various communities under the canopy of a tree. Prince Miloš, Andersen's note informs us, resigned in 1839 in favour of his elder son, Milan (who died after a

few weeks on the throne), his second son Mihailo reigning now. His foundation of a royal house is likened to a branch striking roots and proceeding to
grow so boldly that, if permitted, it could stand among the most glorious kingly
trees of Europe.

No need to explain the metaphor, even if Andersen, both in text and foot-
note, seems unaware of some of the far from pleasant facts behind it: Prince
Miloš's despotic tendencies and ruthless arrogation of riches. For trees seemed
to Andersen to have complete sovereignty in the wild country bordering the
Danube which now, followed upstream, would lead them to the famous Iron
Gates, the gorge with mighty rapids and whirlpools marking the frontier of
Wallachia and Serbia; the next stage of the journey would be Serbian entirely.
He felt he was entering the domain of the Dryads, those tree spirits who would
command one of his greatest late stories. Was he not now making his way
through one vast oak forest that had permeated the songs and tunes of its denizens? Whoever fells a tree takes a life, say the Serbians. To the Serbian male, be
he prince or poet, the green tree is of more importance than the woman who
waits on him so humbly. (Perhaps it was because he envisaged the ubiquitous
Dryads as feminine that Andersen found this last observation romantically
and morally palatable!)

Andersen's style has so engaged with his subject that we feel not just with
our senses but with our whole bodies the great oaks that both dominate and
define existence for the indigenous people, the perpendicular rocks, the
swirling treacherous currents of the Danube, above all in the Iron Gates[55],
against which the ship has to make its often difficult way, the golden wild
laburnum that speckles the great cliffs, the sudden interruption of the richness
of Nature by red-painted houses, minarets, even a pasha's seraglio. And in
doing so we experience – whatever the intellectual doubts that may assail us
when we stand back from these pages, with our burdensome twenty-first-
century knowledge of what destructive tragedies Serbian nationalism has
brought in its wake – an emotional repudiation of all governmental yokes for
peoples who belong to the rural, the natural, and not the bureaucratic or the
commercial worlds.

The dreaded, spectacular Iron Gates, having been successfully negotiated,
there remained Orşova on the Wallachian shore. This meant a spell of
protracted quarantine.[56] Andersen conveys in hypnotic prose the effect on him
of this twelve-day imposition. But then, he ruminates, could not life itself be
regarded as a form of quarantine, the only reprise from which comes from that
inevitability, death? Memorably he recaptures the extraordinary tedium of this
enforced sojourn, the oppressive monotony of the few views obtainable (the
sunlight on the whitewashed walls was bright enough almost to blind one),
the claustrophobia of the place of confinement itself. He did however have a

source of solace here, for he shared the two rooms with two men, Mr Ainsworth and an old guardian of the establishment, a survivor of the great Battle of Leipzig, and now employed to keep his eye on this pair of foreigners. Andersen also makes us appreciate the way in such conditions that thoughts perpetually turn on themselves: for example, he found himself repeatedly visiting that hell to which Heiberg had satirically consigned his plays (amused, despite himself, by the notion). Worse, he also fell ill and had to be prescribed medicine more suitable perhaps for Wallachian horses than for thirty-five-year-old Danes, and then the Pasha came to visit them. But eventually the spell of (benign) imprisonment ended (it was Andersen's second of the expedition, and he minded it more than he had that in Piraeus) and he was able to resume the voyage up the Danube, this time on the steamer *Galathea* which conveyed him all the way to Pesth.

What release, what relief it was to be back in the world of woods and water again, and, after the boring monochrome existence he had been forced to lead, how he relished the romantic country on either bank, far surpassing the Rhine in his estimation, and animated by the glorious May weather. He got off the boat to do justice to woods, rocks, cliffs, caverns, noticing the gypsies, the villages, still largely Wallachian in population and poor but more attractive than their earlier equivalents, and the groups of soldiers. The boat itself was extremely comfortable, and after his ordeal Andersen was wholly prepared to do justice to its beds and provisions of food and drink.

In one of his solitary wanderings off the boat into a forest bordering the river,[57] Andersen encounters, among the bushes, a peasant boy who greets him in German, clearly under the impression that any foreigner must have this as his native language. When Andersen questions him the boy admits that he himself normally speaks only Wallachian. And here we have one of the book's most emotionally affecting episodes.

The boy's face, so clean, so amiable, strikes Andersen also as a singularly wise and good one. Immediately friendly, the lad comports himself with natural, modest dignity that cannot but make a favourable impression. Asked about his probable future, the lad tells him that he must serve as a soldier, all the local boys have to and, that being the case, he wants to be an officer. Andersen asks him if – by any chance – he knows Denmark. The boy says yes, he has heard of it, isn't it a long way away, somewhere near Hamburg? He then goes off into the forest at the older man's request to gather flowers; he makes these into a fine bouquet, for which Andersen pays him. Only in this way can he reward him for the courtesy he has shown. But Andersen also gives him his visiting card, and the boy for his part tells him his name is Adam Marco. If he ever becomes an officer and is sent to Denmark, says Andersen, then he must call on him. They will rejoice together in his good fortune. They shake hands;

the boy does not immediately move away but stays on the quay, looking long at the ship after Andersen has boarded.

Andersen tells us that he has written about this meeting in the hope that some readers of his book will be able to find and help Adam Marco, than whom he has never met a more nobly mannered boy.

A stay in Pesth, 31 May–2 June, was followed by river travel to Vienna where he remained until 23 June. *A Poet's Bazaar* delights in the sheer urbanity of these cities: the pictorial shop-signs, the lively theatres (though Andersen thought that Denmark exceeded both cities in this respect), the abundance of books and newspapers. He visited Prague (where his chief interest was the gravestone of the great Tycho Brahe) and Dresden before arriving at Leipzig. Here he renewed acquaintance with Mendelssohn,[58] who entertained him in his home and therefore passed into the category of friends, and called on his German publisher, the Dane Carl B. Lorck.

In Leipzig, on the very organ that Johann Sebastian Bach (1685–1750) himself had used, Mendelssohn played Andersen one of the composer's great fugues, which he personally was responsible for bringing back into general repertoire. It is tempting to see in that music – whose beauty depends on the sheer logic of its language, which has solemn and antique origins and which eschews the length and the deliberate seeking after effect of later compositions – an analogue of the art of those stories that Andersen would begin work on in the year of his travelogue's publication. They too – even the longest of them, 'The Snow Queen' – never stray from the self-appointed task, never resort to displays of language for its own sake, and deserve, for both their seriousness and their immediacy of emotional address, the epithet 'religious'.

But turning back to the travelogue out of which, in a sense, these great tales arise, one is reminded of later music. You could liken it to a Lisztian tone-poem – or to some successor of his, to Smetana's famous river portrait, *Vltava* (1874) perhaps, even if the journey there is in the opposite direction, beginning at its source – in the mounting movement of its prose through to the great climactic of the Danube adventures to calm into mellower, more contemplative mood at its close. Or you might remember the topographical associations of Mendelssohn's two fine symphonies, the 'Italian' of 1833, the 'Scotch' of 1842, which end with resolutions of key and thematic material.

Back in Northern Europe again he was moved to contemplate what kind of reception he would have in Denmark,[59] where everybody (it seemed to him) was always so keen to criticise him, to pick holes in his character and in its literary expression. But to think about Denmark was not only to think negative thoughts. You couldn't say, except in a literal sense, that Denmark had no mountains, for it had literary ones: hadn't Holberg, Oehlenschläger, Grundtvig,

Ingemann, Christian Winther, and, for that matter (he generously or perhaps expediently adds) Hertz and Heiberg mountainous proportions and impressive features? And, by extension, he implies, hadn't he himself these too?

On 12 July Andersen was on a Denmark-bound steamship and interestingly he went to his birth-city of Odense before going back to Copenhagen.[60] He need not have feared; *A Poet's Bazaar* had a warm critical reception, an indication of the recognition of his greatness that awaited his new book of fairy stories in winter 1843. The next chapter analyses these canonical works, canonical not only in Andersen's *oeuvre*, but in nineteenth-century prose literature.

CHAPTER 8

The Canonical Stories

1

'Den grimme Ælling' ('The Ugly Duckling')

Like 'The Emperor's New Clothes', 'The Ugly Duckling' has passed into proverb. In its proverbial form its account of an unprepossessing, unsatisfactory member of one species evolving into a beautiful, admired member of another encourages us to expect for ourselves an eventual transformation of situation and self for the better, whatever the restrictions of our early circumstances and the current low opinion of others. Obviously this is of irresistible appeal to insufficiently appreciated children, and few of us have not at some point seen ourselves in this category. Here is a story which seems to assure us of our right to a future consonant with our instinctive hopes during our unhappy times, and probably exceeding them, while confounding all those fault-finding authority figures who have given up on us or showed us downright hostility. More, it suggests that we will be granted our rights by a natural process. Bruno Bettelheim in *The Uses of Enchantment* contrasted Andersen's fairy story with folk tale,[1] where the hero generally arrives at happiness only after he has successfully carried out dangerous, difficult, even disgusting tasks: 'No need to accomplish anything is expressed in "The Ugly Duckling". Things are simply fated and unfold accordingly.' This statement is, in truth, far nearer the mark than the popular view of the story, but it contains, as we shall see, two not insignificant oversights.

Many have found it ironical that 'The Ugly Duckling' – the most constant favourite with the young of all its author's tales – appeared in Andersen's first book of fairy stories to drop from its title the designation 'for Børn' ('for children'): *Nye Eventyr, Første Samling* (*New Fairy Tales, First Collection* 11 November 1843).[2] But this deliberate omission is surely appropriate. 'The Ugly

Duckling' enjoins us to leave childhood with its many bitter-tasting episodes far behind, to discount the uncongenial roles it forced on us and to dismiss those enforcing them as ultimately unnecessary to our lives. Instead we should concentrate on the harmoniousness that maturity and independence bring. Children, it hardly needs saying, actually find such an attitude to their own state greatly to their tastes; it is not they, as a rule, who reverence childhood or make a cult of it. Nostalgia is foreign to them.

But all this, even making room for Bettelheim's observation, is only a partially accurate description of the story. Yes, 'The Ugly Duckling' honours natural growth, but the growth it so meticulously presents follows, and very precisely, particular laws which at times coincide with larger, more general ones, but yet are not to be confused with them. So empathic and strong are Andersen's renderings of his central character's desolation – and, too, of his one strange glimpse in its midst of later joy – that we are tempted to see the entire work as expressing a truth universal in application (as well as, undoubtedly, in resonance). But it would be a mistake to do so.

The idea for 'Story of a Duck' came to Andersen on a walk in July 1842[3] during a stay at Gisselfeld,[4] an aristocratic estate in Sjælland. Depressed by the poor reception of his recent 'Dramatic Jest with Music', *Fuglen i Pæretræet* (*The Bird in the Pear-Tree*),[5] and possibly more psychologically uneasy at being the guest of his social superiors than he cared to admit, he felt instantly revitalised by all the summer beauty round him. Three weeks later, after moving to Bregentved,[6] another manor in the locality and equally to his aesthetic taste, he began writing 'Duck or Swan?', which he later called simply 'Svaneungen', 'The Cygnet'. Sadly we do not possess Andersen's notes for his best-known tale, but we do know that he worked very intensely on it, as it progressed in his mind over many months. Hence the concentrated artistry of the final version, every line of which counts, as much as in a Keats ode or a Hopkins sonnet, not reached until 7 October of the following year, 1843, and which appeared in book form two months later.

'Der var saa deiligt ude paa Landet.'[7] 'It was so beautiful out in the country.' The story's opening words reflect Andersen's feelings for his surroundings at the time of the work's inception, and recall the yearning for the Danish rural scene that *A Poet's Bazaar* recounts as overwhelming him when approaching Mantua. They suggest furthermore that the physical world – that which conditions every phase of our lives – is a major source of pleasure and well-being for us, and, whatever the distress and pain it metes out, worthy of salutation and full immersion.

The whole first paragraph, still diffusing this sentiment, establishes typically Danish well-husbanded countryside at the height of summer, the wheat ripe, the hay already stacked. To the back of the fields and meadows evoked are 'store Skove,'[8] but we are ourselves standing in the precincts of 'en gammel Herregaard'; English language translators, including the very best, have rendered these as, respectively, 'vast forests' and 'an old castle', thus bringing their readers into the regions of the Brothers Grimm or Nordic legend instead of the humdrum scene on which Andersen is intent, with, to hand, entirely common flora and fauna, devoid, or shorn, of all folkloric/romantic associations. 'Large woods' does perfectly well for the first phrase, 'an old manor-house' for the second, and both would serve the story far better. (See M.R. James's version!)[9] True, Bregentved, with its moat, can be discerned behind the text, and current online information in English about both Gisselfeld and Bregentved does use 'forest' and 'castle' for publicity purposes, but only in the context of visiting Sjælland, the landscape of which is of comparatively intimate proportions, having yielded centuries ago to human domination. Not that we should be concerned with precise topography; what is important is the positioning of ourselves in a workaday farmyard – in 'Andegaarden',[10] 'the duck-yard', where a maid regularly feeds the birds and an old duck has a red ribbon tied round one leg. Beyond it lies open country where fauna move freely (though not without menace from hunters) merging in places into marshland.

This same first paragraph draws our attention to one duck in particular. She is trying to hatch young from a clutch of eggs which she has placed under a burdock beside the moat. For children and birds the patch of burdocks is as impressive and near-impenetrable as the thickest forest, and in reminding us of this, Andersen demonstrates that easy movement between a creature's (or a child's) vantage-point and an omniscient narrating adult's which will persist until the tale's conclusion, and which he first achieved in 'Thumbelina'. In itself it is emblematic of the whole territory of the tale where the wild and the domesticated thrive simultaneously, and humans have access to both. What is more, they have *need* of both, as the ending will make clear. If ducks are practically useful to us, swans engage us aesthetically, even spiritually, and thus are just as essential to satisfactorily lived human lives.

The eggs duly hatch, all except one, the biggest, and distinctive enough in shape for an experienced old duck to pronounce it a turkey's. Had Andersen stuck to his earlier plan of entitling the tale 'The Cygnet', we would naturally have identified this egg from the first and known the genus of the young bird to emerge from it. But the work gains incontestably from its subject being referred to as 'ælling', 'duckling'. This completely consistent device enables us both to view him in the light of the prevalent misperception of his true nature, one shared by himself, and to witness his seemingly eccentric development, as though we were naturalists scrupulously recording the successive stages of this.

For the creature's history is factually verifiable, like the swallow's in 'Thumbelina', its details contributing in themselves to the tale's overall meaning.

A swan's egg is huge compared with any duck's,[11] and takes between thirty-four and forty-five days to hatch, as opposed to twenty-eight. It differs in colour from most duck eggs too, being of greenish hue. Taxonomically swans and ducks are closely related, both species existing within the family *Anatidae*, both aquatic, both upending when feeding. Thus given the not so very unlikely inclusion of a swan's egg in a duck's clutch, the story's confusions are not just possible, they are probable. Whereas ducklings take to water soon after being hatched, a cygnet requires twenty-four hours to do this, exactly as in Andersen, where our 'duckling' enters the water one whole day after his emergence into the world. Once in the water he swims easily enough, indeed every bit as well as his so-called siblings.

For it is not his lack of abilities but his outward appearance that earns the 'duckling' his ubiquitous unpopularity. His awkward bigness, his irregular shape, his 'dirty' colouring (blackish-grey, as in reality), his comparative lack of grace on land, all beget ridicule, contempt, even dislike. Superficially he is able to participate in the life around him, but his divergence from others in looks and behaviour is sufficiently strong to arouse antipathy and aggression, resulting in his bemused embarrassment at his own physical existence. To understand what it is that 'The Ugly Duckling' is striving to communicate, even at this early stage, one obvious truth cannot be repeated enough: *Only a cygnet can hatch from a swan's egg. Our protagonist's evolution was determined long before even that belated 'Pip! Pip!' with which he freed himself from the shell. It absolutely could not have proceeded other than how it did, whether he met with kind encouragement (as at first from his adoptive mother) or with spiteful enmity.* His sufferings therefore have a single cause: he belongs to a different species from that to which he is assigned, and thus is supposed to conform to, but neither he himself nor any being in his vicinity knows this fact of nature.

Weary of persecution, the 'duckling' leaves the farmyard and encounters his apparent cousins, the wild ducks, which are noticeably more friendly. They too think him hideous, but will accept him provided he doesn't marry into their family. Interestingly Andersen informs us that the duckling had entertained no thoughts whatever of marriage, was not thinking of doing anything more than lying among the rushes in peace and drinking the marsh water. More friendly to him still are two wild geese, both ganders,[12] encountered on the marshes; they are positively attracted by his looks, as, they suggest, some neighbouring female geese will be. Country sport interrupts these words, the kindest our hero has yet been given. Hunters shoot, and his two new friends fall down dead. The water becomes red with their blood. Such is the young bird's first experience of humanity en bloc. Feeling truly alone, he now enters the house of an old woman[13] living by herself with a cat and a hen, and here is given a taste of another kind of domestication than a farmyard's: of a pet's ambiguous (and therefore ultimately uncomfortable) status. The cat and the hen, but particularly the extremely articulate hen, make him feel as inept and useless as the ducks and the maid had done back in the farmyard. And now intense yearnings beset him – which he expresses in words highly characteristic of that distinctive conversational kinaesthesia that Andersen had, as we have seen, already perfected in 'The Little Mermaid': 'Men det er saa deiligt at flyde paa Vandet. . . saa deiligt at faae det over Hovedet og dukke ned paa Bunden.'[14] 'But it's so beautiful to float on the water. . . so beautiful to get it over your head and dive down to the bottom'. After quitting the cottage out of sheer misery, just as he had his native duck-yard, he does indeed experience the joy of these desiderata – but in solitude.

This is the experience to which the whole tale has been building up. Those wild ducks on the marshes were more congenial to him than the tame kind – quite naturally, for neither he nor they can be classed as poultry. The wild geese who also befriended him were in ornithological terms even closer kin to him than any duck could be. The remarks of both about mating were, in truth, redundant, for no cygnet can mate with duck or goose. The marshland on which he met these birds was that transitional territory between land and water, between tame and wild, of such peculiar significance to Andersen the 'swamp-plant'. Immediately we remember Antonio's mandatory crossing of the Pontine Marshes in *The Improvisatore* where his maturity begins, as the duckling's does here. However clumsy otherwise, our protagonist has always been very proficient at swimming. Now in his first voluntary surrender to the water we see that this activity gives him an unprecedented feeling of fulfilment, transcending all utilitarian function. So in this episode we have our first intimation of the story's prime concern. The ugly duckling's antics in the water constitute a *spiritual* experience, the kind associated with innate artists' first contact with the medium proper to them.

Autumn comes, with its high winds always a hard, sometimes lethal season for swans. Our protagonist sees a flock of birds – in fact swans – bound for a warmer climate, without either identifying them (for he has not knowledge enough to do this) or communicating with them (a procedure of which he is not yet capable). But the very sight of them makes him spin round in sheerest excitement, and even cry after them, for he has had his first glimpse of his own kind.

Winter proves harsher even than autumn, the ice closes in on him and he has to be rescued by a farmer, whose wife revives him, though she turns out no better-disposed than the old crone who preceded her in the bird's life. The couple have children, both of whom want to play with the ugly duckling and, after he has flown from them in terror – into, successively, the milk-pan, the butter-tub and the flour-bin – to catch him, showing themselves as at once lively and insensitive to others, a not infrequent combination of qualities in Andersen's children. But, after he has endured yet further sufferings, not in fact specified, spring arrives, and lifts his spirits. One day he sees before him on the water three birds of that same species which had so delighted him months before. He makes towards them, half expecting them to rebuff or even attack him, and in a passage that has disturbed, even repelled, many – eminently Professor Jack Zipes in his brilliantly contentious *Hans Christian Andersen, The Misunderstood Storyteller* (2005)[15] – declares to himself it would be better to be killed by these fine birds than to suffer any longer the cruelties of other species. So he lowers his head towards the water as if for execution by them.

Georg Brandes, in his 1869 critical appreciation,[16] declared that the story should end with the death of the 'duckling' at this point; he saw it, in light of the miseries contained, as essentially a tragedy (which it is not). Or else, thought Brandes, the bird should make one last, proud, solo flight. Modernist though he was, Brandes failed to perceive the stubborn originality of Andersen's mind and art here. Both endings would have gone clean against the whole deter- mined tendency of the tale so far. Andersen makes the moment of the duck- ling's surrender to death the moment when he sees on the surface of the water his own reflection and comprehends, for the first time, his identity: he is a member of the very same species as the magnificent birds whom he has been bold enough to approach. This decisive action on his part Bettelheim also over- looked when he stated that the hero of this tale does not have to accomplish anything, as he had similarly ignored the protagonist's earlier initiative in exchanging native duck-yard for alien great marsh. These new birds, far from slaughtering him, glide towards him, welcoming him as one of their own. And so to the story's most famous pronouncement, the full effect of which, in its teasing simplicity, comes only from the original Danish. 'Det gjør ikke noget at være født i Andegaarden, naar man kun har ligget i et Svaneæg!'[17] 'It doesn't matter being born in a duck-yard, as long as one has lain in a swan's egg.'

For Zipes this dictum promulgates elitism,[18] and, in the conventional sense of that (pejorative) term, it is hard to disagree with him. But for him, as for Brandes before him, there is yet worse to come. Andersen not only gives us the caressing of his hero by the other swans, not only informs us that these moments would not have been such happy moments without all the past tribulations, he introduces child spectators of this reunion of kindred beings. So delighted are these children by what they see that they call out to their parents to look at the 'new swan', surely the loveliest of them all (though, forgotten by some illustra- tors, he will lack the matured swan's dazzling whiteness). Fellow swans seem to agree with this estimation, for they incline their heads respectfully before him.

For Zipes all this admiration bestowed on the protagonist – proper to a 'royal' swan in some parkland (not too unlike Gisselfeld or Bregentved!) far from normal duck-yards and frequented by only the well-behaved and well-born – exemplifies both the writer's essentially bourgeois outlook and his ultimate dependence on aristocratic (or plutocratic) patronage.

But paradoxically – in the light of its author's increasing psychological reliance on association with the famous and on hospitality from the nobility – the more we see 'The Ugly Duckling' in the autobiographical terms Andersen himself considered appropriate for it, the more complex and moving a work it appears, and the undeniable truth contained in Zipes's strictures, while by no means dispelled, takes a secondary place.

In Jens Andersen's words 'The Ugly Duckling' soon became Andersen's 'calling-card',[19] something he invariably read aloud on his many celebrity tours at home and abroad. In May 1861 the English poet Elizabeth Barrett Browning (1806–61)[20] wrote to a friend from Rome: 'Andersen (the Dane) came to see me yesterday. . . . He is very earnest, very simple, very childlike. I like him. Pen [the Brownings' twelve-year-old son][21] says of him: "He is not really pretty. He is rather like his own ugly duck, but his mind has DEVELOPED into a swan." – That wasn't bad of Pen, was it?'[22] Not bad at all, for Pen Browning was surely right to see as the story's concern the 'development' to swan-hood, the progression through preordained, irreversible, and often trying stages to a condition, a mental state, which is a joy to inhabit and which the swan on the water physically embodies.

Of course Andersen's triumphalism, broadcast not least through his autobiographies of 1846 and 1855, his view that his life constituted a journey from humblest beginnings to the heights of literary fame and international society (details of which he was only too happy to supply), only added to the story's enormous public appeal over the years. For example, Andersen read 'The Ugly Duckling' to King Maximilian II of Bavaria beside the Starnberger See (summer 1855),[23] and His Majesty was so moved he broke off a bough of overhanging elder to hand to the author. The mid-nineteenth century was far more admiring of (often substantially sanitised) narratives of upward progress than we now find acceptable: *Jane Eyre* and *David Copperfield*, not to mention Andersen's own *The Improvisatore* and (to an important measure) *O.T.*, can, after all, be so described, nor can their final dispensations of fortune be detached from them. The happy ending gained after so many trials often amounts to a felicitous condition of stasis relished and consciously, gratefully perpetuated.[24] This suggests that an important segment of society believed it deserved to be rewarded for the changes that progress had wrought by receiving a sense of security, which once established could not be broken and which could almost partake of repose. To revert to Bettelheim's thinking, by the last page, the hero of 'The Ugly Duckling' doesn't have 'to do' or 'to perform', only 'to be'.

Andersen the ardent traveller didn't require such stasis, but he unquestionably needed, for all his compulsion to be on the move, to feel he belonged somewhere: hence his untiring fidelity to the whole Collin family, his devotion and regular contacts with almost all his friends from earlier Copenhagen days, and hence and not least, his obsessive co-opting of the illustrious Europeans he met on his travels as a famous writer into the ranks of personal, and, if possible, intimate friends.

There can be no doubt that Andersen meant everybody to see in his ugly duckling's history his own. Those scholars who have identified its sequential characters and incidents with real persons and traumas in Andersen's life have done what he would only have expected. For instance, the two wild ganders so amiably disposed to the duckling have been thought to represent Andersen's comrades from Sorø Academy in his Slagelse days, Fritz Petit (1809–54), who would translate his writings into German, and Carl Bagger (1807–46), Byronic poet and novelist, and dedicatee of *New Fairy Stories, Second Collection*, both of whom tried, without success, to enrol Andersen into the bohemian life they enjoyed themselves, just as Thomas Fearnley would later attempt to do in Rome. Tradition has it that Ingeborg Drewsen, formerly Sophie in *O.T.*, was the prototype for the sharply critical hen in the old woman's house. As for the three swans, must they not be Adam Oehlenschläger, B.S. Ingemann and H.C. Ørsted, Golden Age writers who conferred first friendliness then friendship on the young Andersen, recognising that he was 'one of them'? Did they (figuratively) bend their heads reverentially in realisation of his latent superiority? I suspect that – with the possible exception of the last of the trio (who anyway had other achievements than his writings of which to be proud) – they did not. But they – unlike many lesser literati – did Andersen the honour of appreciating from the start that he was *innately* a literary artist whose creativity was irrepressible.

And if not all Danish artists were warmly inclusive of him, if, on the contrary, they persisted in begrudging him proper recognition of his talents, then there were greater and friendlier artists elsewhere, more affectionate 'royal' swans – in Germany, France and, in the second half of the decade, England. The swan can fly considerable distances, after all. There is a degree to which this story, so rooted in the farmland, marsh and woods of Sjælland and its moated manors, is, of all his work, the most proclamatory of a European fraternity, of artists who spoke to each other across the divisions of nations and political systems, even those of past strife and ongoing tensions. By the time Andersen wrote 'The Ugly Duckling' he felt himself, with some justice, to be an acknowledged member of it.

The artist has obvious similarities to other humans, as cygnets have with ducklings or goslings, but his drives, needs, priorities, self-vindications distinguish him from all except his fellow practitioners. So while admitting, with qualifications, that Bettelheim did the story a service by drawing attention to its hero's accordance with the unstoppable working out of natural laws, he was, I believe, entirely wrong to say that it 'encourages a child to believe he is of a different breed'. It does not. What it promotes in children is something altogether different: the salutation of those rare breeds dedicated to virtue, nobility, beauty, who attempt expression of the ultimately inexpressible. In other words it promotes the love of artists and what has gone into their making. Very few children, if any, to put the case in its most extreme form, are likely to grow up into a Hans Christian Andersen, but a multitude can carry his creations into adulthood for their sustenance – and, not unimportant to Andersen himself, show him their gratitude for these.

For the duckling's early exuberance in the water represents Andersen's precocious delight in acting and story-telling. These arts can never be for solitary consumption; of their nature they reach out to the responses, the feeling lives of others. Therefore in eliciting admiration from both children and adults (the double categorisation in the text must surely be intentional), the ugly duckling is only living up to the dictates of his instinctual nature, and, by logical extension, to his whole *raison d'être*. Andersen shared the intellectual preoccupation of his times in wanting to find explanations for the coexistence of so many different types of human being, so many forms of animal life (and both 'Thumbelina' and 'The Little Mermaid' strongly suggest this). 'The animal is elementary, and takes its external form, or to be accurate, the differences in that form, from the environment in which it is obliged to develop. Zoological species are the result of these differences.'[25]

These lines come from Balzac's introduction to the first collected edition of his *Comédie humaine* (1842). It has already been observed that for 'The Ugly Duckling' Andersen took longer to arrive at a finished version than was usual for him. Roughly half a year after inception he spent two months in Paris where he associated with many leading French intellectuals and artists – for, to return to Elizabeth Barrett Browning's words, while Andersen, despite his omnipresent humour, may have been 'earnest', he was not 'simple' in the least and only superficially 'childlike', as must by now be abundantly clear to readers of this book. On his 1843 visit to Paris the French literati had positively sought him out knowing how responsive *he* was to *them*, Lamartine (whose Oriental travelogue of 1835 Andersen had read before embarking on his own) writing a poem for him,[26] Alfred de Vigny giving him his complete works,[27] Heine (in whose ranks he can be placed) declaring Andersen a true writer, and, perhaps most impressively of all, Honoré de Balzac,[28] finding the time to see him. Balzac's absorption of Buffon and Lamarck had led him to survey humankind in terms of constituent and often conflicting species, and this must have held great interest for the Danish writer with his abiding curiosity about the workings of Nature.

Is there not a resemblance to be found between Balzac's Eugène de Rastignac as he appears in his *Le père Goriot* (1835) and Andersen's 1843 alter ego? Rastignac stands out, because of his aristocratic blood, from the other denizens of that duck-yard which is Madame Vauquer's lodging-house, yet, while canvassing for opportunities, he cannot find his true self in the swampland of Parisian high society. He has imaginative sympathies where more ordinary people deny them, yet he is also gripped by a singleness of ambition born of his own distinction and his acute sense of it; this amounts to sorrowful apartness. When, at the celebrated end of the novel, he addresses the city of Paris 'À nous deux, maintenant!' ('It's between the two of us now!'),[29] our minds can legitimately look forward to Andersen's aquatically gifted, soon-to-be-beautiful duckling confronting the spring in solitude. The latter, however, is fortunate enough to be vouchsafed first the spectacle, then the company of his own kind. Thus, in Andersen's gentler, essentially moralistic *Weltanschauung*, his hero's delayed self-realisation is the first step towards the enhancement of the lives of others. This is less elitism than a curious kind of humility.

Not that the proven artist is exempt from ill-treatment. On that 1861 visit to Rome Andersen listened to Robert Browning reading his 'Pied Piper of Hamelin' (published in 1842, while Andersen's work on 'The Ugly Duckling' was under way). He heard how an artist of odd bi-coloured attire – 'the strangest figure!. . . There was no guessing his kith and kin!'[30] – and of unique and invaluable gifts was cheated of his due by ungrateful, mean-spirited, tight-fisted burghers. But they had underrated his powers: he captured their children by their minds and thereby changed the parents' lives for ever. Andersen must have seen a parallel with himself here.

The widespread love (there is no other word) felt for this story, and from the very first, cannot be explained only by its invitation to respect the once despised artist or its confessed correspondence to a celebrity's (Andersen's) own life. Nor even by its extraordinarily concentrated literary art, endlessly repaying of analytic attention though it is. Separation from, and consequent need for fellow spirits – these are conditions by no means peculiar to practitioners of the arts. All of us know moments of oppressive solitude of the soul. What we want most at such times is the assurance that we are not unique in our emotions, that others have the same yearnings, have suffered similarly. If we only could meet these others – if not in life, then in art – we could be comforted, and, above all else, 'The Ugly Duckling' is an instrument of profound comfort. And if we accept homosexuality as a strong component at the very least of Andersen's emotional make-up, then we can see the duckling's journey as one out of the loneliness of mocked heterodoxy to acceptance by those who knew what he was and who felt as he did, or at any rate sympathised with him. Unfortunately Denmark, as the nineteenth century progressed, would deny homosexuals any show of public unity analogous to this convergence of the swans. By the end of the century, like Britain, like Germany, it had made same-sex relations illegal.[31] But the Andersen of 1843 would not have been able to predict this sad subsequent development. He may well privately have dreamed of such romantic, erotically charged friendships as the one he enjoyed that very same year with young Baron Henrik Stampe[32] – who would go on to marry Edvard Collin's niece, Ingeborg's daughter Jonna, making the older man feel he had been but a pawn in a matrimonial game, and plunging him into depression – as part of the securer, more open communities of a brighter future.

2

'Grantræet' ('The Fir Tree')

'The Fir Tree'[33] is at once a companion-piece to and an inversion of 'The Ugly Duckling'. Like its predecessor it presents with scrupulous fidelity and lyrical sympathy the progression through successive stages of a (non-human) living being. These, when viewed in sequence, shed light on the human condition itself and so contribute, it is hoped, to existential wisdom. But the differences between the two stories' treatment of their common subject matter are such that we could well believe the later came about as a rejoinder, almost a corrective, to the earlier.

The duckling, we saw, was as bewildered by his appearance and seeming deficiencies as any other inhabitant of the duck-yard, and for the same reason: ignorance of his proper identity. Therefore he could only respond to his evolution passively, though this did not preclude suffering or the one recourse open to him, escape. All the greater, then, his joy when maturity brought realisation of what/who he really was. By contrast the fir tree knows its identity perfectly well from its first shoots onwards, surrounded as it is by numerous other firs and pines whose growth it perceives and watches with interest, curiosity – and (that most destructive emotion) envy. The tree notices that in spring and at Christmas-time woodcutters come and fell many of its companions, and it eagerly questions the birds and the sunbeams about where these have been taken to, after they were loaded on to wagons. It doesn't doubt their having been selected for a more interesting existence than its own static one. For instance the stork says that out in Egypt fir trees like those once growing nearby are now ships' masts.

Were it less intent on dreams of a future rivalling theirs, the tree could find much to enjoy in its life: the play of the light and breeze, the sap inside its own healthily expanding body. But, to speak in human terms, it is devoured by a longing for glamour and fame, only intensified by the sparrows' account of how firs (smaller than itself, just to make the news harder to bear) are decked at Christmas-time with all manner of delicious goodies and 'mange hundrede Lys',[34] 'many hundred candles', in the warmth and comfort of town houses. 'The Fir Tree', it will already be clear, is far closer to a parable than 'The Ugly Duckling'. Its central figure differs from its fellows in the forest by character traits we could well label weaknesses, even faults, whereas the duckling was different because of an altogether different species from his associates.

If, after his great 1840–42 journey to Greece and Constantinople and back, Andersen had felt impelled towards a characteristic Danish countryside for 'The Ugly Duckling', 'The Fir Tree' similarly takes us to somewhere quintessentially Northern: the great coniferous forests of Norway, Sweden, Finland and Germany, so different from the huge oak woods of Serbia. And it seems only right to place an emphasis on Germany in particular. The fir forest – think of the Grimms' 'Hänsel and Gretel'[35] – has entered the German psyche, and the trees that comprise it have received de facto consecration in the German home at Christmas-time. The tree at the centre of Andersen's tale is simply referred to as 'Grantræet' (fir tree) but taxonomically is clearly *Picea abies*, the Norway Spruce or Christmas Tree.[36] The German practice of taking it into the house and hanging its branches with objects and lights to celebrate Christ's nativity – Martin Luther is thought to have done exactly this – is probably several centuries older than the mid-to-late eighteenth century when it became so widespread that other societies started to emulate it. Twenty-five years after he had written 'The Fir Tree' (in 1869) a Countess Wilhelmine of Holsteinborg told Andersen that *she* had been responsible for Denmark's very first bedecked tree, in 1809.[37] The diary of the English politician and memoirist Charles Greville (1794–1865) describes three small trees for Christmas 1829 provided by the German Princess Lieven; at Christmas-time 1832 Princess Victoria enjoyed seeing such trees indoors, decorated with candles and 'sugar ornaments'. And, after her ascent to the throne and marriage (1841) to Prince Albert, they would become firm features of royal and commoner family festivities alike; Dickens would even write an essay entitled 'A Christmas Tree' in 1850.[38] Jackie Wullschlager is right to draw attention to Andersen's rich description of the drawing room into which 'our' tree is taken, to stand next to the stove, as the very epitome of Danish Biedermeier.[39] Its furnishings, particularised with admiring accuracy, include chinoiserie, rocking chairs, silk-covered sofas, picture books, heaps of toys, and a rich carpet for the tree's tub to rest on. Yet while we are admiring all these tasteful appurtenances, we can't but ask ourselves: 'Isn't the unmolested forest with its animals and birds roaming

free – for instance, that hare who leaped over the fir when it was but a sapling –
worthier of a (deeper) regard? Ultimately our origins are there; drawing rooms
inhibit appreciation of this truth.

Just as the duckling bowed his head and prepared for death from the three
swans rather than continue with life as constant victim and fugitive, so the fir
tree submits to great pain as its wishes are met, and it is hewed down. Thus its
forest existence comes to an end, and ahead lies the disagreeable transportation
to the place it has dreamed of for so long. But, to its surprise, the pain felt is not
simply a physical affair:

> Øxen hug dybt igjennem Marven, Træet faldt med et Suk hen ad Jorden, det
> følte en Smerte, en Afmagt, det kunde slet ikke tænke paa nogen Lykke, det
> var bedrøvet ved at skilles fra Hjemmet, fra den Plet, hvor det var skudt frem;
> det vidste jo, at det aldrig mere saae de kjære gamle Kammerater, de smaae
> Buske og Blomster rundtom, ja maaske ikke engang Fuglene.[40]

> The axe struck deep into the marrow, the tree fell with a sigh down on to
> the ground, it felt a pain, a faintness, it could not think at all about any happi-
> ness, it was sad at having been separated from its home, from that spot from
> which it had shot forth; it knew well that it would never more see the dear old
> friends, the little bushes and flowers round about, not even the birds.

What we have wished for is by no means always what most deeply suits us.
And our wishes may have been made not only in ignorance of this truth but
with wilful indifference to those around us, who are more important to our
well-being than we have yet understood. Such a message – we will encounter it,
again through the image of an uprooted tree transposed to a more sophisticated milieu, in Andersen's magnificent late story, 'Dryaden' ('The Dryad',
1868)[41] – is not, however, as simple, as pure, as it may superficially appear. Had
the tree not been cut down, as it wanted to be, what satisfaction, we may legitimately ask, would it really have known? How could it have appeased its longings, which cannot originate solely from the wish to keep up with others?
Something else, something very strong, must be at play. And isn't some wider
law being enacted in the very need of human beings to take up the trees and
install them in their houses, even if there are callous aspects of this enactment
we may feelingly regret?

True, any enjoyment of its new surroundings is spoilt for the fir by continuous apprehensiveness about what will happen next. This may obviously be no
more than a further illustration of its inability to live in the present, consistent
with the fable/parable nature of the work. For there is much for it to relish, if
relish it could. Instead – in one of the story's most imaginatively affecting
verbal touches – it feels 'Barkepine af bare Længsel'[42] ('Bark-ache of sheer

yearning') for precisely that forest from which it has been forcibly removed, the proper place for a tree as, until that moment, it had not appreciated. Also it is severely discomfited by the rough hurly-burly of the children of the house as they rush for the goodies tied to its branches. These bring to mind Dickens's contemporaneous picture in *A Christmas Carol* (which appeared the very same month as 'The Ugly Duckling') of the goings-on in the household of the woman Scrooge might have married:

> The shouts of wonder and delight with which the development of every package was received! The terrible announcement that the baby had been taken in the act of putting a doll's frying-pan into his mouth, and was more than suspected of having swallowed a fictitious turkey, glued on a wooden platter! The immense relief of finding this a false alarm! The joy, and wonder and ecstasy.[43]

The tree itself, though at the time proof against these last emotions, does in fact feel them, but, ironically and perversely, not until its banishment from the festive scene to the solitude of the attic where it can relive past times in retrospect. Up there – pathetically expecting a re-entrance newly festooned into revelry no longer going on, and with only inquisitive mice, and some unimpressed rats, for company month after month – it belatedly appreciates all the Christmas jubilation of which it was so central and functioning a part but from which, when in full swing, it recoiled. The audience of mice, particularly struck – a characteristic Andersen detail, the more so now we know his very first fairy story – by the tree's having borne *tallow candles* on its branches, are certainly under the impression that, both in the forest and the drawing room, this discarded object knew a marvellous life.

But a highly significant constituent of the tale is yet to come. While it was downstairs, the tree listened, enthralled, to a story told to the children by a stout visitor to the party, an obvious humorous distortion by Andersen of the tall, lean figure he himself cut socially. This man offered his audience a choice between 'Ivede-Avede' (an unidentified, probably invented title) and 'Klumpe-Dumpe' (Humpty-Dumpty),[44] about an egg-man who fell down the steps yet married a princess in the end. The latter won. And as the fir tree relates to the mice this story, every small part of which it finds it can remember, it thinks that hearing it was, after all, the most interesting event of its entire life. 'Klumpe-Dumpe' is a living entity in itself, as all stories must be, and the fir believes it to be true, which obviously it isn't. But such resonance does it possess that the abandoned tree, whose very needles are now yellowing with decay, is moved to dream – and specifically to dream of a pretty birch tree seen in its forest days.

Here we have one of Andersen's most beautiful metaphors for the power of art. Through 'Klumpe-Dumpe', whose history is infinitely remote from its own, the tree is granted transcendence of circumstance. Presently it will be dragged down to the yard – where for a while it believes it will flourish anew – to be chopped up into firewood. But the story has entered a part of itself independent of time, and so is redemptive.

Nevertheless clock time has to be confronted. The inevitable striking of the hour is why we should never ignore the richness of the minutes before. That is the great error of the congenital daydreamer, of the introspective writer – such as Andersen himself. Eventually the fir sees how different it is from all the burgeoning plant-life elsewhere in the yard, and realises the imminence of its own demise:

'Forbi! forbi!' sagde det stakkels Træ. 'Havde jeg dog glædet mig, da jeg kunde! forbi! forbi!'[45]

'It's over! It's over!' said the poor tree. 'Had I only enjoyed myself when I could! It's over! It's over!'

But, in a partial reversal of the tale's moral, as each log into which the tree has been chopped crackles in the cauldron's flames, the tree – still functioning as a single being – relives those times irrevocably past, and thus relieves the tormenting, terrifying process of extinction.

'Pif, paf!' men ved hvert Knald, der var et dybt Suk, tænkte Træet paa en Sommerdag i Skoven, en Vinternat derude, naar Stjernene skinnede; det tænkte paa Juleaften og *Klumpe-Dumpe*, det eneste Eventyr, det havde hørt og vidste at fortælle; og saa var Træet brændt ud.[46]

'Bang! Bang!' but with every blast that was a deep sigh, the tree thought about a summer day in the forest, [or] a winter night out there, when the stars were shining; it thought about Christmas Eve and Humpty-Dumpty, the only fairy-story that it had heard and knew how to tell; and then the tree was burned up.

That it is the fairy story which, before it perishes for ever, engages the tree's thoughts is of key thematic importance. Fantasy when focused on self and material betterment may be a mistaken displacement of mental energy, but when fashioned into a meaningful artefact it can prove a blessing of inestimable existential solace.

So beautifully is 'The Fir Tree' constructed, with every sentence working towards the harmony of the whole, that we might well wonder why it has not enjoyed the success of 'The Ugly Duckling' to which it so clearly akin in both manner and matter. But the one story ends with affirmation of life – with indeed its unfolding, for the swan is still young and has all before it – the other in death, given here without any of the consolations of faith and with a marked absence of those intimations of immortality that 'The Little Mermaid' promoted. And this is the respect in which the second tale inverts the first.

Delight in life's varieties, sympathy for others, even art in all its profundity are fleeting affairs compared with the eternal annihilation which Andersen himself feared so much and guarded so strongly against. His confrontation of this informs the last sentence, which has that individual conversational ring that became such a stylistic hallmark of his and which distinguishes the famous opening injunctions of his next tale, 'The Snow Queen'. This ending to 'The Fir Tree' is as stark and as musical in its rhythm as such great lines of Shakespeare as Prospero's in *The Tempest*: 'We are such stuff/ As dreams are made on; and our little life/ Is rounded with a sleep.'[47]

> nu var den forbi, og Træet var forbi og Historien med; forbi, forbi, og det blive alle Historier![48]
> now it was over, and the tree was over and the story with it; it was over, it was over, and that's what happens to all stories.

'The Fir Tree' of its nature may lack the captivating charm of 'The Ugly Duckling', its winning promise of redemption both actual and vicarious, but artistically it is as perfectly wrought an achievement, and deserves to be hailed as such.

3

'Sneedronningen' 'The Snow Queen'

In *A Poet's Bazaar* Andersen allowed himself regular flights of the imagination even as he gave us a scrupulously accurate account of the places and times of his travels. In 'The Snow Queen' it is the other way about; here is fantasy with metaphysical implications and spiritual intention, yet the work is thoroughly grounded in topography and in the various cultures different territories beget; it is also informed by the author's sense of the sheer strangeness of our global circumstances. Our psychic states, the story powerfully demonstrates, are correlatives of our physical world. Snow, ice, fire, scorching sun are realities of exterior experience which our inner selves accommodate (though also attempt to reject) by taking them as metaphors for the whole gamut of our intimate feelings – just as our bodily selves have to cope with their exigencies, but cannot always succeed in doing so. The more one reads Andersen's great travelogue of his 1840–42 journey south and east, the more one admires the dignity and interestingness accorded those whose primitive and arcane lives he witnessed: Wallachians, Bulgarians, Turks, Serbs, dotted in communities on huge bleak plains or in mountains clad in deciduous woods. And the more inevitable too appears a work by him dealing with a *northbound* expedition: one made within the huge area of Scandinavia with its vast virginal tracts, rather than through the eastern Mediterranean, its goal not the sites of ancient, widely dissemi- nating civilisations, Roman, Greek, Byzantine, (Rome, Athens, Constantinople) but polar regions inimical to human life and quite unable to support civilisa- tion in any conventional European (or even Oriental) sense of the word.

There was surely an element of national pride here. The territory on earth with the largest portion of surface area *above* the Arctic Circle, Greenland (840,000 square miles, 2,175,600 square km) was Danish, and had been so since 1380 – to this day it is a self-governing region of Denmark – and Andersen had already honoured it, or his idea of it, in his *Picture-Book Without Pictures*. And, even after 1814, both Iceland, the far north of which grazes the Circle, and the Faeroes remained Danish dependencies.[49] As for Norway, taken from Denmark in the post-Napoleonic settlement, but, thanks to centuries of shared monarchy, still emotionally important to Danes, the Arctic Circle cuts through one Norwegian county, Nordland, while two others, vast Troms and even vaster Finnmark (so integral to Andersen's story) lie wholly beyond it. Norwegian too is Svalbard, roughly equidistant from the mainland's northernmost shore and the North Pole. Its largest island, Spitsbergen,[50] holds, we are told, the principal residence of the eponymous Snow Queen herself.

Furthermore 'The Snow Queen' appeared after the publication of the first collection of stories, *Norske Folkeeventyr* (*Norwegian Fairy Tales*) by Asbjørnsen and Moe in 1841, and of the three further volumes in 1842–44. Presented by the collectors in a colloquial language related to the country speech of various districts, these stories frequently revealed features directly traceable back to earlier Norse myth, and, while very much the productions of specific localities, had a demonstrable relationship to folk tales all over Europe and beyond. Peter Christen Asbjørnsen (1812–85),[51] a grazier's son, was a naturalist, and his friend from schooldays, Jørgen Moe (1813–82),[52] a farmer's son, was a poet and clergyman who became Bishop of Christiansand (today Kristiansand). Andersen's great fairy tale will reveal a close fascination with Nature, a poet's capacity for concentration, and a preoccupation with the form of Christianity most conducive, in his view, to humane living. In the *Norwegian Fairy Tales'* famous 'Østenfor Sol og Vestenfor Måne', 'East of the Sun and West of the Moon' (which belongs to the 'Beauty and the Beast' family), a girl undertakes a long journey through lonely country to break the spell cast on a young male, and in her accomplishing this the elements have vital (and saving) parts to play.

This is also the narrative line of 'The Snow Queen', where again the elements are of great importance.

Knowledge of the actual writing procedure of 'The Snow Queen' can help with understanding this most widely admired, critically discussed and divergently analysed of Andersen's works. In a letter to B.S. Ingemann of 20 November 1843[53] Andersen told him that he had two fairy stories as good as ready: one was 'Hyldemoer',[54] 'Elder-mother', the other 'Troldspeilet', 'The Magic Mirror' which he believed would be 'ikke uheldigt', 'not unfortunate', suggesting that he thought from the start that his tale would have a happy outcome. He then gave Ingemann the gist of it:[55] the Devil ('Fanden', 'Old Nick') has amused himself by inventing a mirror in which everything beautiful and good appears ugly and mean, while mistakes and weaknesses are magnified. On its way up to the heavens, where it would distort the reflections of even God and his angels, the mirror, laughing so much at its own abilities, falls out of the devil's hands, and crashes down to earth, breaking into millions of pieces. People who get splinters from it in their eyes or, worse still, shards in their hearts, have their vision changed exactly as if they were looking into the mirror itself.

This is just the beginning of the work. 'Nu kommer Historien i Eventyr',[56] 'Now the story comes into the fairy tale', writes Andersen, which is 'hvorledes Sligt fremtræder og hvorledes kun ved at græde dybt og skue ind i Guds Natur, Glasstumpen grædes ud!' 'how such a thing makes its appearance and how only through weeping deeply and seeing into God's Nature, is the glass fragment wept out'.

But Andersen did not actually start writing the story part – which is the body of the work, occupying six divisions of the completed tale's seven[57] – until the following year when he worked on it in a rush of happiness for only five days, realising what he had been long pondering but also so driven forward by his creative daimon that the rapid modes of transportation (recalling 'East of the Sun and West of the Moon') so important to the tale seem mimetic of the composition process itself. Nevertheless The First Story, 'which treats of the mirror and the fragments', far from being detachable from the rest accounts for and conditions it. Stylistically, however, its matter demands that it stand at a certain distance from, or angle to, the fairy tale proper.

This preliminary chapter shows Andersen at his most brilliant – and mischievous, for its light-hearted manner of presenting serious matter is unsettling. It gives us 'en ond Trold', 'an evil troll', one of the very worst, 'det var "Dævelen" ',[58] 'it was "the devil" '. But note the quotation marks round the name, consonant with Andersen's use of the half-facetious 'Fanden' in his letter to Ingemann. The genus 'troll', well outside any Christian hierarchy of superhuman beings, is a definite pointer to the work's persistent and intentional refusal to distinguish between folklore and those folkloric elements incorporated into popular Christianity (and indeed in many communities actively sustaining it), while at the same time reverencing the figure of Christ as crucial to making life meaningful.[59] This was very much Andersen's own position particularly when, as here, he imaginatively re-entered the world of his Odense childhood, where just such a fusion of beliefs (for instance, in the mind of his own mother) was commonplace.

The First Story enables us to see the characters and events of the following ones all but literally *sub specie aeternitatis*, 'under the mirror of eternity',[60] in Spinoza's phrase, an apt one, for not only is a mirror a vital instrument in the whole work but its final resolution hinges on the very word 'Evigheden', 'Eternity'. Thus we come to our human concerns, the boy Kay, the girl Gerda, from the height of Heaven, and see them caught up in the conflict between the angelic (the life-affirming) and the demonic (the life-denying or death-dealing). We are left in no doubt that before this extra-terrestrial mirror broke, before its fragments entered the systems of so many humans, these two children were full of instinctive benevolence. Can we be sure, however, that we will be privileged to witness a restoration of this state, that the severance from loving, the separation from the loved, and all the consequent fear, desolation and sorrow, will not end in tragedy? Well, Andersen had admitted from the first that this history was 'ikke uheldigt' 'not unfortunate'.

I believe that, both in the relation of the Magic Mirror episode to the body of the tale and in the manner of its presentation, Andersen remembered Goethe's *Faust, Part One*, the third and most seminal Prelude of which is entitled 'Prolog im Himmel' ('Prologue in Heaven').[61] Here The Lord himself, with his Three Archangels, assents – because of his own complete foreknowledge – to Mephistopheles's temptation of Dr Faust. Kay, of course, will not see his various surrenders to negative and destructive urges as any kind of succumbing to temptation, nor, it is important even at this early point to insist, do others around him: the process is too instantaneous. Andersen's witty language in his own Prologue suggests he is offering us a 'pocket' *Divine Comedy*, a miniature *Faust*, its God-given blissful ending – even down here, in our own world – preordained. For Andersen has withheld from us in the First Story what we know to have been in his mind from the very start. The destructive splinters of glass can and do stay in people's eyes – or hearts – till the end of their lives. But they *can* be removed – by altruistic others, by the compassionate tears they weep. The capacity for love is sufficiently strong in us for happy restoration even in our 'fallen' world to occur. (There is an echo here of the benevolent Daughters of the Air in 'The Little Mermaid'.)[62]

Hence we are told that to those afflicted by the shattered mirror the loveliest countryside looks like boiled spinach and many handsome people appear not to have stomachs. What the devil's glass brings about is distention of perspective, decrease in clarity and, in moral terms, an inadequate, uncharitable and therefore restricted *Weltanschauung*. In order to restore vision, the vision proper to the human being who is also a child of God, a journey will be undertaken as long, as full of varieties, as Andersen's real-life one beyond Greece and Turkey into the Black Sea and up past the troubled banks of the Danube. But what made this long, hazard-strewn undertaking unavoidable for both parties, and over what actual terrain does it take us?

'Inde i den store By, hvor der ere saa mange Huse og Mennesker. . .'[63] 'Within the large city, where there are so many houses and people. . .' – These opening words of the Second Story remove us from the world of invisible powers to this world, to a particular (though not particularised) spot in it. Copenhagen comes to mind, for can anywhere else in Denmark be so baldly designated? But certain features – the proximity of the river, the farmers' carts coming so regularly into the town – suggest Andersen's own Odense. Here live 'to fattige Børn',[64] 'two poor children', so poor indeed that their families have their homes up in the attic quarters of adjoining houses, and their garden is a rooftop space by the rain guttering where they grow herbs and roses. (We may well think of Andersen's boyhood home in Munkemøllestræde, Odense.) Curiously we learn nothing whatsoever about the children's parents, and it is hard to attribute this omission to anything other than Andersen's psychological attitude towards his own. Never once do these children miss, or even recollect their parents in their separate solitary wanderings, reflecting surely Andersen's own previously noted absence of regret for his own kin from his departure from Odense onwards. But, however oddly this may strike us, we must take it as a *donnée*, as we must the pair's intense devotion both to each other and to 'den gamle Bedstemoder', 'the old grandmother'. Whose grandmother she is we never learn, but for both of them she is the disseminator of those values essential to a good life. Perhaps indeed she is not a blood relation of either, but a wise old woman such as traditional communities honoured. But once again a psychological factor must be in play: in Bedstemoder Andersen is recreating his father's mother, so potent an influence on him, probably the only relation he truly respected, and whom, to his genuine sorrow, he never saw again once he had left Odense aged fourteen. Ejnar Stig Askgaard, in his essay on the tale, remembering this grandmother's devotion to the plants in the asylum garden, sees her also in the old woman with flower garden of the work's Third Story.[65]

The boy is called Kay, the girl Gerda after the little daughter of Edvard and Jette Collin who had died at the age of four earlier in 1843, the first of three such tragedies to strike that couple until then so blessed by good fortune, not least in Andersen's eyes. His fictional Gerda, older than the deceased Collin child ever became, and whose name has an alliterative echo of Faust's virtuous

Gretchen, will keep her innate sweetness and strength (it is actually called 'Magt', 'power') intact throughout the many dark turns of the long story, without ever realising that these are notable qualities of hers. Her portrait thus amounts to a compensation on Andersen's part for the familial grief of the Collins into which he felt he was not fully admitted. The friendship between Kay and Gerda recalls that of Christian and Naomi in *Only a Fiddler*, but – as he does often, from 'The Dead Man' and 'The Travelling Companion' on – Andersen offers us a significant variation on his earlier treatment of the theme. As in the novel, the beauties of a garden bring the two children together. In wintertime when everything is frozen over, they peep at one another, through holes made by placing stove-heated pennies on the frosted windowpanes, before venturing out of doors to play together again. But here this intent curiosity in one another is presented as something wholesome, valuable, delightful both to witness and to experience, and the foundation of an unselfish relationship which will continue long after the story's ending. (James Massengale in his 2007 essay 'About Little Gerda, and Her "Moratoria" '[66] has a most interesting, even controversial take on this, which will be noted when we come to considering the tale's end.) While Gerda is as strong and energetic as the earlier Naomi, and, like her, galvanic in her vitality, unlike her she is consistent and resolute in moral values, loyalty and affections.

Grandmother ensures their mental lives are informed by a Pietistic Christianity which, as remarked above, sees no discrepancy between folkloric inheritance and its more dogmatic beliefs. (In this respect, though clearly members of a strongly Protestant society, the two protagonists have a not dissimilar childhood experience of religion to Antonio in *The Improvisatore*; I share Massengale's view, in the essay cited, that, when, in the Sixth Story Gerda sees angels assisting her against the attack of the snowflakes, she is reacting like a Catholic child.) As a determining example of the folkloric the old woman tells the children when winter snow falls: 'Det er de hvide Bier som sværme',[67] 'It is the white bees who are swarming'. And when Kay, keen on facts from the first, asks about this particular white swarm, 'Har de ogsaa en Bidronning?' 'Have they also a Queen Bee?' Grandmother tells him yes, the snowflakes do indeed have a Queen, an eminence he will in fact shortly see for himself. (While Kay will not actually meet her until the following winter, it is essential to Andersen's purpose that we early connect the boy, and not the girl, with this dominatrix.) Nor is the likening of snowflakes to bees mere folk fancy. Each cell of a bees' honeycomb is a hexagon, the shape of a snow crystal. Grandmother has imparted to her charges a sense of Christ's love for the earth and all its denizens. An age-old symbol for this is the rose, here appearing in the form of rose bushes, which grow so beautifully – and never more so than during this first summer of the tale – in humble boxes on a rooftop in an

indigent quarter of the city. Gerda is very attached to one hymn she likes to
sing to Kay, extolling the double properties, natural and spiritual, of roses:

'Roserne voxe i Dale,
Der faae vi Barn-Jesus i Tale.'[68]

'The roses grow in the valley,
There we can engage the Christ Child in talk.'

Danish readers may well have recognised these lines as bearing a resemblance
to the hymn 'Den yndigste Rose', 'The loveliest rose' (of which they are a
misquotation) by the Pietistic pastor (later influential bishop), Hans Adolf
Brorson (1694–1764)[69] whose psalms and hymns had been rediscovered and
popularised in the latter part of the Romantic Age, and for whom the rose
represented the beauty of Christ's person. When Gerda is the virtual captive of
an old woman who is a (mostly) benevolent witch, roses are hidden from her,
such is their holy connotation and their inevitable ability to remind her of the
playmate she is intending to rescue. Andersen and Brorson have, of course, a
huge tradition behind them. By the thirteenth century, flowers in general stood
for God's goodness, with the red rose representing Christ, red being the colour
of the blood he shed for humanity.[70] Similarly Gerda, through her dangerous
journeys, sacrifices bodily safety for Kay.

One summer's day, when the roses are particularly profuse and fragrant, the
two children are looking together at a picture book of birds and animals when
Kay is suddenly and painfully assailed by two tiny pieces of glass from the
devil's mirror. One finds its way into his eye, the other into his heart, which will
therefore turn into a lump of ice. Neither child realises what has happened, and
Kay's actual pain soon passes. But almost at once and for no discernible reasons
he starts disparaging the flowers, finding one worm-eaten, another crooked; he
even kicks at the boxes and breaks off the two imperfect roses. Next he derides
both Gerda's picture book and Grandmother's tales, and is soon doing mocking
imitations of the old lady's movements and speech, as well as those of many
other people too. So amusingly observant is he of shortcomings and quirks that
he earns commendation rather than censure for his new caustic wit. And even
Gerda, too often his butt, goes on loving him, a love that will continue after his
disappearance and never wane. Kay is clearly clever, in the manner of ambitious, attention-seeking schoolboys; his preoccupations become noticeably
more cerebral than before, even as chosen amusements turn more demand-
ingly physical, becoming rougher, fiercer, more reckless.

When considering 'The Ugly Duckling' we felt obliged to insist on a most
obvious truth in the face of the various adventures befalling a hero perfectly

ignorant of it: '*Only a cygnet can hatch from a swan's egg. Our protagonist's evolution*. . . *absolutely could not have proceeded other than how it did, whether he met with kind encouragement*. . . *or with spiteful enmity.*' Likewise at this point in 'The Snow Queen' we could say with equal justification: '*Until he was the unwitting victim of those fragments of the mirror, an exterior artefact devised by forces over which he had no control, Kay was a kind, gentle, responsive boy. Whatever sins he now becomes guilty of, we should not look at them as the result of some morally wrong decision of his. Kay is as passive, as fully a "patient", rather than an "agent", as the duckling before him, without any say in his own development.*'

And yet, contrary to the case of the earlier tale, so plain and entirely accurate a statement does not completely satisfy. We feel that while it should not be gainsaid, it leaves out an important element of Kay's situation indispensable to the work's central scheme. Let us therefore contrast the Kay of 'The Snow Queen' with the Ugly Duckling. The latter is, in the circumstances into which he is born, a wholly exceptional creature. What applies to all the birds around him – to other ducks, both tame and wild, and even to geese, closer kin to him though these are – does not apply to him. Both his instinctive responses and the motives behind his actions follow laws seemingly out of kilter (and culpably so) with the world around him. But Kay, despite the sudden truculence he displays to Gerda and Grandmother, does not seem in the least extraordinary to his 'victims' or to what members of his community we meet – or, importantly, to us as readers either. *Everybody*, we are told, laughs at his mimicry; the tougher boys of the neighbourhood take him, for the first time, into their company, and he and they enjoy the various daring games they engage in. I find myself in total agreement here with Wolfgang Lederer in his book, *The Kiss of the Snow Queen* (1986),[71] in which he offers an exemplarily thoughtful and clear summary of Kay's 'transformation':

> If we omit, for a moment, the metaphysics of the situation and concentrate on the observable changes in Kay – on the phenomenology of the situation – then the metamorphosis becomes suddenly quite familiar (one is tempted to say terribly familiar) to all of us, or at least to anyone who has had occasion to watch a boy grow up, or who once was a boy.

It does indeed! Lederer then goes on to list particularities of this 'new' Kay: jeering dislike of anything sentimental or 'soppy'; preference for riskier, not to say danger-courting activities in the company of his own sex over gentle, enclosed, predominantly feminine domesticity; a marked propensity for the factual, the rational, the measurable (which with paradoxical logic leads to the immeasurable, i.e. the philosophical or theological), for the scientific in opposition to the fanciful or romantic-dreamy. And Lederer continues:

> He behaves, in short, like the typical adolescent. At puberty, when a boy is assailed by instinctual-sexual urges, he usually finds to his distress that he is confronted with two tasks for which society – our Western society, at least – provides no guiding ritual or path: To become the man he now begins to feel he should become, he must first of all peel himself out from the world of women in which, so far he has grown up; and he must try to find some activities, generally recognised to be male, that would help him to consolidate his identity as a man.

Lederer then shows us how Kay acts in accordance with both drives. He begins to withdraw from his former female companions, showing them rudeness, 'a callous, aggressive arrogance, which he, evidently, considers very masculine', and, in concurrence with the second, moves in a two-pronged direction. He involves himself with 'the "games bigger boys play": with sports, 'dangerous modes of transportation such as motorcycles and hot-rods' (or in Kay's case wilder sledging effected by tying smaller sleighs behind farmers' carts)

> and with delinquency. Or it may lead into the unsentimental, non-sticky world of mathematics, mechanics, physics, and philosophy – in short, to science and its applications. As Anna Freud has pointed out, such intellectualising is one of the defence mechanisms available to the ego, and is among the chief mechanisms used during adolescence.
>
> The effect of the splinters, therefore, appears to be that they bring about the onset of a perfectly normal, if disagreeable, adolescent phase. To that extent they can hardly be considered detrimental. But we do recall that the splinters are to express sinfulness; in what manner adolescent withdrawal into intellectuality may be a sin is not at all clear. . . .[72]

This last sentence indicates the difficulties 'The Snow Queen' asks us to face. These do not altogether diminish when we remember what the First Story (and behind it Andersen's letter to Ingemann) informed us: not *everyone* got a splinter from the mirror, though millions and millions did/do (and not every adolescent boy either) – one says 'not altogether', because, as Lederer has so well articulated, the majority of young males do in truth behave pretty much like Kay at this stage in the story.

Andersen would definitely *not* have been of their number. We can be certain of this. He disliked other boys when one himself, and refused to play with them. For their part *they* didn't take to *him*. Insofar as he liked other children at all, he preferred girls, who were more favourably inclined towards his own interest in dolls and their clothes. As a youth he was subjected, we recall, to sadistic teasing at work from doubtless entirely ordinary young male employees questioning his very gender; Kay was maybe too intellectual a boy to have inflicted such coarse humiliation on anybody, but in the very ugliness of his recorded antics we can find a link. 'Sinfulness' may well seem to the victim of such unfeeling communal actions an appropriate term for them.

For me, however, Lederer's sensible, textually irrefutable reading of Kay coheres only if we interpret the corrosive results of that shattered mirror as primarily *cultural* rather than pertaining to the individual soul. This fits the already noted biological passivity of Kay who is evolving rather than making decisions, is joining in rather than instigating, is instinctually impelled to criticise or sneer rather than to pass judgement from a new, more objective standpoint. His only too typical unkindness, his hardening of heart against the tenderness of others, result from a wide dissemination of attitudes (for which the flying fragments are a metaphor) about what is and what is not suitable for the young male and which he now shares with his peer group. There will always be comparative outsiders – like the younger Andersen himself – who do not, who cannot, share them, who never (if you like) received any particles from the corrupting mirror, and doubtless Andersen knew, or, better, hoped he knew, others similarly spared these: Christian Voigt or Orla Lehmann may have appeared to him as such.

Any satisfactory interpretation of the tale must pay careful attention to Kay's relationship to the snow, to those white bees which are the snowflakes and to their Queen, who gives her name to the whole work, and to whose palace both the children individually journey. Kay it is, as we have seen, who finds out that these snow-bees have their own Queen. When Gerda expresses fear that this sovereign might come into their house, he retorts, with bragga-docio, that if she dared try, he'd put her on the hot stove so she'd melt. The glass fragments have not yet entered him, yet this boast (so ironic in contrast with how he actually behaves to the Queen when they do meet up) exhibits clearly enough the kind of masculinity he will soon assume: swaggering and offering violence as the answer to any problematic occurrence. Grandmother herself seems to detect his remark as an advance guard of the imminent change in him: she strokes his head, then goes on telling her stories.

But this passage, so perceptive in its smallest detail, leads us to an additional reading of the crucial invasion of the story's main male character: *Kay was ready for the mischievous shards, in fact was an obvious – even a predeter-mined – recipient of them. The mirror in its mirth knew this. Consequently the change in him – great though it might seem – should occasion no surprise, and indeed none is recorded.*

That same evening Kay is back in his own home (for he doesn't live in the same apartment as Gerda) getting ready for bed. 'Halv afklædt', 'half-undressed', i.e. half-naked, he climbs up to look through that little coin-shaped peephole he made in the frozen windowpane – 'tittede ud af det lille Hul'[73], 'looked out through the little hole' – through which he watches the snowflakes, one of which lands on the window box outside. This then expands until it acquires the shape of the Snow Queen in person. How she appears to him at such an early point in the story is significant:

> Den [Sneeflokken] blev tilsidst til et heelt Fruentimmer, klædt i de fineste, hvide Flor, der vare som sammensatte af Millioner stjerneagtige Fnug. Hun var saa snuk og fiin, men af Iis, den blændede, blinkende Iis, dog var hun levende; Øinene stirrede som to klare Stjerner, men der var ingen Bo eller Hvile i dem. Hun nikkede til Vinduet og vinkede med Haanden.[74]
>
> It [the snowflake] eventually became a complete woman clothed in the finest white gauze which was as if made up of millions of star-like flakes. She was so beautiful and elegant, but of ice, dazzling, gleaming ice, yet she was alive; her eyes stared like two stars, but there was no calm or repose in them. She nodded to the window and beckoned with her hand.

If Kay's brag that he would shove the Snow Queen on to the stove if she entered the house was a forerunner of adolescent belligerence, his reaction here is a sign of pre-pubic erotic fascination. Even to pre-Freudian readers 'Hul', 'hole' had sexual connotations. Kay, himself semi-nude, has fastened his gaze on a vagina correlative and found on its far side a mature woman, summoning him and dressed in bridal attire. The conventional young male tends to abhor weddings and their trappings as much as his sisters dote on them. The apparition with her gesture of enticement both intrigues and alarms Kay, who is still after all 'den lille Dreng', 'the small boy'; instinctively he jumps down from the chair by the window.

Spring and summer follow, a summer of particular fullness but witnessing also, thanks to those splinters of glass, the end of Kay's 'small-boyhood'. His sarcastic remarks should be heard as spoken in a voice breaking into untried depths; he will display, when he goes sledging, a typical abundance of that restless energy which also (biologically) coexists with bouts of apathy. That very winter he will yield to the Snow Queen, instead of hiding from her in fear as during the previous one. But before that event we are given an interesting instance of the intellectual side of his new personality. One day he takes a large magnifying glass out of doors, and spreads his coat-tails so that snowflakes fall on to the cloth and he can examine them. He invites Gerda to look through the glass with him:

'Seer Du, hvor kunstigt!' sagte Kay, 'det er meget interessantere end med de virkelige Blomster! og der er ikke en eneste Feil ved dem, de ere ganske akku-rate, naar de blot ikke smelte.'[75]

'Look, how artistic!' said Kay, 'it is much more interesting than the actual flowers! And there isn't a single flaw in them, if only they didn't melt!'

There is an obvious flaw, through, in Kay's comparison: melt snowflakes must, they don't follow the law of growth, decline and rebirth that natural flowers do. But – and he is still fond enough of Gerda to draw her attention to it – the snowflake is a remarkable phenomenon which would have fascinated the Andersen who was so impressed by a drop of water viewed through a magnifying glass in the way Ørsted recommended.[76] Snowflakes are aggregates of snow crystals, which have come together after part-thawing, then refreezing. As no crystal is exactly the same as another, each snowflake too is unique, with incalculable varieties of shape and size. Andersen's descriptions throughout 'The Snow Queen' stress this, and the activities of a boy in America during his own later years would have impressed him. Walter Alwyn Bentley (1865– 1931),[77] or Walter 'Snowflake' Bentley, started serious examination of flakes through a microscope at the age of fifteen, and by the time he was twenty worked with a bellows camera attached to that instrument. Of the almost 6,000 crystals ('ice-flowers' he significantly called them) that he 'captured' (how Kay would have envied him!) he famously declared he'd found 'no two alike'. In truth he had predecessors in other cultures. George Steiner, in his essay-length tribute (2011) to him,[78] reminds us how sinologist and natural scientist, Joseph Needham (1900–95) had, in his great multi-volume sequence, *Science and Civilisation in China* (1954– and posthumously published up to 2008) honoured early Chinese scientists' attention to the phenomena:

> The hexagonal architecture of the snowflake was noted by Han Ying as early as 135 BCE. Characteristically, Needham asks himself what kind of lens, [and] what degree of magnification were available to the Chinese observer. It was the philosopher-sage Chu Hsi, 'perhaps the greatest in all Chinese history', who related the six-pointed snow-flowers to the facets of certain minerals. The mineral here invoked is selenite, translucent hexagonal crystals of gypsum or calcium sulphate.[79]

This triumph of rationalistic scientific dedication is far from inapposite to Kay when domiciled at the Snow Queen's, and is counterbalanced by Gerda's reactions to the flakes when she nears that alarming abode. She is amazed, even horrified, by their many extraordinary shapes – like outsize hedgehogs or clus-tered many-headed snakes or even bear cubs – and has to pray; prayers answered by the angels that appear to rise from her breath in the sub-zero cold air. We have here then two distinct approaches to the enmity, the cruelty not only included in Nature but inextricable from it, which peculiarly engaged nineteenth-century minds like Andersen's, and which long predate Darwin, with whose work he and his literary colleagues would conduct intellectually intense dialogue. A male and a female approach to the issue, the story might appear to suggest, though, on closer inspection, the inferences of the treatment cannot satisfactorily be so reduced.

The upsurge of bodily (testosterone-driven) strength and intellectual inquiry makes it inevitable that the now adolescent Kay will abandon (though not by conscious intention) both the women in his life, Grandmother and Gerda, and head northwards after the anima-embodiment who had beckoned to him the year before. It is now time to look at where she was leading him.

The detail that, after he has accepted her kiss she seems to him no longer a phantasm of ice but an alluringly beautiful woman, is, paradoxical though it may seem, a suggestion that we readers should now turn our thoughts to a real enough region of the world, affecting the lives of real people. While snow and ice will probably disappear from the children's Danish city after a handful of wintry weeks, there are important areas where they hold sway all year round, and whose influence cannot be ignored. Icecap-covered Greenland generates the weather that comes over the North Atlantic and conditions Europeans.

Of the journey Kay makes on the Snow Queen's sleigh we read:

> De fløi over Skove og Søer, over Have og Lande; neden under susede den kolde Blæst, Ulvene hylede, Sneen gnistrede, hen over den fløi de sorte skrigende Krager, men oven over skinnede Maanen saa stor og klar, og paa den saae Kay den lange, lange Vinternat; om Dagen sov han ved Sneedronningens Fødder.[80]

> They flew over forests and lakes, over seas and lands; down below whistled the cold wind, the wolves howled, the snow glittered over which flew black shrieking crows, but up above shone the moon so large and clear, and on it Kay gazed that long, long winter night; by day he slept at the Snow Queen's feet.

In Spitsbergen, where stands the Snow Queen's principal residence, 60 per cent of the terrain is glacier, while pack ice fills the sea all the way up to the North Pole itself. At its very tip, at 81° latitude, the polar night lasts 128 days, with the sun only just visible as a smear of light at midday. However, as it is burgeoning summer in the northern hemisphere's temperate zone, the Queen is now quartering in Finnmark[81] as is her custom – though, when we go there, that appears quite winter-bound and hostile enough. Finnmark is Norway's northernmost province (and its easternmost; its frontier with Russia lies further east than Istanbul) as well as its largest and most sparsely peopled, and exclusively inside the Arctic Circle. At the time of the winter solstice (21 December) even on the Circle itself the sun will not show at all above the horizon; at least one spell of 24-hour-long total darkness can be guaranteed. The wilderness where Gerda is set down by the reindeer on the final stage of her journey to rescue Kay will be part of that vast, lonely plateau, the Finnmarksvidda. Finnmark was known to Finns by the name of Rutja (modern Finnish Ruija), and appears in *Kalevala*[82] as a region where hero/anti-hero 'wanton Lemminkäinen' lures his victims:

> So he sang such men
> one this way, one that –
> into barren glades
> upon unploughed lands
> into fishless pools
> into fishless pools
> ones quite without perch
> into Rutja's steep rapid
> into the smoking whirlpool
> to be froth-crests in the stream
> and rocks amid the rapid
> to smoulder as fire
> and to shoot as sparks.
> (*Kalevala*, Book 12, 'A Bond Broken', translation Keith Bosley)[83]

Even to Finns of the first millennium Finnmark/Rutja seemed remote, intractable. Yet the whole enormous area, seen as divided into two sections – Kalevala, land of the Finns, and Pohjola, Northland, generally thought of the land of the Lapps,[84] now called Sami – had been put on the European cultural map that year of Andersen's real literary debut, 1835. Elias Lönnrot (1802–84)[85] published *Kalevala,* his epic fashioned out of heroic oral poetry collected in the eastern Finnish region of Karelia,[86] on 28 February. It is still celebrated as Kalevala Day in Finland, such has been the extraordinary absorption into national consciousness of his work (revised and expanded to nearly double the original length in 1849), aided, of course, by Sibelius's great music inspired by it.

To arrive at this destination at the top of the world, first Kay then Gerda travel over the vast territory of Sweden's Norrland and northern Finland – over what is nowadays known as Sapmi or Lapland. In fact Gerda meets the 'Lappekonen', 'The Lapp Woman' before she meets 'Finnekonen', 'The Finn

Woman'. It is possible that both women are ethnically Lappish/Sami, and that the second was named for Finnmark where she actually lives; centuries-long confusion has prevailed between these two peoples. Each thought of the other as a repository of magic knowledge; that Finns are still thought of in this way is treated (though not without a touch of parody) in one of the finest Scandinavian novels of the late twentieth century, Kerstin Ekman's *Händelser vid vatten* (*Events by Water* 1993),[87] set in the northern Swedish province of Jämtland. In Andersen's story the message that the Lapp Woman writes (almost certainly in Runes) on dried cod – an authentic medium of communication – for the Finn Woman to read was clearly instantly and completely comprehensible to her. Tacitus, who provides in *Germania* (98 CE) the earliest account of these inhabitants of the Northlands, is also a source of later confusion of the two. The Fenni, about whom he wrote (from which derives our word Finn) probably were today's Sami; certainly Andersen's description of both women's homes suggests great poverty and meagreness of life around them. Tacitus wrote: 'The Fenni are remarkably brutish and appallingly wretched: no weapons, no horses, no dwellings; their food vegetation, their clothing skins, their bed the ground; their only hope is in arrows which, lacking iron, they sharpen with bone.'[88] Andersen's women do have iron, for they have cooking-pots, and they are very far from brutish – being wise, kind, helpful. But the indigence and primitiveness of Tacitus pertain to them. The Lapp Woman's dwelling is 'saa ynkeligt',[89] 'so wretched/pitiful'.

The Sami have inhabited the Arctic and sub-Arctic regions of Scandinavia for 3,000 years and probably, judging by artefacts, for at least 7,000 years before that, and therefore long predate the Finns, who migrated north-westwards from the Ural Mountains to settle some two thousand odd years ago. The languages of the Sami – related to each other and for the greater part, though not entirely, mutually intelligible – are usually placed as an independent branch of the Uralic family, inside which are Finnic (major members Finnish and Estonian), the Samoyedic and Hungarian (with by far the greatest number of speakers). But there is an increasing lack of consensus about the relationship between Sami languages and the Finnic,[90] though the proximity of the two ethnic groups in extensive areas and the Finnish administration of some of the most important of these have resulted in Finnish loan-words in Sami tongues.

Sami – descendants of the Sun whom the daughter of the Sun particularly favours – have a cosmology independent of ancient Finnish myth, and for many centuries have led semi-nomadic lives based on reindeer-herding, the animals themselves being migratory and therefore classed as only '*semi*-domesticated'. Nowadays only 10 per cent of the approximately 70,000 Sami, protected by legislation within all the relevant countries (which includes the Kola peninsula of Russia) actually rely on reindeer for their living, but iconically the animal is inseparable from them. And Andersen makes the reindeer the most actively benevolent character in his whole story, perhaps the only one, Gerda apart (as Grandmother, for all her tales, is as motionless as a figure in Vermeer). We bid him farewell as a happy representative of procreation, of the continuity of life, as seems only right for his invaluable, and indeed highly valued, kind.

If Kay's journey with the Snow Queen is a magically rapid northward one, a result of his adolescent combination of energetic recklessness and passivity to the demands of an Eros figure, Gerda's is slow, time-consuming, danger-strewn – and, unlike his, undertaken altruistically, its aims the finding and rescue of her loved companion.

After Kay's sudden disappearance, reported by the town-boys who had witnessed it, there is a general assumption that he is dead, most probably drowned in the river, and 'mange Taarer flød'[91] 'many tears flowed', another good indication surely that, as far as most people were concerned, Kay was a likeable enough boy, not too truculent or cerebral to be loved and bitterly missed – above all by Gerda herself. But with the end of winter, the certainty of his death weakens.

O, det var ret lange, mørke Vinterdage.
Nu kom Vaaren med varmere Solskin.
'Kay er død og borte!' sagde den lille Gerda.
'Det troer jeg ikke!' sagde Solskinnet.
'Han er død og borte!' sagde hun til Svalerne.
'Det troer jeg ikke!' svarede de, og til sidst troede den lille Gerda det ikke heller.
'Jeg vil tage min nye røde Skoe paa,' sagde hun en Morgenstund, 'dem Kay aldrig har seet, og saa vil jeg gaae ned til Floden og spørge den ad!'[92]

Oh, those were long, dark winter days.
Now came the spring with warmer sunshine.
'Kay is dead and gone!' said little Gerda.
'I don't think so!' said the sunshine.
'He is dead and gone!' she said to the swallows.
'I don't think so!' they replied, and soon little Gerda didn't think so either.
'I will put on my red shoes,' she said early one morning, 'which Kay has never seen, and then I will go down to the river and ask it.'

Clearly Kay – who has vanished in the middle of winter but whose death is denied by the first harbingers of spring (rays of sunshine and swallows) – relates to those figures of mythology, powerfully influential on successive cultures, who, after the full life of summer, die in winter, to be reborn in spring, a process often aided by lamentations, prayers, rites. Andersen would have been familiar with all the most famous instances; study of the West's mythological inheritance as a pursuit vital to its spiritual health was an ever-expanding intellectual tenet in the mid-nineteenth century, and nowhere more so than in the Denmark of Grundtvig. For Grundtvig, myth – and inevitably he was above all others involved with Norse myth – was a divinely overseen foreshadowing of the central dramas of Christianity, the entrance into recordable history of God himself, with which therefore it was deeply reconcilable.

So, anticipating our own Resurrection story and confirming the facts of Nature, we have Osiris, vegetation god, drowned, dismembered, enclosed in a sarcophagus and floated down the River Nile.[93] At the Nile Delta his coffin was discovered by Isis, his wife and sister, who, having opened it, succeeded in bringing her husband bodily back to life (all except his genitals). Osiris and the rites honouring him were intimately connected with the annual flooding of the Nile and the plant cycle dependent on this. We also have Adonis,[94] the boy who remains a boy after being resurrected. Again he is celebrated annually; again he is inextricable from seasonal rotation. Aphrodite (Snow Queen?) fell in love with him and seduced him; he died in her arms (as we might well fear that Kay could do in *his* goddess's). But she sprinkled nectar on his body, as a result of which the anemone came into being, that lovely short-lived flower for ever afterwards associated with his (almost exclusively female) cult. In Adonis's ancestry is the Babylonian Tammuz, object of propitiatory fertility rites to maintain the year's agricultural cycle. Tammuz was thought to be at his strongest at the summer solstice, and to this day the name in the Iraqi Arabic calendar corresponds to our month of July, that month, one infers, when Kay was smitten by the malignant glass shard. When Tammuz was abducted to the Underworld, Ishtar – again wife and sister to the male – undertook a journey of rescue, and secured him for earthly life for six months of the year. The myth is far more ramified than this, and discoveries of Babylonian tablets have cast doubt on the nature of the Tammuz/Ishtar relationship itself, but the previous sentence summarises what parts of it Andersen could have known. These fertility young men/young gods were part of the educated Western consciousness several centuries before such seminal nineteenth-century works of scholarship as *The Golden Bough* (1890,) of J.G. Frazer.[95]

Ejnar Stig Askgaard in his essay, 'Look! Now We'll Begin' (2007),[96] stressing that Andersen 'had a thorough knowledge of Norse mythology', also adduces here, surely rightly, the figure of Balder,[97] banished to the wintry cold and dark of Hel through the trickery of Loki in the *Edda* of Snorri Storluson. He provides a most interesting twelve-part breakdown of the two narratives, which fascinatingly parallel each other – the removal from the world of the living, the northward nature of the journey taken, the rescue journey aided by an animal with supernatural powers – and part company only in the final section: there is no Gerda able to rescue Balder whose good helper, Hermod, fails in his task, leaving him in the hall of Hel to await the post-Ragnarok reordering of the universe.

Kay, recently arrived at puberty only to be enticed to a realm of death by a mature woman: what else could he be but a correlative for Adonis? And Gerda's relation to him, isn't it that of 'wife and sister', with the loyalty, the devotion of the one, and the propinquity, the common past of the other? Gerda's great love for him (whatever name we give to it) causes her, after her long grieving, to ask the river about his whereabouts – its waters not stained anemone-red like Adonis's but a clear artery of existence, possibly the mythic River of Life itself, though those of us who know Andersen's birthplace will have a picture of the Odense River,[98] so near the author's second home with the tiny rooftop garden. The walks beside it through the Munke Mose (Monks' Moor) were very dear to him. ' "Er det sandt, at Du har taget min egebroder? Jeg vil forære Dig mine røde Skoe, dersom Du vil give mig ham igen". '[99] 'Is it true that you have taken my little playmate brother? I will make you a present of my red shoes if you will give me him back again.' And indeed she does this, but the bestowal of her beloved shoes on the river is given a strange twist, not easy to interpret. Thrown into the river the shoes keep returning to her, first to where she is standing on its bank and then to the boat on to which she has clambered, though eventually this picks up speed and the determined little pair cannot keep up.

This odd detail may amount to only a very small episode of the story, but so graphically is it presented that it lodges itself, with pictorial vividness, in the mind; disturbingly so if we are familiar with the troubled 'De røde Skoe'[100] 'The Red Shoes' (1845), written concurrently with this longer work. Here as there Gerda sees the red shoes as pretty appurtenances rendering her attractive; it is a convincing, human touch (a novelist's rather than a fairy-tale teller's) that Gerda remarks to herself that Kay has not yet seen them (i.e. not yet seen – and admired – her wearing them). But for his sake she is prepared to sacrifice even what might appeal to him in her appearance. Gerda thus makes herself barefoot for the first stage of her travels, and, as Maria Tatar observes,[101] will appear to those seeing her as indigent, vulnerable and determinedly persevering, a not inaccurate summary of her present position. Footwear indeed has a decided role to play in the course of the whole story. The friendly prince and princess will provide the girl (appropriately enough) with fur boots for her entry into harsh northern terrain; the robber girl takes these from her, then, obeying one of her erratic, unpredictable impulses of kindness, returns them to her for her ride with the reindeer. However the Finn woman, in her overheated hovel, proceeds to remove them. So when the reindeer at last sets her down at her destination she still lacks these necessities:

> Der stod den stakkels Gerda uden Skoe, uden Handsker, midt i det frygtelige iiskolde Finmarken.
> There stood poor Gerda without shoes, without gloves, in the middle of the terrifying ice-cold Finnmark.[102]

As for the red shoes discarded at the outset of her journey, we should not see them as synonymous with the shoes of the subsequent tale. Red certainly is the traditional colour of passion, and shoes in fairy tales (e.g. 'Cinderella') often connote sexual attractiveness, while Gerda herself is on the threshold of adolescence. But what she stands for is instinctive goodness, original virtue that can withstand original sin. Altruism always involves some self-abnegation, and Gerda's casting of her shoes into the water is a recognition of this truth, their bobbing back to her an indication of how difficult this process can be, and of the strength of one's reluctance, despite good intentions, to pursue the harder course. But Gerda succeeds in doing just this, and without knowing that success or failure has been involved. The Finn Woman will say of Gerda, after the reindeer has begged her to bestow some extra power on the girl, that her very ignorance of her own merits is the key to her considerable strength which will ensure victory:

> 'Jeg kan ikke give hende større Magt, end hun allerede har! seer Du ikke, hvor stor den er? Seer Du ikke, hvor Mennesker og Dyr maae tjene hende, hvorledes hun paa bare Been er kommen saa vel frem i Verden. Hun maa ikke af os vide sin Magt, den sidder i hendes Hjerte, den sidder i, hun er et sødt uskyldigt Barn.'[103]
> 'I cannot give her greater power than she already has! Don't you see how great it is? Do you not see how human beings and animals feel obliged to help her, how she has come so very far in the world on bare feet. She must not know from us her power, it lies in her heart, it lies within, she is a sweet innocent child.'

If the First Story was a Prologue in the Heavens evoking Goethe's masterwork, Gerda and her self-imposed task owe immeasurably to that favourite of Andersen's, *The Heart of Midlothian* to which we paid attention in the book's first chapter. Once the kinship between Gerda and Scott's heroine, Jeanie Deans, is appreciated, much in the authorial intention guiding the narrative becomes clear. Like Jeanie, Gerda has a background of puritan piety whose beliefs and standards alike she maintains – not only during the course of the

story, but, we can be sure, long after its conclusion. (She could even, in educational and economic terms, be thought to be of Jeanie's – numerically large –
social class.) Like her too she undertakes a rescue mission on behalf of someone
incalculably dear to her, (a literal sibling in Jeanie's case, a virtual sibling in
Gerda's) but with a weaker personality than her own, and of whose changed
values and conduct she cannot morally approve. (Both Effie and Kay could be
termed 'worldly' in the word's adverse sense). Both journeys are made with a
life-or-death interview with a queen in mind. True, Gerda does not personally
confront the Snow Queen who, she finds on arrival, has gone off to whitewash
her black cauldrons, that is to say, put snow and ice on the tops of those fiercely
active volcanoes, Etna and Vesuvius. But she nevertheless effects an entrance
into her palace where everything and everybody, including Kay himself, are in
her terrible thrall. Like Jeanie, Gerda triumphs, not least through her own
artlessness (as the Finn Woman had predicted she would) and is rewarded by
being – more happily than Jeanie, and certainly more permanently – united
with the individual for whom she has performed at personal risk so great a feat.

In 'The Snow Queen' – with the sole exception of the reindeer – moral firm-
ness is assigned only to females, to Gerda pre-eminently, but also to
Grandmother, the Lapp Woman and the Finn Woman, even though their great
adversary is also female. Andersen's story is often praised for having given to a
female character the heroic, questing, exacting role generally ascribed to a
male, and among works which would attract a readership of children is often,
legitimately, considered ground-breaking. But Scott's *The Heart of Midlothian*
should be given its full due in this context; here also the woman is depicted as
of infinitely greater moral fibre than any man, even her lover and husband, the
schoolteacher-cleric, Reuben Butler. And there is one section of Gerda's travels
– told in the Fifth Story, and to be dealt with in due course – which bears so
close a relationship to a major strand of Scott's narrative connected with Jeanie
as to place Andersen's remembrance of the 1818 novel beyond all doubt.

Gerda has, however, one other putative predecessor: the heroine of the
Asbjørnsen and Moe's 'East of the Sun and West of the Moon' already
mentioned.[104] But that girl has none of Gerda's composure or sagacity. She
commits two foolish and consequential blunders which amount to grave failures in both understanding and obedience. Also she falls almost instantly in
love with the man (a prince) who at night emerges from the bear disguise cast
on him by his wicked stepmother's magic; there is nothing whatsoever of
Gerda's long, loving knowledge of him whom she is journeying towards. This
Norwegian quest – to the castle of the prince's stepmother lying 'east of the sun
and west of the moon', and home to the long-nosed princess he will otherwise
be forced to marry – is therefore conducted from Eros rather than (Gerda's)
Agape. But she does possess the fortitude we will admire in Andersen's heroine

as she refuses to give up her quest, and turns to the very elements themselves, the Four Winds, to assist her to her goal.

The Third Story of 'The Snow Queen' – 'Blomster-Haven hos Konen, som kunde Trolddom'[105] 'The Flower-Garden of the Woman Who Knows Magic' – and the Fourth Story – 'Prins og Prinsesse',[106] 'Prince and Princess' – break, or at any rate temporarily dissipate, the tension created by Gerda's determination to find her missing loved one, which links her to the girl of the Norwegian tale. Further both are intricately worked, containing so much seemingly autono mous life as to give us an at first somewhat irksome sense of stasis; we have come no nearer Kay and the eponymous Queen, we may feel. But their effect is literary mimesis of what is happening to the heroine herself. She too, like the reader, is being held up, coming surprisingly close to forgetting her objective. Like the unconscious resentment of sacrifice expressed in the persistence of the red shoes, this procrastination, not identified by her as such, is a psychologi- cally inevitable phase of the carrying out of a difficult task. And Andersen makes us appreciate why. Knowing that its successful accomplishment will bring us the only earthly happiness important to us (in this case reunion with a restored Kay), we fear disappointment, and, worse, failure. Postponement, or even abandonment, deflects these disagreeable emotions. Also the acceptance of any challenge is daunting because its very singleness means having to forgo other demands in our lives – springing from different areas of our selves. The comfort of the old woman's home, the wonderful talking flowers in her garden with all their fabular associations, have psychic appeal to Gerda, as do, in the Fourth Story, the newly married prince and princess in their castle.

We can also account for these stopping-places in the narrative topographi- cally. The old woman's garden and the royal castle belong to the temperate zone, in which Denmark lies. We have to reach Latitude 65 to enter uncompro- misingly Northern territory; the Arctic Circle lies between Latitudes 66 and 67 (cutting through Norway, Sweden and Finland), with trees and the usual iden- tifiable flowers becoming sparse, and eventually vanishing. In this country's taiga and tundra there are no farmhouses or manors, only the encampments of semi-nomads or crude accommodation for workers. The old woman herself is, we learn, a basically benevolent witch, antithesis to the Snow Queen in that she is kindly, indeed motherly in her ways, presiding over fecundity – in her garden grow flowers of every climate and season – but she is also an analogue for her, deliberately exercising her powers of control over Gerda just as the title-figure has over Kay, whose recent history she first learns, then misinter- prets in order to keep the girl with her. She even, unsuccessfully, conceals her roses for these are, in popular belief, Christ's flowers, associated with the pious childhood of Gerda and Kay with Grandmother (who provides another point of comparison; the kindness of the flower garden woman is selfish, the other selfless).

Wolfgang Lederer's study of 'The Snow Queen' is percipient on the subject of Gerda's dalliance, though he does somewhat overstate his case. Gerda, after hearing from the roses whose reappearance her warm tears have brought about that Kay is still alive, questions a selection of flowers in the hope of learning where he might be. She listens to stories, but about themselves not the boy, from a Tiger Lily, a Morning Glory (or Trumpet Flower), a Daisy, some Hyacinths, a Buttercup, a Narcissus. Says Lederer '. . . these stories are not interesting. They are overly sickly and sticky; they are kitsch . . . . They are full of *Weltschmerz* and totally lacking in fulfillment. The Narcissus is, appropriately, altogether narcissistic. All this seems like dime-store fiction or true confessions stuff for pulp magazines; we would be tempted to say it is unworthy of Andersen. But we would be wrong. These are exactly the kinds of dreams and stories best suited to the needs and fears of adolescent girls who are so often bewildered by their own budding sexuality and afraid of the world.'[107]

One should qualify this honest, sensible approach by admitting that the stories are only 'not interesting' in the context of the direct narrative advancement so compelling in the rest of the work; like free-standing prisms they also take in and give back light from beyond their fixed positions in the garden. Massengale in his essay reminds us that Andersen himself valued them so highly that he wanted the printer to indent the relevant passages and set them in a different type.[108] His wish was not followed, but it does show that their author saw them as prose-poems whose treatments of yearning and frustration were to be taken seriously. They also constitute a take on the Language of Flowers so popular among girls and women of the more affluent class from the 1820s to the 1880s (with French taste a little in advance of that first date);[109] craftily made-up bouquets and table decorations connoted human emotional conditions. Thus in the stereotypes of this language the Tiger Lily stands for wealth and pride, the Morning Glory for love-in-vain, the Daisy innocence, the beauty of which its possessor is unaware, the Hyacinths for playfulness, the Buttercup for childishness, endurance and riches (this flower brings Grandmother back to Gerda's mind – riches because her kind heart is golden!) and the Narcissus for self-preoccupation and unrequited love.

It is the Narcissus's encouragement to concentrate above all else on one's self that galvanises Gerda into finally exchanging the artifices of the garden for true Nature, and returning (barefoot) into the world which, somewhere or other, contains a still living Kay. Summer, she finds, has now turned to autumn, a Danish or Southern Swedish autumn of mists, yellowing willow leaves and blackthorn with sloes. We can, I think, infer that quite some time passes between the end of the Third Story and the Fourth, for in its first sentence, telling of Gerda's encounter with the helpful crow, the Fourth informs us that snow is on the ground; it must therefore be early winter now. The word 'igjen' 'again' in its opening sentence, 'Gerda maatte igjen hvile sig,'[110] 'Gerda had to rest again', does not necessarily imply that this pause followed on from the one she made after running out through the old lady's garden gate. In truth the timescale of the story is (intentionally) not rendered easy for us, because Andersen makes us pass through psychic as well as sun-time, in the same way that he asks us to travel through psychic as well as geographical territory – and besides, in both categories, including this interim sequence here, he also gives us amalgamations of the two.

Gerda visits the castle in the Fourth Story only because she is convinced by the crow's descriptions that the prince who won the princess through his clever liveliness must be none other than Kay. Wasn't he wearing for the fateful test-interview those new boots she so well remembered creaking? Because of her hopeful belief in this, she is perfectly happy to examine the young man in his bed, one built to resemble a scarlet lily and of a pair with his princess's (whose bed looks like a *white* lily). Lederer's thesis that these two chapters constitute an adolescent girl's awakening to sexuality is surely vindicated by these pages.[111] Gerda is not ready – either in mind or body – for any real consummation, even with a dream-Kay, hence her inability actually to see the bridal pair lying together in the same bed. Yet, even after she has convinced herself that Kay is not the prince, she responds warmly to the couple (even to the point of accepting the groom's offer that she get into his luxurious bed once he himself has vacated it!) as she does to another betrothed pair, for her friendly crow has a domesticated fiancée. ' "Hvor dog Mennesker og Dyr ere gode," '[112] she exclaims, ' "How good people and animals are!" ' Someone with natural virtue sees virtues in others, and receives goodness from them in turn. The prince and princess give her not only boots, mittens and new clothes for the long journey north, for this has to be Kay's direction, but also a carriage to ride in; leave-takings are warm and a little sad, because Gerda feels affection for her helpers, particularly the crows, as will be evident in a moving episode towards the close of the tale. . . . How long does Gerda travel in the carriage before the ambush by robbers? Again this is not clear. The concise, undecorated style of narration traditional to fairy tales employed here suits Andersen's purpose well. It could have happened very soon after the departure from the castle, or after several days (for the carriage is lined with delicious eatables).

Scott's Jeanie Deans, a few days after she has left Edinburgh on her mission to London to save her sister, and at this stage on foot, is accosted towards evening by two thugs who demand 'Your money, my precious, or your life!'[113] Rather than rob her there and then, they lead her off to a hidey-hole of their own, a barn half an hour away from the road, where 'An old woman, who was preparing food by the assistance of a stifling fire of lighted charcoal, asks them, in the name of the devil, what they brought the wench there for, and why they did not strip her and turn her abroad on the common?' The men, rather kinder by temperament for all their lawlessness, call the 'old hag' Mother Blood, not inappropriately for she is armed with a knife which she darts at one of them 'with the vengeful dexterity of a wild Indian', and then throws at him. As difficult to handle is this woman's daughter, who speaks of 'my auld acquaintance the deil'. This turns out, to Jeanie's consternation, to be none other than the notorious Edinburgh criminal's moll, Madge Wildfire; she had had sexual relations with the father of Effie Deans's child, and almost certainly herself had a child (then disposed of) by him. Madge recognises Jeanie. ' "Douce Davie Deans, the auld doited whig body's daughter, in a gipsy's barn, and the night setting in; this is a sight for sair een! – Eh, sirs, the falling off o' the godly! – and the t'other sister's in the tollbooth at Edinburgh! I am very sorry for her, for my share – it's my mother wusses ill to her, and no me – though maybe I hae as muckle cause." ' After further aggression from Meg Murdockson, her deranged mother, Madge, herself far from stable, but greatly preferable to her, proceeds to drag 'Jeanie along with her into a sort of recess, partitioned off from the rest of the barn, and filled with straw, from which it appeared that it was intended for the purpose of slumber.' But Madge remarks, without real irony: ' "Now, saw ye e'er in your life. . . sae dainty a chamber of deas? See as the moon shines down sae caller on the fresh strae! There's no a pleasanter cell in Bedlam, for as braw a place as it is on the outside." ' While Jeanie is alarmed at her unexpected new surroundings, she does in fact have a good night's sleep, and in the morning – partly to spite the others in the gang, and her old hate-ridden mother – Madge is kind enough to escort Jeanie outside into liberty. ' "Did ye never read the Pilgrim's Progress? And you shall be the woman Christiana, and I will be the maiden Mercy . . . ." '

When the robbers fall on Gerda's carriage, they seize the horses and kill the postilions and coachman; Gerda herself they hoist out to meet 'den gamle Røverkjelling',[114] 'the old robber woman', who has a long beard, and eyebrows hanging over her eyes. Impressed by Gerda's plumpness, she exclaims ' "hvor hun skal smage" ', ' "how tasty she'll be!" ' 'og saa trak hun sin blanke Kniv ud og den skinnede, saa det var grueligt', 'and then she drew out her bright knife and it shone so that it looked [was] dreadful'. But her daughter, 'den lille Røverpige', 'the little robber girl', who is both wild and fearless, prevents her using the cruel implement, partly because she wants to appropriate Gerda's carriage. Gerda has no option but to clamber into this with her, but, as Wolfgang Lederer observes,[115] her reluctant acceptance of the girl's semi-erotic responses to her marks a further phase of her sexual maturation. Though capable of rough tenderness the robber girl is emotionally inconsistent, undependable;

she won't let the other gang members or her mother get angry with Gerda and kill her; on the other hand, if Gerda annoys her, she might herself do this.

That night, after drinking soup made in a huge cauldron, the two sleep together in the robber girl's uncomfortable quarters in the robbers' hideout, in a corner strewn with straw and bedding, and with a hundred or so pigeons (both wood pigeons and tame ones) on perches above their heads, and tethered to the wall, her beloved reindeer, Bæ. Her treatment of this animal is only too characteristic of her uncontrolled, uncivilised nature; every night she tickles him with the knife of which he is understandably terrified, and delights in the teasing. The knife itself she always sleeps with, because, after all, you never know what may happen!

But Gerda's story of Kay and his capture by the Snow Queen has appealed to the other girl's imagination. When the wood pigeons inform her they saw Kay riding in the Snow Queen's sleigh over this very land, and the reindeer attests to the likelihood of this because he knows that the Queen's summer quarters lies within the Lapp domain, she decides to help her herself (even while warning her that, if she doesn't lie still, she will stick her knife into her). Consequently she drugs her mother with alcohol, gives Gerda back her boots though not her mittens (substituting the old robber woman's for these), and unties the rope tying the reindeer to his corner. This enables the animal to carry Gerda through those territories his kind (including eminently himself) know uniquely well, all the way to her goal. The robbers' den must therefore lie to the south of Lapland, but be made up of forest and marsh that will shade into its landscape – perhaps some Swedish province like Gästrikland or Hälsingland[116] – and when he arrives in country where the Northern Lights (Aurora Borealis) are visible,[117] those impressive displays in the ionosphere associated with the Arctic Circle and beyond, the reindeer is understandably very happy.

> 'Der er mine gamle Nordlys!' sagde Rensdyret, 'see, hvor de lyse!' og saa løb det endnu mere afsted, Nat og Dag; Brødene bleve spiist, Skinken med og saa vare de i Lapland.[118]
>
> 'There are my old Northern Lights!' said the reindeer, 'look, how they shine!' And then he galloped along still faster, night and day; the loaves were eaten up, the ham too and then they were in Lapland.

The close kinship between the hijackings of Jeanie Deans and Gerda and between the behaviour of Madge Wildfire to the first and the little robber girl to the second will now be quite evident. One feels, however, that the marked similarity in *tone* of these chapters must also be stressed: their combination of somewhat ghoulish humour with a haunting appreciation of the feelings of total outsiders to society. And in this last lies the reason for this kinship, for why

Andersen made such easily discernible use of Scott's novel. The character of Madge Wildfire had already inspired Andersen in 'The Apparition at Palnatoke's Grave' (with the heroine's child-killing mother, Mad Stine of Broby) in his self-published *Youthful Attempts* (1822),[119] though the overwhelming majority of readers of 'The Snow Queen' would not have known this work. But they probably knew – or deduced – that Andersen's high regard for *The Heart of Midlothian* sprang from his gratitude to Scott for his emotionally honest and unshrinking depictions of the humbler sections of society, not merely the badly-off but the marginalised, the helpless, the incapacitated, the criminal. If Gerda's rescue journey is also a pilgrimage towards a full, admirable adulthood, it would have been incomplete without sympathetic experience of the lives of just such persons as these, incurring gratitude and affection not censure and judgement; following, in other words, the example of Christ himself. Gerda has all Jeanie's Elder Son unyielding righteousness, but, unlike that parable figure and to a greater degree than Jeanie herself, she can accommodate the existences and even the personalities of those of less firm clay than herself, of those congenitally inclined to err. These were, after all, to be abundantly found in the milieu, in fact the very family, in which Andersen spent his earliest and most formative years.

Just as Madge Wildfire helped Jeanie back to the freedom of the road to London, so the little robber-girl turns out to be the greatest facilitator of Gerda's travels: the gift of the reindeer ensures rapid and expert coverage of the vast distance between the felons' den and the very precincts of the Snow Queen's palace. Andersen's treatment of the reindeer is of great cultural perception. That the robber girl is as fond of the animal as she declares we can believe, but what to make of her tormenting play with the knife every night?

Here, I think, Andersen has interestingly anticipated the ambivalent attitude of the (principally Sami) reindeer herders themselves to the beasts whose migrations they follow. They tend them unflaggingly, they are intimately knowledgeable about them in all seasons, at all stages, in sickness and in health, they depend on them for milk, and after their deaths, for multi-purpose hides and hair. They may even love them. Yet they also eat their flesh, which means killing them – and this, among nomads, would mean using the knife. Thus there is regular betrayal of built-up trust, a regular infliction by the herders of uncertainty and terror on the reindeer that consorts ill with all the attention given them and their inclusion in belief-systems that go beyond earthly existence. (In fact the Sami accord them a divine protector of their own: Čoarveradien, the Mistress of the Horns.)[120] Thus the robber girl when producing the knife every night and letting it slide along the animal's throat is in, one sense, being more honest, less hypocritical than her more mentally balanced fellows. In our own times the Norwegian Sami, Nils-Aslak Valkeapää (born 1943)[121] is outstanding as interpreter/celebrant in both graphic arts and poetry of Sami traditional life, the greatest exponent of the *yoik*, the unaccompanied song through which for centuries religious myths, legends and historical tales have been presented. Yet, for all his profound feeling of commonalty with his people and respect for their mores, he found himself unable to commit such a turning against a living creature once held in affection as they are prepared to perpetrate. He writes in his moving long poem, *The Sun, My Father* (1988), 'I was expected to/I ought to/kill/ time stopped/my heart pounded/reached my ears/ blood rushed in my head/I saw the eyes of the young female reindeer, in her eyes/tears/or in my eyes. . . . in my eyes fog/in my mind night'.[122]

Only a reindeer, friendly, brave, knowledgeable, efficient, could have carried Gerda over this land still in thrall to winter. Once again Andersen displays his deep understanding of natural history. In the bitter cold the reindeer manages to keep Gerda warm, because he can keep his own body warm: bones within his nostrils increase his body heat before it reaches the lungs. He can root out carbohydrate-containing lichens from the most unpromising places, and move over huge distances fast, the pads of his hooves contracting so they get a grip on frozen or stony ground, making a contemporary TV naturalist liken them to snowshoes.

Capable of speech, Andersen's reindeer shows both 'Lappekonen' and 'Finnekonen' knowledge of the lore which guides lives in such remote habitats and in which he and his kind have a firm part to play. He asks the Finn Woman if she might not influence the winds, knowing that she has the magic to do so. In Sami tradition, the God of the Winds is Bieggolmmái. 'With his shovel, he could force the wind out of its cave, and, with his club, force it back in again. Because of the high north's harsh climate, keeping in good standing with Bieggolmmái was extremely important.'[123] In the Finnish tradition the winds have a goddess, Tuulikki,[124] daughter of Tapio, overlord God of the Forests. Permission has to be obtained from the invariably occluded Tuulikki, who is capable of lifting up without strain any object regardless of its weight, before entering any particular tract of forest. But what Andersen puts into the mouth of the reindeer has the authentic mythological ring, probably because, as Maria Tatar points out, it has quite marked affinities with the central events of 'East of the Sun and West of the Moon',[125] despite the distinct differences between the two heroines. The Finn Woman, the reindeer informs us, can tie the four winds of the world together; thus a sailor unties one of these knots and gets a favourable wind, unties the second and a gale results, undoes the third and the fourth and releases such a storm that it flattens a forest. In Asbjørnsen and Moe the heroine obtains help first from the East Wind, then the West and next the South. But it is the North Wind who has most force and is therefore of most assistance:

Early next morning the North Wind called her, and then he puffed himself out and made himself so big and strong that he was terrible to look at. Away they went, high up through the air at such a fearful speed, as if they were going to the end of the world.[126]

In fact, as we have already seen, the Finn Woman refuses Gerda this kind of 'Magt', for the excellent reason, surely belonging to the explanations of art- rather than folk-literature, that she has already *within* her what can serve her best. And in the event it is a natural living being, a semi-domesticated animal, speedy and lovable, who will take the North Wind's part, transport Gerda to the Finnmark palace, and deposit her at its intimidating threshold.

The snowflakes that fly at her as she stands quite alone in the wilderness are an advance guard of the terrible palace, but she defeats them by praying. Kay, by contrast, as he flew in the face of the snow on the sledge he'd tied to the Queen's, had been able to remember no prayers, only his multiplication tables. The castle walls are built of snowdrifts, the doors and windows of winds, there are over a hundred vast rooms, lit by the Northern Lights. Nothing lovable or enjoyable is to be found here; in the middle of the Queen's own apartment is a vast frozen lake in the exact centre of which the Queen would sit. This is 'Forstandens Speil', the Intellect's Mirror,[127] now broken up into many, many pieces, unique, the best mirror in the whole world – but to readers it inevitably suggests that diabolical mirror also broken into pieces we encountered in the First Story, and Kay is, of course, the victim of both. For the boy into whose eye and heart fragments from the first mirror fell is now, in solitude, trying to arrange those into which the second has been cracked; he is playing 'Forstands Iisspillet', 'Intellect's Ice-game', the object of which is to form the word 'EVIGHEDEN' (ETERNITY). The Queen has offered him a reward, the whole world and a pair of skates, but he cannot work the puzzle out.

No scriptural picture of desolation equals this; it is a terrifyingly potent image of a world from which affection, love, sensibility, the kindly dealings of humans and animals one with another are utterly banished, and the intellect is in sole control, intensified but also reduced to frozen immobility. But in viewing it in terms of the spirit – which needs growth and warmth in all uses of the term – we should not forget that, however much fantasy has gone into the description of the palace itself, its components are real enough. Go to Finnmark or Svalbard (or down south to Antarctica, if you prefer) and you will encounter – with the greatest difficulty, and needing the most elaborate man- made protection – a mineral world, iced over and snowed up, and yet – as we are now peculiarly aware, with the threat of global warming even more urgent than previously estimated – absolutely vital to us and serving planetary laws without which we cannot survive. The Snow Queen's palace and the Arctic materials are geographically verifiable. We cannot, we must not forget them – and yet we cannot survive among them.

Like all animals! Even the reindeer, more adaptable to taiga and tundra than almost any other, needs the kindness of concealed plants and of his human minders – and, for comfort and perpetuation alike, of other members of his own kind. It is a wonderful detail that after Gerda and Kay have left the enormous palace of the Queen, hand in hand, they meet the reindeer who has now brought along his mate who can give them both warm milk to drink. Kindness, pleasant dealings one with another, not excluding the erotic – animals and humans alike require these. Both the intellect – to which Andersen (who kept up with trends in science, the arts and thought, even including the writings of his one-time mocking critic, Kierkegaard) was most certainly a friend – and the cruder approach to sex also so often favoured by the male are insufficient yardsticks for life, appealing though they were to Kay on the threshold of manhood. But now thanks to Gerda the youth's values – and his very existence – will serve deeper forces, those more freely expressed in the world below the Arctic regions.

The comparative speed of Gerda's release of Kay – from the narratalogical point of view – is a masterstroke, and surely corresponds to experiential truth: often the most decisive and consequential acts or episodes of our lives take up astonishingly little clock time. It is by the other time, *psychic* time they have to be measured. Gerda only has to weep with emotional relief at seeing Kay again and the tears go to his heart and melt the lump of ice there. She has only to sing Brorson's hymn and Kay himself cries too, and the devilish glass falls out of his eye. And soon the lumps of ice in the shattered Intellect's Mirror are dancing in joy and forming the word EVIGHEDEN of their own accord.

Just how much time (of either kind) has all this occupied? We cannot know precisely; Andersen does not wish exact knowledge to be ours now, it would vitiate the profound beauty of his story's close, which is more akin to that of Shakespeare's *The Winter's Tale* or *The Tempest* than to those of most nineteenth-century prose works. The fairy tale, as opposed to the novelistic, medium was indispensable to his creative purposes here. It was the beginning of spring when Gerda appreciated that Kay (who had left his home in the winter) was still alive; spring is burgeoning anew when she makes the homeward journey in Kay's loving company. But since we bade goodbye to them – not so long ago, it seems – the kindly crow, we learn, has died, and his domesticated partner wears a black mourning ribbon round her leg; the reindeer has a lactating mate; the Robber Girl now rides a magnificent steed that was once harnessed to the carriage given Gerda by the prince and princess. The royal couple themselves have gone travelling in foreign countries. And – the biggest change of all – when Kay and Gerda arrive back at the house which has been their home and where Grandmother lives, 'de vare blevne voxne Mennesker',[128] 'they had become grown-up human beings'. Grandmother is sitting in Guds klare Solskin', 'in God's sunshine' as though waiting for them, and reads to them: 'Except ye become as little children, ye shall not enter into the Kingdom of Heaven' (Matthew 18: 3). To the pair it is as if the icy thrall of the Snow Queen had never been exerted. Gazing into each other's eyes, they appreciate the truth of Brorson's hymn about the Christ Child. They are at once grown-up and children, adult now in body, but 'Børn i Hjertet', 'children in heart'.

Massengale thinks that up in the Finnmark fastness, Gerda released Kay with her entire body, and that these young people, still innocent in heart, have achieved love in the adult sense, with their new sexuality.[129] This does not mean – as indeed it never should – any contradiction of Gospel Christianity. It is a deeply appealing idea, but I think it highly unlikely that Andersen, at least in the conscious quarters of his mind, could have ever entertained it. There is little evidence that he did not profoundly respect marriage, even though his fiction presents it comparatively seldom. For Ejnar Stig Askgaard in his brilliant essay, the fruit of so much learning and thought,[130] Kay and Gerda have accomplished what Andersen in his 1830 university thesis believed about the relationship of myth and culture in human civilisation. Growing up in Grandmother's monotheistic culture (perhaps 'Christocentric' is a better word), they have to pass through its fragmentation – represented not only by the Snow Queen herself and her magic, but by the successive stages of Gerda's journey, embodiments, all of them, of myths and legends – only to return, and with new understanding, to that same virtue-promoting monotheism. It is a most convincing reading, though one has to add that it is the very syncretism of 'The Snow Queen' and its acceptance throughout its rich course of many different mores and *Weltanschauungen* that have earned it its extraordinary and deserved pre-eminence among nineteenth-century works of the imagination.

For me I find the need to emphasise how Andersen chose to leave readers of this complex, many-layered and many-levelled story, with the simple words of the second half of its final sentence: 'og det var Sommer, den varme, velsignede Sommer.'[131] 'and it was summer, warm blessed summer'. We are back in Denmark, the wiser for travels to regions that belong not to dream but to reality, and the weather here is at its most benign. If we treasure what we have and all that it means, with purity of heart, we will yet be able to accept, to incorporate into our value-systems, so much that is disconcertingly different, even threatening or dangerous. Kay, a conventional enough, if very intelligent, male, and Gerda, a female – like Scott's Jeanie – remarkable for her (nonetheless characteristically feminine) moral strength are doing exactly this, and we should follow their example.

1

'Skyggen' ('The Shadow')

Andersen began 'The Shadow', his darkest and most profoundly autobiographical tale, in Naples on the evening of 9 June 1846.[132] Naples was a city he associated with lively street life and attendant sensuality, his own and other people's. His diary entries for his first ever stay there some twelve years earlier (February/ March 1834)[133] made this candidly plain, recording how the city's climate was affecting his blood and how, with effort and possibly reluctance too, he had resisted all its many temptations, as his companion, Henrik Hertz had *not*. Andersen's diary for June 1846 corresponds so closely with his new story's first pages that we cannot doubt Naples as the setting. The heat is appalling, streets are oppressively noisy, and in the house opposite someone 'practises figured bass or tunes piano'. Yet both the emotional pain at the centre of the story and its all-dominant conceit go back to Andersen's visit to Berlin in June 1831. Indeed, as already adumbrated, 'The Shadow'– its title echoing that of his travelogue, *Shadow Pictures* – is arguably the greatest literary fruit of Andersen's visit to Germany; and for that matter, in its power and refinement of artistry, a nonpareil even in an *oeuvre* as varied and rich as his.

During his stay in Naples Andersen was also at work on his autobiography, for which he had signed a contract with his German publisher Lorck on 19 February.[134] What a lot he had to feel proud of from these recent years! In the year (1844) which ended with the publication of 'The Snow Queen' on 21 December he had made a triumphant visit to Germany (May to August) enjoying social life with such illustrious individuals as the Grand Duke and Duchess of Weimar, Carl Maria von Weber, Robert Schumann and (in Berlin) Jacob Grimm. (He was to see both Grimm brothers for a longer period in December 1845, learning of Wilhelm Grimm's particular admiration for 'The Fir Tree'.)[135] In August/September 1844 he was the holiday guest on Føhr of Queen Caroline Amalie and Christian VIII (who would raise his annuity the following year).[136] He read fairy tales aloud to the royal couple, and on 5 September celebrated the 25th anniversary of his arrival as a hopeful, ingenuous, ambitious youth in Copenhagen from Odense. The year 1845 brought him news of translations into English by Mary Howitt,[137] a major step in his international reputation, while in September his close friendship with the great, already widely celebrated singer, Jenny Lind (1820–87)[138] took off. When during the great European tour on which he embarked in November that year, he stayed in Berlin, he spent a good deal of time with Jenny, at once enamoured and appreciating his own ultimate emotional distance from her, happy at her kindnesses but hurt at her perceived indifference and downcast at her honest admissions that her feelings for him were sisterly only. When he sat down in Naples to get on with his memoirs for Lorck, he did so as one who had to his credit four books of poems (with another imminent at the end of the year); a poetry anthology under his editorship; sixteen works for stage, including adaptations of others' works, and libretti, one of these being the eventually record-breaking *Liden Kirsten* (*Little Kirsten*),[139] put on the month before, May 1846; two substantial travelogues; three widely read novels – and over forty stories. However when he sat down to write 'The Shadow' he was creating a tale of 'et meget godt Hjerte, og særdeles mild og venlig',[140] 'a very good-hearted [man], and always gentle and friendly', who, though successful, indeed famous, through his own exertions and unswerving fidelity to his own principles, undergoes ever-increasing and more cruel humiliations. These climax first in his very selfhood being rejected, then in his life being taken from him.

Remembering his very first excursion out of Denmark in the light of all that he had accomplished since those months of 1831, Andersen could not but reflect further and more deeply on that cruel snub administered him by the individual still more important to him than any other, Edvard Collin, and on the kindly acceptance by him as a fellow writer by Adelbert von Chamisso. So he decided to use the prose masterpiece of the latter – but in a free, idiosyncratic way – to express in succinct literary form his still dormant outrage at the former.

In Andersen's story a young scholar, staying in a southern city, encourages his shadow to investigate the mysterious but inaccessible apartment opposite his own, glimpses of life in which, including a beautiful girl, fascinate him. In carrying out his wish, his shadow disappears, a deficiency the scholar doesn't at first even notice. After eight days he starts growing another one. On his return home the scholar builds up a reputation for his writings about the true, the good and the beautiful. Then, after many years, to his amazement he receives a visit from his former shadow, now outwardly human.

The scholar asks the shadow what he found in that seemingly empty apartment long ago. Poetry itself, is the reply, after which he discovered his own human nature, a mixed experience, involving a good deal of unpleasantness. But it also enabled the shadow to prosper and live well among his fellow beings.

Many more years pass, during which the scholar's fortunes decline. Nobody now wants to read about the true, the good and the beautiful. He has become ill, lost weight. The shadow on the contrary has gained weight, and a great deal of money as well. He now offers to take the scholar on holiday to a spa; the latter accepts. They will travel, says the shadow, as friends, but in truth – 'Skyggen var da Herre, og Herren var da Skygge',[141] 'the shadow was then master, and the master was then shadow'. The scholar, in his innocence, does not properly appreciate this.

At the spa a foreign princess is staying who notices that the shadow-turned-master, to whom she is drawn, casts no shadow of his own. She tells him this, to get the diabolically ingenious reply that he *does* indeed have a shadow, a most unusual one, that looks exactly like a human being; so saying, he indicates his former master now 'shadowing' him. Later the pair travels to the princess's own country. Here the shadow will marry the young woman, but before he does so, he gives the scholar an ultimatum. He will pay him in perpetuity a handsome salary, provided he never admits to being – or ever having been – human. And once a year, on a public balcony, he must lie down at his present master's feet – just as any ordinary shadow would.

This is too much even for the already humbled scholar, who threatens to expose the shadow. But here he makes his gravest mistake. The shadow sees to his arrest and imprisonment. His own grand wedding to the princess follows, but 'Den lærde Mand hørte ikke noget til alt det, for ham havde de taget Livet af –'[142] 'The learned man heard nothing about it all, because they had taken his life from him –'

The departures here from Chamisso's widely known novella[143] point to the essential great differences, in both intention and in overall effect, between the two works. Peter Schlemihl parts with his shadow – to the thin, shadowless Man in Grey, who is the devil – with extreme reluctance, and is sad at its absence. He has his consolations, of course: Fortunatus's Purse from which he delightedly benefits (Andersen's scholar by contrast is unmaterialistic), and his loyal servant, Bendel (though he is not to stay the course). Bendel's unflaggingly ingenious ability to keep the world from seeing what has happened to Peter is, however, parodied in Andersen, since public appearance is what the shadow-turned-master forces from his former owner both in the spa and in the princess's country. Again Chamisso's Peter is enamoured of a girl Mina, whereas the scholar, unable to contact the apparition in the apartment opposite, is curious about, but never develops real feelings for, the other sex. To his chagrin Peter's second and dishonest servant marries Mina, but this episode *does* find its way into 'The Shadow', with the eponymous figure's marriage. The hero is not to be dispatched in Chamisso's story, as he is in Andersen's; on the contrary he goes on to lead the peripatetic life of a naturalist, not dissimilar to the many productive years his creator had spent as this. *Peter Schlemihl* is ultimately a blithe work; 'The Shadow' is nothing of the sort.

Andersen converts Chamisso's story, then, into his belated reckoning with Edvard Collin and his letter of refusal, without flinching from his own agony and resentment of the other's disregard of his feelings. Even more than *O.T.*, and the more effectively so for being such a short, concentrated artefact, is 'The Shadow' a history of the second person singular. This provides a paradigm for the whole subject of social orders, their seeming fixedness, the problems – at all stages – of pain in their interrelations, the possibilities of their loosening or even breaking up, and even of their transcendence. There is an ontological dimension to all this. For the situation in which the central pair is initially placed is a *donnée* of earthly existence itself for both parties – as drily witty authorial turns of phrase emphasise; the shadow's movements on the house wall opposite repeat his owner's, 'for det gør den' ('because that's what it does').[144]

The scholar calls his shadow 'Du' when ordering him inside the intriguing apartment opposite, the correct form for lifelong companions (which one's shadow is!), or addressing one's own self (which surely includes one's shadow). The formal 'De' would be unthinkable in these cases. But 'Du' is also for children, animals, and, in Andersen's own times, servants; indeed to all perceived inferiors of the speaker. So, is the scholar asking his shadow to go through the balcony door as a mate, an intimate, or as one of the lower orders who simply has to do what is asked of him? Or (the more troubling possibility) is there a fusion – *con*fusion – of the two?

When, all those years later, the shadow returns and the scholar wants to find out, at long last, what lay over there in the house across the street, the shadow refuses to tell him unless the informal 'Du' is dropped for the formal form 'De'. Isn't he now a mature, prosperous man who should be addressed like one? Fair enough, the scholar thinks, and apologises for his tactlessness and agrees. The two are therefore now on formal terms, the same terms that Edvard Collin and Hans Christian Andersen were always to be, despite so many shared experiences.

Years later, however, when the scholar in decline accepts the shadow's offer to take him to the spa, they are to travel, he is explicitly assured, as friends. Yet Andersen prepares us for the blow to come by that all-important authorial statement which can be read as the story's kernel: 'Og saa reiste de; Skyggen var da Herre, og Herren var da Skygge. . .'[145] 'And so they travelled; the shadow was then master, and the master was shadow.' It is in language like this that the biblical parable nature of the tale is most apparent; the significant events and their consequences are clear to God, and exemplarily so to us, but not at all to the protagonist. Deceived by the bonhomie that prevails during their journeys, with the two of them continually together, the scholar proposes they use 'Du' to one another: 'skulle vi saa ikke drikke Duus, det er dog mere fortroligt.'[146] 'Shall we not say "Du", it is much more friendly.'

He surely never envisaged any reply other than an affirmative. It is not what he gets, however. The shadow refuses his request. It's a sensible enough one to have made, he concedes, so he will give a candid answer. Some people feel nauseous when touching grey (wrapping) paper, others can't bear hearing a nail scrape across a pane of glass. Well, somebody calling him 'Du' is painful in just that kind of way! The echo of Edvard Collin is loud and unmistakable, and, of course, absolutely deliberate. The perpetrator of the original snub would undoubtedly read the story – though it didn't make him relent over this protocol. But, continues the shadow, he'd be perfectly happy to meet the scholar halfway, and call *him* 'Du' (which so far he hasn't done!)

'Og sa sagde Skyggen Du til sin forrige Herre.'[147] 'And so the shadow said "Du" to his former master.'

The relations of master and servant, of superiors and inferiors are at the centre of the tale, and it's very important that we pay close attention to the master-figure, the scholar who, for obvious reasons, must be some kind of analogue to the author. As concise and dense as a poem, the story demands close textual examination.

It opens with a wry yet grave reminder: 'I de hede Lande, der kan rigtignok Solen brænde!'[148] 'In the hot countries the sun can really burn!' Andersen maintains this *faux naïf* note for the rest of the paragraph, to stress the innocence (or ignorance) of his central figure: a young 'lærd Mand',[149] 'learned man' (sometimes baldly 'den Fremmede', the 'stranger' or 'the foreigner') from the north, 'fra de kolde' and 'fra de kolde Lande', 'from the cold' and 'from the cold countries'. The scholar may want to behave 'ligesom derhjemme', 'as if he were at home', but, exhausted by the sun's heat, and with his very shadow shrinking, he is unable to do this, and perforce remains inside most of the day.

We can envisage here Andersen's fellow Scandinavian artist friends, particularly those of his 1834 Italian visit, who, in homage to Bertel Thorvaldsen, and guided also by Goethe's *Italienische Reise* (1816–17: *Italian Journey*), took themselves to Italy for the sake of brighter light and ampler life. But so often they passed their time, lounging about together, as they do in that famous painting of them all from 1837, by a portraitist of Andersen himself, Constantin Hansen (1804–80), *Et Selskab af danske Kunstere i Rom (A Company of Danish Artists in Rome)*,[150] which we looked at in Chapter 7. We feel from this work that, however ardently these Northern Europeans relish the Southern atmosphere, they are clearly strangers in this environment, behaving neither like their normal selves nor like native citizens.

After dark, his day of enforced lassitude over, our young scholar sits out on his balcony, with the light burning in the room behind him. This means that his shadow falls on the balcony of the house directly opposite. Now the street below becomes animated – cobblers and tailors ply their trades, tables and chairs are put out into the street for meals al fresco, people talk and sing, street urchins let off fireworks, even funeral possessions pass by far more inclusively public than in the North: 'jo, der var rigtig nok levende nede i Gaden',[151] 'yes, it was really lively down in the street'. But, significantly, the scholar never descends to participate in any of this, nor even seems *tempted* to do so. Andersen must have been thinking of the Neapolitan boys of his diary, following him everywhere, pimping for their sisters, and occasionally for themselves, quite without success.

Far more alluring to his hero is the apartment directly opposite. A door, always ajar, leads from the balcony into a room permanently dark. Yet the place cannot be quite as empty as it looks; the flowers on the balcony are freshly watered, and from the interior comes music, some piece being tirelessly practised. This music the scholar finds 'mageløs', 'wonderful', but his landlord, who, when questioned, does not know to whom this house belongs, finds the reiterated phrases 'kjedelig',[152] 'tedious'. This seemingly small detail – which originated in Andersen's own 1846 experiences of Naples – establishes the existence of the music outside the scholar's own head – important, because this story is *not* overtly concerned with subjective states of being, but, like the proper fairy tale, and like Chamisso's *Peter Schlemihl*, is presented as a record of actualities, however remarkable. And this obviously endorses its parable quality. It will report its central character's internal responses if they are vital to the situation presented, but we will not be asked to enter into them.

'En Nat vaagnede den Fremmede',[153] 'One night the foreigner woke up': Andersen has not told us how long the scholar has been staying in the southern city, for like 'The Snow Queen', this is not a narrative primarily concerned with clock time, though inextricably linked to the seasons and the march of years. But thrice in its course an event occurs so decisive that it creates a 'before' and 'after' as irreversible as the executioner's fatal axe-blow which provided the tale's original explicit conclusion (in the published version *implicit* only). . . . What the scholar wakes up to that night is the balcony opposite flooded in a strange light, and a beautiful girl glowing in the midst of the flowers. The young man jumps out of bed, the brightness hurting his eyes. But no sooner does he look across than the girl vanishes, and with her the light. But from deeper inside the house more music issues, the whole piece now (one assumes), towards which the earlier piano exercises were striving: 'saa blød og deilig, man kunde ordentlig falde hen i søde Tanker derved. Det var dog ligesom en Trolddom, og hvem boede der?'[154] 'so soft and beautiful, one could well doze off into sweet thoughts because of it. It was really like an enchantment, and who lived there?'

Flowers, the female form, music – all these are conspicuously absent, if not consciously excised, from the scholar's carefully organised life. Being remote, however, they have become translated into the extra-ordinary, the seductive, and therefore potentially dangerous: 'Trolddom' is a far from comfortable state, whatever its appeal; we succumb to it at our peril. The scholar would like forthwith to enter the apartment, but this is impossible: the floor below consists of shops, all now shut.

A few evenings later – and again Andersen is deliberately unspecific as to how many – the young man is again sitting out on his balcony, and again his shadow extends to his neighbour's wall on the other side of the street; 'ja, der sad den lige over for mellem Blomsterne paa Altanen; og naar den Fremmede rørte sig, saa rørte Skyggen sig ogsaa. . . .'[155] 'yes, there he sat right opposite among the flowers on the balcony; and when the stranger [scholar] moved, so the shadow moved also. . . . This sight of his shadow so at ease on the balcony, from which proceed alluring emanations of strange power, makes the scholar suddenly regard his appendage as enviably *separate* from himself, free from his own restrictive conditions of being, even though (as yet!) subject to his wishes, his commands. He therefore grants his shadow liberty, for the express purpose of gratifying his own too-long-constrained self. He thus engineers – without at all knowing he is doing this – a split in his identity, an operation that cannot fail to have grave consequences. But so in thrall to his present yearning is he, and so ignorant about the limitations of his elected way of life, that he has no inkling of these, let alone of their inevitability.

His shadow is, he thinks, 'den eneste Levende',[156] 'the only living thing' over on the balcony, 'snild', 'clever' enough to carry out a given task: that of penetrating the sanctum of the empty flat and reporting back to him. No sooner has he articulated this surprising observation than it is given literal realisation: the idea becomes flesh. The scholar has stepped, if only for an instant, over the boundaries of his usual persona, and has set in motion something that proves unstoppable – and appalling. And so the shadow himself, in that selfsame instant, becomes 'living', with, so to speak, a life story of his own ahead. The scholar, we might note, is now in the old folk-tale predicament of having made a wish without understanding what it is he has asked for, and then having it fulfilled, to his own serious detriment. . . . ' "Ja, Du skulle gøre Gavn!" sagde han i Spøg',[157] ' "Yes, you shall make yourself useful!" ' he said in jest.' And then he nods to the shadow and the shadow nods back. The scholar next gets up from his seat and turns away; the shadow does the same.

> . . . Skyggen gik ind af den halvaabne Altandør hos Gjenboen, lige idet den Fremmede gik ind i sin Stue og lod det lange Gardin falde ned efter sig.[158]
>   . . . the shadow went in through the half-open balcony door to the opposite neighbour's just when the stranger went into his own room and let the long curtain drop down behind him.

The shadow's actual disappearance has a dramatic effectiveness easily imaginable on the stage, and I believe we are right to think of this scene, indeed of the whole relationship of the pair who enact it, in terms of drama, with which Andersen had an insider's familiarity.

His Italian setting must anyway have made Andersen imaginatively turn to Italy's popular arts, the vitality of which had long fascinated him. If the performances of *improvisatori* inspired his very first novel, he had had childhood experience of another Italian dramatic art, the *commedia dell'arte*, when Giuseppe Casorti's pantomime troupe visited Odense.[159] At the age of ten Hans Christian had felt the fascination of Harlequin, whose masked figure stalks his *oeuvre*.

The *commedia* was developed, in sixteenth-century Italy, by just such travelling players as Casorti's, improvising dialogue for stock situations involving a handful of prescribed characters (in Jungian terminology, archetypes). Of the great literary dramatists, Molière (1622–73) from his early days with l'Illustre Théâtre onwards, learned much from the *commedia dell'arte*, as did the 'Danish Molière', Ludvig Holberg (1684–1754), one of Andersen's role models. But more important for the writer of 'The Shadow' were the later Italian dramatists, the Venetians Carlo Goldoni (1707–93) and Carlo Gozzi (1720–1806)[160] who, drawing also on fairy-tale sources, fashioned sophisticated variations on *commedia* personae and themes, if from radically different angles, stimulating extremely bitter and public disagreements between them and between their supporters. We remember how Andersen adapted Gozzi's *Il Corvo* (1762) for the Danish theatre as *Ravnen* (*The Raven*, 1832), delighting in using real *commedia* costumes for his production, for the tradition-hallowed cast to put on.

Master–servant dealings are absolutely pivotal to the *commedia*. The servant (Arlecchino/Harlequin) is invariably astute, resourceful, cunning. He pursues his master Pantaleone's advantage when the latter is *inamorato*, often setting in train complications and disasters, and sometimes in devious fashion serving himself as much as his employer. Both these features are present in Andersen's fictive variant. The shadow himself bears interesting, and surely intended similarities to Arlecchino – who mutates into Truffaldino in both Gozzi/Andersen's *The Raven* and in Goldoni's still popular *Arlecchino, servitore di due patrone* ([*Harlequin*] *Servant of Two Masters*, 1743).

Arlecchino descended from Zanni in the very earliest *commedia dell'arte*, crafty servant in dark, usually black attire. Arlecchino himself wears a black mask, and diamond-patterned motley with black the dominant colour. Andersen's shadow, obviously dark by his very nature when we first meet him, is, on his reappearance, dressed entirely in black, from top hat to patent-leather boots. Again, Arlecchino is very thin but always hungry; sometimes his remorseless appetite (obviously paralleling his social ambition) leads to his becoming grossly fat. In our story the scholar opens the door to his former shadow, 'og der stod for ham saadan et overordentligt magert Menneske, saa han blev ganske underlig',[161] 'and there stood before him such an extraordinarily thin man that he felt really strange'. But when after many years' interval the shadow makes his second return, he himself remarks: ' "Jeg bliver feed, og det er det man skal see at blive." '[162] 'I am becoming fat, and that is what one should try to become." ' Lastly, Arlecchino is frequently rewarded in *commedia dell'arte* by a partner, a wedding; in both the Gozzi and Goldoni plays cited he gets the saucy Smeldarina. 'The Shadow', too, ends with its Harlequin being married – to the princess in the cruellest twist of the entire tale, a twist which paradoxically is ruthlessly present in the story's very first scenes. The princess is not at all attracted to the poor scholar, whom nobody has ever wanted to marry.

The master–servant relationship in drama must always have had appeal for those in its audience (surely not so few) who, however conventional outwardly or in professed opinions, found the social hierarchies, and all the duties and pieties enjoined by church and rulers for their maintenance, distasteful, irksome, even oppressive. But as society became more fluid, as the mercantile and manufacturing classes grew more affluent and consequently more powerful, the ability of the serving class to ape, match and even outdo those born into privilege considerably expanded. Demonstration of the possibilities of this were warmly welcomed, however subversive. The two best-known plays of Pierre-Augustin de Beaumarchais (1732–99), *Le Barbier de Seville* (*Barber of Seville*, 1775) and *Le Mariage de Figaro* (*Marriage of Figaro*, 1778),[163] give us a servant far cleverer and more sympathetic than his lord, and Rossini's sparkling opera (1816) based on the former, was a particular favourite with Andersen, who after all came from servant stock himself, with both his mother and his sister washing other people's laundry.

Therefore we should bear in mind that while our young learned man is gentle, refined, good-principled, all excellent things, he is acting when asking his shadow to enter the flat opposite and investigate – calling him 'Du' as always – exactly like any young master anywhere, like Pantaleone himself indeed: issuing a command to a presumed inferior who has no option but to obey. His nod of the head is in effect peremptory, and the shadow's reciprocation ostensibly servile, and, like the *commedia dell'arte*'s 'straight lead', the scholar gives his order because he is *inamorato* of a beautiful girl (even if, in his case, the love object is more apparition than flesh-and-blood). That he has spoken 'i Spøg', 'in jest' only compounds his unthinking assumption of superiority. For, even when merely amusing themselves, members of the owner class expect – and invariably obtain – subservience. They also beseech, flatter and exploit those in their service, while never properly admitting their (superior?) abilities and potential. There is no evidence that, without having been commanded that evening, the shadow in this story would have been anything but the docile servant he was seemingly put on earth to be. Abuse of power, even of an apparently benevolent variety, leads to revolt, and this in turn leads to revolution.

There is one further parallel in world drama to the scholar–shadow situation which was surely in Andersen's mind as he wrote his story: once again, Goethe's *Faust* (1808/1832). If the debt to *commedia dell' arte* leads one to see its subject in social terms, its relation to Goethe encourages psychoanalytic and metaphysical readings, tying in with the most famous of all intellectual usage of the shadow when discussing the total human personality and its likely sicknesses, that by Carl Gustav Jung (1875–1961). *Faust* itself was of enormous importance to Jung (who rejoiced in the possibility that he might have been its author's great-grandson!) In *Erinnerungen, Träume, Gedanken* (*Memories, Dreams, Reflections*, 1962) he wrote: 'Faust struck a chord in me and pierced me through in a way that I could not but regard as personal. Most of all, it awakened in me the problem of opposites, of good and evil, of mind and matter, of light and darkness. Faust, the inept, purblind philosopher, encounters the dark side of his being, his sinister shadow, Mephistopheles, who in spite of his negating disposition represents the true spirit of life as against the arid scholar who hovers on the brink of suicide. My own inner contradiction appeared here in a basic outline and pattern of my own conflicts and solutions. The dichotomy of Faust–Mephistopheles came together within myself into a single person, and I was that person.'[164]

In Andersen's tale it is the writer – and consequently the reader – who is 'that person'. The scholar, whose pitiable one-sidedness has intensified since the separation of the pair, proves unable to receive the shadow into himself, and is therefore subjugated by it; worse – he is destroyed and killed by it. For Jung (and he was by no means an unlikely reader of Andersen!; fairy-tale and fantasy continually absorbed him) the shadow came to represent what the conscious self casts off from the total personality and its multiform experiences. It therefore, in its own right, on its own, undergoes development. As a consequence, whenever the primary self encounters it, it feels fear, disturbance, the troubling possibility of disintegration. All these can be healed only by full, guilt-purged acknowledgement of this long-exiled but continuously present component. As Jung himself says: 'The shadow personifies everything that the subject refuses to acknowledge about himself, and yet is always thrusting itself upon him directly or indirectly – for instance, inferior traits of character and other incompatible tendencies.'[165]

The scholar fails to notice his shadow's absence till the day after the disappearance, so much does he take his adjunct for granted. His principal thought when he makes the discovery is regret that there already exists a story about a man losing his shadow, a totally unmissable reference to Chamisso's *Peter Schlemihl*. Attempts by the scholar to entice a new shadow to his person are unavailing. But after eight days, he finds he is growing another, starting at the feet. For the old shadow has left his root behind, and however many human properties he has acquired during absence from his one-time owner, he still lacks certain essential ones: he cannot cast a shadow himself, and cannot grow a beard. The implication here is that he, as much as the scholar himself, lacks desirable and 'natural' completeness. Only the writer's literary self and his ideal reader possess this last.

Andersen informs us that by the time of the scholar's return north this second shadow of his has grown extensively, 'saa at den tilsidst var saa lang og saa stor at det Halve var nok',[166] 'until in the end it was too long and too big by half'. This is one of the most perplexing details of this closely worked tale. Being a secondary growth, the new shadow presumably lacks the primary's capacity to contain (and develop) what the scholar ejects from his conscious self, and is therefore an exaggerated form of this last. The distorted shape, then, that the scholar takes back north with him as his shadow not only implies the distortions of his prevailing *Weltanschauung*, it actually assists its furtherance. The scholar, as he matures and ages, isn't so much as fleetingly interested in the sensuous which plays such a vital role in normal human lives.

However, his life back in his own country is a rewarding and rewarded one, and estimable too – especially when compared with what his shadow's has been like without him. This last even before his evil actions, is revealed by his own words as vulgar, greedy and amoral. The scholar, we hear, writes admired books about 'hvad der var Sandt i Verden, og hvad der var Godt, og hvad der var Smukt',[167] 'what there was true in the world and what there was good, and what there was beautiful'. The second half of this sentence, that following the word 'Verden', contrasts with the first, surely suggesting that while the true (or real, or discernible) is by no means coterminous with the good and the beautiful, these two last can, and should be, sought in it. The scholar's idealism here stems from Immanuel Kant's desideratum of a world united by belief in peaceful coexistence but not forgoing rigorous legal definition of its needs and expectations, with appropriate provisos.[168]

When the scholar finds himself confronting his former shadow, now human, very thin (like Chamisso's Man in Grey), very fashionably dressed, there is one thing he wants to know from him more than anything else. What (or whom) did he discover in the mysterious apartment across the street in that southern city? 'Poesien',[169] 'Poetry', is the answer he gets, making him remember that female beauty he glimpsed in those split seconds between sleep and full waking-up, shining like the Northern Lights. Eagerly he inquires of his former shadow, who has apparently been in the very antechamber of Poetry, unable to get nearer because of the sheer brightness of the light: 'Var der som i den friske Skov? Var der som i en hellig Kirke? Vare Salene som den stjerneklare Himmel, naar man staar paa de høie Bjerge?'[170] 'Was it like a fresh wood? Was it like a holy church? Were the halls like the starry sky when one stands on the high mountains?' In Kant's *Beobachtungen über das Gefühl des Schönen und Erhabenen (Observations on the Feeling of the Beautiful and Sublime*, 1764) just such exalted numinous experiences are instanced as not merely conducive to moral awareness but an actual part of the moral process itself.[171] Maria Tatar has correctly commented that the phrase 'den stjerneklare Himmel', 'the starry sky/heaven' closely echoes Kant's famous dictum from the conclusion of *Kritik der reinen Vernunft (Critique of Pure Reason*, 1781), to be engraved on the philosopher's tombstone and memorial plaque: 'Two things fill the mind with ever new and increasing admiration and awe, the more often and steadily reflection is occupied with them: the starry heaven above me and the moral law within me.'[172]

But there are anyway valid reasons for thinking of Kant at this point in the story.

Our scholar's chaste industrious bachelorhood is conspicuously in accord with Kant's famously routine-bound life in Königsberg,[173] the city from which he never travelled further than ten miles, with his total absence of emotional entanglements, with habits so regular that neighbours could set their clocks by his walks, his high reputation locally and abroad as a thinker both so difficult he required initiation to be understood and yet of enheartening, uplifting universal application. (And if we assign to the younger scholar Kant's strict Pietistic upbringing, we see how unthinkable it would have been for him to join in Neapolitan street life, with its appeals to carnal appetites.)

'Father' Jonas Collin had studied Kantian philosophy at the University of Copenhagen; he had also, as noted, written about Kant's disciple (later only a qualified one), Johann Gottlieb Fichte (1762–1814). The Kantian belief in reconciling 'Das Verstehen', 'understanding', and 'Der Verstand', 'intellect' and in the aesthetic as an invaluable assistant of the moral faculty underpinned the elder Collin's work as a counsellor of such incalculable importance to Andersen's own life.

Nor, it should be pointed out, is the Kantian echo 'starry sky' merely an indication of noble sentiments. Kant was a dedicated, independent-minded astronomer. In the *Critique of Pure Reason* he likened himself to Copernicus, who, having realised that he could progress no further in explaining the movement of the heavens if he went on assuming that 'the whole starry host' revolved around their observers, decided that he must reverse the assumption – and then a successful explanation would ensue. Kant's own inquiries into 'the whole starry host' had already led him to believe (and write) that the cosmos was evolutionary: 'the creation is never finished or complete. It has indeed once begun, but will never cease.'[174]

In answer to the scholar's eager, even excited questions about his adventures long ago, the shadow tells him that, after three weeks in the antechamber of Poetry's court, (*antechamber* only, it should be observed), 'Jeg saae Alt, og jeg veed Alt',[175] 'I saw everything, I know everything.' But the scholar prefers to go on begging him for details appropriate to so exalted an encounter. 'Gik gennem de store Sale alle Oltidens Guder? Kjæmpede der de Gamle Helte? Legede søde Børn og fortalte deres Drømme?'[176] he imploringly asks, 'Did all the ancient gods walk through the great halls? Did the old heroes fight there? Did the sweet children play and describe their dreams?'

Contemporary readers would have caught the allusions in these three queries easily enough: 'Oltidens Guder' would have brought to mind *Nordens Guder* (*Gods of the North*) by Adam Oehlenschläger,[177] and 'Gamle Helte' such heroes of that writer's as Vaulandur (Wayland the Smith) and Hakon Jarl. And his lyrics might well be thought analogues to the sweetness of children with their play and dreams. Andersen, while always grateful for Oehlenschläger's friendliness and approval, had, virtually from the outset, sought to occupy his eminence, as the older man appreciated. High-minded Kantianism and high-minded Romanticism, dedication to pursuits of the mind and moral principle, these then are the leading characteristics of our scholar – by now, it would seem, a man of mature years – but are more or less incomprehensible to his humanised shadow. They are also, it will be obvious, the outstanding, indeed defining, qualities of Jonas Collin, B.S. Ingemann, H.C. Ørsted, Andersen's father-figures, the very pillars of Denmark's Golden Age which, even though it had not yet been granted that name, was recognised, even while being lived through, as an epoch in the nation's history distinct from any previous one. Collin and his fellow sustainers of it combined the rational idealism, the belief in basic human trustworthiness and virtue, of the Enlightenment – Kant's *Die Aufklärung*,[178] when humanity, he thought, could arrive at last at its balanced maturity – with the Romantics' emphasis on feeling, imagination, the importance of childhood and youth, the encouragement of creativity. Through this synthesis they arrived at a high evaluation of the arts as spiritual essentials for any healthy society and therefore – and nowhere more so than in Golden Age Denmark – as already presented, paid scrupulously close attention to their enablement.

The scholar's expression of surprise at seeing his former possession is untranslatable, and yet – in a prose story as dependent on the value of each carefully chosen word as any poem – the Danish phrase contributes inestimably to the overall meaning: 'Nej, jeg kan ikke komme til mig selv!' ('No, I can't come to my self!' i.e. 'I can't get over it!').[179] If the scholar really *could* come to himself, then he would be 'coming' to his own shadow as well, would be having to embrace and take back that former inseparable adjunct of his very being – this servant who will later turn master, and even now flashy in appearance and manner, redolent of crude materialistic success, even sexy, with plans for marrying. In truth, the only way 'our' scholar will ever admit the shadow is through the demeaning and painful coexistence that the shadow eventually forces on him, allegedly to ensure his very survival. *But we should never forget that the severance of the two was entirely brought about by the scholar and his whim.* This explains the notes of both rancour and contempt for his former boss that we hear in the requested description the shadow gives the scholar of his time in the apartment (those three weeks that seemed as long as a thousand years).

Perhaps the most puzzling passage of the story now follows. Of his experience the shadow says truculently, 'havde De kommet derover, var De ikke blevet Menneske, men det blev jeg!'[180] 'Had you been over there, you would not have become a human being, but I became that.' Of course on one level he is stating a truism: the scholar wouldn't have become a man in the apartment opposite because, unlike the shadow, he was a man already. But the sentence clearly has another, darker meaning. The shadow has already told the scholar that, when the two of them knew each other, he was never an ordinary man. Yet, oximoronically, it is this non-ordinary one whom the reader will now take as not just the more admirable, but as the more likeable of the two – for he has kindness and largeness of spirit, qualities the other entirely lacks. The humanity the shadow is so proud of having attained appears ignoble, mean-spirited, amounting to a lowest common denominator of the activities human beings carry out – money-making, sexual assertion, all a far cry from the Platonic, Kantian, loftily Romantic activities the scholar was expecting to hear about. And in fact the shadow himself – who after leaving the halls of Poetry, embarked on a squalid, peripatetic life, hiding in an old woman's skirts, acting like a peeping Tom, and learning what disgusting activities people of every sort, even apparently sweet children (a dig here at Romantic poetry) get up to all the time, fodder for journalists and the popular press – is moved to exclaim: 'Det er i Grunden en nedrig Verden! jeg vilde ikke være Menneske, dersom det nu ikke engang var antaget at det var noget at være det!'[181] 'It is really a nasty world. I would not want to be a human being if it were not always assumed, that it was something to be one.' But the rewards for such an embrace of humanity are, and will continue to be – for they are more conspicuous still on the shadow's second visit (after a long period) – those the 'ordinary' continue to aspire to, not just material security but wealth, celebrity, rank (including professorships) and women.

In terms of the art consequent on such a lowering view of human life we are invited to move on, I think, from the lofty literary tributes to gods and heroes and the innocent young of Oehlenschläger, Ingemann et al., to the cynical, worldly, proto-realist anti-romantic creations of (often French) writers, such as the tremendously popular Eugène Scribe (1791–1861),[182] whose works Andersen had adapted for the Danish stage. *Le mariage de raison* (*The Marriage of Reason*, 1826), for instance, cocks a snook at infatuations of the heart in favour of hard-headed alliances. His plays abound (while mindful of their boulevard audience) in adulterers, seductions, and those cunning and unrepentant cover-ups of infidelities and lies which nonetheless keep the wheels of society well oiled and turning, the very stuff of the shadow's conversation.

Mocking cliché, the shadow says to his former master: 'her er mit kort, jeg bor paa Solsiden og er altid hjemme i Regnvejr,'[183] 'Here is my card, I live on the sunny side and am always at home in rainy weather.' No profundities, no depths in him. In this sense, he is *still* a shadow – and one doesn't see one's shadow when it's raining.

By the time of the shadow's second visit, the scholar is doing badly; the world has gone the way of humanity essentially as the shadow described it. Says the scholar, now old, sadly: ' "Jeg skriver om det Sande og det Gode og det Skjønne, men ingen bryder sig om at høre Sligt, jeg er ganske fortvivlet, for jeg tager mig det saa nær," '[184] "I write about the true and the good and the beautiful, but nobody cares to hear such a thing, I am really in despair because I take it so to heart." By 1846 the most significant figures of Denmark's Golden Age were themselves ageing, not to say aged; their deaths could not be, and indeed were not, so far off in time, and one of the very dearest to Andersen, Thorvaldsen, had died on 24 March 1844. Moreover the palpable movement towards social change everywhere was not only a matter of hastening on a wider, fuller democratisation, which the majority of Golden Age intellectuals would have welcomed. There was an equally palpable (and not unrelated) increase in the power of business and of accumulated and shrewdly invested capital. Is 'The Shadow' therefore a valediction to a Golden Age (and not only in Denmark) embodied in the downfall and demise of the good and gentle learned man?

Not entirely. Certainly the last pages of the tale could scarcely be starker, as my earlier summary of them will have made plain. The shadow, now fat, as he thinks everyone should be, makes his proposition that the two go to a spa together not out of generosity but to complete their reversal of roles. Now he can put the scholar in a position of such servitude that if judged expendable or an irritant he can be (literally) done away with. Yet the shadow isn't properly human either – his whiskers haven't adequately grown. So there's a sense in which both men are shadows, the one a shadow of himself, the other of a true human being. And this last was something, because of his one-sidedness, that the first man also in truth failed to be. The tale would seem therefore to have the grim cathartic completeness we find in such gems of Andersen's admired Scottish literature of the early nineteenth century: it has noteworthy similarities to James Hogg's terrifying study of what we now would call a 'split personality', *The Private Memoirs and Confessions of a Justified Sinner* (1824).[185]

And to think of this masterwork is to bring ourselves back to a point I believe of supreme importance: our scholar, for all his virtues, has played his own part in the change-round, and therefore in his own destruction; he is *not* a wholly innocent figure. Only the attentive and disinterested writer and reader, aware of all shades of ambiguity, can do appropriate justice to the predicament so scrupulously delineated. Andersen's feelings even about Golden Age Denmark, for all his gratitude and personal loves, were inevitably coloured by resentment – of its prevalent acceptance of rigid and divisive class distinctions. Judged by these (as too many had, and sometimes to his very face, judged himself) he was a nobody who associated with somebodies, and had in his youth had the temerity to think that he was a somebody too. He was a shadow of the better-born who then went his own way, if not defiantly or proudly (for he was not temperamentally disposed to do this) but obstinately. And the memory of that opinion of him was still alive in his mind, still rankled, still brought distress and fear of dissolution. But – as manifested in the scholar's own snobbishness – he cannot acquit himself of having, in his wish for self-advancement, and indeed in his success here, been guilty on his own part of arrogant social assumption. He had acquiesced in, even shared if not adopted, the unkind mindset of Edvard Collin which had made him suffer so. That is why it is impossible finally to make an equation between Edvard Collin and the shadow of the story, for Andersen himself keeps creeping in and rendering it unworkable.

'The Shadow' was first to appear in April 1847 in *Nye Eventyr. Andet Bind, Første Samling (New Fairy-tales. Second Volume. First collection)*, Andersen's second book of stories to drop the designation '*for Børn*', 'for children'. This was to be the year when he realised his success in English-language translations and paid Britain a three-month visit. England for its part was to give Andersen a reception it had never before accorded any foreign writer, society hostesses vying for him, and Thackeray and Dickens leading the superlative praises. In Scotland, to his enormous pleasure, he was acclaimed as 'the Danish Walter Scott'.

The same year saw the appearance of an English masterpiece to which 'The Shadow' bears marked and interesting affinities: Emily Brontë's *Wuthering Heights*. Its pivotal character, Heathcliff, the foundling of unknown provenance and incomprehensible native speech, has dark skin, black hair and black eyes, and exhibits feral qualities from the first, but is made to share the two young Earnshaws' childhood, to the jealous resentment of the boy Hindley but to the delight of Cathy, who roams the moors with him as her inseparable companion. When later the question of her marrying Edgar, the local landlord's son arises, Cathy realises that her true affinity (though she cannot act on it) is not with him but with Heathcliff, 'more myself than I am. Whatever our souls are made of, his and mine are the same. . . . Nelly, I *am* Heathcliff – he's always, always in my mind – not as a pleasure, any more than I am always a pleasure to myself – but, as my own being – so don't talk of our separation again – it's impracticable.'[186]

Nevertheless, actually to marry Heathcliff would degrade her, and it is after hearing this statement that Heathcliff disappears – where to we never learn, any more than we learn the shadow's real whereabouts after leaving the foreign apartment. But when he makes his, again sudden, wholly unexpected, return, he appears 'a tall man dressed in dark clothes, with dark face and hair', possessing 'a deep voice, and foreign in tone', as articulate as any educated man in the neighbourhood, and, crucial to his present identity, obviously wealthy. His feral nature has not subsided, however; indeed his prime purpose, similar to the shadow's after *his* second visit, is to wreak vengeance on those who abused or betrayed him: Hindley, even Cathy, his true twin. Like Andersen's shadow he does so by systematically putting them under his control. They simply do not know how to escape his power. The devil in tradition comes as a gentleman wearing black, and the notion, it would appear from both Andersen and Brontë, as well as their readers, still applies to cast-off members from the lower classes – and thus to the cast-off half of the self, intent on compensatory assertion.

It is justifiable, I think, to see 'The Shadow' as the culmination of Andersen's art since the publication in 1835 of his first novel and his first collection of fairy tales. The pressures first from Andersen's experience of Britain in 1847 and then from the revolutions of 1848 and the continent-wide changes they brought about inevitably impacted on his creative works. These demand what they have not always received: appraisal in their own right, at once as part of their author's *oeuvre* and yet of a new order of achievement, the author's aims, both moral and aesthetic, having changed.

PART TWO

FROM 'DET GAMLE HUUS' ('THE OLD HOUSE') TO 'TANTE TANDPINE' ('AUNTIE TOOTHACHE')

CHAPTER 9

Britain, Dickens,
Revolutions and Wars

1

On Wednesday 23 June 1847 Andersen wrote in his diary:

'At 7 o'clock I was on deck and saw England's east coast. – Our ship was sailing slowly; we didn't arrive in London until 5 o'clock. – The Thames bears witness to the fact that England rules the ocean. From here its servants sally forth, whole hosts of ships. Every minute a courier (steamer) arrives; the others have decked out their stovepipe hats: that one over there had a long smoke-crepe with a red fire-flower peeking out. – The long white wake trails behind them. – The coast, probably fifteen to twenty miles wide. The ships come running under full sail, pluming themselves like swans. Thousands of fishing-boats, like a teeming marketplace, like a brood of chicks, like confetti. Steamer after steamer, like rockets in a great fireworks display. – At Gravesend it looked like a big marsh fire, and it was the smoke from the steamers! – The pleasure yachts of rich, young gentlemen. A splendid thunderstorm, lightning struck several times to the north, and a railway train raced along with its blue smoke against the black clouds – these things appealed to me more than the massive, sooty buildings on the other side of the Thames. "They know you're here and bid you welcome!" an Englishman said to me. Indeed, I thought, the Lord knows – he's the one making it thunder.'[1]

Surely no travel writer is Andersen's superior in presenting the salient, culturally telling features of a place, especially as it first strikes the visitor. Or in the ability to convey their immediate sensory impressions on an individual, the emotional or imaginative chords they sound. What could be more vivid to the inner eye as well as the outer than the three similes found here for the increase of fishing boats as Andersen moves up the estuary, for all of which we can find counterparts in his fiction? Nor is he afraid to admit to the feelings of most travellers arriving somewhere new, that conditions have somehow been stage-managed for their own personal benefit (the God-given thunder). One is very aware from this opening diary-entry onwards – much material would, suitably adapted, be incorporated into *My Fairy-Tale Life* – of Andersen's consciousness that he is now visiting a superpower, a country of immeasurable world-consequence attributable both to geography and to a complex social structure, inherited from its long past and arcane to the outsider. Andersen would esteem London as a greater city (and not just in area or number of inhabitants) than Paris or even than Rome, for all its unsurpassable grandeur and his personal associations with it. If Rome, he will pronounce, is the city of night providing rich dreams of the long-gone past, London represents bright busy daytime, a comparison he was to reiterate, even recycle, a fair number of times.[2]

A visit to Britain was all but overdue by the time Andersen made it. William Jerdan,[3] influential editor of the *Literary Gazette* and ardent promoter of Andersen's work, had warmly proposed it back in November 1846. He had ever-growing admirers there.

In February 1845 Richard Bentley, London published Mary Howitt's translation of *The Improvisatore*, subtitled *Life in Italy* and including a thirty-seven-page essay on Andersen by the translator herself based on Xavier Marmier's 'biography'. In August that year the same publisher and translator brought out Andersen's other two novels – *Only a Fiddler,* followed by *O.T.* – in a three-volume edition, with the complementary subtitle *Life in Denmark*. It was designated as 'by the author of *The Improvisatore; or Life in Italy*', but presumably many readers could easily supply the author's name for themselves. Andersen is in good measure responsible for the bad press Mary Howitt (1799–1888)[4] has suffered in accounts of him and his works in Britain. No doubt their relationship, professional, social and personal, suffered severe, ultimately irreparable strains. Certainly she was imperious, regarding him (initially anyway) as her own rightful property and nobody else's. But by citing in full the disagreeable, retaliatory, ad hominem remarks Mary Howitt made about him ('but an average sample of a numerous and giant race' [the Danes])[5] Andersen craftily ensured that any European reader would take *his* side against her. (Nobody, he could be certain, would think him an 'average sample' of any 'race'!) Now, however, as we follow Andersen upriver to his destination, we can let all still lie before us, and try to see Mary Howitt more objectively.

Born into a Quaker family, like her husband and many-times collaborator, William (1792–1879), Mary Howitt was an indefatigably productive writer, of novels, poems (verses for children mostly: ' "Will you walk into my parlour?" said the Spider to the Fly', memorably parodied by Lewis Carroll, was hers), of well-informed apologias for Scandinavian literature and a fine, truthful and posthumously published (1889) *Autobiography* (edited by her daughter). The titles of some of her novels, suitable for a young readership, indicate their serious, sober, puritan interests: for example *Hope On, Hope Ever* (1840) and *The Two Apprentices* (1844) which bring to life real, working communities of provincial England like the weavers of Dentdale on the Yorkshire/Lancashire border. A stay in Heidelberg in 1840 awoke Mary Howitt to interest in Scandinavian culture, and she taught herself Swedish and Danish, proceeding to render into English works by the proto-feminist novelist Fredrika Bremer whose admiration for Andersen, and particularly for *Only a Fiddler*, we encountered in Chapter 6. She brought Bremer the fame she deserved in England. Not at all averse to pushing herself (and her husband) forward in the literary/social world (Dickens, Mrs Gaskell and Tennyson were among the friends Mary Howitt cultivated) and with contracts never far from her mind, she has too often been subjected to doubts and disparagement. Did she always translate from a Scandinavian language as she definitely led publishers and readers to suppose, or did she rely (even chiefly?) on German versions of texts? Well, possibly! And she certainly made mistakes. But she commands (for the most part) a flexible English prose style, that of someone familiar with the art of fiction-making, of holding her readers' attention. Besides, it is through her unstinting efforts that Andersen's work first became known in Britain, and because of them that these Danish productions won the admiration, affection and, more, the creative emulation of Charles Dickens himself.

In February 1846 Mary Howitt brought out her own selection of Andersen's fairy tales, *Wonderful Stories for Children* (ten in all), her publisher this time Chapman and Hall, with, unfortunately, the author's surname given as 'Anderson'! But 1846 was altogether an *annus mirabilis* for Andersen in the English publishing world.[6] Also in February there appeared, from Joseph Cundalls, London, a collection of his stories translated by Charles Boner. May saw versions of Andersen's fairy-tales by Caroline Peachey, issued under the title *Danish Fairy Legends and Tales* (William Pickering, London), and June a further selection by Charles Boner (same publisher as his February volume). In October Richard Bentley, who after all had begun the whole trend and whom Andersen would greatly take to, brought out a translation of *A Poet's Bazaar* by Charles Beckwith Lohmeyer, and in December Chapman and Hall produced a *third* collection of Charles Boner's translations of Andersen. The month (May) before Andersen's actual arrival in England, *Picture-Book Without Pictures* came out in an English translation from the German, and during the actual course of his stay Mary Howitt's version of *The True Story of My Life* appeared (this time, of course, legitimately from the German, since, as we have seen, that was the language in which it had been issued). Andersen could thus arrive in

England as one eagerly awaited by many, his enthusiastic admirers led by Dickens and Thackeray, the latter declaring himself 'wild' about him.

Of all the above book people, Richard Bentley – to be, in due course, the very *first* publisher of certain Andersen works, editions in English preceding those in the original Danish – became the one with whom Andersen enjoyed the warmest relationship.[7] He liked Bentley's handsome house in Sevenoaks, liked his family – and they him – and later was both moved by, and grateful for, Bentley's sincerely worded feelings for the Danes in their dark war-time.

'"You must surely be able to see whomever you wish!"' – "It wouldn't do; people all over England would take exception. . . . This is the land of freedom, where you die from etiquette."[8] This conversation Andersen reports in his Diary as offering an alarming window on to English society, but his autobiography *My Fairy-Tale Life* likewise stresses its ubiquitous cliquishness, though a good deal of his information (and, for that matter, his empirical experience of it) he owed to the Danish ambassador to the Court of St James's, Count Reventlow (whose family would appear in the new novel he had already begun by the time of his arrival). Reventlow was a strenuous escort,[9] quite determined that his country's greatest international literary celebrity should see the best people, and the best people only: Lord and Lady Palmerston, the Duchess of Suffolk, already 'delighted with *The Improvisatore*, the *first* book about Italy!' and the Duchess of Sutherland, 'who is supposed to be the richest lady in England'. There were so many possible pitfalls, Andersen knew, awaiting an innocent such as him. Lady Blessington was well known as a novelist even in Denmark, and was clearly overjoyed at the opportunity to entertain the author of *A Poet's Bazaar,* extolled in her own last publication as 'a literary treasure such as is not to be found in many books taken together'. But Lady Blessington, alas, was not accepted by key sections of the beau monde on account of her scandalous love-life. 'Her!' scornfully 'lisped' a young lady to whom Andersen was rash enough to mention visiting her house, with its beautiful balcony where a Tasmanian blackbird warbled specially for him. Again – 'Dickens had written in *Punch,* and therefore you couldn't talk with him.' It was emphatically borne in on Andersen – and emphatically he repeats it to his readers – that in England the aristocracy and those eminent figures they were prepared to admit into their ranks did *not* consort with artists. But in Andersen's case they were prepared to make an exception, and more, go out of their way to invite and welcome him. Well-born ladies vied with each other to praise 'The Ugly Duckling' and 'The Top and the Ball' to his face – just as the king and queen of his own country had done. Andersen vindicated their collective, possibly convention-defying decision by being captivatingly charming wherever he went. 'Many presented me their cards, and most of them offered me invitations. "This evening," said Count Reventlow, "you have made a leap into high society in which people need years to be accepted! But don't be too modest. You must put on a bold front if you want to advance!"...' Here then Andersen was, that individual to whom (as he had apotheosised fictionally only the year before) Edvard Collin refused to use 'Du', being feted by glittering socialites in the world's richest (and possibly most snobbish) country.

Outside all the receptions and 'at homes' Andersen noted again and again the general politeness of the English; when you asked directions from them, for instance. Policemen set a wonderful example here. You only had to go up to one in the street and 'he will go with you and show you the way'. People in shops were memorably kind and helpful.[10] As if to redress his comments about its enslavement to etiquette, Andersen declares in his autobiography: 'Here one is in a nation, which at the present is perhaps the only religious nation on earth; there is a respect for morals and good manners. It is no use dwelling upon occasional excrescences and excesses that are always to be found in a great city.'[11]

This last clause is another instance of Andersen's disingenuousness, this time about the workings of his own mind. Even if he did not morbidly 'dwell' on them, Andersen was made morally uncomfortable by many disagreeable features of London life and duly noted them; 'the windows had so much soot on them that my sleeves were blackened. The sun is shining on the bed to show there is a sun here.'[12] He observed the coal dust even on the public statues. As for commercialism, 'here you must demand an exaggerated price for everything', and 'religion', however admirable, was also responsible for the oppressive Victorian sabbatarianism which led him to write: 'Sundays are terribly boring in London.'[13]

Even at his most euphoric he could not deny his distress at London's poor, and, though tempted, did not try hard to play it down. The passage in his autobiography where he expresses this is one of the most powerful in the entire book: he discontinues his effusive (and now decidedly wearying) apostrophes to English Society and offers instead an indictment of the culture which has produced not only large-scale wretchedness but also large-scale refusal to accept responsibility for it, or even pay it the attention any foreigner could see it demanded.

I have seen 'high life' and 'poverty'; these are the two opposite poles of my memory. 'Poverty' I saw personified in the form of a pale, hungry girl in miserable, ragged clothes hiding in a corner in an omnibus. I saw 'wretchedness' and yet it never uttered a word in all its misery, for that was not allowed. I remember those beggars, both men and women, carrying on their breasts a large, stiff piece of paper on which were written the words: 'I am dying of hunger! Have pity on me!' They dare not speak, for they are not allowed to

beg, and so they glide past like shadows. They stop in front of people and
stare at them with an expression of hunger and melancholy on their pale, thin
faces. They stand outside the cafes and restaurants, choose one of the people
sitting there and stare fixedly with such eyes – oh such eyes as only misery can
show. A woman points to her sick child and to the words which are written
across her breast: 'I have not eaten for two days.'[14]

It is scarcely surprising that Andersen should be so moved and so appalled
by such sights.

Two years earlier he had been a guest of Duke Christian August of Augustenborg,
whom he had met through the royal couple, at Gråsten Castle, from 12 to 21
November 1845. He had been saddened by the temper of the political talk
there, not least because of the prevailing attitude to Schleswig-Holstein encouraged by the Duke's friend (and later political-military associate) Prince Frederik
of Nør. So Andersen turned to a picture recently sent him by the painter, Johan
Thomas Lundbye (1818–48) and was inspired by its subject to write one of his
best-known stories, 'Den lille Pige med Svolvstikkerne' ('The Little Girl with
the Matches', usually known in English simply as 'The Little Match-Girl'); it
was published the following month (December 1845) in *Dansk Folkekalender
for 1846*.[15] And it is surely in pictorial terms, like a swift magic-lantern sequence,
that this heart-wringing work lives on in the mind. Andersen scarcely needs to
give us any detail extraneous to his visual images. Yet what details he does
provide add hugely to its devastating effect. It is hard, here as on other occasions, to know Andersen's state of mind as, surrounded by ducal splendour, he
wrote feelingly of extreme poverty. (Likewise episodes of *The Two Baronesses*
dealing with crippling rural misery were written at the luxurious manor of
Glorup.) All one can say is that write them he did, and that he rated 'The Little
Match-Girl' high among his creations.

The setting is New Year's Eve in a city, a time of forward thinking and festivities for most citizens – and therefore too of conspicuous waste, since such
occasions are celebrated with luxury goodies – and also, of course, this being
Northern Europe, a time of bitter cold. The little girl at the picture's centre
stands totally outside all the happy plans and gatherings, yet is the victim of the
economic prodigality behind them just as she is of the winter cold. With such
lavish expenditure on family meals and table decorations (of all of which she is
aware), what can be left with which to relieve the discomforts of those outside
the doors? And how, lacking even essentials of clothing and food, can she and
her kind survive snow and cutting winds? The slum home she has emerged
from has, Andersen informs us, walls these winds whistle through despite the
cracks having been stuffed with straw and rags. If she goes back there without

having sold a single match, her father will beat her, though he must know – as she herself does – that the odd skilling from a sale will scarcely solve their economic ills.

We first see the little girl walking along a frozen city street barefoot, in fairy-tale terms a favourite posture of brave venturesome innocence; think of Gerda on her winter journey to find Kay. But in literal terms the condition is only too probable; shoe-leather, as Andersen the cobbler's son knew, was expensive. When she left home, the match-seller did indeed have slippers on, her mother's and therefore much too big for her, and inevitably one came off as she dashed across the road to avoid being run over by two carriages. The other slipper was snatched from her by one of the many pert, waggish street-boys who populate Andersen's *oeuvre* and who derive from his juvenile persecutors back in Odense. This specimen – a relation too of the cobbler's apprentice in 'The Tinder Box' – jokes that he can use the girl's slipper as a cradle when he comes to have children of his own. Including this item of crude humour so early on in the text means that we take this street along which the match-girl makes her difficult way as a *real* one. We cannot dismiss the central character's misfortunes as merely fictional and remote from ourselves. Its reality makes it seem a more ineluctable place from which to make the ascent from the harsh sufferings produced by Mammon into the kindly sphere of God's love.

This ascent constitutes the body of the story, and each of its four – or is it five? – stages can be seen in both physical terms – consequent on bodily actions of somebody so beside herself with cold and fatigue she scarcely knows what she is doing – and spiritual ones. Andersen leaves it open as to whether the girl's successive visions are hallucinations brought on by her overwhelming hunger. But every vision except the last derives from the tangible world from which the match-seller has been, through fate and not through any shortcoming of her own, banished. In truth, many of our most treasured spiritual/emotional experiences are inextricable from secure material circumstances. A warm stove in which a fire cheerfully burns; a table set for an ample family feast; a Christmas tree ablaze with candles – these, domestic, cosy, assuring, are the very stuff of our childhood experience of joy. And these are what the girl sees as she strikes the matches she knows there's no point in selling. We should make a correction here; these items are the very stuff of *other* children's experience of joy. They are all way beyond *this* child's reach. Each vision fades out; the stove vanishes to leave one burnt-out match behind, the feast parodies itself like the end of some nightmare, the roast goose leaping up from the platter with a knife and fork stuck in its back, and the Christmas candles rising in the sky until they turn into a constellation of stars, a single one of which tumbles downwards.

' "Nu døer der Een!" '[16] ' "Now someone is dying there!" ' thinks the little girl, for her grandmother, who, when alive, was her only true friend, used to tell her that when a star falls towards earth a soul is simultaneously rising up to God. Andersen confessed that when beginning his story his own 'Mormoer', mother's mother, was much in his thoughts.[17] For all her shady past and the Odense Tugthus, he had been fond of her and still treasured her fund of stories. One had been about Anne Marie, his own mother who, as a young girl, had been forced to go out on the streets begging.

This little beggar-girl, obviously, doesn't realise that she herself is dying. Eagerly she strikes a fourth match against the wall, and on seeing her grand-mother, begs her not to disappear like the stove, the goose on the platter, and the candlelit Christmas tree. In her anxiousness that this old woman, 'saa klar, saa skinnende, saa mild og velsignet',[18] 'so clear, so shining, so gentle and blessed', will stay, she strikes all the matches she still has. They reward her by casting a radiance round her envisioned grandmother, who takes her in her arms and bears her – to where else but Heaven? This sight, and indeed this destination are perfectly consonant with what we now know can occur in the human mind at the moment of death. But we hesitate to describe it as a fifth mental stage of the heroine's journey because life has now departed from her; in earthly terms she no longer exists. But her glimpse of Heaven is truly part of the belief-system which has sustained her when alive and thus redeemed her last moments.

The people who, early next morning, find the little girl dead with the bunch of spent matches beside her think she expired while trying to warm herself against the freezing night. 'Ingen vidste, hvad Smukt hun havde seet, i hvilken Glands hun med gamle Mormoer var gaaet ind til Nytaars Glæde!'[19] 'Nobody knew what beauty she had seen, in what radiance she had gone with her old grandmother into the joy of the New Year!' The gloomiest manifestation of urban poverty can be but the screen behind which spiritual joy awaits; appre-ciation of the universal capacity to attain this means never writing off any indi-vidual, however remote from us. Think about the following:

> Jo is in a sleep or a stupor today, and Allan Woodcourt, newly arrived, stands by him, looking down upon his wasted form. After a while, he softly seats himself upon the bedside with his face towards him. . . . The cart had very nearly given up, but labours on a little more.
>
> '. . . It's turned wery dark, sir. Is there any light a-comin?'
>
> 'It is coming fast, Jo.'
>
> Fast. The cart is shaken all to pieces, and the rugged road is very near its end.
>
> 'Jo, my poor fellow!'
>
> 'I hear you, sir, in the dark, but I'm a gropin – a gropin – let me catch hold of your hand.'
>
> 'Jo, can you hear what I say?'

'I'll say anythink as you say, sir, fur I knows it's good.'
'OUR FATHER.'
'Our Father! – yes, that's wery good, sir.'
'WHICH ART IN HEAVEN.'
'Art in Heaven – is the light a-comin, sir?'
'It is close at hand. HALLOWED BE THY NAME!'
'Hallowed be – thy –'
The light is come upon the dark benighted way. Dead![20]

These are the last moments of Jo, a crossing-sweeper – a juvenile underclass Andersen was intrigued by in London 1847 – in the slum quarter, Tom-All-Alone's as famously rendered by Dickens in *Bleak House* (1852–53). Dickens was outraged by social abuses and cruelties above all because they offended against the whole vision of humanity, and its great, if elastic capacity for fellow feeling, which he imaginatively entertained and tried to express – and to encourage. Andersen, while far less involved in practical politics than Dickens, was also possessed of such a vision, apparent from *The Improvisatore* all the way to the very last tales. Furthermore he shared with Dickens manic depressive spirits – probably each soon recognised this in the other – so that the heights and depths of the society they lived and worked in corresponded with, and appealed to, the highs and lows in themselves. And in both cases only humour and, at times, a fierce willed sentimentality could enable them to achieve the equilibrium essential to ambitious creativity.

Andersen first met Dickens in the home of none other than that Lady Blessington whom so many more proper members of Society chose to shun. (Wasn't she, Andersen had heard, having an affair with her own son-in-law, Count d'Orsay, 'the most elegant gentleman in London'?) Not that fashion and elegance were exactly absent from the dinner of hers Andersen attended at which guests, including the Duke of Wellington's son, were served by waiters with silk stockings and powdered hair ('as in other grand houses'). Andersen was signing copies of Mary Howitt's translation of *The True Story of My Life*, with suitable personal inscriptions, when Charles Dickens made his entrance: 'young and handsome, [he] had a kind, intelligent face with a mass of beautiful hair, that fell on both sides. We shook hands, looked deep into each other's eyes, spoke to each other and understood each other. We went out on to the veranda, and I was so moved and delighted to see and speak to the living English writer whom I love more than any other that tears came into my eyes. Dickens realised my love and admiration. Among my fairy tales he mentioned "The Little Mermaid" which Lady Duff Gordon had translated for "Bentley's Magazine"; he also knew *The [A Poet's] Bazaar* and *The Improvisatore*.'[21] This last fact is of particular interest to the present study, for Dickens, I feel sure, remembered Andersen's first novel (and possibly Andersen himself, his whole compelling persona, ingenuous, transparent-seeming on the one hand yet mysterious, unfathomable) when he came to write his most purely personal and perennially popular book *David Copperfield* (published 1849–50).

Dickens – who on 1 August, because unable to visit Andersen, left for him 'all of his works beautifully bound and inscribed inside: "To H.C.A. from his friend and admirer C.D." '; 'I was ecstatic!'[22] – was fittingly to be the last person Andersen saw in England. But breaking into his English stay was a carefully planned and much looked forward to trip to Scotland.

Walter Scott was present in Andersen's mind throughout his Scottish visit, and the novel now taking shape in his head and to come out in English (September 1848) before it did in Danish, *The Two Baronesses* (*De to Baronesser*) is permeated by Scott, to the extent of containing a fully acknowledged adaptation of the central episode of *The Heart of Midlothian*. 'I was full of the thought that I was in Scotland, the land of Walter Scott,' wrote Andersen in his first Scottish diary entry.[23] And re-appreciation of what Scott had achieved must have made him view Dickens anew, for who but 'Boz', 'the author of Pickwick', 'the Inimitable', was the true successor – in Britain, Europe (including Russia) and America – of 'the author of Waverley', 'the Wizard of the North'? Much of what Andersen had in common with and had part-learned from Scott applied to Dickens too: a profound reverence for Shakespeare; a high regard for Fielding with his imposition of the picaresque on to deep-rooted situations; a restless curiosity about the different, indeed diverse component groups of their societies and the traditions and world-pictures upholding them; a sense of how the past, with its flaws as well as virtues, went to make the present; a lively interest in lore of all kinds and an ability to harness the forms of fairy tale with their bottomless psychic address to more domestic or workaday situations. And all three men were driven by an awareness of the childhood self deep within, born of sufferings in early years never fully overcome, when they felt they were apart from other children (Scott through his lameness, Andersen and Dickens through the often squalid ups and downs of their families entailing hopelessly erratic schooling for exceptionally talented sons). And all three possessed the steeliest will to excel, to surpass their erstwhile superiors.

The drama of Edinburgh, its fusion of a speaking past with geographical features of impressive singularity, struck Andersen from the first, from when he was brought there by the railway that so amazingly cuts right into the middle of the city through that 'immense trench' (Andersen's phrase) containing Princes Street. He saw on the one side the New Town created by the Adam brothers (perhaps too regular and geometric for his tastes), and on the other, scaling the left-hand hillside, the Old Town 'so picturesque and magnificent, so old, so murky, so distinctive. . .,' its medieval tenement buildings rising up 'nine and eleven storeys'.[24] Views of Edinburgh from various elevations Andersen likened to the magnificent prospects of Constantinople and Stockholm he had already honoured in prose.

> Where the town slopes down towards the sea there is the hill called Arthur's Seat, famous from Walter Scott's novel, *The Heart of Midlothian*. The whole of the old town is like a mighty commentary on these great works. And the Walter Scott monument is situated so beautifully in a spot in the new part of the town where there is a panorama of old Edinburgh. It is in the shape of a mighty Gothic tower, under which is a statue of the poet seated in a chair. His dog Maida lies at his feet, and in the topmost arches of the tower there are figures from his works, figures who are now known the world over, *Meg Merrilies*, the *Last Minstrel* and so forth.[25]

Andersen was so intimately familiar with these creations of Scott's that he tracked their movements down in Edinburgh, though he was far from unmindful of the frequent filth and squalor of their present-day context, and he would take such characters with him when he went on a tour of the city – to Loch Lomond and Loch Katrine, to Sterling and the Highland Line, and to both sides of the Firth of Forth. He was keen to see, but frustrated by not being able to do so, Ravenswood Castle, the ancestral home of Edgar its Master, and where Lucy Ashton went mad for love of him, in *The Bride of Lammermoor*, the opening chapters of which are reworked in those of *The Two Baronesses*.[26] In this new novel a male character, who has personally seen it, will even give the heroine a welcome description, down to the dog Maida, of the Scott Memorial itself (actually inaugurated 1846, only a year before Andersen's visit).

Andersen was back in London by 26 August. On 30 August he left for Ramsgate to take the Ostend steamer next day. But on arrival at the Royal Oak, his hotel there, he found a note from Dickens saying that he and his family would expect him for dinner (at five o' clock) in their house at nearby Broadstairs. The quality of this occasion and its sequel next day Andersen celebrated in his autobiography:

> [He] and his wife gave me a hearty welcome. It was so splendid to be with them that for a long time I did not notice what a beautiful view there was from the dining-room where we were sitting. The windows faced the Channel, and the open sea rolled in just below. The tide went out while we were eating, and the water receded extremely quickly. The great sandbank there, on which

lie the bones of many a sailor, could be seen in all its splendour, and the light-house was lit. We talked of Denmark and Danish literature, and about Germany and its language, which Dickens wanted to learn. An Italian organ-grinder happened to come and play outside while we were eating. Dickens spoke in Italian to the man, whose face beamed with delight at hearing his native language.

After dinner the children came in. 'The house is full of them!' said Dickens. There were no fewer than five of them; the sixth was not at home. All the children kissed me, and the smallest of them kissed his own outstretched hand and then gave it to me. . . . We parted late in the evening, and Dickens promised that he would write to me in Denmark.

But we were to meet once more before I left. Dickens surprised me by going to Ramsgate the following morning, and was standing on the jetty when I arrived to go on board. 'I had to come and say a final farewell to you!' he said and went on board with me, and there he stayed until the ship's bell gave the signal for departure. We shook each other's hand, and with his sincere, wise eyes he looked at me in such a friendly way, and as the ship sailed, he was standing as far out as he could go, by the lighthouse. He waved his hat. Dickens was the last one to send me a greeting from the coast of my dear England.[27]

One very significant result of these occasions of friendship (testifying, for all their amiable warmth, to a histrionic quality in both men) was Andersen's first break with his previous publishing precedent. In December 1847, following the agreement made with him, Richard Bentley issued a collection of new fairy stories in English (versions by Charles Beckwith Lohmeyer) *before* its appear-ance in Danish called, appropriately enough, *A Christmas Greeting to my English Friends*. There was, it must be said, commercial as well as sentimental reasons for this; Andersen would be paid for both volumes rather than having the translated one ride free on the back of the original. In fact two out of the seven tales *had* already appeared in Denmark: 'The Shadow' and 'Den gamle Gadelygte' ('The Old Street Lamp').[28] But the other five were fresh from the writer, as announced. Andersen explained his conviction that England should get his latest book before anywhere else, in his heartfelt but decidedly gushing preface (addressed, as one might have expected, especially as Bentley was the publisher, to the first of his English-language readers, Charles Dickens):

Whilst occupied with a greater work [one assumes the novel, *The Two Baronesses*] there sprung forth – as the flowers spring forth in the forest – seven new short stories. I feel a desire, a longing to transplant in England the first produce of my poetic garden as a Christmas greeting: and I send it to you, my dear, my noble Charles Dickens, who, by your works had been previously dear to me, and since our meeting have taken root for ever in my heart.

Your hand was the last that pressed mine on England's coast: it was you who from her shores wafted me the last farewell. It is therefore natural that I should send to you from Denmark, my first greeting again, as sincerely as an affectionate heart can convey it.[29]

Of these stories one, 'Historien om en Moder' ('The Story of a Mother')[30] Andersen would later declare pleased him, 'Barnet i Graven' ('The Child in the Grave', 1859),[31] with its similar theme excepted, more than any other of his productions. 'It came to me without any apparent reason while I was walking down the street.' With its uncompromisingly dominant theme of infant mortality – so prevalent, indeed virtually inescapable, in every social class at this time; both the Dickenses and Edvard and Jette Collin suffered its almost unmanageable pain – this tale struck a raw contemporary nerve, and its imagery is correspondingly bold and universal, deriving as it does (like 'The Little Match-Girl') from popular notions of what lies beyond human death. A mother pursues Death who has taken away her child, on a bitterly cold winter's day, after an illness agonising to witness. On her journey to catch up with him she sacrifices her eyes to a speaking lake and her (still youthful) dark hair to an old woman guarding Death's strange greenhouse. This last, a contrast to the freezing forest and the cavern-studded mountain that is Death's residence, is full of exotic plants which she is unable to see until Death returns and – in order to prove a grim point about his very being – gives her back her eyes. All the many plants there throb with the heartbeats of real people, but in some growths the hearts of the newly dead pulsate, and naturally the mother recognises those of her own late child. In her desperation she grabs hold of two flowers, but Death asks her with her restored eyes to stare down into a well and view the futures of a young life that these plants contain, the one happy, the other wretched. One of them must obviously be the future of her child were he restored to life, but Death refuses to tell her which. Rather than let him face (the fifty-fifty possibility of) a lifetime of anguish, the woman relinquishes the flowers and consents to Death taking her child into a yet more distant realm. She herself goes back to our world, allowing that all that happens there is ultimately for the best, because we have such limited knowledge of existence.

For all the intensity of the rendering of the mother's grief and the tactile vividness of the forested wasteland through which she ventures, 'The Story of a Mother' traffics in major theological problems it has not scope enough to tackle adequately, let alone answer. In the first version the story ended happily, with the woman waking up and finding her child better, and normal life awaiting her. Obviously the second ending is an improvement artistically – after the mother's purgatorial experiences, how could the humdrum have had any kind of solidity? And from the standpoint of truth too, for children *do* die however much we love them; there is no value in making a story suggesting otherwise. Even so, the final verdict on accepting sad events as part of God's scheme which must *ipso facto* be good can't but read tritely.

It was 'Det gamle Huus' ('The Old House')[32] that Dickens liked best of the stories of *A Christmas Greeting*; he admired it enormously and wrote to Andersen: 'I read that story over and over again, with the most unspeakable delight.'[33] Certainly its art is strikingly close to Dickens's own, while also very much its author's. For us it also seems interestingly prescient of the changes now under way all over Western societies. It is at once valedictory of a past with mores that can and will never be revived and prognostic of an ampler, perhaps kindlier future.

2

'The little boy, the old man, and the Tin Soldier are especially my favourites,'[34] said Dickens, and 'The Old House' can be thought of as a fugue on these three characters, with the last named in a different key from the other two. The theme itself is nothing less than Imagination (including the art of narrative) as our only weapon against Time, even if, as with the Tin Soldier himself, we can allow it to turn destructively against us. Significantly the story is named not after any member of the trio but after what subsumes them, illustrating in its history even more forcefully Time's inexorability. It stands opposite the small boy's home, it is where the old man spends his last years, and it retains the Tin Soldier, even after its demolition. As in 'The Shadow' the house beckons alluringly to the individual with whom we identify (the boy) and surely proves to be the dwelling-place of 'Poesie'.

It was built almost three hundred years earlier, according to the date on its central beam, (mid-sixteenth century), and is now the only old house in the street. 'I had never before seen,' Andersen wrote of York, 'such picturesque houses as these with their carved beams in their gable-ends and bay windows.'[35] In the story he emphasises the house's jutting upper storey and abundant wood carvings, and so brings to mind buildings like those we still can see in York's famous Shambles. The nineteenth century's belief in itself, leading to replacement of the old by the modern, is a given here, the fine house despised as an anomaly by its neighbours, whom Andersen wittily and characteristically makes articulate: ' "hvor længe skal det Skrummel staae til Spektakel her i

Gaden" ',[36] ' "how long will that monstrosity remain as a blemish here in the street" '. (That the age also, whether in the Gothic Revival or later on, in Art Nouveau, also sought to reproduce and even outdo Middle Ages decorativeness perhaps provides an ironic subtext to the tale.)

Fittingly, this solitary house is home to a solitary and very old man. Apart from an aged factotum coming in to assist him every morning, he is alone all day. And just as the house announces its antiquity by its replete appearance, so the old man involuntarily advertises his years: leather knee-breeches, brass-buttoned coat, indisputably eighteenth-century-style wig – sartorial appurtenances long since discarded, rejected.

The small boy opposite is fascinated by the house which provides him with images of the past, of soldiers, and creatures of once-popular fantasy like dragons. No less is he interested in its single inhabitant, nodding to him through his window, to be nodded back to: 'og saa vare de Bekjendtere og saa vare de Venner',[37] 'and thus they were acquaintances and thus they were friends'. Yet they don't exchange a word. Communication exists on so many levels, and culture from the Industrial Revolution forward has unduly exalted speech and writing over other, yet more instinctual forms. But when the boy hears his parents say: '"den gamle Mand derovre har det meget godt, men han er saa skrækkelig ene!"'[38] '"that old man across the way is very well off, but he is terribly lonely!"' he knows he must make more real his bond of friendship with him: he will relieve his loneliness by giving him one of his two tin soldiers. So across the road he goes and presents the soldier, wrapped up in paper, to the man's factotum, explaining why it is he is making this gift.

Here Andersen was drawing on personal experience, charmingly related in *Notes for My Fairy Tales and Stories* (1862), and showing his rapport with children, his understanding of their mindsets. He had been staying with the German writer (poet, verse-dramatist, novelist, apologist for German-Jewish culture and friend of Tieck and Wagner), Julius Mosen (1803–67) in Oldenburg in Lower Saxony, Mosen having become dramaturg at its Court Theatre.[39] His small son gave Andersen on his departure one of his tin soldiers, precisely so that he would not be lonely. In the story the soldier does not belong to a toy army – as he did in 'The Steadfast Tin Soldier' (of which this new tale is in part a remake). He is one of a pair, and when taken away from the boy's home to the old house, he feels desolate, missing his mate acutely. More resonantly even than in the earlier story, we sense the autocracy of the young over their loved possessions because they have endowed them with so much of themselves, and their concomitant disregard of them as free-standing individuals. This situation extends well beyond that of child and toys, as an analogue of graver and central social relations: landlords and tenants, masters/mistresses and servants, employer and employees, humans and animals, patrons and artists.

The boy's kindness to the old man is much appreciated, and his esemplastic mind (to use Coleridge's term), so notable in the pre-pubic young, is exercised on the interior of the house into which he is now invited. It is in a lamentable state – rickety balcony, creaking chairs and cupboards, floors full of holes, courtyard walls and flowerpots choking with excess vegetation – yet to him exuding romantic grandeur. He hears the wooden trumpeters carved on the doors blowing him a fanfare, the suits of armour clinking as if worn by real warriors, the silken dresses of the women in the pictures on the wall rustling, and he relishes the objects the old man produces for him – a picture book, playing cards more gilded than present-day ones, a piano which sounds hoarse when his host plays on it. The old man also shows him a portrait of a beautiful but cheerful-looking woman who, the boy thinks, looks at him with 'sine milde Øine',[40] 'her gentle eyes'. Who is she? In an anti-romantic masterstroke Andersen reveals that this picture is no souvenir of the past but something the old man bought in the junk shop down the way because he once knew the subject, dead for half a century. Whether there was ever an emotional connection between the two is unclear, unimportant; the connection exists *now*, for this junk-shop purchase, by appealing to memory and imagination, keeps the old man's evaporated past alive, and lightens up his present, enough to make his loneliness bearable.

Memory does not at all alleviate the misery of the Tin Soldier, rather it intensifies it, making it impossible for him to forget the liveliness of the small boy's home in contrast with the torpor of the Old House. During the boy's two visits to the Old House the Tin Soldier leaves him in no doubt about his sufferings, and the tears of tin he has shed, and impassionedly evokes the life from which he has been forcibly (as he sees it) removed – particularly the doings of his former owner's siblings, like his little sister, Maria, not yet two years old.

Here again – according to the writer's *Notes*[41] – Andersen drew on the family of a friend, of the composer J.P.E. Hartmann (1805–1900): 'It was the composer Hartmann's little daughter Maria who as a two-year-old always had to dance whenever she heard music. Once she entered the room while her older sisters and brothers were singing a hymn. She started to dance, and her musicality was such that it did not permit her to change the rhythm, so she danced by standing first on one leg and then on the other as long as the measure of the hymn demanded.' (There is, as we shall see, a tragic sequel to this episode.)

This anecdote finds its way into the pining complaint to the boy of the Tin Soldier who then continues: ' "... Siig mig, om I synge endnu om Søndagen? Siig mig Lidt om den lille Maria! og hvordan har min Kammerat det, den anden Tinsoldat! ja han er rigtignok lykkelig! – jeg kan ikke holde det ud!"

' "Du er foræret bort!" sagde den lille Dreng, "Du maa blive. Kan Du ikke indsee det?" '[42]

' ". . . Tell me, whether you all still sing on Sundays? Tell me a bit about little Maria! and how my comrade there is, the other Tin Soldier! Yes he is really fortunate! – I cannot stand it!"

' "You have been given away as a present!" said the small boy, "you must stay. Can you not see that?" '

This (a repetition of a previous exchange) convinces as a dialogue between one in a superior position and his perceived inferior; while kind-hearted, the former sticks rigidly to an authority he has done nothing to deserve but accepts, dismissing the latter's feelings as irrelevant. (The contemporaneous *The Two Baronesses* also includes effective instances of this.) The inferior, on the other hand, emphatically does not accept the argument's justice, but loudly and indignantly repeats an earlier declaration: '*Jeg vil i Krig! Jeg vil i Krig!*' '*I will go to War! I will go to War!*'[43] He was made in warrior mould, but while living in the family had been able to accommodate his nature easily enough. Now in his lonely impatience he refuses to do so any longer. Having delivered his *cri de coeur*, he throws himself down in anger on the rotten floorboards, to fall down through one of the many cracks in them. Not even the old man can find him! This is, in quiet miniature, an earnest of 1848 revolutionaries. All over Europe, we feel, in the tumultuous years still to come of 1848 and 1849, there were young men, angry at their present lot and disappointed by treatment from their superiors, who realised their inherent aggression and went off to war – to disappear (often before seeing the combat they sought).

The day of the Tin Soldier's disappearance is the boy's last visit to the Old House. A week goes by, then many weeks; winter sets in, snow covers the decorated exterior of the house, and the boy – like Kay in 'The Snow Queen' – makes himself a hole in the frozen windowpane to look out from. The house appears very empty, and indeed *is* so; in the cold spell the old man has died. (And in his first outburst against his prison-like life, the Tin Soldier had predicted that the only thing that would ever happen to the Old Man would be his funeral.) In beautifully economic sentences the boy watches his coffin being taken from the house to the family grave in the countryside, noting the absence of mourners: the old man has survived his friends. Within a few days the auctioneers are stripping the Old House, even down to cupboards and flower-pots, while the once-loved portrait of the beautiful lady is bought back by its former junk-shop owner. With the spring – season of newness – the Old House is pulled down. And nobody is sorry – we do not hear of any regret even on the boy's part; children are resilient.

Endorsing the already created impression that the building long survived the meaning of its identity, Andersen gives us popular sentiment again: ' "det var en Skrummel," sagde Folk',[44] ' "it was a monstrosity," said people'. . . . And this being the beginning of an age which value development per se, before long a new building goes up, 'et deiligt Huus',[45] 'a splendid house' with large windows and 'hvide, glatte Mure', 'white, smooth walls', in contrast to medieval elaborations and jutting Shambles-like upper storeys. Instead of abutting directly on the street like old town houses, the new one is set back from the road from which it is separated by a garden with railings and an iron gate over which people like to look. We are now in the present bourgeois age when privacy demands a certain decorous ostentation, no question now of nodding to the occupant of a house opposite, or of those upstairs shaking hands across the street with their neighbours.

Andersen makes the years pass as rapidly, as gracefully as he did that winter in which the old man died. The boy has now grown into 'en dygtig Mand',[46] the Danish epithet denoting excellence, competence, reliability, of whom his parents are proud. Newly married he has come to live in the house built on the site of the old one that had once intrigued him so. He stands beside his young wife as she plants a wild flower in the garden, signifying her exemplary natural-ness, her unaffected spontaneity of response, so needed in changing times. She pricks her finger on something that sticks up out of the soft soil, a Tin Soldier, which, pleased with her unexpected *objet trouvé*, she dries with first a green leaf, then her scented handkerchief. We readers are in no doubt as to who this is: the very toy soldier who had fallen through the rotten floor never to be found, and who therefore had spent at least a couple of decades unnoticed. Let me see him, asks the young husband, but his memories do not automati-cally come back in full: 'Ja ham kan det nu ikke være, men han husker mig paa en Historie med en Tinsoldat jeg havde, da jeg var en lille Dreng!'[47] 'It can't really be him, but he reminds me of a story about a tin soldier I had when I was a small boy!' And he relates to his wife what we already know, how he had given the old man across the way one of his two soldiers to relieve his loneliness. And his wife is moved to tears. She is sure this must be the very same Tin Soldier, and for that reason will take great care of him. She would also like to visit the old man's grave, but her husband has no idea of its whereabouts so long ago was the man's death.

This (morally) beautiful episode, for all its domestic Biedermeier charm, is resonant with truths uncomfortable but necessary to accept. First we face up to the fact that, important though they may have seemed at the time, the small boy's dealings with the old man and the Tin Soldier have not retained their stature over the years. Time has reduced them, or broken them up, even inside the head of the person to whom they were of most significance. It is clear that he hasn't thought about them this long while, and even now is uncertain – despite the undeniable geographical evidence – that this really *is* his old Tin Soldier. We have a strong impression, indeed, that the young husband is not even certain of the actuality of these past occurrences: 'en Historie med en

Tinsoldat jeg havde', 'a story about a Tin Soldier I had', nothing more specific or concrete. Yet – and this is the second truth, one more significant for a period of rapid change like the late 1840s than for a more settled, conservative one – we have the capacity to fashion our memories, or the fragments they have been reduced to, into meaningful wholes to assist us in our present and future lives. (Equally we are able to distort memories into agencies of destruction.) We feel here that the finding of the toy and the release of the past it contains will work creatively on the newly married couple. Does the discovery of the toy not make them think tenderly about the old man and his loneliness in life and in death?

Yet in the last paragraphs of the tale Andersen sounds the discordant notes used for the presentation of the Tin Soldier. Whatever has *he* been feeling all this long, long time? A kind of wry, ultimately stoical vindication of himself, it would seem at first, for he echoes the wife's view that the old man was 'skrækkelig ene', 'terribly lonely', but then, after hearing the pair go over his own story, 'men deiligt er det, ikke at blive glemt',[48] 'but it's splendid not to be forgotten'. In whatever incomplete form, and after whatever discontinuity, he and the old man *have* been remembered at last, as has the old vanished house which brought them all together. A further truth, and, if sensibly accepted, a reasonably assuring one.

Yet a fourth, less agreeable truth awaits us; once again the Tin Soldier is its medium. The gilded hangings on the walls of the Old House had a little rhyming motto which a bit of rag, all that's survived of them, now repeats: ' "Forgyldning forgaaer,/Men Svinelæder bestaaer." Dog det troede Tinsoldaten ikke'.[49] ' "Gilding perishes,/But pigskin endures." But that the Tin Soldier did not believe'. And he was right not to do so. Finally everything must and does perish.

Why did the contemplation of tin soldiers bring Andersen to such heights of literary achievement? Perhaps admiration of their sterling qualities, of their neat mimesis of human beings at their most disciplined and hard-tested was united in his mind with overwhelming pity. All their orderliness and regimentation, all their smart appearance in the end got them nowhere, because – there was nowhere for them to go, at least nowhere commensurate with their innate (endowed) expectations? Whatever the explanation, among Andersen's unitary fairy tales – those proceeding by unswerving development of a single theme; 'The Ugly Duckling' and 'The Fir Tree' are other major members of this group – 'The Steadfast Tin Soldier' and 'The Old House' seem to me Andersen's most perfect achievements, the profoundest and the most extensive in their charity. But we could legitimately debate whether we should call 'The Old House' a fairy tale at all. Except for the talk of the Tin Soldier – easily accountable as a projection of the boy/the husband – its only supernatural element is its communication of the mystery of Time.

Did Dickens remember Andersen's Old House when, two years later, he described so vividly that of Mr Wickfield and Agnes, his hero's wife-to-be, in *David Copperfield*? It stands in Canterbury, a city decidedly similar to York:

> At length we stopped before a very old house bulging out over the road; a house with long low lattice-windows bulging out still farther, and beams with carved heads on the ends bulging out too, so that I fancied the whole house was leaning forward, trying to see who was passing on the narrow pavement below. It was quite spotless in its cleanliness. The old-fashioned brass knocker on the low arched door, ornamented with carved garlands of fruit and flowers, twinkled like a star; the two stone steps descending to the door were as white as if they had been covered with fair linen; and all the angles and corners, and carvings and mouldings, and quaint little panes of glass, and quainter little windows, though old as the hills, were as pure as any snow that ever fell upon the hills.[50]

Mr Wickfield's house represents goodness and learning to David, newly released from the tyrannies of the Murdstones and his inadequate, broken schooling, yet the widower Mr Wicksteed is to feel lonely there, his situation undermined evilly by his clerk (and factotum, very unlike the one in Andersen's tale), Uriah Heep.

Again one wonders if the last pages of Andersen's story came into Dickens's head when, at the close of *Great Expectations* (1860–61) he sent Pip into the garden occupying the site of the extraordinary, rambling Satis House, the emotional and imaginative lodestar of his earlier years, and long since pulled down:

> There was no house now, no brewery, no building whatever left, but the wall of the old garden. The cleared space had been enclosed with a rough fence, and looking over it, I saw that some of the old ivy had struck root anew, and was growing green on low quiet mounds of ruin. A gate in the fence standing ajar, I pushed it open and went in. . . . I could trace where every part of the old house had been and where the brewery had been, and where the gates, and where the casks. I had done so, and was looking along the desolate garden-walk, when I beheld a solitary figure in it. . . . The figure of a woman. . . . I cried out: 'Estella!' '[51]

But all these, interesting, even thought-provoking though they might be, are incidentals. Far more importantly, *David Copperfield* shows real affinities of concept, presentation, structure, vital subjects and themes to *The Improvisatore* which we know, from no lesser an authority than Andersen himself, Dickens read and admired. But we should reaffirm here that the pressures of industrialisation and the urgent related movements for political change – in England expressed in the Poor Law Board of 1847 and the Third Chartist Petition of 1848 – caused writers to re-examine their past, the effects of early years on the later formed personality. Their attempts to do so are, of course, correlatives for the transformation, at once stimulating and terrifying, of British society. The childhood memories contain possibly redemptive cameos of a more innocent world, but also pointers towards the harsh circumstances yet to come but now ubiquitous. Charlotte Brontë's *Jane Eyre* came out in 1847, Thackeray's *(The History of) Pendennis* in 1848 (completed 1850). It is more than possible that these writers too had read *The Improvisatore*, to which, however, *David Copperfield* bears a closer resemblance, closer in a literal sense than it does to either of the English novels.

Andersen's and Dickens's novels are both first-person accounts of the subject's life from birth to eventual fulfilment in happy fruitful marriage, in both cases to a second (more mature) love. Dickens's own favourite among his books – entitled, in emulation of Thackeray, *The Personal History of David Copperfield* – opens: 'Whether I shall turn out to be the hero of my own life, or whether that station will be held by somebody else, these pages must show. To begin my life with the beginning of my life, I record that I was born (as I have been informed and believe) on a Friday, at twelve o'clock at night.'[52]

Despite the deliberate nod here to Sterne's *Tristram Shandy*, this announcement by David of the circumstances of his birth begins an infinitely fuller treatment of growing-up from infancy onwards and of the subject's realisation, often blocked by difficulties and obstacles not of his making, of innate expectations of fulfilment than any made in English prose to date; the similarities here to Antonio's in *The Improvisatore* must already be clear to readers. Like Antonio, David is a posthumous child (Antonio knows nothing about his father, and we know extremely little about David's); like Antonio again, David loses his mother ('bewitching Mrs Copperfield') at an early date, leaving the author free to explore child–adult relationships through a series of surrogate parents, one of whom, Peggotty, with her unstinting practical affection, surely recalls Domenica, the countrywoman whom Andersen would always declare was based on his own mother. Then Andersen and Dickens rely on *deus ex machina* figures – the Eccellenza, Betsy Trotwood – to make points about the benevolence to be found even in a largely hard-hearted and class-ridden society, and also about false or even detrimental mentors: Antonio's despicable headmaster Habbas Dahdah, David's terrible, sadistic Mr Creakle. Both Antonio and David are sensitive boys, unafraid of their own sensitivity – here their kinship to Romantic poetry rather than to eighteenth-century fiction is apparent – and they give us ample evidence of it in their frequently lyrical responses to places, events, even works of art (literary rather than visual in

David Copperfield's case), as well as to kindly or admirable persons. David, like Antonio, relishes the theatre, while his love for the Norfolk he visits with the Peggottys and for its denizens, is decidedly reminiscent of Antonio away from Rome in the Campagna.

But the most important resemblance of all comes in the trio at the emotional centre of both novels: Antonio–Bernardo–Annunziata in *The Improvisatore*, David–Steerforth–Little Emily in *David Copperfield*. Antonio had known and been drawn to Annunziata when he was a boy and she a winning little girl, David knew Little Emily (in Norfolk) when both were at similar ages to those of Andersen's characters. This childhood familiarity will complicate their reactions to what happens at a later stage. Again Bernardo, the Senator's son, and Antonio from penniless obscurity are both at the same school, as are Steerforth and David, and the older boy accordingly wins the younger's grateful admiration, which the former cynically exploits. This situation continues when the older of the pair turns into a Byronic man about town, Steerforth making use of David to further his amorous designs, which involve the object of his friend's childhood daydreams. Furthermore, that amphibious streak in Antonio which Bernardo pronounces on is something in the schoolboy David that Steerforth is aware of:

> 'Good night, young Copperfield,' said Steerforth, 'I'll take care of you.'
> 'You're very kind,' I gratefully returned. 'I am very much obliged to you.'
> 'You haven't got a sister, have you?' said Steerforth, yawning.
> 'No,' I answered.
> 'That's a pity,' said Steerforth, 'If you had one, I should think she would have been a pretty, timid, bright-eyed sort of girl. I should have liked to know her. Good night, young Copperfield.'[53]

The two school-friends meeting after an interval of some years is one of the great scenes in *David Copperfield*, indeed in all Dickens, and it may well remind us of Antonio and Bernardo meeting during the Roman Carnival after a far shorter length of time:

> I was so filled with the play, and with the past – for it was, in a manner, like a shining transparency, through which I saw my earlier life moving along – that I don't know when the figure of a handsome well-formed young man, dressed with a tasteful, easy negligence which I have reason to remember very well, became a real presence to me. But I recollect being conscious of his company without having noticed his coming in – and my still sitting, musing, over the coffee-room fire.
> At last I rose to go to bed, much to the relief of the sleepy waiter. . . . In going towards the door, I passed the person who had come in, and saw him

plainly. I turned directly, came back, and looked again. He did not know me, but I knew him in a moment.

At another time I might have wanted the confidence or the decision to speak to him, and might have put it off until next day, and might have lost him. But, in the then condition of my mind, where the play was still running high, his former protection of me appeared so deserving of my gratitude, and my old love for him overflowed my breast so freshly and spontaneously, that I went up to him at once, with a fast-beating heart, and said:

'Steerforth! Won't you speak to me?'

He looked at me – just as he used to look, sometimes – but I saw no recognition in his face.

'You don't remember me, I'm afraid,' said I.

'My God!' he suddenly exclaimed. 'It's Little Copperfield!'[54]

This could hardly be better or more honestly done. But one might wish that Dickens had followed Andersen in granting Steerforth a less melodramatic and therefore more open ending than the death by drowning eventually accorded him, involving as it does the death of the seduced girl's affianced and an over-written pathetic fallacy of violent weather. Though Dickens shows far greater knowledge of young men's dealings with the opposite sex in *David Copperfield* than Andersen does in *The Improvisatore*, he is, probably for that very reason, more guilty than the older writer of distorting truth to suit pharisaic elements in his society: not just Steerforth's death but the treatment of Little Emily and Martha, the prostitute, flying in the face of likelihood. But both *The Improvisatore* and *David Copperfield* fail in their endings, and in similar ways for, I suspect, ultimately similar reasons. To make an 'I' narrator tell of the happiness to which he has won through and praise the woman who has made it possible is a hard enough task in any instance, but it is made harder by the writer having no experience at all of sustained union with a woman (Andersen), or failing to feel for a wife (and even children) that committed devotion in which he professed to believe (Dickens). *David Copperfield* ends, like the earlier Dickens's novels, in a familial stasis which might have met the self-deceiving dreams of middle-class readers but which would fiercely have dissatisfied their creator. Yet isn't this also true of our final pictures of Antonio himself? Antonio's character, as we have seen, responded to an improvisatore's life, to wandering, random encounters, adventures and to the art which drew on his temperamental qualities; the protracted idyll was never part of his life. Dickens was less like the comfortable middlebrow novelist David Copperfield becomes (a successful one too, though it's hard to envisage his books) than he was like the compelling, fitful Steerforth.

Andersen's copy of *David Copperfield* was sent to him by Dickens himself. It must have brought back warmest memories of England. He read the novel with enormous and deeply felt admiration. 'I often think I live in the same house as you,'[55] he told Dickens in his letter of thanks. But that remark was even more true than Andersen appreciated, for both writers faced the difficulties consequent on the admiration their work had engendered – and their own apparent need for it, coexisting with psychological needs of a different, infinitely less amenable nature.

The first fourteen chapters of *David Copperfield* constitute an unassailable mythopoeic masterpiece which has entered the English psyche and spoken to generations of readers all over the world on account of its intensity and truthfulness. After these David makes a 'new beginning' and, for all its beauties, the novel lowers its emotional temperature considerably, and (even remembering the unforgettable Uriah Heep) reduces its confrontations with what in life is hard, even impossible to assimilate. Dickens's later novels, under pressure from personal problems and overpowering social change, eschew the forced serenity of his most directly autobiographical novel. To take the supreme example, *Great Expectations* (1860), told, like *David Copperfield*, in the first person, demands and receives a very different resolution from that accorded the hero of the earlier novel, and both the endings Dickens wrote for the novel do justice to the tragic elements which have engulfed Pip.

Andersen too surely demanded in the depths of his nature something in addition to all the generous attention and hospitality from the royal couple, from the Hereditary Grand Duke of Weimar, from Mendelssohn, the Schumanns and Liszt with his Princess Consort, and all the many other high-born and famous folk he was disposed to mingle with. In the tragic war years for Denmark so soon to come, Andersen faced challenges the meeting of which, if it gave him indisputable anxiety, pain and sadness, brought out something strong, even tough in him. He had already in the depths of his psyche anticipated them, because he had seen the dark occurrences of the war manifested, if in miniature, long before they were reality, in scene after scene of his early years, informed as they were by suspicion, fear and aggression. He had sensed these as perpetually latent in human, indeed animal experience, and he would never forget the confirmation of this harsh truth that the dreadful events afforded him. The major works still ahead of him would, like *Great Expectations*, not forfeit the tragic in their resolution. At their pinnacle stands a novella virtually the contemporary of Dickens's masterpiece, 'Iisjomfruen' ('The Ice Maiden', 1861). Though it nowhere deals with the sorrows of the Three Years' War – his most flawed novel, '*At være eller ikke være*' ('*To be or not to be*', 1857) will do this, in its striking and memorable pages of reportage, which form perhaps its most completely successful section – it is fair to say that this short masterpiece could not have been written without first-hand experience of them.

3

In April 1848 William Jerdan, editor of the *Literary Gazette,* printed an impassioned open letter signed Hans Christian Andersen. This is its second paragraph:

> You know how it is at this moment in Denmark. We have war! but a war that is carried on by the whole enthusiastic Danish people; a war wherein the noble and lowly born, inspired with this just cause, voluntarily places himself in the ranks of battle. It is this enthusiasm that I must paint to you: this love of our country, which fills, and elevates the whole Danish nation.[56]

His diary, however, sees the war in less generic and more painfully individual terms, as in this entry for 13 May:

> Heard a good deal about the battle: the men shot in the chest or head had lain as if they were asleep; those shot in the abdomen had been unrecognizable because their faces were so convulsively distorted with pain. One had lain literally 'biting the dust' with his teeth; his hands had clutched at the turf. . . . Lundbye [the Danish artist responsible for the picture that inspired 'The Little Match-Girl'], the officers told me, had been standing dejectedly leaning on his rifle; some farmers were passing by close to where the other rifles were propped up in front of him and happened to knock them over. They heard the shot and saw Lundbye fall to the ground, shot from below upward through the chin, his mouth torn and a piece of flesh with a beard on it shot away. He emitted a few weak sighs; was wrapped in the Danish flag and buried. Lieutenant Høst, who is staying here, wept.[57]

1848 was indeed a watershed year for Europe, for Denmark, and psychologically for Andersen himself, and it would have the profoundest effects on his later art. Andersen wrote in his autobiography: 'The year 1848 arrived, a strange year, a volcanic year, in which the great waves of time also swept with murderous force across my native land.'[58]

On 20 January 1848 King Christian VIII died of blood poisoning aged sixty-one. Andersen had maintained the good relations with him cemented by his stay on Føhr, and indeed had accepted an invitation in early January to take tea with him 'and bring something with me to read'. The King seemed animated enough, though he had to lie down during the visit, laughing as before at some of the tales and hearing 'a couple of chapters from my [unfinished] novel, *The Two Baronesses.*' But he deteriorated, as became publicly known, and Andersen, feeling anxious and fearing they were imminently to lose him, went out every day to the Amalienborg Palace to find out about his health. When he heard of his death he felt disconsolate 'and so painfully moved I became ill'.[59] A man of very different character, Søren Kierkegaard, recorded in his *Journal* only warm, laudatory memories of Christian VIII: 'He said many flattering things to me and begged me to visit him. . . . He also said something about my having so many ideas, and so couldn't I give him some.'[60]

What kind of king, though, had Christian been? He had succeeded his cousin Frederik VI (1768–1839), who, though just as progenitive as himself, had left no heir. Frederik, on account of his father's mental instability, had been for twenty-four years Crown Prince Regent of Denmark and Norway (1784–1808) and for thirty-one years King of Denmark (six of them as King of Norway also). Andersen was to put Frederik's character and death into his principal literary production of 1848, *The Two Baronesses*.

Half British on his mother's side, Frederik had both his regency and his reign made difficult by Britain, which carried out devastating pre-emptive onslaughts on Danish shipping for strategic reasons. By 1814 and the defeat of the Napoleonic France with which he had been forced to side, Frederik was monarch of a bankrupt country stripped of any international bargaining position, epitomised above all by the handing over by the victorious powers of Norway to Sweden. This led to an increased authoritarianism on his part, and of abjuration of the liberal policies he had followed as Regent, the most famous of which was the ground-breaking abolition of slavery in 1788. The court of Frederik – which, we must remember, Jonas Collin served and of which Andersen had been a young beneficiary – imposed censorship on the press and brooked little overt criticism, though by the later 1830s, after an upturn in the economy, the Estate Assemblies were set up to articulate concerns of the different regions.

The far more appealing figure of Christian VIII, of whom his cousin Frederik had been generally somewhat suspicious, seemed to promise a more thorough modernisation, and liberal elements were hopeful that he would steer Denmark towards democratic Constitutional Monarchy. A good-looking, charming man, he was devoted to literature and science, as was his second wife Caroline Amalie, herself a passionate admirer of Grundtvig and disposed to discuss dreams and spiritual intimations with Andersen during his stay on Føhr. (He was to keep up a friendship with her after her husband's death.) Christian held principles in advance of his ability (or possibly even his whole-hearted inclination) to act in support of them. Hopes placed in him were disappointed. Over the dominant Schleswig-Holstein question – *Spørgsmålet om Sønderjylland [Slesvig] og Holsten* – Christian displayed indecision until 1846, and then took a clear stand only over Schleswig.[61]

By now the Liberal faction in Denmark wished the legally anomalous position of the two duchies to end. Schleswig (Sønderjylland, South Jutland) where
there was a clear, nationalist-minded Danish-speaking majority should be
incorporated into Denmark. This would mean, however, its abandoning its
medieval Salic law blocking any heir to the Danish throne through the female
line, and bringing its administration into step with that of Denmark proper.
Holstein, closely affiliated under international law to Schleswig though it was
and sharing its law of succession (and, like its fellow duchy in connection
specifically with the *Danish* king), presented a morally and empirically more
difficult situation. Here the majority, a sizeable one, was German-speaking,
and indeed, as a former constituent of the Holy Roman Empire, Holstein was
also a member of the German Confederation (to which the King of Denmark
was therefore a signatory). Post-Napoleonic nationalism encouraged pride in
regional history and lore everywhere, and in the German lands this was stimulated by the pronouncements of such pundits as Jacob Grimm who considered
Jutland original German territory and the Danes but arrivistes. All this intensified Holsteiners' feelings about their identity and the future appropriate to it,
and greatly complicated the issue of the duchies' presence in any reformed
'new' Denmark. Holstein being anyway a profoundly conservative society, the
more straightforward-seeming proposals seemed likely to result in a veritable
tangle of legalistic paradoxes. No wonder Lord Palmerston famously said that
only three persons understood the Schleswig-Holstein Question, one of whom
was himself – and he had forgotten it!

On Christian VIII's death, Frederik VII (1808–63) was expected to accomplish what his father had failed to achieve: Denmark would become a
Constitutional Monarchy (and indeed proclamation to this effect was made on
28 January while the late king was still lying in state) and Schleswig-Holstein
would be accorded a proper working settlement, the two appearing a single
matter in progressive minds. On 20 and 21 March crowds demonstrated in
Copenhagen, to make their views plain to the King in Christianborg Castle,
and Andersen was one of those chosen by the Committee of Order to be a
steward and see that the marches and meetings didn't get out of hand. Such
expressions of popular feeling were made in the wake of the much-bruited
protests by the French in Paris on 22–24 February, against which Louis
Philippe's government had employed military force, and also of the subsequent
revolutions that followed the Parisian example: Vienna on 13 March, Berlin on
18 March. In all instances, and notably in Denmark, the professional classes
made up a good section of those voicing their principled discontent and
expectations.

Their claims and the royal response to them were over-interpreted in Kiel,
the main city of Schleswig-Holstein and centre of German nationalism, where

it was thought that the separation of the two duchies had actually been decided. A provisional Kiel government was proclaimed on 24 March, and while the Duke of Augustenborg (Andersen's several-times host whose views had so disturbed him) went off to seek aid from Prussia, his friend (and Andersen's co-guest) Prince Frederik of Nør headed a rifle corps and students from Kiel University seized the duchies' armoury at Rendsburg. By 31 March the port of Flemsborg in Schleswig was occupied by soldiers from both duchies, 7,000 of them, to be assailed by a matching number of soldiers from the Danish army proper. Andersen published in the newspaper *Fædrelandet* ('The Fatherland') patriotic verses 'Slagsang for de Danske' ('Battle Song for the Danes').[62] The consequent Battle of Bov on 9 April was a victory for Denmark under General Hans Hedemann. But when the Prussian troops arrived bringing with them soldiers from other parts of the German Confederacy, the character of the conflict changed.

The second battle of the war, the Battle of Schleswig on 23 April, begun on a cold, wet morning, saw a terrible defeat for Denmark. The Prussian forces under General Wrangel (who believed in the war offensive far more strongly than his comparatively equivocal king, Friedrich Wilhelm IV), were, at 18,000 strong, three times the size of the Danish, who suffered 170 men dead (as opposed to 41 Prussians), 463 wounded and 258 taken prisoner. Prussia – in this year of change and people's power – believed it was helping a genuine democratic uprising, a sympathetic attitude in ironic contrast to its stances elsewhere. Sweden, Russia and Britain, on the other hand, all anxious not to see Prussia a major Baltic power, took the part of Denmark. The Battle of Schleswig enabled the Prussians to invade Jutland.

Nevertheless, with auxiliaries from Norway and Sweden arriving in Fyn, their warm reception by the locals glowingly described by Andersen in his autobiography, and a stiffening of Danish morale after the Schleswig defeat, the war went quite well for Denmark in 1848. By the end of May the Germans began evacuating soldiers from Jutland. There was a strong Danish victory at Dybbøl Mølle on 5 June, and by 26 August, Prussia, under a king very anxious not to antagonise other European powers, acceded to many Danish demands, to the indignation of the Estates of Holstein. The ceasefire of 1 September held for eight months, but realists must have seen that it would never prove durable.

Andersen's fairly prompt apologia for his country in the *Literary Gazette* had been published and circulated in international periodicals, including German ones, as were his poems. He had expressed his great grief at public events to the German friend by now emotionally dearest to him, the Hereditary Grand Duke of Weimar;[63] he had befriended and celebrated Danish and Swedish participants in the war, and his novel that year could certainly be viewed as the work of a patriot, indeed of a patriot committed to the new

Denmark. This didn't stop him being the target of snide remarks the following year – by Jonas Collin's daughter, Ingeborg Drewsen among others – to the effect that he wasn't sufficiently whole-heartedly patriotic, as he stilll maintained close relationships with Germany. There was always an edge to his compatriots' reception of him as a public figure, which derived ultimately from an unwillingness to recognise his international standing, let alone that it might be deserved.

But might Andersen's attitudes to the war not in truth have been entirely consistent? Maybe he did not always feel as he did when he wrote his exhortatory verses? Remembering his not infrequent derogatory statements about his own country, he may well have entertained thoughts not dissimilar to those of his 'antagonist', Kierkegaard, who in his *Journal* for early 1848 wrote:

All this fear of Germany is imagination, a game, a new attempt to flatter national vanity. One million people who honestly admitted that they were a small nation, and each, before God and on his own account, resolved to be no more would constitute an enormous power; here there would be no danger. No, the disaster is something quite different; it is that this small nation is demoralized, divided against itself, disgustingly envious man to man, refractory towards anyone who wants to govern, petty-minded with anybody who is somebody, impudent and undisciplined, dredged up into a kind of mob tyranny. This gives people a bad conscience, and that is why the Germans are feared. But no one dares say where the trouble truly lies, and so one flatters all these unhealthy passions and acquires self-importance by taking on the Germans.

Denmark is facing a nasty period. The market-town spirit and mutual petty meanness: it will end with one being suspected of being German if one doesn't wear a certain kind of hat, etc.[64]

4

'I made great progress on my novel;' wrote Andersen in his diary on 22 May, only a week and a day after he had recorded those agonising war scenes and about a book that would come out during the long lull in the conflict; 'later in the day a title for it occurred to me – *The Two Baronesses*. Today is a great day for ushering a novel into the world!'[65] To us now it is hard to believe his title wasn't (as in the case of *The Improvisatore*) present in Andersen's mind from the very start of work on the book, so completely do the two eponymous women not only give it shape but endow it with artistic and thematic unity. They are not blood relations, neither comes from the aristocracy herself, and neither significantly espouses it once having joined it. By the end of the novel these two outsiders in eminent social positions are mother- and daughter-in-law. The harmony of the ending confirms that ambivalent exclamation in the diary just quoted. *The Two Baronesses*, started before the war, written during some of its bloodiest months and completed after the ceasefire, is, to an important extent, a novel celebrating Denmark as a nation state, a refutation of the kind of opinion of the country held by Kierkegaard above and by Andersen himself (if far less dogmatically) in his darker moods. It gives us the diversity of its landscapes and peoples in a virtually *e pluribus unum* spirit. It also forms (though it ends when Christian VIII has been on the throne four years) a tribute to the country's progression towards socio-political modernity, about which Kierkegaard was suspicious. The enlightened new constitution bringing the Absolute Monarchy to an end would come into full effect on 5 June 1849. Certainly this novel contains incidents and speeches more uncompromisingly and overtly critical of the Danish *ancien régime* than anything Andersen had written so far. And it implies that, if gradually, these can be consigned to the past.

The novel's beginnings in Andersen's mind date, as we have already noted, from summer 1847, before the death of Christian VIII and the Three Years War and contemporaneous with his visit to Britain. Scotland and his appreciation there of how Scott did literary justice to an entire country stand behind the book, and interestingly he reread two Scott novels while in the thick of work on it (May 1848): *The Heart of Midlothian*, which directly inspired its central action, and *Rob Roy*, which must surely have confirmed his desire to cover large tracts of territory in its course. And that book's distinction between life below and above the Highland Line informs, I believe, Andersen's own between the body of Denmark on the one hand – above all Sjælland and Fyn – and, on the other, southern Jutland, with the wild, sparsely populated Halligen Islands off its west coast doing service for the Hebrides and Orkneys which had so captured Scott's imagination.

Andersen noted that Scott reserved his greatest creative energies for novels set in, and interpreting, the past – though *St Ronan's Well* (1823),[66] which he had read as recently as November 1845, has a contemporary setting, a spa reflecting current fashions. His own fiction-writing instincts led him to follow his characters' fortunes from a given date in the past up to the present day, at which point he will examine how they are faring. Once again Andersen is exemplarily specific about dates. Written as it was in the year of Christian VIII's death, Andersen's book includes, as it moves towards its close, the death of his predecessor, Frederik VI, on 3 December 1839. On 14 August the following year, the older baroness's birthday, her grandson, Herman, and Elisabeth, the novel's heroine realise their mutual love, and we learn that Elisabeth is only sixteen years of age. Because we were present at her birth in sad, harsh circum-stances, this amounts to a confirmation for us of its date: 1824. After Elisabeth and Herman's marriage we move on, we are told, four years. Therefore when the old baroness dies, at peace but still mindful of the terrible injustices of the not so distant past, we have arrived at 1844, that period of great creative and social achievement for Andersen. This must have have seemed all the more worth treasuring in view of the tensions and tragedies of these months of the Three Years War, which had not, for all the welcomed respite, come to its conclusion. It was also the year when Andersen stayed on Føhr, one of the places most vital to the novel.

Both baronesses come from a social obscurity not so far removed from Andersen's own. The elder is the daughter of a peasant-smallholder or share-cropper, 'lange' (long) Rasmus, who, for complaining about the drudgery he was forced into, to pay the Fyn landowner, the Baron, his rent, is given a grotesquely cruel punishment.[67] He is compelled to ride a 'wooden horse', a thin plank on two poles across which he is placed with two heavy bricks on his legs that pull him perpetually towards the ground, which he is nevertheless unable to reach. His strong-willed three-year-old daughter, Dorothea, horrified at seeing her father's sufferings, tries to slip stones into the gaps under his feet, but the old baron sees her doing this and slashes her savagely with a whip. Her pregnant mother, Hannah, tries to intervene and the Baron kicks her, causing injuries from which she dies. (This appalling punishment, preserved in Fyn lore, made such a great impression on Andersen when he heard about it that he uses it also in his fine historical late story, 'Hønse-Grethes Familie', ('Chicken Grethe's Family', 1870).[68]

The Baron drinks himself to death from apoplexy, and his reckless-living son proves almost as bad a character, but not cruel. He falls in love with Dorothea, who, after her parents' death, has been brought up by the village schoolmaster, and the two marry. After his early death, she comes into her own as Baroness of a large estate, able through her position and wealth to indulge in, even cultivate, her wilful eccentricity. None of her children survive her, but her grandson Herman does. Her coolness to him over the years, refusing to see him – he is a talented, largely kind-hearted young man of handsome appearance with jet-black eyes – has a rational explanation. On her travels through Italy the Baroness's late daughter was assaulted by an Italian, who made her pregnant. It will thus be clear that, for all her attractive defiance of convention, and awareness of what the high and mighty do to the lowly, the Baroness is not immune to the faults of the rank she has entered; her capricious taking up and dropping of people she owes to a rich Copenhagen hostess, Fru Bügel who turned against Andersen socially for reasons he never discovered. She also points up the disagreeable truth that sufferings do not always make their victim sympathetic or tolerant; they can often have the opposite effect.

The arrival in this world of Elisabeth, our second Baroness, is the business of the arresting and atmospheric first chapters of the novel, which are a creative 'take' on those of *The Bride of Lammermoor*. Stormy weather makes three well-born young men from Copenhagen, amateur sailors, and their tutor, Moritz, a Holsteiner, put up on the coast of Fyn opposite the island of Langeland, though their destination was the estate of Count Frederik's father between Svendborg and Fåborg. Count Frederik decides they should instead take shelter that night in a tumbledown property close by, which is being done up for him by order of his father: 'en reen Røverkule at see til, men ganske romantisk',[69] 'a real Robber's den to look at, but quite romantic'. This is a virtual reworking of the arrival at near-ruinous Ravenswood in Scott's novel, and in Christen the caretaker we have a modified version of its Caleb Balderstone. But Andersen's young men – though they have a certain class hauteur – show themselves as far more civi-lised than Scott's, as their talk while bedding down for the night reveals. They tell hunting and shooting anecdotes, bringing to mind the exploits of Scott's characters which feature a repellent, indeed nauseating description of a stag kept long and ruthlessly at bay. By contrast Andersen's young men admit that, while they take pride in their marksmanship, depriving an animal of life can trouble their hearts and consciences. Herman, more the hero of this novel than anybody else, the older Baroness's grandson, relates how once he looked into the large brown eyes of a seal he'd just shot 'og det var, ligesom jeg havde skudt et Menneske'.[70] 'and it was as if I had shot a man'. And, very significantly, it is precisely as he makes this sympathetic confession that a strange sound in the ruin is heard.

A young woman – recognised by the old servant as the wife of a local peri-patetic musician – has entered the manor-house courtyard to escape from the storm, and collapses, giving birth before she dies to a child, a girl. This is Elisabeth, the heroine. All the young men and Moritz, their tutor, take a solemn oath that same night to look after her, to be her godparents, but one of them – Herman, who has just voiced fellow feeling for animals – will become her husband, making this girl, born of misery and poverty, the second Baroness of the title.

In fact Elisabeth spends her first five years with Herman's aunt, the Baroness, and falls foul of her. Every year, on her birthday, the Baroness retreats into a special chamber in her country residence, greatly arousing speculative gossip. Little Elisabeth determines to find out what she is doing, appropriates her key, and enters the secret room to see dominating it a portrait of an old man – the former Baron, the Baroness's own father-in-law, apoplectically red in the face and angry in expression. The Baroness pays him an annual visit to remind herself of the enemy whose son she married and whose estate she inherited. But when she discovers Elisabeth out in her clandestine room, she has the little girl expelled from the household. The eventual result of this piece of imperious cruelty – for which Andersen, faithful to his scheme, forgives her a little too comprehensively – is that Elisabeth goes to live with the oldest member of the group present at her birth, Holsteiner and widower Moritz Nommesen, pastor, whose sister keeps house for him, on one of the Halligen archipelago: 'Halligerne, de stille Øer i den stormende Nordsø', 'the Halligen, the calm islands in the stormy North Sea.'[71] The setting of her formative years – for which Andersen drew on his memories and diary entries from his time on Føhr with the royal couple- – is vital to the novel's meaning.

Andersen back in 1844[72] took the keenest interest in the geography and traditions of these islands, obviously, off the Schleswig-Holstein coast as they are, of greater political significance in the year in which he was writing than when he had stayed there. Linguistically they fascinated him; you could hear Danish, German, a dialect of Danish so heavily influenced by German it was hard to understand, Frisian (which he noted as close to English, indeed together they form the Ingweonic branch of Germanic languages) and Fering, a North Frisian dialect in use both publicly and privately on Føhr itself. Thus the Halligen form a microcosm of Schleswig and Holstein, and a paradigm, even a template for the kingdom of Denmark itself, where North Jutland (Otto's ancestral home in *O.T.*) hosts interesting independent dialects, and Bornholm, far to the east of both Denmark proper and the south of Sweden, speaks *born-holmsk*, which, with its three genders and an archaic phonology, is closer to dialects of Skåne, Sweden than to ordinary Danish. Elisabeth's foster-father is a Holsteiner who has grown up near Itzehoe, the Duchy's oldest city with a castle built by Charlemagne and set in country comparatively rich agriculturally. But he feels, as he nears the islands he is to serve as a cleric, an affinity with their culture, with the gables of their houses, the layout of their farms with their big gateways.

The islanders clung tenaciously to their traditions, which Andersen noted down on his visit, often with less immediate attraction to them than he conveys in the novel. In the first Frisian-speaking village he arrived at 'people were not very polite, not a single hello; and if you said hello to them you got a brusque nod; no one took his hat off'.[73] He wrote that life could be very hard, and this we appreciate from the context of Elisabeth's, comfortable and protected though she herself is. The fields in which cattle graze are flooded by seawater for many weeks of the year; most of the men have to turn to the sea for their livelihood, risky fishing or whaling expeditions as far away as Greenland (and here Andersen shows a commendable transcendence of time and location by making one of the islanders feelingly evoke the intelligence of whales and their ability to care for one another). Many of the women on the island are widows.

Elisabeth grows up in an atmosphere of puritan devotion (at prayer meet-ings the women dress in mourning-style garments with linen kerchiefs half concealing their faces), home education and, encouraged by this, the reading of

Walter Scott who, she feels, expresses the truths about existence itself. But she isn't proof against sexual attraction. The Commander's son, Elimar, appeals to her heart, at fourteen a seaman and an active sportsman with a gun, something of a rip, some of whose mischievous antics – the teasing of the tame jackdaw and the cat, ending with the death of the former – are downright unkind. But Elisabeth misses him greatly while he is away, and the dreams and fantasies she entertains about him in his lengthening absence are based on an unreal, not to say erroneous, picture of his personality. He joins a Dutch ship to acquire a more scientific grasp of navigation and sea-craft, spends time in Holland itself, where he is extremely happy, and then – after several rumours of scapegrace activities have travelled back to the Halligen – becomes Second Mate on a large vessel bound for North America. For a while there is silence about his doings, then appalling news. No, not that he is dead, but that he is in a Copenhagen prison, in fetters, for having killed the First Mate in a brawl. Elisabeth, trying not to listen to stories of the wild Frisian ancestry of Elimar's that includes killers who suffer both remorse and punishment, is filled with sorrow until she remembers her best-loved book: Walter Scott's *The Heart of Midlothian*. She will do as its heroine Jeanie Deans did, make a journey across country (an equally long and strenuous one, as it happens) and beg from her king (Frederik VI) a reprieve for her convicted loved one.

And here Andersen has an ingenious surprise awaiting us. Elisabeth is indeed granted an audience – not with the King as hoped, for he has seen too many people that day – but with the object of her journey itself. Here is Elimar Leyson, she is told – but it is not he. She insists that he isn't Elimar, and finally gets the truth out of the prisoner (whom in fact she knows): he is Jes Jappen, a servant's son back in the Halligen, who has used Elimar's papers. Elimar himself is about to get married to a rich widow in the United States. What was set up to be a grand emotional scene has, in truth, a quality of dark farce, because, for Jappen, his life is every bit as important as Elimar's.

There are two further surprises. Elisabeth is taken up by a shady widow and a twenty-year-old seamstress assistant of hers, Adelgunde. Their principal business is persuading men to part with money ostensibly for charity or small services, an exertion not so far removed from those of Andersen's Copenhagen aunt and her attendant girls as they would profess themselves to be. In the course of her association with the widow and her girls Elisabeth calls at an apartment where she finds two friendly men, both connected with the day of her birth on the Fyn estate: Baron Holger, now a roué who likes the company of girls and women of diverse kinds, and his great friend Baron Herman, the eccentric Baroness's grandson, who, for all his bohemian streak, is an honourable, kindly, sensitive man. That day the love of Herman and Elisabeth for each other begins. The second surprise is that, while she is still in Copenhagen, the object of her ambitious venture, King Frederik, who has in his long regal career raised and dashed so many hopes, and, qualifiedly, raised them again, dies. In the mythology of the young, kings and queens cannot die; that this one does provides an awakening in Elisabeth to life's realities outside even the admirable pages of Scott.

Elisabeth like Gerda in 'The Snow Queen' and Scott's Jeanie Deans stands at her story's centre, performs its most adventurous and praiseworthy feat, of a kind usually reserved in both literature and life for males, and is its most sympathetic and fully drawn figure. She differs from Jeanie and Gerda in being intellectually inclined, in fact an embryonic literary artist. Though, when her lover reads and comments somewhat critically (and to us patronisingly) on her writings and she protests that she is only writing for herself – how many gifted and original nineteenth-century women must have felt themselves obliged to make this reply! – we are left in little doubt that she will continue her literary endeavours. Whatever its application to Elisabeth's own efforts, Herman's remarks about the novel form have impressive resonance: 'I Romanen vil jeg ikke have Begivenheder alene, men Charakteer og Poesie. . .'[74] 'In the novel I will not have events alone, but character and poetry.'

Poetry – especially in the description of the Langeland coast and the Halligen islands – The Two Baronesses does contain, and humour too, that constant and individual presence in Andersen – notably in the figure of the Kammerjunker (Chamberlain), a rootless artistic jack of all trades fuller of plans than attainments, and, though inspiring affection, often treated as a social inferior. He is a parodic version of the author himself. The activities of the widow-lady and her young companion are portrayed with a refreshing freedom from the mounting bourgeois morality of the age. But 'character' – by which we means the portrayal of human beings in depth so that their emotions, behaviour and experiences alike address our own being – no, here The Two Baronesses is deficient. Even the heroine we feel is schematically manipulated into, to use Herman's essentially pejorative term where novels are concerned, 'Begivenheder', 'events'. Not only does she fail to partake of Jeanie Deans's individuality and culture (Scott is at pains to show his heroine's Covenanter roots), but we have the uneasy feeling that the action in which she emulates Scott's heroine has been decided by the author too long in advance so that it does not fully accord with her whole personality as it has developed. Most of the other dramatis personae are brief walk-on parts: Count Frederik, Baron Holger, even Elimar, and the more sympathetic Moritz and Herman lack the sollity and hence the significance intended for them. Maybe then the whole book is too voulu, its fundamentally amiable intentions too conscious and thus too near the surface for this to match Andersen's work in his now-preferred medium, the tale. Maybe too – despite that near-jocular entry of his in his diary – the times were too demanding for

Andersen to give his mind and his heart to a full-scale work of this kind. And maybe negative mental rumblings – if not as disagreeable as those of Kierkegaard's *Journal* – did prevent a sustained mood of confidence.

5

On 23 February 1849[75] the truce ended with the result that on 2 April fighting resumed. At January's London Conference which had seemed to be acceptable not only to Prussia but to the German Confederation as a whole, Denmark refused to give way on the Duchies' unbreakable tie to the Danish crown. This was to be a year of victories for the Danes, but each victory came with severe losses: Adsbøl (3 April over Schleswig-Holsteiner troops), Dybbøl Mølle (13 April over troops from the German Confederation), Vejlby, 31 May preventing another Prussian advance into Jutland, and decisively Fredericia on 6 July. All this ended in a truce on 10 July as doomed as the first: Schleswig to be administered separately from Holstein, which would be ruled by a German vice-regent.

Andersen travelled in Sweden from 17 May to 16 August, gathering the material he would use for his lyrical travelogue expressing faith in humanity, *I Sverrig* (*In Sweden*, 1851),[76] which would come out in Britain and Germany as well as Denmark. When he returned, it was to a country not only thankfully enjoying a temporary peace but able to congratulate itself on having become a democratic Constitutional Monarchy: universal male suffrage, a two-chamber parliament, freedom of speech and of religious worship. From lagging behind Western Europe Denmark advanced to its vanguard in respect of civilian rights.

The Schleswig-Holstein question, however, was still not settled. Prussia, not of one mind anyway on the matter, was exhausted and therefore prepared to postpone demands for the Duchies indefinitely. So 2 July 1850 saw the signing at Berlin of a peace treaty between Denmark and Prussia which – at least in its own eyes – gave the former the ability to deal with the recalcitrant in Schleswig-Holstein as it judged best. The Battle of Isted (Istedt) fought on 25 July from the very earliest hours until evening and inspiring a poem by N.F.S Grundtvig himself, 'Det var en Sommermorgen',[77] 'It was a summer morning', effectively smashed the Holstein army. One of the fallen on the Danish side was Frederik Læssøe, officer-son of Andersen's friend and mentor Signe, and Andersen mourned the cutting off of a talented individual's life.[78] Andersen would commemorate the battle in '*To Be or Not To Be*' Essentially the tide had turned against the Duchies, and attempts by the Schleswig-Holstein commander, General Karl Wilhelm von Willisen, to provoke other German states into rallying against the Danes failed. The Danes were successful at the Battle of Lottorf, 24 November 1850, but decided not to pursue their enemy; there were no Danish dead and only one Schleswig-Holsteiner fatality. In early

1851 the Danish troops started to come home, and Andersen joined in all the jubilations: 'Life has been rekindled in people,' he wrote in his diary on 9 February, 'the old despondency is gone. They're on the move; they get together; they have been restored to an awareness of themselves and a sense of brother hood.'[79] He listened with fascination to the stories of returning men, celebrated them in verses of his own and edited a compilation of poems and songs written during the Three Years War for distribution to the soldiers. Peace itself was to be confirmed in the (second) London protocol of 8 May 1852 affirming the integrity of Denmark (the Royal Danish Federation) as a 'European necessity and standing principle'; Schleswig and Holstein were to be treated as separate entities, the one not enjoying any closer relation to the Danish crown than the other but each bound to it, as its head.

Whatever the good outcome of *Treårskriget,* Andersen was frequently depressed in its aftermath. To have known that peaceful, respectable members of his nation had ended up with blood and faeces streaming out of their shot-punctured abdomens or their nerves shattered by their witnessing of these horrors naturally affected the equilibrium of his mind. Besides, 1850 and 1851 were sad personally for Andersen, for reasons adumbrated in our Introductory section: figures of the Golden Age who had been both mentors and friends were coming to the end of their life. On 20 January 1850 Adam Oehlenschläger died, peacefully with his children around him, listening to the testimony of Socrates about eternal life. For all his younger man's rivalry with him, and the doubts he had sometimes expressed on the universal merits of all his works, Andersen had admired him and been fond of him, noting that relations between them had greatly improved of late, and besides he believed him to be the first among Nordic poets. His death was 'a great sorrow for me, – a sorrow too for Denmark and the realm of art'.[80]

Dearer still in a personal sense, and a constant inspiration as writer and thinker, had been H.C. Ørsted. He had fallen ill in the early days of March 1851, but believed he would get better; Andersen did not think so. Ørsted died on 9 March; Andersen had been in his house all day, and had slipped out to walk to the Collins' when the death actually occurred. 'It was almost too much for me to bear. . . . Ørsted, whom I had known and come to love through almost all the years I had been in Copenhagen. He was one of those most interested and understanding throughout the varying fortunes of my life. . . . It felt as though my heart were going to break.'[81] Jens Andersen in his *Life* is particularly strong on Andersen's relationship with the man who had perceived qualities in Andersen that not even Jonas Collin had done, who was sure that his extraordinary imagination would create works (far from being runners-up to the productions of Oehlenschläger and Ingemann) of altogether unique, and in truth immortal quality. Ørsted's great last work, *Aanden i Naturen (The Spirit*

in Nature, two volumes, 1850/51),[82] seemed to Andersen the very consummation of his chief intellectual guide's profound thinking about existence: that the
human mind mirrors the complexities the scientist can scrutinise in all forms
of Nature, serving to illustrate the workings of a spiritual force both in and
behind the universe itself. Jens Andersen believes that Ørsted saw Andersen as
the chief literary representative of his ideas. And indeed his 'spirit in Nature',
both before and after its final two-volume exposition, profoundly informs
Andersen's writings – as must already be evident to the reader of this study: all
those many literary syntheses of human, animal and plant life infused with
emotions, very frequently articulated to mutual satisfactory comprehension.

  Four days before Ørsted's death Andersen had lost another dear friend, the
composer Hartmann's wife Emma.[83] Nor was this all:

> At the very time of her mother's death, the youngest of the children, a little girl
> called Maria, suddenly fell ill. I have preserved some of her features in one of my
> fairy-tales, 'The Old House'. It was this little girl who, as a child of two, always
> had to dance when she heard music or singing, must dance to it; and when she
> came into the room on a Sunday while her brothers and sisters were singing
> hymns, she would start dancing. But her sense for music would not allow her
> not to do what was correct, and so she automatically stood throughout each
> hymn, first on one leg and then on the other, involuntarily dancing to its rhythm.
>
>   In the house of her mother's death this little head bowed down, it was
> almost as though her mother had prayed to our Lord, 'Let me take one of the
> children with me, the smallest, for she cannot do without me.' And God heard
> her prayer.[84]

The Denmark of the early 1850s was far nearer to the country later generations
are familiar with – in its unifying values, in its priorities and social temperament – than that before 1848. And it is hard not to attribute this, to a very
considerable extent, to the powerful figure of N.F.S. Grundtvig.[85] The Collins
may have disliked him, Andersen been at times equivocal, but he still remains
a pivotal member of the culture he helped to bring into coherent shape. His
study of Nordic myth, his translation of myths into learned volumes and poems
proved not just inspiriting but harmonising for Danes developing their national
consciousness after years of difficulty. His view that the Bible possessed a spirit
greater than its varying parts, together with his often-quoted dictum that
people were human before they were Christians, helped create a non-divisive
church for Denmark. He himself was a practical as well as a practising Christian,
as pastor of the chapel of the Vartov Hospital from 1839 till his death in 1872.
The achievement for which Europe has remembered – and even sought to
emulate – him is the establishment of Folk High Schools, popular education to

stimulate the mind and imagination of all, irrespective of background. (They were to take off in Sweden too.) Queen Caroline Amalie was an ardent supporter of this wide-scale project, and we would surely be right to see Andersen's own tales as an expression of the same endeavour, of the Danish *folkelighed* he sought to encourage.

Two fairy tales from the early 1850s seem to me worth examining more closely now: ' "Alt paa sin rette Plads!" ' (' "Everything in Its Right Place!" ', 1852)[86] and 'Nissen hos Spekhøkeren' ('The Goblin at the Grocer's', 1852).[87]

6

It was Just Mathias Thiele (1795–1874) who suggested that Andersen write a fairy tale about a whistle that could blow everything into its right place. 'In these words lay the plot of the story and from that the fairy tale sprang.' But what does 'sin rette Plads', 'its right place' really mean, and what constitutes 'Alt', 'everything'? Changes cannot be made in one corner without radically, and visibly, affecting the whole vicinity. Andersen, in common with thinking people all over Europe from 1848 on, had been giving intense thought to this question. He would come to his conclusions by following through transpositions made via a fairy-tale conceit, and for his purposes would jettison the kind of chronology so dear to the social novel, now in thorough literary dominion. His brief tale, in contrast, leaps over blocks of years and spans more than a century, to end with a characteristic saw-like one-liner, half sending up the mental exercise in which the whole piece has engaged: 'Evigheden er lang, længere end denne Historie.'[88] 'Eternity is long, longer than this story.' Also Andersen will employ magic with its own consistent laws to convey a universal truth more sharply than any plot device used in realist fiction could ever do.

A young tutor to a rich baronial family makes the operative whistle out of the branch of an old willow tree. He does so at the request of the boy who is his youngest charge, but also to please the baron's oldest daughter who loves the willow tree and cherishes stories of its history. Later there is a grand reception in the baronial household and the young man has no alternative but to play publicly on the whistle, even though he first declined to do so; a mocking young 'Cavaleer', in effect laughing at him because of his social position, was too insistent. But – 'Det var en underlig Fløite! der lød en Tone, saa udholdende, som den klinger fra Damp-Locomotivet, ja meget stærkere',[89] 'It was an extraordinary flute! There issued a sound, so penetrating, as if it rang out from a steam-locomotive, yet much stronger.'

The simile is very much one of the Andersen of these years of change ('Thousands of Years to Come', with which our study opened, is this tale's contemporary); this magic whistle both resembles and outdoes the marvels of the day – resembles because we should never forget what ingenuities modern humankind is capable of, outdoes because there are forces greater even than science at play in our world. And these are what our flute is serving. As a result of the notes played on it, a storm wind arises, which cries out what it is about to effect: 'Alt paa sin rette Plads!'[90] 'Everything in its right place!'

The young baroness – who will be, with the tutor, one of the two chief beneficiaries of the whistle-blast – is the only person in all the ensuing repositioning – or is it restitution of rights? – to know enough not to be surprised by it. The history of the willow tree from which the flute was whittled has long seemed important to her, and it was with the most relevant part of this that the tale itself opened. These first pages show that Andersen had put neither the matter nor the moral questions of *The Two Baronesses* behind him. The willow tree in question – it hasn't been pruned so grows freely, and though twisted by a storm hosts many plants in the cleft in its trunk – is itself an offshoot of a larger willow tree that once grew beside the manor-house moat. Breaks or irregularities in genealogical lines are absolutely integral to this tale. This willow tree – known as 'vort Stamtræ',[91] 'our family tree' – manifests both the importance and the unimportance of them.

More than a hundred years before there stood on the site of the family's present property an earlier manor house, an *ancien régime* establishment whose master lived in complete disregard of social classes other than his own – though in his work-free life he lived off their backs. Coming back from one of the hunting expeditions that fill his ample leisure time, he sees the estate's goose-girl – 'Halv Barn var hun endnu',[92] 'Half a child was she still' – hurrying her flock over the moat-bridge to avoid the galloping horses. It amuses him to poke her in the chest with his whip, making her lose her balance, and to shout the story's motto at her, adding: 'i Skarnet med Dig!'[93] 'into the mud with you!' ('Skarnet' could equally well be translated as 'the shit'.) He laughs at his own crass humour, as do his sycophantic, wastrel companions. And into the mire the girl would have fallen had she not clutched the branch of the willow tree. But in doing so she causes it to snap off, and she would have fallen down into the moat had not a man who witnessed the whole ugly business given her a strong hand. He is a pedlar, a wandering stocking-seller, and he plants the broken willow branch in the ground, begging it to grow so a flute could be made from its wood. This could play a tune the lord of the manor and his friends would dance to. Shortly afterwards the pedlar himself suffers at their hands. Inside the manor house plying his wares, he is subject to more cruel practical jokes, forced to drink out of one of his stockings.

Leaving the manor, and likening it to Sodom and Gomorrah, he realises that it was no place for him. Literally true, ultimately untrue. For while the

Baron and his friends – hell-raisers like the older Baroness's father-in-law and husband in Andersen's previous novel – drink and gamble their way into bankruptcy, the pedlar himself works hard and builds up enough trade to buy the property from them. As Andersen puts it: 'Ærlighed og Driftighed, de give god Medbør, og nu var Hosekræmmeren Herre paa Gaarden.'[94] 'Honesty and enterprise, give good fair wind (i.e. prosperity), and now the pedlar was lord of the manor.' The prevalent values of the nineteenth century have asserted themselves betimes, almost half a century before the French Revolution: thrifty, middle-class, evangelically disposed and hard working. These prevail over the unthinking acceptance of high rank and the consequent self-indulgent hedonism of so many members of the squirearchy. Appropriately the new-type squire, the pedlar-landowner, bans cards in his household, reminding us of Andersen's own strong anti-gambling stance.

He also takes himself a wife, and who else but the goose-girl with her undiminished sweetness of nature? She looks as beautiful in fine clothes as any young lady born into the upper classes. How did their fairy-tale-like union come about? Andersen, in complete mastery of his own matter and manner, verbally shrugs: too long to explain in such busy times as the present, and it isn't important to the story anyway. But he vividly conveys what *is* important: that under this pair the manor prospers very thoroughly. Wealth produces more wealth, particularly if the homestead itself is well cared for, the land husbanded, the house always orderly and clean, the mistress spinning with her maids in the long winter evenings, and the master – who rises to the rank of Justitsraad, Privy Councillor – reading aloud from the Bible every Sunday evening.

We now move on a hundred years, and the carefully loaded descriptions of what has replaced the manor and moat that the pedlar bought up – alongside the strange events that cause such upheavals in them – amount to a miracle of condensed social history. As in 'The Old House', a new edifice has gone up on the estate of the old manor, standing on an eminence, proudly modern and with glass windows of such transparency it looks as if there are no panes in them at all. The house is grander as well as smarter than its predecessor, far more comfortable, far fuller of luxuries, and the garden is correspondingly much more orderly, even to the point of being rather manicured-looking, with its smooth-cut lawns, and trellised roses above the front steps. Its owners are evidently rich people, and titled ones too, so can they really be descendants of a resourceful erstwhile pedlar and his goose-girl wife?

Certainly their portraits – an obviously eighteenth-century man with a powdered wig and his obviously eighteenth-century wife with powdered hair – have been relegated to the passageway in the servants' hall where present-day little barons have been amusing themselves shooting arrows at them. The pictures themselves, unlike so many others in the house, are surely worthless junk, and their subjects, so unlike their own papa and mamma, aren't really members of the family; how could they be when he sold wares and she kept geese? Yet they are their own great-grandmother and great-grandfather.

It is clear that this establishment stands at far more of a tangent to the countryside than either the original old manor or the manor when the pedlar and his wife developed it. This is an urban, indeed urbane atmosphere; new money – trade, banking – has obviously gone into the place's design and upkeep. The titles of its owners have probably been purchased, or as good as this. The omnipresent baronial atmosphere extends not only to the resident family themselves but to their many guests and employees. This is nowhere more apparent than at a ball and concert they hold. Clergymen sit modestly in a corner and the clergyman's son who is the young tutor, enamoured of the young baroness, even speaks – a bit pompously and sycophantically – of the beauty of true nobility, of how wrong those social critics are who deny the aristocracy its proper merits, though he hasn't a drop of blue blood himself.

And then he plays the flute, and the forceful wind starts to blow. 'Everything in its right place!' is the order, and the snooty young gentleman who insisted on the tutor playing the flute finds himself, with not a few of his friends, flying head over heels into the chicken-house. Papa, the Baron is blown into the shepherd's cottage, and the shepherd himself is promoted to the servants' hall. Some of the noble guests unconsciously prove their nobility by remaining in place, while the flautist and the young baroness go to the top of the great dining table. They are in love, and where love is, nobility is, as the pedlar and the goose-girl once proved.

Is it an improved, an egalitarian or Grundtvigian society Andersen is presenting to us now? Not exactly, because after everything the different stations remain in place: it is their occupants who are changed round. And we know Andersen to have been far from averse to some of the things that go with nobility – refinement, cultivation of conversation and interests that exceed the utilitarian and are carried out for their own sake. Nevertheless, the very transportations have their own point to make. Absolutely nobody has the right to take their own rank, let alone their right to it, for granted. And when they contemplate it, they should remember the less fortunate, the victimised salesman, the abused servant-girl.

'The Goblin at the Grocer's' is a delightful *jeu d'esprit*, but serious enough, and the one-liner saying at its end presents a quite undeniable truth about our lives. A 'Nisse',[95] or goblin, widespread in Scandinavia, has his equivalent in British folklore: he is the hob or lob who does helpful work about the house and garden in exchange for a dish of food (porridge more often than not) left out for him by the householders. And it is porridge – with a large pat of butter floating in the middle – which Andersen's goblin receives from the grocer with whom he makes his home. A student lives in the house too, up in the attic. He buys his provisions from the grocer, coming in the back door to do so. But one day he is so intrigued by a leaf from a poetry book he spies at the base of one of the grocery casks that he asks to have the whole book instead of his usual cheese. For the student, poor and unimportant though he is, passionately loves poetry, and when the goblin creeps up to his garret, he sees him engrossed in the torn pages the grocer has given him. Reminding us of 'The Shadow' and the apartment across the way where 'Poesie' dwelled, the goblin now sees the dreary little upstairs room transformed by emanations from the poetry book: a great tree springs up with green leaves and blossom, and each blossom is a beautiful girl's head. No wonder the goblin likes being in the student's quarters. And yet – the dull, incontestable fact remains: *the student has no porridge*. And hasn't he himself to be where the food is? Yes, but even so his total satisfaction with the main part of the grocer's house diminishes after his glimpse of the Poesie-filled room.

One night the goblin wakes up to hear appalling sounds: a fire has broken out, and the grocer's household must be evacuated. Everybody wants to save the possession dearest to him/herself. The goblin leaps up the stairs to the student's attic, and finds him standing quietly by the window gazing at the conflagration. It is the goblin who seizes the poetry book and takes it to rooftop safety. As he sits there, reading it himself in the glare of the street fire, he realises that he shares the student's priorities, that poetry is what he himself cares for most. And then he thinks of the part of the grocer in his life:

'Jeg vil dele mig imellem dem!' sagde han, 'jeg kan ikke reent slippe Spekhøkeren for Grødens Skyld!'

Og det var ganske menneskeligt! – Vi andre gaae ogsaa til Spekhøkeren for Grøden.[96]

'I will divide myself between them!' said he, 'I can't completely let go of the grocer because of the porridge!'

And that was perfectly human! – We others also go to the grocer's because of the porridge.

This beautifully crystallises the basic nineteenth-century tussle between material need and spirituality, between commercialism and culture. It is even a pointer towards the Wilcox–Schlegel dichotomy of E.M. Forster's *Howards End* (1910).

But Andersen's most considerable imaginative undertaking of the mid–1850s was the novel *'At være eller ikke være'* (*'To Be or Not To Be'*). He began

preparations for it in November/December 1855, and the book came out –
simultaneously in Danish, German and English – in May 1957. It is a remarkable and too little known work.

7

Before the Jutland clergyman, Japetus Mollerup sets out on his first visit to
Copenhagen in thirty years, his daughter begs him to bring her a good book,
while his wife requests as her present a bad boy – 'en slem Dreng'[97] – out of
whom she can make a *good* Christian. Japetus does indeed return from the
capital with a boy – Niels Bryde, the novel's protagonist – and though he cannot
be described as 'bad', he exhibits enough wilfulness to distress this God-fearing
couple. Chief among these is his inability to accept Christianity as a matter of
faith. Instead he moves through religious doubt into science-based atheism,
and this despite following Japetus's example and studying for the ministry.
Increasing alienation from his adoptive parents culminates in a twelve-year
period of never seeing them at all. Yet at the end of the novel Niels returns to
the Jutland parish for their diamond wedding, and finds himself, in the depth
of his soul, reciting 'Fader vor',[98] 'Our Father'. After so long a time – which
includes the terrible 1848–50 War – the prayer of the clergyman's wife has been
answered.

The scheme of the book will already be clear: Niels, orphaned at age eleven,
is fortunate enough to be taken into a good, Christian home but, resisting its
tenets to the point of renunciation, he knows true homecoming, spiritual as
well as literal, only in maturity. By this time, thanks to the hard lessons of experience, he has overcome stumbling-blocks to the quietude of genuine belief.
The trajectory of his life thus partakes of the closing of a circle.

That this is the novel's underlying design is apparent when we compare a
salient early passage about Niels as a child with one near the close. In Niels's
early years the two books most important to him were the Bible and the
Thousand and One Nights, just as they had been for Andersen himself. The
stories in both compendia shed light on existence for him. Aladdin in particular has such appeal for Niels that, even later on in life, he sees as significant a
childhood dream in which he emulated him:

Han drømte nemlig en Nat, at han som Aladdin steeg ned i Hulen, hvor
tusinde Skatte og skinnende Frugter næsten blændede ham; men han fandt
og fik den forunderlige Lampe, og da han kom hjem med den, var det – hans
Moders gamle Bibel.[99]

He dreamed namely one night, that like Aladdin he descended into a cave,
where a thousand treasures and shining fruits nearly blinded him; but he

found and took the wonderful lamp, and when he came back home with it, it was – his mother's old Bible.

And in the final chapter – actually entitled 'Den nye Aladdin', 'The New Aladdin' – we revisit this dream with him. Niels has been moved by his reunion with Jutland folk of his past, all showing their age now, and thinks also of those he has lost during the course of his life: his blood parents, the Jewish girl, Esther, whom he had come to love. Pain and death are inseparable from exist-ence and should be our chief instructors, a truth which makes him recall his long-ago dream of going down into the cave, picking up Aladdin's wonderful lamp and discovering later that it was his mother's old bible. But his reflections don't end there:

> Ja, tilvisse! som en ny Aladdin var han steget ned i Videnskabens Hule, for mellem dens vidunderlige Frugter at finde Livets Lampe, og han holdt – sin Moders gamle Bibel, ikke dens Legem, men dens guddommelige Sjæl.[100]
> Yes, indeed! Like a new Aladdin he had descended into the cave of science, in order to find among its wonderful fruits the lamp of life, and he held – his mother's old bible, not its body, but its divine spirit.

Enough has been said already of the imaginative importance of Aladdin to the Danish psyche, and of its personal meaning for Andersen himself. Didn't he write in his diary for Christmas 1825 when staying with the Wulffs: 'Oh, what hasn't God done for me! It is going for me as it did for Aladdin. . .'?[101] But he can now see himself as 'a *new* Aladdin'. He has in recent years climbed down into the cave not for precious minerals to make him rich (the normal reading of the *Arabian Nights* tale, for doesn't every hero, especially one of humble provenance, want to end up prosperous?) rather in the hope of finding among the fascinating discoveries of science the very key to the mystery of existence. Out in the light of common day, of reviewed empirical experience, these turn out to be part of the lessons of the Bible.

But we note it isn't the Bible *tout court*, as in his original dream. The new Aladdin's lamp is not a literal book but the spirit immanent in it. Readers know now just how much of time and energy Niels has spent on rigorous current German biblical scholarship. Yet just as scientific discoveries cannot diminish his faith, but are splendid complements to it, neither can this Higher Criticism of Holy Writ. The Bible can now be seen – as many Grundtvigians did indeed see it – as an *imperfect* vehicle for perfect truths, however full the text might be of impurities and inconsistencies; as a repository of matchless moral and spiritual truths, humankind's strongest illuminator. Niels, newly appreciating all this, stands not just for Andersen – whom he resembles far less closely than any of the heroes of his other novels – but for every thinking Dane of the times.

Importantly, the new Aladdin we salute on departure is an *adult,* not just a resourceful youth; he has the right to think of himself as a member of a sore-tested but successful new country. He has not only come through the appalling trials of the Three Years War but has acquitted himself well in it, experiencing its tragedies and its victories at first hand and personally contributing to relieving its pains and sorrows. Niels is admiringly cognisant of recent achievements in science and learning – in Denmark and elsewhere, perhaps in the German lands most of all – and is prepared to build on them. But equally he wants to be at one with the country's longest-held creed, Christianity, which has undergone civilised evolution until it can now be viewed in its essence: the core teachings of its founder.

In the new Constitution of 1849[102] – probably through the exertions of Grundtvig himself – the exact position of the State Church was not rigidly defined. As a result it was able to accommodate – like another state Protestant organisation, the Church of England – a diversity of religious opinions and to be respected for its social role by those unable to accept traditional Christianity at all. Thus – though there are some less than complimentary remarks about Grundtvigianism in the novel – Niels, back at home with a pastor foster-father he once found too narrowly doctrinaire, can feel part of this man's family (he has a devout daughter, Bodil), even of his flock, with no sense of psychological or intellectual strain. Or so we are asked to believe. The novel doesn't show us Niels after these moments of spiritual reconciliation.

'To Be or Not To Be' then gives us a threefold Aladdin's journey, rewarded by reunion with the loving guardians of a *Weltanschauung* once spurned. Andersen spoke of his immense labours on the novel, and truly the territory covered, societal, geographical, emotional, intellectual, historical, must have made enormous demands on him (though it is hard not to detect a certain hastiness in the last chapters). But both at the time and subsequently it has not been one of Andersen's most admired – let alone loved – productions, something easily enough accounted for. The task of presenting religious doubt and its resolution in a narrative that also strives to bring to life individuals in a specific society is a hard one, and the novel – like *The Two Baronesses* – suffers as a result from an imbalance of attention. As a serious man of his day Andersen was interested in, maybe even knowledgeable about, the religious controversies preoccupying so many. But they did not enter the creative components of his mind; he was respectful of theses and disputes, but not mentally at ease with them. Earnest respectful endeavour replaces imaginative engagement, and this is why even those critics and biographers well-disposed to Andersen as a novelist,

Bredsdorff or Jens Andersen, have paid the book comparatively little attention. Before a closer examination, then, why not cite those merits it possesses, for all its undoubted unevenness, over its predecessors? They are, in this critic's view, far from inconsiderable.

In Niels Bryde, Andersen has created a male character with little obvious resemblance to himself, while not being in any way a compensatory stand-in. His maleness is not just firmer than that of his counterparts in the other novels, it comes across as something we don't question. And it reveals and exercises itself, both interestingly and credibly, in action within the public arena, without shirking the challenge of combat. Niels is intelligent, with a questioning intellect never lightly satisfied, and is therefore eminently representative of that egregiously questioning European generation which participated in – or at least found sympathetic – the upheavals of 1848. He is also – which helps us to accept him in sociological and historical terms – quite blessedly free from shoots of genius: the improvisational gifts of Antonio, the wayward Byronic temperament of Otto Thostrup (though he, a fellow Jutlander, is the hero to whom Niels is closest), the thwarted musical talents of Christian in *Only a Fiddler*, or even the rare literary powers of Elisabeth the younger Baroness – to say nothing of the spectacular capacities of the prodigy Peer in Andersen's last novel of all.

Allied to this is another welcome absence in the novel – that of excursions into high society, and likewise of protectors/patrons of dazzling eminence to whom gratitude must constantly be expressed. You could argue that, together with 'Everything in its Right Place', no work of Andersen's displays the post-Constitution, Grundtvigian *folkelighed* of Denmark more than '*To Be or Not To Be*'. Niels comes from good working-class stock, his saviour Japetus Mollerup is an ordinary enough clergyman (and, paradoxically, the more credible as an idiosyncratic individual for being this), of no social consequence outside his remote Jutland area. The Jewish Arons family are drawn with a confidence and verisimilitude (for all the ideational matter foisted on them, especially the daughter, Esther) that allows us to see them as likely inhabitants of a *real* Copenhagen. It is as if Andersen – having shed his authorial self of the type of obeisance to grandees that dominated his social calendar – felt at liberty to exercise that natural sharpness of observation and psychological assessment we encounter in his diaries. The characterisation here of Herr Svane, the perennial student who is Japetus's friend and Niels's godfather, or of Julius Arons, the spoilt son of an affluent father (his background consequently moving us the more keenly when he fights in the war – and loses his life) illustrates Andersen's truth-telling shrewdness superbly.

Then this fifth novel develops more fully and impressively what we have already admired in key sections of the earlier fiction: Andersen's ability to understand and bring to life the ways of a nameable community, with its particularities of belief, custom and conduct. He knew Jutland and its

Silkenborg area more intimately than he obviously did the Campagna (*The Improvisatore*) or the Halligen islands (*The Two Baronesses*), which explains the greater solidity here of both landscape and the characters who arise out of it. And they are rendered without the hovering clouds over them of private, still-resented distress which at times obfuscate comparable scene-painting in *O.T.* and *Only a Fiddler*. Perhaps this should be attributed to Niels's moving through places as a full specimen of male humanity, not as an androgynous being, a marsh-plant on legs.

In the book's first chapter Japetus Mollerup goes back to his old Copenhagen college, Regentsen. Its caretaker, Poul is also janitor of the adjacent observatory with its Round Tower, where he lives with his son Niels. At the reunion party held for Japetus, Herr Svane introduces him to his godson; this is Niels, clearly a great favourite with the whole company, 'livlig og opvakt',[103] 'lively and quick-witted', with 'Læselyst', 'a passion for reading', qualities that will never forsake him. Herr Svane suggests that the following day the boy should show Japetus the way to his own apartment; when he fails to turn up to do so, this seems greatly out of character. The two men soon find out the reason; Niels bursts in on the two of them and tells them his father has just been killed.

Poul had gone out into the city streets earlier that morning on a shopping errand, undecided whether he should turn first to the right or to the left to discharge it. After a moment's deliberation he went left, and almost as soon as he did so, a window crashed down on top of him from the third storey of a building. It didn't kill him outright, but he died shortly after his arrival in hospital. This abrupt and strange happening accords with Andersen's constant preoccupation with the relationship between blind (or seemingly blind) chance and the Christian God's foreknowledge and will.

Finding out that Poul was a widower and that his son has no living relations, Japetus – remembering his wife's request – decides to take him to Jutland and give him a home. Up until the previous day Niels and he had no knowledge whatsoever of each other's existence, and the whole episode is surely a correlative for the mystery of how we are placed in life as we are. It too is a matter of chance. Niels – who will share some of his foster-father's intel-lectual interests – is no more like or unlike Japetus than many a son is like or unlike his true father; than, say, Hans Christian Andersen, that epitome of motivation and unswerving concentration on self-imposed tasks, was to Hans Andersen.

Herr Svane – who will appear and reappear as a kind of wayward guardian angel of Niels (he has a certain resemblance to the peripatetic musical *Kammerjunker* in *The Two Baronesses*) – is sure that the right decision for both parties is being made when Japetus takes Niels with him. But is he 'bad' enough to meet Japetus's wife's requirement? Herr Svane assures him: ' "Drengen er hæderlig – og Trold er der i ham" ',[104] ' "The lad is honest – and there is [a] troll in him." ' Certainly both halves of this statement are true – but in a novel with frank theological concerns it is difficult to know quite how we should take this last sentence. If we are to infer from it that Niels is no freer from original sin than any other human, and that this will manifest itself (and by no means always to old Japetus's liking), well and good. But if we are to see this troll as representative of Niels's propensity to evil, only routed by his saving return to the Church, then it holds up less well. In truth Andersen's inclination was to take a psychological, inclusive attitude to behaviour, however disagreeable, especially a child's or young person's. And this is what we find in the case of Niels Bryde, even taking into account certain darker aspects of his behaviour.

After this first chapter bringing foster-father and -son together, we travel back in time for a brief overview of Niels's young life to date: 'Rundetaarn',[105] 'Round Tower', the pages, like the years they deal with, take colour from the remarkable structure after which the second chapter is named. Built to cater for the scientific needs of Denmark's greatest son (in Andersen's estimation), Tycho Brahe, the tower enjoys spectacular views of Copenhagen, of its historic sites and its contemporary bustle alike. A feat of architecture and engineering, and a dramatic, stalwart landmark, it is often alarmingly at the mercy of the elements, regularly battered by mighty winds. And, to suit Brahe, it stretches up towards the heavens, the night patterns of which so intrigue little Niels. Though characteristic enough of Andersen's predilections in life and literature, this chapter suggests – as does the whole boyhood sequence following it – the influence on him of *David Copperfield*, revealed in manner as well as matter, making the relationship between Andersen and the great English novel, when viewed with hindsight as a whole, one of give-and-take. Consider the details Andersen gives us of Niels's imaginative life.... Until Godfather Svane puts him right, he believes the dark spots on the moon are all you can see of a man who stole cabbages and was then placed right up there so all the world below could view him. Couldn't Dickens's David have entertained a similar mythopoeic fancy? And when we move on to Chapter 3 and Niels's arrival at Hvidingedalsbanker, near Silkeborg in Jutland, there is more than a little of the excited, bewildered, ever-curious response of David to Yarmouth when he makes his (temporary) home with the Peggottys. Musician Grethe, the old tailor with his fanatical, self-destructive honesty, the gypsy woman with her special magical tree and her deformed baby, all these come across charged with the mystery that the impressionable Niels instinctually imposes on their existences.

No episodes bring Niels more fully to life or show us Andersen's kinship with Dickens as a recorder of a boy's complex, unpredictable passionate life better than those concerning a cat and (further into the novel) a dog.

Niels is allowed to choose a kitten from the litter of a favourite cat of the manse, and he delights in watching its antics, seeing it play with a brass button like a child with a toy. Then a little gold-and-silver vinaigrette goes missing. The pastor's wife, knowing all other persons near the object would be completely innocent of theft, thinks Niels is the culprit. He is not, and is both hurt and enraged by the very notion that he could be suspected. Obviously – as far as readers are concerned, though Andersen is too subtle to state it – his still fragile sense of security as an adopted boy is threatened. If others cannot see what kind of person he is, someone who would never steal anything and never tell a lie, what hope can there be for him of ever belonging here?

And then the thief is revealed. It is the little cat which, having taken a fancy to the brightness of the vinaigrette, had rolled it into a hole in the skirting-board. Niels, who has been feeling like a pariah, is suddenly seized with blind rage, picks up the kitten and hurls the poor creature against the kitchen stove. This injures the cat so severely that it has to be put down. Of course Niels is appalled by his own action, and the emotional fit in which he performed it makes him feel as though – says Andersen – he has committed the crime of Cain. But it tells us that Herr Svane was not wrong in his remarks to Japetus: there *is* a troll somewhere in Niels; his is a fierce, not an easy-going, adaptable nature, and may well get him – and others too – into trouble. All the same he is sufficiently alarmed by what he has done to watch himself more closely thereafter. What Andersen does not state – but surely intends us to infer – is the limitations of vision of what Burns would have called the 'unco' guid', of the pastor and his wife. Their very virtue makes them see vice too readily, and Niels, innocent of the crime they accused him of, accordingly went on to perpetrate a far worse one.

Niels's impetuosity – this time working for good – is shown in his relation to his dog. One of his own attributes that Andersen did bestow on the young Niels was terror of dogs; he will go any length to avoid them. However in Jutland he soon takes to the manse's beloved watchdog, and his fear leaves him so completely that, when he is in Copenhagen, he acquires a puppy he calls Hvaps (a play on the word 'Hvalp', 'whelp'). This dog becomes his dearest companion. Returning with him to Jutland on the ferry, the dog falls overboard. Niels implores the captain to stop the boat, otherwise Hvaps will be drowned. The captain refuses – to stop a boat for the sake of a dog? But you would stop it for the sake of a man, retorts Niels, and jumps overboard himself, to rescue the animal. Later in their lives, when Niels lies wounded and semi-conscious on the battlefield where he has been serving as a medic, it is Hvaps who finds him and is responsible for his survival, a beautiful, haunting scene.

David Copperfield is also an apt point of comparison in an unfortunate sense, since, just as the vitality in the English novel ebbs after the hero's young boyhood, so here; after the vivid chapters of Niels's Jutland years – taking him to the age of eighteen – the novel loses focus and therefore intensity. It remains, though, always worthy of attention, and in the account of Niels's experiences as an army surgeon in the war shows aspects of Andersen's mind and art which may well have taken critics by surprise. But Niels as a social animal in Copenhagen does not greatly interest us; indeed he interests us far less than the not dissimilarly placed Otto in *O T*, and for two reasons.

If Niels has a masculinity more acceptable, more recognisable by conventional criteria than Andersen's other heroes, this does not take a sexual form. He is a keen sportsman, liking to go out with a gun on the Jutland heath, he has a taste for dialectical argument in which he can more than hold his own. But to passion he is a declared stranger; he is a cerebral, hard-working intellectual with no time for the erotic; he has the opportunity to visit the dance halls of Hamburg but they don't appeal to him. Though he has a circle of friends, he is not preoccupied by comradeship – even with Julius – as Andersen's other young men are. All this means that, after his boyhood, he is difficult either to identify with or even properly to see and hear. And when we are asked to believe in his late love for Esther – who has largely represented opposite points of view to his during their seemingly interminable discussions on religion – we cannot really comply. Esther is a concept rather than a character, as, we rather feel she was to Niels himself. However, we have to add to this criticism the literary success of the account of her death in the terrible cholera epidemic of 1853. Perhaps this gains in effect because the author makes us understand that, tragically, she is but one of many whose sufferings Niels unflaggingly confronts as a doctor.

Religious debates being so heatedly to the fore in the Europe of the 1840s and '50s, nothing is more believable than Niels's intent wish to come to grips with them, and, especially as he is actually reading for the ministry, absorbing current ideas to the point of (temporary) discipleship. Those of two in particular engage him: David Friedrich Strauss (1808–74)[106] and L. Feuerbach (1804–72).[107] For a while Niels resists reading Strauss, until fellow students tell him *Das Leben Jesu* (1835–36) is an indispensable work, and then he does apply his mind to it. It would have been an irresponsible budding theologian of the 1840s who did not feel obliged to do so; Niels feels he almost *becomes* this book, which uses a historian and a textual critic's exacting methods to examine the Gospel accounts of Jesus. (George Eliot translated it into English from the German in 1846.) Andersen himself, moved by his own father's utterances that Jesus may well have been a man like any other, if an inspired man, repeatedly held and expressed – sometimes to the annoyance and distress of acquaintances – essentially Unitarian views (which were also those of Charles Dickens). He can have been neither astonished nor shocked by *Das Leben Jesu*, unlike old

Japetus, who is both. Feuerbach is an altogether more revolutionary spirit (in more ways than one; he was influential in the events of 1848 and importantly on Karl Marx himself, despite his turning his critical apparatus on him), and Andersen – perhaps to give his words more authority, perhaps simply to insulate them – includes a quotation from him in the thinker's original German. For Feuerbach – as is pithily clear in these incorporated sentences – Christianity (indeed God himself) was a construct of the human mind devised to answer deep emotional and intellectual needs. Theology should therefore be considered anthropologically; we should seek to determine what these components of human nature and experience are that it is attempting to administer to, and analyse accordingly. The true trinity was that which existed *within* the human being: reason, love and will. Immortality was not to be thought of: indeed his first major book, written only in his twenties, took the form of a fierce attack on the very concept of it: *Gedanken über Tod und Unsterblichkeit* (*Thoughts on Death and Immortality*, 1830). One wonders how Andersen of all people would have reacted to one of its most quoted epigrams: 'Man is a cobbler, and the earth is his last'. In *Das Wesen des Christentums* (*The Essence of Christianity*, 1841) Feuerbach proclaimed God a human creation, and Christianity a myth designed to gratify humankind's longing for perfection. Impassioned pages of '*To Be or Not To Be*' supply a heartfelt rejection of Feuerbach's own rejection – of life after death.

Unless the protagonist is someone of extremely strong and unusual personality who can convert ideas into arresting yet representative actions, like Ivan or Alyosha Karamazov in Dostoevsky – or, dare one say it, since it is *his* soliloquy that provides the book's title and numerous points of reference: Hamlet? – the battle between ideas and flesh-and-blood humans to engage writers' and readers' attention in a form as earth-bound as the nineteenth-century novel is a most unequal one. And Niels, externally, behaviourally so lively, appears inwardly rather a blotting-pad. He has nothing of his own to contribute to the arguments he instigates, and how indeed could he have? He is no Feuerbach. To us – especially when confronting Esther as she passes from Judaism into Christianity – he seems merely to be going through set paces. What one has to term the philosophical aspect of the book is interesting primarily for what it tells us about both Andersen and Danish society in context.

Jens Andersen in his biography makes an interesting case for the novel being in certain respects a posthumous and eminently respectful dissociation, if not precisely from Ørsted himself, then from the ideas expounded in his influential book, *The Spirit in Nature*.[108] Certainly we are led to perceive that Niels's awed study of anatomy and of the power of electricity, far from confirming the theism of Andersen's mentor, sets him on the dangerous course of Feuerbach-like denials of a supreme force external to the *monde visible*, one not merely responsible for the enthralling complexities of Earth's micro-socie-ties (inside the human body, inside a mere drop of water) but capable of loving absorption of the individual into Life Everlasting. For, if you conflate the world of physics and the world of spiritual inquiry too thoroughly might you not conclude terrifyingly and - for Andersen - insupportably, as Niels comes for a while to do, that with annihilation of the brain, the soul too is extinguished?

Though Andersen claims in his autobiography that he and Kierkegaard (who died in 1855) had become, after their much-trumpeted hostilities, civil, even friendly to one another,[109] and though there is some evidence to support the fact that socially they could meet without embarrassment and with a show of friendliness, we can find in the novel only ambiguous regard at best for Denmark's most controversial, indeed notorious theologian, for his desire that Christianity be individually experienced as existential truth. Esther, the questing Jew, who becomes, for an important later section of the novel, Christianity's greatest apologist, does not care for his works - unlike all those Danish society women, says Andersen, who claim to understand him. His writings are described as 'dette Humorets og Forstandens Drypsteens-Væld',[110] 'this collection of stalactites of humour and reason', an implication (I take it!) that aphoristic brilliance is too big a part of them, and that ironically they lead back to 'orthodoxe, gothiske Kirkebue',[111] 'orthodox, Gothic church arches', away from the hurly-burly of quotidian nineteenth-century life. (Considering Kierkegaard's inestimable influence on twentieth-century thought, Esther's evaluation - which is presumably Andersen's own - seems rather wide of the mark, to say the least, but that is not our concern here.)

There are some references to Grundtvig in the novel that are not precisely complimentary. Niels is unconvinced by his 'Edda-Christianity', that is, Grundtvig's determination to see the whole line of pre-Christian myth, espe-cially the Nordic, as though it were divinely approved route to Christianity. As we will find in one of his most ambitious tales, 'Dyndkongens Datter' (The 'Marsh King's Daughter', 1858)[112] and in his story/essay 'Det ny Aarhundredes Musa' ('The New Century's Muse', 1861),[113] Andersen became ever more morally apprehensive of too much reverence for civilisations outside the Graeco-Roman, Judaeo-Christian aegis. Perhaps a more telling qualification of admiration for Grundtvig comes in the scene where Niels, as surgeon, is quar-tered in the house in Schleswig of a strongly anti-Danish, pro-German young woman, Hibernia, with whom he argues. He concedes that Grundtvig, with his articulated patriotism and war songs the greatest champion of the Danish cause, is perhaps letting himself be carried away by partisan fervour. Perhaps he should fight a duel with his German counterpart while the rest of the popu-lation - Danes, Germans and Schleswig-Holsteiners of both denominations - attended to the matter of just getting on with one another.

But this apart – Niels is joking here but pleased to be doing so – '*To Be or Not To Be*' seems impregnated with the essentials of Grundtvigianism, even if it is never acknowledged as such. Instead of a mystic fusion of science, poetry and theology *à la* Ørsted, instead of arrival at a Christian faith through an intellectual assault on its cardinal documents (German scholars still within the Christian fold), we come to a kindly symbiosis of intellectual pursuit and quiet conviction, of acceptance of the past and energetic application to the present, of belief in the importance of the individual soul and a loving commitment to other people and to the best forms of society for them to flourish in. The novel's deeply felt evocation of gypsy life and religion, the solemnity with which the gypsy woman's magic tree, Ma Krokone, is presented, further exhibit a positively Grundtvigian inclusiveness of approach to differing cultures and faiths.

The proof of Andersen's own concordance with all this is the novel's marvellous war sequence, which, together with the childhood chapters, provide the best reason for a restitution of '*To Be or Not To Be*' in the Andersen canon. For its peers we have to turn to the Thackeray of *Vanity Fair* (1847–48)[114] or the Stendhal of *The Charterhouse of Parma* (1839),[115] while reminding ourselves that Andersen is not recreating a war from annals and reminiscences of the elderly but from the still raw experiences of combatants and from his own impressions. And it is warfare at its most uncompromisingly modern.

Niels has changed his studies from theology to medicine, and, virtually at the outbreak of the Schleswig-Holstein war, enlists as assistant surgeon in the regiment that his friend Julius Arons has joined. Julius's conduct here carries complete conviction; long bored by his rich-boy dissipations, he now discovers as a non-commissioned officer an energy in himself that had hitherto been only latent. Danish victory at Bov (9 April 1848) raises spirits generally, but Julius and Niels then move on to Schleswig the city, which the Prussian General Wrangel has been ordered to occupy. After nine hours of intense fighting the Danes are unable to take it from the Prussians (23 April) but Niels has remained on the outskirts of the town and so is able to answer a call to go on to Isted (later the scene of a major Danish triumph). There he has to work with the wounded until he all but drops – the sense of exhaustion is conveyed in Andersen's most kinaesthetic manner – and he has to be roused by mates from the deep sleep into which he falls. Next he makes his way towards the Danish headquarters established on the island of Als. As the enemy army advances into Jutland, the blaze of its fires can be seen all the way over to Fyn. At this difficult, dispiriting period of the war, Niels goes over to Augustenborg to see Julius Arons who is dying from typhus, these soldiers' scourge. Julius asks Niels whether he believes life awaits him after this war, and Niels, to his own surprise, cannot bring himself to give a negative reply. But he knows, only too well as he watches the death throes, that this is the one he makes in his heart.

Weeks pass. Andersen warns us that he is not offering a history of the Schleswig-Holstein war, just a picture of its effect on an individual mind. But with a lively insistence he makes us appreciate the movements of the Danes just before the encounters at Sundeved and Nybøl (28 May) that marked the turning-point and culminated in the victory of Dybbøl Mølle. It is almost midnight on 28 May when Niels, standing on the wall while working with the hospital vans, suddenly experiences a stab of pain, like a hornet's sting, and all goes black. When he comes to – and this with incomplete consciousness – he is lying in a ditch, 'i Overgang til Ting',[116] 'in transition to [being] a thing', as his progressive student self would have said. But he is aware of something in him demanding that this does not happen. He is also aware to an acute degree of his surroundings, the damp grass, the moonlight, a horse dying from war wounds nearby. And his mind continues to play on the difficulties of ascribing spirituality to a failing body such as his own now, the mortality of which will surely shortly be proved.

Just as he is giving himself up to nothingness, he is aware of movement close to him, of two eyes gazing down at him. These eyes belong to Hvaps, his dear dog, who has been looking for him and now has found him, out of love, and now in that love is offering him comfort. The beautiful lines that come next suggest – to me very strongly – that Andersen's now stated belief in the soul, in virtuous forces that can transport us beyond death, does not confine itself to humans:

> Hunden kom til ham-! var dette kun Instinct? Var dette kun Hjernens Function, Nervernes og Blodets Bevægelse, der førte til denne Slutning og Handling, eller var der noget Høiere, og skulde Dyret her, imellem Liv og Tilintetgjørelse forkynde ham det?[117]
>
> The dog came to him! Was this only instinct? Was this only the function of the brain, the movement of the nerves and the blood, which led to this end and action, or was there something higher, and would the animal here, proclaim it to him between life and extinction?

And this is what Hvaps surely does, for two paragraphs later we read of Niels:

> Han laae stille, udstrakt; hans Hund sad klynkende ved hans Hoved, og klart skinnede Maanen hen over Valpladsen, det store Blad med Døds-Hieroglypher, der gjemte Nøglen til Spørgsmaalet:
>   '*At være eller ikke være!*'[118]

He lay still, outstretched: his dog sat whimpering by his head, and the moon shone clear over the battlefield, that great page with death's hieroglyphics, which hide the key to the question:

'To be or not to be!'

It is, of course, Hvap's sounds that draw passing soldiers to Niels, who rescue him so that, in a literal sense, he *is* rather than is *not*. But spiritually too he has passed from the negative stage which has occupied so many youthful years to one of affirmation that he is the possessor of an eternal soul.

8

'*To Be or Not To Be*' was dedicated to Charles Dickens, and at the very time of its reception in Britain, Andersen was – after a ten-year gap and a warmly pressing invitation – the guest of the dedicatee, staying at Dickens's country home near Rochester, Kent: Gad's Hill ('This is the exact spot Shakespeare used as a setting for *Henry IV [Part 2]*').[119] On 28 June 1857 Andersen, alone with Mrs Dickens (Catherine) and the children, was writing in his diary:

Slept restlessly, dreaming. The review in *The Athenaeum* lay upon my heart like a vampire. I'm still sitting this morning heavy at heart. – Letter from Mrs Scavenius. Today in *The Examiner* another not so very good review of *To Be*. They don't seem to have understood the book. I'm not content, cannot be so and feel myself a stranger among strangers. If only Dickens were here! – To exist without being able to express oneself, always fixing one's thoughts on the same dark point without being able to erase it. Lord God, it must be Thy will that I endure this! – Let me bear in mind that I must be friendly and kind to strangers. The forsaken are sent to me by God so that when we meet I can try to help them forget it's an alien land they're in, a language foreign to me they speak. Lord, teach me to be as Thou art – loving. After lunch I talked to Mrs Dickens about my mood. She read the two newspapers, said it was 'stupid' and that her husband never read what the papers said about him. ('Without his knowledge or consent, M. Andersen may deceive some young intelligence, some susceptible heart. In one word, the book is dangerous.') When Dickens came home, he heard about it from his wife and said at the dinner table: 'You should never read anything in the newspapers except what you yourself have written; I haven't read criticism of me in twenty-four years!' – He had brought along with him a Mr Shirley Brooks, one of the foremost contributors to *Punch*, the one who had produced that article about me. Later Dickens put his arms around me, saying, 'Don't ever let yourself be upset by the newspapers; they're forgotten in a week and your book will live on! God has given you so very much; follow your own lead and give what you have in you; go your own way; you're above all those petty things!' – And when we were walking on the road, he wrote with his foot in the sand. 'That's criticism,' he said and rubbed it out, 'and it's gone just like that!' – 'A work which is good survives on its own merits. You've experienced it before; see what the verdict is.' We lay by the monument all evening. A mist was rising from the sea; the sun shone in the windows in Rochester. We drank mixed wine up there. Later there was lightning. – The visitor gave me two issues of *The Times* from a long time ago. When I went to bed, Dickens said he hoped everything had now been forgotten and that I would sleep well. When I was asked at dinner how long I was staying in England, I answered, 'Long for Mr Dickens, short for me!'[120]

Among other things this entry (deliberately quoted in full) reveals what a superb diarist Andersen is, lively, unashamedly personal, with a keen eye and ear, fluid in style, moving from the inward to the external world and back again with an instinctual ease – and ingenuous (surely a virtue rather than otherwise in a diary-writer). In contrast, he was but an indifferent autobiographer, *disin-genuous*, sometimes to the point of psychological dishonesty, and too often unwilling to impose adequate control on self-indulgently over-abundant material. What a lot we learn from this record of 28 June. We have a vivid impression of Dickens's own open, manly, masterful charm, and of his confident approach to writing, his own and that of authors he admired; we have an excellent example in the quotation from his critic, given by Andersen, of English pharisaism, more redolent of journalistic self-importance than true religious conviction, and a lightly executed cameo of the Kentish scene. It also tells one a good deal more about Andersen's behaviour in the Dickens household and its attitude to him than he intended or realised. Which is not to say that he was unaware of the nature of these.

Andersen's stay with Dickens (11 June–15 July) has entered literary history, and we encounter it principally for two reasons: to show the tragicomic extent of Andersen's naïve egotism, and to illustrate the last stage of Dickens' s strained marriage which would end in a publicly announced separation the following year. This is the biographer's territory, not the literary critic's, but I believe Andersen's unhappy experiences of summer 1857 were not without effect, even considerable effect, on the course his work would afterwards take. And it is the diaries, written for himself, that best provide us with intimations of this.

'Long for Mr Dickens, short for me!' Mercifully Andersen never knew what Dickens would famously write after he had gone, words placed on the guestroom mantelpiece: 'Hans Andersen [*sic*] slept in this room for five weeks – which seemed to the family AGES!' But Andersen's own records show that he would not have been wholly surprised, that he was all too aware he was outstaying his welcome – if, after the very first, welcome was what he was given – and yet unable to do anything about the situation, either to save it or to remove himself from it.

Andersen's curiosity never forsook him, even if it were exercised from an extremely self-centred viewpoint, and he was observantly interested by Dickens's sons, recording the not insignificant names their father had chosen for them: 'Charles Dickens, Walter Landor, Francis Jeffrey, Alfred Tennyson, Sydney Smith, Henry Fielding, Edward Bulwer Lytton,'[121] a real roll-call of distinguished English men among whom Dickens clearly counted himself and which he hoped that his offspring would in some measure join. Andersen didn't endear himself very greatly to these boys – his paper-cuts pleased them only at first and they giggled at his making little nosegays of flowers – and this he realised, but he took his own side rather than theirs, as was his general habit. Perhaps, on reflection, he was right to do so here. The Dickens boys strike one all too clearly as the casual-mannered products of a culture (England itself rather than that generated by Dickens personally) too pleased with itself by half. Andersen's often detailed accounts of his time with the family convince one as accurate, for all the note of self-pity. Charles (Charles junior, eldest son) was obviously irritated at having to drive the guest to Rochester to be shaved, though he did later try to be affable and make up for his bad grace ('he must have his moods'). Walter, second son, then sixteen and in a few weeks' time to set out for seven years in India as an officer in Calcutta, was even less disposed to be hospitable.[122] Deputised to be Andersen's escort in the country and the town, he clearly was bored by the role, as he was by the distinguished visitor himself. 'At Gravesend [after returning from central London] I saw Walter Dickens; at Higham he [and a friend] came; neither of them showed any particular attentiveness or interest in helping me by taking my luggage.'[123] Seeing the youth later at an al fresco lunch, Andersen noted: 'Young Walter Dickens asinine! I'm thinking of his father.' In point of fact the life ahead of Walter is sad to think about. He was an unsatisfactory officer; Indian army life didn't suit him. He got badly into debt and had a breakdown. He died in Calcutta of an aneurysm before he could be invalided home. Somehow Andersen's portrait of him in his diary pages suggests the possibility of this fate: through the prism of his own private complaints he saw what he was like.

Though to Dickens's exasperation Andersen would publish a laudatory article about the Dickens family in his publisher's magazine, Bentley's Miscellany,[124] likening Catherine Dickens to Agnes in David Copperfield, that serene model of wifehood and motherhood, in his diary he unmistakably suggests an air of unease in the household. Catherine's sister Georgina who was in fact later to remain with her brother-in-law and his children after Catherine's legally arranged departure comes across as watchful, unfriendly, potentially subverting, actually resenting Andersen's presence. Andersen's own misery during his visit may surely have been caused by his realisation that something was gravely amiss in the family set-up, and his inability to get at it, hampered not just by his clumsy, faltering English but by something in his own temperament. None of his writings, after all, show any insight into marriage, or even into sustained relationships between the sexes. The same goes for the complexities of connections within a family. The underlying tensions of the Dickens boys' relationship with their extraordinary, magnetic father eluded him. And he lacked those robust, extrovert capacities that would have enabled him to join in their more ordinary recreations and entertainments and to establish easier communication with them.

All his life the only family he ever *properly* knew were the Collins. To them he had laid heavy emotional siege almost from the first, and we have observed in the course of this book the problems – the possible resentments, jealousies and competitiveness – that this had involved, though with the years there grew between himself and the family members a steadiness of acceptance, and of reciprocal affection too. The next decade and a half were to see Andersen spending considerable amounts of time with Jonas Collin's grandsons – to whom he was a benevolent, not always tactful but basically concerned de facto godparent. But his experiences of Dickens's family life almost certainly confirmed some melancholy inner knowledge of himself, of just how much he was one of the world's loners.

For that matter, though he always writes in laudatory and grateful terms about Dickens himself in diaries, letters, and published work, the personality of the greatest English writer of his times as he watched it manifest itself in all its varieties must also have uncomfortably overwhelmed him.

Though I have suggested in my account of their 1847 dealings with each other that the two men probably had more affinities with one another imaginatively than either had with any other contemporary, yet their temperaments – and where these led them in social and emotional life – were significantly dissimilar. Dickens's propensity to heartiness has almost nothing in common with Andersen's publicly vaunted super-sensitivities, as that entry for 28 June showed. Dickens must (unwittingly) have reminded him – as the very different Edvard Collin and his novelistic stand-ins did in a different way (the Bernardos and Vilhelms of literature and life) – just how apart he was from most other men, of the uniqueness of the haunted, spirit-populated chambers of his own mind.

Dickens made his London house in Tavistock Square open to him, and Andersen was mesmerised by his friend's acting in his collaborative work with Wilkie Collins, the melodrama *The Frozen Deep*.[125] The audience he was invited to join couldn't fail to impress him either; Queen Victoria and the Queen of Belgium headed its luminaries, and Dickens told Andersen that Victoria knew him to be there. Nobody thrilled more to the spell of the stage or had been more successful in a national theatre than Andersen in Copenhagen, yet his theatre activities there, with his difficult relationship with the Heibergs and his belief in an aesthetic world complementary to the ordinary one, did not resemble the barnstorming performances of Dickens and his team.

In fact I conjecture that something in the whole strident philistine vigour of English life, in contrast with his feted Society sampling of it ten years previously, jarred on him. Certain it is that the literary works he applied himself to when he returned from an English sojourn he knew, deep down, to have been a failure, are outstanding for their involved artistry, their intricate experimentation, their pursuit of the spiritual roots of culture (and indeed of the cultural roots of spirituality), their comparative retreat from the pressures of the humdrum. I cannot believe this to be altogether coincidental, any more than I can that Andersen did not *au fond* understand why, after a polite reply to his thank-you letter, Dickens never wrote to him again and never agreed to any of his requests (to meet Danish visitors to London, etc.). Of course he knew why he didn't, knew too that the reasons were profound ones, inseparable from the nature of his own creativity, from his mysterious heightened sensitivity to pain and joy, rendering hearty extroverted social participation an ultimate impossibility.

And did the protracted and difficult company of Andersen make no impact on Dickens the writer? I believe that in what is for me our greatest novelist's supreme (and certainly most artistically harmonious) masterpiece, *Great Expectations* (1860–61) we can find (conjectural) evidence that his contact with the Danish writer passed through the crucible of Dickens's imagination. Pip is after all from a humble background without any parents, and is transported – through (unknown and mis-identified) patronage – into a world of prosperity and comparative refinement which he, with his complexity of nature, at once admires to the point of eager emulation and sees through. As Andersen's tended to be, Pip's saints are from the economic background he came from (literally in the case of his brother-in-law, Joe Gargery) and his villains from the sneering hyper-confident upper class, like Bentley Drummle who marries and mistreats his *princesse lointaine*, Estella. At the same time – cf. *O.T.* – there is pervasive fear of the more disorientated members of the lower class destructively asserting themselves to wreak their worst (Orlick, and the convict Compeyson, and, for much of the book, Pip's benefactor, Magwitch himself). It is not hard to see the correspondences in the novel of landscape to the complexities and travails of human emotions as strongly reminiscent of Andersen's own use of Nature. And is it wholly a coincidence that the landscape in question is a huge tract of marshland? Andersen himself after all was a 'marsh-plant' (indeed, his next significant work will take us to marshes again), and we have to remember that two works of his that we *know* Dickens to have admired, *The Improvisatore* and 'The Ugly Duckling', offer us unforgettable descriptions of this geographical feature.

But more important is the type of work *Great Expectations* is: a mythopoeic novel for which 'romance' as employed by Hawthorne is as good a term as any. Without sacrificing acute observation of people and society, it operates on a psychic level; that is, it presents its characters primarily in their (utterly convincing) psychic affect, above all for the narrator himself and the course he is trying to steer through the maze of life. Does it not belong to the same genus of literary achievement – not so much as *Madame Bovary* or *L'Education sentimentale*, in other ways its peers – as 'The Snow Queen' or, as we shall see, its contemporary 'The Ice Maiden' (1861)? Its extraordinary events, its characters like Miss Havisham or the lawyer Jaggers who possess the solipsistic powers we associate with fairy-tale persons, combine to form a unified metaphor about existence, of deepest visual and aural impact, and the same can be said for Andersen's masterworks.

CHAPTER 10

What the Wind Tells:
Stories 1858–59

1

Andersen knew the stories written in the two years following his return from England marked an innovative departure from his previous work, demanding refinements in technique and style to meet the challenge of their audacious subjects. He would always believe that the best among them equalled (to say the least) his most celebrated earlier productions, and was irritated by the conservatism of critics and some readers, who would insist on the superiority of the earlier Andersen – the one they knew – without always remembering correctly what was written when![1] Four stories in particular from 1858 and 1859 are particularly rewarding, and they have enough differences from their predecessors and enough in common with each other to be placed in the same chapter. All are overtly Denmark-orientated (indeed three out of the four take us firmly to Jutland) but it is a Denmark which occupies a visible, not to say prominent, place on the historical-cultural European map (stretching back into the first millennium, and further if one thinks in terms of natural life). The tales we are concerned with here then are 'Dynd-Kongens Datter' ('The Marsh-King's Daughter', to call it for the time being by its usual English name, published in *Nye Eventyr og Historier. Anden Samling, New Fairy-Tales and Stories. Second Collection*, 15 May 1858); 'Vinden fortæller om Valdemar Daae og hans Døttre' ('The Wind tells of Valdemar Daae and his Daughters') and 'Anne Lisbeth' (both in *Nye Eventyr og Historier, Tredje Samling, New Fairy-Tales and Stories. Third Collection* published 24 March 1859) and – the fruit of his tour of Jutland, especially its northern parts, 20 June–12 September 1859) – 'En Historie fra Klitterne' ('A Story from the Dunes', in *Nye Eventyr og Historier. Fjerde Samling, New Fairy-Tales and Stories. Fourth Collection*, 9 December 1859).

Andersen – for whom the composition of his surely most ambitious story to date, 'The Snow Queen', had flowed along with miraculous-seeming ease – found the writing of these tales difficult; unprecedentedly so. 'The basic story – as has been the case with all my fairy tales –,' he confessed of 'The Marsh-King's Daughter', 'occurred to me in a single moment, in the same way as a well-known melody or song can sometimes come into one's mind.'[2] He did as he usually did, wrote it down, then worked on it, 'but even after the third version lay before me,' he could not feel satisfaction. In this instance, not with the others, he wanted to do more reading round and research to see the story in the depth it needed and deserved, and all that inevitably gave rise to new questions, new answers: 'this story was rewritten six or seven times, until finally I was convinced that I could not improve upon it'.

The writing went no more easily for a story Andersen rated particularly highly: 'The Wind tells about Valdemar Daae. . . ': 'It is one of the stories that I have revised most for the sake of style, so that the language would have the tone of the blistering, whistling wind, who tells the story.'[3]

This last admission gives us a key to what Andersen was embarking on in these new works: the nature of the narratology itself. Who should present the incidents and people of the story to us to do them the justice the author felt was their due? Through whose eyes – if indeed anybody's – should they be seen? (For eyes will always be part-clouded by their owner's personality and concomitant prejudices.) Our principal guides to the complex events of 'The Marsh-King's Daughter', which involve emanations of primordial evil and virtue, and conflicts for domination between rival cosmogonies, are a pair of storks on their nest. Their chatter has an amusingly domestic quality (the father-bird a touch vain and over-inquisitive, the mother-bird rather too practical and pragmatic in her approach to life) yet what they have to relate takes us away from the certainties of familial duties into conflicts that literally have rent continents asunder. The storks do not comprehend all that they witness – in this sense, they anticipate the modern concept of the unreliable narrator – and to complicate matters they actually intrude into, and play a part in, central events. Indeed the most crucial occurrence of all – Helga's adoption by the Viking woman – is effected by the father-stork. And the narrative device is further complicated at the close of the tale when we are left uncertain as to which age the storks have been talking to us from.

In 'The Wind Tells . . .' it is the wind who, with onomatopoeic effects and not a little pride in its own being, gives us the tragic history of a Sjælland nobleman and his three daughters. Yet here too it is a case not merely of impartial, non-human witness (and even the impartiality isn't total, since the wind has value-based preferences among the daughters), but of a narrative voice which is also an agent in the history concerned. Of Ide it says: 'Tidt tog jeg fat i hendes lange, brune Haar, naar hun ved Æbletræet i Haven stod tankefuld. . .'[4] 'Often I took hold of her long, brown hair when she stood by the apple-tree in

the garden full of thought.' And of her sister Johanne, its favourite who has run
away to sea in disguise, it boasts: 'Den Raskeste af Søstrene tog jeg mig af!. . .
blæste jeg hende overbord. . . ."[5] 'The liveliest of the sisters I took care of!. . . I
blew her overboard', thus saving her from scandal.

What I consider the masterwork in this 1858–59 quartet, 'A Story from the
Dunes' reads like a history, told with both factual objectivity and feeling and
sober acceptance of its tragic outcome, such as the old saga-writers or professional keepers of stories might have had in their repertoire. Yet at the close we
learn that this too has been airborne, has come to the author via the ever-
present winds of north Jutland:

> Ingen forstyrrer den Dødes Hvile, Ingen vidste eller veed det, før nu, –
> Stormen sang det for mig mellem Klitterne.[6]
>   Nobody disturbs the peace of the dead man, nobody knew or knew about
> this before now – the gale sang it to me among the dunes.

'Anne Lisbeth' makes use of no such experimental narrative devices, yet it too
relinquishes conventional presentation of characters in time and space.
Although it proceeds chronologically, it defies linear procedure by deliberately
leaping over a decade and a half of its central character's life, and leaving a not
inconsiderable number of years a blank. There are any number of questions
about Anne Lisbeth we could not answer: Why did she move to the town? Who
did she marry, and what happened to her husband? Why did they have no
children? Was it her marriage that made her well-off, or were there subsequent
relationships? But – paradoxically, and this is one of the story's remarkable
triumphs – by such restricted concentration on but one aspect of his heroine's
life, on an episode of her youth which she herself chose to regard as unimportant and which, against her will, comes back to haunt her, Andersen gives us an
entirely satisfying picture of the person she is, of the ways she will have spent
the years of which we are factually ignorant. What Andersen accomplishes
here is a demonstration of how the human mind moves, at the profoundest
level, independently of clock time. Yet it is housed within a system – the body
– wholly subject to this, to the successive stages of growth, maturity, ageing,
decline. Therefore pressures from deep within, when they rise to the surface,
can erupt into the temporal, spatial sphere, and even affect and change it. Anne
Lisbeth is, we can work out, entering middle age proper when her crisis occurs
– she must be thirty-five.

> Anne Lisbeth gik og tænkte ikke paa nogen Ting, som man siger, hun var
> borte fra sine Tanker, men Tankerne vare ikke borte fra hende, de ere aldrig
> borte fra os, de ligge bare i en Døs, baade de levendegjorte Tanker, der have

lagt sig, og de, som endnu ikke have rørt sig. Men Tankerne komme nok frem, de kunne røre sig i Hjertet, røre sig i vort Hoved eller falde ned over os.⁷

Anne Lisbeth went on and thought about nothing at all, as they say, she went away from her thoughts, but her thoughts didn't go away from her, they are never away from us, they exist even in a snooze, both the vitalised thoughts which have settled, and those which as yet have not stirred. But the thoughts still come forward, they can move into the heart, move into our heads or fall down over us.

It's impossible not to see this as an account of the Freudian unconscious and its workings *avant la lettre*. Except, as we will see, conscience, in the Christian sense, operates through it; deeds and feelings, long suppressed for reasons of 'worldly' expediency, eventually surface for moral acknowledgement. Andersen said in his Notes: 'In "Anne Lisbeth" I wanted to show that all virtues lie in every human breast;'⁸ He likened these to seeds, from which nutritious plants grow.

How to define identity while recognising the extent, the complexity and the inconsistency of consciousness is central to the stories of this quartet. In 'The Marsh-King's Daughter' – far the nearest of them, in both overall effect and component parts, to fairytale – the eponymous main figure is, for the greater part of the narrative, under a curse, like the princess in 'The Travelling Companion'. She alternates between vicious (hyperactive) aggression and a pained, bewildered, beseeching gentleness. For most of the tale the division is immutable, though one presumes that the anguish of the second state owes much to awareness of conduct in the first. The eponymous nobleman in 'The Wind Tells . . . .' is shown as descending through obsession into a madness that sets comfort, health, hygiene, food, clothing, and obligations to other human beings, at naught. Finally he will die in a seizure consequent on a delusional triumph. The alchemist is convinced he has made gold. 'Anne Lisbeth' and 'A Story from the Dunes' show their protagonists becoming (for want of a better word) 'simple-minded'. In Anne Lisbeth's case, as summarised above, it is the final stage of an obsession-dominated guilt-driven psychosis whose roots lie in uncaring youthful action, which she has done her best to expunge from her mind. The tale demonstrates that trying to bully the memory in this way is doomed to failure. In 'A Story from the Dunes' the pitiful mental state is brought about by a trauma consequent on a physical calamity, though behind that trauma itself lies Jørgen's whole scarred history (including that of his birth). Attempting the rescue during a disaster at sea in which he and Clara, the young woman he loves, are involved, he is defeated by the force of the waves and arrives back on the shore bearing the body of his dead sweetheart:

Fjollet kaldte man Jørgen, men det var ikke det rette Udtryk; han var, som et Instrument, hvorpaa Strængene ere løsnede og ikke længer kunne klinge, – kun i et enkelt Øieblik, faa Minuter, fik de en Spændkraft, og de klang, – gamle Melodier klang, enkelte Takter; Billeder rullede op og hentaagede, – han sad igjen stirrende tankeløs . . .⁹

People called Jørgen daft, but that was not the right term; he was like an instrument of which the strings have got loosened, and can no longer sound, – only for one single moment, no more than minutes, would they get elasticity, and give out sound – old tunes rang out, single measures; pictures rolled up and vanished; he sat again staring mindless . . .'

'A Story from the Dunes' comes from the same year as *The Origin of Species*, which would both gather up and stimulate debates about what the English Darwinian Herbert Spencer was famously to call 'the survival of the fittest'.¹⁰ An interesting passage in 'A Story from the Dunes', adjacent to the one just quoted, attempts to contextualise – in biological terms – the hero's terrible fate unjustifiable by any narrowly moralistic or behavioural view of existence. Here we have a boy, conceived, back in Spain, as the welcome heir to privilege, position and wealth, who survived the accident that killed his parents and grew up in Denmark talented, strong and handsome enough to expect a long and fulfilled life and seemingly overcome hazards in the path of this. And then at thirty he loses all ability to manage for himself, even to entertain coherent thoughts. Andersen proceeds to remind us of an earlier cameo in the tale showing a box of bulbs that had drifted onshore from a stranded ship. Shouldn't all of them have grown into beautiful flowers, that being what they were created to do? But the majority rotted on the sand, and some were eaten by fishermen (who mistook them for onions, one assumes). Is that how we should see Jørgen's life – as a wasted flower-bulb? Andersen, as soon as he has imposed the interrogative simile on us, passionately rejects it. No, no! Every human being is made in the image of God. (And possibly every living being, according to a divine concept?) But the image remains, however blighted. Likewise Anne Lisbeth was egregiously attractive. Yet she doesn't stay her course as a well-heeled, well-respected middle-aged woman but degenerates – not a slow process – into a possessed halfwit scrabbling in the hard earth until her fingers bleed from the nails in her efforts to dig a grave. . . . Nevertheless somehow we respect her and feel for her more in this dreadful last development than ever we did earlier on. Her final apotheosis inside the church before the altar seems therefore entirely right.

Andersen's art opposes in every fibre of its being that rejection of imperfect or impaired lives which major belief-systems in the post-Darwin age developed with such infectious thoroughness: laissez-faire capitalism, Social

Darwinism, the eugenics-favouring utopian socialism of Wells, the Webbs, the Myrdals, Marxist-Leninism mutating into Stalinism, as well as Fascism, Nazism, the various avatars of the Free Market with its doctrinaire refusal to find room for those who cannot bring in good money. We shall return to this major strand (arguably *the* major strand) of Andersen's literary achievement in the final chapter when we attempt a summarising overview. But it is undoubtedly this group of stories that first and uncompromisingly embodies Andersen's detestation of a utilitarian attitude to human beings (and to their non-human kin: there is a beautiful plea for a donkey's soul towards the beginning of 'A Story from the Dunes'). The corollary of this is dignified representation of the jumbled thoughts, the unarticulated emotions of those for whom utilitarianism put into practice could find no room.

Their technical adventurousness, their new philosophical emphasis do not mean, however, that these tales eschew Andersen's grammar of images which was inextricable from his language as a writer. Storks, swans, storms, the transitional country between water (sea, fjord) and the land, marshy terrain home to secret amphibious life, all recur. Even more important, all these tales give us children, orphaned or abandoned and having to survive in a world without the support of kinfolk, that motif with its origins in Andersen's earlier moments of self-awareness, and often with heart-touching parallels in the creature world.

Helga, the Marsh-King's daughter is the result of her monstrous father's rape of her Egyptian princess mother who came to the bog-country of north Jutland as a swan in order to find a healing plant for her sick father. Deposited like Thumbelina as a miniature humanoid in the bud of a flower, she was found by the father-stork, who took her to be brought up by surrogate parents, a Viking chief and his wife. The chieftain, away on raids for much of his foster-daughter's young life, is proud of her beauty, her tomboy's strength and daring and knows nothing of her other side – her nightly existence as a wounded, mournful frog. Her foster-mother, on the other hand, is repelled by Helga's wilful, often cruel audacity, and responds to her sad tenderness when she appears in her hideous amphibian form.

Valdemar Daae's daughters are certainly his – by his proud, well-born beauty of a wife, compared (by the wind) to a tulip, magnificent, showy and without scent. But they might as well not be, since after her death he has little thought, let alone affection, for them. The acquisition of gold is his consuming interest, and when it doesn't come his way after his extravagant building of a ship, then he turns to alchemy, to the transmutation of other material into gold, and this fills his days and nights. Meanwhile his daughters lead neglected, unfulfilled lives, and face dereliction after his death. The rose, the lily and the hyacinth they were called when young. But the rose, Ide, ends up married to a peasant, living in penury and harsh servitude, the lily Johanne runs away to sea disguised as a boy (like Naomi in *Only a Fiddler*) and falls to her death from the ship's deck (blown by the wind, as we have seen), while Anna Dorthea, the most sensitive of the three – the only one to grieve for the birds made homeless by trees felled to build her father's grandiose ship – ekes out her days in a hovel all by herself, watched over only by storks, whose relatives she had once protected.

In 'Anne Lisbeth' the abandoned (or to be more precise, the given-away) child is all-pervasive. In the note already cited Andersen proclaimed: 'This is the story of mother love and how it is given life and strength by experiencing fear and terror.'[11] This mother love was originally – and indeed for many, many years – repudiated, denied. Or was it? It may well have undergone a transposition into a never-recognised substitute or correlative.

Of pretty, popular Anne Lisbeth when young we hear: 'Foden var let i Dandsen og Sindet endnu mere let!'[12] '[Her] foot was light in the dance, and [her] mind was even more light!' Almost inevitably Anne Lisbeth becomes pregnant, we never know who by; that is unimportant to the tale. What *is* important, one assumes, considering the insistence on it, is the child's ugliness. Anne Lisbeth feels no inclination to keep him – would she have done had he been a bonny little baby who would have drawn forth compliments? – but hands him over to the local ditch-digger's wife for a modest regular payment. She never visits her son, nor is tempted to do so, especially after she has moved away to the town. It is an indigent, uncaring, loveless home in which she has deposited him. The lad has a big appetite for food, and so is early put out to work to get money for his keep – minding Mad Jansen's red cow, for instance – but his physical growth is stunted, and his appearance is repulsive enough for all the farm-hands and servants where he is employed to cuff and insult him. His is truly a case of 'aldrig elsket',[13] 'never loved', and what happens, asks Andersen, to those for whom 'aldrig elsket' is the order of the day?

They do not love themselves, for a start. And they leave the home country where they have been unhappy, for miserable jobs they would have been better off not taking. Anne Lisbeth's boy joins a barely seaworthy boat, sitting by its helm while its skipper drinks himself legless. Of course when a storm comes the boat gets into severe difficulties, and for all the boy's shouts, the skipper cannot cope. It sinks, and Anne Lisbeth's son is drowned. The only survivor of the wretched vessel is one bottle, the broken base of which rests on a piece of blue-painted wood; this is borne on the current towards the shore.

How different has his young mother's life been. While her son is only a baby she becomes nursemaid to a count's child, and is quartered in a castle in greatest comfort. She dotes on her nice-looking, well-born charge, and, long after she has left her post, has married and gone to live, in good material circumstances, in the town, her mind and conversation often turn to him. We readers see that the boy has become the receptacle for the strong maternal instincts Anne Lisbeth stifled, but without doubt, Anne Lisbeth herself does not. It is less a case of self-deception than of a mechanism in the mind having been effectively set up that only some shock can put out of action. And such a shock she receives, though it follows a course of action her conscious self has decided on (however, we may well reject this last interpretation of her decision).

So often has she thought and talked about her first charge that she finally takes it on to herself to go to the Count's castle and see again 'sin søde Dreng',[14] 'her sweet boy', who must now be fourteen. She is granted an interview with him, after he has had dinner. But – the whole economically presented scene resembles some bitter, ironic moment in de Maupassant – he looks at her, doesn't speak to her, and clearly fails to recognise her. (It would of course have been strange if he had done so; she has preserved him in the chambers of her mind, but he cannot be expected to have done the same with her.) Desperate, for her whole carefully nurtured identity has been struck at, she seizes his hand and presses it to her, lips, whereupon he says 'Naa, det er godt!'[15] (a convincing translation of which would be a graceless 'All right, all right!' or 'Steady on!') and promptly leaves the room.

Devastated, humiliated by this snub, Anne Lisbeth makes her way towards the ditcher's cottage, guided by some compulsion, only emphasised by the croaking raven that flies down to land on the road in front of her. The ditcher's wife, commenting how well off in her plumpness Anne Lisbeth looks, gives her the news she didn't know: that her real son was drowned at sea. She need send no more money for his upkeep. So now Anne Lisbeth has lost two sons – the real and unprepossessing one, whom she chose to cast out of her life, and the surrogate one who had lived for years a fantasy life in her head. Her psyche cannot stand such upturning of the premises on which a whole life has been built, and it takes swift revenge on her entire being – first through an over-whelming dream of an emissary from Heaven trying to take her there for her son's sake but unable to do so, and next, and repeatedly, through hallucinatory demands that her unburied son should receive Christian burial. During the course of the strange phantasmagorical wandering it insists she takes, she will stumble across – indeed, cut her hand on – the bottle with the blue wooden base, sole survivor of the rotten hulk which saw the last of her unfortunate bastard son.

The motif of the foundling, the adopted child, is elaborated still further in 'A Story of the Dunes', set in the late eighteenth century, and as in 'Anne Lisbeth' bad weather at sea is a major agent. The protagonist's actual birth, attributable to this, is also reminiscent of that of Elisabeth in The Two Baronesses. There is a further echo of that novel, in that he has Southern European parentage, like (the admittedly only half-Italian) Baron Herman. Born to his mother after a shipwreck on the Jutland west coast that kills her as it already has his father, Jørgen is brought up by a fisherman and his wife whose own child had died at just five years of age. Theirs is a hard life, in a poor community used to adversity. 'Granatkjærnen fra Spaniens Jordsmon blev Marehalmens Plante paa Jyllands Vestkyst.'[16] 'The pomegranate seed from the soil of Spain became a lyme-grass plant on Jutland's west coast.'

Such reversals of fortune, such transpositions of living beings, happen all the time, Andersen reminds us. Nature versus Nurture is obviously a dominant theme of the tale, as in so much of Andersen, from 'The Ugly Duckling' (emphatically Nature) to 'To Be or Not To Be', where civilising, Christianising Nurture certainly scores some impressive points (as, it could be argued, if with a little ingenuity, it also does in 'The Marsh-King's Daughter'). But something else comes into play in 'A Story from the Dunes', apparent in Andersen from *The Improvisatore* onwards: that the circumstances and experiences of the first years shape the individual immeasurably. The kinship to Wordsworth and Dickens (and to Andersen's own first novel) is seen in his authorial assertion about his hero: 'til dette Hjem klamrede han sig med sin Livs aarlange Rødder,'[17] 'to this home he [Jørgen] clung with the years-long roots of his life'.

Destiny, whether seen as the logical outcome of innate inner qualities when pitted against the obstinate realities of external life or as the (no less logical) consequential development of choices – or of actions demanding choice – is a major feature of the 1858–59 stories. The storyteller's task is seen in these tales in the workings of Destiny manifested in individual lives through epiphanies, dreams, meaningful encounters, recurrent objects or phenomena of psychic significance to the persons concerned but not necessarily yielding to conscious interpretation on their part. In October 1858 Andersen gave an intentionally inspiriting lecture to the Mechanics' Association in Copenhagen: 'far more people than there were places for in the great hall: the crowd outside pressed close up to the windows and clamoured to have them opened'.[18] The words he offered his enthusiastic listeners are very germane to the stories he was engaged on at this time:

'Among the instructive readings which are given at the Mechanics' Association there is one that it has been thought should not be omitted, and that is one from the poetic, the art that opens our eyes and our hearts to the beautiful, the true and the good.

'In England, in the Royal Navy, through all the rigging, small and great ropes, there runs a red thread, signifying that it belongs to the crown; through all men's lives there runs also a thread, invisible indeed, that shows we belong to God.

'To find this thread in small and great, in our own life and in all about us, the poet's art helps us, and it comes in many shapes. Holberg let it come in his comedies, showing us the men of his time with their weaknesses, and their amusing qualities, and we can read much of these.

' "In the earliest times the poet's art dealt mostly with what are called Wonder Stories; the Bible itself has enclosed truth and wisdom in what we call parables and allegories. Now we know all of us that the allegory is not to be taken literally by the words, but according to the signification that lies in them, by the invisible thread that runs through them.

'We know that when we hear the echo from the wall, from the rock, or the heights, it is not the wall, the rock, and the heights that speak, but a resounding from ourselves; and we also should find [in the parable, the allegory] ourselves – find the meaning, the wisdom, and the happiness we can get out of them.

'So the poet's art places itself by the side of Science, and opens our eyes for the beautiful, the true and the good; and so we will read here a few Wonder Stories.' [19]

And indeed in each of the stories here we do follow the thread by which the characters, self-ignorant though they may be, and terrible the route they have to take and terrible too the destination, attain some state of Grace. Crazed Anne Lisbeth, missing from home but this time not to be found on the seashore, is discovered by herself in a church where she will shortly die. Jørgen too, possessed by pictures of splendid reconciliation with people from the past, ends up in a church, which is itself buried by huge drifts of sands from the dunes. That is his resting-place to this day. These Wonder Stories, which emphatically are *not* mere parables or allegories, but which serve the Kantian 'the beautiful, the true and the good' are nevertheless contributions to Christian culture.

Andersen in *My Fairy-Tale Life* could not resist relating what followed after that last-quoted pronouncement: 'And I read and was followed with close attention; a single heartfelt burst of applause was heard. I was glad and satisfied to have read. Afterwards I gave still a few more readings. . .'[20] A few paragraphs on, he names 'The Marsh-King's Daughter' among his Wonder Tales. Like 'A Story from the Dunes' it requires further attention.

2

Andersen observes that there are two stories in the storks' repertoire which are outstanding for antiquity and length. One of them is universally known, that of Moses, found in the bulrushes by Pharaoh's daughter and growing up to be a great man; the other – to be substantially given us by the storks themselves, even while its events are unfolding – is not, as yet. Thus this second unknown story is offered as a companion-piece, if not as a complement, to a mythic history that became a cornerstone of Western civilisation itself. 'The Marsh-King's Daughter' is also concerned with the movement and home-seeking of peoples, with the faiths that sustain them for these purposes, and the necessary and inevitable yielding of older creeds, born of earlier circumstances, to innovative, forward-looking ones. In both stories the transitional stage – between departure and arrival, between obscurity and fulfilment – is a major area of interest. We should therefore briefly remind ourselves of what Exodus tells us of Moses's start in life.[21]

The descendants of the Hebrew Joseph and his brothers multiplied and prospered in Egypt to such an extent that the host nation resented them, imposing restrictions and harsh working conditions and treating them largely as a servant class. All to no avail. Consequently the King of Egypt determined on elimination. First he tried the unworkable policy of getting midwives to kill any male Hebrew children, then he ordered the drowning of all male babies in the river (Nile). But a husband and wife of the tribe of Levi – ironically, one of Jacob's two sons denied his father's good wishes – produce a child so 'goodly' that his mother refuses to kill him and instead hides him for three months. When this is no longer practicable, she places him in a little ark made of bulrushes and 'daubed' with 'slime', which she puts among the reeds at the river's brink, to be found. It is Pharaoh's daughter herself who, to her joy, discovers it, recognises the baby inside as Hebrew, and asks a girl nearby – in fact, the baby's sister – to fetch a nurse for him; she does this, and brings their own mother, who then cares for the child until Pharaoh's daughter is ready for him, 'and he became her son', and she called him Moses because he was 'drawn out of water'. But years later, despite growing up a member of the royal household, Moses takes his own Hebrew kinsman's side in a quarrel with an Egyptian and kills the aggressor. Consequently – for Pharaoh learns of the incident – he is forced to leave Egypt for the land of Midian. So begins Moses's heroic history, culminating, after acute sufferings for both nations, in his leading his own people out of Egypt in the direction of Canaan and giving them a code of law, so simple in its moral directives, so free of the clutter of tradition, and so generally benevolent in its tendencies as to supersede all predecessors.

It is easy to see how Moses's infancy with its confusions of provenance, its translations of familial membership and domicile, and its subsequent unstoppable movement towards his acceptance as moral spokesman for a whole people would have appealed to Andersen, with his own segmented life, his divisions in loyalty, never more tested than in the 1850s, and, despite all the misery experienced, his now widely established fame. Moses was superficially an awkward human being, 'slow of speech, and of a slow tongue', a stammerer, and Andersen too had been ill-spoken, gauche, comical and stork-like in society, and yet had – by some inner power – become a success. To this 'swamp-plant' the scriptural context of Moses's start in life, river, river-brink and reeds as appropriate cradle for a genius of national and international significance, must have had potent psychic resonance. Also he would have been quick to see the Pentateuch story in suprapersonal terms as evidencing the emergence of a country (his own) from obscurity (the 1813 impositions, and subsequent bankruptcy) into a confident nation state that could defeat its enemy. Certainly the biblical images recur in this 'second' storks' tale, reinforced by emphatic circumstantial details: the watery country is actually named for us: Vildmosen (Wild Marsh) in Vendsyssel in the county of Hjørring near Skagen in northern Jutland.[22]

At this point comment on the title chosen by Andersen for his story is necessary, the more so as its usual English rendering, 'The Marsh-King's Daughter' – though employed for readers' convenience throughout this book – is neither accurate nor adequate, failing to do justice to the author's – later explicitly conveyed – purpose. The story's first sentence does indeed speak of 'Sumpen og Mosen',[23] 'swamp' and 'marsh', the second Danish noun recalling the northern English word 'moss' (as in Holme Moss, Derbyshire/Yorkshire and Moss Side, Manchester) and connoting moorland with its many, treacherous patches of 'bog', another term by which 'Mose' is often translated. But 'Dynd', which occurs in the subsequent text, means 'mud', 'slime', even 'ooze', referring to the basic and (to warm-blooded animal life) the most dangerous element of which marsh/swamp/bog is compounded. As we have seen in *The Improvisatore*, marshland has in its duality of earth and water much to teach us, challenging the limitations of singleness, and thus (as for Antonio, and indeed for Moses himself) offering new life, rebirth. In Andersen's own language there is wordplay here, which there cannot be in ours, but, by inference, so there was in the ancient original ('his name Moses. . . Because I drew him out of the water'); Moses is 'of [the] marsh'). But in Andersen's story 'Dynd', if an inextricable ingredient of all marshes, is certainly not coterminous with them. It is what renders them perilous, capable of sucking us in to our deaths and reminding us of that primordial slime from which every living being had to emerge if it was to know existence at all.

In an intellectual climate obsessed with the beginnings of life, Andersen clearly saw 'Dynd' as at once indispensable and destructive. You can see it too as an analogue for chaos, for the formlessness which precedes forms and into which they are forced to return. The King of Slime is a terrifying, malignant, indescribable being, yet creation somehow needs him: after all, he begets Helga, the story's central figure. The intention of 'The Marsh-King's Daughter' is nothing less than the essentially biblical one of showing how chaos can be held off, first through self-protecting energies which include concern for others (embodied here by the stork parents, with their concern for the young and their enormous, valiant, migratory flights at specific seasons), and next through religion, which addresses itself to the whole question of beginning and ending. But religion, like life itself, undergoes continuous evolution. Whatever faith the Hebrew descendants of Jacob practised in Egypt, it underwent a tremendous transmutation when Moses received the Commandments on Sinai.

Standing back from this long fairy tale, we will not find it difficult to discern its bottom line, of growth and concomitant moral progress. But above that line weave intricacies of subject, abetted by an unusually elaborate manner of presentation, which demand concentration. As was made clear at the beginning of this chapter, nowhere is Andersen's new artistic desire for experimentation more testingly demonstrated than in his narratological methods. The married storks most certainly do not recount occurrences from any factual certainty of knowledge. Furthermore, the stork father is the bemused, dismayed witness of the first gravely seminal event and – some while later – becomes an actual instrument of the second. But regularly we hear the voice of the author as well, summarising the storks' conversation or commenting himself on the birds and on the sequence of events in which they have interested themselves.

This sequence in itself involves an intricate union – or conflation – of various archetypal situations and deeds from past legend. Andersen who, as we have seen, read so widely for, and worked so immensely hard on, this story must have decided – or arrived at – this apparent concertinaing of motifs for an overall purpose. We have perhaps to call to mind here the many usages the Moses story has been subjected to – religious, nationalistic, historical. So, is Andersen, by thus bringing together so much diverse folk material, not reminding us that, if the subject of the development of physical life forms has attracted many differing schools of mythological, theological and scientific thought (some susceptible to reconciliation, others mutually antagonistic), so too has the development of our souls, our psyches, been addressed in numerous myths and lore? And while they often exhibit interesting cultural distinctions, they have an underlying kinship, not to say unity, illuminating in itself and helpful to us in the present age of ontological uncertainty.

Certainly as we review the story itself, we shall constantly hear echoes or see shadows of widely regarded and culturally influential others.

An Egyptian lord is gravely ill, and his daughter, believing that that he could be restored by a marsh-flower that grows in a northern country, journeys there with two other princesses who know the area; all wear swanskins enabling flight. Once she has arrived in the wateriest part of the marsh in question – Vildmosen in Vendsyssel – she alights on an alder log, casts off her swanskin, asking her companions to take care of it for her, and dives down to pluck the desired flower. But when she comes up again, the other two princesses – for no reason that is stated – tear her feather-skin into shreds, telling her that now she will never see Egypt again. They then fly back there themselves. In her distressed state the princess weeps until she animates the alder log, which, it transpires, is nothing less than the body of Dynd-Kongen, the Slime King. He rolls himself over, taking the girl down into the dark depths with him. As our stork-narrator at this point doesn't know what has happened to the Egyptian princess after her disappearance into the mud, his account here is vividly redolent of atavistic fear:

> Hun sank strax i, og Elletrunten gik ned med, det var ham [Dynd-Kongen] der halede; der kom store, sorte Bobler og saa var der ikke Spor mere. Nu er hun begravet i Vildmosen, aldrig kommer hun med Blomst til Ægyptens Land.[24]
>
> She sank immediately, and the alder log went down with her, it was him [Slime-King] who tugged; there came large black bubbles and then there was no more trace. She is now buried in Vildmose, she will never come with the flower to the land of Egypt.

The image here is at once excremental and crudely priapic, all that we strive upwards away from. . . . The stork, despite his solemn words, doesn't altogether give up hope, and regularly inspects the wild marsh for signs of the princess's survival. One day he sees on the marsh-lake's bed a green shoot. This grows into a bud, and the bud opens into a flower in the very middle of which he can see lying a tiny beautiful infant girl. Remembering that the woman in the house high atop the roof of which he has built his own nest has long been wanting a child, Stork Father carries this diminutive human in his beak over to her house (thus fulfilling his species's folkloric role of childbringer, which Andersen made us aware of in *Only a Fiddler*). The woman's happiness at his gift is alloyed, however, when it turns out that at night-time the child undergoes a change of form, from lovely girl into hideous frog. Nor is this the only troubling feature of her being, as it develops under the foster-mother's care, for she has, as we have seen, a double nature: as a human outwardly fair, but spiteful, uncontrollable, and as a frog gentle, kindly, but sorrowful. It is the author, and not the uncomprehending Stork Father, who has to give the explanation here: 'her var to Naturer, der skiftede om, baade udad og indad'; 'here were two natures which changed round, both outwardly and inwardly' – her father's destructive temperament inside her mother's externally pleasing body, her mother's kindly temperament inside just such an ugly shape as her father's.

In the above procession of situations major themes of universal fairytale are immediately detectable, closely interwoven: the arcane plant that can heal and the difficult journey to find it; the metamorphosis (or part-metamorphosis) of human into bird; the inexplicable malignity of two siblings (so often sisters) to a third, the foundling of unknown or mysterious provenance, and its kinship to the wild; the gift of a child to the long-childless – and finally, and most impor-tantly, the double self-presentations, or separate diurnal/nocturnal manifesta-tions, of a single individual. This last – the marsh-king's daughter who is at her best at night as a frog – is a variant, whose idiosyncrasy has intellectual, ideo-logical causes, on that large group of tales that Bruno Bettelheim (in *The Uses of Enchantment*, 1977) calls 'The Animal Groom', with a subsection 'The Frog King'[25] in which (for the gender is most commonly male) the handsome prince, desirable socially and sexually, is at night a misshapen, repellent creature, so often a frog, who has somehow to be (re-)humanised. 'There are,' says Bettelheim, 'direct associations between sex and the frog which remain unconscious. Preconsciously the child connects the tacky, clammy sensations which frogs (or toads) evoke in him with similar feelings he attaches to the sex organs. . . . Repulsive as the frog may be, as vividly described in "The Frog King" [the Brothers Grimm],[26] the story assures us that even an animal so clammily disgusting turns into something very beautiful, provided it all happens in the right way at the right time.' True enough of 'The Marsh-King's Daughter', with one extremely important proviso: that it is the clammily disgusting (female) frog who is both virtuous and appealing, the outwardly perfect human being (female also) who repels and terrifies. Andersen's extraordinary mind always demanded reworking of given conventions.

Not only can many familiar folk tales be discerned in the narrative so far but much-read Andersen *Eventyr* also: 'The Wild Swans', 'The Snow Queen' (the girl as quest-maker); 'Thumbelina' (the miniature human girl found in the flower); 'The Travelling Companion' (the female bewitched into an evil self); 'The Little Mermaid' (the fraught passage between two elements). Such an omnium-gatherum of his own images suggests, when placed beside that from folklore, and remembering the unusual length of time spent working on the story, that the intention was to create a compound metaphor for nothing less than the growth of civilisation itself.

From the précis so far, one key fact has been omitted. The storks have built their nest on top of a *Bjælkehuus*[27] – a log house, three-storeyed, with a tower and a stone-lined cellar, erected and lived in by Vikings. For the adoptive mother of the marsh-king's daughter is a Viking woman; at the time of the child's arrival her husband and the other menfolk are away on one of their raids. In the middle of her hall burns a fire, and tapestries depicting Norse gods, Odin, Thor and Freia hang on the walls. 'The Marsh-King's

Daughter' – the finished version of which was the fruit of the author's deep immersion in history, lore and the Norse sagas themselves – is Andersen's most sustained imaginative engagement with Viking culture, interest in (indeed admiration for) which had been for so long virtually de rigueur for Danish intellectuals, following the examples set by Grundtvig and Oehlenschläger. Snorri Sturleson (1179–1241)[28] the authority in whom Andersen immersed himself, and a widely consulted source of reference for those pursuing Norse studies, viewed his subject matter from a Christian perspective, whatever imaginative and emotional ambiguities he retained. That Andersen himself had doubts about Grundtvig-style 'Edda Christianity' we have seen in 'To Be or Not To Be'. For this reason possibly Andersen has chosen to set *his* Viking presentation at the time when the Vikings's conversion to Christianity is, with bloody travails, well under way,[29] and to highlight in his narrative the Apostle of the North, (Saint) Ansgar, (801–865), whose mission was the Christianising of the North. Ansgar made at least two recorded expeditions on behalf of the faith to Jutland, and later became Archbishop of Hamburg-Bremen, the see specifically established for northern proselytising. The dualism of marsh-king and Egyptian princess, of heartless girl and feeling frog, of northern summers and southern winters, climaxes in the oppositions of Norse and Christian (there can be no dialectic here) but there is an interesting, highly significant foreshadowing of this, to which we should address ourselves.

Not long after he has brought the Viking woman the marsh-king's daughter, our principal informant of events, Stork Father, his wife and fledglings take part in their great late summer migration, programmed by Nature, southwards from Jutland and winter. The Egypt they journey to is not, obviously, the biblical land of Moses's persecuting pharaoh, but an Islamic society, part of the sophisticated Abbasid caliphate ruled from Baghdad, a society, religious and virtuous, with which dialogue is possible and desirable.[30]

As I read this story and ponder its emphases (the more striking because made within the boundaries of a severe and *sui generis* structure), I cannot but be reminded of a passage in a much later masterpiece: Boris Pasternak's *Doctor Zhivago* (1946–57, in English 1958). The speaker is Zhivago's metaphysician uncle, Nikolay Nikolayevitch:

'[It] is possible not to know if God exists or why He should, and yet to believe that man does not live in a state of nature but in history, and that history as we know it began with Christ, it was founded by Him on the Gospels. Now what is history? Its beginning is that of the centuries of systematic work devoted to the solution of the enigma of death, so that death itself may eventually be

overcome. This is why people write symphonies and why they discover mathematical infinity and electromagnetic waves. Now, you can't advance in this
direction without a certain upsurge of spirit. You can't make such discoveries
without spiritual equipment, and for this, everything necessary has been
given us in the Gospels. What is it? Firstly, the love of one's neighbour – the
supreme form of living energy. Once it fills the heart of man it has to overflow
and spend itself. And secondly, the two concepts which are the main part of
modern man – without them he is inconceivable – the ideas of free personality and of life regarded as sacrifice – Mind you, all this is still quite new.
There was no history in this sense in the classical world. There you had blood
and beastliness and cruelty and pock-marked Caligulas untouched by the
suspicion that any man who enslaves others is inevitably second-rate. There
you had the boastful dead eternity of bronze monuments and marble columns.
It was not until after the coming of Christ that time and man could breathe
freely. It was not until after Him that men began to live in their posterity and
ceased to die in ditches like dogs – instead, they died at home, in history, at
the height of the work they devoted to the conquest of death, being themselves dedicated to this aim.'[31]

    This approach to Christianity's role in the history of civilisation informs the
story's account of the coming of the new religion to Vildmosen, the accord it
finds in the heart of the Viking woman already drawn to loving-kindness and
gentleness as cardinal virtues. And she responds to the very idea of the 'Hvide
Christ', 'White [pure] Christ' even before she finds herself invoking his miraculous name.
    Its thematic and artistic ambitions and their hard-won union in its course
certainly justify Andersen's pride in 'The Marsh-King's Daughter' and the high
reputation it has subsequently enjoyed. Yet, for all its abundant merits, I find
the story less than wholly satisfactory. One way of accounting for this is an
admission that, returning to Andersen's statement about the basic story coming
to him in a moment of inspiration, I have difficulty in knowing just what that
first germinating idea would be. Though the strange, beautiful, melancholy
ending bringing home to us the immensely distant past to which Helga belongs
resembles a symphonic coda, gathering up and rounding off the thematic
material of the whole, 'The Marsh-King's Daughter' fails to cohere as an organic
whole. This failure is due less to the palimpsest-like complications of both
construction and the narration than to the virtuosic brilliance of the individual
sections, which vie for supremacy in the receiving mind, and even more so in
the critical-adjudicatory memory. The evocation of the three Egyptian princesses' flight to Jutland, say, competes with the later story of the Christian priest
and his death, and they refuse altogether to gel. But there are two further and

graver obstacles to giving the story the admiration the others in this chapter truly deserve.

A heroine like Helga who for most of its course alternates between two complete and contrasting states (active viciousness and passive virtue) cannot satisfactorily exist in a work of this length (virtually a novella). In the tightly controlled world of folktale, and its derivatives like 'The Travelling Companion', she can be a plausible enough representative of opposing spiritual forces; in the far more detailed and at the same time far larger fictional world of 'The Marsh-King's Daughter', spanning continents and centuries, she defeats belief, and ironically the richly written passages of her evolution into a kindly, full human being only increase one's inability to credit her with reality, inner as well as exterior. The vitiating imbalance between features proper to the fairy tale and those more appropriate for a work of ampler dimensions is even more apparent in its use of instruments of redemption – Christ's name, the Christian Cross, the golden censer of the Mass. The virtuous efficacy of these is only acceptable if one assumes the moral superiority of the religion to which they belong, even in its outward forms. This could scarcely be done with any adequacy in a fairy tale where they perforce coexist with mud-bound monsters, evil flying princesses and beneficent plants in the Jutland marshland. Perhaps the problem inherent in this is what caused Andersen such immense trouble and so many rewritings.

3

'The Marsh-King's Daughter' pays rich tribute to Jutland's landscape and its long past. How much Jutland meant to Andersen as both traveller and writer will already be clear to readers: he had after all spent his first literary earnings in 1830 on a trip to Jutland, partly because of his enthusiasm for the writings of poet and short-story writer, Steen Blicher (1782–1848). The impression made on him by the region was tremendous, and fuller knowledge only strengthened his feelings – with the 'German Ocean' (North Sea) on one side and the Baltic on the other and, at its very tip, marking the Skagerrak from the Kattegat, Skagen of the dunes and quicksands. Otto in *O.T.* was heir to a Jutland estate, where he grew up after his traumatic beginning in Odense Tugthus; his friend Vilhelm loved to hear him tell tales of the rough, venturesome lives of ordinary people on Jutland's west coast, not dissimilar to those accounts of Cornish wreckers that have exercised a pull on the British mind. Niels in '*To Be or Not To Be*' became absorbed in Jutland country life after he moved to his foster-father's parish as an eleven-year-old boy, taking to its pursuits and fascinated by its more primitively cultured inhabitants. One presumes that he will spend the rest of his life there. Certainly what one carries away from the novel most strongly is the evocation of Jutland's free, untrammelled land- and seascapes, and Niels's ardent, if sometimes perplexed response to them. But no work of Andersen's is more imbued with Jutland, is a more fulsome homage to its long history and to its present robust culture, to its indigenous people and to its amazing natural features than 'A Story from the Dunes', the writing of which followed a major exploration of the region by the author.

Andersen, that summer of 1859, crossed by barge the Limfjord, which bisects the peninsula making northern Jutland a de facto island. He visited administrators (including the commissioner for the prevention of sand drifts), clergymen (one of them Kierkegaard's elder brother), musicians and painters, thus deepening his knowledge of the province's mores and constituency. He went to see the famous Kloster (Cloisters) at Børglum (the setting for an 1861 tale of his evoking late medieval times and struggles for power within the Church),[32] the sand dunes at Rubjerg, and – the culmination of his visit, as it is of Jutland, of the nation state of Denmark and of mainland Europe itself – Skagen.

The hero of 'A Story from the Dunes' is born on Jutland's west coast, near the shore on to which his mother was tossed from her wrecked ship by the waves. So metaphorically the sea, which plays such a determining part in Jørgen's life, was also his womb. He grows up strong, intelligent, good at committing songs and stories to memory, skilled at making pictures of ships out of shells, carving sticks into diverse shapes, and singing a melody as soon as he hears it. You could liken him to a fine instrument whose range would be known the world over had it not been confined to a remote corner of Jutland – and, as we have already noted, it is to such an artefact Andersen compares him when his mind has gone: one with loosened strings. All these abilities and demonstrations of a refined taste probably derive from his Spanish antecedents about whom he knows nothing (and whose *palacio* he unwittingly sees when a sailor-boy going on shore into a Spanish port). On the other hand he is also very much a vigorous young male of Jutland's west coast; hardship and setbacks he takes in his stride. Yet his identity is put to severe tests.

He goes to sea, against his protective affectionate foster-mother's wishes, and suffers not just storms and bad weather but bullying masters whose cruelty he fiercely resents. When he returns he finds that his foster-mother has died. For the next couple of years his working life alternates between strenuous fishing and, together with his pal Morten, signing on as crew-member for ships bound for Norway and Holland. The period also includes his foster-father's death after a fever, and rivalry with Morten over a girl, Else: she prefers Morten, and, after an act of real generosity to them both, one carefully thought out but maybe screening darker feelings (for does he truly wish them well?), Jørgen decides he must leave the neighbourhood. He makes for the house of his foster-mother's uncle, a favourite of his from boyhood when he relished his jokes and anecdotes; this man is an eel merchant in Bovbjerg.

But before he reaches the narrow channel that connects Nissum Fjord with the sea (as always, Andersen is punctilious over geography, of which he had a keen sense), he is arrested for Morten's murder: his friend and rival has been found with a knife in his neck, and Jørgen is the obvious suspect. He is taken to Ringkøbing and imprisoned in a cold, damp jail, where, though he can't understand why such an unjust and terrible thing has happened to him, he comes to feel the grace of God on him and certainty of an existence beyond this earthly one. Maybe this is in part an acknowledgement of the hostile, quasi-murderous emotions he had entertained for his one-time best friend. For Jørgen is not of a cool disposition, he is lively, adventurous, passionate, proud. But we are led to understand that, even in the further tribulations to come, this new knowledge, this comparative serenity will not leave him.

He remains in prison in Ringkøbing for a year before the real killer of Morten is apprehended. Then Jørgen is set free. Even inside the cell he is able to hear the sea and he thinks that just as a man can be carried over its most furious surface and yet survive, so can he endure appalling, unanticipated disasters and remain essentially intact. The story proves this reading of the natural world and our relation to it to be literally untrue – the hero's girlfriend Clara does not survive disaster, and Jørgen himself will also be, to outward perception, an irreparable casualty of the elements. But spiritually – looked at *sub specie aeternitatis* – one can come through, to attain states of reunion and bliss that to us in our humdrum condition defy imagining.

To show that the world is not all injustice and suffering, a man Jørgen has always liked and admired, Kjøbmand Brønne (Merchant Brønne), takes him into his business and his home – in Skagen.[33] He suggests they burn the calendar of the previous year; Jørgen must build a new life for himself in a spot others think of as regrettably remote but which, for all its underdeveloped, primitive aspects, is a place to love and respect. And Jørgen is indeed happy with the merchant and his wife, who grow truly fond of him. Nor do they resent the tenderness that grows up between the young man and their daughter, Clara. One Sunday in particular when the family goes to church and takes Holy Communion makes an indelible impact on him; never will he forget Clara and himself sitting beside each other at the altar to receive the bread and wine. This togetherness confirms his love for her: and somehow strengthens his resolve to follow her to Norway. And indeed the pair do meet up in Christiansand; it is on the way back from there to Skagen that the ship runs aground (as had, so many years earlier, that carrying Jørgen's parents). Clara dies – and with her Jørgen too; that is, he dies to the world as a rational human being able completely to fend for himself.

For his rich, well-born Spanish parents, Andersen tells us, 'Som en Fest glede Dagene hen, for dem,'[34] 'Like a banquet the days glided past for them.' That's how in privileged circumstances, life can seem. But it is an illusion. It was an illusion for *them*; they died as a result of Nature's ineluctable power, long before their planned arrival in St Petersburg. Maybe the uncertainties that beset the fisher communities of Jutland are better guides to what to expect of life, and the dunes of Skagen and the roar and beat of the breakers on its shores better analogues for existence than charming pomegranate gardens in Spain.

The thread we have followed through Jørgen's life history has taken us finally (but Andersen would surely dispute the adverb) to a realm of unmerited suffering. Yet deep within Jørgen's unfathomable mind, images keep themselves alive through the years, ones we have received into our hearts ourselves – above all of himself kneeling beside Clara in the church, of the tears of devotion and love running down her face. So that on the day the catastrophic storm rages and he takes shelter in the church, little knowing that sand will bury it, with himself inside, his mind is a veritable treasure-house of beauties, of moments in earthly life informed by divine spirit – or 'Sjælens Lys der aldrig vil udslukkes,'[35] 'light of the soul which will never be extinguished'.

In a piece he wrote for the Copenhagen paper *Illustreret Tidende, Illustrated News*, Andersen recommended distant-seeming Skagen as a place to visit: 'If you are a painter, follow us here, because you will find a profusion of subjects to paint. Here are scenes to inspire poetry. Here in the Danish environment you will find images of Africa's deserts, of Pompeii's ashes.'[36]

He wrote prophetically, since Skagen was to attract and give its name to a group of remarkable Danish *plein-air* artists, who by the late 1870s had cohered into a 'school' with shared ideals and artistic practices: Holger Drachmann (1846–1908), Michael Ancher (1849–1927), Anna Brøndum Ancher (1859–1935) and the painter who most famously celebrated them as a fellowship (with erotic currents between them), P.S. Krøyer (1851–1909).[37] If we can find much that is harsh and sombre in their canvases, there is also much that is breathtakingly beautiful, recalling the scene-painting of the dunes and the windswept little town in Andersen's story, and often saltily human also. After all, Morten in the story who came to so ugly an end, was also a jolly, libidinous youth of whom one of the older men observed: 'Morten maatte nok gaae med et Andenæb syet i Buxerne,'[38] 'Morten must go around with a duck's bill stitched to his trousers.'

The solemn events of life in a fishing community, involving struggle against great odds, which the Skagen painters recorded, earning repute for themselves, could all be found in 'A Story from the Dunes', so that taken together they form a wonderful coincidence of Danish genius animated by the intensity of folk life.

Look at Michael Ancher's great paintings *Will He Round the Point?* (1879) and *Taking the Lifeboat through the Dunes* (1883),[39] or read his fellow painter, Holger Drachmann's account[40] of the Skagen lifeboat man, Lars Kruse who organised the rescue of the foundered Swedish brig *Daphne*, in winter 1862 (published 1879), and one is back in the cruel but inspiring world of Jørgen and the Brønne family who loved him.

And in his concentration here on a locality within a region intensely interested in its own history and lore, Andersen showed himself very much the European Witness of our title. The modern European nation, as it shaped itself, at once appealed to, and put strain on, those areas with long-standing identities of their own. As Patricia G. Berman writes in *In Another Light: Danish Painting in the Nineteenth Century* (2007): 'By mid-century, and particularly following the German annexation of Schleswig and Holstein in 1864, a rising sense of nationalism impelled some intellectuals to seek what they considered to be people and places so untouched by foreign influence that they might be identified as symbols of an essential Denmark. Skagen's fishermen provided romantic nationalists with such figures. By the 1870s a core group of these painters had attracted others to Skagen each summer and by the 1880s an art colony had coalesced.'[41]

All that lies well in the future. In the summer and autumn of 1860 Andersen travelled to Germany and Switzerland, and was distressed when in the former to hear strongly anti-Danish sentiments expressed. In the spring and summer of 1861 he travelled with Edvard Collin's son Jonas, increasingly an important figure in his life, to Italy and Switzerland. The creative links with Germany and its culture (including Swiss-German writing) continue in his works, however. The subject of our next chapter could well be seen – as indeed 'The Story from the Dunes' itself can be – as an example of that German genre *c.*1840–80, of which Gottfried Keller and Theodor Storm were masters, *Poetische Realismus:*[42] fiction, usually in the form of the novella, that makes its impact through a deft weaving of poetic episodes and images, is interested in the life of the imagination, in dreams, uncanny occurrences, etc. and yet does not forswear surface fidelity to life or the sociologically convincing portraiture of a believable community.

CHAPTER 11

'Iisjomfruen', 'The Ice Maiden', 1861

1

'Lad os besøge Schweiz',[1] 'Let us visit Switzerland', opens 'Iisjomfruen', 'The Ice Maiden', and Andersen himself was visiting (or rather *revisiting*) Switzerland when he started work on this arguably most ambitious and searching of all his tales. He had arrived in the country from Italy, with Jonas Collin junior as his rather wearing companion, via the Simplon Pass and St Maurice in the Canton Valais to the town of Bex in Canton Vaud. Here on 18 June 1861[2] he recorded beginning 'Alpejægeren', 'The Alpine Hunter'. The working title is interesting to us as we reflect on the finished work, since it shows that Andersen's mind was from the first exercised by the plight of its protagonist, Rudy, which, he felt, had something strong and interesting to tell about Switzerland itself. The Simplon and the Rhône valley in which both St Maurice and Bex stand will appear in the final story, and Bex itself will play a determining role. From 18 to 22 June Andersen and Jonas Collin stayed in Montreux on Lake Geneva, ever afterwards associated in the writer's mind with the early stages of composition.

Yet the Swiss features he first directs us to in the tale are the two glaciers between Schreckhorn and Wetterhorn near Grindelwald. His friend Thomas Fearnley[3] – Johan Christian Dahl's pupil and a companion of Andersen's in his first stay in Rome, he who had tried to make his life a little more sexually adventurous – had painted splendid oil canvases celebrating these. Schreckhorn, 13,379 feet, 4,078 metres high, would anyway have resonated with many of Andersen's readers since fascination with it virtually initiated the mid-nineteenth-century craze of Alpinism, though a complete ascent was not made until the summer of 1861 itself.

If 'The Ice Maiden' is to have a metaphoric application to the development of Switzerland as a nation state, then specificity about place will be vital to it, and indeed the story does repay being read with a map to hand. Dates are no less important. The climax of 'The Ice Maiden', Rudy's death, occurs, Andersen informs us, in 1856. And the paragraphs bringing the reader towards the present – a present in which Rudy has no part – paint a country in which tourism is exponentially increasing, with railway lines extended through areas once remote, even secretive.

Rudy's childhood, we learn, belonged to a period 'for nogle og tyve Aar',[4] 'twenty-some years before' the writing of this story. Therefore it's possible to work out that he would have been born – in Canton Valais/Wallis[5] – in 1833, actually the year of Andersen's own first, long-treasured visit to Switzerland. So with this in mind, we can begin a close examination of the novella by going through Rudy's biography, attending to its changes in place and time.

When just one year old, Rudy loses his father, a mail-coach driver whose job connects different – often culturally self-contained – regions of this mountainous country. He himself came from the Rhône valley, where his brother still lives. But after his death his widow decides to take their son back to her native Bernese Oberland.[6] Her father is a successful wood carver from Meiringen whose home now is close to Grindelwald. Chamois-hunters from the Valais accompany mother and child on their journey, which proceeds over the high mountains rather than along the valley roads. But high on the Gemmi Pass a disaster occurs. Newly fallen snow has covered up a chasm, and the mother slips and falls deep down into it with her child. After strenuous rescue work – ropes and poles are brought from the nearest human habitation – both bodies are retrieved from the crevasse; the mother is dead, but Rudy is revived.

He emerges from the traumatic experience unlike his former self. Before, little Rudy had been noted for his perpetual smile. Not any longer. He grows solemn, mirthless: only when beside a rushing waterfall does he ever smile.

> den Forandring var nok skeet med ham i Gletscher-Spalten, i den kolde, underlige Iisverden, hvor Sjælene af de Fordømte ere lukkede ind til Dommens Dag, som Schweizerbonden troer.[7]
> this change took place in him inside the crevasse, in the cold, strange iceworld where the souls of the condemned are locked in till Judgment Day, as the Swiss peasant believes.

These words must be kept firmly in mind when considering those critical interpretations of the story which seek to relate Rudy to personal/psychological issues of Andersen's own and speak of 'innate' or 'congenital' qualities. A popular belief such as that adumbrated above, if brought to bear on a terrible occurrence hard in itself to assimilate, would undoubtedly affect a child's entire being – and, of course, its development, for it will know that others have *not* gone through the same ordeal. And so it is with Rudy; he feels cut off from other children, even when associating with them, and in him natural competitiveness takes the form of excelling at essentially solitary pursuits.

His maternal grandfather lives higher up on the mountainside than the village proper. The traditional art he practises recalls the carpentering abilities of Andersen's paternal grandfather (for all his mental impairment), and also those of Thorvaldsen's wood-carver father and grandfather. Yet Rudy is never deeply won over to his art. Yes, he is singled out by visitors (tourists) when, together with other children, he offers for sale the beautiful wooden objects of the locality, but that's because of his 'alvorligt Ansigt',[8] 'serious face'. In truth, when inside his grandfather's house, his eye is always on the rifle up among the rafters and not on the many examples of his kinsman's craft: nutcrackers, carved boxes decorated with images of leaves and even of leaping chamois. He is not his paternal uncle's nephew for nothing. But maybe there's some inner compulsion he himself doesn't understand which makes him prefer instruments of death to those of domestic harmony.

Rudy always wants to be alone. Even when herding the goats, he likes exceeding his charges' nimbleness and climbing up to high, inaccessible places, encouraged in doing so by his grandfather's cat, his chief instructor and friend. (He can converse with him, as he can with the dog, Ajola, Andersen claiming this an attribute of almost all small children, one later denied, forgotten or repudiated: the relationship, more, the intimate connection between humans and other animals, is absolutely integral to the story.) With the cat Rudy sits on the ridgepole, in the treetops, on rocky precipices up to the very edge, and ventures too up slopes beyond the treeline. The keen air of the higher altitudes, fragrant with mountain herbs, is his favourite drink; the very swallows recognise him as being like themselves.

When he is eight years old, his father's brother asks that he return to the Rhône valley. For the second time Rudy makes the escorted journey *over* the mountains instead of *through* the valleys; his route is precisely given, and therefore easily traceable, and essential to the story's paradigmatic nature. The formidable ascent involved of the massif's north side – 'Opad, altid opad gik det . . .'[9] 'Upward, always upward it went . . .' – does not exhaust the little boy as much as he feared, though for a moment he looks up at the great glacier, remembering that fateful journey of his infancy and the loss of his mother to a crevasse. Even so he maintains his balance 'fast som en Gemse',[10] 'steady as a chamois'. This is the first time Rudy has been likened to the chamois he will become so adept at hunting with his gun, our first intimation that when he's stalking them it's a case of a predator pursuing his own kind, his own kin, to their deaths.

In front of Rudy stand those three great peaks so emblematic of Switzerland's national image and with which he has been familiar all his childhood though has never before seen close to: the Jungfrau, the Eiger, the Mönch.[11] The first and highest of these Andersen calls by the Danish rendering of its German name: Jomfruen, the Young Girl or Young Virgin (for there is a strong current of abjuration of warm human sexuality throughout the story), the major residence of the Ice Maiden/Virgin herself. Interestingly – and we know how Andersen loved to gather information about places he wrote about – the party who first reached the Jungfrau's summit on 3 August 1811 consisted of two brothers from Aarau (the Meyers) plus two *chamois hunters from the Valais*.

As in 'The Snow Queen', spiritual forces, taken into and then dominating our psyche, specific places traditionally identified with them, and the immutable laws of physical geography are indivisible, interpenetrative. The Eiger and two peaks beyond it as seen from this route, the Wetterhorn and the Schreckhorn, cradle a formidable instance of Nature's destructive capacity, the Föhn[12] wind which will resound through the novella. The men accompanying Rudy hear this in its early stage in their stopping-place high on the pass, and tell him not to fall asleep but be ready to move off. When the Föhn descends, its ferocity intensifies; down in the valley it can break trees like reeds and shift houses from one side of the river to the other like chess pieces, so Andersen tells us, faithful to facts.

Rudy's journey to his uncle (his father's family) takes him out of German-speaking (Protestant) Switzerland down into a strongly francophone and Catholic region. 'Alt var Nyt for Rudy, Paaklaedning, Skik og Brug, Sproget selv. . . .'[13] 'Everything was new for Rudy, clothes, common practice, speech itself. . . .' ' "Her er ikke saa slemt i Canton Wallis," ' sagde Farbro'er.[14] ' "It's not so bad here in Canton Valais [Wallis]",' said his uncle (his father's brother). (Andersen uses throughout the tale the German form of Swiss names, despite the key importance to the tale of the fact that in Valais/Wallis most people speak French.) His uncle vaunts pro-French views, has married a French wife, and in conversation commends the French (under Napoleon) for many enterprises: 'saa sang Farbro'er en fransk Vise og raabte Hurra for Napoleon Bonaparte',[15] 'then Uncle sang a French song and yelled out Hurrah for Napoleon Bonaparte' – just as Andersen's own father might have done.

Uncle and nephew get on well, and become good mates. His uncle soon realises Rudy's aptitude with a gun, and takes him chamois hunting. Under his expert guidance the boy becomes, within a comparatively short time, an accomplished hunter of these animals with their acrobatic ability to leap, land on precarious ledges and then leap away again. Rudy's own movements emulate theirs, but if the chamois are clever, he has to be cleverer still. His uncle teaches him a useful trick: by hanging coat and hat on an alpenstock a hunter can fool chamois into bounding away in the direction that suits his purpose. This method of decoy is of great significance to the novella; many years later it crops up in the dream Rudy's troubled fiancée, Babette has on the eve of her marriage to him, seemingly questioning his very identity. But the attentive reader will have had doubts about this even in the early chapters.

It is when the two of them are out chamois hunting that Rudy's uncle meets his death. They have climbed to a high altitude, the older man is crawling upwards on his stomach towards their quarry, scattering loose stones into black depths below, Rudy is a hundred paces behind him, the rock still firm underfoot. The uncle has eyes only for the chamois, who has her kid with her. Rudy, on the other hand, can see a vulture swooping down towards the man, clearly intending to dislodge him and turn him into carrion. Rudi aims for the bird while his uncle aims for the chamois, which he kills, though her kid runs away, free. Rudy, however, fails to hit the vulture; terrified, it speeds off. Older and younger man begin a cheery enough descent, feeling a good day's hunting has been had, when a dreadful noise makes them turn round: an avalanche is coming towards them. It kills the uncle, smashing his head in, but Rudy preserves his own life by pressing himself down to the ground. This is the first time he experiences real fear. From this episode we can surely infer two truths contributory to the work's overall meaning but not apparent to Rudy himself.

In bringing about the separation through death of a young being from his mother, his uncle has perpetrated a tragedy identical to Rudy's as an infant (also in the company of chamois-hunters). Misfortune when it befalls the non-human animal causes no less distress and sorrow than when it befalls the human. The second truth is that, for all his undoubted, indeed remarkable skills, Rudy can never attain superiority over indomitable Nature itself. Thematically it has to be *his* shot at the vulture (fired higher into the air than his uncle's) that dislodges the snow ridges and thus sets the deadly avalanche in motion.

As his French aunt-by-marriage/foster-mother tells him on hearing of her husband's death, Rudy is now the breadwinner of the household, at an early age (but by no means unprecedentedly or improbably). This important fact alone – and it is one never forgotten, but regularly, if lightly, insisted on – brings 'The Ice Maiden' (on one level anyway) far nearer mainstream nineteenth-century fiction than any other major fairy tale of Andersen's. The marriage of a credible external world to an equally credible inner or fantasy one is a characteristic of the German *Novelle* to which category, in length, construction and style, this can legitimately be thought to belong. We gather that Rudy acquits himself in his new role reliably, conscientiously and with a certain aplomb, which earns him a reputation in his community. Nevertheless there is a discrepancy between his social and his naked selves that will widen and occupy our attention. The desire, the psychic need for overreach so characteristic of his earliest years do not significantly abate, his predicament relating him, however loosely, to a long line of nineteenth-century novel protagonists from Stendhal to Mark Twain. (Both Tom Sawyer and Huck Finn would surely have understood Rudy perfectly):

'Hvem er den bedste Skytte i Canton Wallis?' Ja, det vidste Gemserne: 'Tag Dig iagt for Rudy!' kunde de sige. 'Hvem er den kjønneste Skytte?' 'Ja, det er Rudy!' sagde Pigerne, men de sagde ikke, 'tag Dig iagt for Rudy!' det sagde ikke engang de alvorlige Mødre; thi han nikkede ligesaa venligt til dem som til unge Piger, han var saa kjæk og glad, hans Kinder vare brune, hans Tænder friske hvide, og Øinene skinnede kulsorte, en kjøn Karl var han og kun tyve Aar.[16]

'Who is the best shot in the Canton Valais?' Yes, the chamois knew it: 'Be on your guard against Rudy!' they would say. 'Who is the most handsome shot?' 'Yes, that's Rudy!' said the girls, but they didn't say, 'Be on your guard against Rudy!' not even the serious-minded mothers said it; for he nodded just as friendlily to them as to the young girls, he was so good-spirited and cheerful, his cheeks were tan, his teeth a clean white, and his eyes shone coal-black, a handsome fellow and only twenty years old.

Yet even in this apparent encomium, built up from local chit-chat, we can detect the seeds of Rudy's ultimate inability to accommodate his whole self to his society, of his instinctual choice of the wilderness over civilisation, of – for it surely amounts to this – Thanatos over Eros. Why this decorum with girls where one might have expected more dash, more adventurousness (though we are to learn that, clandestinely, he has in fact kissed the schoolmaster's daughter, Anette, and other girls too after village dances)? What we learn of other aspects of his life shows him to have these qualities pre-eminently. His uncle was a cooper and has taught him the trade, but he has no interest in it. By common consent he is the best mountain guide in the area, the beneficiary of lessons from the cat in his Oberland childhood and, of course, from the chamois – and from his late uncle who also worked as a guide. But it is hunting to which he devotes his attentions and which brings in income.

His lack of real interest in the girls of his neighbourhood is offset by his sudden aspiration – paralleling his persistence as a mountain hunter – to win a girl outside his village, the daughter of a rich miller in the town of Bex. Just as chamois alight on ledges far beyond normal human range, so Babette stands outside Rudy's own economic and social milieu. Babette has been well educated, and brought up in a house reflecting her father's social position: large, three-storeyed, turreted, close to a rushing stream and surrounded by walnut trees. Nevertheless, though they have never had a proper conversation, a current of attraction has passed between the youth and the girl. He has business in Bex, and decides to pay the miller's house a visit.

We can work out from later details in this same chapter – IV, 'Babette' – that Rudy lives in or near Leuk, in the upper stretch of the Valais section of the Rhône valley. His west-bound route to Bex is once again made guidebook-clear to us: no work of fiction better justifies the explorations of Franco Moretti's admirable *Atlas of the European Novel 1800–1900* (1998)[17] than 'The Ice Maiden'. There being no railway then, Rudy takes an ever-narrower road from Sion following the valley with its bend like, he thinks, an elbow (the map will show how right this observation is) – and so up to St Maurice and the border with the next canton, Vaud;[18] this frontier is marked with an old tower on the one side and on the other, at the end of the river-spanning stone bridge, with a tollhouse. Whereas Valais does have, in its eastern valleys, a sizeable number of German-speakers, Vaud, with its capital Lausanne, is far more predominantly French-speaking, and some of its most famous towns – which we will visit in the latter part of the story – Vevey and Montreux, both on Lake Geneva (Lac Léman) are flourishing representatives of long-established French-Swiss culture. Even today Valais is Catholic; Vaud – partly by influence from Calvin's city of Geneva – strongly Protestant.

Bex itself, the place, as we have seen, where Andersen actually began writing 'The Ice Maiden', is virtually a character in this novella. The francophone town is deftly evoked, culturally a cut above any community Rudy has hitherto known, and no house in it more so than Babette's home. He is daunted by his self-imposed social challenge as he has never been by his many harsh physical ones. The mill-house would appear to lie on the far side of Bex from the Rhône bridge. To reach it Rudy takes the road out of the town, passing beneath the snow-capped peaks of Les Diablerets, in fact, at 10,531 feet, 3,210 metres the highest point in Canton Vaud.

Rudy learns that the miller and his daughter are away in Interlaken, for a shooting contest that will draw sportsmen and their followers from all over Switzerland's German cantons. He decides to go there. Interlaken is a long way off by road, but as a chamois-hunter he knows a far shorter if extremely precip-itous route there, across the mountains, essentially that taken in his infancy to Grindelwald and then retraced when he was eight years old. He has no doubt he will win the shooting contest (he does!) and the admiration of Babette (he wins this too), so to Interlaken he makes his hunter's way: over the Gemmi Pass (as Andersen specifically informs us), above Kandersteg, with prospects of the Schreckhorn – the highest peak wholly in the Bernese Oberland, the northern-most in the Alpine block, capped by ice and the hardest to climb: 'det løftede sin hvidpuddrede Steenfinger høit i den blaae Luft',[19] 'it lifted its white-powdered stone finger high in the blue air'. He then follows the course of the two fast-flowing glacier-fed Lütschine rivers, Schwarze and Weisse, to their union at Zweilütschinen, where he has the satisfaction of seeing his destination, the famous resort between the lakes of Thun and Brienz before him, full of hotels and tourists, German-speaking, praised by Goethe and frequented by Andersen's friend, the late Felix Mendelssohn.

At the marksmanship contest Rudy makes a great impression on everybody, spectators and performers alike. He acquits himself spectacularly as a shot; people want to know who he is: ' "Han taler det franske Sprog, som det tales i Canton Wallis! Han gør sig ogsaa ganske godt tydeligt i vort Tydsk!"[20] ' "He speaks French as it's spoken in Canton Valais! He also expresses himself clearly enough in our German!' This is a telling detail; to an important degree Rudy straddles both major components of Swiss culture, the French and the German, a great advantage to him initially, but also perhaps – as we shall see – an instrument in his eventual failure. The miller himself identifies Rudy as coming from the Valais, which, here in the Oberland, he chooses to regard as brother-canton to his own Vaud, and therefore takes a local patriot's pride in Rudy's performance. His enthusiastic reception facilitates Rudy's acquaintance with Babette, who enchants him close to as much as from a distance; she chatters away to him freely, and the two stroll pleasantly through the avenues of the resort. Before long he is admitting to her that he really came to Interlaken on her account.

Andersen gives us a convincing enough précis of Babette's talk which Rudy finds so irresistible: its subjects the many absurdities in dress and gait of the visiting foreign ladies, her elegant English godmother, the brooch that lady gave her, which is now on her own bodice. The marksman has entered a very different sphere from that of pursuing chamois or even snatching kisses from the girls in Leuk, and it is hard to believe that, the physical charms of the speaker apart, it is at all congenial to him. Wouldn't it be right to remember here the mock human being of coat and hat on an alpenstock set up to deceive the chamois?

Triumphant, laden with trophies, Rudy now makes the arduous mountain journey back home, edging the great Jungfrau/ Jomfru, following the Lütschine upstream now, and passing close to the Schreckhorn. This chapter – V, 'Paa Hjemveien', 'On the Journey Home' – is the most difficult to grasp on first reading, yet it surely contains the key to the work's central preoccupation. For it presents the first direct confrontation by Rudy of Iisjomfruen, the Ice Maiden (or, more literally, of one of her representatives, or servants). Behind the history we have followed of a young man leading a recognisable enough life, we have already been made aware of an unquenchable malignant power, which has expressed itself in the two deaths so consequential to his history. We must now look at what Andersen has told us so far about the Ice Maiden, and the portents in his descriptions of what is devastatingly to come.

We hear of her first in the opening chapter, after Andersen has revealed how Rudy's mother died. Though her son did not perish, but was rescued and restored by the men of the party, the Ice Maiden has not forgotten him. Her palace may lie within the fatal glacier, but she is also 'et Luftens Barn',[21] 'a child of the air', able to scale the iciest, tallest peaks with the grace of a chamois and to sail down rapid Alpine rivers. She declares: ' "min er Magten! . . . En deilig Dreng stjal man fra mig, en Dreng jeg havde kysset, men ikke kysset til døde. Han er igjen imellem Menneskene . . . min er han, jeg henter ham!"[22] ' "Mine is the power! . . . A handsome boy they stole from me, a boy I had kissed, but not kissed till dead. He is again among human beings. . . . he is mine, I will get him!" ' She has minions to carry out her will, chief among them Svimlen (Giddiness or Vertigo), an unfortunate enemy for the intrepid climber, Rudy to have. Thanks to the lessons of the cat – and the example of the chamois them-selves – he manages to evade her attentions, not least as the beloved of the force within Nature actively opposing her, represented by 'Solstraalernes Døttre',[23] 'the sunbeams' daughters' and manifest in the celebrated alpenglow on the mountains in the evening.

The second presentation of the Ice Maiden occurs, in the same topograph-ical context, during eight-year-old Rudy's return journey to the Rhône Valley. For a moment, no more, he remembers what he has been told about his moth-er's death and his own narrow escape. The terrain all around awes him; he appreciates its deadliness when he sees the butterflies and bees which have flown too high up as little corpses among the snows, and thinks the glaciers look as if they are holding hands (that is, united in their hostility to living beings): 'hver er et Glaspalads for Iisjomfruen, hvis Magt og Villie er: at fange og begrave',[24] 'each was a glass-palace for the Ice Maiden whose power and wish are to capture and to bury'. This fresh experience of the forces that rule the mountains enters the boy's ineradicable sense of what life entails, just as his infantile one has been incorporated into his psyche. 'Indtrykket af den hele Vandring, Nattekvarteret heroppe, og Veien videre frem, de dybe Fjeldkløfter, hvor Vandet, i en tankesvimlende lang Tid, havde gjennemsavet Steenblokkene, heftede sig uforglemmelig i Rudys Erindring'.[25] 'The impression of the entire trek, the night-camp high up, and the path going onwards, the deep mountain clefts where the water, for a mind-dizzying length of time, had sawn through the stone blocks, fastened itself unforgettably on to Rudy's memory.' These indelible features can be all classed as appurtenances of the Ice Maiden, a personification of what in Nature we find hardest to grasp – and also to avoid.

By the time of Rudy's third encounter (Chapter V) he is more man than boy, tested by severe misfortune and by his own consistent pitting of his wits against Nature at its most dangerous. Moreover, he believes himself mature enough for love, and with the daughter of a socially well established man. Once more he is

making the Bernese Oberland /Canton Valais crossing, at a great altitude with
the river Lütschine roaring beside him.

Tæt ved Rudy gik pludselig en ung Pige, han havde ikke bemærket hende, før
hun var lige tæt ved ham; ogsaa hun vilde over Fjeldet. Hendes Øine havde en
egen Magt, man maatte see ind i dem, de vare saa selsomt glasklare, saa dybe,
bundløse.

    'Har Du en Kjæreste?' spurgte Rudy; al hans Tanke var fyldt med at have en
Kjæreste.

    'Jeg har ingen!' sagde hun og loe, men det var, som hun talte ikke et sandt
Ord.[26]

Suddenly a young girl was walking beside Rudy; he hadn't noticed her before
she was quite close to him; she too was bound over the mountain. Her eyes
had a peculiar power, one had to look into them, they were so weirdly crystal-
clear, so deep, fathomless.

    'Do you have a sweetheart?' asked Rudy; all his thoughts were filled with
having a sweetheart.

    'No, I do not!' she said and laughed, but it was as though she didn't speak a
true word.

She laughs, one assumes, because she intends her sweetheart to be Rudy himself.
And in asking so bold a question wasn't Rudy soliciting her? Next she proposes
they take a short cut over the pass which Rudy knows only too well will lead to
a crevasse. The girl tells him she knows the mountains better than he does; he
belongs essentially to the valley. ' "Heroppe skal man tænke paa Iisjomfruen,
hun er ikke Menneskene god, siger Menneskene!" '[27] ' "Up here one should
think about the Ice Maiden, she is not good to people, the people say." ' He
protests, ' "Jeg frygter hende ikke" ', ' "I am not frightened of her." ' But perhaps
it would have been better for him had he allowed himself to be so; fearlessness is
too often attained at the expense of proper knowledge, including *self*-knowledge,
and so makes for catastrophe. The matter central to this close-worked, perplexing
short chapter will reassert itself in Chapter XII, 'Onde Magter', 'Evil Forces'.

    Nothing in this strange incident refuses to yield to a subjective interpreta-
tion. Here is a young man homeward bound who, for the first time ever, has
won himself a sweetheart who really appeals to him. His conscious mind is too
much under the influence of custom and convention for him to admit to
anything less than wholehearted joy over this. But his unconscious has reacted
very differently. The erotic charge of the encounter with this mountain maid
can scarcely be doubted, and seems stronger still when taken into conjunction
with what we will find in Chapter XII. Babette – as has been made only too
clear to us – is still immersed in adolescent romance about jewellery, beaux,

engagements and weddings, and while this is for the moment delightfully attractive to him, she has not managed to reach the deeper, darker regions of his being, part-formed by those very features of Nature he is now facing again.

What truly has happened is that he has successfully met a social challenge that satisfies his self-image as a male in exactly the same way as winning the marksmanship contest did. Andersen means us to take the two triumphs in tandem – and to see the hollowness behind them. Just as the shooting in Interlaken was not of the endangering, morally debatable kind in which Rudy excelled up in the Alps, so his courtship of Babette has bypassed the fiercer, hard-to-tame aspects of his own sexuality. But here – in the anti-human desolation of the Alpine pass – he sees them, face to face, probably for the first time ever . . . It grows dark, the girl offers to help him; he needs no girl's help, not yet, he says, and turns his back on her.

Behind him in the gathering blizzard Rudy hears her laughing and singing: 'det klang saa underligt. Det var nok Troldtøi i Iisjomfruens Tjeneste; Rudy havde hørt om det, da han som Lille overnattede heroppe paa sin Vandring over Bjergene'.[28] 'it sounded so strange. It was some magic creature in the Ice Maiden's service. Rudy had heard about that when as a child he spent the night up here during his trek over the mountains.' Exactly so; he can import material from his childhood both to endorse and to exteriorise his present bewilderment. But then, gaining the eminence after which the path descends towards his home valley, he sees in the clear sky towards Chamonix two bright stars. The known physical universe has asserted itself, leading him to think with mistaken complacency about Babette – and the second half of his history can begin. We can follow this in the knowledge that Rudy has now at last become aware of the Ice Maiden – externally and, terrifyingly, internally. This being the case, we see that the course of his life could never meet the desiderata of the norm.

The miller, happy to see Rudy in his home on account of his sporting prowess and delighting in his tales of this, is, on the other hand, unsure of him as a suitor for his beloved only daughter. Once more this novella is dealing with the very stuff of conventional fiction, and entirely accurately. He makes a wager with him. Rudy has admitted to turning down an Englishman's offer of gold, the reward for bringing down alive an eaglet now occupying a remote lofty nest on a Canton Valais mountainside. Madness to try, he'd thought, there's a limit to everything. Now the miller tells him, half in jest, that if he attempts the feat and succeeds, he can certainly have Babette. Rudy accepts the challenge, performs the task he himself declared impossible, and thus wins the miller's consent and Babette's hand. This constitutes what Ludwig Tieck called the *Wendepunkt*, essential in his view to the novella, its surprise turning-point. It surprises because what should constitute the start of Rudy's progress to the desired state of fulfilment marks instead the victory of those dark forces of which we have been only intermittently aware – and he himself, until that last episode, aware only vicariously. If, however, we look more closely at the chapter entitled – as Andersen had once intended the whole work to be – 'Ørnereden', 'The Eagle's Nest', we can see that the history's dark conclusion is nothing less than an inevitability.

The first stage of the eaglet's capture – against which his friends, while impressed by his daring spirit, advise Rudy – has to be carried out at night. Then, when day breaks, the fierce eagle guarding the nest can be shot, and, at enormous bodily risk, Rudy will be able to reach out into the nest – defying, as he does, the Ice Maiden's minion 'Svimlen', 'Giddiness/Vertigo' – to get the young bird who is the object of the whole operation.

For the second time – the first preceded his uncle's death from the avalanche – Rudy has deliberately, following his own hunter's code, brought about the orphaning of a wild creature, depriving it of the relation to a caring mother indispensable to every animal, bird or mammal, inflicting on it his own fate dealt him en route to Grindelwald. Furthermore, the undertaking reveals the omnipresence of cruelty in earthly existence, a cruelty Rudy is now himself compounding. As he peers into the nest itself, he chokes on the stench of the carrion there, all the rotting corpses of lambs, chamois, other birds that the eagles have preyed on. His deed – without his realising it – has placed him on the side of his apparent enemy, the Ice Maiden, and against the harmonious life available in Bex. Paradoxically, by first risking his life and then saving it, he has, in the longer run, lost it. His victory wins him the miller's kindness and the hand of Babette, but, ironically, it ensures that he never enjoys the warmly human reward he believes he is seeking. He will continue to belong to the wilderness to the point of abandoning the living for the realm of death itself.

og nede i det sorte, gabende Dyb, paa det ilende Vand, sad Iisjomfruen selv med sit lange, hvidgrønne Haar og stirrede med Dødsøine som to Bøssepiber.
   'Nu fanger jeg Dig!'[29]
and down in the black gaping deep, on the rushing water the Ice Maiden herself, with her long, pale green hair sat and stared with eyes of death like two barrels of a gun.
   'Now I will get you!'

When he comes down from the Valais mountainside back to the house in Bex, the miller and his daughter are so impressed that Rudy and Babette are as good as affianced. But Andersen's account of the arrival of the captured bird in the miller's house is a vivid and disquieting one, and surely constitutes the novella's very kernel:

'Her er det Forlangte!' sagte Rudy, der traadte ind hos Mølleren i Bex og satte paa Gulvet en stor Kurv, tog saa Klædet af, og der gloede frem to gule, sortkransede Øine, saa gnistrende, saa vilde, ret til at brænde og bide sig fast hvor de saae; det korte, stærke Næb gabede til Bid, Halsen var rød og dunet.'[30]

'Here is what you asked for!' said Rudy, as he entered the miller's house in Bex and set down on the floor a large basket, took the cloth off, and there glared out two yellow, black-rimmed eyes, so flashing, so wild, ready to burn and to fasten on to whatever they saw; the short, strong beak opened to bite, the neck was red and down-covered.

What pity we feel for this wild bird brought into a world he cannot understand or escape because of a faux-romantic whim! But the interest of this paragraph doesn't end there. We have been enabled at last to 'place' Rudy in the scheme of things: the resentful eaglet he has orphaned is an analogue of himself. In truth he is as thoroughly an outsider in this bourgeois home as the bird of prey, and this despite the subsequent billing-and-cooing with Babette during the ensuing winter cosiness as the two plan their wedding. Not only this! Rudy is essentially an outsider in society itself, as it is establishing and confirming itself in this ever more progressive and affluent country, whose career has parallels with that of Denmark. Rudy's dilemma is, in Andersen's view, inseparable from the complex development of Switzerland, as he had followed it over three decades.

2

By the time Andersen was writing 'The Ice Maiden', Switzerland was considered a template for socio-political development within Europe. For all the antiquity of its traditions, it represented an American-style federation of peoples differing from one another in language and faith but bound together by common belief in what nationhood should signify, by firm moral priorities and by centuries-long shared experience of geographically unique territory. Switzerland appealed to the thinkers of the Enlightenment, while the historians contemporaneous with them stressed the pivotal importance to the country's identity of the fourteenth-century hero commemorated in ballads and folk drama, William Tell. In the next century Schiller's great drama, his last, *Wilhelm Tell* (1804) and Rossini's opera *Guglielmo Tell* (1807)[31] emblazoned this charismatic figure more fully on the European consciousness: his being compelled by representatives of Austrian Hapsburg tyranny to shoot an apple placed on his own son's head, his killing of the cruel enforcer of this test, not as part of a personal vendetta but out of desire for his country-folk not to suffer any longer. In 'The Ice Maiden' the miller has a weathervane on the turret of his house in the shape of Tell's apple.

It is absolutely central to Andersen's thesis that Rudy, who combines in his own person the two dominant ethnic groups of Switzerland, should be, like its national hero, an expert marksman, winning championships and bringing down its most elusive and prized fauna, quintessential to Alpine life (chamois and eagle) The question we are invited to ask ourselves is what could be the meritorious advantage, let alone the societal relevance, of such accomplishments – and the deeds proving them – to the vanguard society Switzerland had become by the 1860s: prosperous, neutral, internationalist, sophisticated, and thriving on that most internationalist and sophisticated activity: tourism?

Already the country's more turbulent recent history had receded from popular view,[32] though Andersen takes great care to remind us of key features still discernible. Victorious Revolutionary France dismantled the Swiss cantonal structure in 1798, replacing it with centralised government. The Helvetic Republic was not popular with the majority of its subjects, who subsequently refused to fight for it against France's enemies when the Russians and Austrians invaded. In 1803 Napoleon's Act of Mediation gave back to the Swiss their canton system. And the Congress of Vienna of 1813, so detrimental to Denmark, worked favourably for Switzerland, recognising its independence and neutrality and bringing back into the Confederation three cantons not included in the Helvetic Republic, one of them being the Valais. Rudy's uncle was pro-French, we recall, with a French wife; he sang songs honouring Napoleon and liked to speak of French achievements, above all the construction of the Simplon Pass in the Valais, which transformed travel into Italy. However, disputes between cultural blocs were stressful, and led to the formation of the Sonderbund by seven Catholic and conservative states, – and to the brief Sonderbundskrieg, the Sonderbund war of November 1847, only a month long and with only a hundred casualties.

This conflict, resolved by the new Swiss Constitution of 1848, which, while allowing for certain canton rights, was strongly federalist, has definite relevance to Rudy's personal history. The Valais was not just a member of the Sonderbund but the last to give in to central military force. Its government built fortifications at St Maurice, on the opposite bank of the Rhône to Bex, as we have seen, from which it intended to launch an attack on Vaud, that historical stronghold of Protestantism. This was called off. But when the miller and Rudy encounter one another at Interlaken in the early 1850s, armed opposition between their cantons is a comparatively recent experience. The miller's heartily expressed feeling that men from the Valais in general, and Rudy the champion in particular, are brothers because of the French language they share, is not therefore without inner qualification. For his part Rudy would have realised this, and been pleased and relieved at the man's friendliness – perhaps indeed, on this very account, overrating his bonhomie. In truth there is ambivalence on Rudy's side too, not just about the Vaudois, whom he may well think of as 'stuck-up', but about French culture generally. After all, Rudy had had to be informed that the Rhône he saw every day later flowed past the great sophisticated city of Lyons, which his uncle was so proud of having visited. And he will remain throughout his short life not only a (francophone) Valais youth and backwoodsman, but a boy of the Bernese Oberland, reared in a remote German-speaking wood-carving and goat-herding community. Even there he had been more at home in the wild than in the village.

During the harsh winter that follows, the Ice Maiden keeps her eye on a seemingly changed Rudy. For all the power of Andersen's personification, which includes the credible rhetoric ascribed to her, we can legitimately regard her as an interior force begotten on the psyche by exterior forces and phenomena that most modern belief- or value-systems find hard to accommodate:

> Iisjomfruen red paa den susende Vind hen over de dybeste Dale. Sneetæppet var lagt heelt ned til Bex, hun kunde komme der og see Rudy inden Døre, mere end han var vant til, han sad hos Babette.[33]
>
> The Ice Maiden rode on the howling wind across the deepest valleys. The blanket of snow lay right down to Bex, she could go and see Rudy indoors, more than was usual for him, he was sitting at Babette's.

Is it she who is stalking him, as the literal reading would indicate, or are we, in truth, seeing into a Rudy stifled by this uncharacteristic and interior way of passing time, and thus unwittingly compelled to find an external correlative for his condition? The second interpretation is by no means vitiated by the next chapter, IX, actually entitled 'Iisjomfruen', which presents her particular *Weltanschauung* (but is it also – were he able to intellectualise his position – Rudy's own?) while insisting that we view her – as we are now viewing Rudy and Babette – as components of Switzerland itself.

It is spring, traditionally the time of courtship, love and weddings, and the Rhône – river of the French Cantons of Valois and Vaud – is rushing along in fullest spate, swollen with melting glaciers, effluvia from the Ice Maiden's Palace in the high Alps of the German cantons. Up there she sits and looks down, and what she sees of human activity infuriates her. For in the sunlight of the new season people are on the move, hard at work, breaking up rocks: the construction of roads and tunnels and railways is under way, to diminish Nature's power, facilitate communication, ease some of the hardships of life in so stubborn a land – and, not least, to enable more and more human beings from elsewhere to look wonderingly at the stupendous mountain scenery. All this fills the Ice Maiden with violent loathing: ' "Aandskræfter, som solens Børn

kalder Eder! . . . Kryb er I! En rullende Sneebold, og I og Eders Huse og Byer
ere masede og udviskede!'"³⁴ ' "Intellectual powers, as the sun's children call
you! . . . Vermin you are! One rolling snowball, and you and your houses and
towns are crushed and obliterated!" '

Time and time again, every year of our lives, are her words vindicated – and
yet isn't there something splendid and virtuous about enterprises that counter
this perpetual threat? These human endeavours – which Andersen now lets us
see more closely – and those planning and carrying them out, the engineers,
builders, architects – we remember Dickens's celebrations of these dedicated,
new professional men in *Bleak House* and *Little Dorrit*³⁵ – and those toiling
intently, tirelessly, even selflessly, on their behalf, are in fact serving the creative
forces of Nature, visible everywhere in the capabilities of animals and birds, and
at no season more so than spring. (They are morally preferable, we feel, to the
stalking of chamois to their deaths, or the violation of a nest, which make up
Rudy's greatest achievements.) ' "De lege Muldvarp",³⁶ ' "they're playing moles," '
observes the Ice Maiden, ' "de grave Gange" ', ' "they dig passages" '. And again,
' "De lege Herrer dernede, Aandskræfterne! . . . Naturmagternes Kræfter ere
dog de raadende!" ', ' "They are playing at gods down there, the intellectual
powers! The powers of Nature's forces are still the controlling ones." '

But the Ice Maiden is speaking only of those she has under her sway. Nature
also contains benign generosity, and the powers that represent these aspects
applaud and bless all creative undertakings. 'Men Solens Børn sang endnu
høiere om Menneske-Tanken, der raader, der spænder Havet under Aag, flytter
Bjerge, fylder Dale; Menneske-Tanken, der er Naturkræfternes Herre.'³⁷ 'But
the children of the sun sang even louder about Human Intelligence, which
prevails, which hitches the sea to its harness, shifts mountains, fills valleys;
human thought which is the master of Nature's forces.'

And even as the Ice Maiden speaks her scorn, a party of well-equipped
travellers, perilously near her glacier palace, manage to evade her elemental
expression of it, and a train comes along through the valley she is grimly
surveying. She can see every passenger on it – and they include Rudy, Babette
and the miller himself (in jovial mood). The eastern end of the Rhône valley
now has a train service – we have reached the 1850s – which will undergo
improvements to everyone's benefit by the end of the decade, which is also the
end-point of the novella itself. ' "Der sidde de To!" ' fumes the Ice Maiden,
' "Mangen Gemse har jeg knust, Millioner Alperoser . . . jeg sletter dem ud!" '³⁸
' "There sit those two . . . Many chamois have I crushed, millions of Alpine
roses . . . I wipe them out" '

With seamless artistry Andersen moves from invisible forces rendered disturbingly visible and articulate to a topographical presentation perfectly consonant

with his own factually immaculate travelogues; it brings to mind on the one hand Baedeker, on the other the whole line of nineteenth-century novelists intent on limpid descriptions of recognisable places, from Flaubert and Turgenev, through de Maupassant to Henry James. It is a deft transition too since we have arrived where that train, which so incensed the Ice Maiden, was bound: the resorts which make a garland, as Andersen puts it, on the north-eastern shore of Lake Geneva (Lac Léman): Villeneuve, Vernex (for seeing the Château de Chillon made famous by Byron), Clarens, Montreux where Babette's English godmother is staying, the reason for the trip, and Vevey. 'At Montreux,' wrote Andersen, 'was wrought my Wonder Story "The Ice Maiden" . . . in which I would show the Swiss Nature as it had lain in my thoughts after many visits to that glorious land.'[39] And indeed, as we have seen, thinking about Switzerland – its constituents, its progress, its likely future – is what has promoted the whole novella, which now takes a new turn, just as it does topographically: we watch Rudy the victor translated into Rudy the loser, the discarded.

Babette's English godmother has brought to her Montreux *pension* her daughters and their cousin, a foppish, flirtatious young man who lays instant siege to Babette. A friendly woman, keen to make friends with her goddaughter's fiancé, the Englishwoman generates an atmosphere of well-to-do culture – books, sheet music and drawings spread out on the table in her room! – with which Rudy simply cannot cope. 'Rudy, der ellers altid var kjæk, livsfrisk og freidig, følte sig slet ikke i sit Es. . .'[40] 'Rudy, who normally was always bold, lively and confident, felt himself not at all in his element. . .' Being so ill at ease affects even his usually lithe movements. While his companions stroll leisurely about like the sightseers they are; he becomes apathetic. Looking at tourist high spots like the Château de Chillon[41] bores him, and he is downright irritated when the English cousin presents Babette with Byron's poem, 'The Prisoner of Chillon' (translated into French). Normal enough male jealousy is obviously one reason for his objection, but so too is his own utter indifference to the romantic appeal of both place and associations. He sees Chillon, says Andersen, as merely the site of an execution in the past, he has a severely literal mind, and therefore longs to be away from all the civilised chatter and Babette's obvious enjoyment of it – to be for example out on the lonely little island in the lake with the three acacia trees. And yet, could he understand or tolerate them, the opening lines of Byron's sonnet are not inapplicable to Rudy himself:

> Eternal Spirit of the chainless Mind!
> Brightest in dungeons, Liberty! Thou art,
> For there thy habitation is the heart –
> The heart which love of thee alone can bind;[42]

Rudy's reactions to these English visitors – and to Babette's very different response to them – are conveyed with a shrewd sensitivity; Turgenev, Henry James, Theodor Fontane come to mind as we both feel for Rudy's emotional states and place them sociologically and psychologically. The reactions intensify, and when later he not only discovers that the English cousin is a guest at the mill in Bex, but that he has climbed up to have a view of Babette in her bedroom, his fury turns violent. Convincingly, Andersen portrays Babette as not wholly guiltless in all this business, but it is an innocent kind of complicity; at nineteen years old, she is, perhaps a little too easily, flattered by the young Englishman's advances, and the idea of seeing Rudy jealous amuses her (and pleases her vanity). Babette is presented throughout the chapters of their courtship as a normal enough, indeed not especially interesting, specimen of young womanhood; it is only on the last page that she will undergo her unforgettable transfiguration.

In truth Babette has not connived at the Englishman's foolish venture to her window, but Rudy chooses to believe the worst of her, and goes off in dudgeon. He takes the path over the mountains from Bex to his home village, partly to assuage his anger with strenuous exercise; this is territory which he feels is his own, the southern range of the Berner Alps. With its uncannily inspirited side he is already familiar. Up here – Chapter XII is specifically entitled 'Evil Forces', 'Onde Magter' – he meets one of the Ice Maiden's minions, but is she this? Maybe she is a mere country girl who, like Rudy himself, belongs to the untamed rather than the tamed world. Certainly she bears more than a passing resemblance to that first girl towards whom Rudy was drawn sexually rather than through romantic convention or social aspiration: the schoolmaster's Anette. She may even *be* Anette, Rudy for a few moments believes. As on the way home from the marksmanship contest, Eros asserts itself to Rudy in elemental rather than domestic or social terms. This Eros is less an opponent of Thanatos than its concomitant. ' "Du er kjaek!" '[43] ' "You are bold!" ' Rudy tells the girl; " 'Du ogsaa!" ' ' "You too!" ' is her reply, endowing him with that quality he temporarily lost while at Montreux with the cultured English. And bold he immediately proves himself, as he possibly never could be with Babette, with whom he always had to refine away parts of his real self. After he has accepted the strange girl's surprising offer of wine:

> hans Øine straalede, der kom et Liv, en Glød i ham, som om alle Sorger og Tryk dunstede bort; den sprudlende, friske Menneskenatur rørte sig i ham.[44]
> his eyes shone, a liveliness, a glow entered him, as though all sorrows and stress [had] evaporated; sparkling, hearty human nature stirred within him.

Of this, raw sexuality is a component, irresistible, overwhelming. When the girl says she will let Rudy kiss her if he gives her his engagement ring, symbol of the socialisation, the downscaling of Eros, he complies – without realising the gravity of his action:

> Pigen her paa Bjerget var frisk som den nysfaldne Snee, svulmende som Alperosen og let som et Kid; dog altid skabt af Adams Ribbeen, Menneske som Rudy. . . . ja, forklar, fortæl, giv os det i Ord – var det Aandens eller Dødens Liv, der fyldte ham, blev han løftet, eller sank han ned i det dybe, dræbende Iissvælg, dybere, altid dybere; han saae Iisvæggene som et blaa-grønt Glas; uendelige Kløfter gabede rundt om, og Vandet dryppede klin-gende som et Klokkespil og dertil saa perleklart, lysende i blaahvide Flammer, Iisjomfruen gav ham et Kys, der iisnede ham igennem hans Ryghvirvler ind i hans Pande, han gav et smertens Skrig, rev sig løs, tumlede og faldt, det blev Nat for hans Øine, men han aabnede dem igjen. Onde Magter havde øvet deres Spil.[45]
>
> This girl here on the mountain was fresh like the new-fallen snow, full as an Alpine rose, and as nimble as a kid. Yet she was created from Adam's rib, human as Rudy. . . . Yes, explain, recount, give it us in words – was it the life of the spirit or of death that filled him? Did he become raised up or did he sink down into the deep, deadly ice chasm, deeper always deeper? He saw ice-walls like blue-green glass; fathomless canyons gaped all around and water dripped ringing like a Glockenspiel and so crystal clear, shining in blue-white flames; the Ice Maiden gave him a kiss that froze him through his verte-brae into his forehead, he gave a scream of pain, tore himself free, toppled and fell; it became night in front of his eyes, but he opened them again. Evil forces had played their game.

What to make of this? Has their game resulted in victory for the evil forces? When he returns, after a six-day interval, to the mill, he feels that his extraordi-nary experience up on the mountain has given him some new insight into himself, something surprising in one whose life has so depended on the exterior world and physical acts. Now, however, he appreciates that the hunt can be pursued inside his own heart, that the Föhn wind can blow through his own spirit. In the light of this new knowledge should he confess all to Babette when back at her father's mill? But he cannot, it would be a duty impossible to discharge; in this sense the novella is true to the conventions of man/woman relations in the society of the times with which the ordinary novel makes us familiar. But he wants first to hear from Babette, for whom he feels a fresh rush of love, that she is sorry for flirting with the Englishman, then he for his part will tell her how repentant he is for ever having doubted her fidelity. And indeed a great reconciliation between them follows – though Andersen implies (this being more apparent on rereadings) that it is of a somewhat over-sentimental kind, corresponding, as so much of their courtship has done, to a code that popular romances and ballads have done their best to promote. The previous chapter has made only too clear, in its near-hallucinatory poetic prose, that Rudy in the depths of his being is unable to enter into a world of domesticated loving. He belongs to the boundless, captivity of any kind is inimical to him, and in this context it will not be wedding and marriage that await him but death.

And yet in the final sentence of Chapter XIII, 'I Møllerens Huus', 'In the Miller's House' everything would appear to be turning out well in romantic storybook fashion, and the couple are sitting together for the very last time before the wedding day:

> Udenfor var Alpegløden, Aftenklokken klang, Solstraaernes Døttre sang, 'Det Bedste skeer!'[46]
> Outside was the alpenglow, the evening bell rang, the daughters of the sunbeams sang, 'The best things will happen!'

When we have reached the tragic conclusion to the novella, and been able to reflect on it in relation to the whole work, with its beautifully wrought palimpsest of emotional epiphanies, we find – whatever our preference for even qualified happiness in this hard life – that the sunbeams' daughters' pronouncement is a true and fair one. In the end we see that justice *is* done, any future different from the one actually granted was always a chimera; and, interestingly, this would seem to be Babette's final verdict too.

In Chapter XIV, 'Syner i Natten', 'Visions in the Night' the Föhn arises, and clouds develop threateningly over the Rhône. The Ice Maiden has come from her glacier palace because the wedding of Rudy and Babette is imminent. And that young Englishman in Babette's life – seemingly routed for good and all by Rudy – turns out to have a psychic, if not a social or a physical, presence in her life. . . . Babette has an astonishing and deeply disturbing dream. She has been married to Rudy for years, and he is now away hunting chamois, just as you might expect. She is sitting next to the Englishman about whom she has, it seems to her dream-self, long stopped thinking. She feels attracted to him (as, one assumes, she did in recent reality). She takes his hand and descends with him from the house, but, as she does, she feels she is committing a sin against Rudy (as we know *he* already has against *her*); worse, a sin against God. As she goes down the path, thorns rip at her clothes, and her very hair, she realises, has turned grey, she is no longer young. She raises her eyes to the crest of the mountain and sees him, Rudy. She stretches out her arms to him, but he turns out to be not his flesh-and-blood self but just such a form as his uncle and he used to construct to decoy the chamois to their deaths, with the hunting-coat and hat hung on an alpenstock. Babette cries out that she would like to have died on her wedding day because that would have been a merciful act of God, 'da var det Bedste skeet, der kunde skee for mig og Rudy',[47] 'then the best would have happened that could have happened for me and Rudy'. In her agony at this situation she throws herself into the crevasse, the Ice Maiden's habitat, repeating, without knowing it, the tragic fate of Rudy's mother. She hears a string snap (the thread of life), and the note of a lament (death, to which Rudy belongs).

This dream, the description of which is one of the highlights of Andersen's art at its most visionary and psychologically penetrating, disperses as dreams do, though Babette knows it was of an appalling nature. Yet she remembers that the Englishman featured in it. She was truthful in her reply to Rudy that she hadn't been seeing or even thinking of him for months, yet, now that her unconscious has brought him back to her, she can't help wondering whether he is still in Montreux, and whether she might not see him at her wedding. And – 'Der gled en lille Skygge hen om den fine Mund.'[48] 'There passed a little shadow across her refined mouth.' Could anything reveal more tellingly her deep-down unlikeness to Rudy and her equally deep-down awareness of this? Yet soon she is smiling again and thinking of the glorious wedding day ahead.

In the evening the bridal pair walk out to Chillon, and Babette is possessed by a great desire to go out to the little island of acacias. They see a small boat and Rudy, a natural oarsman, rows out there, to find just enough space for the two of them to dance. The two are as happy as a couple in their position should be, delighting in each other's existence, while beyond them the lake and its shores are lovely in the sunset; and after the shadows have lengthened they see, higher up, an alpenglow the like of which they have never witnessed before playing on the famous Dents du Midi:

> 'Saa megen Deilighed! saa megen Lykke!' sagde de To.
> 'Mere har Jorden ikke at give mig!' sagde Rudy.[49]
> 'So much loveliness, so much joy!' said the pair.
> 'Earth has nothing more to give me!' said Rudy.

And after reaffirming the blessings of existence, his own delight in them and the goodness of God, he reiterates this last declaration, making us aware of its disquieting ambiguity. Isn't what makes them feel so blissful now but an overture to their happy life together? Rudy, for the moment anyway, thinks this. ' "Imorgen er Du ganske min! min egen lille, yndige Kone" ,[50] ' "Tomorrow you're completely mine! My own lovely little wife" .'

It is then Babette notices that the small boat has come loose from its moorings and is drifting away. Seemingly a chance occurrence, this is, we come to realise, on one level or another, the operation of those secret powers the story has made us aware of. Rudy behaves now as the complete storybook hero, and of course takes off his coat and boots, and jumps into the water to catch hold of it.

Why then does he feel compelled to give 'kun et eneste Blik',[51] 'just one single glance' into the lake? He sees there in the cold turquoise water fed by the mountain glaciers the ring he gave away to the troll girl (Anette?). And inside the ring, a circle which expands and expands, Rudy can see the glacier and whole troupe of 'Unge Jaegere og unge Piger', 'young hunters and young girls', and a parodic wedding service going on, and on the lake floor the Ice Maiden herself who rises up to meet him: ' "Min, min," '[52] ' "Mine, mine" she echoingly claims, ' "Jeg kyssede Dig, da Du var lille! kyssede Dig paa din mund." ' ' "I kissed you when you were little! Kissed you on the mouth!" ' Now she will kiss him all over, he is all hers at last! And as he hears these words he disappears into the depths of the water.

Pre-Freudians though they were, there surely could have been no readers of the novella unaware of the sexual symbolism and implications of this culminating section, at once folksong-like stark in what is actually narrated, and yet laden with significant, suggestive detail. The young man meeting his death has not consummated his relationship, he is leaving his loved one marooned on the island a virgin, and what meets him are vaginas self-enlarging enough to absorb him and take from him his life. Is Rudy himself a virgin, even after the mountain encounter with the magical 'Anette'? Did what happened up there – gaining him, Andersen specifically tells us, insights into his own nature – fill him with horror, such horror indeed that he never wants to repeat the act – let alone with Babette, for whom he feels such tenderness?

This is possible, even arguable, but – considering the proofs of his susceptibility to the opposite sex we have been given – I do not believe that Rudy's moments anterior to death amount to a repudiation of female sexuality. Rather they constitute a fervent psychic and physical rejection of all *domesticity*, of being appropriated and tamed – which goes to the heart of the cultural debate of the novella. Rudy draws back from consummation with Babette and makes a sexual entrance into a cold, destructive world because he is incapable of being the lover, the husband, the father all so necessary to harmonious social living.

And perhaps it was best that he died before he could bring Babette and himself painful confirmation of this profound inability of his, this instinctual turning back to very different, atavistic priorities. The most extraordinary words of the whole tale are still to come, and when we read them we must again remember Andersen's obsessive yet determined preoccupation with immortality.

Deiligt at flyve fra Kærlighed til Kærlighed, fra Jorden ind i Himlen.

Der brast en Stræng, der klang en Sørgetone, Dødens Iiskys beseirede det Forkrænkelige; Forspillet endte for at Livs-Dramaet kunde begynde, Misklangen opløses i Harmonie.

Kalder Du det en sørgelig Historie?[53]

How beautiful to fly from love to love, from earth to Heaven.

A string snapped, a mourning tone rang out, death's icy kiss conquered the corruptible [flesh]; the prologue ended before the drama of life began, discord was dissolved into harmony.

Would you call this a sad story?'

Apparently the author does not. Of course Babette suffers terribly, as is mirrored in the fearful storm which proceeds to take over the island while she is alone there. But even in her distress she realises – itself surely curious – that Rudy will be lying as if under the glacier where his mother once lay before him, and that the Ice Maiden has taken him. And *then* she sees the Ice Maiden herself in all her majesty, with Rudy at her feet, and, agonised, begs God for enlightenment. Her enlightenment is to appreciate the truth of her own dream, which concluded with her wishing the best for herself and Rudy. Has Rudy died because her hopes for the two of them were sinful? No, surely not! Rudy felt – in a rush of joy – that the earth had no more to give him (that he was not made for the kind of happiness that civilisation brings) and so there is a rightness in his death.

All this happened in 1856. But Andersen gives us a glimpse of Babette's present life, a tranquil one, not in her father's mill but in this same considerably developed part of the canton in which we took leave of her. Now greatly extended railways bring travellers down the Rhône valley, from Bex down to Chillon and the Lake of Geneva, and she herself can many times enjoy from a safe position, as they all do, the wonderful alpenglow and take comfort from it.

The novella poses questions almost impossible to answer. That is why it is such a powerful and successful work, artistically, emotionally, intellectually.

Do we prefer a civilised life, emphasising peace and harmonious coexistence, to a more primitive one with its premium on self-acquittal in struggle? Of course! How could we not? How could readers of such refined, intricately wrought literature as Andersen's tales not have this preference? Do we prefer the Switzerland of resorts and comfortable hotels, of well-appointed homes and efficient transport (and the opportunity to be at our ease as we contemplate the magnificent scenery) to those mountain valleys of eastern Valais and the Oberland where life can still be hard and is much more closely bound up with the difficulties each season brings? Answers to this question come far less readily. We may even feel, with Rudy-like atavism, that the first place lacks something that the second transmits to the deeper regions of our being. But then how much do we really value the intrepidity, the unflinching strength and determination of a Rudy? We may well not esteem the purposes for which he exercises these qualities, but neither can we quite dismiss them, even if we have built up a society in which they seem redundant, and are proud to have done so. Come any threat of danger – an attack, an invasion, a war – and we find we are not only grateful for them but admire those who possess them, especially those who possess them unreservedly. We may forget this uncomfortable fact later on, but time, history, will see that its hour comes back.

Thus 'The Ice Maiden' refuses to make pat judgements about self and civilisation, even as it compels us to face up to the questions about them which it dramatises. We face up to them by means of the tale's complex verbal richness, its controlled abundance of psychically penetrative imagery, its narrative that never once loses metaphoric force and its haunting ambivalence of sympathy. If we feel for Rudy, we also feel for Babette; if we are basically at one with Babette and admire the serenity she wins through to, we cannot forget the adventurous, bold, irrepressible Rudy and banish him from our hearts and our lives. If we are with Rudy, however, then we remember innocent Babette alone and vulnerable there on her island, without the one she loved and with the elements beating at her furiously.

3

On 2 March 1862, Andersen had published another speculation on the future, 'Det nye Aarhundredes Musa', 'The New Century's Muse',[54] far more essay than fairy tale. The Muse here is the summation of our own (and our predecessors') better tendencies, which have however to be first identified and then analytically discussed. There is much that is working against these, powerful reductive elements in both science and commerce which threaten the imagination and are therefore injurious to the Muse's health. The present age is far too busy making money and over-dependent on the roar and clatter of machinery to give poetry (synonym for all genuine artistic endeavours) the requisite attention. Instead, in its crass utilitarianism, it prefers to ascribe creativity and altruism to mere automatic responses of the nervous system.

'Al Begeistring, Glæde, Smerte, selv den materielle Stræben er, sige de Lærde os, Nervesvingninger. Vi ere Enhver – et Strængespil.
   Men hvem griber i disse Strænge? Hvem faaer dem til at svinge og bæve? Aanden, den usynlige Guddoms Aand, som lader, gjennem dem, klinge *sin*

Bevægelse, *sin* Stemning, og den forstaaes af de andre Strængespil, saa at de klinge derved i sammensmeltende Toner og i Modsætningens stærke Dissonanser. Saaledes var det, saaledes bliver det i den store Mennneskeheds Fremadskriden i Friheds Bevidsthed![55]

All [one's] enthusiasm, joy, pain, even physical exertions are, the learned tell us, nerve vibrations. We are every one of us – a stringed instrument.

But who moves these strings? Who makes them vibrate and tremble? The Spirit, the unseen Divine Spirit, which lets its emotion, its feelings, sound out among them, and it is understood by the other stringed instruments, so that they ring out in synthesising tones or in the strong dissonances of contrast. So it was, so it will be in humanity's great forward march in conscious-ness of freedom.

The Muse is thus not only a guardian angel of humanity but a functionary of the Divine Spirit. We are to imagine her having a father, a mother and a nurse, all of whom contribute to her nature and to her growth. On her father's side she is a child of the people, earnest yet humorous also, and practical. Her mother, by contrast, is high-born, academy-educated, an emigrant's daughter, with golden rococo memories. But independently of her parents, this New Century's Muse has to develop an awareness of a far vaster universe than any known to previous generations. Humankind would, in the foreseeable future, have expanded the heavens themselves.

Through her nurse, songs and tales from earlier (pre-literate) cultures have become part of the Muse's self. But this author with an international reputation for fairy-tale interestingly doesn't regard the legacy of primitives or ancients with unqualified admiration, any more than he automatically values all things childish. Yes, the infant Muse should be familiar with the Icelandic Eddas, the Persian *Shah-Nama* (*Book of Kings*), the Minnesingers, those medieval ballads so inspiring to Andersen's friend and mentor, Heinrich Heine, and, obviously, *The Thousand and One Nights*, that rich and gratefully valued quarry for Andersen himself. But just remember the savage horrors that fill the Eddas! These should never be repeated, in art or life. Even stories for the very young, making use of ancient folk material, should be moral improvements on their ancestors, however respectful of them.

When the Muse exchanges cradle for nursery, she can explore such bequests from earlier phases of civilisation as Greek tragedy, Roman comedy, successive schools of art and literature, the music of Beethoven, Mozart and Gluck. But will even this *embarras de richesses* withstand the exponentially increasing strains and contradictions of the Western world as it evolves towards the next century? Andersen reminds us that while this Muse of the new century is still at her educative play, whole nations are busily engaged one against another in power games, there are cannons sounding, and pens issuing implacable, belli-cose commands, and the real purpose behind all this activity is, like many old runes, still indecipherable. (And, of course, four years hence the second Dano-Prussian War over Schleswig-Holstein would break out.)

Rising to meet pressing contemporary conflicts Andersen pictures the Muse donning a Garibaldi hat (a sign perhaps of some optimism about Italy) and reading the perennially inspiriting Shakespeare and also the perennially wise Molière, further tribute to Britain and France at the expense of the German lands.[56] By this time the Muse should have achieved the desirable quietness of soul, matching the more serene and Nature-loving of the biblical Psalms, while not forgoing hopeful expectations of what lies beyond this mortal life. She will have a Homeric courageousness, her soul fusing the finest qualities of Ancient Greece and Judaeo-Christianity.

Therefore Andersen now, bolder than many of his intellectual associates, asks whether the emergent Muse of the new century will actually be Christian? Which, obviously, is also to ask whether twentieth-century *Europe* will still be Christian and will have succeeded in its various missions to Christianise the rest of the globe.

> Hvorledes staaer det sig med hendes Christendom? – Hun har lært Philosophiens store og lille Tabel; Urstofferne have knækket een af hendes Melketænder, men hun har faaet nye igjen, Kundskabsfrugten bed hun i paa Vuggen, aad og blev klog, – saa at 'Udødelighed' lynede frem for hende som Menneskehedens genialeste Tanke.[57]
>
> How does it stand with her Christianity? – She has learned the great and the little tables of philosophy; the elements have broken one of her milk teeth, but she has grown them [a] new [one] again, the fruit of knowledge she bit in her cradle, ate and became wise, – so that 'Immortality' shone out from her as humanity's happiest idea.

In her fine essay examining Andersen's ideas, 'The Toll of Andersen's Bell' (2005),[58] the critic Vera Gancheva views 'The New Century's Muse' as an expression of belief in the immanence of Spirit within Nature – in distinction to the older Romantic view that Spirit and Nature are coterminous. She thus sees it manifesting a Neoplatonism long congenial to Andersen and reinforced by H.C. Ørsted's synthesis of science and cosmology. 'Neo-Platonists advo-cated their view that the soul's function is to fuse *the situated above and the situated below in creation*, as well as the belief that love is the power guiding and directing the soul. Their ambition was to create a universal philosophy and a universal language, which would express the subtlest shades of human thought and discourse; a language that would be beautiful and gratifying to people all over the world. Some Neo-Platonists went even further than that and suggested the possible unification of all world religions.'[59]

Returning to the culture of the next century Andersen admits that he does not know *where* its Muse will arise, and that he can think of her principal attributes only in terms of desirable negatives. He feels confident that she will *not* be divorced from technological progress for all its dangers; she will indeed be borne to us by modern means of transport, thus endorsing the enthusiasm for modernity of 'Thousands of Years to Come', with which we opened our study. But from which country will airship or speedboat bear her? Not from America surely where the native inhabitants have been so mercilessly hunted down and Africans so cruelly enslaved – though California's incomparably venerable redwood forests suggest themselves. From Australia? Egypt? Britain, where Shakespeare still reigns? Or his own Denmark, land of Tycho Brahe, even though it eventually dismissed the great astronomer?

Andersen feels on surer ground when listing what the Muse will *not* concern herself with. She will *not* be expressive of times long past, will *not* employ the conventions and vocabulary of bygone art. Neither will she distort human language to suit tastes for novelty. She will fuse the poetry of High Culture and the plain prose of ordinary speech; not for nothing is she the result of union between her two contrasting parents. She will *not* chisel from Icelandic saga-blocks celebrations of old gods, for the excellent reason that 'de ere døde, der er ingen Sympathie for dem i den nye Tid, intet Slægtskab',[60] 'they are dead, there is no sympathy for them in the new age, no kinship'. On the other hand she will have *no* interest in the modern French novel, she will bring us an elixir for living, not the chloroform of preoccupation with everyday materialism. She will *not* go down the road of callow nationalism, for there will be such an inter-mingling of the West and East – thanks to the advance of railways and other means of transport – as to arrive at a luminous cultural syncretism that will enhance and stimulate all mental activity.

Power, Andersen concludes, may seem now to reside in the machine – even the Great Wall of China itself is vulnerable to it – but the truest power dwells within. One should not, however, think of this as only benevolent. If it is the soul that wields ultimate authority, and not 'Mester Blodløs', 'Master Bloodless' (Andersen's name for the 'mind' of the machine, a pejorative term he will use memorably again), then it has to be in first-class health, otherwise it is capable of initiating hideous acts of destruction. One of his greatest, most resonant later stories 'Det Utroligste' ('The Most Incredible Thing', 1871) will demon-strate precisely this, and has had a significant posthumous life accordingly.

Therefore we Europeans – for who else are this essay's addressees? – must not indulge in facile enthusiasms and expectations. There is biblical sternness in the essay's last sentences which we – knowing that war not only between

Denmark and Prussia, but between France and Prussia will have scarred the continent in ten years' time – cannot but find ominous:

> Vær hilset, Du Musa for Poesiens nye Aarhundredc! Vor Hilsen, løfter sig og høres, som Ormens Tanke-Hymne høres, Ormen under Plovjernet skæres over, idet et nyt Foraar lyser og Ploven skærer Furer, skærer os Orme sønder, for at Velsignelsen kan groe for den kommende nye Slægt.
>
> Vær hilset, Du det nye Aarhundredes Musa![61]
>
> Greetings, you Muse of Poetry's new century! May our greeting rise and be heard as the thanksgiving hymn of the worm is heard, the worm to be cut up under the iron plough, as a new spring gives out light, and the plough cuts furrows, cut us worms to bits, so that the blessing can extend to the coming new generation.
>
> Greetings, you muse of the new century!

4

'The situation looks very bleak,' Andersen wrote in his Diary on 12 December 1863. 'It is as though Denmark faces her final hour. All I can think of now is war and rebellion. . . . It's all over for Denmark and for the existence of my happiness – the night of death draws near.'[62] On the last day of the year he would pronounce, 'the outlook is pitch-black, sorrowful, bloody [for] the New Year.'[63]

By 1 April 1864 his mood was no less dark: 'The past year of my life has been full of trials and tribulations. First Jonas Collin was mean to me – he is now out of my heart. . . . The king died. The war is threatening Denmark with destruction. I've got old. I have false teeth that torment me. I'm not in good health. I'm heading for death and the grave.'[64]

Of these lamentations let us deal first with young Jonas Collin (born 1840),[65] the companion of the European tour that resulted in 'The Ice Maiden'. Edvard's son was named after his grandfather, and, as it happened, 'Father Collin', Andersen's single greatest benefactor, died as Andersen and Jonas junior were making their way homewards from their European expedition on 28 August 1861.[66] Andersen was overcome with feelings of inconsolable sadness, attended the funeral (2 September) and had a commemorative poem on him published in *Dagbladet* the same day. Later, even during the mourning period, Andersen would feel that the older man had not understood him quite as completely as he could have wished, and that his own anxiety to please him had had a certain inhibiting effect on his imagination.

Certainly his relationship with his young namesake was to be very nearly as complicated and fraught with misunderstandings, rows and reconciliations as that with the youth's father, Edvard. In photographs Jonas looks very like

Edvard, the same kind of masculine, well-set-up figure, and handsome, intelligent face. He was moody, irascible, argumentative, even truculent, capable of affection (he was genuinely moved when Andersen proposed they used 'Du' to each other, and he agreed to it, as his father had not) but also wilful, over-conscious of his own social standing (and of Andersen's lowly provenance) and thus capable of arrogant unkindness. Andersen took Jonas, as he had done his cousins Harald, Viggo and Einar Drewsen, on long tours abroad, partly to repay the past generosity of the Collin family (not only patron Jonas senior but Edvard also, his constant business manager and literary agent). He did so because he himself was apt to become intolerably lonely and bored on his travels even though these were often the only answer he could find to his gnawing compulsion to alleviate restlessness, melancholy or dissatisfaction. Edvard and Jette Collin, who saw rather clearly the difficulties of their son's temperament (and behaviour), were warmly articulate in their gratitude to Andersen for his kindness – and munificence – to Jonas, from whom they doubtless heard many stories of Andersen's impossible ways when he was his travelling companion.

And, to a young man, impossible they must often have seemed. One can detect in Andersen's attitude to him far too much of those pleading, possessive, over-emotional, self-preoccupied qualities he had shown over the years to Edvard (to the latter's exasperation), too fulsome and embarrassing a pleasure when well disposed towards him, too injured and complaining a displeasure when upset. Here are two consecutive entries from his diaries, 14 and 15 May 1861, when Andersen and Jonas Collin were staying in Rome. Jonas had just irked Andersen by volunteering that he rated his first cousin Viggo Drewsen (who would later, in fact, become his brother-in-law too) more highly than the distinguished Norwegian writer Bjørnstjerne Bjørnson[67] whom Andersen had just introduced him to – because he was more his own man!

> It's approaching 12 o'clock at night, and I'm still up! Jonas hasn't come home yet; I don't want to write down what I'm thinking and feeling. – Now it's 12.30, and he isn't here yet. Everyone all around is asleep; I am nervous. My legs are shaking under me; my head is burning hot. I'm not going to think any more!
> *Wednesday 15 May.* He didn't come home until after 12.30. He'd been at the club and later with the others at the café. He seemed sorry that I was still up. I left him with a less fond heart than usual and went to bed; was very nervous and upset. Today it was around 9 o'clock when we got up; he later than I. My mood is not pleasant. What will he do now? What will the day bring? It may well be me who gets unpleasant this time. . . .[68]

Saturday 18 May was even worse. Jonas 'has no consideration for me, just like Drewsen's sons; I was grieved and offended' – so much so indeed that he found himself 'jumping out of bed, and ranting'.[69] The next day, though, brought comparative and very welcome tranquillity. 'Later, when Jonas came home, I put my arms round him, said a few kind words; and he was moved and agreeable. It made me happy.'[70] All this would surely have driven even a less irritable and self-regarding young man than Jonas Collin stark crazy. One would never suspect from all these pitiful words that they were written by a writer of quite literally unequalled world fame aged fifty-six about the twenty-one-year-old son of an old friend far less eminent than himself. But Jonas never ceased to remind Andersen how enormously indebted he was to Jonas Collin senior, indeed the whole Collin tribe, and in a moment of more than usually blunt honesty Andersen wrote down that he was repaying this harped-on debt to 'a presumptuous conceited cashier'.[71] One cannot help thinking that, even at this late stage of his development, Andersen would have been happier and healthier psychologically if he could for once have insisted that proper respect was due to him simply as a successful middle-aged male.

The longest journey on which Jonas accompanied Andersen was to Spain and back from late July 1862 to March 1863, though they arrived home in Denmark separately. There was much intermittent tension between them, and the situation worsened as time progressed. Jonas, for all his immersion in natural history, was keen to revisit the bullfight, which Andersen had utterly detested, deploring the cruelty to horses as well as to bulls. *I Spanien* (*In Spain*, 1863)[72] was the fruit of these travels which included crossing over to Tangier and covering mountain territory on horseback. Surely the enterprising Jonas must have enjoyed all that, and been grateful to Andersen for providing him with such exotic experiences? But gratitude was not something Jonas found easy to express, assuming that he ever really wanted to. On Thursday 15 October 1863 Andersen wrote:

At Edvard's today there was a little of the Collin brand of unpleasantness. Jonas is really an insolent twerp on whom I have wasted the kindness of my heart etc.[73]

But as with Edvard himself, the friendship the two enjoyed was surely more complex than any letter or diary account can indicate, and fuller of mutual affection and sense of kinship than the many expostulations and hostile judgements on both sides would suggest.

The apocalyptic terms in which Andersen viewed the imminence of a second Schleswig war are far from mere hyperbole. They can, on the contrary, be seen as realistic, as only too prophetic. He understood, with a mind more sharpened than most by long experience of representative Germans, not least in the previous decade, that another conflict over Schleswig-Holstein – against a stronger, far more resolute Prussia, led by a Bismarck determined on some major show of military might, and, in the event, joined by Austria – would mean certain disaster for his country. And indeed it did; Danish defeat led not only to deaths and casualties themselves in distressing numbers but to removal of about 40 per cent of the crown territory, to a loss of face in Europe, and to a profound damage to self-image that would not truly recover until the mid-twentieth century.

In one sense the war was provoked by what seems now something of a *folie de grandeur* on Denmark's part, part-stoked by too great and unthinking a national self-confidence after the victories of the First Schleswig War. In another sense Prussia was waiting for just such provocation as it was given (as in 1870 with Napoleon III and France), and a victorious campaign against Denmark provided an opportunity to demonstrate the nature of its authority. Also, since the Prussian defeat in the Three Years War, the cause of German nationalism had greatly intensified, and Holstein provided a suitable (and in many eyes eminently justifiable) rallying-point.[74]

Under the late Frederik VII, the death of whom was a great sorrow to Andersen, a constitution had been drawn up integrating the Duchy of Schleswig, with its majority Danish population, into the Kingdom of Denmark. Frederik's heir, Christian IX, expressed serious reservations about the wisdom of this but felt compelled to put his signature to a document that went completely against the London Protocol of 1852. This, while, as we have seen, affirming the Danish federation as a 'European necessity and standing principle', also insisted that the two duchies were autonomous, and that Schleswig had no tighter constitutional link to Denmark than Holstein had. The 'November Constitution', however, violated this agreement, and on 1 February 1864 Prussian forces crossed the border into Schleswig.

In appalling wintry conditions fighting concentrated on the long linear earthworks called the Danevirke, dating from Viking times and thus having deep cultural meaning for the kingdom. Stretching from the marshes of the Eider estuary to the town of Schleswig, it protected the neck of the Jutland peninsula. For Danes to be forced by Prussians and Austrians to withdraw from the symbolically and strategically significant Danevirke, in snow-carrying gales for four days and nights without respite, made them compare themselves to Napoleon's soldiers in their winter retreat from Moscow. It was in the conflicts that followed, though, that they began to suffer heavy losses, at Dybbøl especially, the site of such success in the first war. Here Viggo Drewsen, a Collin grandson taken on a trip by Andersen, and hero to his cousin Jonas, was captured by the Prussians. Andersen, deeply upset as he was by the deaths of so many friends' sons, worried about him greatly. To the relief of all, Viggo had come off comparatively lightly, with a leg injury.[75]

On Bismarck's orders the Austrians now pushed up into Jutland. Prussians also fought northwards. To hear that the Prussian General von Falckenstein signed his name in the book of Skagen church must have made very bitter, poignant news for Andersen. The decisive battle was at Als (now reincorporated into Denmark) from 29 June to 1 July 1864, which cost the Danes 3,000 men, killed, wounded or taken prisoner.

On 20 July 1864 there came the ceasefire, and on 1 August the Danes prepared a preliminary peace treaty. Britain, France and Russia had taken a greatly more detached stance to the Second Schleswig War than they had done to the First, and had then announced that they would stay neutral; Norway and Sweden did not send military help as expected, something which so shamed and angered Henrik Ibsen that it brought about his years-long dissociation from his native country. On 30 October the Treaty of Vienna was signed, and Denmark lost both duchies and also enclaves inside western Schleswig that were properly and legally part of itself. It was deprived of some 200,000 Danish-speakers, a community that would not be returned to its natural homeland till the 1920 plebiscite after the First World War, when it voted to join it.

The rest of this book should be read with the Danish defeat always in mind, like a ground-bass in music. How it could be other than an abiding sorrow – a hostile aggressive neighbour invading areas of the country beyond the disputed territories, a disproportionately large number of dead and wounded, a sense of friendless isolation in Europe that would lead to political insularity (Denmark would be neutral in the First World War and occupied in the Second)?

Yet posterity can justifiably entertain a more sanguine reading of the situation alongside the one expressed above, especially if the result of the later 1920 plebiscite is taken into consideration. As historian Knud J.V. Jespersen says:

> What little remained of Denmark was as close-knit as could possibly be imagined in terms of a perfect nation state. There was a single nationality with a single language: Danish. The modern small homogenous nation state of Denmark is thus the product of the catastrophe of 1864.[76]

Beginnings and Endings.
From 'Dryaden' ('The Dryad') to 'Tante Tandpine' ('Auntie Toothache')

1

On 28 October 1868 the up-and-coming critic, Georg Brandes[1] paid a call on Andersen, who then read out to him his most recent story, 'Dryaden' ('The Dryad'), to be published later that year. Brandes responded with great enthusiasm, which Andersen found particularly gratifying. Brandes, only twenty-six and dazzlingly self-confident, was already known as a missionary for new movements in European culture, for Realism and Naturalism, for the ideas of Hippolyte Taine and John Stuart Mill.

The two men had, to our certain knowledge,[2] already met twice that year, at a theatre on 12 March, and then, on 20 April, at dinner chez Edvard and Jette Collin, who, always open to youth, would invite them both, again for dinner, on 2 November. This last occasion was to be important emotionally and socially for Brandes. During the evening he fell for Caroline David, wife of one of the other guests. Later Caroline would leave her husband to stay with the Collins, subsequently marrying Brandes. Coexisting with Brandes's championship of the European vanguard was his deep admiration for Hans Christian Andersen – as a writer of fairy tales, an art form he prized and which he believed Andersen to have elevated to rare heights. (He had, however, only limited regard for the novels, which this study cannot but regret.) He felt, and said, that Andersen's now *sui generis* art made the literary critic redundant; nevertheless, he would, in the summer of the following year, publish a seminal and insightful three-part essay on Andersen's stories, in *Illustreret Tidende*, on 11, 18 and 25 July 1869. Dealing as it does with the psycho-social problems of a modernity that entices and disorientates but which cannot be held back, 'Dryaden' ('The Dryad' or 'Wood-Nymph') must have struck the listening Brandes as peculiarly apposite for a critical reassessment of Andersen.

Appearing as a single booklet on 5 December 1868, it had virtually sold out in two print runs by Christmas. Its subtitle, 'Et Eventyr fra Udstillingstiden i Paris 1867' ('A Fairy Tale from the Paris Exposition 1867') doubtless added to its commercial appeal. Andersen later supplied his own account of how it had come into being:

> In 1867 I had been in Paris to see the Paris Universal Exposition; never before or since have I been so delighted or so overwhelmed as I was on that occasion. The exhibition had already been officially opened when I came, although the marvellous and amazing wonders were not yet all completely built. In France and throughout the world, newspapers wrote of this splendour. One Danish report claimed that no author except Charles Dickens had the ability to describe it. It occurred to me that I, too, might have the necessary talent, and how pleased I would be if I were to do it so well that both my countrymen and others would have to acknowledge it.[3]

The story's first sentences sweep us alongside the writer as he travels from Denmark to Paris – by steamship, by railway – all with an ease, a velocity, unthinkable to previous generations, and exemplifying that technological progress celebrated in the *Exposition universelle* itself. We now make such journeys, the author of 'The Snow Queen' reminds us, 'aldeles uden Trolddom', 'quite without sorcery'.[4] What need of that now when '*Vor Tid er Eventyrets Tid*',[5] '*Our time is the time of the fairy-tale*'? This was an idea that Andersen would develop in his story of December 1871, 'Den store Søslange' ('The Great Sea Serpent'),[6] a tale he himself related to 'The Dryad' because both of them confronted the truly modern.

What distinguished this magnetic Exposition, galvanising Andersen into writing a fairy tale in which it occupies the commanding centre?

The Exposition[7] opened on 1 April 1867 and closed on 31 October, but it really came into being four years before, on 12 June 1863 with Emperor Napoleon III's decree that Paris should host a Great Exposition in 1867, in direct response to London's 1862 World Exposition. (Britain indeed was the first nation to accept the Emperor's invitation to participate.) From its inception its prime intention was to display France's current scientific, technical and industrial triumphs, so integral to Napoleon III's vision of his Empire. Massively endorsed by plebiscite in a country that, unlike Britain, enjoyed universal male suffrage, and embodied in Paris by the spectacular creations of the architect Georges-Eugène Haussmann (great boulevards, housing for workers close to the factories employing them, a renovated sewerage system), the Second Empire proclaimed itself the first-ever French administration to give economic success priority. Reforms of 1860–61 had resulted in a comparative liberalisation of society, countering protectionism and giving workers the right to strike. The Emperor, 'completely committed to the needs of the great majority', himself submitted a model workers' house for an Exposition competition – and became a prize-winner. The venue for the Exposition (as we learn from Andersen's text) was the Champ de Mars, but so many and big were its displays that it spilled over to the Île de Billancourt. Visitors could arrive by special trains or riverboats, and within the precincts could move about by steam-driven buses. A new electric lighting system, with 50-metre-high light-towers, enabled night-time opening and gave the sky above the city that alluring, shimmering glow Andersen would make so much of in 'The Dryad'.

At the heart of the Exposition stood a gigantic oval iron building, its shape the 'rational spatial solution' to the problem of how best to give visitors inclusive overall views of its contents, from an interior network of raised causeways. In appearance the edifice was reminiscent of Rome's Colosseum but bigger and, unlike the classical monument, designed and constructed for *peaceful* purposes: Harmony – between human activities, between components of society, between nations – was its watchword. Beyond it the many pavilions showcased the different contributing nations, trades and inventions. The Champ de Mars also included a *Jardin reservé* containing imported meadows and trees, man-made grottoes and man-made waterfalls tumbling down into little man-made lakes. Greenhouses, aviaries and cages displayed plant and animal life from all quarters of the globe. Most remarkable of all these attempts to accommodate Nature in unmitigated urban surroundings were the subterranean grottoes filled with aquaria. Visitors descended by flights of steps to peer into domains of both fresh and salt water, and observe their denizens, animal and vegetable. Surely it was a given that this underwater construction would so appeal to Andersen that he would honour it with some of his most memorable and stylistically virtuosic paragraphs. Characteristically he will imagine the fishes bemusedly looking out on successive troupes of human beings. After all, hadn't he already depicted in 'The Little Mermaid' a genus which perceived birds as fishes and humans as the strange creatures of an overworld? It's likely that these state-of-the-art aquaria forged in Andersen's mind the very palpable link between his popular earlier story and this latest one dealing with present times; also that their inhabitants suggested the fish and cetaceans of 'The Great Sea Serpent'.

More than a political regime's self-advancement animated the Exposition; a world-view pervaded its culture: a belief in advantageous classification to empower the human mind in its relations to the external world. (Almost a majority of Andersen's ensuing tales reveal a fascination with systemisation, in which both distaste and admiration are present.) The programme for the

Exposition divided human achievement into ten categories and provided multiple examples of each from different times and societies: *objets d'art*; material and its application in the liberal arts; furniture and domestic appliances; clothing, fabrics, and wearable objects such as jewellery and even weapons; industrial products and machinery for the extraction and processing of raw materials; equipment for the applied arts; foodstuffs; agricultural products; horticultural products; objects for the improvement of the physical and moral condition of nations (which included teaching aids). France itself also offered a History of Labour (referred to in Andersen's tale), beginning with Stone Age workmen and their primitive implements, and ending with the exponential developments of the host country in the last decade.

'Nutidens Aladdinslot er reist!'[8] 'A present day Aladdin's castle has risen up!' we hear in Andersen's story; the author's very Danish identification with the *Thousand and One Nights* hero that has not yet run its course. (*Lucky Peer*, 1870 will end with its apotheosis.) Out of the barren 'desert-like' expanse of the Champ de Mars, above the problem-ridden quarters of a huge city, above all the difficulties and quarrels of the Second Empire and the Europe in which it was a major player, stood a magnetic palace of wonders capable of transforming countless lives. And yet – interesting both technically and for its implications – Andersen the well-known travel-writer gives us no account of the Exposition through his own eyes. Instead he ensconces himself and his readers in a well-appointed hotel in a typical Paris square, where a new-leafed young chestnut tree is being planted in an older discarded one's place and then promptly abandons use of the first person singular. Objective recorder now, he gives us this new arrival's history. According to Andersen himself this procedure accords with the movement of his own mind after he had stepped out on to his hotel balcony:

> Down in the square I noticed a tree that had died and been uprooted. Nearby in a cart was a fresh, young tree which had been brought that morning from the country to take its place. The idea for a story about the Paris Exposition was hidden in the young tree. The Dryad (wood nymph) waved to me. Every day during my stay in Paris, and long after, when I had returned to Denmark, there grew and sang through my mind the life story of the Dryad and it was interwoven with the Paris Exposition. But I had not seen the entire exhibition, and if my story were to be a true and complete picture of the exhibition I would have to return to Paris, which I did in September. In Copenhagen, after I came home again, the tale was finally finished . . . .[9]

Illuminating as it is of the story's unexpected vantage-point and its emphasis, this account is less than accurate. Andersen visited Paris from 29 March to

13 April 1866[10] – a whole year before the Exposition opened – and appears to have thought of a Parisian/Dryad story at this time. After his fortnight in Paris he went on to Spain and from there to Portugal, where he stayed three months with friends, gathering material for a new travelogue (also published in 1868). On his way back to Denmark, Andersen visited Paris again – 30/31 August 1866, two days of intense personal significance with irrefutable psychological and artistic repercussions. And during 1868 itself Andersen paid Paris yet another visit, from 11 to 18 May; it was during this last visit, it would seem, that the greater part of the writing of the story was done.

The history of the Dryad before and after her removal to Paris constitutes the body of this tale. After taking us to his Paris square, Andersen speaks only once *in propria persona* before the Dryad nears death and his story its tragic close, and then but briefly. The result is that the *Exposition universelle*, so purposefully highlighted in the subtitle, is presented first through the words of an invisible chorus, a multiform 'they' who regale the young chestnut tree's country home with news of the exciting, unprecedented things going on in Paris, and then secondly through the Dryad herself, naïve, bewildered, attracted and impressed by what she confronts, though her experience is very artfully manipulated. As the true chronology of the story's writing might suggest, the Exposition, while delineated with a fascinated accuracy, is less central to the fable behind the fairy tale than its site: Paris itself, Paris as the capital of Second Empire France and Paris as representative megalopolis expressing the confusions of the last third of the nineteenth century, its strengths and seductions on the one hand, its weaknesses and snares on the other.

Before a wagon brought her to Paris, the spring morning of Andersen's own arrival there, the chestnut tree was growing towards maturity in a village that prompts images of *la France profonde*, except that Paris appears discernible from it on the far horizon. In the daytime the vineyards and forests fill the vision, but at night-time 'den straalende Taage',[11] 'the glittering haze' indicates the great city. The day/night distinction has obvious yet satisfying resonance; Paris flourishes at night, through science and therefore through artifice, and thus can exert power over the rhythms of Nature herself. In the country human beings and domesticated animals work during the day and rest at night.

The Dryad has coexisted with the chestnut tree ever since her sapling days, and understands birdsong, animal language and human speech itself. Her greatest delight is to listen to the old village priest talking about the glories of France to the children assembled under the venerable oak tree nearby. He is surely a singularly inclusive teacher since he speaks affirmatively of both Joan of Arc *and* Charlotte Corday, both Henri IV *and* Napoleon I! France herself is 'Snillets Jordbund med Frihedens Krater',[12] 'the soil of [technical] accomplishment with the crater of freedom'. The Dryad pines to see more of this wonderful country in which she has been so fortunately placed, and she is not alone in her yearnings. One of the poorest village children, a pretty little girl who wears red flowers in her hair, experiences them too. The old priest warns Mari (*sic*) 'Kom ikke til Paris! Stakkels Barn! kommer Du der, det bliver din Fordærv!'[13] 'Don't go to Paris. Poor child, if you go there, it will be your ruin!' But as Andersen remarks with the tart brevity of his style at its most effective: 'Og dog gik hun derhen',[14] 'And yet she went over there!'

Mari returns to the village just when, significantly, the Dryad's tree is putting forth its first chestnut blossoms (expressing arrival at puberty). The girl too has blossomed – she is elegantly dressed now and drives her own coach. To the priest all these trappings only confirm his worst fears: 'Du kom derind! det blev din Fordærv, stakkels Mari!'[15] 'You went there! It was your ruin, poor Mari!' But the Dryad can't agree with him. She rightly connects the glittering haze on the horizon with Mari's rise from literal rags to self-evident riches, and from now on a longing to emulate her begins. And towards its realisation Nature itself becomes, ironically, the principal instrument. That summer a terrible storm breaks out, destroying the fine old oak tree, and with it communal village life. The priest, the village school and its children suddenly become the irrecoverable past. When spring comes round again after the desolations of autumn and winter – we readers realise it is now April 1867 – that brightly shimmering horizon beckons more irresistibly even than before, its allure augmented by the Dryad's own sense of loss and her awareness of an increase in activity generated by those now more lustrous city lights over in Paris:

Ud fra den fløi Locomotiv ved Locomotiv, det ene Banetog ved det andet, efter det andet, susende, brusende, og det paa alle Tider; ved Aften og Midnat, ved Morgen og hele den lyse Dag kom Togene, og fra hver og ind i hver stimlede det fra alle Verdens Lande med Mennesker; et nyt Verdens-Under havde kaldt dem til Paris.

Hvorledes aabenbarede sig dette Under?'

'En Kunstens og Industriens Pragtblomst,' sagde de, 'er skudt frem paa Marsmarkens planteløse Sand . . .'[16]

Out from it sped locomotive after locomotive, the one train after another and another, whistling, roaring, and all the time; in the evening, at midnight, in the morning, and throughout the day, the trains came, from which and into which people from all countries of the world crowded; a new wonder of the world had called them to Paris.

How did this wonder manifest itself?

'A magnificent flower of art and industry,' they said, 'has shot up on the plant-less sand of the Champ de Mars.'

In place, then, of any attempt at a comprehensive picture of the Exposition, Andersen selects some of its most singular features, the most extraordinary of the man-made petals on this 'Pragtblomst', 'magnificent flower' as they strike the gossiping humans and passing birds – from the machines clanging away in the grand hall of technology to Denmark's own contribution to the characteristic buildings of the nations, a little thatched cottage flying the Danish flag; from those grottoes underground where polyps move among stalactites to the various oriental cafés, until the Dryad is sick with desire to see the whole thing, a desire which grows so strong that it dominates her entire existence. 'En mægtig, lysende Skikkelse' ('a great shining shape') appears,[17] warning her of the dangers inherent in her present obsession. Yes, it announces, she will go to Paris, but she will not live nearly as long there as out here in Nature and, far from satisfying her longings, the city will only intensify them until she comes to resent the very tree in which she dwells, craving to leave it and roam at will. And once she yields to *that* desire, her whole lifespan will shrink to that of half a mayfly's, half of one day. The shape then echoes the words of the late village priest to Mari: 'Stakkels Dryade, det bliver din Fordærv!'[18] 'Poor Dryad, it will become your ruin.'

But the Dryad's longings do not diminish, and she welcomes the (in truth, sad) moments when her chestnut tree is uprooted and tied to the wagon. She does not even trouble to say farewell to the beautiful place she has known all her life, the grasses and flowers that have been the context of the tree's growing-up. By failing to do this, she seals her own dark fate. Or, rather, Andersen seals it for her.

In Paris it turns out as the shape predicts. The evocative paragraphs of the Dryad's reactions to Paris – its enormity, its diversity, its vitality – can well stand, with their onomatopoeia and mimetic rhythm, their nervous thrust, any comparison with later literary confrontations with cityscapes of apparently measureless dimensions and inhabitants – with the distressed appreciation of severance from Nature and History ('Unreal City. . . . A crowd flowed over London Bridge, so many,/I had not thought death had undone so many') of T.S Eliot's *The Waste Land* (1922)[19] to the awed, hectic modernist apostrophes to Brooklyn and Harlem in Federico García Lorca's *Poeta en Nueva York* (*Poet in New York*, 1931). We can hardly wonder, given the linguistic excitement of these passages, that the Dryad is not content to stay imprisoned (as she sees it) inside a single tree in a single square. She must extend her experience and therefore her own identity, even if her life-span undergoes inescapable contraction. Now the parallels with 'The Little Mermaid' become clearer to the reader. What is the Dryad's cry that she is not wholly alive where she is, and that, to become so for one mere night, she is prepared to give up all the years stretching ahead of her but the Little Mermaid's cry that she wants human love and the prospect of possessing a soul rather than those three hundred years guaranteed her as a member of the mer-folk?

Except, of course, that in the Dryad's case there is *no* possibility of eternal life. We cannot find here that all-embracing non-dogmatic Christianity that animated 'The Little Mermaid' in particular – though it will resurface in 'Hvad hele Familien sagde' ('What the Whole Family Said', 1870)[20] with its apostrophe to the Bible as the Book of Life. The wood-nymph escapes from the chestnut tree knowing that the power which has granted her prayer (a power given, it must be said, no satisfactory literary definition) won't permit her survival after this very night: she has been doomed, she knows full well, to only *half* a mayfly's allotted span. Except too that there has been no struggle to speak of over this, only the reception of ominous warnings themselves uninteresting compared with the many activities about her in which the rest of the world is allowed to participate. The absence of such a struggle is surely why 'The Dryad', for all its admirers, has failed to enter readers' hearts as 'The Little Mermaid' has, though its descriptions of Paris life are as brilliant as anything in Andersen's *oeuvre*, and their allure strikes generally sympathetic chords. All of us have, at some stage and in some form, had to make choices between the sophisticated/ contemporary (whatever its ethical deficiencies) and the natural/custom-hallowed (whatever its limitations). The Mermaid's dilemma – however factitious the metaphysical context imposed afterwards – seems real to us because true to both inward and outwardly lived human experience. Likewise we feel, and empathise with, her galvanising love for the prince, so movingly expressed in her acceptance of the princess he marries. However, in 'The Dryad' there is neither a values-challenging dilemma nor any question of love. But in what words could one convey incarceration in a tree as the most desirable of conditions? Equally hard, however, is it to present a purposeless, haphazard tour of an unknown city as some sort of spiritual imperative. For this is how the Dryad undoubtedly views it.

Once at large in Paris the nymph is shown as exposed to some James-Thomson-like *City of Dreadful Night*, a virtually contemporaneous work, written between 1870 and 1873. As she moves at night, like one propelled, with the inevitable morning denied her, down the grand boulevard, past pavements on to which expensive cafés spill out, past all the traffic and the motley customers, women and their patrons, masters and their servants (despite the human heterogeneity we find no egalitarian democracy here), we are irresistibly reminded of Thomson (1834–82) himself:

The City is of Night, but not of Sleep;
There sweet sleep is not for the weary brain;
The pitiless hours like years and ages creep,

A night seems termless hell. This dreadful strain
Of thought and consciousness which never ceases,
Or which some moment's stupor but increases,
This, worse than woe, makes wretches there insane.[21]

But our Dryad's 'strain of thought and consciousness' *does* cease: she perishes earlier than even those driven literally insane by city ways. Her circumnavigation of Paris takes in the marvels of the Exposition and of the lauded new sewerage system (a typical Andersen touch here is her hearing the indigenous rats regret the filth of the good old days) – and, among older monuments, the church of La Madeleine (St Mary Magdalen),[22] thus leaving us in no doubt as to the fate, predicted by her priest, of poor Mari from her own village and of thousands like her. (And maybe the enforced planting of trees for this grand urban show brought to Andersen's mind the destruction of all the Liberty Trees that heralded Napoleon III's *coup d'état*.) The Dryad is borne along to many nightspots of this bright, unsleeping city, the girls out in the streets flaunting their prettiness and then gravitating to a lurid place called MABILLE,[23] which echoes to the rocket-like uncorking of champagne bottles, and recalls the cancan-dancing Underworld with which Offenbach, to Andersen's contempt, had vulgarised the legend of Orpheus. It is, significantly, in Mabille that the Dryad's disembodiment begins in earnest. Her half a mayfly's span is now approaching its end, even as the revels grow stronger and more bacchanalian. By the time she gets to the famous *Jardin reservé*, she is in a state of terror at her imminent extinction, but can find no solace in the artificial landscape, as she would have done in a real one. She is compared – tellingly, disturbingly – to a woman who has slashed her wrists in her bath and then watches the blood flow from her body while hoping against hope to survive her suicide.

The Dryad's adventures and death are inextricable from the erotic, that omnipresent feature of the culture Paris was proffering an eager world, and of the strength of which Andersen had been aware even during his visits to the city as a much younger, less sophisticated man. We should now review his experiences of erotic Paris in the second half of the 1860s.

Andersen's hosts in Portugal had been the O'Neill brothers,[24] of whom George (Jorge), merchant and Danish consul, was an old friend able to elicit from him admissions of an egregiously intimate nature, just as, earlier, Theodor Collin and his nephew, Einar Drewsen, had done. Theodor and his medical mates had repeatedly told Andersen that regular sexual intercourse was necessary for unattached males, and that prostitutes were by and large the only means for this release. Jorge O'Neill, on learning how tormented Andersen was by strong sexual desires, expressed the same view. What the man indubitably needed was 'kneppe', to fuck (diary entry of 12 July), and Jorge recommended a trip to a Lisbon brothel to 'flush out the waterworks'. His remarks struck home, and though Andersen did not go to a brothel in Lisbon, on his return journey home he stopped for two nights in Paris, where almost the first thing he did was to find one (written up as diary entry for 30 August 1866):

> During this entire trip [the months in Portugal] I have been urged to seek out a prostitute. However tired I was, I did, all the same, decide to see one of these creatures. I approached a house; there appeared to be a woman in the business of selling human flesh, and four prostitutes paraded for me. The youngest was 18, or so they said. I asked her to stay. She wore almost nothing but a shift, I felt so sorry for her. I paid 5 francs to the madam, gave her, when she asked me for it, 5 francs, but I did nothing; merely looked at the poor child, who undressed completely and seemed surprised that I merely looked at her.[25]

He was relieved to be leaving Paris the very next day because 'the flesh is vulnerable', as he noted then, and as he discovered anew when in the city for the Exposition 15 April–9 May 1867. His regular companion was Robert Watt,[26] adventurous young journalist who, as editor of *Figaro*, Copenhagen, had published in December 1867 an extract from *Et Besøg i Portugal 1866* (*A Visit to Portugal 1866*).[27] Watt was similar in temperament to Andersen's friend, Henrik Hertz from those distant Rome and Naples days, but his libidinousness proved more contagious. For 3 May Andersen's diary reads: 'Went out to see Watt, who was with his compatriots yesterday evening at the Mabille' (to be rendered in 'The Dryad' as the very entrance to the Underworld, the place of literal disintegration), 'all of them rather drunk. Some of them spent the night with some wenches – a wild life.'[28] His own vicarious enjoyment of Watt's 'wild life' led Andersen two days later – after running into his dissolute young friend at the Café de la Recange, and listening to his new stories about his 'adventures with the ladies', while wondering if they could really all be true – to his second brothel. So for 5 May he could record:

> After having dinner I walked about in unfulfilled desire, then went suddenly to a shop which traded in human beings. One was painted with powder, the other plain-looking, a third quite a lady. I spoke with her, paid 12 francs, and left without having sinned in action, but probably in thought. She asked me to come again, said that I seemed to be very innocent for a gentleman, I felt so light and happy when I emerged from this house. Many would call me a spineless fellow, am I this here?[29]

Why 'so light and happy'? Because he had managed to behave like Watt and other virile (but youthful) compatriots and visit such a 'shop'? Or because he had left with still intact that innocence remarked on by the whore who was 'quite a lady'? The terminology of the diary entry certainly reveals troubled ambivalence about what his visit *meant* (as regards himself, as regards the behaviour of the average male), yet he felt able to repeat it on his return to Paris and the Exposition in September (from the 7th to the 22nd). This time he actually went inside the brothel with Robert Watt himself, but, as on his first visit, was drawn to a very young girl, 'the poor child' for whom he felt so sorry that, to her surprise, he once again did nothing, merely talked.

Not that this was his last brothel venture. He needed to go to Paris again the following year to carry out further research for 'The Dryad'; indeed back in the city he worked on the tale very consistently between 11 and 18 May 1868.[30] In Paris Einar Drewsen,[31] son of Ingeborg (née Collin) and Adolph Drewsen was now posted. Though years earlier, when Andersen had taken him on holiday, the two had not got on well, Einar being sulky and uncooperative, they had subsequently enjoyed a warm, intimate relationship, with Andersen confiding in him in 1862 his 'erotic time' with Harald Scharff. By now a rising young banker, Einar was delighted to see his old friend in Paris, and for his part Andersen had never seen the young man so happy. He wrote to Jonas Collin telling him so; Paris had brought about a transformation in his cousin. The two were sufficiently at ease with one another for Andersen actually to accompany Einar to a brothel. By now the relevant diary entry (for 17 May) has a decidedly déjà vu quality:

[I] merely sat and talked to Fernanda, the little Turkish girl, while E. amused himself. She was the prettiest, really. We spoke about Constantinople, her home town, and about the illumination there on Mohamed's birthday. She was very eager 'pour faire l'amour' but I said I was just there to talk, nothing else. Come soon, she said, but not tomorrow as that is my day off.[32]

All these biographical details only confirm one's sense that 'The Dryad', while certainly 'from' the Exposition, is less *about* it than about Parisian culture generally, a culture in which the commercialisation of sex was dominant. Certain attributes of Andersen's behaviour are immediately striking, and find their way transmogrified into his story: his selection of the youngest and/or the most refined females in the establishment; his pity for them and interest in – more, curiosity about – their provenance; his finding no difficulty in refraining from sexual activity with them (the last entry surely makes clear that he had no intention of indulging in it) – and the girls liking him enough to be willing, possibly keen, to pleasure him. There is also the curious fact that Andersen seems, on his own admission, to have been propelled to the brothel by the advice, talk and examples of other men, and, further, actually visited and chose the girls on two occasions in their (young) company. Andersen obviously felt that, compared with Jorge O'Neill, Robert Watt, Einar Drewsen, Jonas Collin and many another, he was incomplete as a male, and that to attain completion he had at least to go through the motions of doing as they did, even if deep-down he had no intention of fully doing so.

Einar Drewsen's father, Adolph, presumably ignorant of what Andersen had been up to in Paris, remarked, if half-humorously, that 'The Dryad' gave one second thoughts about Andersen as the wiser older companion of youth, of Jonas Collin for example. Andersen laughed to himself here as the disparity between himself, elderly, timid, inexperienced, and wilful young Jonas came into his head. Perhaps, though, Adolph Drewsen discerned – as Brandes, for all his favourable first reception, must also have done – the fundamental (and ultimately detrimental) prurient evasiveness of 'The Dryad', which its structural ingenuity and stylistic brilliance temporarily disguise.[33]

The village girl Mari, whom the Dryad consciously emulates, is depicted as quite flagrantly going against her wisest teacher, the priest, and the good life of her rural community, opting instead for a life of self-flattering luxury, as empty as it is immoral. The Dryad herself is treated with more imaginative sympathy, not least perhaps because (like Andersen) she only *vicariously* participates in the life of the flesh for which Mari has fallen, epitomised by the dance hall, Mabille. But who is it who frequents Mabille? We know the real-life answer – Robert Watt and his friends from Denmark. Who else but he and his like pay for the luxuries which Mari in her village (and the Dryad in her chestnut tree) aspires to, then pass unheedingly on elsewhere after satisfaction has been obtained?

Nothing is more impressive in this tale than its description of how her immediate surroundings fail the dying mayfly/Dryad, because they are entirely man-made. The passage stands as an affecting indictment of a culture that has, if not downright rejected Nature (as one of its best-known members a decade and a half later proudly proclaimed – J-K. Huysmans's *À Rebours* [*Against Nature*], 1884),[34] at any rate substantially reduced her place in the lives of countless human beings through its own seductive artefacts. But as the fate of one erring, basically ignorant individual, it is hard to acquit the writing of punitive relish.

And seeing these pages as Andersen chastising himself for his own lust and inquisitiveness about what could staunch it in no way exonerates them. As an artistically sophisticated appreciation of a major contemporary vortex, 'The Dryad' is impressive. But Andersen chooses to retreat from his authorial self as diagnostician (hence his early abandonment of the first person) into other roles doubtless preferable to his wide readership: apologist for the old virtues, as evidenced in a most imprecisely rendered France, which Mari and the Dryad have reputedly betrayed, represented by two French heroines (Joan of Arc and Charlotte Corday) yoked together by a stern Roman-like code, and by that model of altruism and chastity, Napoleon I. As he did in the notorious 'The Red Shoes' he is also issuing moral warnings that would not have disgraced a writer for the SPCK. Did Andersen feel a warning was necessary, or even desirable, for Robert Watt or for Einar Drewsen? We know that he did not. In fact we can here use an appropriate Tolstoyism. The characters of *War and Peace* are virtual fictional contemporaries of Andersen's, even if placed by the author in the Napoleonic period. We remember the light-hearted attitude to their own carnality of the likeable, even lovable Count Nikolai and his friend Denisov, and how Tolstoy views their behaviour as part of their *samodovolnost*, their animal satisfaction in simply being themselves. Andersen did likewise with his own young friends, and envied them for it. In *Lucky Peer* the hero's opera is a triumph and will prove how lucky he is to possess such great talent. But it is his foil, Felix, who, as his name suggests, is the happy one of the two friends. And he will live a life containing normal dissipation.

Aage Jørgensen in his essay 'Andersen between Rootedness and Modernity' (2005) shrewdly points out another irresolution in 'The Dryad': 'Why does this narrator assure us that the present age is the age of fairy-tales at the same time that his narration argues overwhelmingly that the present age is doomed and destructive? And why does the curse and the self-destruction so strikingly relate itself to sexuality and godlessness?'[35] The only answer would seem to be that the fairy-tale as the now ageing Andersen fashioned it was increasingly as concerned with danger, threat, the aversion of catastrophe as with positive matters. And while modern inventiveness continued to elicit respectful wonder from him (as from most visitors to the Paris Exposition), he knew it was also responsible for providing easy opportunities for flouting traditional moral values, for gratifying sensual whims and sexual urges on a scale and of a sophistication and comparative refinement new in human experience. In *Only a Fiddler* the sailors seek out Steffen-Karreet in a squalid slum street; in 'The Dryad' the women are relished in the setting of Haussmann's squares and boulevards, the *ne plus ultra* of planned urban elegance.

Whatever the prurience of his own approach to the subject, Andersen was making a serious point in insisting on venality as a cardinal attribute of the Second Empire, which was then approaching, though he could not, of course, have known this, its spectacular and terrible demise. Paris had established itself as a world capital for the flesh, epitomised by the well-known, lubricious extramarital antics of Napoleon III himself. Its writers seem to have taken positive pride in its reputation.

As the establishment Mabille is so luridly highlighted in 'The Dryad', we can use it as an index of Parisian life reflected in two of its most eminent literary figures, the Brothers de Goncourt,[36] with whose critical values Brandes was in full accord. Back in November 1852 Jules de Goncourt was recording: 'We are supping out a great deal this year; mad suppers where they serve mulled wine made from Leoville and peaches à la Conde costing 72 francs the dish, in the company of trollops picked up at Mabille and shop-soiled sluts who nibble at these feasts with a bit of sausage they had for dinner stuck in their teeth. One of them once exclaimed naively: "Why, it's four o'clock. . . . Ma's just peeling her carrots." We make them drunk, and strip the animal that lives inside a silk dress.'[37] In October 1857 he was noting 'young men from the Stock Exchange, Rothschild's clerks, who have brought along some high-grade tarts from the Cirque or Mabille to offer their little appetites the satisfaction of some fruit or a cup of tea. . .'[38] A diary entry from 26 May 1861, and therefore written only five years before Andersen's first Paris brothel visit, brings 'The Dryad' to mind more closely. A friend tells the de Goncourt brothers he's been chatting up a tart who, 'bored and unhappy' in the country, has come to the city to better herself. She first gets a job as a gentleman's maid, and then realises that by spending a bit of money on a silk dress, she could better herself rather more thoroughly. So 'she finds a dressmaker who rigs her out on tick. Off she goes to Mabille . . . and there's another in circulation.'[39]

The casual, frank cynicism of the de Goncourts makes one more appreciative of the dark tones of Andersen's story, which, however hypocritical or collusive, is at least free of their callousness, their nonchalant contempt. But if we wish to find a contemporaneous work dealing with sexual mores in Second Empire Paris both complementary and corrective to 'The Dryad', then we must turn to a novel by a friend of the two literary brothers, a writer only in his late twenties, published in the Exposition year itself and reprinted in the year of 'The Dryad' (1868) with an almost impudently self-confident introduction that is now literary history: *Thérèse Raquin* by Emile Zola (1840–1902).[40] It shocked, appealed and impressed in equal measure. Zola's first significant novel, a masterpiece of tension, soon became the very pattern of the Naturalism under way, thanks principally to the de Goncourt brothers themselves (with, for example, their novel *Germinie*, 1864, a case study of a late cherished servant who, unknown to them during her life, had not only been sexually debauched but had systematically cheated them). Towards the end of *Thérèse Raquin* both the central female character and her lover (now husband) Laurent go out into the infinitely corrupt-seeming world of prostitution, the world of Mabille, to seek release there from their appalling and erotically motivated crime.

Thérèse is the niece and ward of Madame Raquin, a widow with one son, Camille, a spoilt, pathetic, conceited, low-sexed young man. In their sequestered life in the Seine-side town of Vernon, Thérèse, quiet, passive, but aware of unnameable pent-up longings, has no real alternative to marrying her cousin. The quiet ménage continues. But then Camille, bored, decides to get a job in Paris with the Orléans railway company, and so the trio moves to the capital. Madame Raquin opens a little haberdashery shop, where Thérèse serves, and, for social diversion, instigates Thursday evening gatherings. One Thursday Camille brings home from the office a young man, Laurent, whom he had known years before in the Vernon days, son of a peasant-made-good, with law qualifications and a certain (limited) aptitude as a painter. 'You'll stay to dinner?' Madame Raquin asks him. He does:

'Thérèse had never seen a real man before. Laurent, tall, strong and fresh-faced, filled her with astonishment. She stared with a kind of wonder at the low forehead, from which sprung black bushy hair, the full cheeks, red lips, and regular features which made up his handsome, full-blooded face. . . . Beneath his clothes you could make out the well-developed, bulging muscles and the firm, solid flesh of his body. Thérèse looked him up and down with great curiosity, from his fists to his face, and a little shiver of pleasure ran through her when her glance settled on his bull's neck.'[41]

From then the course of events runs with an unimpeded naturalness, whatever the havoc its movement causes, but then doesn't that apply to other natural phenomena? Laurent frequents the Raquins not only on Thursday evenings but on most others. Thérèse and he become furtive lovers; it would have been biologically impossible, we feel, for them not to become this, and the foolish, chatty, unaware Camille is daily more of an irritant and, worse, an obstacle. The idea of his being killed comes to Thérèse and is articulated by her quite spontaneously, almost lightly, an inevitability which, once it has arisen in the brain, cannot be un-thought; the notion is in itself an irreversible act. Thérèse and Laurent murder Camille on a pleasure outing on the river, a hideous and distressing scene. Ever afterwards Zola will refer to 'the *two* murderers', justly, though in a literal sense only Laurent was Camille's killer. The lovers are cautious, keep a distance from each other, and when they marry, it is – it would outwardly appear – at the insistence of Madame Raquin herself and her Thursday evening friends. But, having attained their goal, they know no peace, the strong mutual sexual attraction disappears, they come to feel loathing not love for each other, and a wish to wound. Madame Raquin's stroke further breaks down the barriers they have erected between themselves and others, until, paralysed, the woman at last understands what it is they did to her loved son. The conclusion astonishes but has a dark logic to it: before the mute incapacitated woman's eyes the pair murder each other.

Zola's somewhat truculent defence of his book against hostile critics (whom he, never averse to publicity, may well have orchestrated himself) makes tacit appeal to two of Georg Brandes's principal mentors (and fellow diners at Magny's Restaurant[42] with the de Goncourts and Zola himself) Charles Augustin Sainte-Beuve (1804–69) and Hippolyte Taine (1828–93), but his essential tone is that of the Young Turk with science on his side, and a duty to make an over-comfortable bourgeoisie aware of laws guiding their lives:

> In *Thérèse Raquin* I set out to study, not characters, but temperaments. Therein lies the whole essence of the book. I chose to portray individuals existing under the sovereign domination of their nerves and their blood, devoid of free will and drawn into every act of their lives by the inescapable promptings of the flesh. . . . I hope it is becoming clear that my objective was first and foremost a scientific one. When I was creating my two characters, Thérèse and Laurent, I set myself a number of problems and then solved them for the interest of it: I tried, for instance, to explain the strange union that can come about between two different temperaments, and to show the profound disorders wrought in a sanguine nature through contact with a nervous one . . .
>
> [The novel is] 'an example of the modern method, an application of the universal investigative tool which our century is using to lay bare the secrets of the future. Whatever might be their conclusions, they would accept my starting-point, the study of the temperaments and the profound modifications brought about in the human organism by the pressure of surroundings and circumstances.[43]

Georg Brandes espoused the Naturalism somewhat stridently adumbrated here, even while he was seeking to give Andersen the critical stature which he thought – probably because of his enormous popularity – he had been largely denied but strongly deserved. Is there a paradox here? I think not. *Thérèse Raquin*, to confine one's arguments to this seminal and artistically accomplished blow in the new movement's cause, eschews almost everything the reader of a conventional novel (even well into the twenty-first century) expects: protagonists easy to identify with, events and adventures it is a vicarious pleasure to embark on, an appeal to life's varieties of mood and incident, and to the desiderata and the anathemas of the times. Instead it is a work of extreme concentration, making for an end which also sheds light retroactively on what has gone before. Likewise the Andersen fairy story (though not the Andersen novels, for all their many merits). All the best *Eventyr/Historier* succeed because they eschew circumstantial detail interfering with rigid development of their theme. Moreover, the persons at their centre could be called 'not characters but temperaments' and could be seen as 'acting under the sovereign domination' of one or two overriding qualities, compared with those of the psychological or social novel. And *Thérèse Raquin* itself, with its inexorable forward movement, its cast of four characters of whom only two command our whole attention, and its ending beyond which one can travel no further, is nearer kin to, say, 'A Story from the Dunes' or 'The Ice Maiden' than to the fiction of another patron of Magny's, Ivan Turgenev (1818–83),[44] one of the most interesting features of whose novels is the author's overviews of people both before and after the action recorded. Something else needs to be said too. The Naturalists' insistence that life should be looked at as through a micro-scope, with, for scientific accuracy's sake, no feature once spotted omitted but all held in severe focus, means that they can admit into their ken phenomena, – superstitions, fears, dreams – that the more conventionally realistic novelist would not include. To return to *Thérèse Raquin*. . . . Before Laurent chucks his friend, strangled but not completely dead, into the river waters, Camille bites him, tearing flesh from his arm. Ever afterwards, even as weeks turn into months and months into years, Laurent can feel that wound, can see it on his body in all its livid fury, and during their doomed married life Thérèse notes its sinister glow too – and is appalled. There is a degree to which this relates to the fairy tale rooted in common humanity rather than to facts-and-figures documentary realism.

Pleased as he was by Brandes's initial reception of 'The Dryad', Andersen was disappointed that he didn't include it in his three-part article for *Illustreret Tidende*. But in fact Brandes *did* pronounce on the story, connecting it to Andersen's other major fairy tale of 1868–69, 'Hønse-Grethes Familie' ('Chicken-Grethe's Family') of which he had made a clean version only five days after the appearance of the first part of Brandes's essay. Both 'The Dryad' and 'Chicken-Grethe's Family' pushed the fairy tale, said Brandes, to its extreme limits, a perilous undertaking since it was precisely on limits that the genus throve, both of subject and of manner.[45] Expand the subject too broadly, and the language peculiar to the medium seems inappropriate, even abused. Was it really wise of Andersen (wondered Brandes) to free his Dryad from the tree that mythology accorded her, and set her roaming the Paris streets of 1867, even taking in a contemporary hot-spot like 'Mabille'? Was a fairy-tale of the kind that 'Chicken-Grethe' formally and stylistically belongs to a suitable vehicle for the presentation of one of Danish history's most controversial figures, Marie Grubbe (1643–1718)?[46] In this second instance, continued Brandes, any attempt on the author's part at analysis – which so extraordinary and document-attested a personality cried out for – would only undermine the medium chosen; there would be set up, in his words, 'et Misforhold mellem Gjenstanden og Formen',[47] 'a discrepancy between the object [of Andersen's interests] and the form'. While believing this to have occurred, he does concede that the lapses are comparatively infrequent, and by inference unimportant.

To us, greatly as we applaud the general modernist direction of Brandes's tripartite essay, we can say that he is perhaps holding 'Chicken-Grethe's Family' too close to his mostly very sensible definition of the fairy-tale with its own laws of inclusion and exclusion, development and resolution. It is not insignificant too that the tale was the acknowledged part-inspiration for the first truly *modern* Danish novel, one which can hold its own with contemporaneous French achievements, which we will be looking at briefly. 'Chicken-Grethe's Family' first came out in book form in *Tre nye Eventyr og Historier* (*Three New Fairy-Tales and Stories*) in December 1869, dedicated to Edvard Collin himself. As in the case of 'The Dryad', it is important to know the genesis of 'Chicken-Grethe's Family' to appreciate its complexity.

2

Before Andersen, only Norwegian-born Ludvig Holberg (1684–1754) among Danish writers had known wide international fame. His creations like Jeppe paa Bjerget (Jeppe on the Hill) or Erasmus Montanus entered popular lore just as Andersen's Big Claus and Little Claus or Little Mermaid were to do. Sooner or later Andersen was bound to look to Holberg for a subject. Then he lighted on a passage in his letters (Epistle 89 in the *Epistles 1748*)[48] in which the great dramatist described his youthful encounter, wholly by chance, with the notorious Marie Grubbe, when she was an elderly woman living under another name in conditions of hardship. Andersen will give us the meeting of these two now famous persons (albeit enjoying very different kinds of fame), but only after recounting for us – as viewed from a distance through a curious prism – Marie's sensational earlier history. (Or, at any rate, a substantial portion of it.) Nonetheless, it is with Holberg that we should begin examination of this powerful tale.

Holberg was a young student in Copenhagen with no literary works to his credit, when, in 1711, plague broke out. So he fled the city, like many another, travelling by ferry from Hårbøllebro on Møn to the island of Falster. This meant crossing the Grønsund strait with its treacherous shallows. Once on the Falster side, on its north-eastern tip, he looked for accommodation and was put up in Borrehuset, the scantily furnished dwelling of the ageing wife of the Grønsund ferryman. This man, Søren Sørensen Møller, was not at home, however, but in prison in Nykøbing Falster for having killed a captain from Dragør in a brawl. He had, the woman's neighbours told Holberg, a reputation as a fighter – and as a regular wife-beater too. Asked for his own name – ' "Ludvig Holberg," sagde Studenten, og det Navn lød som ethvert andet Navn, nu lyder i det et af Danmarks stolteste Navne; den Gang var han kun en ung, ukjendt Student.'⁴⁹ ' "Ludvig Holberg," said the student, and this name sounded like any other name, [which] now resounds as one of Denmark's mightiest names; at this time he was only a young, unknown student.'

The nature of fame – its unpredictability, its tardiness in arrival and its speed in departure, its power, its questionable desirability, and, in some cases, its obstinate endurance for better or worse – is an important subtext of the tale. The ironic point here, of course, is that at this time, Marie Grubbe's name, which she had discarded for her socially valueless married one, was of the two greatly the better known. The obscure young student was to become very famous indeed, while the old woman had been, and under her own name was to remain, positively *infamous*. When Holberg admits to her that he has heard that her jailed husband beats her, she does not repudiate him but says that she probably deserves such treatment, not least for the wrongs she's committed in the past. Besides, her husband is for the most part a good man, and she goes on to paint a vivid picture of his strength and bravery when, some years back, he found and rescued her, and saw to her recovery. This leads her on to a summary of her truly remarkable earlier years:

' "Jeg er ikke skabt til at ligge syg og saa kom jeg mig. Hver har det paa sin, Søren paa sin Led, man skal ikke dømme Øget efter Grimen! Med ham har jeg i alt Det levet mere fornøielig, end med ham, de kaldte den galanteste og meest fornemme af alle Kongens Undersaatter. Jeg har været ud i Ægteskab med Stadholderen Gyldenløve, Kongens Halvbroder; siden tog jeg Palle Dyre! Hip som Hap, hver paa sin Viis og jeg paa min. Det var en lang Snak, men nu veed I det!" Og hun gik ud af Stuen.'⁵⁰

' "I was not created to lie sick and so I got well. Everybody has sin in him, Søren has his, but we should not judge the horse by its harness! With him I have in all lived more happily than with him who was called the noblest of the most elevated of all the King's subjects. I have been married to the Viceroy Gyldenløve, the king's half-brother; afterwards I took Palle Dyre! Hobson's Choice, each with his vice and I with mine. That was a long talk, but now you know." And she went out of the room.'

(Marie Grubbe's casual rounding-off of her confession is of a piece with Andersen's own demotic and idiosyncratic endings to his tales. Brandes – like Edvard Collin in his book on his friend, and many another – had enormous regard for such lively storyteller's devices of Andersen's.)

Andersen calls Marie Grubbe's progress through life a 'Tumleklode,'⁵¹ a 'tumbling orb', a world whose movement through time and space is downward.

Hers is an extremely strange story, especially in regard to her time, its code and its laws, and only admission of the sheer brute force of sexuality, in this case a woman's (manifested in both irresistible attraction and incurable repulsion) can go any way towards understanding it.

Marie Grubbe was born in 1643, the daughter of an aristocrat Erik Grubbe (1605–92) and his gentle, pious wife, Maren Juul (1608–47) who died too early to be an active influence on her strong-willed and wayward younger child. Marie was married off to Ulrik Frederik Gyldenløve (1638–1704) whose very surname proclaims his part-royal identity, used as it was for illegitimate sons of Danish monarchs. Something of a rake, with, behind him, a love-match to an older woman forced into dissolution by a disapproving court society, he distinguished himself as a soldier in the Dano-Swedish wars (especially in the Battle of Nyborg, 1659). In 1664 he was appointed Viceroy of Norway, based in Oslo (Marie accompanied him here) and applied himself to government with commendable thoroughness, simplifying the country's tax system, establishing a new appeals court, and building fortifications along the Swedish border. Marie was many times unfaithful to him – with Gyldenløve's secretary, with the court's French representative and, most scandalously, with her brother-in-law, Stygge (Sti) Høeg. In 1667 the couple separated. Adultery was punishable by death, but Gyldenløve (with marital indiscretions of his own to his name) was lenient; the settlement allowed Marie to remarry and to retain her money. All this, as we shall see, fascinated one of the early readers of 'Chicken-Grethe's Family', young J.P. Jacobsen (1847–85)[52] into researching Marie Grubbe's history and deciding it warranted a whole novel to itself, *Fru Marie Grubbe*,[53] two chapters of which were published by Georg Brandes's brother, Edvard, in October 1873 in the monthly magazine he edited, *Det nittende Aarhundrede* (*The Nineteenth Century*). But this wealth of lurid and dramatic material Andersen himself preferred to bypass.

Now divorced, Marie returned to her father's estate, where she was far from welcome; Erik Grubbe decided the two of them could not live at close quarters. So for a second time she was married off, in 1673, to a nobleman, Palle Dyre. Andersen's thumbnail portrait of him appears close to historical truth: a heavy-drinking braggart with high blood pressure whose only real interest was hunting. But their marriage lasted – drearily, lovelessly – seventeen years. Then in 1690 Marie started a sexual relationship with a much younger man, their coachman, Søren Sørensen Møller. When this was discovered, Erik Grubbe weighed in, insisting his daughter be disinherited and imprisoned. But once again a husband was to show himself more merciful than Society. All Palle Dyre wanted was divorce, so Marie became free to to marry Søren, the man banged up in jail at the time of Holberg's stay with her, though for some time, the couple, who had issue, were extremely hard-up, surviving mainly on charity. Then the Queen Dowager herself took pity on Marie, giving her a house, Borrehuset, to live in, from which Søren could work as the Grønsund ferryman. When Marie provided Holberg with hospitality, she was sixty-eight, and her third (and vastly preferred) husband – who did not spend long in prison – about fifty.

When we compare this authenticated story of Marie Grubbe with Andersen's version (which Jacobsen proceeded very considerably to redress in favour of both historical truth and frankness about the carnal), we are struck first by the size and ruthlessness of the omissions, and by an interpolation if anything even bolder, and executed in the face of the facts. In 'Chicken-Grethe' Marie Grubbe does not, as she did in reality, become the Viceroy's consort in Oslo; instead she walks out of the marriage to Gyldenløve after a mere four months, before indeed her personal goods have arrived in Copenhagen by boat from her father's Jutland estate. By telling us of Marie's immediate visceral dislike of her husband-to-be when she was only a child – she slapped his face at her father's dinner table for presumptuous pseudo-gallantry to her – Andersen makes it clear that her marriage to Gyldenløve is dead before embarked on. The marriage to Palle Dyre – which in 'Chicken-Grethe' comes about as a result of the pair meeting out on the heathland, where Marie, a young amazon, has gone hunting herself – is presented, with deft brevity, as one protracted episode of tedium, brought to an end by Marie's long overdue running away. No scandalous relationship precipitates this, which brings in its wake a serious illness from which she is rescued by the man she goes on to marry, Søren Sørensen Møller. Here lies the greatest change Andersen made to the history Holberg presented in his Epistles, under the appropriate enough heading 'Peculiar Marriages'.

Andersen has given Marie a virago's childhood alleviated by one playmate, Søren, son of a peasant on her father's estate. This boy, her own age, often fetches birds' nests for her from high branches, and Marie shows one of her rare moments of tenderness (but also her characteristic fearlessness) by heeding his piteous request that his father, Jon, be spared the cruel punishment commanded for him by Erik Grubbe for some unspecified trivial offence: this entails being tied and forced to straggle a stone-weighted wooden horse, the same penalty to which, in *The Two Baronesses*, the old Baroness's father was condemned by her subsequent father-in-law. When, after her brief marriage to the King's half-brother, Marie returns home, she asks – of the birds – what happened to her childhood companion, to learn he is working on ships, climbing tall masts instead of high trees in search of their eggs. If we ever doubt that the two Sørens in Marie's life are one and the same, then we should read more carefully the information Andersen gives us, semi-casually, about the birds flying back to Jutland to broadcast news of Marie's death who give details about Søren when he was young, and Marie first knew him:

'. . . ham, der som lille Dreng tog deres Æg og dunede Unger, Bondens Søn, der fik Hosebaand af Jern paa Kongens Holm . . .'[54]

'. . . him, who as a little boy took their eggs and down-covered young, the peasant's son, who got an iron garter on the King's Island. . .' (that is to say in the prison on Falster, the situation common to both narratives.)

No question therefore of Andersen's Marie absconding with a man in her husband's stables almost twenty years her junior and then sharing his rough life-style, even to accepting his beatings – so much the norm among men of his class.

All the above may seem like a wanton distortion and, worse, a bowdlerisation of history, and in a literal sense these charges can't be refuted. Even so, one would have to offer in retaliatory defence the already quoted justifying account of her life that Marie gives Holberg, a wonderful précis of decades of tribulation within social conventions and of psychological release outside them, showing a Shakespearean fusion of economy and richness of suggestion. But the best defence is that this carefully wrought fairy tale – and Brandes was right to locate it still within the genre – is not *about* Marie Grubbe as a historical personage, but has been *inspired* by her in pursuit of purposes entirely of Andersen's own. Unlike Jacobsen to come, Andersen does not call his story after her, but names it for the character with which it so intriguingly opens:

Hønse-Grethe var det eneste bosiddende Menneske i det ny stadselige Huus, der var bygget for Hønsene og Ænderne paa Herregaarden; det stod, hvor den gamle ridderlige Gaard havde staaet, med Taarn, takket Gavl, Voldgrav og Vindelbro.[55]

Chicken-Grethe was the only resident human in the splendid new house, which was built for the hens and ducks on the manor; it stood where the old noble manor-house had stood, with tower, crow-stepped gables, moat and drawbridge.

The story's opening paragraphs give us a picture of sustained decline. The only clue to the elite status before its onset is a polished brass plate on top of the chest of drawers in Chicken-Grethe's own room, bearing the name 'Grubbe'. It is this name which enables authorial movement into the past of the estate and the family it belonged to, a vision of which is likened to the mist that plays on the adjacent marsh: sometimes obscuring the immediate scene with its mirages, but then evaporating so that it is hard to believe one has ever seen anything else. But in all the dramas that ensue in Marie's descent from her class, from her marital, familial and fiscal rank, Andersen will not allow us to forget the eccentric old woman of the present. Chicken-Grethe's current life acts as the prism through which we see Marie Grubbe's history, and constitutes its ultimate and logical conclusion. Andersen expresses at key points in his tale his fear that we may focus too closely on the celebrity, and even on Holberg, our principal literary link to her, and so be in danger of losing its central point:

> Og vi ville høre hvorledes det gik Marie Grubbe, derfor glemme vi dog ikke Hønse-Grethe, hun sidder i sit stadselige Hønsehuus i vor Tid, Marie Grubbe sad i sin Tid, men ikke med det Sind som gamle Hønse-Grethe.[56]
>
> And however we want to hear how Marie Grubbe fared, we must nonetheless not forget Chicken-Grethe, she sits in her splendid chicken-house in our time, Marie Grubbe sat in her time, but not with that disposition of old Chicken-Grethe.

And again:

> Den danske Historieskriver Ludvig Holberg, der har skrevet saa mange læseværdige Bøger og de morsommme Comedier, af hvilke vi ret kunne kjende hans Tid og dens Mennesker, fortæller i sine Breve om Marie Grubbe, hvor og hvorledes i Verden han mødte hende; det er nok værd at høre, derfor glemme vi slet ikke Hønse-Grethe, hun sidder glad og godt i det stadselige Hønsehuus.[57]
>
> The Danish historian Ludvig Holberg, who has written so many readable books and amusing comedies, through which we are truly able to know his time and its people, tells in his letters about Marie Grubbe, where and how in the world he met her; it is really worth hearing, so we won't at all forget Chicken-Grethe, she sits happy and well in the splendid chicken-house.

Because Marie Grubbe's union with the ferryman produced offspring, her tempestuous history cannot simply end with what Holberg glimpsed and posterity has ferreted out: it too must have issue. By a tragicomic irony, simple-minded Chicken-Grethe, Marie's own *granddaughter* is totally unaware of her illustrious (and infamous) forebears. For her existence quite simply means the birds she lovingly tends.

  How are the mighty fallen (for through Marie there is royal blood), we might exclaim. Yet Marie Grubbe herself, as we have heard, gloried in her fall, and this tale, surely one of Andersen's very finest, invites us to glory with her, even to the point of accepting her life with Søren and his crude habits. Perhaps we are enabled to accept this invitation far more completely than we would have done had we been more fully (and accurately) informed about all Marie's lapses from accepted morality. As it is, we leave her feeling that she was amply justified in repudiating the life into which she was born, with its hideous expectations that any woman, however individualistic, should comply with whatever demands male hegemony saw fit to impose. One curious aspect of Marie's curious history owes nothing to Andersen's powers of invention, however, though it may well have played a part in its appeal for him: her two husbands were sufficiently sympathetic to their wife to flout contemporary mores on her behalf, even in the face of her own father's wishes.

If, like 'Valdemar Daae. . .' this is a story of familial decay to the verge of extinction, there is significantly no lament in it. Chicken-Grethe's peculiar kind of obscurity is informed by a beautiful justice when we remember the cruelty that in their heedless youth Marie and Søren inflicted on birds, for she carries out her caring tasks on the very site of them, the former Grubbe estate. If, to make his *Eventyr* express the need to put the cruelties of time-hallowed tradition firmly behind one, Andersen felt he must go against verifiable records at certain points, then the result wholly vindicates him.

'Just think,' wrote J.P. Jacobsen to Edvard Brandes (1847–1931), editor, critic, journalist, playwright and Georg's younger brother: 'I get up every morning at eleven and go to the Royal Library, where I read old documents and letters and lies and descriptions of murder, adultery, corn rates, whoremongery, market prices, gardening, the siege of Copenhagen, divorce proceedings, christenings, estate registers, genealogies, and funeral sermons. All this is to become a wonderful novel called *Fru Marie Grubbe, Interieurer fra det syttende Aarhundrede*. You may remember, she is the one who is mentioned in Holberg's Epistles and [in 'Chicken-Grethe'] by Andersen, and who was first married to U.F. Gyldenløve and afterwards to a ferryman.'[58]

As the subtitle might indicate, *Interiors from the Seventeenth Century*, Jacobsen's novel is built up of *tableaux vivants* (or *scènes historiques*) connected one to another by Marie Grubbe not only as a central figure but as the fleshly source of both centrifugal and centripetal force, experiencing (to the point of virtual helplessness) sexual attraction to certain men, not necessarily those society proffers her, and arousing this in others, more often than not in further defiance of social codes. The author's debt, to and divergence from, Andersen can be seen in those first two chapters published in Edvard Brandes's magazine and written when Jacobsen was closest in time and reading experience to 'Chicken-Grethe's Family'. Like Andersen, Jacobsen gives Marie a lonely but natural Rousseauesque childhood, marked in his case by emphasis on her closeness to flowers. There is an irony here: as we have noted already, Andersen's own reverence for flowers had a strong impact on the youthful Jacobsen, even heightening his dichotomy over whether to become a natural scientist (especially botanist) or a writer. The former won, and by the time the young man began writing *his* story of Marie Grubbe, he had completed his biologist's training and had made the first translation into Danish of Darwin's *Origin of*

Species.[59] Marie Grubbe's feeling for the plant world, which exhibits sex so openly and in such lovely forms, permeates her own intimate being, in contra-distinction to the little tomboy Andersen gives us, waging war on the estate's birds.

Both instigator and victim to far higher degrees than in Andersen, Jacobsen's Marie Grubbe can in part be explained by the lovelessness of Erik Grubbe's menage, with his concubine by whom he has a child, Marie's half-sister Anne-Marie. Marie's first passion is for the illegitimate half-brother of the king (the bastard son of Denmark's most celebrated king, Christian IV, and the half-uncle of the first man she will marry), Ulrik Christian Gyldenløve. This invol-untary choice reveals truths about her nature that the domestic/marital career arranged for her cannot cover up. As a daring soldier U.C. Gyldenløve was known as Colonel Satan, but his love-life was equally ferocious, and when Marie has most to do with him, he is a dying man; from syphilis, one conjec-tures. Throughout the novel Jacobsen will spare conventional sensibilities few details, not only of the turbulence that unchecked eroticism can lead to, but of the dizzying satisfactions it can bring, that put the humdrum into drab relief. Not for nothing was Jacobsen, to become possibly the most distinguished crea-tive writer of the Georg Brandes-led movement, Det moderne Gennembrud (The Modern Breakthrough),[60] widely considered the first Naturalist among Danish writers, with his command of detail, his preoccupation with societal veracity, his unflinching yet non-sensationalist attitude to sex and violence. *Fru Marie Grubbe*, for all the distance from the writer's day of its subject matter, is clear and worthy kin to the contemporaneous novels of Zola so dear to Brandes's critical heart: in its portrayal of Marie's marriage to Ulrik Frederik, with the husband exercising his marital rights despotically, betraying her with licen-tiousness of his own, yet periodically falling in love with her again; in Ulrik Frederik's deformed pander friend, Daniel Knopf, catering for his lowlier tastes; in the melancholy, compulsive temperament of Sti, the brother-in-law with whom she has her most protracted affair, and in her approaches to her second husband's coachman, to Søren, with his mixture of awe and contempt for the gentry. And the entrance of Holberg, the quiet, reliable, innocent witness, in the last pages beautifully seals the work; no longer does it seem a caravan procession of often torrid episodes but a unity, with a profound moral purpose behind it, to make us face the complexity not only of human behav-iour but of the human condition itself, both animal and nervously sentient. Brandes was enormously impressed when, already a very sick man, Jacobsen neared the end of his first novel, published in 1876. He wrote to him:

> What an excellent and lasting work! One might almost think that the superb quality of the first chapters could dampen down your own hopes of being able

to attain the same heights in the later chapters; every section was as it were a challenge to you to maintain the next at the same level – and behold you have succeeded. . . . My thanks for each individual scene, but especially for the conversation about the secret company of the melancholy, for the scene in which the dying Ulrik Christian breaks his sword and cries out for pardon, for the whole of Daniel Knopf, for the description of Sti Høeg. O man! You are great![61]

And in a letter to Bjørnson, Brandes emphasised the acknowledged strength of Andersen's influence on Jacobsen, modernist in orientation though he was. Thus Andersen's contribution to the direction of the Danish novel is inestimable.[62]

The two stories other than 'Chicken-Grethe' which appeared in *Three New Fairy-Tales and Stories* in December 1869, dedicated to Edvard Collin, are interesting glosses on the art of fairy-tale, especially in light of Brandes's observations. These are 'Hvad Tidselen oplevede' ('What the Thistle Experienced') and 'Hvad man kan hitte paa' ('What One Can Think Of').

The thistle grows outside the fencing of a manor-house garden, yet attracts the attention of one of its visitors because, being Scottish, she is gladder to see her national flower than any of the other – and rarer – trees, shrubs and flowers there. Hitherto, only the donkey drawing the milk wagon has taken an interest in the plant, and this because he would like to eat it, something he cannot do owing to the shortness of his tether. Now, however, the son of the manor steps over the fence and fetches the girl one of the thistle's flowers, which she promptly puts in his buttonhole as a sign of her favour. This makes the thistle bush very proud, and, when later it learns that the couple have got married, it regales all its floral neighbours with the anecdote, boasting of probable Scottish connections of its own. (Here again Andersen showed his knowledge of botany, for the 'Scotch' thistle is distinct from other kinds, taller, thicker, creamier in its flower, and thriving on just such sandy soils as Jutland's.) When the young couple, now husband and wife, view the thistle bush again, they notice that it's no longer in bloom; the one flower-head it bears is thistledown, 'Spøgelset', 'the ghost' of a flower. But the young bride thinks of a way of perpetuating it. Just as in the manor house there now hangs a portrait of the groom wearing the thistle bloom in his lapel, so its ghostly kin should be painted into her frame. Art is our best defence against decay, against ubiquitous death. The sunray tries to encourage the bush to be optimistic about the future, because its home then will be not as it has been hoping in a flowerpot, but in a fairy-tale.

Yet, with biographical hindsight, we today cannot help seeing more in 'What the Thistle Experienced' than just a philosophic statement about the durability of story in transient time. The thistle bush reveals herself as a mother:

Naar ens Børn er vel inde, finder en Moder sig i at staae uden for Stakittet.[63]
   When one's children are well inside, a mother puts up with staying outside
the fence.

Andersen's mother had one child who went very far outside the fence of
Odense's working class, and paradoxically found himself *inside* the houses of
some of Copenhagen's best families – the Collins' 'Home of Homes', to name
the dearest to him among them – while she lived in an asylum suffering from
delirium tremens. Yet her ultimate home would be a fairy-tale – if obliquely
presented: the infinitely compassionate 'She Was No Good'.
   The third significant story in this collection, 'What One Can Think Of', is
an engaging, somewhat mischievous tale of a young man who very much wants
to become a writer – before Easter if possible, since that is the traditional time
for weddings, and he hopes that being a writer will give him enough money to
marry on. He consults an old wise-woman who tells him that everything, even
the most humdrum-seeming, is material for imaginative writing: for example,
the potato patch near her cottage and the blackthorn bushes still to produce
their best berries. When she lends him her spectacles, the young man can see
just how interesting – with pasts, presents and futures of their own – these
commonplace items are, and even more is he impressed by her beehive. But
with the spectacles off, he can't see or hear anything that inspires him. So he has
to give up his hopes of being a writer before Easter, and indeed of being a writer
at all. The wise-woman suggests that instead he go down to the Shrove Tuesday
festivities, buy some masks and make faces at the poets. ' "Hvad man kan hitte
paa!" sagde den unge Mand, og saa slog han af Tønde hver anden Poet, da han
ikke selv kunde blive Poet.'[64] ' "What one can think of!" said the young man,
and so he [literally] knocked off the barrel every other poet, seeing that he
could not become a poet himself.' He thus becomes a literary critic, a reviewer.
Those who can write, do the writing; those who can't, criticize those who do.

3

med sit fulde, varme, unge Hjerte elskede han Konsten, den var hans Brud,
hun gjengeldte hans Kjærlighed, løftede ham i Solskin og Glæde;[65]
   . . . with his full, warm, young heart he was in love with art; she was his
bride; she returned his love and lifted him into gladness and sunshine;

This is Peer, reviewing his position after having been told by his friend, Felix,
born on the same day as himself and in the same house, but to its rich owners
rather than to its warehouseman and his wife, that he doesn't understand what
being a young man is like. We who have read through Andersen's *oeuvre* think

of Antonio defending himself against Bernardo (*The Improvisatore*), or Otto Thostrup contrasting himself with Vilhelm (*O.T.*). Peer's achievements to date, the fruits of ardent self-dedication, already justify his lofty reading of himself, and there are greater things yet to come. Throughout his story we are reminded of a traditional sobriquet for a lucky person: Lykke-Peer. Endowed with prodigious talents, not prosperous circumstances, Peer is driven by his very nature to realising them; all other activities are in comparison uninteresting distractions. That's how it was with Andersen himself in youth, we might think. But *Lucky Peer*, in size the slightest of Andersen's six novels, and in tone the lightest (enabling delicacy of satire in its treatment of Danish upper-class society) is also the most disconcertingly ambiguous. Its shock ending, with the final bitter-sweet authorial comments, demand of us instant re-examination of Peer's linearly presented history. Death has struck a still young artist after his most triumphant work of self-vindication. Isn't then the reiterated word 'lykke' ironic? And, to what extent, in terms of the art he so single-mindedly serves, is he to be judged exemplary? Beneath the book's pleasantness of surface lurk real doubts about the direction of the contemporary arts, and about the author's relationship to this.

The single most important aspect of this short *Künstlerroman,* deliberately obscuring obvious autobiographical parallels between Andersen and his central figure, is that the latter is a member of the younger generation, closer to, say, Jonas Collin or Einar Drewsen in age than to himself or Edvard. Care is taken, for all the plain fabulist's style employed, with its repetitions echoing the *Arabian Nights*, that readers realise in which years the story is set. To take a conspicuous example, Peer grows up in the Denmark of railways. He travels by train from Copenhagen to the town of his schooling, patently the Slagelse of Andersen's own. Even his old grandmother, fearful of the very idea of such speed, goes by train to visit Peer after he has fallen severely ill, enjoying her ride and the company it provides. '"Gud være lovet for Jernbanen!"'[66] '"God be praised for the railway!"' she exclaims. Denmark entered the railway age, as already recorded, in 1847 (Copenhagen to Roskilde), while the Copenhagen–Korsør line that would have taken Andersen to his old school was constructed in 1856. Again when his Capelmester (singing teacher) suggests an opera with a part especially suitable for Peer's burgeoning career, he chooses *Hamlet* (1868) by Ambroise Thomas (1811–96),[67] a performance of which Andersen had admiringly attended in Paris in February 1870, with the great Swedish diva Christina Nilsson as Ophelia. The novel praises *Hamlet* because the music concentrates on character, but Peer doesn't stay with Ambroise Thomas, becoming instead an enthusiastic Wagnerian. Wagner embodied the future in the arts – *Das Künstwerk der Zukunft* (*Artwork of the Future*) as the composer's own 1849 manifesto has it, and – what Peer himself probably read – his 1861 essay

Zukunftsmusik (*Music of the Future*)[68] – which essentially meant Music-Drama, fusing the genius of music and poetry as indeed Lucky Peer's own opera will surely do. Around the time of the novel many of Andersen's friends, the Collins among them, were intelligently making themselves better acquainted with Wagner; thus Peer is involved with the contemporary, and annexing himself to this future, though he debars himself from full entry into it by dying.

He does so, we can assume, in the year of the novel's composition itself, 1870, aged eighteen or nineteen. *Lucky Peer* is (like Andersen's previous novels) thoroughly scrupulous in its recording of the passage of time. Central to Peer's development are the two (ordinary enough) life events of confirmation and voice-breaking (the audible onset of puberty); in his case the second antedates the first by a month or so, which takes place at the traditional time of Easter. He would then surely have been thirteen or fourteen. For Peer, so promising a young singer, his voice breaking brings on a crisis, and his teacher recommends he gives singing a complete rest for at least two years if he is, as hoped, to make successful professional career. During these two fallow years he is a pupil at a boarding school. It is just Whitsun and he has all but completed his time there, when he suffers from the life-threatening illness which brings his grandmother to see him. In his fever he has a remarkable hallucinatory dream, and on waking, discovers his voice to have returned to him, as beautiful as before it broke. After a month he can return to Copenhagen to resume singing lessons of one regular hour a day, Schubert Lieder to begin with, while being further initiated by his teacher into the riches of music in general. But a whole year has to pass before he is judged ready to sing opera in public and give his reputation-making performance as George Brown in Boieldieu's Scott-inspired *La Dame blanche* (from 1825).[69]

The year after this debut he starts composing on his own account while also taking the title role in *Hamlet*. Wagner follows, Peer's choice being *Lohengrin*,[70] another huge public success for him; Copenhagen society takes him to its bosom. But the Wagner opera has motivated him creatively, and he proceeds to occupy a further year in writing an opera of his own, its subject Aladdin. He decides on this because it concerns a boy from a poor background making good; subliminally readers have been thinking of this work from the outset of the novel: in its *Arabian Nights* original, in Oehlenschläger's version, and in its echoes in Andersen's own writings. Its composition, however, inflicts the gravest wear-and-tear on the young man, and its rapturous reception literally kills him. If then we (very reasonably) take his school-leaving age to be sixteen, he is only nineteen at the time of his unexpected, premature death.

The tale of a lucky person? Solon's 'Call no man fortunate till he's dead!'[71] is quoted. His singular blessings made Peer a readily religious youth for whom confirmation was a definitive event; he gave repeated thanks to God, and the first real use he put his restored voice to was singing Psalms. His is largely a steady, good-hearted, generous nature, able to cope with setbacks: his father's death in war; his voice-breaking and the horrible uncertainty about his whole future that it brought. He is attentive to the advice of others (the Capelmester, his mother and grandmother), and he never lets his (eventually spectacular) triumphs go to his head, something that must have amused Andersen's more elderly readers. If, in *O.T.* Andersen was asking himself what he would have been like if born into a noble family, and in *Only a Fiddler* if he had lacked perseverance and unstoppable drive, in *Lucky Peer* he is posing the question: 'How would it have gone for me if I had been as humble in origins as I was in reality but had had the familial stability I lacked? Would my own temperament as a young man have been correspondingly more stable? And, if so, what kind of art would I have produced?' Then, he must have added, remembering all the multitudinous wounds and humiliations which this study has recounted as determinants of his art, he might truly have been considered 'lykke'. Though a certain amount of Society malice is (lightly) set down in this novel, bearing out what Felix tells him, half in jest, that everybody in these circles is a *little* spiteful, his brief progress through the world seems basically an agreeable one. Not least because between Felix and himself there are none of the tensions that grow up between Antonio and Bernardo, Otto and Vilhelm – or Andersen and Edvard Collin. We are told, on good authority that jealousy stalks the world of the theatre, and another kind of jealousy is apparent when Felix's mother, wife of the well-to-do merchant, wonders how anyone of such humble parentage and limited education as Peer could rise to his attainments, but the majority of people wish him well and applaud his achievements. (Andersen had well-connected well-wishers too. In this novel he gives them their due and lets them oust all those others from the reader's attention.)

Of the two boys, it is the son of the rich *Grosserer* (merchant, wholesaler and, it is implied, a self-made man; this is post–1849 Denmark) who is christened Felix ('fortunate' 'happy'), the other being given an ordinary enough name, though one, as noted, with demotic and proverbial connotations of hopefulness. Both pairs of parents are good, caring people; however, the rich couple employ a nurse, so Felix makes his infant outings in her company not his blood mother's. Felix and Peer don't speak to each other until they are two years of age, and do not really become friends until, through his celebrated performances, Peer himself has made it in Copenhagen Society. There is a genuine sympathy between the two, but character and economic circumstances alike separate them. Amiable as he is, Felix lacks depth, and despite his favoured provenance – symbolised by the shining glass fragments in the walls enclosing his home – he is basically ordinary, before long a *(jeune) homme moyen sensuel* and proud of being such. He can't understand why Peer doesn't care for parties with dancing-girls or is indifferent to the baroness and her attractive daughter, who are so palpably interested in him. Felix will hold a distinguished position in the world; he becomes, in his late teens, an equerry, the acknowledged first step to becoming court chamberlain, but there is nothing, apart from the social confidence associated with the upper crust, to distinguish him from scores of other intelligent, well-adjusted males. Peer, in contrast, has been selected by destiny, endowed with talents with the potential to affect many lives. Felix will acquire a literal golden key because he's a court official but Peer has an invisible one: 'Geniets Guldnøgle, som lukker op for alle Jordens Skatte, og Hjerternes med,'[72] 'the gold key of genius which opens up all the treasures of the earth and all hearts too'.

This comparatively mild treatment of the friendship between two boys who contrast in both hereditary wealth and hereditary make-up is consonant with the general serenity with which Peer's life story is portrayed. We could even suspect Andersen of a certain compensatory whitewashing. Up in the garret of the merchant's house, Peer's family lives contentedly enough until the 'sad years of war', clearly the Dano-Prussian Schleswig-Holstein conflict (a further means of dating the story to within easy reach of its composition year). Then his warehouseman father is called up for military service (it is not suggested that he volunteered – he is no Hans Andersen or the Tailor from *Only a Fiddler*) and is killed when fighting the overwhelming enemy. He is bitterly mourned, but the merchant and his wife being good, principled people, permit his widow to stay on at reduced rent. She takes in washing but only for well-paying, well-born gentlemen, and besides, to help keep the home running, there is Peer's grandmother, a tribute to Andersen's paternal grandmother whom he admired so much; she appears the very pattern of unselfish devotion. Peer, for his part, is pleased with his lot, glad he goes to an ordinary city school and isn't isolated with a tutor like Felix. He can even deal with tiresome fellow pupils, and when, after his voice has broken, he is sent away to school like the privileged merchant's son, he finds much to satisfy him there as well. The headmaster, Herr Gabriel, for all his self-importance and affectation, is depicted without the rancour Andersen felt towards his obvious original, Simon Meisling (cf. *The Improvisatore.*) And his wife, Mette Gabriel, is not, as she is in Andersen's first novel, a Potiphar's Wife.

Peer proves a diligent, popular student who finds favour in his mentors' eyes, and in the household of the local pharmacist, a lover of amateur dramatics with whose daughter he falls in love. This is the weakest strand of the novel, though the scene where Felix comes up to the provincial town for a ball held at its Councillor's house, and gazumps Peer for his dance with this girl, has a certain credible sharpness; convincing is our complaisant hero's surge of resentment, here tinged with hatred. Nevertheless, not only has the girl herself no fictional presence, Peer's feelings for her are so perfunctorily done that when we hear how desolate he is that she has married the fat middle-aged Councillor (as Sophie in *O.T.* did the Kammerjunker), we have all but forgotten he ever had them in the first place; Andersen must have felt obliged to pay Riborg Voigt and Louise Collin further tribute, but the episode doesn't come to life.

Nor, despite those warnings of ubiquitous jealousy, do Peer's successive entries into the world of music – from ballet and theatre orchestra to singing lessons with the Capelmester, comparable with Andersen's travails in Copenhagen 1819–22 and fictionalised in rasping manner in *The Improvisatore*. Penury here is of an almost acceptable kind, with the merchant and his wife constantly to hand, and as a native Copenhagener Peer knows none of Andersen's indignities of lodging with Fru Thorgesen or of being deceived by her dubious lodgers, of being at the mercy of Giuseppe Siboni's rages or the conditional patronage and displeasures of Professor Guldberg.

Andersen's low-key representation of his hero's experiences is, however, artistically justifiable, for they are of secondary importance to his theme: the evolution of Peer's relationship to art free from the emotional impedimenta he himself had known. Art is a Platonic absolute we apprehend through intima-tions (as in Wordsworth's 'Immortality Ode'); it is a parallel world, awareness of which illuminates and gives meaning to our own, while showing up its flaws and limitations. It can also be likened to a mansion among the many rooms of which the true aspiring artist must make a choice if s/he is to realise inherent capabilities most completely. Thus, just as young Hans Christian initially thought of himself in terms of dance, acting and stagecraft before discovering the profound appeal of the written word, so Peer – with the Capelmester's help – has to find the appropriate form for his individual creativity. But first the very nature of that individuality must be perceived. While Peer's search amounts to a tour through the musical/artistic culture of the 1860s, it is preceded by disquieting (not least to himself) glimpses into the arcanum of his psyche. In childhood Peer has 'lucky' finds in the dirt of the backyard; one of these is an amber heart which his grandmother threads on a string for him to wear round his neck, telling him never to part from it. This *objet trouvé* surfaces in the dream he has on his first night at boarding school, by which time he has passed through ballet and vocal training, and is having to face both temporary loss of voice and a more formal education than he has been used to:

Hvad man drømmer den første Nat, man sover i et fremmed Huus, har Betydning, havde Faermoer sagt. Peer drømte, at han tog Ravhjertet, han endnu bestandig bar, lagde det i en Urtepotte, og det voxte til et høit Trae, gjennem Loftet og Taget; det bar i tusindviis Hjerter af Sølv og Guld;

Urtepotten revnede derved, og der var intet Ravhjerte meer, det var blevet
Muld, Jord i Jorden – borte, altid borte.[73]

What one dreams the first night one sleeps in a strange house has significance, Grandmother had said. Peer dreamed that he took the amber heart,
which he still constantly wore, laid it in a flowerpot, and it grew into a tall
tree, through the ceiling and the roof; it bore thousands of hearts of silver and
gold; the flowerpot cracked because of this, and there was no amber heart any
more, it had become mould, earth to earth – gone, gone for ever!

We fully understand this mysterious passage only when we reach the book's
last chapter. Then we see that indeed it is possible for something simple, beautiful and ancient to expand into something else, something too luxuriant and
ostentatious to be borne as amber can be, in the hand or round the throat,
something increasingly not merely cumbersome but destructive and self-
destroying, serving death, not life. . . . Death also features in the second
recorded dream of Peer's boarding-school days. Now in his second year, he is
contented enough save for the fact that there's no sign of his singing voice
coming back.

One night he dreams that he is in a forest at springtime and a cuckoo calls.
It's an old tradition that one asks one's first cuckoo of the year how long one will
live. Peer's bird returns with a single 'Kukkuk!'[74] Peer pleads with him for a
different answer, so the bird responds by cuckooing without stopping. Peer
joins in his song, as do all the many other songbirds in the forest, to feel a flow
of happiness that doesn't leave him on waking. He now has, he thinks, divine
assurance that his voice will return, but days, weeks, months go by and it does
not. This dream episode is less a harbinger of Peer's early death than a reminder
that the household and the body one is born into, the nature of one's gifts and
of one's physical condition, let alone the length of one's life, are not under one's
control, but subject to laws ultimately beyond even one's comprehension. Peer,
understandably, wanted to hear that his lot would be good, but no confirmation or intimation of good fortune was forthcoming. In fact when what he is
hoping for – the return of his voice – happens, it takes him by surprise as he
emerges from fever.

But the half-delirious dream scenes which precede the happy moment are
peculiarly discomfiting, shot through with foreboding about trials to come.
They derive from the old ballad of Ridder Oluf (Knight Olaf) who rode out to
invite guests to his wedding but was detained by elfin maidens who drew him
into their dance, from which he doesn't return alive. This is the story told in the
fine cantata of 1854 by the novel's dedicatee, Niels Gade (1817–90), Elverskud
(Elf-shot but usually known in the English-speaking world as The Elf-King's
Daughter).[75] Reminders of its sombre theme act as a cultural signifier here to

the debates that will preoccupy both Peer and his Capelmester when the former has re-entered Copenhagen musical life. In the meantime, in his dream, the subjects of *Elverskud* undergo threatening transformations in which the dancing elf maidens claustrophobically engulf him; the one nearest in appearance to the girl of his choice, the pharmacist's daughter, turns into a Huldra, that Nordic female monster, beautiful in front and completely hollow at the back, as castle walls, having glided towards each other, then close in upon him, keeping him prisoner from the whole human world. Finally he can take no more:

Og Væggene rørte sig, og Luften derinde blev som en gloende Bageroven. Han fik Stemme.

'Vorherre! Vorherre! Har Du forladt mig?' raabte han i den dybeste Sjælesmerte.

Da stod Faermoer hos ham. Hun tog ham i sine Arme, hun kyssede ham paa Panden, hun kyssede ham paa Munden.

'Min egen søde lille Ven!' sagde hun. 'Vorherre slipper Dig ikke, han slipper Ingen af os, selv ikke den største Synder . . .'

Og hun tog frem sin Psalmebog, den samme hvoraf hun og Peer mangen Søndag havde sunget. . . . alle Elverpigerne lagde deres Hoved til Hvile, de trængte dertil. Peer sang med Faermoer, som han før havde sunget hver Søndag, hvor var hans Stemme med Eet kraftig og stærk, dertil saa blød: Slottets Vægge rørte sig, bleve Skyer og Taage . . .[76]

And the walls trembled, and the air became like that of a glowing baking-oven. He got his voice [back].

'Our Lord, our Lord, have you forsaken me?' he cried from his deepest pain in his soul.

There stood his grandmother beside him. She took him in her arms, she kissed him on the forehead, she kissed him on the mouth.

'My own sweet little friend! Our Lord will not let go of you, he doesn't let go of any one of us, not even the greatest sinner . . .'

And she took out her psalm-book, the same out of which she and Peer had sung many Sundays. . . all the elf maidens laid down their heads for a rest they were in need of. Peer sang with his Grandmother as he had sung before every Sunday – how strong and powerful his voice was all at once so sensitive, what's more: the castle walls trembled, became clouds and mists. . .

On one level this can be taken as a rite of passage through the hectic sensual torments of the pagan (pre-Christian myth) into the sober realistic rationale of gentle non-dogmatic Christianity. But we note that Peer has needed the folk legend in order to accomplish it. Artistically the composition behind the sequence, Gade's Cantata, belongs to the mainstream of European culture, thoughtfully uniting the achievements of pre- and post-Christian humankind in the manner approved by Bishop Grundtvig, and one of Grundtvig's spiritual ancestors, Erasmus himself.

Once back in Copenhagen, with voice restored but in need of conscientious nurturing, Peer is given a thorough induction into serious musical history, especially the masterpieces of the quartet form, in his implicit admiration of which Andersen proves himself among the critical elite, responding to the high estimations of the form by Schumann, Mendelssohn, Gade himself: 'Øre, Sjæl og Tanke fyldtes af Beethovens og Mozarts herlige Tonedigtninger,'[77] he tell us, 'Ears, soul and thought were filled with the glorious musical poetry of Beethoven and Mozart.' What is being championed here is plain enough: pure music, in a medium encouraging concentration of intellect and emotion; intricate artefacts and spiritual documents far distant from the programmatic tone-poems and chromatic audacities of Liszt.

Peer also attends a performance of Beethoven's Sixth Symphony, the Pastoral, the ineffably beautiful second movement, Andante, 'Scene by the Brook':

> Den bar ham ind i den levende friske Skovnatur; Lærken og Nattergalen jubilerede, Kukkeren sang ind deri. Hvilken Naturpragt, hvilken Vederqvægelsens Væld! Fra denne Stund kjendte han hos sig selv, at det var den malende Musik, hvori Naturen afspeilede sig og Menneskehjertets Strømninger gjenklang, som slog dybest an hos ham, Beethoven og Haydn bleve hans Yndlings-Componister.[78]

> It carried him into the living fresh woodland scenery; the lark and the nightingale rejoiced, and the cuckoo sang there. What magnificence of Nature, what a wellspring of refreshment! From that hour he knew in himself that it was the graphic music, in which Nature was reflected and the feelings of men's hearts met, that struck deepest into him, Beethoven and Haydn became his favourite composers.

But this, it could be objected, is praise of a symphonic movement given a specific title (and even including bird-calls to live up to it) and part of a larger work (Beethoven's manuscript bears his inscription: 'We give Thee thanks for Thy great Glory') which moves through peaceful country landscape to village revels, a thunderstorm and a shepherds' song of thanksgiving. Isn't this 'programme' rather than 'pure' music? But then Beethoven himself said in 1808: 'The Pastoral Symphony is not a painting, but an expression of those sentiments evoked in men by their enjoyment of the country, a work in which some emotions of country life are described.'[79] He might even, one feels, have worried about Andersen's word graphic. In truth the Pastoral Symphony is, in the literal sense, a *classical* symphony, not a forerunner of Liszt or Franck, let alone Richard Strauss. The distinguished composer and critic Robert Simpson's comments on this movement are instructive: 'The simple texture of the [symphony's] first movement are offset by the proliferation of the *andante molto mosso*, elaborate in detail as it is expansive and leisurely, a sonata organism that finds time even to stand still. . . . Throughout the development, which shares with that of the first movement a predilection for long stretches at a time in one harmonic region, the scoring and the modulations are miraculous, conveying a depth of sound that suggests visual perspective. The imagination is so sensitively precise that the sounds of nature seem to be coming from different distances; the superb changes from G major to E flat and thence to G flat, C flat, and the home dominant, accompanied by constantly varying orchestration of astounding beauty, seem to change the direction in which we are facing without moving us from the enchanted spot.'[80]

The libretto for the Boieldieu opera, *La Dame blanche* (by the popular dramatist Eugene Scribe and based on Walter Scott's *Guy Mannering* and *The Monastery*), in which he will score his first (and sizeable) public hit, seems to Peer 'som noget Selvoplevet, et Kapitel af hans egen Livshistorie; den melodierige Musik fyldte ganske denne Stemning',[81] 'like something personally experienced; the richly melodious music absolutely filled this mood'. Its story is of a lively young officer coming to his ancestral castle without knowing that it is this, and roused into memories of distant childhood by an old ballad (there are surely echoes here of Otto Thorstrup with his half-forgotten childhood moving from Odense to Jutland in *O.T.*). Yet there is no question of Peer having anything but the most humdrum (and humble) ancestry; we are talking here of an instinctive appreciation of the noble and the tradition-hallowed which amounts to a sense of birthright, to, if you like, an aristocracy of the spirit (which Felix, the well-off merchant's son, most definitely does not have). As for Ambroise Thomas's *Hamlet*, well versed in Shakespeare as Andersen was (and also, we are expressly told, Peer himself too) the Capelmester is right to say (approvingly) that the opera should have been called *Ophelia*. Her madness and death by drowning occur actually on stage; we hear the girl singing the old ballad about the mermaid beckoning humans into the water, we hear a dialogue between Ophelia and the river to which she will surrender. This is not Shakespeare's *Hamlet,* as Gounod's *Faust* wasn't Goethe's, but a creditable and moving work of art nonetheless. Says his singing teacher: 'Det Speculative er ikke Stof for Musiken, det er Kjærlighets-Forholdet i begge disse Tragedier, der løfter sig til en Digtning i Toner',[82] 'The speculative is not material for music, it is the love-relationship in both these tragedies that raises them to tone-poetry.' Moreover *Hamlet* and its kin are judged superior to unspecified

Italian operas (presumably the bel canto works of Donizetti and Bellini) where the various singing parts are thought of principally as vehicles for the singer and not integrated into an interactive whole.

But, whatever the merits of Boieldieu and Thomas, Peer wishes to move on from them, and even adduces the dream of the silver- and gold-laden tree growing from the precious amber heart (quite forgetting how the tree broke the pot and turned into mould) as justification for his doing so. A musical composition, not excluding opera, has to be an integrated breathing whole, of an intensity and organic intricacy that neither of these composers had achieved. 'Fremtidsmusiken, som den nyere Retning i Operaen kaldes og for hvilken særlig Wagner er Bannerfører, fik en Forsvarer og Beundrer i vor unge Ven',[83] 'The music of the future, as the new movement in opera is called and of which Wagner is standard-bearer, had a defender and an admirer in our young friend.' He is impressed by the forward-movement, the rich seamless continuity of a Wagner opera, never broken up into arias. His singing teacher can't quite agree with him here, thinking of the incomparable effect of arias in a masterwork like *Don Giovanni*. 'Jeg bøier mig for Dygtigheden i den nye musikalske Retning, men jeg dandser ikke med Dig om dens Guldkalv!'[84] 'I bow to the skill in the new musical movement, but I do not dance to its Golden Calf.' And he wonders if his gifted pupil has properly understood its significance or is merely going in the direction of the modish, of the resolute pursuers of the new.

Undeterred, Peer is determined to take part in a Wagner opera. He decides on *Lohengrin*, with its young knight travelling in a swan-drawn boat down the river Scheldt to deliver Elsa of Brabant from evil. On completing this in 1848, Wagner himself had declared: 'With that work, the old world of opera comes to an end. The spirit moved over the waters and there was light.'[85] Vision of oneself as supreme creator could hardly come stronger. *Lohengrin* was the work that made Ludwig of Bavaria so passionate a Wagnerian that he became the composer's devoted patron. Peer achieves, as the eponymous knight – with his bridal chamber love song and his farewell song before his mysterious disappearance attended by the white dove of the Holy Grail – yet greater success than earlier. Even his teacher is won over to his cause, or almost. 'Denne Aften var . . . for Syngemesteren et Skridt frem til Erkjendelse af Fremtids-Musiken. – "Med Betingelser!" sagde han',[86] 'This evening was . . . for the singing teacher a step forward towards acknowledgement of the music of the Future' (that all-important phrase again) ' "With qualifications!" he said.'

Andersen's own respect for Wagner's work certainly also had qualifications. In 1852 he recorded in his diary that Liszt no longer wanted to perform Mozart at the theatre; he thought it old hat, so concentrated instead on 'Wagner and other sensation-mongers'. The composer/impresario and by now friend of Andersen arranged – Andersen liked to think it was for his own benefit –

performances of Wagner's two most famous operas, *Tannhäuser* and *Lohengrin*, so when writing of Peer's ardour for Wagner he was doing so remembering his own two-year-long familiarity with his music. In 1855 he visited Wagner himself,[87] in Zurich, and in his autobiography reports him as being friendly, interested in Danish composers, among whom he knew only Gade well. Andersen therefore spoke to him about the long history of Danish music; Wagner listened most attentively, and Andersen left the man with warm feelings for him that never quite translated into their equivalent for his operas. On 2 May in the year of *Lucky Peer*'s composition, 1870,[88] however, he attended a performance of *Lohengrin* itself in Copenhagen, and this time was so moved that he not only sent Edvard and Jette Collin tickets for it but saw it again himself. Wagner divided musical opinion in Denmark as elsewhere. While Edvard and Jette were interested by it, Andersen's friend the actress Johanne Heiberg was against it, and indeed was to level the criticism against *Lucky Peer* that it treated Wagner far too favourably.

But does it? It certainly gives a compellingly vivid portrait of a young man enthused by Wagnerian ideals: the complete fusion of text and music, so that, as he embarks on his own opera *Aladdin*, scene succeeds scene in his head with words and music equal claimants to his attention. And, when it is performed, the stage itself will reveal an inspirited world: Aladdin standing in a garden where the very flowers and stones suggest music, as do the springs and caverns, 'forskjellige Melodier smeltende sammen i en stor Harmoni',[89] 'different melodies blending together in one great harmony'. It is a syncretism of arts, purportedly appropriate for the iconic story of the poor boy, Aladdin. Both Oehlenschläger's classic realisation of this, referred to by some early readers of *Lucky Peer* by way of disparaging Andersen, and Andersen's own revisiting of the tale in 'The Tinder Box' allowed characters and events to stand out as remarkable singularities, but each making a contribution to the whole. Peer's welding everything into some tremendous unity manifests his own musical powers and his modern sensibility, and altogether overwhelms the first-night audience with its scope, power and invention. Nor can one doubt the young composer's deep feeling for the *Thousand and One Nights* youth who'd come to represent the Danish psyche and Denmark's rebirth among nations, and who was his own surrogate. But can't we also think of Peer's composition – to judge by its effects – as an imposition of overheated artistry on material fascinating in its own right and in no need of lavish novelties of treatment? And Peer dies as a result of its reception, the orgasmic quality of which brings to mind only too readily the swooning and adulatory hysterics of excited spectators at Bayreuth.

'Død!' gjenlød det. Død i Seiersglæden, som Sophokles ved de olympiske Lege, som Thorvaldsen i Theatret, under Beethowens Symphoni. En Aare i

Hjertet var bristet, og som ved et Lynslag var endt hans Dage her, endt uden Smerte, endt i jordisk Jubel, i Kaldet af sin jordiske Mission. Den Lykkelige fremfor Millioner![90]

'Dead!' resounded [through the theatre]. Dead in the joy of victory, like Sophocles at the Olympic Games, like Thorvaldsen in the theatre during Beethoven's symphony. An artery in his heart had burst, and as by a stroke of lightning his days here were ended, ended without pain, ended in earthly joy in the call of his earthly mission. The lucky one in comparison with millions!

At the time of writing, Andersen, we know from diaries and letters, was feeling his age, constantly brooding on how long he had to live, how he would die, and what he would suffer before he did so. He was also increasingly mindful – perhaps Brandes's essay only heightened this – that death might come before Denmark gave him his full due purely as a literary artist. Or worried that he might not survive such esteem (it was, as he knew, on a great scale) as he had actually been given. Perhaps dying when experiencing unbridled enthusiasm for the first full fruits of your talents was not such a bad thing; Peer was spared ageing, decrepitude, the long wait for death to come sooner or later, the fading out of public recognition of works it had once applauded, never mind of the creative gifts themselves. But, to offset this, the two greatest figures in Andersen's pantheon, Sophocles and Thorvaldsen, lived long and productive lives. Thorvaldsen, we have already seen, is a ceaselessly evoked point of reference in Andersen's work. So it is most unlikely that he would have wanted all promising youngsters to die, and, interestingly, a diary entry of 29 November 1870[91] apropos reception of *Lucky Peer*, tells us that were he young again, he would embrace life more physically, with more bodily enthusiasm than he had done in reality, and commends his own delightful tale of 1845, 'Springfyrene',[92] 'The Jumpers', as a template. Nor surely, considering the fable-like direct impetus of the narrative, can Peer's sudden end be dissociated from the direction we have watched him taking, his choice of vehicles for his own particular promise having such obvious resonance for contemporary readers. In his diaries Andersen, noting that critics complained of Peer's weakness (above all, in his dropping dead on his great first night) observed, not without bitterness, 'our age has no use for weakness, only strength', and in this value-system Wagner, whose new morality celebrated the strong loving the strong, and perhaps *only* the strong, held a major place. Though, of course Peer, in pursuit of his vocation, had shown – as Andersen himself had done – enormous strength, and that without the pushiness or vanity which so many had been keen to point out in his creator. One critic (on 2 December) wrote: 'Lucky Peer shouldn't have died but experienced adversity and remained Lucky Peer.'[93] The view has something to be said for it, and Andersen was pleased to record it, but it misses out the

obvious point that Peer did die, and precisely as a consequence of his achievement. It seems to me possible therefore, especially when we compare Andersen's
instinctual artistic preferences with those of the fashionable world of the time,
to read the tale as telling us that Peer, in seeking the right direction, chose a
wrong turning, leading not to new fullness of life but to death.

There are two reasons, I submit, for doing this, though both take us into extra-
literary areas. The first is the loving delineation of the Singing Master; the second
is the novel's dedication.

The Singing Master is one of Andersen's most attractive creations, a wise
and good man with a convincing living presence. His goodness is above all
shown in his paying for Peer's education without wishing this fact to be known,
concealing it indeed from the beneficiary for as long as he can. His wisdom is
demonstrated in his advice that Peer rests his voice, and in the thorough
grounding in musical culture he gives the youth after its return. Even though
he somewhat relents in his suspicions of Wagner, especially after Peer has sung
Lohengrin, he yet retains his qualifications and reservations. No episode in the
novel is more moving than that in which, after speaking to Peer of the inex-
haustible depths of the Talmud, he tells him he is Jewish. The Singing Teacher,
revealing himself as the literary descendant of, among others, Naomi's 'grandfather' and the holy pedlar Joel in *Only a Fiddler*, is surprised by Peer's own
surprise, but a little later, seeing Peer's sadness at the marriage of the pharmacist's daughter, takes him slightly further into the intimacy of his own religion.
He had once loved a girl, he says, and wanted to marry her, but could only have
done so if he were converted to Christianity. This he found himself unable to
consent to. Peer, somewhat ingenuously, asks him if he has any faith at all. The
musician beautifully replies in almost untranslatable words: ' "Jeg har mine
Fædres Gud! han lyse for min Fod og min Forstand" ;[94] ' "I have my father's
God! He gives out light for my feet and my understanding." '

In view of Andersen's strong and consistent philo-Semitism, it is hardly
likely that he would not have known of Wagner's polemic, directed against the
(never named) Jewish Meyerbeer (who had befriended him) and also taking in
the work of Mendelssohn, *Das Judenthum in der Musik* published in September
1850 in the *Neue Zeitschrift für Musik* under the name K. Freigedank (K. Free
Thought). Wagner revealed himself as the author in 1869, the year before *Lucky
Peer*. It was dangerous, this deplorable article argued, for Germany to take the
Jewish sensibility as its cultural model, when it was demonstrably incapable of
that great 'heart-searching effect' required of music; Mendelssohn could not
manage an opera, and the emotion most characteristic of him was melancholy.
Doesn't this exhibit that very tendency Andersen deplored in his diaries, to
regard what was tender and compassionate as 'weak', and to celebrate power
and so-styled 'majesty' instead?[95]

The political situation in Prussia had forced Niels Gade to leave Leipzig where he had succeeded his friend and (perhaps overly perceptible) mentor, Mendelssohn as principal conductor of the famous Gewandhaus orchestra. Instead Gade became Director of the Copenhagen Musical Society, and played until his death a leading, arguably *the* leading, role in the life of musical Denmark. Gade was the composer of eight symphonies, three violin sonatas, oratorios (a form that Wagner despised), a string octet, sextet, quintet and quartet. Melodic, the tunes in his essentially classically structured works increasingly having a decided Nordic tang to them, a conventional yet imaginative orchestrator reminiscent at his best (in the Fourth and Fifth Symphonies) of what Dvořák would do more impressively, Gade gave his country a body of satisfying if basically self-restrained compositions. He produced no work remotely like Lucky Peer's *Aladdin* (though his pupil Carl Nielsen[96] was to compose memorable music for a production of Oehlenschläger's drama). Yet Andersen greeted him on his last novel's dedication page: 'Componisten/ N.W. Gade/med Venskab og Beundring/tilegnet', 'Dedicated to the composer N.W. Gade with friendship and admiration.'

Here, however, we surely have one of the two teasing ambiguities that hang over this limpid and deftly constructed novel and contribute to a niggling dissatisfaction with it. Gade's ambitions and achievements alike are so much less adventurous than Wagner's that acknowledgement of the fact amounts to a value judgement in itself, one which posterity has abundantly confirmed. Those younger composers who resented, disliked or disapproved of Wagner – Sibelius or Debussy, for instance – invariably had to come to terms with him, and work *through* him, to attain their own originalities of artistic personality. If *Lucky Peer* does contain an anti-Wagnerian message, then it is inadequately conveyed, or, rather, the story of Peer as a new Aladdin and of his own *Aladdin* as a self-inflicted *coup de grâce*, don't really carry enough weight.

The second ambiguity ruffling the smooth surface of the novel comes from the opposite direction, not from art and its demands but from life in all its unavoidable and frequent roughness. Isn't there more to be said for Felix's type of happiness and less for Peer's exceptionalism than Andersen allows? Uneasily we cannot suppress the feeling that Andersen in his heart agrees. Felix comes across as real, likeable, vigorous, and we cannot but think of the many virtual contemporaries of his in whose company Andersen, whatever his irritation and awareness of their deficiencies, found warm contentment. When, only five years later, he was dying, Jonas Collin and Viggo Drewsen took turns in sleeping in the next room.[97] So might the good-humoured Felix have done. Peer could not have met this challenge. High art, with his collusion, would have long since done away with him.

4

While *Lucky Peer* was still at the printer's, Andersen wrote on 5 September 1870 to Jette Collin (to whom he expressed his most intimate feelings) 'people seem not to favour reading poetic works this year. . . . What a ghastly bloody time this is!'[98]

He spoke truly. On 15 July 1870 (the day in fact on which he had completed the draft of *Lucky Peer*) war between France and Prussia had broken out.[99] Andersen was writing to Jette only five days after the Battle of Sedan, that bloodstained watershed in not only this war's but Europe's history. Napoleon III had himself accompanied the massive French army commanded by Marshal Patrice de Mac-Mahon, while with the Prussian army went King Wilhelm I and the Chancellor, Bismarck. The Prussians encircled the French, whose ensuing casualties were of spectacular proportions: 120,000 dead to the Prussian 9,000. By nightfall Napoleon III declared an end to the fighting, and next day ordered the running up of the white flag. He gave himself up in person to the Prussians, and after captivity in Germany would go to live in England (he died in 1873). This was the ignominious end of the grandiloquent Second Empire. Danes, like Andersen himself, were constantly reminded by events of their own hubris in knowingly provoking Prussia, and the consequent loss of lives and reputation (and, it was popularly felt, honour).

Napoleon III might have surrendered, but France itself had not. A Government of National Defence continued the war with engagements on the northern and eastern fronts, and even in the Loire Valley; Paris was besieged from 19 September 1870 to 28 January 1871. During the Siege of Paris the King of Prussia was proclaimed in the Hall of Mirrors at Versailles, on 18 January 1871, as Deutscher Kaiser (German Emperor), a title chosen for him after careful thought by Bismarck as that most suitable for the head of the new Deutsches Kaiserreich (German Empire, the name for the united German Confederation since 10 December 1870).

Nor did the sufferings of the French come to an end with the armistice. President Adolphe Thiers headed a highly conservative government based in Versailles because Paris itself was too unstable, too animated by resentments difficult to assuage, such as that of having to pay the lion's share of France's heavy indemnity payments to the Prussians. A socialist-style government ruled Paris – the famous Paris Commune – from 18 March (officially 28 March) to 28 May 1871. Its leadership was split, but many of its social ideals and practices were progressive, humane, imaginative. It was finally put down by the 'Versailles army' with enormous brutality, deaths through street killings and executions running into tens of thousands, followed by vicious government reprisals afterwards; it became a crime to have so much as supported the Commune at all. Thiers hoped such bloodshed would teach people a lesson.

And this was the fate of what Andersen had repeatedly called 'Europe's crater', the crater of civilisation itself. The city that had so thrilled him – admittedly with some moralistic qualifications – and whose Exposition he had counted as one of the greatest experiences of his entire life, had witnessed cruelty and misery on a medieval scale, indeed in the man-made instruments that promoted them exceeding all times past.

As so often before, Andersen had already created a work of uncanny presci-ence, the unforgettable fairy tale 'Det Utroligste', 'The Most Incredible [Thing]'. Its debut was a somewhat incongruous one: in September 1870, in English (as 'The Most Extraordinary Thing') in an American children's periodical, *The Riverside Magazine* edited by his admirer Horace Scudder, who was keen for him to visit the United States in person. It came out in Danish the following month, October, in *Nyt dansk Maanedsskrift, The New Danish Monthly Review,* and in book form two years later, on 30 March 1872.[100]

What *is* the most incredible thing: what would truly exceed normal expec-tations? A king sets a competition to find out, and appoints a board of judges too, ranging from infants to folk in their nineties, and the reward – a double one – is in the very best folk-tale/fairy-tale tradition: the king's daughter and half his kingdom. Andersen with typical humour describes the ideas of some of the competition's entrants: street-boys, never a class Andersen was fond of though they may have amused him more than he liked to admit, tried to spit on their own backs; they could think of nothing more extraordinary than that.

But when the most incredible thing actually appears, there is universal agreement as to its merits, itself a significant endorsement of the submitted artefact's properties, for the truly miraculous can never be faked; by definition it surpasses all conventional criteria and expectations. It is a clock in a case, and as each hour strikes, 'levende Billeder', 'living pictures', appear with 'bevægelige Figurer', 'lifelike figures'.[101] At the stroke of one comes Moses with the First Commandment; at two, the First Pair (Adam and Eve) in the Garden of Eden. Three sees – what else? – the appearance of the Three Wise Men (one of whom is black) bearing their gifts; four, the Four Seasons, spring with a bough of beech and a cuckoo, summer with a grasshopper on an ear of corn, autumn with an empty stork's nest and winter with an old crow who likes to tell stories behind the stove. When five strikes, then it's time for the Five Senses: sight represented by spectacles, hearing by a coppersmith, smell by violets and woodruff, taste by a cook and feeling by a mourner dressed in black. Six is honoured by a gambler casting a dice with a 'six' uppermost. Seven is itemised for us with another piece of characteristically piercing Andersen humour. Were the figures for this hour the Seven Days of the Week or the Seven Deadly Sins, it is asked. People couldn't agree, for who can tell them apart? Eight o'clock brings a choir of monks for the evening anthem, and nine the Nine Muses. Andersen's elaboration again displays his incorrigible humour (as well perhaps as his idiosyncratic preferences); instead of the Greek presiding spirits of each art, *these* Muses consist of an historian, an archivist and seven spirits all concerned with the theatre! Ten brings back Moses, this time with all ten of the Commandments. Eleven is introduced by eleven children singing a traditional Danish rhyme featuring the word 'elleve', 'eleven'. The stroke of twelve gives onlookers the most wondrous living picture of them all. A night-watchman sings a song peculiar to his uniformed calling: 'Det var ved Midnatstide,/Vor Frelser han blev født',[102] 'It was in the midnight hour,/Our Saviour he was born.' And as he gives voice to this carol, roses unfurl and turn into angels with rainbow-coloured wings.

> 'Det Hele var et mageløst Konstværk, det Utroligste,' sagde alle Mennesker.'[103]
> 'The whole thing was a matchless work of art, the most incredible thing,' said all the people.'

And how could they not? For the great construction, the winning entry in the competition for sure, amounts to a synthesis of all the arts (all the most refined appeals to our senses and our emotions), and a syncretism of the cultures, blending representatives of belief-systems and mythologies so that they accord with each other and with needs and satisfactions deep within the collective psyche. Natural humankind is addressed by the four seasons and the five senses, the classical and the ultra-contemporary worlds meet in the Muses, while the first tableau and the last, the Alpha and Omega of the clock, recall us to the profound truth of the Judaeo-Christian religion, about which the elderly Andersen would argue, with irritable persistence sometimes against too dogmatic an approach but always maintaining his core of personal spiritual adherence. Doesn't the great timepiece show us what Europe has managed to harmonise in its progressive intellectual tolerance? Its astronomers, its little children and its night-watchmen following the old customs of their society are as one: all components, if you like, of the same mind.

And what of the maker of 'Det Utroligste' 'the most incredible thing'? He is an ordinary-seeming young man of solid virtue: 'hjertensgod, barneglad, tro Ven og hjelpsom mod sine fattige Forældre',[104] 'good-hearted, happy as a child, a faithful friend and helpful to his poor [i.e. impoverished] parents'. Nobody has any doubt that he will be the winner of the competition, and the judges even wink at him before they officially proclaim him victor. And then 'en lang knoklet Kraftkarl',[105] 'a tall strapping fellow' roars out that *he* will be the one who will do the most incredible thing, and with an axe he breaks the wonderful clock. The ingenious mechanism is smashed into bits and pieces that go flying everywhere in no time at all. Nobody can deny this act of total *de*struction is absolutely incredible, even more so than the act of *con*struction which had produced the clock. Certainly all the judges, though gasping with shock, think this, and they have, after all, to honour the terms of the competition; this raw upstart will win the hand of the princess and half the kingdom.

Brawn has won over brain, but that isn't all; more sinister truths lie behind this episode. Isn't society, possibly humankind in general, really more impressed by use of force than by creativity? Doesn't it settle all its problems through inflicting damage – including loss of life – rather than through triumphs of the intellect and the imagination? Copenhagen is bombarded by the British, old towns like Als or Schleswig, the culmination of centuries of cooperation and endeavour, even great Paris itself with all its richness of culture, are harassed and turned into scenes of carnage by Prussians – and the rest of the world agrees not with the bullied but the bullies. Even the more apparently peaceable countries of Europe – Sweden, for example – have behaved much as the princess in this tale has done, by self-accommodation, for all the disappointment and cherished contrary values, to the will of the oppressor.

But the people of this kingdom are to have a further moment of incredulity, and the disagreeable situation which has come to pass will change as a result, and infinitely for the better. The mechanism, the body of the young man's clock, may have been shattered, 'men ikke Aanden',[106] 'but not the spirit'. The wedding ceremony of the princess and the strapping fellow, attended by syco-phantic, time-serving knights and court ladies, is interrupted by every single part of the great clock marching up the aisle and imposing itself between the bridal pair. And each component expresses indignation at the groom in actions and words. The groom, however, is not in the least ashamed. How could he be? His is not a *Weltanschauung* that acknowledges pity, so shame is not an emotion he could ever entertain. It is left to the night-watchman, to him who honoured Christ in his carol, to fell the groom with his club. This done, the figures disap-pear, the candles become flowers, the organ plays of its own accord, the prin-cess asks for the man who made the work of art that has reanimated itself; he and nobody else will be her husband and rule half the kingdom. So the kindly young man is the winner after all. But Andersen has a further moral twist on which to end his tale:

> Alle velsignede ham; der var ikke Een, der var misundelig, – ja, det var det Utroligste![107]
>
> Everybody gave him their blessing; there was not one who was envious, – yes, that was the most incredible thing.

Humanity is capable of rising above its usual tangle of conflicting feelings, to feel united in happiness when it recognises what is truly good. The old Kantian hope! Just as in '*To Be or Not To Be*' Aladdin's lamp was transformed for Niels into his mother's old bible in his first dream, and in his second into a bible possessed by a spirit greater even than its pages, so this clock is greater than its constituent parts, representing the spirit behind the world that promotes universal love.

'The Most Incredible Thing' itself enjoyed a deserved and influential resurrected life. During the Nazi Occupation of Denmark, Elias Bredsdorff and other Danish scholars organised a newly and topically illustrated, clandestinely published edition of the tale, and it became a kind of holy text for the Resistance. Here we should restate the truth that Andersen's *oeuvre* espouses every value which Nazism and its totalitarian kin opposed, in particulars as well as in general. The writer had been friendly with Jewish children at his infant school and remembered them warmly, he kept up Jewish friendships all his life, introduced a pogrom rendered in all its hideousness in *Only a Fiddler*, and the last years of life were irradiated and made comfortable by friendships with two highly cultured Danish Jewish families, the Henriques and the Melchiors;[108] indeed it was at the Melchiors' that Andersen died, and Fru Melchior, at his request, wrote the last entries of his diary for him. He was sympathetically interested in gypsies, and some of his liveliest passages evoke their customs and beliefs with no degree of cultural condescension at all. Quite the reverse. He had an extraordinary empathy with the mentally and physically impaired, and it is possible, I think, that this aspect of his work will become even more important to future generations of readers than it was to previous ones. We have seen, these last decades, a terrifying return of Utilitarianism, of the estimation of human beings in terms of earning capacities and cost, and a dismissal of any beliefs and practices at variance with this. Andersen's own sexual leanings are a subject fraught with difficulties, containing so many seeming (but probably not actual) contradictions, yet he made no distinction in literature or in life between same-sex and opposite-sex emotional and erotic relationships, and the ambivalent (amphibious) figure is, as we have repeatedly seen, central to his imagination. Far from banishing women to child-minding, kitchen and church, he sent his most memorable female characters on quests, in the carrying out of which they surpassed their male peers. He detested cruelty to blacks and indigenous people and unequivocally spoke up for them. His attitude to children, animals and plant-life was always infused with respect and tenderness, for the weak as well as the strong, for the healthy and normal as well as for the remarkable and obviously interesting. He rejected arrogance and any kind of contemptuousness; he revered and promoted friendliness, kindness, freedom in religion, politics, and social and familial existence.

On 1 and 2 August 1872 Andersen stayed with Georg Brandes,[109] to whom he had now become very attached, and read out to him and his family a new story 'Tante Tandpine', 'Auntie Toothache', its title a reminder that Andersen had suffered appallingly from his teeth all his life,[110] – and his new false teeth were an acute problem for him too. Brandes was greatly entertained by the story, which appeared in book form, along with three others, on 23 November of the same year in *Nye Eventyr og Historier. Tredie Række. Anden Samling (New Fairy-Tales and Stories. Third Series. Second Volume)*. By this time Andersen's mortal illness had struck him: cancer of the liver, perhaps brought about by increased consumption of strong spirits (a growing habit of his about which Jonas Collin had been pleased to tell his family). He never got better, he never wrote another fairy-tale. So it is fitting that it is with 'Auntie Toothache', a modernist tour de force which nobody could have appreciated better than Brandes, that we end our study of Hans Christian Andersen.

He had continued his virtual mania for travelling until the onset of his illness, and had enjoyed the companionship of younger, progressive-minded journalists and writers, Nicolai (or Nikolaj) Bøgh and Robert Watt (the lively editor, the lusty patron of 'Mabille', the compelling narrator of lubricious anecdotes). Now he would be far too unwell to travel. Of course Andersen's last years are sad, but friends and both the Danish and the international reading public never ceased to express their reverence for him and his art; his birthdays were handsomely celebrated, and his funeral would be a huge state occasion with the King himself in attendance.

On 22 May 1873, from yet another visit he had made to Switzerland, weak though he was, he wrote to Edvard Collin:

> I have many friends, indeed some who are so vividly kind and sympathetic to me as if I belonged among their close relatives, for instance the Melchiors; but you, my dear friend, are the earliest of my friends, right back from the time you helped me with my Latin composition. . . . On every occasion your many wonderful qualities stand out, and I am not the only one to see you in this light. You are infinitely dear to me, and I shall pray to God for you to survive me, for I cannot think of losing you. What I am writing here flows from the heart, you will understand me. It is wonderful to have friends in this world, friends as I have.[111]

'Auntie Toothache', sombre though in many ways it is, relates to that delightful tale of 1853, 'The Goblin at the Grocer's', and has something of its common-sense empiricism, mutating here into stoical acceptance of things as they are, as perforce they have to be. In the earlier work, it will be remembered, a student, whose great interest was poetry, discovered, in the grocer's shop above which he was a lodger, sheets from an old book of poems used for wrapping up cheese; he forwent the cheese for the sake of having the poems. Andersen opens his last story with an almost Borges-like reminder of the usual (one might say invariable) fate of all intellectual/imaginative endeavours involving the written word: the rubbish bin – though the papers in the bin may well have been used as wrapping-paper beforehand. Andersen/the story's author is handed some sheets – covered in clear, beautiful handwriting – of a composition by a student who has recently died. It is called – as is the entire story – 'Auntie Toothache'. This unfinished effort is now presented to us readers as a *mise en abŷme*.

The student, kin to the young inventor in 'The Most Incredible Thing', is really quite ordinary, and honest about his ambitions and his talents. 'Der er Noget i mig af Poeten, men ikke nok',[112] 'There is something in me of the poet, but not enough.' Andersen's art therefore ends not with a genius like Lucky Peer but with a kindly, imaginative but, in a literary sense, quite ungifted man who can represent us all. He has always been fond of his great-aunt – whom he knows simply as 'Tante', 'Auntie' ('Auntie Mille'). When he was a child he loved her for all the sweets she insisted on giving him, so detrimental to his teeth. Now he is only too frequently a victim of raging toothache. She also shows sweetness in her attitude to his writing, likening him to the great German writer Jean Paul and even to Dickens, obstinately clinging to the idea that he will be a distinguished man one day. How difficult it is to tell kindness from indulgence, reassurance from foolishness, especially when an individual is important in your life. And Auntie *is* a little foolish, it has to be admitted, with her long stories of a man who courted her without ever marrying her, Brygger (Brewer) Rasmussen, another person with tooth problems. One night the student goes to the theatre to escort his auntie home; a fierce snowstorm arises, and he decides that the two of them had best spend the night at his own lodgings. During the wild snowy night the student's toothache flares up and he has a (waking?) dream in which he is a visited by a spectral woman, Fru Tandpine ('Madam Toothache'), 'hendes Forfærdelighed',[113] 'her Frightfulness', who insistently and rhetorically assures him that a great poet must have 'great toothache', and encourages him to admit her power in exchange for the ability to write verses in all manner of remarkable metres. But all the student wants is for her to go away and leave him to lie in peace, with no toothache. So he declines her gift, and his slumbers are correspondingly deep and gentle.

When he wakes in the morning, he has almost forgotten that Auntie Mille was there, but when he sees her, he recalls the dream. Were the two women possibly one and the same? Wasn't Madam Toothache the same as Auntie Toothache who even now reaffirms her sweetness by asking him kindly if he has written any poetry during the night? He shouts out a heartfelt negative reply to this.

And there his manuscript comes to an end.

The author comments:

Bryggeren er død, Tante er død, Studenten er død, ham fra hvem Tankegnisterne gik i Bøtten.

Alt gaaer i Bøtten.[114]

The brewer is dead, Auntie is dead, the student is dead, him whose sparks of ideas ended up in the rubbish-bin.

Everything ends up in the rubbish-bin.

True? Ultimately, perhaps. We have no real alternative to thinking this as far as physical existence is concerned, and Andersen – despite his belief in immortality – could not accept the idea of the resurrection of the body. Perhaps he had always had too strong a sense of the (as he viewed it) God-given quiddity of every living being – and of individual objects too. But Andersen's writings for their part have defied the destructive forces of time. They are as vital now as when they first appeared, and they continue to enchant, fascinate and touch the heart not only in their continent of origin – whose moods and problems, multifarious peoples and many-sided cultures he so appealed to and served – but in all the continents of the globe, about which he was ceaselessly curious. If we ask ourselves why and how, then we can answer by thinking of two fairy-tales whose messages have such startling clarity they almost defy analysis: 'Nattergalen', 'The Nightingale' (1843),[115] and 'Hun duede ikke', 'She Was No Good' (1852).[116] The nightingale – his tribute to the 'Swedish Nightingale', Jenny Lind for whom he felt so much – wins out over her artificial mechanical rival, wondrous and amazing though it is, because her natural song, in tune with the whole diverse living world of which it is a part, addresses itself to people of every degree and sort, and does not avoid tidings of pain and suffering, even as it assures its listeners of the beauty and overall goodness of life. Cannot the same be said of Andersen's stories? 'She Was No Good' was inspired by the defence by his mother against these very words about a drunken old Odense washerwoman who was a friend of hers. Andersen was his mother's son in this measurelessly important respect: he, too, never thought a person no good – not even the most obscure and unprepossessing of tippling washer-women – and therein lies the supreme and enduring merit of his still living corpus of work.

Chronology

1805 2 April. Hans Christian Andersen born in Odense to Hans Andersen and his wife, Anne Marie.

1810 HCA attends Fedder Carstens' infant school primarily for Jewish children.

1812 Hans Andersen conscripted as musketeer fighting for Napoleon. He returns from Holstein January 1814 mortally weakened. Dies 26 April 1816.

1818 8 July. Anne Marie remarries.

1819 18 April. HCA confirmed at St Knud's Church, Odense.

4 September. Leaves Odense with testimonial letter from Herr Iversen.

6 September. Arrives in Copenhagen at end of last-ever pogrom in Denmark.

18 September. Meets Singing Master Siboni, also composer Weyse and writer Baggesen.

1820 June. Voice breaks; Siboni ends lessons. HCA joins Court Theatre Dance School.

1821 25 January. First walk-on theatre part.

March. Pays visit to Royal Theatre Director Jonas Collin; solicits his help 2 April.

1822 12 June. *Youthful Attempts* published by Villiam Christian Walter.

13 September. Jonas Collin heads board decision to have HCA formally educated.

26 October. Starts at 'Latin' school at Slagelse; headmaster Simon Meisling.

Christmas. Meets Jonas Collin's family.

1822–1826 HCA studies under Meisling, following him to Elsinore, May 1826.

1827 HCA's complaints result in his leaving Meisling in April for private studies in Copenhagen and expanding his social circle.

25 September. 'The Dead Child' (poem) published.

1828 22 October. 'Studentereksamen' – HCA acquits himself successfully.

1829 2 January. *A Walking Tour from Holmen Canal to the Eastern Point of Amager in the years 1828 and 1829* (fantasy travelogue) published.

25 April. *Love in Nicholas's Tower* (vaudeville comedy) performed at Royal Theatre.

30 June–16 August. Travels in Denmark with lively social life.

21 October–19 November successful 'Anden Examen' for university studies (not pursued).

1830 2 January. *Poems* published.

31 May–12 June. First trip to Jutland.

July. Meets Riborg Voigt, his first love, in Fåborg, Fyn.

27–29 July. 'Les trois glorieuses' July Revolution in Paris.

1831 16 May–24 June. Travels through Germany.

19 September. *Shadow Pictures* (travelogue) published.

1832 2–17 July. Visit to Odense and last-ever meeting with his mother.

October. Writes memoir for Louise Collin, never completed, published in 1926.

18 December. *The Twelve Months of the Year* (poems) presented to King.

1833 22 April. Departs Copenhagen for long, ambitious tour of Europe.

10 May–15 August. In Paris, with meetings with Hugo and Heine.

15 August–15 September. In Switzerland.

15 September–18 October. Travels in Italy during which (7 October) his mother dies.

18 October–12 February 1834. In Rome, where he makes friends with fellow-Scandinavian artists, most notably Bertel Thorvaldsen.

1831 16 February–20 March. In Naples, then back to Rome until 1 April. After travels through Italy and Austria, HCA stays in Munich and Berlin.

3 August. Arrives back in Copenhagen.

1835 9 April. *The Improvisatore* (novel) published.

8 May. *Fairy-Tales Told for Children, First Booklet* published. It contains 'The Tinder-box', 'Little Claus and Big Claus', 'The Princess on the Pea', 'Little Ida's Flowers'.

16 December. *Fairy-Tales Told for Children, Second Booklet* published. It contains 'Thumbelina', 'The Naughty Boy', 'The Travelling Companion'.

1836 21 April. *O.T.* (novel) published.

1837 7 April. *Fairy-Tales Told for Children, Third Booklet* published. It contains 'The Little Mermaid' and 'The Emperor's New Clothes'.

22 November. *Only a Fiddler* (novel) published.

1838 26 May. Receives an annuity of 400 rigsdaler from the king.

6 September. Søren Kierkegaard: 'From the Papers of a Person Still Alive' (critique of *Only a Fiddler*) is published.

17 September. Thorvaldsen returns to Copenhagen.

2 October. *Fairy-Tales Told for Children, New Collection, First Booklet* is published. It includes 'The Steadfast Tin Soldier' and 'The Wild Swans'.

1839   19 October. *Fairy-Tales for Children, New Collection, Second Booklet* is published. It includes 'The Storks'.

20 December. *Picture-Book Without Pictures* (a sequence of stories) is published.

1840   3 February. *The Mulatto* (play, his most successful) is published.

31 October. Begins journey to Greece and Constantinople.

1841   13 July. HCA returns to Denmark.

20 December. *Fairy-Tales for Children, New Collection, Third Booklet* is published. It includes 'The Swineherd'.

1842   30 April. *A Poet's Bazaar* (travelogue of journey to Constantinople and back) is published.

1843   8 March–8 April. HCA in Paris meeting many illustrious people.

9–20 August. Falls in love with singer Jenny Lind.

11 November. *New Fairy-Tales, First Collection* is published, which contains 'The Ugly Duckling', 'The Nightingale', 'The Sweethearts' and 'The Angel'.

November/December. Falls in love with Henrik Stampe, which intensifies in the spring of the following year.

1844   24 June–1 July. Visits Weimar; friendship with the Hereditary Grand Duke, Carl Alexander begins.

29 August–9 September. Stays on island of Føhr as guest of Royal Couple.

21 December. *New Fairy-Tales, Second Collection* is published, which contains 'The Fir Tree' and 'The Snow Queen'.

1845   17 April. *New Fairy-Tales, Third Collection* is published, which includes 'The Red Shoes', 'The Jumping Competition'.

22 November–14 October 1846. Travels in Germany and Italy, including important May/June stay in Naples.

1846   February onwards. Successful translations into English, building on Mary Howitt's translation of *The Improvisatore* February, 1845.

1847   January/February. *The True Story of My Life*, an autobiography commissioned by Lorck to accompany the German Collected Stories and published in German version.

6 April. *New Fairy-Tales, Second Volume, First Collection* published, which includes 'The Shadow'.

23 June–30 August. Visit to England and Scotland. Feted in Society. Meets Dickens.

1848   22 February. Revolution in Paris, which spreads throughout Europe.

4 March. *New Fairy-Tales, Second Volume, Second Collection* is published. This includes 'The Old House', 'A Drop of Water', 'The Little Match Girl', 'The Story of a Mother'.

23 March. *Treårskrigen* (Three Years War), greatly to preoccupy HCA, begins.

28 September. *The Two Baronesses* (novel) published in English.

25 November. *The Two Baronesses* published in Danish.

1849 17 May–16 August. Travels in Sweden.

5 June. Denmark becomes a Constitutional Monarchy.

1851 2–26 February. Soldiers start coming home from the Three Years War, resolved in Denmark's favour.

9 May. *In Sweden* (travelogue) published.

1852 5 April. *Stories, first booklet* published, which contains 'The Swan's Nest'.

17 May–8 June. Returns to Weimar after five years' absence.

30 November. *Stories, Second Collection* published, which includes 'Everything in its Right Place', 'The Goblin at the Grocer's', 'Thousands of Years to Come', 'Under the Willow-tree'.

December. Story 'She Was No Good', published in Danish Folk Calendar for 1853.

1855 12 July. *My Fairy-Tale Life* (autobiography) published.

1857 20 May. *'To Be or Not to Be'* (novel) published simultaneously in Danish, English, German.

11 June–13 July. Stay with Dickens detrimental to their friendship.

1858 2 March. *New Fairy-Tales and Stories* published.

15 May. *New Fairy-Tales and Stories, Second Collection* published, which includes 'The Marsh King's Daughter'.

October. Addresses the Workers' Association, the first Danish writer to do so.

1859 24 March. *New Fairy-Tales and Stories, Third Collection* published, which includes 'What the Wind Told about Valdemar Daae', 'Anne Lisbeth'.

20 June–10 September. Travels in Jutland.

9 December. *New Fairy-Tales and Stories, Fourth Collection* published, which includes 'The Dead Child', 'A Story from the Dunes', 'The Two Brothers'.

1860–1861 Many readings to the (new) Workers' Association of 1860.

1861 2 March. *New Fairy-Tales and Stories, Second Series* published, which includes 'What Father Does is Always Right', 'The Snowman', 'The New Century's Muse'.

4 April–20 June. European travels with Jonas Collin junior.

28 August. Jonas Collin senior dies.

25 November. *New Fairy-Tales and Stories, Second Series, Second Collection* published, which includes 'The Ice Maiden'.

1862 February. An emotional/'erotic' friendship with dancer Harald Scharff begins.

23 July–31 March 1863. Travels to Spain and back with Jonas Collin junior.

1863 9 November. *In Spain* (travelogue) is published.

1864 1 February–30 October. War between Denmark and Austro-Prussian alliance, ending with defeat of Denmark and surrender of Schleswig-Holstein.

1865 17 November. *New Fairy-Tales and Stories, Second Series, Third Collection* published, which includes 'The Bishop of Børghum Kloster'.

1866 31 January. Extensive travels begin. Stays in Lisbon 6 May–14 August, and on return journey spends 30/31 August in Paris, where he visits brothels.

11 December. *New Fairy-tales and Stories. Second Series, Fourth Collection* is published, which includes 'The Janitor's Son'.

1867 15 April–9 May and 7–22 September. Two visits to Paris to see the Universal Exposition.

6/7 December. Andersen awarded Freedom of Odense and sees town illuminated in his honour.

1868 12 March. First meeting with Georg Brandes.

11–19 May. In Paris.

5 December. The Dryad published (single volume).

1869 11, 18, 25 July. Georg Brandes's three-part critique of HCA in *Illustreret Tidende*.

17 December. *Three New Fairy-tales and Stories* published, dedicated to Edvard Collin and containing 'Hønse-Grethe's Family', 'The Adventures of a Thistle', 'A Question of the Imagination'.

1870 19 July–10 May 1871. Franco-Prussian War.

11 November. *Lucky-Peer* (novel) published.

1872 30 March. New *Fairy-Tales and Stories Third Series*, including 'The Most Incredible Thing', 'The Great Sea-Serpent'.

25 July–31 August. In Scandinavia (Sweden and Norway).

November–December. HCA seriously ill with liver cancer.

23 November. *New Fairy-tales Third Series, Second Collection* published, including 'The Story Old Johanne Told', 'Auntie Toothache'.

1873–1874 Life increasingly taken up by illness, HCA spending more and more time at Rolighed with the Melchiors.

1875 2 April. HCA's 70th birthday celebrated nationally and internationally.

4 April. HCA dies at Rolighed.

11 August. Funeral with King, Crown Prince and many hundreds of other people attending.

Notes

References and Abbreviations

Original texts of all stories quoted can be found on www.adl.dk (Arkiv for Danske Litteratur) and on www.andersen.sdu.dk. Numbered notes also refer readers to the pages of the Collected Reitzel (Det Reitzelske Forlag) edition of 1893, *Eventyr og Historier*, abbreviation: *E og H* Vols *I-V*. The website www. andersen.sdu.dk is also the source of Johan de Mylius's *Year by Year*, biographical tables of Andersen's life and works, abbreviation: *Y by Y* + Year, an online version of Johan de Mylius's day-by-day biography, *Hans Christian Andersens liv. Dag for Dag (The Life of Hans Christian Andersen Day by Day)*. Copenhagen: Aschehoug, 1998, itself an expansion of his *Hans Christian Andersen, liv og værk: En tidstavle (Hans Christian Andersen, Life and Work: A Timetable)*. Copenhagen: Aschehoug, 1993. Johan de Mylius is also the author of an invaluable study of the fairy-tales *Forvandlingens pris: (H.C. Andersen and his Fairy-tales) H.C. Andersen og hans eventyr (The Price of Transformation)*. Copenhagen: Høst & Søn, Gyldendal, 2004/2005.

The text of the novels quoted is from the following editions, to which notes also refer; the abbreviations used throughout the notes are in parenthesis:

Improvisatore (Imp). Copenhagen: Gyldendal, 1900
O.T. (O.T.). Copenhagen: Gyldendals Trane-Klassikere, 1948
Kun en Spillemand (KES). Danske Klassikere/Det Danske Sprog- og Litteraturselskab/Borgen, 1988
De to Baronesse (DTB). Copenhagen: Gyldendal, 1903
'At være eller ikke være' (AVEIV). Danske Klassikere/Det Danske Sprog- og Litteraturselskab/ Borgen, 2001
Lykke-Peer (LP). Danske Klassikere/Det Danske Sprog- og Litteraturselskab/Borgen, 2000
En Digters Bazar (EDB). Danske Klassikere/Det Danske Sprog- og Litteraturselskab/Borgen, 2006
The English quotations from *My Fairy-Tale Life* are from the new translation of *Mit Livs Eventyr* by W. Glyn Jones. Sawtry, Cambs: Dedalus, 2013; abbreviation: *MF-TL*. Quotations from the Diaries are from *The Diaries of Hans Christian Andersen*, selected and translated by Patricia L. Conroy and Sven H. Rossel. Seattle & London: University of Washington Press, 1990 – abbreviation *D*. For the travelogue *Skyggebilleder*, etc. they are from *Shadow Pictures*, translated by Anna Halager and edited by Sven Hakon Rossel and Monica Wenusch. Vienna: Praesens Verlag, 2011. Abbreviation in Notes *SP*.

Abbreviations for regularly cited secondary material:

Jackie Wullschlager *HCA*: Jackie Wullschlager, *Hans Christian Andersen: The Life of a Storyteller*. London: Allen Lane, The Penguin Press, 2000
Jens Andersen *HCA*: Jens Andersen, *Hans Christian Andersen: A New Life*, translated by Tiina Nunnally. New York: Woodstock, London: Duckworth, 2005
Elias Bredsdorff *HCA*: Elias Bredsdorff, *Hans Christian Andersen*, London: Phaidon, 1975
Tatar AA: The Annotated Hans Christian Andersen, edited by Maria Tatar. New York: W.W.Norton, 2008

All other books referred to, Danish English, primary or secondary, are given full titles in text or notes.

Danish is a member of the Scandinavian group of Germanic languages (of the Indo-European family) and descends from the East Norse dialects of Old Norse. It is as good as mutually intelligible with Norwegian and Swedish, certainly in written form, but Danes and Swedes find it somewhat harder to understand each other than either does Norwegian. Norwegian, in this case, means the far more widely used of Norway's two official languages, *bokmål* (rather than the West Norwegian-based *nynorsk* (formerly known as *landsmål*), since it is actually derived from Danish as Norway's administrative language for centuries under Danish ownership (Dual Monarchy). Unlike Norwegian and Swedish, Danish is not tonal, but has a sound system markedly different not only from these two languages but also from most other languages in the world – a tendency to engulf or assimilate consonants, and the vocal 'stød' ('push'), halfway to the glottal stop, which give it its strong aural character. Dialects have waned since the middle of the last century, though they do survive, especially in Jutland and on Bornholm. Standard Danish is in spoken use throughout this nation of 5.6 million. Danish reformed its spelling/orthography in 1948.

Introductory: Europe, Denmark, the World

1. *Fædrelandet,* founded in 1834 as a weekly, became a regular newspaper at New Year 1840, with Andersen's friend, the Liberal politician Orla Lehmann (see Chapter 1, note 69) on its staff. A progressive paper, it was instrumental in its demands that Denmark have a proper Constitution (as it did in 1849) and was a great supporter of the Danish cause in Schleswig. The editor at this point was the National Liberal supporter, Carl Plougmand.
2. With its first issue dated 3 January 1749, *Berlingske Tidende* is one of the world's oldest newspapers. It has been, and is, of conservative tendency and has a circulation (2013) of *c.*103,000.
3. For a clear summary, see Knud V. Jespersen, *A History of Denmark,* translated by Ivan Hill and Christopher Wade. Basingstoke and New York: Palgrave Macmillan, 2011, pp. 21–26.
4. Published in *Fædrelandet* on 5 March 1850.
5. Jespersen, op. cit., p. 66. This protocol was a revision of the earlier one of 2 August 1852; its signatories were Austria, France, Prussia, Russia and Britain, together with Denmark and Sweden.
6. Both stories were published in book form in the year of their first appearance, 1852, 'The Swan's Nest' on 5 April as one of the stories in *Historier;* 'Thousands of Years to Come' on 30 November in *Historier. Anden Samling* (Stories. Second Collection).
7. *E og H Vol II* p. 266.
8. H[ans].C[hristian]. Ørsted (1777–1851). A major figure in Andersen's life (see throughout this study), than whom, at his own declaration, Andersen loved nobody more. Physicist, chemist, writer and prominent public intellectual, he was born in Rudkøbing on the island of Langeland (off Fyn), and he and his brother Anders, sons of a pharmacist, were largely educated at home before going on to the University of Copenhagen, where both did brilliantly. A Kantian dedicated to the supreme importance of investigating and understanding the natural world, he became involved with problems in physics after meeting the German physicist Ritter. Through Ritter he developed research leading to his discovery – on 21 April 1818 – that electric currents create magnetic fields, a key aspect of electromagnetism. He became a professor at the University of Copenhagen in 1806, and was deeply involved in Danish cultural life and the pursuit of philosophical, religious and literary matters.
9. *E og H Vol II* p. 268.
10. 'Locksley Hall', a long poem by Alfred Tennyson. Andersen later admired Tennyson sufficiently to include an image of him on the decorated screen he made in his last years. Though published in 1842, this poem probably dates from 1837–38, and takes the form of a monologue by a man revisiting the house by the sea where he and his cousin fell in love. His unhappiness that she married another is projected on to the present-day world, so that progress, which the poet himself followed keenly, is viewed as a series of occasions for alarm. In Alfred Tennyson, *The Major Works,* edited by Adam Roberts. Oxford: Oxford World's Classics, 2009; 'Locksley Hall' 119–138, pp. 106–107.
11. *Y by Y* 1853 for 31 May ff. It appears that the previous year Andersen was actually given demonstrations of the telegraph line by those working on it. The writer Carsten Hauch (1790–1872) was also on the Board of Directors for the Royal Theatre, Copenhagen. Born in Norway, he returned to Denmark as a boy, and at age 17 was a volunteer against the British invasion. He became friendly with Oehlenschläger (see note 18) whom he was to succeed in 1851 as Professor of Aesthetics at the University of Copenhagen. He studied science, and while pursuing studies in France had a foot amputated. His earlier poetry and plays were not critical successes; the five novels beginning with the still highly regarded patriotic romance *Vilhelm Zabern* (1834) and ending with *Robert Fulton* (1853), so admired by Andersen, fared far better. So did the tragedies he wrote between 1841 and 1866, though the lyrical poems of the 1850s and 1860s are the works of his that have survived the best.
12. *D* p.48.

13. David Gilmour, *The Pursuit of Italy.* London: Penguin, 2011, pp. 176–191.
14. 'Billedbog uden Billeder'. Copenhagen: Reitzel (Det Reitzelske Forlag), 1845 edition, pp. 29–31.
15. *E og G Vol II*, p. 230.
16. *Tatar AA* pp. 168–192, which actually appends a translation of Mathias Winther's version – from his *Danske Folkeeventyr* (*Danish Folk Tales,* 1823) – to an illuminatingly footnoted translation of Andersen's magnificent story, far more concerned with the feeling life than the transcribed folk tale. Winther (1795–1834), like Andersen from Fyn, and like him too in having a difficult family background with financial hardship, was a seminal figure for the serious examination of Danish folk inheritance. It is possible, despite the popularity of some of his publications, that he never had his proper literary due on account of the chaotic nature of his personal life with its extramarital scandals.
17. Tycho Brahe features recurrently in Andersen's writings, becoming for him not just a supreme representative of the Danish genius for inquiry, for studies transcending immediate worldly concerns, but also for the country's less than wholehearted gratitude to its most remarkable sons. Repeatedly Andersen draws attention to Brahe's departure from the country as an illustration of this. After receiving handsome royal patronage – enabling the construction of the Uranienborg observatories on the island of Hven – Brahe fell out with the new king, Christian IV, and went to work for the Holy Roman Emperor, Rudolph II in Prague, where he was assisted by Johannes Kepler.
18. Adam Oehlenschläger (1779–1850), a writer vital to the whole culture of his times, whose character he played a pre-eminent part in forming, and vital too to Andersen's own life and career; at times we can almost believe that Andersen based his career on the older man's. Their backgrounds, however, were very different; Oehlenschläger and his sister grew up in Frederiksberg Castle, and he was given a childhood of freedom without formal education until he was 12 years old. Adam then went to the college known as Posterity's High School. Its principal was the poet Edvard Storm who taught a course in Scandinavian mythology, thus setting the boy on course for his life's work. Though he was first attracted to the stage, he followed the advice of the Ørsted brothers to pursue studies instead at Copenhagen University, but never completed them. A meeting with the Norwegian/Danish philosopher, Henrik Steffens (1773–1845) was a turning-point in his life, and from then on he dedicated himself to poetic drama and poetry, celebrating the great religious and mythopoeic traditions of the Norse. By 26 he was able to collect, in two volumes, his *Poetiske Skrifter* (Poetic Writings) among which is the long verse-play *Aladdin,* which gave the Danes a hero with whom to identify. He met Fichte in Berlin, Goethe in Weimar, Tieck in Dresden; major works contemporaneous with these friendships are *Hakon Jarl* and *Baldur hin Gode* (both 1807). In 1810 he became Professor of Aesthetics at Copenhagen University. In 1829 he was publicly crowned – by Sweden's Esaas Tegnér – as 'King of Nordic Poetry', and has the best claim of any to be regarded as Denmark's foremost Romantic poet.
19. Bertel Thorvaldsen (1768–1844). Thorvaldsen, like Andersen, came from a poor background. His father was an Icelandic shipyard woodcarver with an alcohol addiction. Thorvaldsen would work for him even after he had been admitted, with the financial support of friends, to the Copenhagen Academy at the age of 11. A prize-studded Academy student, he was awarded a royal bursary to pursue studies in Rome, and henceforward would celebrate the day of his arrival in Rome – 8 March 1797 – as his real birthday, the proper beginning of his life. Guided by the Danish archaeologist resident in Rome, Georg Zoëga, he concentrated on Greek rather than Roman antiquities, and became an authority on them. His statue of Jason (1802–03) was his first acclaimed work, praised by Antonio Canova (1757–1822), together with whom he would become the leading sculptor of Neoclassicism. He was a central figure in Rome's artistic colony, and became the only non-Italian commissioned to create a monument in St Peter's: the tomb of Pius XII (begun 1824, completed 1831). His years in Rome saw such masterpieces as the bust of Lord Byron – Andersen would take down verbatim an account Thorvaldsen gave him of the poet 'sitting' for this – and the equestrian statue of Poniatowski, and also in 1820 the great works for the Vor Frue Kirke (Church of Our Lady) in Copenhagen, now Copenhagen Cathedral, perhaps his most impressive legacy. By 1833 he had been appointed Director of the Academy of Fine Arts in Copenhagen and was making plans for the Thorvaldsen Museum, work on which, under the architect M.G. Bindesbøll, would begin in 1837. In 1838 he made an official and triumphantly received return to Copenhagen, where he mixed in circles Andersen would also frequent, such as the estate of Baron and Baroness Stampe. See Dyveke Helsted, Eva Henschen and Bjarne Jørnæs, *Thorvaldsen.* Copenhagen: The Thorvaldsen Museum, 2003. Also see John Henderson, *The Triumph of Art at Thorvaldsen's Museum, 'Love' in Copenhagen.* University of Copenhagen: Museum Tusculum Press, 2007.
20. Valdemar Vedel (1865–1942), poet and literary critic. In 1890 he would publish *Studier over Guldalderen i Dansk Digtning* (*Studies of the Golden Age in Danish Writing*). Copenhagen: P.G. Philipsens Forlag. Also see Patricia G. Berman, *In Another Light: Danish Painting in the Nineteenth Century.* London: Thames and Hudson, 2007, pp. 18 and 192–193.

21. Immanuel Kant (1724–1804). Kant's influence on Danish Golden Age intellectuals – refracted in Andersen's own thought and works – is of incalculable dimensions. Born in East Prussia's Königsberg (today's Kaliningrad) into a strong Pietistic household, he spent his entire life in that city, entering the university there at age 16 and remaining in the institution throughout his whole career. He published his first philosophical work when he was 23, but distinguished himself early as an astronomer and anthropologist, and it was only after a silence that he produced the first of the great critiques which made him a figure of unassailable intellectual magnitude: *Kritik der reinen Vernunft* (Critique of Pure Reason, 1781), followed by *Kritik der praktischen Vernunft* (Critique of Practical Reason, 1788) and *Kritik der Urteilskraft* (Critique of Judgement, 1790). Kant held that morality proceeds from reason and that the structure of our minds determines our *Weltanschauungen*. There is the noumenal – the world of things outside the self, with autonomous existences – and the phenomenal – the world of our experiences. Morality/reason justifies belief in God (and in divine virtue), even though we can have no empirical knowledge of such a being.

22. Johann Gottlieb Fichte (1762–1814). It was principally through Oehlenschläger that Fichte's ideas entered Danish culture. A student of Kant's philosophy in 1790, he sent his own tract on 'subjective idealism' to Kant himself, who published it in 1792. He became Professor of Philosophy at Jena in 1794, and wrote a series of influential treatises, though controversy over his alleged atheism led to his being removed from his position. He became Rector of the new University of Berlin in 1810. Existence was viewed in the subjective terms of Ego, with God as Absolute Mind – or Ur-Ich – and the world beyond the self as the Non-Ego. His ideas were of a strongly nationalist tendency, with the latent ascription of the Ego, the moral being, to the entire German people.

23. Thorvaldsen's is the beautiful Twenty-Fourth Evening of the 'Picturebook-Without-Pictures' (*Billedbog uden Billeder*, Copenhagen: Reitzel, 1845, pp. 55–57), which commemorates his boyhood in poverty, his artistic successes in Rome and his triumphant return to Denmark. Ørsted is the subject of 'To Brødre' ('Two Brothers', 1859) together with his brother, Anders Sandøe Ørsted (1778–1860), jurist, politician and Prime Minister 1853–54 (but forced to resign for his ultra-conservative policies). He is also honoured in 'Oldefader' ('Great-grandfather', 1870). And the kind of experiments in natural science he approved of – and which Andersen had himself carried out – occasioned 'Vanddraaben' ('A Drop of Water', 1848), showing the teeming life this minute particle contains; Andersen dedicated the tale to him.

24. The term is Ørsted's, though he also coined a purely German alternative, *Gedankenversuch*. A hypothesis is followed through so that all its potentials as well as likely consequences become apparent. It need have no practical significance, but often by showing up validity or invalidity within any theory, it can be of great use in a variety of fields.

25. This poem-sequence was intended to span science and poetry, showing that science's latest and most adventurous inventions had all the imaginative appeal of a poem. The picture-boards of the original edition depicted hot-air balloons.

26. The three newspapers in question were *Fædrelandet*, *Berlingske Tidende* and *Kjøbenhavnsposten*. The verses, in a setting taken from the music of composer C.E.F. Weyse (1774–1842), were sung as the cortège paused by Oehlenschläger's birthplace.

27. *E og H Vol II* p. 232.

Part One: From *Skyggebilleder* (*Shadow-Pictures*) to 'Skyggen' ('The Shadow')

Chapter 1: William Christian Walter

1. Ejnar Stig Askgaard, 'The Lineage of Hans Christian Andersen', www.museum.odense.dk.
2. See Chapter 4, *O.T.*, note 20.
3. *MF-TL* p. 12. 'I was an only child, and was extremely spoiled, but my mother constantly told me how very much happier I was than she had been, and that I was being brought up like the son of a count.' Of course, Andersen could legitimately have retorted that by this sentence he meant he was the only child of both his parents, but nevertheless this and similar passages do give an impression that he was an only child *tout court*. Likewise he recalls parties held in Odense Tugthus – certainly occasions most of his readers would not have shared – but bowdlerises them. His parents become mere friends of the jailer; there is no mention of the familial connection with the institution.
4. *MF-TL* pp. 12 and 18. See also Ejnar Stig Askgaard. 'The Lineage of Hans Christian Andersen', www.museum.odense.dk.
5. *MF-TL* pp. 12–13.
6. Jean de la Fontaine (1621–95). A learned man, deeply versed in the classics and brought up in the country, he spent his adult life in Paris, associating with both Racine and Molière. Drawing on his fund of literary knowledge – and Aesop – his work is remarkably original, giving readers a new,

witty and thoughtful way of relating humankind to animals, and vice versa. Fontaine's fables first appeared in six volumes in 1668: *Fables choisies mises en vers* (*Selected Fables Put into Verse*).

7. Ludvig Holberg (1684–1754). Only Andersen has created characters who have entered the Danish national consciousness as thoroughly as those of Holberg's comedies, expressly influenced by Molière and the Italian *commedia dell' arte* – from *Jeppe paa Bjerget* (*Jeppe on the Hill*, 1722), which portrays a 'transformed peasant', through the eponymous *Mester Gert Westphaler* and *Erasmus Montanus* (1723) to *Den forvandlede Brudgrom* (*The Changed Bridegroom*, 1753). Holberg was born (at the time of the dual monarchy) in Bergen, Norway, but spent most of his life in Denmark; he was, however, a great traveller, and made a significant stay in England, including a spell at Oxford. He was a humanist, a deist, a historian and a moralist who expressed his thoughts through the essay much in the manner of Montaigne.

8. Askgaard, Lineage, op. cit.

9. *Y by Y* 1810.

10. Askgaard, Lineage, op. cit. *Y by Y* 1818, which contains Professor de Mylius's observations.

11. Askgaard, Lineage, op. cit.

12. Andersen's own Notes, *E og H Vol V*, pp. 318–319.

13. *E og H Vol II*, pp. 308–318.

14. 'Odense', a poem published in *Illustreret Tidende,* 21 February 1875.

15. *MF-TL* p. 14.

16. Det kongelige Teater (The Royal Theatre) was built by the court architect Niels Eigtved in 1748, with major renovations in 1772. The company based there visited Odense annually. See Frederick J. Marker, *Hans Christian Andersen and the Romantic Theatre.* Toronto: University of Toronto Press, 1971, pp. 3–5.

17. Giuseppi Casorti (1749–1826). Italian actor and troupe-leader, born into a theatre family. He spent his last twenty years in Denmark, based at Prices' Teatret in Vesterbro, but maintaining Italian traditions. See Marker, op. cit. pp. 15 and 29. Andersen was much taken with his *Harlequin Foreman of the Threshers. MF-TL* p. 23.

18. See the tribute in *MF-TL* p. 27 to Madame Bunkeflod, to whom Andersen would read aloud and for whom he made a white pincushion which she preserved, and to Herr Iversen, ibid., p. 34. The actors from Copenhagen whenever they were in Odense would call on Herr Iversen every day, as the young Andersen noted. So it made good sense for him to ask the printer for a letter of introduction that would be useful to him on arrival in Copenhagen. The letter Herr Iversen actually gave the boy, in good faith, to Madame Schall from the Royal Ballet, did not have the desired result.

19. *Y by Y* 1818. *Y by Y* 1819.

20. *Y by Y* 1819, Askgaard, Lineage, op. cit.

21. *MF-TL* p. 44.

22. Giuseppe Siboni was born in Forlì, Italy, and sang with Italian opera companies throughout Europe – in Genoa, Prague, Milan (La Scala), London (The King's Theatre), Rome (Teatro Argentina), Naples (Teatro San Carlo). Between 1810 and 1814 he was a friend of Beethoven's in Vienna. King Christian VIII invited him to Denmark, where he joined the Royal Theatre Company in 1829. He founded the Royal Conservatory of Music in Copenhagen in 1825 (to be re-founded by the composer Gade in 1867), and was made Kongelig Kammersanger (Royal Chamber Singer).

23. C[hristoph] E[rnst] F[riedrich] Weyse (1774–1842) the most famous composer of his day, and an arbiter of Danish musical taste. As a young man he had enjoyed the friendship of Mozart's widow, who had likened him to her husband. Like Mozart, he was a brilliant pianist much in demand. Weyse remained always true to the classical style, rejecting the advanced compositions of Beethoven; this is shown in his seven symphonies and, even more markedly, in his piano pieces. He became a professor at the University of Copenhagen in 1816, and in 1819 composer at the Royal Court, which had a special relationship with the Royal Theatre.

24. Jens Baggesen (1764–1826). His life and literary career have significant affinities with Andersen's own. Born into poverty, he passed an unhappy childhood and youth, and several times attempted to kill himself. Yet his first successful writings – and they were *very* successful – were comic verses. His opera *Holger Danske* (1789) was attacked as being insufficiently patriotic and too influenced by German writing. This upset Baggesen sufficiently for him to spend the next twenty years out of Denmark, and even to write in German. However in 1792–93 he published his two-volume account (in Danish) of his travels, *Labyrinten* (*The Labyrinth*), which had enormous influence on Danish prose: see Chapter 2. From 1806 to 1820 Baggesen was back in Denmark, usually in a state of feud with its writers and cultural figures, so Andersen was lucky to have seen him as he did, not least because the following year he departed his native country once more. His last years were marked by familial tragedy, debt and acute melancholia. He died in Hamburg in a Freemasons' Hospital.

25. *Levnedsbogen* – which Andersen wanted published only in the event of his early death but which was then thought to have been lost – was discovered and published by the scholar Hans Brix in

1926. It was later issued, annotated and edited by H. Topsøe-Jensen, in 1962. The autobiography commissioned by Carl Lorck – and translated into English by Mary Howitt as *The True Story of My Life*. London: Longman Brown Green and Longmans, 1847 – was not put out in Danish until 1942 as *Mit eget Eventyr uden Digtning!*, edited by Helge Topsøe-Jensen. Copenhagen: Nyt Nordisk Forlag/Arnold Busck. *Mit Livs Eventyr* (*My Fairy-Tale Life*) came out from Reitzel of Copenhagen in 1855; revised edition 1859. Andersen's American translator, Horace E. Scudder (working with the English Mary Howitt), asked – for his English-language version published in New York and London, Paddington Press in 1871 – for additional chapters covering the years 1855–67, which Andersen supplied. These did not appear in Danish until the new edition (Reitzel also) of the book in 1877, after Andersen's death.

26. B[ernhard] S[everin] Ingemann (1789–1862). A clergyman's son, Ingemann began his literary career as a poet, publishing while still a student, and then as a dramatist, before launching himself as a prose-writer with a story about Bornholm (1820) and tales influenced by Hoffmann. In 1822 he was appointed instructor in Danish Language and Literature at Sorø Academy, and from then on played a strong part in Danish literary culture. In 1826 he began his series of Scott-inspired novels, successful in their own time, about the Danish past. He also wrote a sequence of poems for children, *Morgen- og Aften-Sange* (*Morning and Evening Songs*, 1837) and hymns which became popular. He was a close friend of N.F.S. Grundtvig, whose interests and ideals he shared. In his diary for 5 October 1825 Andersen describes visiting Sorø and going a walk with Ingemann: 'he told me that once when he was recovering from an illness a gremlin came in to him that was stranger than anything he had ever seen before and bowed and grimaced at him, and sat by his bed. . . . It is his idea that I was born to write novels in order to describe the lower class' (*D*. p. 9).

27. Grundtvig. All thinking Danes, Andersen included, had to define their views on religion, culture and society in relation to this all-embracing thinker and public personage. For an excellent appraisal of his work and legacy see Knud V. Jespersen, *A History of Denmark*, translated Ivan Hill and Christopher Wade. Basingstoke and New York: Palgrave Macmillan, 2011, pp. 112–122 and W. Glyn Jones, *Denmark: A Modern History*. London: Croom Helm, 1986, pp. 52–58. Also *passim* in this study.

28. Just Mathias Thiele (1795–1874), a pivotal figure in the Danish Golden Age. From 1817 he worked in the Royal Danish Library, during which period he collected Danish folk tales by travelling round the countryside: *Danske Folkesagn* (*Danish Folk Legends*, 1818–23), I–IV. A scholarship took him to Rome, where he became a close friend of Thorvaldsen's, writing on him, editing him and in due course being responsible for his biography – in four volumes 1851–56. He was Secretary of the Royal Danish Academy of Fine Arts 1825–71. For his work as a folklorist see Timothy R. Tangherlini, *Danish Folktales, Legends and Other Stories*. Washington: University of Washington Press, 2013, pp. 22–23 in particular. 'Thiele's role in Danish literary life should not be underestimated.'

29. Knud Lyne Rahbek (1760–1830). In addition to his own writings and influential translations, especially from the English, Rahbek is credited with having founded the study of literary history in Denmark with his five-volume *Bidrag til en Oversigt over den danske Digtekonst* (*Contribution to a survey of Danish Poetry*, 1820–29), in collaboration with the scholar Rasmus Nyerup. His wife Kamma, an artist and great letter-writer, enjoyed a reputation as a *saloniste*, and so some of the success of *Bakkehuset* gatherings must certainly be attributed to her. Andersen when a young guest there very much liked talking to Kamma Rahbek, but said that her husband, in contrast, never brought himself actually to address him (*MF-TL* pp. 50–51). Rahbek also wrote a good many drinking and club-life songs.

30. Marker, op. cit. p. 30. (Taken from Søren Kierkegaard, *Samlede Værker*, xiv, Copenhagen, 1963, p. 118.)

31. Jonas Collin (1776–1861). Though he is remembered primarily for his work in cultural matters, and his unflagging assistance to artists and scholars (not only Andersen) – on the board of directors of the National Theatre; responsibility for the royal fund *ad usus publicos* – this highly educated lawyer, linguist and philosophically trained intellectual was a key public official, one of the most enlightened and influential administrators of the Absolute Monarchy in its last phase. His sense in fiscal matters derived from his work in the Finance Secretariat; he understood banking in detail. He was involved with public works and exhibitions in Copenhagen, and took a practical and reformist interest in agriculture. He largely welcomed the liberalising reforms of 1848/49 and had friends among its strongest advocates. He married Henriette Christine in 1802; she had previously been married to his teacher, Michael Gottlieb Birckner (1756–98), by whom she had two daughters.

32. *Robbers of Vissenburg in Fyn*. A scene from this was actually published at the time, in A.P. Liunge's magazine, *Harpen*, on Friday 9 August 1822. Says Marker, op. cit. p. 31, 'the melodramatic dialogue in the robbers' den gives ample evidence of the drama's exaggerated *Sturm und Drang* tendencies'. Readers today can judge for themselves because it is included – in modern Danish orthography – in Johan de Mylius's excellent *HCA et livs digtning* (*HCA: A Life's Writing*), Aschehoug, 2005.

33. *Die Räuber* (*The Robbers*, published 1781). Schiller's prose-drama concerns the fate of a young nobleman, Karl von Moor, a reckless young student, done out of his inheritance by his cunning, materialistic, dishonest brother Franz. Believing his father has died (in fact he is imprisoned in a dungeon by Franz), and hating all the injustice of the conventional world, he goes out into the Bohemian forest and becomes leader of a robber band. Though Karl succeeds in finding his father, in arranging for Franz's capture (Franz eludes this by committing suicide) and in retaining the love of Amalia (whom Franz has pursued), he cannot break free of the robbers, but is deeply ashamed of the crimes the band has committed. In the end he gives himself up to justice. Its dialectic of liberty (which contains anarchy) and a controlling civilisation (which inevitably entails both convention and corruption) had deep appeal for the century ahead. We can detect the direct influence of *Die Räuber* on both Scott and Andersen (see Section 5 of the present chapter). Tolstoy was to make a list of literary works particularly important to him and cited Schiller's *The Robbers* as a 'very great influence' (Henri Troyat, *Tolstoy*. London: W.H. Allen, 1968, p. 56), and we can see this in his early work, *The Cossacks* (1852–53).

34. *Alfsol.* Andersen took the subject matter for this play from P.F. Suhm, *Nordiske Noveller* (*Nordic Novelle*, 1783).

35. *MF-TL* p. 57.

36. Simon Meisling (1787–1856). Meisling has had such a spectacularly bad press, above all from his most distinguished pupil, that it is worth emphasising that Collin, Rahbek et al. had perfectly good reason to believe good of him and think that the Grammar School Board had done well to appoint him to the Slagelse headship. He was an established classical philologist and translator of classical poetry, who went on to produce a verse translation of Virgil's *Aeneid*. He was a humanist, largely progressive and enlightened in his views on education, and in addition to classical works, translated Shakespeare, Gozzi and Goethe. Sincerely interested in his students, he sadly found it almost impossible to get on well with them, few of them liking him, while his home life was unhappy and disorderly.

37. *Youthful Attempts.* While Andersen himself used the form 'Villiam', I have used Shakespeare's name 'William' correctly in my chapter title, to point up the loftiness of Andersen's view of and ambitions for himself.

38. *D* p. 7.

39. Skælskør. *MF-TL* pp. 68–69, including the quoted sentence.

40. A couple researching family history had been loaned one of the four cases, and there came across the manuscript. However, it was Esben Brage who took the matter up, with the results outlined. Professor Jørn Lund, a philological expert, points out that the word 'for[m]fuldendt' ('flawless'), doesn't occur in Andersen's writings untill thirty years later (www.*avisen.dk*, 21 December 2012). Professor Christian Graugaard, Professor of Sexology at Aalborg – author, and a regular contributor to *Politiken* – considers it a story about the phallus and ejaculation, and I would not substantially disagree with this reading (*Kultur*, Danish Broadcasting Corporation, 22 December 2012).

41. All quotes from 'Tællelyset' are from its first publication, in the 12 December 2012 issue of the Danish newspaper, *Politiken*.

42. This poem was first printed in *Kjøbenhavnsposten* on 25 September 1827, side by side with a German translation by Ludolph Schley.

43. *MF-TL* pp. 76–77.

44. 'Fritz' Petit (1809–54) and Carl Bagger (1807–46): see Chapter 5, discussion of 'Ugly Duckling'.

45. For a detailed and largely sympathetic (to both parties) account of the friendship of Andersen with Edvard Collin, see the whole of Chapter 4 in Jens Andersen *HCA* pp. 148–212, which not only puts it into the context of Romantic friendship and the expression of male–male relations acceptable to the times, but also analyses Edvard's 1882 book about his friend.

46. Ejnar Stig Askgaard: 'En akademisk borger', in Ejnar Stig Askgaard, editor, *Anderseniana* 2000 Odense: Odense bys museer, 2001, pp. 79–90, together with a transcription of the Andersen 1830 dissertation: 'At udvikle de græske og nordiske Mythers Forskjellighed i Lighederne og deres Overeenskomst i Forskjelighederne' ('To explain the difference between Greek and Nordic myths in the similarities and their common basis in [the] differences').

47. Johan Ludvig Heiberg (1791–1860). As critic and arbiter of Danish cultural opinion, Heiberg's standing and influence in his own times can scarcely be exaggerated. Throughout his life Andersen would consider his views as a touchstone, a benchmark (if sometimes of questionable merit where he himself was concerned). Son of a political writer and a novelist, he spent his early years in France, to which he returned after studying at the University of Copenhagen. From 1822 to 1825 he was an influential Professor of Danish Language at Kiel University, publishing lectures on Danish/Norse themes. He wrote vaudeville, serious plays and poetry, much of it satirical. He was editor of *Flyvende Post* (1827–30), which published Andersen when young, *Interimsblade*

(1834–37) and *Intelligensblade* (1842–43). In 1831 he married Johanne Luise Pätges (1812–90), the greatest Danish actress of her day and a friend of Andersen's, like him from a poor background, and, like him too, a protégée of Jonas Collin.

48. The print run of the self-published *Journey on Foot*, 500 copies, sold out speedily, and C.A. Reitzel then agreed on Andersen's original terms to issue a second edition. *Y by Y* 1829.

49. See Roger Paulin, *Ludwig Tieck, A Literary Biography*. Oxford: Oxford University Press, 1987. See also much of Chapter 2 of this study.

50. E.T. A. Hoffmann (1776–1822). See the introduction, text and notes to *The Golden Pot and Other Tales* edited by Ritchie Robertson. Oxford University Press, Oxford: Oxford World's Classics, 1992.

51. See the introduction by Leopold von Loewenstein-Wertheim to his translation of Adelbert von Chamisso, *Peter Schlemihl's*. London: Oneworld Classics, 2008, and Chapter 2 *passim* of this study.

52. Johan de Mylius, *HCA et livs digtning*. Copenhagen: Aschehoug, 2005, p. 117.

53. *Love on St Nicholas's Tower* was premièred on 25 April 1829 and ran for three performances only. Frederick J. Marker (op. cit.) amusingly juxtaposes conflicting reports by critics for the Royal Theatre (pp. 34–35), one saying 'It is high time to stop the boyish foolishness that more and more dominates our stage', another saying 'the fine, flowing verse, and the vigorous action throughout speak in its favour . . . one of our best vaudevilles'. Unfortunately, in this instance, the negative opinion won.

54. Marker, op. cit. p. 62.

55. *The Bride of Lammermoor* had its first night on 5 May 1832 and ran for eight performances. Elaborately staged in Gothic style using a moonrise machine and a 'Eidophusikon' to show thunderclouds passing over the moon, it was generally judged a success. Ivar Bredal was a viola player who had by this time written a 'potpourri' for his instrument with orchestral accompaniment. From 1835 he was concertmaster at the Royal Chapel, and from 1849 to 1863 choirmaster at the Royal Theatre. Despite Weyse's considerable fame and Andersen's friendship with him, *The Bride's* successor, *The Feast at Kenilworth*, pleased the librettist far less; he was angry that Weyse insisted on a happy ending with Amy Robsart united with Leicester. Even so, the opera – première 6 January 1836, seven performances – was very well received, Weyse was declared to have produced a masterpiece and Andersen's libretto was also praised.

56. Jane Austen, *Mansfield Park*, edited by John Lucas. London: Oxford University Press, 1970, p. 306.

57. Commodore Peter Frederik Wulff (1774–1842). Distinguished naval officer, rising to admiral and chief of the annual naval cadet ships, he was engaged in significant strategic engagements, not least in seeing off British warships. His happy marriage to Henriette Weinholdt stimulated his interest in artistic matters, and he opened his doors early to the young Andersen, making him feel at home. His disabled daughter Henriette Wulff (1804–1854) became a greatly beloved friend of Andersen's and remained so until her tragic death on a ship bound for America. Wulff took over the translations of Shakespeare from the actor Peter Thun Foersom, and from 1818 to 1825 produced Volumes 6–9.

58. John Sutherland *The Life of Walter Scott: A Critical Biography*. Oxford: Blackwell, 1995, p. 220. For the impact of Scott's novels on Denmark, see the essay by Jørgen Erik Nielsen, 'His pirates had foray'd on Scottish hill' (Danish reception of Scott) in *Reception of Walter Scott in Europe*, edited by Murray Pittock. London: Bloomsbury Academic, 2007.

59. Donizetti's *Lucia di Lammermoor* premièred on 26 September 1835 in Andersen's beloved Teatro San Carlo, Naples.

60. *D* p. 181, and for Andersen's rereading of the novel (17 May 1849) ibid. p. 212.

61. *D* p. 196.

62. 'Galoshes of Fortune'. This delightful story of galoshes that transport a person wearing them to the largely incongruous times and places of their expressed wishes appeared in *Tre Digtninger* (*Three Pieces of Writing*) in 1838. The title of the story has passed into common Danish usage to signify a happy reversal.

63. *Nussknacker und Mausekönig* appeared in Vol. I of Hoffmann's *Die Serapionsbrüder* (*The Serapion Brothers*) in 1819.

64. 'top Danish novelist'. See *Y by Y* January 1836 and Chapter 6: *Only a Fiddler*, note 1.

65. Walter Scott, *The Heart of Midlothian*'. London: Everyman edition, 1906, pp. 61–62.

66. Ibid. p. 249.

67. Ibid. p. 425.

68. Heinrich Heine (1797–1856). Born into a Jewish family in the Rhineland, with rich family connections but not rich himself, and rejected by the girl with whom he was in love, Heine turned his feelings of outsider status, his longings for love and inclusion on the one hand, and his contempt for moral dishonesty and timid bourgeois values on the other, into the ravishing poems of his young manhood – his first collection, *Gedichte*, in 1822, with his *Buch der Lieder*, 1827 clinching his growing reputation. In 1824 he went on a walking tour of north Germany and then of the Harz, which provided the material for his *Reisebilder* (see Chapter 2). Friendly with leading intellectuals in Berlin, some of whom – Alexander von Humboldt, Chamisso – Andersen would meet himself,

Heine was sufficiently disappointed in the state of Germany and his life there, and enough encouraged by news of the July Revolution in Paris, to move to the French capital in 1831, where he stayed for the rest of his life. This is the Heine that Andersen read raptly as a young man, emulated in his own verses and travelogue, and eventually had significant conversations with in Paris.

69. Orla Lehmann (1810–70), so strongly identified with the Danish National Liberal Party and the concept of Denmark's inviolability (the country's southern frontier being the Eider River), was in fact half German, his father being a Holsteiner. (Hence his easy familiarity with German poetry, especially Heine.) His family were friends of Oehlenschläger and H.C. Ørsted. Studying law at Copenhagen University, he entered radical politics early, contributing to the liberal *Kjøbenhavnsposten* and for three years (1839–42) co-editing *Fædrelandet*. He was imprisoned for three months for intemperate radicalism, and was prominently involved with the protests of 1848. He entered the Cabinet in 1848, but resigned the same year out of impatience with the speed of reform. He held positions in the new constitutional Danish Parliament from 1851 to the year of his death, 1870, being Danish Minister of the Interior 1861–63. Liberal in every respect, including supporting women's rights, he was so committed to the Danish position over Schleswig-Holstein that the country's loss of the Double Duchy in 1864 made him bitter, even pessimistic. In 1864 he wrote a widely read study of the issue, *Om Aarsagerne til Danmarks Ulykke: et historisk Tilbageblik* (*On the Causes of Denmark's Misfortunes: A Historical Retrospect*).

70. *MF-TL* p. 90.

71. Andersen has contracted the actual lines in his quotation from this poem in 'Die Nordsee' section of Heine's *Buch der Lieder*. It should read: 'Thalatta! Thalatta!/Sei mir gegrüßt, Du ewiges Meer!' 'Thalatta! Thalatta!/Give me greetings, you eternal sea!'

72. Initially, *Digte* was surprisingly generously received by critics, for all its glaring mistakes, even eliciting a review in the prestigious *Maanedsskrift for Litteratur* (*Monthly Review of Literature*).

73. *Christian den Andens Dvarf* (*Christian II's Dwarf*) probably dates from as early as 1825, though he went on writing it until at least 1829. It was posthumously published in *Anderseniana 3*, Odense, 1935, pp. 59–111.

74. The relevant letters for 13 July 1830, 14 July 1830, 22 July 1830 and 28 July 1830 can be read in *Breve* (*Letters*) on www.andersen.sdu.dk. They also – in modern Danish – are included in Johan de Mylius, *HCA en livs digtning*, pp. 168–174. All the quotations here are taken in original Danish from the sdu online collection.

75. Fåborg (Faaborg): Lone Mouritsen, Roger Norum and Caroline Osborne, *Rough Guide to Denmark*, London: Rough Guides/Penguin Books, 2010, pp. 172–174. The Voigt family were eminent rich merchants there.

76. *MF-TL* p. 89.

77. *Phantasier og Skizzer* (*Fantasies and Sketches*), published 10 January 1831 at Andersen's own expense.

78. Henrik Hertz (1798–1870) was a Danish poet and playwright particularly associated with J.L. Heiberg. His *Gjengangerbreve* (*Letters from a Ghost*), published anonymously in December 1830 (though authorship was known in literary circles), mockingly attacked Andersen for lacking the formal qualities in his poetry that the Heiberg circle demanded. Hertz enjoyed a successful literary career. His novel *Stemninger og Tilstande* (*Moods and Conditions*, 1839) allegedly features Kierkegaard, and his romantic drama *Kong Renés Datter* (1845) in the translation of T. Martin as *King René's Daughter* (1850) was very well received in England.

79. *MF-TL* pp. 91–92.

Chapter 2: Germany 1831 and After

1. *MF-TL* p. 92.
2. HCA, *The True Story of My Life*, p. 63.
3. *MF-TL* pp. 93–94.
4. *MF-TL* p. 92
5. There were four *Reisebilder*, each volume blending original poems, often ones now important in the poet's *oeuvre*, into the prose: Volume I, *Die Harzreise* (*Journey to the Harz*), 1826; Volume II, *Die Nordsee* (*The North Sea*), 1827; Volume III, *Die Reise von München nach Genua* (*Journey from Munich to Genoa*) and *Die Bader von Lucca* (*The Baths of Lucca*), 1830; Volume IV, *Die Stadt Lucca* (*The City of Lucca*) and *Englische Fragmente* (*English Fragments*), 1831.
6. *D* p. 24.
7. It cannot be definitely asserted that the Christian mentioned in the Diaries is Riborg's brother, but in the context – Christian was in Andersen's confidence about his love for his sister and an admired friend in his own right, and the other companions cited in the seeing-off include Orla Lehmann (see Chapter 1 note 69) from Fyn – it seems far more likely than not.

8. *SP* pp. 27–28.
9. Ibid. p. 28.
10. Ibid. p. 29.
11. Ibid. p. 111.
12. Ibid. p. 56 and Heinrich Heine, *Selected Verse*, Harmondsworth: Penguin, 1967, p. 30.
13. Jens Andersen *HCA* pp. 163–180; and for letter p. 167, Tiina Nunnally's translation capturing the tone of the original incomparably well.
14. *SP* pp. 35–43.
15. Heine's rather caustic observations on Goslar, which he thought had been overrated by guide-books, did not go unnoticed by its residents. Andersen, who went there metaphorically armed with Heine's travelogue, records, 'worthy citizens of Goslar . . . always looked glum when I mentioned Heine.' *SP* p. 60. This is understandable, considering the acidity of Heine's prose account of the place.
16. Both the achievement and the influence of Johan Christian Dahl (1788–1857) can scarcely be overestimated; he is widely accredited as *the* opener-up of the Norwegian landscape for serious artists. Born in Bergen of humble parentage (into a fishing family), he was given financial help to complete his artistic studies at the Copenhagen Academy, and here he first appreciated, through attention to the Dutch artist Ruisdael, his own inclination towards landscape painting. In 1824 he became a professor at the Academy at Dresden, the city he made his home for the rest of his life. In Dresden he enjoyed the friendship not only of Tieck (celebrated in Andersen's travelogue) but of Caspar David Friedrich (1774–1840), though the two men, personally so close to each other, disagreed about the relation of science to art. For all their Romantic qualities, Dahl's Danish and Norwegian landscapes pay great attention to geographical accuracy and to the effects of history and culture on the scene being depicted. Among Dahl's many students were Norwegians Thomas Fearnley and Peder Balke (1804–87), who specialised in Norway's more intractable mountain- and seascapes, Dahl made regular visits back to Norway and was a co-founder of the Norwegian National Gallery. See Christopher Riopelle with Sarah Herring, *Forests, Rocks, Torrents: Norwegian and Swiss Landscapes from the Lunde Collection*. London: National Gallery Company, distributed by Yale University Press, 2011.
17. J.M. Roberts, *The Penguin History of Europe*. London: Penguin, 1996, pp. 400–410.
18. *SP*, 45.
19. Ibid. p. 102.
20. Heine, *Selected Verse*, op. cit., p. 6.
21. We have noted in Chapter 1 the immense influence of this complex-structured fantasy, anchored in a specific place (Dresden) on Andersen. Hoffmann did not actually move to Dresden until 1813, and left the following year. See Ritchie Robertson's introduction and chronology to *The Golden Pot and Other Tales*, Oxford: World's Classics, 1992.
22. Ibid pp. 2–3.
23. *SP* p. 136.
24. Ibid. p. 135.
25. Ibid. p. 146.
26. Ibid. p. 149.
27. Ibid. p. 156.
28. Matthias Claudius (1740–1815) was a successful, productive poet, a journalist and an editor, with a special link to Denmark, where he worked as secretary to Graf Holstein in Copenhagen (1764–65) and later – from 1785 on – received a Danish pension. He was a friend of Herder and Goethe.
29. Ibid. p. 27.29. The librettist was Johann Friedrich Kind (1768–1843) and Andersen's travelogue contains a fuller tribute to his imagination and relationship to the 'Teufelsbrücke' (Devil's Bridge') gorge in *SP* pp. 128–130. Andersen adds a verse commentary of his own on *Der Freischütz* (1821), which exercised a great pull on his mind as it did on so many of his contemporaries. (In London three theatres simultaneously staged performances.) It has been generally considered, not least by Richard Wagner himself, the masterpiece that initiated German Romantic opera.
30. Smollett, dissimilar as his temperament largely was to Andersen's, felt, as the Dane regularly did, the need to leave the country in which his books first appeared because of controversy and (as he felt) inadequate appreciation (despite also enjoying considerable success). At 42 he transferred his wife and household to France and Italy, and then, after an unsatisfying return to Britain, left again for Italy, where he died at his house near Livorno in 1771. Perhaps the youthful Andersen sensed, and already recognised in himself, something of this irritable restlessness. Andersen would have read Smollett's novels in the translations made from English by Johan Clemens Tode (1736–1806).
31. His nephew, Jeremy Melford, perhaps the novel's most sympathetic character, writes: 'My uncle is an odd kind of humourist, always on the fret . . . his being tortured by the gout may have soured his temper, and, perhaps, I may like him the better on further acquaintance. . .' Tobias Smollett, *Humphrey Clinker*. London: Penguin Classics, 2008, p. 36. He does, and his readers with him.

32. *SP* p. 46.
33. Ibid. p. 29.
34. Ibid. p. 86.
35. Ibid. p. 87.
36. Ibid. p. 47.
37. Ibid. p. 47.
38. Ibid. p. 61.
39. Heinrich Heine, *Travel Pictures*, translated by Peter Wortsman. New York: Archipelago, 2008, p. 28.
40. *SP* p. 42.
41. Ibid. p. 68.
42. Heinrich Heine, *Travel Pictures*, op. cit., p. 25.
43. Hoffmann's *Nutcracker*, see Chapter 6, note 56.
44. *SP* p. 139.
45. This novel's first person narration, as of an autobiographer telling us his emotional life, can be seen as a progenitor of Andersen's *The Improvisatore*, if of a less marked nature than Tieck's *Franz Sternbalds Wanderungen*. Incest is there, in that the hero becomes engaged to a girl who turns out to be his sister.
46. It is worth noting that the first volume contains two fairy-tale plays (*Märchendramen*), one of which the lively, humorous *Der Gestiefelte Kater* (literally *The Booted Cat*, but we know it as *Puss-in-Boots*) is intended for children, and takes the ingenious form of a play within a play.
47. For a fuller plot summary, see Henry and Mary Garland, *The Oxford Companion to German Literature*. Clarendon Press: Oxford, 1976, pp. 238–239.
48. This view of him has lasted: e.g. Lord David Cecil speaks of Scott as sharing Shakespeare's sense of what is truly, rather than obviously, heroic. 'So also in the work of Scott, the novelist likest to Shakespeare, the humble Highland gillie Evan outshines the lordly head of the clan.' Lord David Cecil, *Library Looking-Glass*. London: Constable, 1975, p. 118.
49. Novalis (1772–1801) the pseudonym of Friedrich, Freiherr von Hardenburg, son of the Director of the Saxon Salten Mines in which business the poet himself worked. This was after university studies in Jena and Leipzig, where he became friendly with the literary critic/pundit Friedrich Schlegel and deeply influenced by Kant and Fichte. His personal life then took an extraordinary turn, inextricable from his art and subsequent reputation: he fell in love (in November 1794 – it can be precisely dated) with 12-year-old Sophie von Kühn who, some months later, contracted pulmonary tuberculosis. Novalis did all he could to effect a cure, but she died in 1797, as did a loved younger brother. The tragedies precipitated a crisis from which the poet emerged with a religious vision of his own, developed in remarkable works of literary art: *Hymnen an die Nacht* (*Hymns of the Night*, 1799) begotten by his double bereavement, the visionary extended prose-poems, *Die Lehringe zu Sais* (*The Novices of Sais*, 1800), and the unfinished novel *Heinrich von Ofterdingen* in which appears the symbol of the Blue Flower, so meaningful to subsequent Romantic poets. Schlegel and Tieck, as close friends, were responsible for collecting and editing his work after his early death (also from tuberculosis).
50. Heinrich von Kleist (1777–1811). As with Novalis, it was Ludwig Tieck who was responsible for the posthumous collected works of his friend, whose life had been a strained and difficult one with a tragic, if self-sought, ending. From an old military family, Kleist was both involved in, and repelled by, military life. A student of the works of philosophy of Kant and Fichte, he reacted against the faith in the future associated with the *Aufklärung*, and both his restless life – which included joining Napoleon's army when it was preparing to invade England, and later trying to join in a Prussian plot against Napoleon – and his works in several genres display a dark reading of man's ability to control his impulses or, by extension, his destiny. In drama his greatest work is his last, *Prinz Friedrich von Homburg* (1810), in the novel his proto-modernist novellas, *Michael Kolhaas* and *Die Marquise von O. . . .* (also 1810) and *Der Zweikampf* (*The Duel*, 1811). His friend Henriette Vogel asked him to kill her to spare her sufferings from a terminal illness; he shot her and then himself by the Wannsee, near Berlin.
51. Friedrich von Schlegel (1772–1829) and his elder brother August (1767–1845) were distinguished intellectuals, associated with the University of Jena, and with the definition of the Romantic, especially through the journal *Das Athenäum*, which they edited.
52. *SP* pp. 49–50.
53. *SP* p. 144.
54. 'And then – as always, in this extraordinary year [1840] – Schumann celebrated by working out another set of songs. This time, he drafted in the afternoons of just two days (11 and 12 July) his masterpiece for the female voice, the solo cycle *Frauenliebe und Leben* (Op. 42), in which a woman sings of her love and her loss. He set three more songs in the two days following (Op. 31); and then, between 16 and 18 July, in another astonishing rush of work he completed four more songs, the set

of translations by Chamisso of four Hans Christian Andersen texts published as Op. 40.' John Worthen, *Robert Schumann Life and Death of a Musician*. New Haven and London: Yale, 2007.

55. Jackie Wullschlager *HCA* p. 105. Her lively rendering of the correspondence cannot be bettered.

56. Ibid. p. 106.

57. Ibid. pp. 108–109.

58. The *locus classicus* for these major features of Norse mythology is *The Prose Edda* (written before 1223) of Snorri Sturluson (1179–1241). See Snorri Sturluson, translated with Introduction and notes by Jesse Byock. *The Prose Edda*, London: Penguin Classics, 2005, *Ragnarök* (also *Ragnarokr*) is briefly defined in its Glossary of Names, p. 172 as 'Darkness or Twilight of the Gods'. A.S. Byatt has brilliantly woven the ancient accounts of this eschatological event with a memory of her youthful self trying to comprehend world war, wholescale destruction and ideas of ending, in *Ragnarok*. Edinburgh: Canongate, 2011.

59. Glossary definition in Snorri Sturluson, *The Prose Edda*, London: Penguin Classics, 2005, p. 161, '*Gimle* (Gimlé: Protected from Fire) place where the righteous men will live after death.'

60. Though Andersen probably later modified his enthusiasm for this seminal Danish cleric, thinker and reformer, it will be remembered from Chapter 1 that he sent Grundtvig copies of his early poems.

61. Snorri Sturluson, op.cit., p. 71.

62. Ibid. p. 28.

63. Jens Andersen *HCA* pp. 143–147.

64. In conversation with the author.

65. See Marker, op.cit., especially pp. 42–43 and 78–83.

66. Ibid., especially pp. 44–45. Essentially 'an adaptation of Carlo Gozzi's play *Il corvo* (*The Crow*, 1761)', a work much admired by E.T.A Hoffmann, the 'production of *The Raven* in October 1832 was [notable] for its fine score by Denmark's foremost romantic composer, J.P.E Hartmann' (1805–1900). In a significant six-page review in *Neue Zeitschrift für Musik* (1840) of the publication by Musikforeningen of piano selections from *The Raven*, Robert Schumann warmly praised both Hartmann's music and Andersen's text: 'While all of Hartmann's music is permeated by depictions of the sea, *The Raven* in particular can basically be called an opera of the sea. Violent storms and ocean waves were vividly portrayed in Hartmann's score and in the staging.' Students of Andersen's imaginative writings will be interested in the importance to the work of the mermaids' choric warnings.

67. J[ohan] P[eter] E[milius] Hartmann came from a musical Copenhagen family of German origin. Andersen's almost exact contemporary (born 14 May 1805), he produced his first symphony (in G minor Op. 17) in the same year (1835) as Andersen's first novel and first book of fairy tales. Founding the Danish Musical Association in 1836 and chairing it his whole long lifetime through, he stood at the very centre of Danish musical activity, though he also enjoyed close association with German composers. Another operatic collaboration with Andersen, *Liden Kirsten* (*Little Kirsten*) Op. 44, 1844–46, was to prove the most successful Danish opera of the century.

68. A delightful lyrical suite of poems, this was published on 18 December 1832 (though dated 1833), the edition, illustrated in black and white, being dedicated – and indeed handed over in person – to His Majesty King Frederik VI. The poems make use of dialogue and of articulations by characters suitable for the time of year – e.g. a young gentleman on horseback for April. In the verses for the Christmas month, December, Ingeborg Drewsen (née Collin)'s children (lifelong favourites of Andersen), Viggo and Jonna make appearances, as does Louise Collin. The first complete reprint of the sequence is in Johan de Mylius's edition of *Samlede Digte* (*Collected Poems*). Copenhagen: Aschehoug, 2000.

69. *Y by Y*. Letter to Henriette Wulff, 16 February 1833.

70. *Y by Y* 1833/1834.

71. *D* p. 42.

72. Sven Hakon Rossel, *Do You Know the Land, Where the Lemon Trees Bloom? Hans Christian Andersen and Italy*. Rome: Edizioni Nuova Cultura, 2009. This rich, rewarding book covers, with great attention to detail, all aspects of Andersen's relationship to Italy, showing the many Italian motifs recurrent in his works, and discussing plays and poems as well as novels and tales. Readers are directed to its chapter on Andersen's last Italian journey of 1872 as especially illuminating. Also recommended by Sven Hakon Rossel: *Hans Christian Andersen: Danish Writer and Citizen of the World*. Amsterdam: Rodopi, 1996.

73. Thorvaldsen is inseparable from Andersen's reception of Italy, the kindness he showed him, the exceptional understanding of his social and professional position with its strong resemblance to his own of earlier years. Their friendship seems to have grown very quickly after their first meeting on 19 October 1833 (*D* p. 50). Four days later Thorvaldsen was one of those listening to Andersen read: 'Thorvaldsen seemed delighted, praised the harmony, the beautiful verses and the central idea of the work; asked me to read it for him at my leisure' (*D*, p. 54).

74. Hertz's attack on Andersen went on rankling for some time. In his diary for 22 September 1833 (*D* p. 47) he was writing, 'Hertz is, so to speak, a kind of poetical tinsmith, a tinker, although I don't want to go so far as to say that he tried to pass off on Copenhageners his highly polished tinny piece as gold.' So he was not best pleased to learn that Hertz was coming to Rome – he arrived on 21 November 1833 (*Y by Y*). But in fact he warmed to him, and they enjoyed each other's company, Hertz marvelling at Andersen's innocence – though the latter was intrigued and even titillated by Hertz's anecdotes and activities, this being especially true when the two of them were together in Naples in February 1834. But by 21 December 1833 he was recording: 'Hertz quite the confidant this evening! Gossiped about the theatre management and lechery' (*D* p. 62).

75. One of the invisible presiding spirits of *The Improvisatore*, in my view, and in his actual work as a painter, even more strongly of 'The Ice Maiden', as we shall see. We can, I believe, find something of Fearnley personally in the character of Bernardo in the first work, and, in the second, Andersen's intense, detailed yet atmospheric evocations of the Alps have a real correspondence to some of the artist's greatest works. For a fine survey and appreciation of Thomas Fearnley, his disposition as traveller and man of Europe, his Nordic background, his artistic 'apprenticeship' to Dahl, and his painterly discovery of, and homage to, Italian, Norwegian, English (he was hailed as a man of 'genius' on his 1836–38 visit to England, painting the Lake District with especial enthusiasm), and Swiss landscapes, see *In Front of Nature: The European Landscapes of Thomas Fearnley*, edited by Ann Sumner and Greg Smith. London: The Barber Institute of Fine Arts, University of Birmingham in association with D. Giles Ltd, 2012. There we can also get a picture of the man himself: 'this most avuncular and sociable of men' (ibid., p. 20), 'a serious artist who brought pleasure and a sense of well-being wherever he went. A man whose endearing qualities transcended boundaries, just as his work found popularity across the continent, making him in every sense a truly European artist.' These words could apply to Andersen too. But, unlike Andersen, 'well-being' went in Fearnley's case with a lively appreciation of the sensual, the carnal, and, like Hertz, he was positively worried by Andersen's virginal ways and thought he ought to be taken in hand. Andersen records for Christmas Eve 1833, 'Fearnley talked to Thorvaldsen about seducing me, about my innocence' (*D* pp. 63–64).

Chapter 3: *The Improvisatore*

1. *D* p. 65.
2. *D* p. 59.
3. Georgina Masson, *The Companion Guide to Rome*. London: Collins, 1965, pp. 41–42.
4. *D* p. 59.
5. See Avriel Goldberger, 'Introduction' to Madame de Staël, *Corinne or Italy*. New Brunswick, NJ: Rutgers University Press, 1987, pp. xxix–xxx.
6. 'Fata morgana' is a term for a mirage or illusion, especially on the sea, deriving from the Italian attribution of the phenomenon to the fairy Morgan le Fay, thought to be responsible for its appearance on the Straits of Messina. It has haunted many writers; in the 20th century. Eudora Welty called the Mississippi community in *The Golden Apples* (1949) 'Morgana' because of the illusions that dominate the lives of its inhabitants.
7. *D* p. 65.
8. William Wordsworth, *The Prelude* (1895 version), lines 305–306.
9. See Henry and Mary Garland, *The Oxford Companion to German Literature*. Oxford: Clarendon Press, 1976, p. 238–239 for a detailed plot summary.
10. *Imp* p. 33.
11. *Poems of Robert Browning 1842–1864*. London: Oxford University Press, 'The World's Classics', 1907, pp. 88–89.
12. *Imp* p. 133.
13. *Imp* p. 134.
14. *Imp* pp. 117–118.
15. *Imp* p. 133.
16. David Gilmour, *The Pursuit of Italy*. London: Allen Lane, 2011, especially pp. 137–147.
17. Laura Bandiera and Diego Saglia (eds), *British Romanticism and Italian Literature*. New York: Editions Rodopi, 2005, p. 176 ff.
18. *Imp* p. 182.
19. Ibid. p. 182.
20. David Gilmour, op. cit., p. 143.
21. *D* p. 75.
22. Andersen pays tribute to her in *MF-TL* p. 161.

23. 'Under the Willow-tree' (1853), rather diffusely made up of autobiographical elements and inspired (a little too obviously) by Andersen's relationship to Jenny Lind, centres on a young man, Knud, a cobbler by trade, who, as a boy in Køge, had fallen in love with his girl playmate, and maintained his love for her even after she had moved to nearby Copenhagen and already launched herself on her acting career. Johanne, though warmly disposed to him, feels for him as a sister feels for a brother. Learning this, Knud chooses not to stay in Denmark but instead travels on the Continent, working at his trade in various German cities. Eventually he comes to Milan and, after three peaceful industrious years there, is taken to the theatre and sees Johanne, the performance's incontrovertible star and, according to gossip, soon to make a society marriage. Knud forthwith journeys back to Denmark, but dies in winter snows, dreaming of a wedding to his loved one, before he reaches his homeland.

24. *D* p. 73.
25. *Imp* p. 184.
26. *Imp* p. 206.
27. *Imp* p. 219.
28. Thomas Fearnley also honoured both Vesuvius and Capri in some of his finest canvases. See the magnificent oil painting *Night View of Vesuvius Erupting*, 1834, reproduced in *In Front of Nature: The European Landscapes of Thomas Fearnley*, edited by Ann Sumner and Greg Smith. London: The Barber Institute of Fine Arts, University of Birmingham in association with D. Giles Ltd, 2012 p. 101. This brings Andersen's prose to mind. For Capri, look at *View at Capri (the Marina Piccola)* 1833 (ibid. p. 45) and *Coast Scene*, tentatively identified as Capri, 1833–34 (ibid. p. 47).
29. Giacomo Leopardi, *Canti,* translated by Jonathan Galassi. London: Penguin, 2010, p. 286.
30. Ibid. p. 306.
31. Ibid. p. 308.
32. Andersen based this fable about the ubiquitous craftiness of Cupid on a poem by the Greek lyricist Anacreon (6th century BCE). The poet taken by surprise by the naughty boy's arrow is surely a projection of the author himself (who, at that time particularly, had good reason to think of himself as a poet) as a kindly, cautious, elderly man.

Chapter 4: *O.T.*

1. *O.T.* p. 17.
2. *O.T.* p. 10.
3. *O.T.* p. 11.
4. Jens Andersen *HCA* p. 208.
5. *O.T.* p. 37.
6. The friendship between Arkady and Bazarov, between the essentially easy-going son of the gentry and his fellow student, a self-proclaimed nihilist, forms the axis of the novel and its most resonant metaphor. The two young men, who get on splendidly, provide significant contrasts in their attitudes to the opposite sex and love, to parents, to science and art, and to the future of their own society.
7. Far more even than his decidedly self-punishing obsession with Estella does Pip's relationship to his contemporary Herbert Pocket stand for the discrepancies within Victorian society. It shows how affection and common sense (and the firm good nature of one of the pair) help these to be borne and overcome. Herbert Pocket is an unflagging friend to Pip when faced with Magwitch; Vilhelm is never permitted the chance to be as helpful to Otto over *his* socially embarrassing connections.
8. *O.T.* p. 11.
9. This whole exchange to be found in *O.T.* p. 25.
10. *O.T.* p. 70.
11. *O.T.* p. 72.
12. *O.T.* p. 101.
13. *O.T.* p. 102.
14. *O.T.* p. 116.
15. *O.T.* p. 136.
16. *O.T.* p. 137.
17. *O.T.* p. 231.
18. *D* p. 96.
19. Jens Andersen *HCA* pp. 390–395.
20. Ibid. p. 391, with diary entry 8 February 1842. 'When I came home I found a letter from my mother's daughter; I experienced what I had described in *O.T.*'

21. *O.T.* p. 247.
22. Osvald says in *Ghosts* that everything he has painted turns on 'Livsglæden. Altid og bestandig om Livsglæden.' 'The joy in life. Always and without exception the joy in life.' And the word is taken up by his own mother, who realises what has been absent from the conventional Norwegian life around her.
23. *O.T.* p. 251.
24. *O.T.* p. 132.
25. *O.T.* p. 256.
26. *O.T.* p. 98.
27. *O.T.* p. 99.
28. *O.T.* p. 101.
29. *O.T.* p. 102.
30. *O.T.* p. 156.
31. The sensational success of *Hernani* was seemingly self-perpetuating, objectors and enthusiasts loudly interrupting its first hundred performances often to the point of making the actors inaudible. The eponymous Hernani is a Spanish outlaw whose rival for the hand of Donna Sol de Silva is, among others, none other than Don Carlos, later King of Spain and Holy Roman Emperor. After scenes of romantic excitement and clamorous verse, Hernani and Donna Sol achieve a *Liebestod.*
32. *O.T.* p. 255.
33. Stendhal, *The Red and the Black,* translated by Catherine Slater, Oxford: Oxford World's Classics, 1991, p. 26.

Chapter 5: *Eventyr, Fortalte for Børn* (*Fairy-Tales told for Children*)

1. 'Fyrtøiet' *E og H Vol I* p. 1.
2. 'Das Blaue Licht', 'The Blue Light' in the Brothers Grimm, *Kinder-und Hausmärchen,* 1815 and 1857. Here the soldier is, at least initially, a far more overtly sympathetic character than Andersen's, actually spurned (in so many words) by the king he has served, and then in his distress throwing himself on the witch's mercy afterwards. Again the witch herself is more thoroughly unkind, playing deceitful, malicious tricks on the young man. When the soldier has gained the lamp and the little man who emanates from it, he wants the wicked woman tried properly in a law court; her subsequent death, by hanging from the gallows, is none of his doing. But when he comes to the capital city he displays a thirst for revenge on the King far more explicit than anything in 'The Tinder Box'. The King's daughter will be his maidservant. The little man from the blue lamp grants him his wish, and this is only thwarted – the trick with the peas failing as in Andersen – by the shoe the princess has left behind being found in the soldier's room. As later in Andersen, the soldier is thrown into jail, and then appeals out of the cell window to a passer-by, in this case a comrade, to retrieve his bundle of possessions (with the lamp in it) from his lodgings. The soldier produces the lamp at the trial at which he has been condemned to death. Thanks to the little man, all the judiciary fall down, but the soldier yields to the King's pleas for mercy, on the condition (which is met) that he gets his kingdom and his daughter in marriage. Two good new English versions are to be found in Grimm, *The Juniper Tree and Other Tales,* translated by Anthea Bell. London: Pushkin Press, 2011, pp. 235–241 and *Selected Tales of the Brothers Grimm* translated by Peter Wortsman. New York: Archipelago Books, 2013, pp. 120–125.
3. *Tatar AA* p. 157.
4. *E og H Vol 1* p. 6.
5. Ibid. p. 6.
6. Ibid. p. 7.
7. Ibid. p. 9.
8. *D* p. 15.
9. 'Clumsy Hans'. Clumsy Hans has two wonderfully clever older brothers who decide to enter the competition set by the king's daughter: she will take as husband the man who has most to say to her. The two young men set out on fine horses to present themselves but, to their scorn, Clumsy Hans insists on going with them, mounted on a goat, to enter the contest. While his brothers are preparing their witty speeches, Hans is finding odd, seemingly insignificant, things on the roadway: a dead crow, a discarded broken shoe, the best kind of mud. . . The princess receives her suitors in an overheated room with aldermen and clerks to hand, to write everybody's amusing words down. She explains that the heat is caused by her father roasting chickens. All the young men, including Hans's two brothers, become tongue-tied on hearing this, but not so Hans himself. He says he will roast his dead crow alongside the chickens, will cook it in the shoe that has a tin heel he can use as

pot-handle, and he will use some of the mud as sauce. The rest of the mud he flings at the officious aldermen who don't respect him. He wins the princess.

10. 'What Father Does . . .' A happily married farmer decides that he must sell or barter their horse, and his wife agrees, because she believes that whatever he decides will be the right course. He swaps the horse for a cow, the cow for a sheep, the sheep for a large goose, the goose for the toll-keeper's clucking hen, the hen for a sack full of rotten apples (to feed pigs with). On this last he makes a bet with two Englishmen, who have been observing the transaction, that his wife will not be furious with him when he gets home. In fact she herself has been through a chain of swaps to make her husband an omelette on his return, and, for her own reasons, is happy to have the sack of rotten apples. The two Englishmen very happily hand over the money they now owe him, which is quite a tidy sum – so all's well that ends well if your wife really loves and admires you. Andersen presents the story as one he had heard when a little boy.

11. Jackie Wullschlager in her notes for *Hans Christian Andersen Fairy-Tales*, translated by Tiina Nunnally, edited and introduced by herself. London: Penguin Books, 2004, p. 424.

12. Paul Binding, *Imagined Corners: Exploring the World's First Atlas.* London: Hodder Headline, 2003, pp. 48–50.

13. 'Dødningen', 'The Ghost' is a prose story with the same plot as 'The Travelling Companion', which Andersen inserted into *Digte* (*Poems*), published on 2 January 1830.

14. 'Thumbelina', for all its coy sound thanks to the musical *Hans Christian Andersen*, is in fact as good a rendering of the Danish 'Tommelise' as you could have, the Danish for 'thumb' being tommelfinger.

15. Ancient Greek used the word 'psyche' to connote both the soul and the butterfly, for obvious reasons – its metamorphosis through caterpillar and chrysalis, its beauty, its ascent.

16. *E og H Vol I* p. 63.

17. This classic children's book (Part One 1906, Part Two 1907) by the Swedish Andersen-admirer Selma Lagerlöf (1858–1940) describes the adventures of a 14-year-old boy, Nils Holgersson, who because of his malicious conduct to an elf is metamorphosed into a midget. Trying to stop the farm gander from joining a migrating flock of wild geese, Nils jumps on its back, forgetting his stature, and thus makes a journey all the way up to the north of Sweden and back, learning the ways of birds and animals, and achieving a new compassionate moral sense as a result. His nickname among the geese is 'Tummetott' – *tumme* being the Swedish for thumb. A timely new and complete translation of *Nils Holgersson's Wonderful Journey through Sweden* by Peter Graves, was published by Norvik Press, London in 2013.

18. *E og H Vol 1* pp. 68–71.

19. Denmark's Lutheran Church retained the books of the Apocrypha, of which The Book of Tobit is one as part of the scriptural canon, unlike the Calvinists who rejected them.

20. *E og H Vol I* p. 68.

21. Ibid. p. 69.

22. In the very first moments of *A Doll's House*, Helmer playfully (and insensitively) likens his wife to a skylark and a squirrel, and the imagery persists, signifying that his possessive domestication of her is the same living death that captivity would mean for these wild creatures.

23. *The Oxford Ibsen Vol. VII*, edited by James Walter McFarlane. London: Oxford University Press, 1966, p. 62.

24. Ibid. p. 450.

25. Ibid. p. 449.

26. Jens Andersen *HCA* pp. 497–499.

27. See especially the whole of Act III of this masterpiece, with Alfred Allmers's accounts of his enlightenment up in the lonely mountains.

28. *The Oxford Ibsen Vol VII*, op. cit. pp. 449–450.

29. Katharine Briggs, *Dictionary of Fairies*, London: Allen Lane, 1976, pp. 287–289.

30. *E og H Vol I* p. 109.

31. Fouqué was also the author of a mythological trilogy, *Der Held des Nordens* (*The Hero of the North*, 1810), romantic plays in verse based on the Icelandic Eddas, which he read in the original. Fichte was the dedicatee.

32. *Undine*, translated by F.E. Bunnett. Milton Keynes: Lightning Source UK, 2011, p. 37.

33. Ibid. p. 42.

34. Ibid. p. 42

35. Ibid. p. 75.

36. Ibid. p. 84.

37. *E og H Vol I* p. 128.

38. Ibid. p. 130.

39. Ibid. p. 130.

40. See *Tatar AA* p. 120.
41. Heinrich Steinhöwel's *Esopus*, 1476, in Latin and German, is generally agreed to be the first inclusive scholarly compilation of Aesop in Europe.
42. Interestingly, Infante Don Juan Manuel also wrote a didactic novel he did not finish and an educational work for his own son, giving him advice on, among other matters, love.
43. Annette Madsen's essay is to be found in Johan de Mylius, Aage Jørgensen and Viggo Hjørnager Pedersen (eds), *Hans Christian Andersen. A Poet in Time. Papers from the Second International Hans Christian Andersen Conference 29 July to 2 August 1996*, Odense: Odense University Press, 1999.
44. *E og H Vol I* p. 136.
45. Ibid. p. 135.
46. Ibid. p. 141.
47. These two poems of Wordsworth's are placed side by side in *Lyrical Ballads*, 1798. In 'Anecdote for Fathers' the child finally tells his father why he prefers Liswyn farm to 'Kilve by the green sea'; it is because the first has a weathercock that fascinates him. The little girl in 'We Are Seven' refuses to make a distinction between her living siblings and her deceased ones. The closing stanza of the first of the pair is particularly apt for the Romantic/early 19th-century evaluation of the wisdom of the uncorrupted child: 'Oh dearest, dearest boy! My heart/For better lore would seldom yearn,/Could I but teach the hundredth part/Of what from thee I learn.'
48. *E og H Vol I* p. 141.

Chapter 6: *Kun en Spillemand* (*Only a Fiddler*) and 'Den Standhaftige Tinsoldat' ('The Steadfast Tin Soldier')

1. *Y by Y* 1836.
2. *Y by Y* 1836.
3. Jens Andersen *HCA* pp. 340–342.
4. *KES* p. 9.
5. Ibid.
6. Svendborg, now linked to the islands by a bridge, is virtually a recurrent character in the novel. The larger of the two ports on the southern coast of Fyn, it has a thriving, lively feel to it; see *The Rough Guide to Denmark*, London, 2010.
7. *KES* p. 62.
8. *KES* p. 78.
9. *KES* p. 273.
10. Knud V. Jespersen, *A History of Denmark*, translated by Ivan Hill and Christopher Wade. Basingstoke and New York: Palgrave Macmillan, 2011, pp. 61–63.
11. *KES* p. 62.
12. For a full study, see Jesse Russell and Ronald Cohn, *The Battle of Bornhöved* (1813) – German spelling of the Danish name used – VSD (Book on Demand) Publishing, 2012.
13. Hugely influenced by the thought and writings of Ludwig Tieck and Wilhelm Heinrich Wackenroder, the Nazarenes – also known as the Lukasbund or Lukasbrüder (the Brotherhood of St Luke) – were a group of German painters who believed in a return to the art and values of the German and Italian Primitives, revered Dürer and admired the earlier Raphael. Founded in Vienna in 1809 by Friedrich Overbeck (1789–1869), a painter Andersen himself considered 'probably the greatest painter of our day', (*D* p. 63), and Franz Pforr (1788–1812) – a writer whose early death affected the group's development – they moved to Rome the following year (1810). Here they were joined by Peter von Cornelius (1783–1867) and resided for a while in a monastery. They interested themselves greatly in the art of fresco, Cornelius in particular striving for a revival of ambitious, publicly prominent painting (see his *Last Judgement* in Munich's Ludwigskirche). The affinities, both ideological and actual, with the group of the English Pre-Raphaelites (founded 1848) will be obvious even from this brief description.
14. *Y by Y* 1810. The little Jewish girl at Fedder Carsten's school in Odense especially for Jewish children who stands behind Naomi was called Sara Heimann.
15. *KES* p. 18.
16. Ibid. p. 19.
17. Ibid. p. 23.
18. Ibid. p. 60.
19. Emily Brontë's *Wuthering Heights* was published in 1847. Perhaps Q.D. Leavis was the first to argue (in 'A Fresh Approach to Wuthering Heights', *Lectures in America*, 1969) that behind this great novel stands Shakespeare's tragedy *King Lear*, and an attempt, never completely carried out by the author, to transpose it into northern English life at the turn of the 18th/19th centuries. Thus

Heathcliff, brought back from Liverpool by Mr Earnshaw, is his son, the bastard he favours above his legitimate one, just as Shakespeare's Gloucester does his bastard Edmund. Hence he is Cathy's half-brother. The related themes of half-siblings and incest fascinated the 19th-century mind; the age became more determinedly respectable as society, under the pressures of progress and urbanisation, grew at once more tangled and more ruthlessly divided.

20. *KES* p. 30. In Greek mythology, Amphion was a musician who built the walls of Thebes by charming the stones into position with his (Orphic) lyre.

21. See Daniel M. Grimley, *Grieg Music, Landscape and Norwegian Identity.* Woodbridge: The Boydell Press, 2006. Emphasising the profound effect of Bull as musician and cultural icon for Grieg, Grimley draws attention to important ambivalences within Bull which apply not only to Grieg himself but also to Andersen in his double role of both promoter of Nordic (Danish) tradition and European innovator: 'As a historical musical figure, Bull reflects many of the tensions and oppositions within the idea of a Norwegian musical identity. His career as a virtuoso classical violinist placed him very much within a cosmopolitan context as a touring international professional. From this perspective his interest in Norwegian folk music was simply another form of exoticism. . . . But his enthusiasm for French revolutionary politics and his direct support of folk musicians . . . also had a catalysing influence on folklorism in Norway itself, where Bull was increasingly seen as a national hero' (p. 35).

22. The letter from Andersen to Bull of 8 December 1838 is reproduced on Peter Sheppard Skærved's webpage: Ole Bull in H.C. Andersen's 'Billedbog', posted 16 October 2012. Address: www.peter-sheppard-skaerved.com.

23. Nøkken (Nøkk)/Nix/ Nixie/Neck/Näck are all Germanic names found in Germany, the Nordic countries and Britain for a shape-shifting water spirit, usually male and related to the Kelpie and the Water Horse (who assumes humanoid disguises). Nøkken haunts lakes, streams and waterfalls and likes to play seductive music on the fiddle, principally to entice women and girls, not necessarily for malevolent purposes. See Katharine Briggs, *A Dictionary of Fairies.* London: Allen Lane, 1976. Andersen, in linking Christian's godfather (and Ole Bull) to this spirit, is being entirely consistent with known folkloric beliefs.

24. *KES* p. 66.

25. Ibid. p. 103.

26. Ibid. p. 104.

27. For information and critical insight into Fredrika Bremer, see Sarah Death's translation and commentary on *The Colonel's Family* (in Swedish *Familjen H****, 1831). Norwich: Norvik Press, 1995.

28. Jens Andersen *HCA*, p. 345, comments illuminatingly on the significance of the name, saying that the word *Karreet* ('cart') would have signalled her membership of the prostitute class to most Danish readers of the day.

29. *KES* p. 123.

30. Ibid. p. 125.

31. Ibid. p. 126.

32. Ibid. p. 43.

33. For English-language readers, *From the Papers of One Still Living* (ironically subtitled 'Published Against His Will') was included in *Early Polemical Writings* by Søren Kierkegaard, NJ edited and translated by Julia Watkin. Princeton: Princeton University Press, 1990.

34. Op. cit. p. 99.

35. Ibid. p. 98.

36. Ibid. p. 99.

37. Ibid. p. 100.

38. *KES* p. 247.

39. *O.T.* p. 30.

40. Stendhal, *The Red and the Black,* translated by Catherine Slater. Oxford: Oxford World's Classics, 1991, p. 195.

41. *KES* p. 156.

42. Ibid. pp. 187–188.

43. Ibid. p. 196.

44. Théophile Gautier, *Mademoiselle de Maupin,* translated and edited by Helen Constantine with an introduction by Patricia Duncker. London: Penguin Classics, 2005, p. xii.

45. Op. cit. p. 166.

46. *KES* p. 225.

47. *MF-TL* p. 171.

48. *KES* p. 247.

49. The first night was an enormous success with its audience; this included Frédéric Chopin, who declared Meyerbeer destined for immortality. The libretto of this first French 'grand' opera – set in

medieval Sicily – was by the acclaimed and influential dramatist, Eugène Scribe (1791–1861). By citing Naomi's presence at this great occasion – which ushered in a tremendous run of successes for the work – Andersen is signalling Naomi's embrace of all that is triumphantly fashionable.

50. Possibly the creation of the celebrated international Danish choreographer Pierre Jean Laurent (1758–1831).

51. These two operas, written in succession, were, though Andersen could not have known it, the culmination of Rossini's life as an opera composer. *Le Comte d'Ory*, a comedy opera, dates from 1828, *William Tell*, a heroic one, from 1829. Born in 1792, Rossini lived until 1868. He wrote no operas but occasional pieces, including, for piano, a Stabat Mater (completed 1842) and a *Petite Messe Solonelle* in 1863.

52. *Y by Y* 1833 and 1841. Andersen's own first meeting with Victor Hugo was on 19 August 1833. His friendship with Alexandre Dumas (père) flourished in March and April 1841.

53. *KES* p. 257.

54. Ibid. p. 275.

55. *E og H Vol I* pp. 191–192.

56. E.T.A Hoffmann, *The Nutcracker and the Mouse King* included in *The Nutcracker & The Strange Child*, translated from the German by Anthea Bell. London: Pushkin Press, 2010, pp. 17–20.

57. *E og H Vol I* p. 193.

58. Ibid. p. 194.

59. Ibid. p. 196.

60. Ibid. p. 196.

61. Ibid. p. 196.

62. Thomas Mann, *The Letters of Thomas Mann 1889–1955*, selected and translated by Richard and Clara Winston. Harmondsworth: Penguin Books, 1975, p. 472.

Chapter 7: *En Digters Bazar* (*A Poet's Bazaar*)

1. *EDB* pp. 26–27.

2. *Y by Y* 1840.

3. *EDB* p. 26.

4. Ibid. p. 27.

5. Ibid. pp. 26–27.

6. This is amusingly both contradicted and confirmed by the anecdote Andersen tells (Chapter X) of seeing in a bookshop window a copy of *The Improvisatore* in German and going inside to ask the bookseller for a copy. He is handed a slim volume containing only the first part. When Andersen observes that the book isn't complete, the vendor assures him it is – and that modern writers (French writers, he cites) delight in not concluding their novels conventionally and leaving the readers to use their imagination. 'Jeg har *læst* den!' says the bookseller (*EDB* p. 43), 'I have *read* it!' 'Men jeg har *skrivet* den!' replies Andersen. 'But I have written it!'

7. 'Metalsvinet' ('The Bronze Pig') forms Chapter III of Part Two 'Italien', 'Italy' of the travelogue, pp. 62–72. This is a somewhat sentimental story about an embryonic artist, a poor slum-boy, child of a harsh, slatternly mother forced by hunger into begging. Given to affectionately embracing the bronze cast of the statue of a pig, the latter comes to life to give the child a magical nocturnal tour of Florence. The tour includes the great monuments of the city's Renaissance culture, but nothing impresses the boy more than a painting by Agnolo Bronzino (1503–72) in the Uffizi, showing Christ surrounded by children as if to assure them they will all go to Heaven. Removed from his background, the beggar-boy is adopted by a glover and his wife, though the latter demonstrably prefers her pet pug Bellissima to him and is angry with the boy when he captures the dog in order to draw her. Befriended by an older artist – like Antonio in *The Improvisatore* – the boy grows up to be a great painter but dies young. His two best-known works, we are told, depict Bellissima and a ragged small boy leaning against the Bronze Pig.
   The other two stories are 'Venskapspakten' ('Friendship's Pact'), see note 40, and the extended prose-poem – or rhapsodic essay – in Part IV, 'En Rose fra Homers Grav', 'A Rose from Homer's Grave', which Andersen liked sufficiently to include with the other two in the first German edition of his *Collected Stories*, then in the Danish.

8. *D* p. 96.

9. Karl Gutzkow. Their mutual mounting literary fame apart, Gutzkov, as later shown, was an unlikely friend for Andersen to make. A radical by conviction from the lower ranks of society (his father was a groom), Gutzkov was inspired by the July Revolution of 1830 into a career of polemical journalism, with writings that provoked prosecution for blasphemy – his 1835 novel about an emancipated woman, *Wally die Zweiflerin*, and plays (18 in number) challenged political and social orthodoxies and often drew on his own complicated, sometimes hectic, sexual/emotional life,

including a charged triangular relationship. He was a supporter of, though not an active participant in, the 1848 Revolution in Prussia, which provided the creative impetus and indeed the subject matter for a 9-volume novel of enormous ambition, *Die Ritter vom Geiste* (*The Knights of the Spirit*) which he believed marked a new departure for fiction, and is, by its admirers, seen as crucial to the German social novel. All in all, it is not surprising that he cared little for Andersen's writing, and when the two were both guests at the Danish aristocratic estate of Maxen, he was bold and unkind enough to tell him so. 'Irked by Gutzkov,' wrote Andersen on 18 June 1856 (*D* p. 245): 'At the dinner-table Gutzkov tried to pick a quarrel with me about "Under the Willow-tree" – it was sentimental, forced; Christian [hero] was stupid; I had no understanding of children! I defended myself and said he hadn't understood the work or read it deeply enough.' The two men seem to have made it up next day. Gutzkov's later years were marred by depression and paranoia.

10. Franz Liszt (1811–86). A prodigy, Liszt was playing the piano in public at the age of nine and was sent to Vienna to study. By the time Andersen met him, he had composed his still popular two piano concertos (No. 1, 1830, revised 1849; No. 2, 1839), lived in Paris, made three spectacularly successful tours of England, and had cohabited with the Comtesse d'Agoult, fathering three children by her, one of whom Cosima, would marry (1870) Richard Wagner as her second husband. Andersen was to get to know Liszt when he became a frequent visitor to Weimar, where the composer directed opera and gave and organised concerts, as well as pursuing his own work

11. Regiomontanus (1436–76), the name by which the great German mathematician and astronomer Johannes Müller became known. He settled in Nuremberg in 1471 where he acquired a rich patron, founded algebra and trigonometry as academic studies in Germany, and worked on the *Alphonsine Tables* and the *Ephemeride,* which Christopher Columbus consulted. He inspired the same admiration in Andersen that he had felt for his great countryman Tycho Brahe.

12. Hans Sachs (1494–1576). It was only to be expected that Andersen would have a fellow feeling for this extraordinarily creative man, accredited with 6,300 literary compositions. He was reared to be a shoemaker, and for five years practised his trade as an itinerant throughout Germany, then establishing himself as a cobbler back in his native Nuremberg, where he rose to become a master of his guild. He was also a youthful member of the Guild of Meistersingers, and his enormous output contains many *Meisterlieder* as well as probably 200 verse-dramas in many categories: tragedies, comedies and *Fastnachtspiele* (plays for Shrovetide). Like his friend Dürer, Sachs was a strong Protestant: his poem *Die Wittenbergisch Nachtingall* (*The Wittenberg Nightingale*) celebrates Luther; he wrote proselytising dialogues; and the poem he composed when he thought he was dying, *Summa all meiner Gedicht* (*The Summa of all my Poetry*, 1567), stresses the religious purpose of his creations. Interest in him was revived by Goethe, and he was apostrophised in Wagner's opera *Die Meistersinger von Nürnberg* (begun in 1848 but finished in 1868: *The Mastersingers of Nuremberg*).

13. Albrecht Dürer (1471–1528). It is tempting in view of Andersen's great admiration for Dürer to see some correspondences between the two men, and to think that Andersen appreciated them. Both were masters of all forms of their art, and in both cases posterity has treasured their innovative contributions to a smaller-scale genre rather than the initially more acclaimed larger-scale ones, for all their acknowledged merits. Dürer's engravings *Melancholia 1, St Jerome, The Knight, Death and the Devil* and his woodcut *Apocalypse* have become part of the Western mind's treasury in much the same way as Andersen's best-known fairy tales have. Dürer was a man of wide curiosity and a great traveller, and he associated with many of the most distinguished men of his day, including Erasmus and Melanchthon, whose portraits he painted.

14. On 7 December 1835 the steam-hauled Bavarian Ludwig Railway was opened between Nuremberg and Fürth, and with it German railway history. The locomotive in use – 'Adler', ('Eagle') – was actually built in Britain, by Stephenson & Co. in Newcastle upon Tyne. It is pleasing to think that the first German railway, celebrated here, and the first of Andersen's fairy stories date from the same year.

15. See note 13 of Chapter 6, above; Cornelius's devotion to monumental public art was outstanding and trend-setting.

16. Enormously admired though his large-scale cartoon *Hunnenschlacht* (*The Battle of the Huns*) was, Kaulbach's fame has not survived his death in 1874. From 1849 he was Director of the Munich Academy of Art, and a son, a nephew and a great-nephew of his all became established painters.

17. 'Engelen' ('The Angel'), first published separately on 11 November 1843, and then in *Nye Eventyr. Første Bind. Første Samling* (*New Fairy Tales. First Volume, First Collection*), 1844.

18. Mantua suffered repeatedly in the Napoleonic Wars, surrendering to the French for two years, being retaken by the Austrians, and then retaken in 1810 by Napoleon again before returning to Austrian control in 1814. Reaction against Austrian rule intensified in the 1840s, swelling to sustained revolt in 1851–1855, that was brutally put down. Andersen, therefore, in lighting on Mantua's feelings of unease is giving us a cameo of proto-Risorgimento Italy. Of course the city would have interested him for cultural reasons, as the birthplace of Virgil and seat of the Gonzaga

family, patrons in the course of time of such major artists as Andrea Mantegna, and later the composer Monteverdi.

19. *Y by Y* 1840 and 1841.
20. *EDB* p. 88.
21. Ibid. p. 110. It is 6 January, Epiphany, celebrated in Italy – still – with the figure of La Befana, an old lady, distributing presents to children. Andersen, remembering his previous stay in Rome and literary tribute to the occasion, had expected to be delighted, but this time felt disgust. It shows perhaps a commendable maturing in Andersen as observer, no longer carried away by enthusiasm simply by being abroad.
22. In *EDB* he describes this charming-sounding ceremony as more comic than uplifting. The description actually uses many of the words of his diary entry for 17 January 1841. Though he thought the sight of the peasant boys seated near the tails of the donkeys about to be blessed to be picturesque, he didn't like their pricking an animal belonging to an old lady with long pins, hurting the poor creature so much that soldiers had to intervene. This must have reminded him of the cruelty of street-boys in many societies – for instance, those in Odense who had so teased his demented grandfather.
23. In fact *The Moorish Girl*, first night 18 December 1840, ran for only three performances. The whole episode of its poor reception and Andersen's attempt to justify himself and his creation in a printed apologia for it brought a renewal of ridicule down on the author's head. Frederick J. Marker, *Hans Christian Andersen and the Romantic Theatre*. Toronto: University of Toronto Press, 1971, judiciously concludes: 'Separating evidence from outraged sensibilities, however, *The Moorish Girl* is clearly inferior to most of Andersen's other plays. Although the dramatist styled this five-act drama a "tragedy", its theme and use of background music composed by Hartmann bring it closer to the category of conventional melodrama. Raphaella, a Spanish Saint Joan figure, who wins the love of the King of Cordova after saving his life in a battle against the Moors but who flees from his proposal of marriage on patriotic grounds, is basically a stock melodramatic heroine with "ugly duckling" overtones' (p. 51).
24. This squib, 'En Sjæl efter Døden', 'A Soul After Death' appeared in J.L. Heiberg's *Nye Digte* (*New Poems*), available in December 1840, though officially not published until January 1841.
25. The first 20 stories of *Billedbog uden Billeder* had been published on 20 December 1839. 'What the Moon Saw' was (appropriately enough) the title under which the sequence appeared in English: *What the Moon Saw and other Stories*, translated by H.W. Dulcken. London: Routledge, 1866.
26. *Billedbog uden Billede.* Copenhagen: Reitzel, 1845, pp. 3–4.
27. Ibid. pp. 5–6.
28. Ibid. pp. 11–12.
29. Ibid. pp. 49–51.
30. Ibid. pp. 13–15.
31. Ibid. pp. 23–25.
32. Ibid. pp. 39–41.
33. Harlequin (Arlecchino), Columbine (Colombina, 'little dove') and Pulcinella (anglicised as Punch) are all stock central characters in Italian 17th-century *commedia dell' arte* and had a major bearing on Andersen's 1846 story 'The Shadow', in the commentary and notes on which further details about them will be found. Harlequin is the canny comic servant, Columbine his wife or mistress, of the upper servant order, who often aids her employer, the *inamorata*, in the pursuit of her love-object. Pulcinella is characterised by his large, unsightly nose and his attire mimetic of the conjunction of life and death, white garments surmounted by a face masked in black. Stravinsky made him the central figure in his eponymous ballet for Diaghilev of 1920, based on music by Pergolesi (or ascribed to him).
34. Constantin Hansen (1804–80). Though he grew up in Copenhagen, Hansen was actually born in Rome, the son of a Danish portrait-painter. His christening, though, took place in Vienna where Mozart's widow was his godmother. Family tragedy made establishing his career in his twenties a hard task, but, like Andersen himself, he received stipends to travel abroad, and became one of the best known of Denmark's Golden Age painters. He spent eight years in Italy altogether, associating with Bertel Thorvaldsen and Christen Købke among others. He married in 1846 and had thirteen children, five of whom died young, four as babies, one at the age of 19. His deep interest in nation-building Norse-based mythology informs his historical and public paintings.
35. Albert Küchler (1803–86). Born and educated in Copenhagen, Küchler went to Rome in 1830, and established himself as a member of the Scandinavian colony there, being popular and lively. His portrait of Andersen dates from Andersen's own sojourn in Rome (1833–34) and strongly conveys the impression of a sensitive, spiritually minded but determined young man. His own work at this time chiefly consisted of genre pictures of local life. In 1844 he became a Catholic convert, and

eventually went to live in the San Bonaventura Monastery in Rome. Here he was visited by many of his compatriots, including fellow artists and members of the Danish royal family.

36. Michael Gottlieb Bindesbøll (1800–51) a pre-eminent architect of the Danish Golden Age, responsible for one of Copenhagen's greatest monuments, the Thorvaldsens Museum (constructed 1838–48). Influenced by H.C. Ørsted, and himself a nephew of Jonas Collin, he went to Rome and joined the Scandinavian colony in 1834, also visiting Greece to study ancient architecture. Jonas Collin was one of the champions of his design for the museum, mooted as early as 1833. He served as Royal Buildings Inspector in Copenhagen in 1851.

37. Ditlev Conrad Blunck (1798–1853), a Golden Age Danish painter who, like Hansen, also celebrated the Scandinavian colony in Rome – in his painting (c.1836) *Danish Artists on the Osteria La Gensola in Rome*. Influenced by the Nazarenes, he increasingly turned to religious motifs. A homosexual scandal caused him to leave Denmark in 1841, never to return. A Holsteiner, he supported Schleswig-Holstein in the Three Years War.

38. For all details of the itinerary see *Y by Y* 1841.

39. Athens had suffered considerably as a city under Ottoman rule, and was largely chosen as capital of a free Greece because of its incomparable past. It probably had at the time about 12,000 inhabitants. Both the modest size and the squalor of many parts surprised visitors unfavourably. But when Andersen stayed there, the University (1837) had been built, and the National Gardens were open, while the National Library and Royal Palace under construction. Andersen's response to Athens is evoked in *EDB* pp. 175–221 and his rather rosy impression of the king pp. 204–207.

40. 'Venskapspakten', 'Friendship's Pact' is probably most memorable for its evocation of the countryside near Delphi where a stream descending from Mount Parnassus itself flows near the peasant hut which is the narrator's childhood home. Also it vividly sketches what life in an occupied country is like – Turkish-ruled Greece – and the discontent and disruptions that result. But psychologically the story is of the greatest interest to a student of Andersen's psychology. It centres round the pact of the title, an oath of brotherhood between two friends taken in a solemn ceremony presided over (as priestess) by whichever girl of the neighbourhood is judged the most virtuous and beautiful. In the case of the vow taken by the young sailor Aphtanides and the narrator, the girl in question, Anastasia, is the latter's adopted sister whom he has loved – with an ever-increasing intensity – since she was brought naked into the house after being rescued by his father from a Turkish massacre. The reader is half led to expect a tragic outcome to the dilemma posed by the fact that Anastasia is also the object of his pact-friend's love. But Aphtanides is generous – literally so – he gives the narrator money to facilitate his marriage. It's as if – by an ingenious twist of the personnel – Edvard Collin had facilitated Andersen's marriage to his sister, Louise or Christian Voigt had bestowed Riborg on him.

41. *EDB* pp. 239–231.

42. By the end of the decade, 1850, Constantinople was estimated to have 785,000 inhabitants, and was cosmopolitan, progressive, expanding.

43. For *Tanzimât*, see James L. Gelvoin, *The Modern Middle East*. Oxford: Oxford University Press, 2008.

44. *EDG* pp. 165–166.

45. Ibid. p. 257.

46. Kustendje, the name for the Black Sea port once called Tomis – a Greek colony in Scythia, where reputedly Jason and the Argonauts landed after capturing the Golden Fleece, later taken over by the Romans. Ovid was banished there in 8 CE by Emperor Augustus and lived there, writing, until his death in 17 CE. The city was then named after Constantia, the half-sister of Constantine the Great. Largely Romanian (Wallachian)-speaking in Andersen's day, it is now not only Romania's largest port but the largest of all Black Sea ports.

47. Jason and his companions sailed across the Black Sea in their ship *Argo* to Colchis (in today's Georgia) in order to seize the Golden Fleece. This task was accomplished partly due to the aid of the Colchian princess, Medea, whom Jason proceeded to marry. She avenged herself on Jason when he deserted her, by killing her rival and their children. Jason died when a fragment of the *Argo* fell on his head. His adventures were commemorated in the Alexandrian-Hellenic epic by Apollonius of Rhodes (*fl.* 3rd century BCE), For an account of *The Argonauts* see Peter Levi: *A History of Greek Literature*. Harmondsworth: Viking Penguin, 1985, pp. 420–423 ff.). It contains enough geographical details and oddities to have delighted Andersen, who evokes Jason and the Argonauts rhapsodically in accounts of his Black Sea voyage. Andersen was naturally very pleased when the ship taking him up the Danube turned out to be called the *Argo*.

48. Ovid (Publius Ovidius Naso) 43 BCE–17 CE). Ovidn had already written six books of his *Metamorphoses* and tried to regain favour with the Emperor Augustus when he was sent into permanent exile by the latter in Tomis on the Black Sea. The reason for the expulsion is still unclear. See R.O.A.M. Lyne on 'Ovid'. *The Oxford History of the Classsical World* edited by John Boardman, Jasper Griffin and Oswyn Murray. Oxford/New York: Oxford University Press, 1986.

49. *EDB* pp. 285–289.
50. For the outlined itinerary see *Y by Y* 1841.
51. Following, unrest, Wallachia was placed under Russian military administration by the Treaty of Adrianople, 1829, without removing it from suzerainty to the Ottoman Empire. By the time of Andersen's visit, Wallachia traded outside the Empire, and had grown economically and demographically. The years ahead were difficult: Gheorghe Bibescu, elected to the throne, proved less than supportive of 'Romanian' language-based clamour for national independence (union with the Moldavians), and the popular dissatisfaction culminated in the Wallachian Revolution of 1848. The Wallachian language (of the Romance group) – which Andersen's young friend Adam Marco speaks – is what today would be termed Romanian, but was written (until 1860) in the Cyrillic, not Latin, alphabet.
52. *EDB* pp. 297–308.
53. Rustzuk is today Bulgaria's fifth town in size, and connected to Romanian Giurgiu by the Ruse-Giurgiu Friendship bridge, the only bridge spanning the Bulgarian and Romanian stretch of the Danube. Rustzuk was to be the birthplace of Elias Canetti (1905–94), who came from a Sephardic (Ladino-speaking) family.
54. *EDB* pp. 308–313. For further information about Serbia and the Balkans, see Misha Glenny, *The Balkans 1804–1999*. London: Granta, 1999.
55. The Iron Gates is the gorge on the Danube that forms the frontier of Romania (to the north) and Serbia (to the south) separating the Carpathians (Romanian) from the Balkans (Serbian). Navigation of this narrow stretch of river was severely impeded by rocks and not improved until the late 19th century.
56. *EDB* pp. 315–321.
57. Ibid. pp. 327–328.
58. Felix Mendelssohn-Bartholdy (1809–1847), co-dedicatee with Tieck of the German section of this travelogue, would in the year of his entertaining Andersen publish four books of his famous *Songs Without Words* for piano. His Symphony 2, *Lobgesang*, 'Hymn of Praise' had come out the previous year (1840) and his engaging Symphony 3, 'The Scotch', today still firmly in the concert repertoire, would appear in the following one (1842).
59. *EDB* p. 365.
60. *Y by Y* 1841.

Chapter 8: The Canonical Stories

1. Bruno Bettelheim, *The Uses of Enchantment*. London: Thames and Hudson, 1976; Harmondsworth: Penguin 1978, pp. 104–105.
2. The others are 'Engelen' ('The Angel'), 'Nattergalen' ('The Nightingale') and 'Kjærestefolkene' ('The Sweethearts'). The print run (850 copies) sold out immediately, as did the reprint the next month (December 1843).
3. *Y by Y* 1842.
4. *My Fairy-Tale Life*: 'At the homes of what are called the leading families in the country I met a number of cordial, friendly people who valued the good qualities they found in me and accepted me in their circles, allowing me during the summer to share in their good fortune . . . It was there I really got to know the Danish countryside. . . . Here, I was not a poor child of the people: no, I was a guest who received a kindly welcome.' pp. 235–236. Gisselfeld had formerly been a monastery, Christmas in the big house was hospitable and Nordic in style, and Andersen, like its owners, loved the beech-woods all around. Visit www.gisselfeld-kloster.dk.
5. *The Bird in the Pear Tree* debuted on 4 July 1842 with a total of six performances, and despite the good initial response aroused vitriolic reactions, some of it orchestrated by Heiberg, even though his wife Johanne was taking the leading role of Henriette. Frederick J. Marker in *Hans Christian Andersen and the Romantic Theatre*, Toronto: University of Toronto Press, 1971, considers it one of 'Andersen's most delightful plays' (p. 133), a vaudeville calling for ingenious staging. '[The] quarrel of two neighbours provides the comic background for the amorous intrigue of Herman and Henriette; here, too, love surmounts all obstacles, including a fence erected between the feuding neighbours' gardens and figuring prominently in the action. A high point in this atmospheric genre sketch is Andersen's rich characterization of Counsellor Arents, who in spite of his basically friendly nature becomes entangled in the neighbour['s] dispute over the pear-tree' (p. 36).
6. The chapter of *My Fairy-Tale Life* quoted in note 4 continues: 'From Gisselfeld I went to the splendid, charming manor of Bregentved, where I was invited by Count Wilhelm Moltke, Danish Minister of Finance of beloved and blessed memory. The hospitality I met there, the happy, domestic life in which I shared, brought sunshine into my life.' Visit www.bregentved.dk.
7. *E og H Vol 1* p. 365.

8. Ibid for both phrases.
9. Hans Andersen [*sic*], *Forty-two Stories* translated from the Danish by M. R. James. London: Faber, 1930. From 'The Ugly Duckling': 'Round the fields and meadows there were large woods and within them deep lakes; indeed, it was pleasant out in the country. Full in the sunshine, an old manor house stood.'
10. *E og H Vol I* p. 368.
11. See *The Complete Book of British Birds*. Basingstoke and Sandy: RSPB, 1988/1998, pp. 96–97.
12. The two wild geese have been identified as two companions of Andersen's, see p. 201. See also *Tatar AA* p. 107. Bagger's somewhat reckless life, marked by alcohol addiction and marital upheaval, was indeed to end sadly, like his surrogate here, in early death, brought about by recalcitrant elements in his very nature, so the incident here is uncomfortably prophetic.
13. Marie Tatar points out (*Tatar AA* p. 108): 'The old woman plays a subordinate role in the household, with the purring cat and egg-laying hen serving as master and mistress.' This only compounds the claustrophobia of the cottage from which the duckling has, for his own sake, to escape.
14. *E og H Vol I* p. 375.
15. Jack Zipes *Hans Christian Andersen The Misunderstood Storyteller*. New York and London: Routledge, 2005, pp. 69–70. Zipes goes so far as to say, 'The fine line between eugenics and racism fades in this story where the once-upon-a-time dominated swan reveals himself a tame but noble member of a superior race.' It is hard to argue against this, but I hope my argument – that the conceit is primarily about the artists and art in an increasingly philistine world – does something to mitigate the charge.
16. Georg Brandes's three-part examination of Andersen in the summer of 1869, 'H.C. Andersen som Æventyrdigter' ('H.C. Andersen as fairy-tale writer'), appeared in *Illustreret Tidende* on 11 July, 18 July and 25 July. See Elias Bredsdorff, *H.C. Andersen and Georg Brandes*. Copenhagen: Aschehoug, 1994, pp. 40ff.
17. *E og H Vol I* p. 379.
18. Zipes, op. cit. p. 70. 'In appealing to the "noble" sentiments of a refined audience and his readers, Andersen reflected a distinct class bias if not classical racist tendencies.'
19. Jens Andersen *HCA* p. 231.
20. Elizabeth Barrett Browning (1806–1861) wrote her own poetic tribute to Andersen. Dated 'Rome, May 1861', 'The North and the South' was in fact her last poem. In its dialogue between the two opposites it stresses the need of the North (Northern Europe) for the sun and fecundity of the South (Southern Europe). Its last two stanzas read: ' "And O, for a steer to discern the same!" ' Sigh'd the South to the North;/"For a poet's tongue of baptismal flame,/To call the tree or the flower by its name!"/ Sigh'd the South to the North.' 'The North sent therefore a man of men,/As a grace to the South;/And thus to Rome came Andersen,/"Alas, but must you take him again?"/Said the South to the North.'
21. Pen Browning (1849–1912) was the Brownings' only child, surrounded in his precocious Italian childhood by an over-protective solicitousness. This ended after his mother's death in 1861. He devoted himself to sport at Oxford University (he left without a degree) and later became – promoted by his father – a moderately successful painter and sculptor.
22. Quoted in Wullschlager *HCA* p. 374. Letter from *Letters of Elizabeth Barrett Browning* edited by F.G. Kenyon. London: Macmillan, 1897, Vol. II, p. 448.
23. *Y by Y* 1855.
24. Consider the final pictures we are given of the comfortable, eventless married life of the hero and his wife in *Nicholas Nickleby* (1838–39) and *David Copperfield* (1849–50).
25. From Balzac's *avant-propos* (foreword) to the 1842 collected edition of his *Comédie humaine*, translated by George Sainsbury, 1901. This fascinating profession of authorial intention actually states: 'The idea [i.e. of the *Comédie*] originated in a comparison between Humanity and Animality.'
26. Alphonse de Lamartine (1790–1869). As restless in temperament as Andersen himself, Lamartine experienced religious crises and passionate love affairs in his earlier years. Fame came with poems (1817) inspired by the death of his lover Mme Julie Charles, who had died in 1817. After marriage, service as a diplomat, and election to the Académie française, he embraced the July Revolution of 1830. By the time Andersen met him, he was espousing a spiritual, somewhat pantheistic notion of progress. The travelogue of his that Andersen read was *Souvenirs d'un voyage en orient* (Bredsdorff, op. cit. p. 158). Andersen's need for friends like him is well put by Sven H. Rossel in his preface to the *Diaries* (p. x): 'Travel was Andersen's life-blood. It put him in touch with the great masterpieces of Western civilization – its monuments, its statuary, its paintings, its music, and not least, its theatre. In Paris he could speak with Hugo, Lamartine, and Heine about life and art, as he never could with colleagues in the feud-ridden, claustrophobic Copenhagen of his day.'
27. Alfred de Vigny (1797–1863). From a noble family, and the author of romantic drama and poems, de Vigny did not respond favourably to the 1830 July Revolution. His most popular work is perhaps

his prose recapturing of his ten-year-long military experiences *Servitude et grandeur militaire* (1835). At the time of Andersen's meetings with him he had embarked on *Poèmes philosophiques,* published between 1838 and 1844 in *La Revue des Deux Mondes.*

28. See *D* for 1843 pp. 129–130: 'Thursday, March 23. . . . That very day there had been a big argument, Buntzen [Danish surgeon resident in Paris] told me, among the ladies about whether Balzac or I was the greater writer. . . . Saturday, March 25 . . . I was picked up by Buntzen at 10 o'clock, and we walked to Countess Pfaffin's on rue Sainte-Anne for the soirée. There I met Balzac, to whom I paid some compliments. He was a short, broad-shouldered stocky fellow.'

29. Honoré de Balzac, *Père Goriot,* translated by A.J. Krailsheimer. Oxford: World's Classics, 1991. p. 263.

30. 'The Pied Piper of Hamelin' was published in Part Three ('Dramatic Lyrics') of Robert Browning's *Bells and Pomegranates* (1842). It, like Andersen's earlier tales, was explicitly 'told to children', addressed to Willie Macready, the great actor's son.

31. A prime mover towards the criminalisation of homosexuality was H.C. Ørsted's brother, the eminent jurist and politician Anders Sandøe Ørsted (1778–1860). Comparatively liberal during the Absolute Monarchy, he became progressively more reactionary afterwards. His term as Prime Minister (21 April 1853–12 December 1854) ended in forced resignation because of his attempts to get a new, ultra-conservative constitution through. Denmark completely decriminalised homosexuality in 1933, only the third European country to do so, and now stands in the very vanguard of gay rights, with the age of consent at 15.

32. *Y by Y* 1844. The affair with Henrik (Baron) Stampe is not recorded in any diaries, but letters and almanac entries testify to what Professor de Mylius calls 'a close and passionate relationship': 'The almanac from the first few months of 1844 is extremely ambiguous, containing a great deal of initials, rather than names. . . . marked by jealousy, anger, desperation and sensuality.' By the summer, however, he wrote to Jette Collin of 'Stampe's intense love for me which then evaporated once he had used me as a ladder by which to reach Jonna.'

33. 'The Fir Tree' came out in *Nye Eventyr, Første Bind Anden Samling* (*New Tales, First Volume, Second Collection*) on 21 December 1844, together with 'The Snow Queen'. Andersen relates in his Notes – *E og H Vol V* pp. 312–313 – that the idea came to him in the Royal Theatre, Copenhagen, during a performance of Mozart's *Don Giovanni.* Perhaps the fir tree learning harsh truths about existence after pining for luxury and then finding luxury insouciant about his real needs can be attributed to Mozart's opera, or rather to Andersen's reception of it.

34. *E og H Vol 1* p. 384.

35. 'Hänsel und Gretel' appeared in the Brothers Grimm, *Kinder- und Hausmärchen,* 1812 and 1857.

36. For characteristics of the Norway Spruce and also for the German/European Christmas festivities associated with the tree, see Richard Mabey, *Flora Britannica.* London: Sinclair-Stevenson, 1996, pp. 19–25.

37. Christmas 1808; the tree in question was indeed a Norway Spruce.

38. Christian Hole, *English Custom and Usage.* London: Batsford, 1941–42, pp. 14–25, including a reference to Charles Greville.

39. Jackie Wullschlager *HCA* pp. 247–249.

40. *E og H Vol 1* p. 384.

41. See Chapter 12.

42. *E og H Vol 1* p. 386.

43. Charles Dickens, *A Christmas Carol,* in *A Christmas Carol and Other Christmas Books.* Oxford: World's Classics, 2006, p. 40.

44. The rhyming titles 'Ivede-Avede' and 'Klumpe-Dumpe' both suggest the story of them being known in English as Humpty Dumpty, who had a great fall, irreparable because he is essentially an egg (though Andersen's wins the princess). See *The Oxford Dictionary of Nursery Rhymes,* edited by Iona and Peter Opie. Oxford: Oxford University Press, 1951, pp. 213–16. Andersen's friend J.M. Thiele; see Chapter 1 notes 28 and 44) included in *Danske Folkesagn* (1820–23) 'Lille Trille laae paa Hylde; Lille Trille ned af Hylde; Ingen Mand i hele Land/Lille Trille curere kan', which nursery-rhyme compiler J.O. Halliwell (1820–1889) in *Popular Rhymes and Nursery Tales* (1849) translated as 'Little Trille lay on a shelf; Little Trille thence pitch'd himself; Not all the men in our land, I ken; Can put Little Trille right again.' Op. cit. p. 215.

45. *E og H Vol 1* p. 391.

46. Ibid. p. 392.

47. William Shakespeare, *The Tempest,* Act IV, scene i, lines 156–158. New Penguin Shakespeare, 1968, edited by Anne Righter (Anne Barton), p. 120.

48. *E og H Vol 1* p. 392.

49. See W. Glyn Jones, *Denmark, a Modern History.* London: Croom Helm, 1986, Appendix 1: The Faeroe Islands; Appendix 2: Greenland, pp. 216–217.

50. Spitsbergen is the largest island of Svalbard, though formerly the name (often incorrectly spelled by the British as Spitzbergen) was often used for the whole archipelago. It lies roughly midway between the north of Norway and the North Pole, has an Arctic climate and contains considerable wilderness areas. It is the habitat of polar bears and reindeer, and breeding-ground for many seabirds. Its Dutch name is descriptive, meaning 'pointed mountains'. Andersen would rightly have thought it uninhabited, though a base for fishing and whaling expeditions; Longyearbyen did not exist, even as a very small community, until the late 19ᵗʰ century. Denmark claimed the island after its explorations of 1617, and retained it (as part of the Dual Monarchy) until 1814, when, together with Norway itself, it was handed over to Sweden. When the Union between Norway and Sweden was dissolved, it returned to Norway, and from 1925 has been a fully integrated part of that country. One could say that Andersen's story tells us that the Arctic power (Snow Queen), is Dano-Norwegian (or even Swedish-Danish-Norwegian).

51. Peter Asbjørnsen (1812–85) collaborated so closely with Jørgen Moe in working methods and style, that the two are usually spoken of as a single entity, Asbjørnsen-and-Moe, though Asbjørnsen did publish a collection of his own, *Huldre-Eventyr* (*Tales of the Huldre*, 1845). Asbjørnsen had begun to write down folk tales he had collected as a 20-year-old student of zoology at university (Christiania). He made extensive expeditions on foot throughout Norway in search of material. He was also active on behalf of Norwegian forests in protest against deforestation, becoming Forest Master until his retirement in 1876. *Norske Folkeevntyr* was hailed all over Europe as a work of literature as well as of socio-anthropology, and there were two further collections in 1844 and 1871.

52. Jørgen Moe (1813–82) was 14 when he became friendly with Asbjørnsen, the two studying for the same exam, though it was some years before they appreciated just how coincident their interests and their pursuit of them were and joined forces. Moe too travelled a good deal in search of material, particularly in the mountains of southern Norway. He studied theology and took orders in 1853, eventually rising to a bishopric. He was also a distinguished lyric poet, and one of his most famous songs 'Sæterjentens Søndag' was set to music by Ole Bull (see Chapter 6).

53. C.S.A Bille and N. Bøgh, *Breve fra H.C. Andersen*. Copenhagen: Aschehoug, 1877, pp. 475–478.

54. 'Elder Mother'. This is one of Andersen's most delightful stories with its sensitive, subtle depiction of the small boy who has caught cold, the amusing old man who lives in the apartment at the top of his house and who entertains the boy, in his indisposition, with a story, its feeling for the way one generation succeeds another, and for the gentle, fertile charms of the Danish countryside. Limpid and conversational in style, it also looks back to the complex Chinese-box devices of Hoffmann and forward to the *mise-en-abŷme* of 20ᵗʰ-century modernist writing. The elderly man, who needs fairy stories to knock on his forehead and enter him, spins a tale round the teapot in the room; the pot turns out to be full of elder, in which lives an old woman, presiding over an old couple's golden wedding anniversary. But then she in turn transmogrifies into a young girl, who takes the hand of the invalid boy and escorts him through successive stages of life until he reaches the age and circumstances of the old, long-gone anniversary couple. Of course he is brought back to plain 'reality' in the end, and as for Elder-Tree Mother, just let her stay in the teapot!

55. C.S.A. Bille and N. Bøgh, *Breve H.C. Andersen*. Copenhagen: Aschehoug, 1877, pp. 475–478.

56. Ibid. pp. 475–8

57. The actual publication date was 21 December 1844. See note 33 for further details.

58. We remember that the author's father, Hans Andersen, expressly did not believe in the devil, only in bad impulses in the individual.

59. Perhaps Andersen's deep feeling for this inclusiveness goes right back to his early childhood and his encounter with Spanish soldiers quartered in Fyn during the Napoleonic War: 'One day a Spanish soldier took me up in his arms and pressed against my lip a silver image which he wore on his naked breast. I remember that my mother was angry about this, for it was something Catholic, she said, but I liked the image and the foreign soldier' (*MF-TL* p. 15). The image was indubitably a crucifix, a representation of Christ.

60. 'sub specie aeternitatis' 'under the mirror of eternity': Baruch (Benedict de) Spinoza (1632–77), Dutch-Jewish philosopher, in *Ethics* V xxxi (1677).

61. Goethe *Faust Part One,* translated by David Luke. Oxford: Oxford World's Classics, 1987, pp. 9–12.

62. *E og H Vol I* pp. 133–134.

63. *E og H Vol I* p. 396.

64. Ibid. p. 396.

65. Of his grandmother Andersen wrote: 'She was employed to look after the garden belonging to the hospital [asylum]' (*MF-TL* p. 16).

66. James Massengale, 'About Little Gerda and Her "Moratoria" ', in *Hans Christian Andersen. Between Children's Literature and Adult Literature. Papers from the Fourth International Hans Christian Andersen Conference 2005.* Odense: University Press of Southern Denmark, 2007, pp. 478–504.

67. *E og H Vol I* p. 397 for both Kay's two questions and Grandmother's answer.

68. Ibid. p. 399.
69. H.A. Brorson (1694–1764, a Danish pietist clergyman who began writing his many hymns when he was a pastor in southern Jutland. He rose to become Bishop of Ribe. His hymns – such as the famous Christmas one 'Den yndigste Rose er funden' ('The loveliest rose is found') – have beauty as lyric poems, and, after a period of comparative obscurity, were rediscovered and reappraised by the Romantic generation – by Grundvig and Oehlenschläger, for instance.
70. Jack Goody, *The Culture of Flowers*. Cambridge: Cambridge University Press, 1993, pp. 120–163.
71. Wolfgang Lederer, *The Kiss of the Snow Queen*. Berkeley, Los Angeles, London: University of California Press, 1986. The subtitle of this thoughtful and thought-provoking study indicates its concerns: *Hans Christian Andersen and Man's Redemption by Woman*.
72. Ibid. pp. 26–28.
73. *E og H Vol I* p. 398.
74. Ibid. p. 398.
75. Ibid. p. 401.
76. See 'Vanddraaben' ('A Drop of Water', 1848).
77. W.A. Bentley and W.J. Humphrey, *Snow Crystals*. New York: McGraw Hill, 1931.
78. George Steiner, *My Unwritten Books*. London: Weidenfeld & Nicolson, 2008, pp. 1–30 (Chapter One, 'Chinoiserie').
79. Op. cit., pp. 7–8.
80. *E og H Vol I* p. 403.
81. Finnmark is Norway's largest and most northern county, open to the Arctic Ocean by the shores of which most of its inhabitants live. The Sami, on the other hand, live mostly in its inland area, largely taken up with a vast plateau, the Finnmarksvidda. Here tens of thousands of Sami-owned and -tended reindeer graze. The Sami language has now been given official status and they have their own parliament. Finnmark has land borders with Russia and Finland.
82. *Kalevala* is the name given to an epic poem wrought out of Finnish oral poetry traceable to the first millennium CE, preserving the rhythm of singing and given narrative shape by Finnish scholar Elias Lönrott (see note 85 below). See Keith Bosley's detailed introduction to the edition cited below.
83. *Kalevala*, translated by Keith Bosley. Oxford: Oxford World's Classics, 1989, Book 12, pp. 144–145.
84. The words 'Lapp' and 'Lappish' – though, of course, found in a majority of 19th- and 20th-century books and other printed matter – have now been replaced by the term 'Sami'. The great majority of Sami live in Norway – *c*.42,000. Of the rest, 20,000 live in Sweden, 6,000 in Finland, and 2,000 in Russia. See, for example, www Lapland-travel-info.com.
85. Elias Lönnrot (1802–84) was a Finnish scholar and district health officer, who published his first edition of the *Kalevala* in 1835, the same year as Andersen's first novel and first two booklets of fairy tales. In 1840–41 he produced the *Kantelaar*, a collection of Finnish lyrics from the same oral tradition. He brought out the second massive edition of the *Kalevala* in 1849.
86. The Finnish province of Karelia (Karjala), cradle of Finnic tradition, was divided into two after Finland lost the 1939–1940 Winter War, and the eastern part (11% of Finnish territory) went to Russia. This, now the Republic of Karelia, is part of the federal republic of Russia, and Karelian (closely related to Finnish, and by some thought to be a dialect of it) is widely spoken but not given official status as yet.
87. Translated into English by Joan Tate as *Blackwater*. London: Chatto & Windus, 1995.
88. The quotation from Tacitus is to be found in Keith Bosley's introduction to his translation of *Kalevala* (see note 83 above), p. xviii.
89. *E og H Vol I* p. 430.
90. There are nine extant Sami languages, not all of which are mutually intelligible, due to divisive geographical features; one, Northern Lappish (Norway, Sweden and Finland), accounts for more than 75% of speakers. Scholars are more split than formerly over the relationship of these as a language group to other groups within the Uralic (or Finno-Ugric) family. Commonly it was assumed that it was the closest to the Finnic (which includes Finnish and Estonian) but it is thought that the resemblances may be explained by sustained political/educational influence. Other Uralic groups are Hungarian, Mordvinic and the Samoyed languages. See Pekka Sammallahti, *The Saami [sic] Languages: An Introduction*. Kárásjohka: Davvi Girji, 1998.
91. *E og H Vol I* p. 404.
92. Ibid. pp. 404–405.
93. Andersen would have been familiar with Osiris from Mozart's *Magic Flute* (1791) with its great aria and chorus: 'O Isis und Osiris!' For accounts of Osiris and his cult, see the one-volume edition of Sir James George Fraser's *The Golden Bough*, Oxford: Oxford World's Classics, 1994, pp. 366–374.
94. Ibid. pp. 300–305, 331–334.

95. *The Golden Bough* (1890), then expanded into 12 volumes, 1906–15. In addition to its radical ideas and its vast influence on the modernists, the work is a summation of the long 19ᵗʰ-century obsession with the relationship between myth/folklore and religion, so prevalent a theme in this book.

96. Ejnar Stig Askgaard, 'Look! Now we'll begin. When we have got to the end of the story we shall know more than we do now', in *Hans Christian Andersen. Between Children's Literature and Adult Literature. Papers from the Fourth International Hans Christian Andersen Conference, 2005.* Odense: University Press of Southern Denmark, 2007, pp. 547–569.

97. Balder, son of Odin and Frigg, was so beloved by the gods that Frigg obtained a promise from all living things not to bring any harm to him. The mistletoe, however, because of the way it grows, was outside this oath-taking. Loki, the trickster god, therefore got Balder's blind brother Hodr to shoot an arrow of mistletoe at the handsome, seemingly invulnerable god. He died. Writes Askgaard, 'It would seem as if "The Snow Queen" is a religious version – a "literary myth" – of the fertility myths, so it would seem natural [knowing Andersen's great interest in the field] to investigate a version of such a myth in Norse mythology, e.g. the one found in the tale of Balder's death', ibid. p. 557.

98. Andersen's feeling for the Odense River is exemplified in the beautiful short fairy tale 'Klokkedybet' ('The Bell Deep'), 1856.

99. *E og H Vol I* p. 405.

100. 'The Red Shoes' (1845). This story has fascinated, horrified and morally repelled readers in about equal measure. If, in 'The Snow Queen', Gerda's action with her shoes illustrates her dominant unselfishness, Karen's red shoes – seemingly a perverse choice of footwear anyway, since, in all instances given, the circumstances demand the conventional formal black – show her extreme selfishness, which grows the more its appetites are fed. The shoes are themselves the instruments of her punishment, causing her to dance and dance until she despairs, in pain and fatigue, of ever stopping. Even when the executioner obliges her by severing her feet from her legs, she still doesn't part company from them, since they dance mercilessly in front of her whichever direction she turns. Only when she becomes a modest servant to a pastor and his family, who are sorry for her disability, does her life take a better turn – but she dies within a short time of entering this pious household. The story creates many difficulties; the heroine's name, Karen, is that of Andersen's half-sister, Karen-Marie, who had turned up in 1842, to his dismay – and (modest) financial cost. Karen-Marie's disreputable lifestyle may be reflected in the fairly obvious sexual symbolism of the shoes (both on and off the girl's feet), suggesting the power of erotic desire. The story meets with strong and well articulated moral disapproval from Jack Zipes in *Hans Christian Andersen The Misunderstood Storyteller.* New York: London, Routledge, 2005, pp. 86–89, emphasising Andersen's proneness to insist on subjugation of fantasy and appetite where his female characters are concerned, though he allows Gerda to be a triumphant exception. He does, however, draw attention to a somewhat different approach to the tale by Erin Mackie, 'Red Shoes, and Bloody Stumps', in *Footnotes: On Shoes,* edited by Shari Benstock and Suzanne Ferriss. New Brunswick, NJ: Rutgers University Press, 2001. Here the red shoes are set in the context of 'a socio-religious system fixed against her [Karen]'. I would agree with this, and emphasise the importance of the girl's poverty (Karen-Marie's?) to the tale's opening. The little girl's ankles are red (through being inadequately shod) and old Mother Shoemaker, in order to oblige her a little more comfortably, makes her first pair of shoes out of old strips of red cloth. No wonder she didn't comport herself as respectable girls do – and she does end up, reductive though it rightly seems to our way of thinking, loved, useful and an imminent enjoyer of God's everlasting peace.

101. *Tatar AA* p. 42.

102. *E og H Vol I* p. 433.

103. Ibid. p. 432.

104. See *East of the Sun and West of the Moon* by Peter Asbjørnsen (Moe's name omitted from title page), translated by George Darsent. Ware: Wordsworth Editions, 1995.

105. *E og H Vol I* pp. 404–413.

106. Ibid. pp. 414–422.

107. Wolfgang Lederer, *The Kiss of the Snow Queen.* Berkeley, Los Angeles, London: University of California Press, 1986 pp. 42–43.

108. Massengale, op. cit., p. 488.

109. 'Language of Flowers' in Jack Goody, op.cit., pp. 232–260.

110. *E og H Vol I* p. 414.

111. Lederer, op. cit., pp. 39–44.

112. *E og H Vol I* p. 421.

113. Walter Scott, *The Heart of Midlothian.* London: Everyman edition, 1906, pp. 306–313.

114. All sentences from *E og H Vol I* pp. 423–424.

115. Lederer, op. cit. pp. 52–58.
116. The provinces of Sweden's Norrland not abutting on the Arctic Circle and the Sami domains are Gästrikland, Medelpad, Ångermanland, Hälsingland, Jämtland, Härjedalen and Västerbotten.
117. Displays of Aurora Borealis are most frequent around the equinox, and appear as a greenish glow in the sky, and sometimes as a reddish one. At their most spectacular, they will continue for many hours, but can sometimes be of only a few minutes' duration. They are caused by a collision of particles with atoms in the thermosphere, the particles being delivered into the atmosphere by the Earth's magnetic field. Finnish Lapland perhaps offers the most consistent good opportunities for viewing this phenomenon.
118. *E og H Vol I* p. 429.
119. See Chapter 1.
120. Jens Andreas Friis, *Lappisk-mythologi-eventyr-og-folkesagn*. online.
121. From translators' Preface to *My Sun, My Father*. Guovdageaidnu, Norway: DAT O.S., 1988 in Sami, printed in Vaasa, Finland, 1997 and distributed by University of Washington Press, Seattle: 'Nils-Aslak Valkeapää was born in 1943 to a reindeer breeding family in Sapmi, homeland of the Sami . . . A Finnish citizen, he lives in both Norway and Finland. He studied and received teacher's certification, but instead, devoted his life to the arts. . . . He served as the first cultural coordinator in the World Council of Indigenous Peoples.'
122. *My Sun, My Father.* See above, p. 52; translations by Ralph Salisbury, Lars Nordström, Harald Gaski.
123. Jens Andreas Friis website: see note 120.
124. *The Kalevala* translated by Keith Bosley. Oxford: Oxford World's Classics, 1989, pp. 159–161.
125. *Tatar AA* p. 42, note 38.
126. 'East of the Sun and West of the Moon', op. cit., pp. 195–196.
127. All phrases from *E og H Vol I* p. 436.
128. All phrases *E og H Vol I* pp. 439–440.
129. Massengale, op. cit pp. 496–499.
130. Ejnar Stig Askgaard, op. cit., pp. 547–569.
131. Ibid. p. 440.
132. *D* pp. 159–163.
133. Ibid. pp. 72–85.
134. This was sent off to Lorck on 13 August 1846. *Y by Y* 1846. This, as already mentioned, is the short autobiography rendered into German and published in that language in Leipzig 1847: *Das Märchen meines Lebens ohne Dichtung.*
135. Andersen arrived in Føhr on 29 August and stayed until 9 September (see *Y by Y* 1844). He was personally congratulated on his writings by King Christian VIII, who inquired about his earnings and implied that he would like to raise his annuity. However, Andersen could not bring himself to follow this through. He heard that his annuity had been raised on 8 April 1845.
136. He arrived in Berlin on 17 December 1845 and stayed until 7 January 1846, at the very centre of Berlin's high life as the 'hero of the day'. He greatly appreciated his meetings with Jacob and Wilhelm Grimm, by far his warmest and most satisfactory to date, and the praise of Wilhelm for 'The Fir Tree', with its very German attention to the forest and Christmas ceremonial.
137. This was *The Improvisatore; or Life in Italy*, with a prefatory biography of Andersen made by Mary Howitt from Marmier's essay. Mary Howitt (1799–1888), author of many children's books and translator, with her husband William (1792–1879), of books from German and Scandinavian languages, moved in literary circles in both England and Continental Europe (France, Germany, Austria, Italy). For Andersen's connections with her, literary, personal and social, see Chapter 9.
138. Jenny Lind (1820–87), 'the Swedish Nightingale', the most famous soprano of her times. Jenny was born out of wedlock in Stockholm, though her parents married when she was 14. It was not as hard a childhood as Andersen's own – her mother was an educated teacher – but as dramatic in the opportunities presented and taken, and in the speed of ascent. Jenny was singing on stage when she was 10, sang the lead role in *Der Freischütz* when she was 18, and became a member of the Royal Swedish Academy at 20. Andersen fell in love with her during her tour of Denmark in 1843. She was admired by Meyerbeer, Schumann, Mendelssohn (there has been conjecture that he and she were lovers) and Berlioz, and premièred leading roles in operas by Donizetti, Bellini and Verdi. She also enjoyed an emotional friendship with Chopin. She made a spectacular but exhausting tour of America in 1850–51, arousing wide 'Lind mania'. She married pianist and conductor Otto Goldschmidt in 1852; they had three children and from 1855 made their home in England.
139. *Little Kirsten*: première 12 May 1846 with 310 performances, music by J.P.E. Hartmann. Partly derived from old ballads, and celebrating the rural peasantry and medieval lore, it was rapturously received, *Kjøbenhavnsposten* proclaiming it, on 25 May 1846, 'the loveliest painting we have seen

on the Danish stage for a long time, a picture which leaves a deep and beautiful impression on the spectator.' Frederick J. Marker, op. cit. p. 48.
140. *E og H Vol II* p. 123.
141. Ibid p. 123.
142. Ibid. p. 129.
143. See Adelbert von Chamisso, *Peter Schlemihl,* introduced and translated by Leopold von Loewenstein-Wertheim. Richmond: Oneworld Classics, 2008.
144. *E og H Vol II,* p. 115.
145. Ibid. p. 123.
146. Ibid. p. 124.
147. Ibid. p. 124.
148. Ibid. p. 114.
149. Ibid. pp. 112–113.
150. See Chapter 7, note 34.
151. *E og H Vol II* p. 113.
152. Ibid. p. 114.
153. Ibid. p. 114.
154. Ibid. p. 114.
155. Ibid. p. 115.
156. Ibid. p. 115.
157. Ibid. p. 115.
158. Ibid. p. 115.
159. Casorti. See note 17 to Chapter 1. For *commedia dell' arte,* see note 33 to Chapter 7.
160. Carlo Goldoni (1707–93) was the author of over 200 plays, and believed that Italian theatre should move on from the *commedia dell'arte,* even while drawing from it, substituting witty, thoughtful dialogue for the usual improvisation or stock responses. Carlo Gozzi (1720–1806), though the younger man, was fiercely, even morally opposed to this. His own plays have fantastic elements that endeared them to the Romantic generation of critics.
161. *E og H Vol II* p. 117.
162. Ibid. p. 122.
163. Pierre-Augustin Caron de Beaumarchais (1732–99). An adventurous life involving confidential missions for Louis XV and Louis XVI and writing scabrous plays for private performances in aristocratic households, together with involvement with the works of Voltaire, encouraged him in the complex cynicism which informs both his most famous plays. The trickster servant Figaro is at once menacing and subordinate to the society he ingeniously serves and a figure with whom audiences sympathise.
164. Carl Gustav Jung, *Memories, Dreams, Reflections,* recorded and edited by Aniela Jaffé; translated by Richard and Clara Winston. London: Fontana/Flamingo, 1983, p. 262.
165. Carl Gustav Jung, 'The Archetypes of the Collective Unconscious', 1934/1954, in *Collected Works Vol. 9,* edited by Herbert Read. London: Routledge and Kegan Paul, 1968, pp. 284ff.
166. *E og H Vol II* p. 116.
167. Ibid. p. 116.
168. Immanuel Kant, *Zum ewigen Frieden: Ein philosophische Entwurf (On Perpetual Peace: A Philosophical Project,* 1795).
169. *E og H Vol II* p. 119.
170. Ibid. p. 120.
171. S. Körner, *Kant.* Harmondsworth: Penguin Books, 1955 (particularly Chapter 8, 'Kant's Theory of Aesthetic Taste', pp. 175–195.
172. *Tatar AA* p. 271, note 20. For the quote from the *Critique* see Paul Guyer, 'Immanuel Kant', in *Routledge Encyclopaedia of Philosophy,* 2004: www.rep.routledge.com/article/DB047.
173. Ibid. On the above webpage.
174. Simon Schaffer, 'The Phoenix of Nature: Fire and Evolutionary Cosmology in Wright and Kant', *Journal of the History of Astronomy,* Vol. 9 (1978), p. 186 (includes English translation of Kant's German).
175. *E og H Vol II.* p. 120.
176. Ibid. p. 121.
177. Oehlenschläger: See Introductory note 18, p. 424.
178. The term was given currency through Kant's essay in *Berlinische Monatschrift (Berlin Monthly),* December 1784: 'Beantwortung der Frage: Was ist Aufklärung?' 'Answering the question: What is Enlightenment?' arguing that church and state prescriptions should be replaced by freedom of individual thought.
179. *E og H Vol II* p. 117.

180. Ibid. p. 121.
181. Ibid. p. 121.
182. Eugène Scribe (1791–1861). Immensely successful dramatist, author of over 300 plays, and to whom the commercial ideal of the 'well-made play' is usually ascribed. Ingenious and tight-knit in plot, often lively in scene and dialogue, his plays reflect an anti-Romantic attitude to human behaviour, dealing with familial discord, adultery, difficult liaisons, etc. in a lively and ultimately acceptable manner, stimulating but never distressing his boulevard public.
183. *E og H Vol II* p. 122.
184. Ibid. p. 122.
185. This extraordinary work, by James Hogg (1770–1835), 'the Ettrick Shepherd', is a study in antinomianism: a young man 'saved' according to the tenets of his faith, and seemingly virtuous, is led by a mysterious stranger (a Shadow Self) to commit a series of horrible murders, two victims being members of his own family. In fact the stranger is the devil, and the young man himself commits suicide, his own death being the only logical conclusion to the chain of deaths he has set in train.
186. Emily Brontë, *Wuthering Heights* (1847). London: Chatto & Windus, Zodiac edition, 1947, Chapter 9, p. 75.

Part Two: From 'Det Gamle Hus' ('The Old House') to 'Tante Tandpine' ('Auntie Toothache')

Chapter 9: Britain, Dickens, Revolutions and Wars

1. *D* p. 164.
2. Ibid. p. 174.
3. William Jerdan (1782–1869) became the editor of the *Literary Gazette*, which he co-founded with Henry Colburn, in 1817 and remained *in situ* until 1850. Scottish-born (in Kelso) he came to London in 1806 and worked as a reporter. He became friends with many leading literary figures, including George Crabbe, Samuel Taylor Coleridge and Mary Russell Mitford. He wrote an *Autobiography* (1852–53) and an account of some of his friendships, *Men I Have Known* (1866).
4. Mary Howitt (1799–1888) was born Mary Botham, and married Derbyshire-born William Howitt in 1821. At the start of their married life William ran a chemist's shop in Nottingham, but after fifteen years the couple could support themselves and their children on their writings. Independently and together they produced some 180 books and translations. They travelled extensively, wintering in Rome and summering in Austria, and William and two sons spent time in Australia. William was the author of a book about his Derbyshire boyhood, *The Boy's Country-book* (1839). Later in their lives the Howitts moved from Quakerism to – in William's case – spiritualism, and – in Mary's – Roman Catholicism.
5. *MF-TL* p. 463.
6. *Y by Y* 1846.
7. Richard Bentley (1794–1871). Born into a publisher/printer family, Bentley founded his famous firm in 1819, issuing books of a high production standard and aiming for a wide market while maintaining literary values. The 'Standard Novels' series began in 1831, with one-volume editions of triple-deckers being brought out at an attractive price (six shillings). In 1836 he launched *Bentley's Miscellany,* choosing Charles Dickens as the editon of the series. Sales were excellent as a result of the serialisation of *Oliver Twist*, but the two men did not get on well; eventually Dickens bought the copyright from Bentley, and he withdrew as editor, Harrison Ainsworth taking his place. Bentley was keen on publishing European writers, Lamartine and Chateaubriand among them, and also Americans such as Fenimore Cooper. Andersen greatly preferred the Bentleys' children to Dickens's.
8. *D* p. 167 ff.
9. *MF-TL* p. 381.
10. Ibid. p. 383.
11. Ibid. p. 383.
12. *D* p. 165.
13. Ibid. p. 193.
14. *MF-TL* p. 393.
15. *Y by Y* 1846.
16. *E og H Vol II* p. 71.
17. See Danish commentary by DSL (in the Archive for Danish Literature), www.andersen.sdu.dk.
18. *E og H Vol II* p. 71.
19. Ibid. p. 72.
20. Charles Dickens, *Bleak House*. Oxford: New Oxford Illustrated Dickens, 1948, p. 649.

21. *MF-TL* p. 389.
22. *D* p. 190.
23. Ibid. p. 185.
24. *MF-TL* p. 398.
25. Ibid. p. 400.
26. *The Two Baronesses* was to be published by Bentley in English on 28 September 1848 before its first Danish publication on 25 November 1848.
27. *MF-TL* pp. 414–415.
28. 'The Old Street Lamp' and 'The Shadow' had appeared in *Nye Eventyr. Andet Bind. Første Samling* (*New Fairy-Tales. Second Volume. First Instalment*) on 6 April 1847.
29. Introduction to *A Christmas Greeting to My English Friends*, translation by Charles Beckwith Lohmeyer. London: Richard Bentley, December 1848.
30. Andersen's Notes, *E og H Vol V* p. 315 describe how story came to him.
31. 'The Child in the Grave' is an attempt to reconcile the death of an innocent loved one, still a little child, with God and with goodness as a force in operation throughout earthly existence. Virtually a reworking of 'The Story of a Mother', it gives us a woman out of her mind with grief at the loss of her four-year-old son, and unable to appreciate her husband and her two surviving daughters. She encounters Death himself (a man dressed in black but with youthful eyes) beside her son's newly made grave. He leads her down into the region where the mourned deceased has gone. She learns from him that for her to yield entirely to grief is to inhibit her son's own personal ascent to God along with other children who have also died, and so she returns to her husband and family restored, with the strength to endure the tragedy.
32. First published in Danish in *Nye Eventyr. Andet Bind. Anden Samling* (*New Fairy-Tales. Second Volume. Second Instalment*) on 4 March 1848.
33. Written late January 1848. In *Selected Letters of Charles Dickens,* edited by Jenny Hartley. Oxford: Oxford University Press, 2012, p. 191.
34. Ibid. p.191.
35. *M F-TL* p. 397.
36. *E og H Vol II* p. 131.
37. Ibid. p. 132.
38. Ibid. p. 132.
39. Andersen's Notes, *E og H Vol V* p. 314.
40. *E og H Vol II* p. 134.
41. Andersen's Notes, *E og H Vol V* p. 314.
42. *E og H Vol II* p. 139.
43. Ibid. p. 139.
44. Ibid. pp. 140–141.
45. Ibid. p. 141.
46. Ibid. p. 141.
47. Ibid. p. 142.
48. Ibid. p. 142.
49. Ibid. p. 143.
50. Charles Dickens, *David Copperfield*. Oxford: New Oxford Illustrated Dickens, 1948, p. 218.
51. Charles Dickens, *Great Expectations*. Oxford: New Oxford Illustrated Dickens, 1953, p. 458.
52. Charles Dickens, *David Copperfield*, op. cit., p. 1.
53. Ibid. p. 87.
54. Ibid. p. 287.
55. Letter, June 1847, www.andersen.sdu.dk/service/biblio/date/1847.
56. *Breve fra Hans Christian Andersen*, Vol 11 Copenhagen Aschehoug, p. 558. Translation in Bredsdorff *HCA* p. 219.
57. *D* p. 210.
58. *MF-TL* p. 423.
59. Ibid. p. 424.
60. Søren Kierkegaard, *Papers and Journals: A Selection*, translated and edited by Alastair Hannay. London: Penguin Classics, 1996, p. 355.
61. W. Glyn Jones, *Denmark, A Modern History*, London: Croom Helm, 1986, pp. 33–35. See also for transition of reign and onset of war *Y by Y* 184.
62. Actually published on 31 March 1848. For information about the Three Years War, see Nick Svendsen, *The First Schleswig-Holstein War*. Solihull: Helion & Co., 2008. See also *Y by Y* 1848, 1849, 1850.
63. Hereditary Grand Duke Carl Alexander (1818–1901), Grand Duke of Saxony-Weimar-Eisenach.
64. Søren Kierkegaard, *Papers and Journals: A Selection*, op. cit., p. 289.
65. *D* p. 212.

66. *St Ronan's Well* does, however, deal with heirs to aristocratic titles. Two half-brothers are the sons of the Earl of Etherington, and both love the daughter of the local laird.

67. It is surely noteworthy that it is in this year of revolution that Andersen gives us his first sustained instance of gratuitous cruelty by a landowner able to treat employees as he wishes.

68. See Chapter 12.

69. *DTB* p. 4.

70. Ibid. p. 21.

71. Ibid. p. 92.

72. *D* pp. 142–147.

73. Ibid. p. 141.

74. *DTB* p. 259.

75. W. Glyn-Jones, op. cit., pp 36–40 inclusive. Nick Svendsen, op. cit., *passim. Y by Y* 1849.

76. This was in fact Andersen's fourth visit to Sweden. On 17 May he went by boat from Copenhagen to Hälsingborg. From there he went to Gothenburg and then up the Göta Canal, through Lakes Vänern and Vättern to Stockholm. He was received by King Oscar I and made a public defence of Denmark's right to pursue the Schleswig war. He visited Uppsala, and then, back in the Swedish capital, met Bonnier the publisher/bookseller and Almquist the poet. He next went to Dalarna where the scenery enchanted him (midsummer celebrations at Leksand). His time in Sweden was a consciously sought antidote to the militarism coming from Germany. The travelogue of his journeys and meetings came out on 9 March 1851 simultaneously in Danish, German and English.

77. 'Det var en Sommermorgen', 'It was a summer morning', even before day had begun! Grundtvig's two sons Svein and Johan were involved in the fighting. The song evokes the old hero Holger-Danske and the present place of fray, Isted. It was later (1864) set to music by P.A. Heise.

78. Andersen did not hear of the death of Frederik Læssøe (1811–50) until two days later, 27 July. He was much moved and stirred to thoughts about the friendship of youth.

79. *D* p. 221.

80. *MF-TL* p. 464.

81. Ibid. pp. 484–485.

82. Ibid. pp. 473–476, some of which pages are taken up by a letter from Andersen to Ørsted about his great book and his grateful response to it. His Swedish travelogue reflected his enthusiasm for its first part, even in structure. See particularly Jens Andersen *HCA* pp. 416–420.

83. 'Everything about her was a harmony of beauteous qualities imparted to her by genius. She was one of the people who drew me into the orbit of their spirit, their humour and their heart, and so she was reflected on me like sunlight on a plant.' She was generous, too, to many outside her family and circle, 'the poor, the sick, and the sorrowing', p. 480.

84. Ibid. pp. 481–482.

85. See W. Glyn Jones, *Denmark; A Modern History*, op. cit., pp. 55–58.

86. Published on 30 November 1852 in *Historier. Anden Samling* (*Stories. Second Collection*). Note the starker, more adult titling.

87. Ibid. In this volume also appeared two stories we have considered already: 'Thousands of Years to Come' and 'Under the Willow-tree'.

88. *E og H Vol II* p. 259.

89. Ibid. p. 258.

90. Ibid. p. 258.

91. Ibid. p. 248.

92. Ibid. p. 245.

93. Ibid. p. 245

94. Ibid. p. 247.

95. *Nisse* is the name given in Denmark, Norway and Skåne, the southern Swedish province formerly Danish, to a miniature humanoid creature who looks after a farm and its inhabitants in return for certain comforts, such as food. The name is the usual (affectionate) diminutive form of the Swedish Nils, hence its use by Selma Lagerlöf in her story: see note 17 to Chapter 5. In other parts of Sweden the creature is known as a *tomte* or *tomte nisse*.

96. *E og H Vol II* p. 265.

97. *AVEIV* p. 11.

98. Ibid. p. 230.

99. Ibid. p. 24.

100. Ibid. p. 229.

101. *D* p. 15.

102. Knud J.V. Jespersen, *A History of Denmark*, translated by Ivan Hill and Christopher Wade. Basingstoke and New York: Palgrave Macmillan, 2011, pp. 114–116.

103. *AVEIV* p. 14.
104. Ibid. p. 20.
105. Rundetaarn (modern Danish Rundetårn). See *Rough Guide to Denmark*, by Lone Mouritsen, Roger Borum and Caroline Osborne Rough Guides. London: Penguin Books, 2010, p. 65, which considers it 'the city's most intriguing landmark', 'built by Christian IV as part of the Trinitas complex'.
106. David Friedrich Strauss (1808–74). Leading exponent of the German 'Higher Criticism' as applied to biblical texts, which resulted in the demythologising of them, as the very title of his most famous work *Das Leben Jesu, kritisch bearbeitet* (*The Life of Jesus, Critically Examined*, 1835–36) proclaims. His studies led him to the conclusion that in the Gospels the historical record had been substantially infiltrated by mythological material, and so there could be no reasonable case for regarding Jesus himself as divine. He studied and taught at Tübingen University. George Eliot's translation of *Das Leben Jesu* was crucial to her own philosophic development since she accepted its basic premise.
107. Ludwig Andreas Feuerbach (1804–72), a follower of Hegel who, though starting out a student of Protestant theology, had by the age of 21 turned against religion itself and embarked on a radical programme of philosophical materialism. This necessitated analytical criticism of the Bible itself. *Thoughts on Death and Immortality* (1830) and *The Essence of Christianity* (1841 pseudonymously, and under his own name 1843) gained many admirers, mostly for their cathartic demolition of ideas that had tended to atrophy in the 19th-century mind. George Eliot translated Feuerbach too, as Marian Evans – *The Essence of Christianity*, 1854–55 – and his ideas permeate her whole creative work. In less negative mode came *Grundsätze der Philosophie der Zukunft* (*Principles of the Philosophy of the Future*, 1843) which, written with the conviction that religion/Christianity has had a deleterious effect on human development, explains deities as products of fear and pleads for a philosophical acceptance of material reality.
108. See Jens Andersen, *HCA*, pp. 438–443. I find his argument largely persuasive.
109. *MF-TL* p. 187. Of Kierkegaard and their initially mutual bristly relations he writes: 'Later I was better to understand this author who has shown me kindness and discretion as I have progressed.'
110. *AVEIV* p. 189.
111. Ibid. p. 189.
112. 'The Marsh-King's Daughter' (see Chapter 10) came out in *Nye Eventyr og Historier Anden Række* (*New Fairy-Tales and Stories*, Second Series) on 15 May 1858.
113. 'The New Century's Muse' (see Chapter 10) appeared in *Nye Eventyr og Historier. Anden Række* (*New Fairy-Tales and Stories*, Second Series) on 2 March 1861.
114. See *Vanity Fair*, Chapters XXVIII–XXXIII inclusive for a portrait of Waterloo from both an un-heroic, 'ordinary' military perspective and a non-combatant one. Thackeray, in due course, would surely have read 'To Be or Not to Be'.
115. *The Charterhouse of Parma* Chapters Three, Four and Five. Tolstoy in *War and Peace* – and in his earlier *Sevastopol Sketches* (1855) – is another point of comparison, Tolstoy having learned from *The Charterhouse of Parma*; the resemblances between Fabrice in the French novel and Pierre in the Russian, at this point, being easily apparent.
116. *AVEIV* p. 159.
117. Ibid. p. 163.
118. Ibid. p. 163.
119. *D* p. 247.
120. Ibid. pp. 254–255.
121. Ibid. p. 248.
122. See Michael Slater, *Charles Dickens*. New Haven and London: Yale University Press, 2009, and Clare Tomalin, *Charles Dickens*. London: Penguin Books, 2011. These two superb biographies are heartily to be recommended as portraits of Dickens, and by no means least in his familial relationships. For Dickens's relationship with Walter, see Slater, pp. 429–430, 441, 500 and 525–526, and Tomalin, pp. 273–274, 280–284, 320, 335. For relations with Andersen, see Slater, pp. 422–429, and Tomalin, p. 281.
123. Both quotes *D* pp. 254 and 262.
124. *Bentley's Miscellany* issue for August 1857.
125. *The Frozen Deep*. Though originally conceived and written by Wilkie Collins, Dickens – chief actor in the play, and stage manager – rather took the work over, as was his wont when in collaboration, and much of the dialogue, as reviewers realised, was his. The theme of the melodrama is the disappearance of the Franklin Expedition, the aim of which was to find the Northwest Passage, in July 1845. The production that Andersen attended on 4 July 1857 included not only Queen Victoria, Prince Albert and their family, together with the Belgian King, but also Prince Friedrich Wilhelm of Prussia, and W.M. Thackeray.

Chapter 10: What The Wind Tells Stories 1858-59

1. See Andersen's own Notes to his stories, dated September 1874, *E og H Vol V* p. 328; here he attributes adverse criticism principally to people enchanted by those fairy stories of his which they read when they themselves were young, and who, for extra-literary, purely personal reasons, cannot find the same magic in the same author's later offerings. He also thinks the great success of his fairy tales all over the world provoked hostile criticism whenever anything new from him appeared.

2. The text here is from Notes to *Hans Christian Andersen: Complete Fairy-Tales and Stories* translated by Erik Christian Haugaard. London: Gollancz, 1974, p. 1,082. For the Danish see *E og H Vol V* p. 322.

3. Haugaard op. cit. p. 1,083; in Danish, op. cit. p. 323.

4. *E og H Vol III* p. 162.

5. Ibid. pp. 169-170.

6. Ibid. p. 318.

7. Ibid. p. 212.

8. Haugaard, op. cit. p. 1,083; in Danish *E og H Vol V* p. 323.

9. *E og H Vol II* p. 313.

10. Herbert Spencer (1820-1903) first used this phrase in his *Principles of Biology* (1864) with reference to Darwin's *On the Origin of Species* (1859), Darwin's own phrase being 'natural selection'.

11. Haugaard, op. cit. p. 1,083; in Danish *E og H Vol V* p. 323.

12. *E og H Vol III* p. 201.

13. Ibid. p. 205.

14. Ibid. p. 207.

15. Ibid. p. 207.

16. Ibid. p. 278.

17. Ibid. p. 178.

18. *Y by Y* 1858.

19. From the additional chapters to the autobiography, dealing with the period April 1855 to December 1867, commissioned by Horace E. Scudder for his American edition (1871) *The Fairy Tale of My Life*, new edition. New York: Cooper Square Press, 2000, pp. 429-431.

20. Ibid. p. 431.

21. Exodus, chapter 2.

22. Lone Mouritsen, Roger Borum and Caroline Osborne *Rough Guide to Denmark*. London: RoughGuides/Penguin Books, 2010, pp. 252-264.

23. *E og H Vol III* p. 75.

24. Ibid. p. 81.

25. Bruno Bettelheim *The Uses of Enchantment*. London: Thames and Hudson, 1976; Harmondsworth: Penguin edition, 1978, pp. 282-309.

26. 'Der Froschkönig', in Brothers Grimm, *Kinder-und Hausmärchen*, 1815 and 1857.

27. Log houses had long had an appeal for Andersen. An early poem of 1829, included in his *Digte* of 1830, honours them: 'Ak, hvor romantisk smiler dog det Bjælkehuus i Dalen', 'Ah how romantic still smiles the log-house in the valley'.

28. See note 58 to Chapter 2.

29. See the chapter 'The Old and the New Religion', in Else Roesdahl, *The Vikings* translated from the Danish by Susan M. Margeson and Kirsten Williams. London: Allen Lane, The Penguin Press, 1991, pp. 147-167.

30. In the 9th century, Egypt was largely ruled by Turks through a governor resident in Baghdad. This situation provoked rebellions in the country not only from the (Muslim) Egyptians but also from the (Christian) Copts.

31. Boris Pasternak, *Doctor Zhivago* translated by Max Hayward and Manya Harari. London: Collins and Harvill Press, 1958, p. 19.

32. 'Bispen paa Børglum og hans Frænde' ('The Bishop of Børglum and His Kinsmen', 1961). A superb evocation of the effect of a sinister, power-hungry prelate on his diocese and beyond, with vivid rendering of the coast of west Jutland. It has something of the detestation of the Middle Ages which we also find in Dickens.

33. Skagen is situated at the very tip of Jutland, where the Skaggerak (leading out to the North Sea) meets the Kattegat (leading into the Baltic). Beyond the little town are amazing sand dunes where the visitor can walk in order to view their convergence. Obviously this is a place much beset by harsh winds, rough seas, and storms involving shipwrecks. The harshness of life there gave the place the elemental appeal which so drew painters to it in the last third of the 19th century. See *Rough Guide to Denmark*, op. cit., pp. 257-262.

34. *E og H Vol III* p. 267.
35. Ibid. p. 315.
36. Quoted (her translation) in Patricia G. Berman, *In Another Light: Danish Painting in the Nineteenth Century*. London: Thames and Hudson, 2007, p. 138.
37. P.S. Krøyer's 1888 painting '*Hip, Hip, Hurrah!*' shows the Skagen painters at a merry outdoor dinner, at one with each other, their art and their surroundings (in fact not always the case) in a manner similar to Pierre-Auguste Renoir's celebrated *Luncheon of the Boating Party*, 1880–81.
38. *E og H Vol III* p. 294.
39. These powerful narrative paintings reproduced in Patricia G. Berman's study, op. cit. – Figs 102 and 103 – convey the harsh lives that Jørgen, his foster-father and his friend Morten lead, and some of the activities Andersen ascribes to them.
40. Holger Drachmann, *Lars Kruse. En Skildring fra Virkelighedens og Sandets Regioner* (*Lars Kruse. A Story from the Regions of Reality and Sand*, 1879). See Patricia G. Berman, op. cit., p. 142.
41. Berman, op. cit., p. 133.
42. This term has often been applied to the Swiss writer Gottfried Keller (1819–90), author of the long novel *Die grüne Heinrich* (*Green Henry*, 1854–55) and to the collection of novellas, *Die Leute von Seldwyla* (*The People of Seldwyla*, 1856) of which the most famous is the second, 'Romeo und Julia auf dem Dorfe' ('A Village Romeo and Juliet'), with which 'The Ice Maiden' bears a distinct affinity. Also to the later novellen (1870s/1880s) of Theodor Storm (1817–88), set in his native Schleswig-Holstein. Though coined by the philosopher F.W. J. Schelling in 1802, the term was made current much later by the literary critic and playwright, Otto Ludwig (1813–65) in his essay, 'Der poetische Realismus'. A work that merits this description 'avoids the monotony of idealism on the one hand, and on the other . . . disentangles the confusions of realistic detail. A wealth of shrewd and sensitive observations of the world, however small, is reproduced by artistic means and techniques of style without sacrificing the sense of permanence which characterises human nature of all ages and environments.' Henry and Mary Garland, *Oxford Companion to German Literature*. Oxford: Clarendon Press, 1976, pp. 678–679.

Chapter 11: 'Iijsjomfruen', 'The Ice Maiden', 1861

1. *E og H Vol IV* p. 54.
2. *Y by Y* 1861.
3. See Chapter 2, note 75. Fearnley's large-scale oil on canvas, *The Grindelwald Glacier*, 1838, pays tribute to the great natural phenomenon that plays so determining a part in this tale. Likewise his painting of 1835, *Near Meiringen*, shows the landscape near Rudy's grandfather's home – on pp. 83 and 93, respectively, of *In Front of Nature: The European Landscapes of Thomas Fearnley*. For more on the relationship between Scandinavian and Swiss painters, see Chapter 2, note 16 and Christoper Riopelle with Sarah Herring, *Forests, Rocks, Torrents*. London: National Gallery Co, distributed by Yale University Press, 2011.
4. *E og H Vol IV* p. 56.
5. Canton Valais/Wallis is in south-western Switzerland and contains the valley of the Rhône from its sources down to its entry into the Lake of Geneva. Its administrative centre is Sion. Some of the very highest and most famous Swiss peaks are here, notably the Matterhorn. French is the majority language of the more populous eastern section, amounting to over 60% of the whole canton. It is overwhelmingly Roman Catholic and in 1845 joined the Sonderbund.
6. The German-speaking Bernese Oberland refers to the Alpine region round Lakes Thun and Brienz, and contains such much-visited towns as Interlaken, Adelboden, Wengen, Mürren, Lauterbrunnen, Grindelwald and Meiringen.
7. *E og H Vol IV* p. 61.
8. Ibid. p. 56.
9. Ibid. p. 67.
10. Ibid. p. 67.
11. The Jungfrau, 4,158 m (13,642 ft) high, the Mönch (Monk) at 4,107 m (13,474 ft) and the Eiger (Ogre) at 3,970 m (13,020 ft), constitute a tremendous alpine massif overlooking the Bernese Oberland; the Jungfrau is spectacularly visible from Interlaken. The notorious and – in the history of climbing, only too frequently fatal – north face of the Eiger, with its formidable glaciers, rises above Grindelwald.
12. The Föhn is a strong, dry, down-slope alpine wind that occurs on the lee side of mountains. The Eiger is a notorious cradle for it, making attempts at ascent particularly dangerous. Capable of melting snow and starting wildfires, the Föhn can have severely deletrious effects on the human nervous system, compounding psychoses and suicidal feelings.
13. *E og H Vol IV* p. 70.
14. Ibid. p. 71.

15. Ibid. p. 71.
16. Ibid. pp. 75-76.
17. Franco Moretti, *Atlas of the European Novel 1800-1900*. London: Verso, 1998.
18. Canton Vaud spans Lake Neuchâtel and the whole northern shore of Lake Geneva, and thus also stretches from the Alps to the Jura. The third most populous Swiss canton, it is French-speaking and has a long history of vigorous Protestantism. It was an active opponent of the Sonderbund. Today, because of Southern European immigrants, the balance has been redressed, with about 34% of Vaudois now Catholic.
19. *E og H Vol IV* p. 81.
20. Ibid. p. 83.
21. Ibid. p. 62.
22. Ibid. p. 62.
23. Ibid. p. 63.
24. Ibid. p. 68.
25. Ibid. p. 68.
26. Ibid. pp. 87-88.
27. Ibid. p. 89. Both parts of the exchange.
28. Ibid. p. 89.
29. Ibid. p. 98.
30. Ibid. p. 100.
31. Schiller's *Wilhelm Tell* – its plot taken from, among other sources, the *Chronicum Helvetium* – is imbued with ideals of freedom and honour of the 18th century post-French Revolution. Tell has killed a bloodthirsty tyrant, but does not necessarily approve of bloodshed, and certainly refuses to welcome the assassin of the Austrian Emperor. He helps him to escape only on condition that he expiates his sin. Rossini's opera had a French-language libretto based on Schiller's play.
32. See J.M. Roberts, *The Penguin History of Europe*. London: Penguin Books, 1997 especially pp. 361-162 and 373; Leo Schelbert, *Historical Dictionary of Switzerland*. Lanham, MD: Scarecrow Press, 2007, *passim*; Wilhelm Oechsli, *History of Switzerland 1499-1914*. Cambridge: Cambridge University Press, 1922.
33. *E og H Vol III* p. 101.
34. Ibid. p. 102.
35. Allan Woodcourt, surgeon, who marries the heroine Esther Summerson, in *Bleak House*, and Daniel Doyce, engineer, in *Little Dorrit*.
36. All phrases in the paragraph *E og H Vol 1V* pp. 102-103.
37. Ibid. p. 104.
38. Ibid. p. 104.
39. From *The Fairy Tale of My Life* as commissioned by Horace E. Scudder for his American edition of 1871, new edition. New York: Cooper Square Press, 2000, p. 464
40. *E og H Vol IV* p. 106.
41. Château de Chillon stands on an island off the shores of Lake Geneva 3 km from Montreux. The Swiss patriot François de Bonivard (1493-1570) was imprisoned there, in a dungeon, by the Duke of Savoy in 1530 but released, by the Bernese, in 1536.
42. From 'The Sonnet of Chillon'. Visiting Chillon in June 1816 with his friend Shelley, Lord Byron was inspired to write this sonnet, which in turn inspired him to write a long narrative poem about Bonivard, as hero in the cause of liberty: 'The Prisoner of Chillon', to which the sonnet acts as an introduction. *The Prisoner of Chillon and Other Poems* was published by John Murray in December 1816.
43. *E og H Vol III* p. 112. Both parts of the exchange.
44. Ibid. p. 113.
45. Ibid. p. 113.
46. Ibid. p. 119.
47. Ibid. p. 121.
48. Ibid. p. 121.
49. Ibid. p. 123.
50. Ibid. p. 124.
51. Ibid. p. 124.
52. Ibid. p. 127. Both parts of the exchange.
53. Ibid. p. 127.
54. In *Nye Eventyr og Historier Anden Række* (*New Fairy-Tales and Stories, Second Series*), published 2 March 1861. 'The Ice Maiden' would be included in *Nye Eventyr og Historier. Anden Række. Anden Samling* (*Fairy-Tales and Stories. Second Series. Second Collection*), published 25 November 1861.
55. *E og H Vol IV* p. 47.

56. Ibid. p. 50.
57. Ibid. . p. 50.
58. Vera Gancheva, ' "The Toll of Andersen's Bell" – From Neo-Platonism to New Age – Ways of Understanding and Appreciating the Great Writer's Spirituality', in Johan de Mylius, Aage Jørgensen and Viggo Hjørnager Pedersen (eds), *Hans Christian Andersen Between Children's Literature and Adult Literature: Papers from the Fourth International Hans Chrsitian Andersen Conference*. Odense: University Press of Southern Denmark, 2007, pp. 570–584.
59. ibid p 578.
60. *E og H Vol IV*, p. 52.
61. Ibid. p. 53.
62. *Y by Y* 1863.
63. *Y by Y* 1863.
64. *D* p. 307.
65. Jonas Collin, junior (1840–1905) zoologist. Son of Edvard and Jette Collin.
66. *Y by Y* 1861.
67. Bjørnstjerne Bjørnson (1832–1910) Norwegian poet, playwright and novelist and a cultural figure of such influence that he earned himself the name of 'uncrowned king of Norway', and became the first Scandinavian writer to receive the Nobel Prize for Literature – in 1903, an honour denied Ibsen and Strindberg, who were both alive at the time. He wrote stories of life among country peasants; *Synnøve Solbakken* (1857) is one of the best known. Like Ibsen's, Bjørnson's plays moved from being historical dramas recreating the Nordic past to attempts to portray contemporary life and its problems. These include comedies and plays scrutinising man's life in society, and dealing with representative yet individualised men and women; *De Nygifte* (*The Newly Married Couple*, 1865) broke new ground at the time. It seems regrettable but inevitable that this and subsequent work should always be compared to Ibsen, and to Bjørnson's detriment. Like Ibsen, too, Bjørnson later moved in his drama towards symbolism and what one can only call spirituality: *Over Ævne* (Del 1) (*Beyond Human Power* (Part 1), 1883) concerns a clergyman who believes he has the power to perform miracles; *Over Ævne* (Del 2) (*Beyond Human Power* (Part 2) 1895) deals with some of the same characters facing the problems of capital and labour.
68. *D* p. 280.
69. Ibid. p. 283.
70. Ibid. p. 283.
71. Diary entry for 25 March 1863, quoted in *Y by Y* 1863.
72. *In Spain* was published on 9 November 1863, and has always been the least regarded of Andersen's travelogues. Andersen's work was hardly known in Spain at that time.
73. *D* p. 298.
74. See in particular W. Glyn Jones, *Denmark: A Modern History*. London: Croom Helm, 1986, pp. 39–45 and 59–62; Knud J.V. Jespersen, *A History of Denmark*. Basingstoke: Palgrave Macmillan, 2011, pp. 22–26 and 66–70.
75. *Y by Y* 1864. *D* pp. 309–310.
76. Knud V. Jespersen, *A History of Denmark* translated by Ivan Hill and Christopher Wade. Basingstoke and New York: Palgrave Macmillan, 2011, p. 25.

Chapter 12: Beginnings and Endings. From 'Dryaden' ('The Dryad') to 'Tante Tandpine' ('Auntie Toothache')

1. George Brandes (1842–1927) was the most influential Danish critic of his time, not only in Denmark/Scandinavia but all over Europe. Espousing Realism and Naturalism at the outset of his brilliant, continuously high-profile career, he was the consistent enemy of any atrophying or reactionary tendencies in both society and literature, waging war against all retreats into aestheticism and fantasy and involving himself in radical movements both inside and outside the arts. He was a friend and champion of Ibsen, a self-proclaimed follower of Hippolyte Taine, and his 1871 lectures – *Hovedstrømninger i det 19de Aarhundredes Litteratur* (*Main Currents in 19th Century Literature*) – later the title of his major four-volume study of European literature (1872–75) – are generally credited with starting the forward-looking Danish literary movement: Det moderne Gennembrud (The Modern Breakthrough, see notes 52 and 60 of this chapter). His belief in progress for humanity – and possibly his espousal of the works of Nietzsche, whose currency can, to a great extent, be attributed to him – led him to fight shy of the results of practical socialism, and later in life to espouse an 'aristocratic radicalism' based on the thought of great, if sometimes aloof, spirits. W. Glyn Jones in his introduction to his translation of *Georg Brandes: Selected Letters* (Norwich: Norvik Press, 1990), writes: 'With the exception of Hans Christian Andersen there can be few Danes who have had such a wide circle of international friends and acquaintances. Brandes'

range from Stuart Mill to Kropotkin, from minor Scandinavian politicians to Georges Clemenceau, from J[ens] P[eter] Jacobsen to Verhaeren, from Ibsen to Shaw. He received vast numbers of letters – between 30 and 40 a day at one stage. Writers deluged him with their works, hoping for a (positive) review, while universities sought him as a distinguished lecturer. . . . For all his deference to Taine, Brandes knew that he himself was brilliant, and it was a constant source of irritation and frustration to him that he was tied to a minor language like Danish, much as he loved it for its intrinsic values' (p. 12). Glyn Jones also admits, apropos of Brandes's move from Copenhagen to Berlin and then back (1877–83), and the numerous controversies and quarrels which marked his career: 'It is difficult not to come to the conclusion that in some perverse way Brandes enjoyed being in conflict. He was soon the *enfant terrible* of the Danish literary scene: appalled by the conservatism and lack of vision by which he was surrounded on all sides. . . . Yet [in Berlin] he soon became aware of reactionary forces, and here, too, he created enemies as well as friends. He was finally prevailed upon to return to Copenhagen when friends and admirers secured a financial basis on which he could continue' (p. 8). His personal life was as tumultuous, marked by marital and sexual/emotional conflicts, involving an affair with the Swedish novelist Victoria Benedictsson that ended with her suicide in 1888, for which Society talk blamed him. Though this event scarred him publicly, he remained a relentless and controversial fighter for sexual freedom. He was also a bitter and outspoken opponent of the First World War and of the imperialism motivating both sides. See also Johan de Mylius: 'The Andersen Legacy: Georg and Edvard Brandes in Dispute on H.C. Andersen' in *H.C. Andersen Old Problems and New Readings*, editor Steven P. Sondrup. Odense and Proo, Utah: The Hans Christian Andersen Centre, The University Press of Southern Denmark, Brigham Young University, 2004.

2. *Y by Y* 1868.
3. Andersen's Notes: *Hans Christian Andersen: Complete Fairy Tales and Stories* translated by Erik Christian Haugaard. London: Gollancz, 1974, p. 1,092. *E og H Vol V*, pp. 334–335.
4. *E og H Vol V* p. 63.
5. Ibid. p. 63.
6. The eponymous Great Sea-Serpent is, of course, the great underwater telegraph cable that connects Europe and America. But, in similar fashion to his technique in the aquarium episode of 'The Dryad', Andersen imaginatively views this revolutionary human achievement through the eyes of the fishes and cetaceans that encounter it. The story first appeared in *Illustreret Tidende* on 17 December with the significant subtitle *Et Nutids-Eventyr* (*A Contemporary Fairy Tale*).
7. www.expositions-universelles.fr/1867-exposition. Roger Price, *The French Second Empire*. Cambridge: Cambridge University Press, 2007, pp. 210–249.
8. *E og H Vol V* p. 70.
9. Andersen's Notes, Haugaard, op.cit., note 3, p. 1,092. *E og H Vol V* p. 335.
10. *Y by Y* 1866.
11. *E og H Vol V* p. 67.
12. Ibid. p. 66.
13. Ibid. p. 67.
14. Ibid. p. 67.
15. Ibid. p. 67.
16. Ibid. pp. 69–70.
17. Ibid. p. 72.
18. Ibid. p. 73.
19. T.S. Eliot, *The Waste Land* (1. 'The Burial of the Dead'), line 60, in *The Complete Poems and Plays of T.S. Eliot*. London: Faber, 1969, p. 62.
20. 'What the Whole Family Said'. In one house live two families, and, above them, on the attic floor, nearest to Heaven, the godfather of the youngest of all the children there, little Marie. All agree with him, despite their own fantasies and favourite stories, that life itself is the best fairy tale of all, but it takes him – a 'stand-in' for the author – to tell them that all the fairy-tale wonders of the world (and of the human brain) are contained in his favourite among his many books, the Bible, which endeared itself to him after he had endured so many trials. It is a rather dull tale, unrelieved by any really interesting touches, though there is charm in the picture of the children. It appeared in *Eventyr og Historier. Ny Samling* (*Fairy Tales and Stories. New Collection*) on 30 March 1872.
21. 'The City of Dreadful Night', lines 71–77. This long narrative poem was published in book form in *The City of Dreadful Night and Other Poems* in 1880.
22. L'église de la Madeleine – a neoclassical building – was originally a monument to la Grande Armée. But after the fall of Napoleon it was decided that it should become a church and it was consecrated in 1842. Requiem masses for many famous men of the arts have been held here, e.g. for Chopin in 1849. Andersen, by using the church, is signalling the uneasy conflation of the statist, the glamorous and the sacred.

23. Mabille. This dance hall and the garden it stood in (Jardin Mabille) were named for a dancing-teacher, Père Mabille, who owned land just off the Champs Elysées, and opened it as a dancing-space for his pupils. His more ambitious sons took it over in 1844, and made it a widely sought place of public entertainment; in the middle decades of the century it acquired a sexy reputation, in both senses of the word.

24. Carlos, José and Jorge O'Neill were sons of the Danish Consul in Lisbon, who had lived in Denmark for four years in the 1820s and stayed with the Wulffs, at whose home Andersen met them. His stay with them in Portugal was only an indifferent success, as Andersen wanted to see places in his own time and on his own terms, while José wanted to whisk him round on proper sightseeing tours, as if, thought Andersen, he were an Englishman.

25. All quotes *Y by Y* 1866.

26. Robert Watt (1837–94) was a writer and journalist, editor of *Figaro* and *Dagens Nyheder* (*Daily News*), and later a managing director of Copenhagen's Tivoli. His lively, rakish journalist's temperament had considerable appeal for Andersen, and Jackie Wullschlager in her biography says shrewdly that Andersen found him a salutary antidote to the class-conscious younger sons of the Collin family.

27. The whole book was published on 19 November 1868.

28. *D* p. 330.

29. *Y by Y* 1867 for both May and September quotes.

30. *Y by Y* 1868.

31. Einar Drewsen (1833–73), son of Adolph and Ingeborg Drewsen, Edvard Collin's brother-in-law and sister. Andersen's relationship with him must surely have been a complex one, in its movement from mutual irritation to an unusual degree of mutual confidence from an older man to a younger one, including, in many writers' opinion, Jackie Wullschlager's for instance, revelations about homosexual practices. Later Einar clearly had a major breakdown, necessitating care in a famous Norwegian hospital catering for mental illness, Oringe Mental Hospital near Vordingborg. Andersen was much concerned with his welfare, and before and after Einar's premature death – at the age of 40 – wrote some of his most caring and selfless letters, to his sister Jonna, perhaps his favourite among all Jonas Collin's grandchildren.

32. *Y by Y* 1866.

33. Jens Andersen *HCA* p. 466.

34. Joris-Karl Huysmans (1848–1907). Originally associated with Zola and the Naturalists, Huysmans is most famous for his provocative novel *À Rebours* (*Against Nature*, 1884) the hero of which, Des Esseintes, pursues unusual sensations and rejects the bourgeois world as stifling, tedious, unspiritual. It became a cult book with the decadents, and, in England, with Oscar Wilde and the aesthetes.

35. Aage Jørgensen, 'Hans Christian Andersen between Rootedness and Modernity, with Special Reference to His Fairy Tale, "The Dryad" ' (2005), in *Hans Christian Andersen between Children's Literature and Adult Literature, Papers from the Fourth International Hans Christian Andersen Conference* edited by Johan de Mylius, Aage Jørgensen and Viggo Hjørnager Pedersen. Odense: University Press of Southern Denmark, 2007, pp. 199–215.

36. Edmond (1822–96) and Jules (1830–70) de Goncourt were art critics and collectors, social commentators and novelists who developed and propagated the *roman documentaire*, which necessitated massive research and to which they themselves made distinguished contributions. The remarkable harmony of interest, ability and temperament between the brothers enabled them to write the *Journal* together for which posterity best honours them, the enterprise being continued by Edmond after Jules's death from syphilis, which he'd agonisingly and precisely described. They knew and associated with many of the most interesting French writers and intellectuals of their time, dining with them, discoursing and arguing with them, recording their percipient remarks, their flaws, their inconsistencies. They proclaimed themselves 'John-the-Baptists of modern neuroses', a self-designation that has, over the years, both impressed and repelled simultaneously.

37. Edmond and Jules de Goncourt, *Pages from the Goncourt Journals*, edited, translated and with an introduction by Robert Baldick; Foreword by Geoff Dyer. *New York Review of Books*, 2007, pp. 7–8.

38. Ibid. p. 30.

39. Ibid. p. 60.

40. Serialised in *L'Artiste* earlier in the year, the novel was published in December 1867, and brought Zola virtually immediate critical attention and, as the reprints testify, commercial success as well, enough to enable him to embark on his ambitious literary project. This was the famous 20-volume Rougon-Macquart sequence which began with *La Fortune des Rougon* in 1871. In a long letter he wrote to Bjørnson on 8 February 1878, Brandes declared: 'Zola is brutal, audacious, so ruthless. . . . But he is a true genius. Just read *La fortune des Rougon*.' *Georg Brandes: Selected Letters* edited and translated by W. Glyn Jones. Norwich: Norvik Press, 1990, p. 78.

41. Émile Zola, *Thérèse Raquin*, translated by Andrew Rothwell. Oxford: Oxford World's Classics, 2008, p. 26.

42. See Robert Baldick, *Dinner at Magny's* (new edition). Sawtry, Cambs: Dedalus, 2006. The literary critic Saint-Beuve and Brandes's admired Hippolyte Taine – critic, philosopher, historian, anti-romantic, Positivist and Determinist – were prime movers of these influential gatherings. Taine was the author of a seminal work of literary criticism, *Histoire de la literature anglaise* (1863), and, after France's defeat in the Franco-Prussian War, *Origines de la France contemporaine* (1873–93).

43. Émile Zola, *Thérèse Raquin*, op. cit., pp. 1–2.

44. As observed in Chapter 4, see note 6, there seem to me decided similarities of both theme and treatment between Turgenev's *Fathers and Sons* and Andersen's *O.T.*, and their delicate but sophisticatedly skilled art, taken together with their overlap in time, has sufficient in common to make one think it likely that Turgenev read and admired at least some of Andersen's work. Turgenev was an influence on the Danish novelist J.P. Jacobsen (see note 52 below).

45. For Brandes's criticism in *Illustreret Tidende*, look under these two proper names on www.andersen.sdu.dk.

46. Andersen's Notes, *E og H Vol V* pp. 335–336. Marie Grubbe's scandalous life with its highs and lows, and its touching that of Holberg, has fascinated other writers and artists as well as Andersen and Jacobsen. The Danish composer Ebbe Hamerik (1898–1951) made an opera of her life, *Maria Grubbe* (1940).

47. As for note 45 above.

48. *Epistler* (*Epistles*) appeared in five volumes, 1748–54. See Sven Hakon Rossel (ed.) *Ludwig Holberg, a European Writer: A Study in Influence and Reception*. Amsterdam: Rodopi, 1994, esp. pp. 67–103.

49. *E og H Vol V* p. 112.

50. Ibid. p. 118.

51. Ibid. p. 118.

52. J[ens] P[eter] Jacobsen (1847–85). Perhaps the leading creative writer of Det moderne Gennembrud (see note 1 to this chapter) and the writer who initiated Naturalism – and who significantly presented and translated Darwin to a Danish readership. Born in Jutland, Jacobsen was divided even as a boy in his interests in natural sciences, especially botany, and literature; he wrote poems when young. His ambition was to bring into his imaginative work the wonders of Nature as apprehended by science. (He always admired Andersen's tales for their feeling for the natural world, particularly flowers.) Georg Brandes, ever his enthusiastic admirer and advocate, described him in a letter to Bjørnson (*Georg Brandes: Selected Letters* edited and translated by W. Glyn Jones Norwich: Norvik Press, 1990, p. 76) as 'a quiet little Jutlandic farmer's son (his father is actually a boat-builder, but his cultural background is entirely that of a farmer) so closely tied to Denmark that he has always felt half in despair when he has been beyond its borders. . . ' For all this apparent lack of sophistication, he became the first Danish translator of Darwin's major works. In 1872 he produced a Naturalist novella of extraordinary artistic perfection, *Mogens. Fru Marie Grubbe* took him four years to bring to the excellence he sought. By this time he had learned that he had advanced tuberculosis, and had little time left. In 1880 he published one of Denmark's supreme modern (modernist) classics, *Niels Lyhne*, a novel, admired by Ibsen and by both Brandes brothers and which had incalculable effect not only on contemporary and subsequent Danish writers but on Rilke, Freud, Hermann Hesse, Thomas Mann, Stefan Zweig and both D.H. and T.E. Lawrence. Jacobsen's sensitivity and his intellectual courage – he was a committed atheist – proved irresistible. From *Niels Lyhne* Frederick Delius created his opera *Fennimore and Gerda* (1908–10, but it was delayed by the war until 1919), writing the libretto himself.

53. *Fru Marie Grubbe*. The first modern Danish novel, despite its historical setting, was published in full in 1876.

54. *E og H Vol V* p. 119.

55. Ibid. p. 99.

56. Ibid. p. 107.

57. Ibid. pp. 110–111.

58. Translated by Hanna Astrup Larsen in her introduction to her translation of *Marie Grubbe*. New York: Boni & Liveright, 1918 (republished London: Forgotten Books, 2012). www.forgottenbook.org.

59. Jacobsen produced the first complete versions in Danish of Darwin's *Origin of Species* and *Descent of Man* in 1876.

60. Spearheaded by Brandes's lecture and publications on currents in 19th-century European literature, the writers who loosely formed this movement were dominant for the rest of the 1870s, and during the 1880s and 1890s, radical in politics and social thought, in the question of women and sexual standards, and defiant of orthodoxy in religion and artistic (and even personal) criteria. As it was a Scandinavia-wide movement, writers from all three countries can be included: Brandes and Jacobsen from Denmark, and also Holger Drachmann (1846–1908) and Herman Bang (1857–1912); from Norway Ibsen and Bjørnson (though the movement cannot adequately contain them), Jonas Lie (1833–1908), Alexander Kielland (1849–1906), Arne Garborg (1851–1924) and Amalie

Skram (1847–1905) who later lived in Denmark; from Sweden, Strindberg (to a certain extent), the eminent educationalist and feminist Ellen Key (1849–1926) and Brandes's lover, Victoria Benedictsson (1850–88). See Hans Hertel, *Det stadig moderne gennembrud: Georg Brandes og hans tid, set fra det 21. århundrede (The Steady Modern Breakthrough: Georg Brandes and his Time, seen from the 21st Century)*. Copenhagen: Gyldendal, 2004.

61. *Georg Brandes Selected Letters* edited and translated by W. Glyn Jones. Norwich: Norvik Press, 1990, p. 66.

62. Ibid. p. 76.

63. *E og H Vol V*. p. 127.

64. Ibid. p. 134.

65. *LP.* p. 73.

66. Ibid. p. 50.

67. *Hamlet* (1868) by Ambroise Thomas (1811–96), composer of the successful *Mignon* (1865), had a libretto based on a version of Shakespeare's play by Alexandre Dumas père, concentrating, fashionably, as *Lucky Peer* makes clear, on the character of Ophelia, and with a striking Mad Scene. Long neglected, it has appealed to late 20th-century/21st-century audiences, and there was a successful revival at the Metropolitan Opera, New York, in 2010.

68. *Zukunftsmusik* – a preoccupation of this novella. In the earlier and longer essay, 'The Artwork of the Future', Wagner stressed the need of the *Volk*, the people, in the present-day vacuum, for an art form that united, synthesised all the arts into a revolutionary whole. The 1861 essay – originally published in a French translation the year before – summarises and restates his previous precepts. In it he praises Weber as the first true German opera-composer and Beethoven as the supreme symphonist. The musician is for him something of a mystic – communicating the 'thing unspeakable', 'the untold mystery'.

69. *La Dame blanche (The White Lady*, 1825) was the most successful opera of François Boieldieu (1775–1834). Its libretto, by Eugène Scribe, derives from two Scott novels, *Guy Mannering* (1815) and *The Monastery* (1820). A young English lieutenant visiting Scotland becomes godfather to the youngest child of his friends, Dickson and Jenny, tenants of a haunted castle. The castle's ghost is a White Lady, a friend to her own sex against fickle men. Dickson is summoned to meet the 'ghost' but George valiantly takes his place. Though she is an imposter – employed by the false owner of the castle to impersonate the legendary spectre for his own purposes – Anna, the White Lady, is also a good, honourable woman whom George knew years back when they were both children. Eventually the falsification of affairs is unravelled, and George himself turns out to be the heir to the castle, and marries the White Lady. Perhaps the theme of inheritance being belatedly accorded to a virtuous, comparatively obscure, individual had significance for both Andersen and Peer.

70. *Lohengrin* dates from 1850, but is imbued with the revolutionary sentiments and ideals of freedom of 1848/49 and drawn from a medieval German romance about Parsifal's son, the Knight of the Swan, which had obvious personal appeal for Andersen. Lohengrin is borne down the river Scheldt to Antwerp by a swan in answer to the prayers of Elsa, daughter of the Duke of Brabant, falsely accused of fratricide. The only condition he gives for aiding her against her enemies is that she never ask him his provenance, family or name. Lohengrin fights – and spares – Elsa's principal accuser, he and she fall in love, and preparations for the wedding get under way. But then Elsa's enemies taunt her for not knowing her husband-to-be's identity, and, her confidence undermined, she puts the forbidden question to him. Lohengrin once again fights and now kills Elsa's enemy, but, because of the broken promise, the power of the Holy Grail demands he leaves Antwerp. But he performs one more service for Elsa. The swan that brought him to her was Elsa's brother transformed. He effects his release from the spell, while himself returning upriver in a boat pulled by a dove. But the double shock has been too much for Elsa and she dies in her re-found brother's arms.

71. *LP* p. 81.

72. Ibid. p. 73.

73. Ibid. p. 31.

74. Ibid. p. 43.

75. Niels Gade (1817–90). Born in Copenhagen and working as an orchestral musician there, he submitted his first symphony to Mendelssohn in Leipzig. Mendelssohn was much impressed and conducted its first performance in 1843. Gade became friends with Mendelssohn, taught at the Leipzig Conservatory, and was assistant conductor of the Leipzig Gewandhaus, with the distinction of conducting the premiere of Mendelssohn's probably most famous work, his Violin Concerto (1844). The war between Denmark and Prussia forced Gade to return to Denmark in 1848, and from then on he was the dominant figure in Danish musical life, Director of Copenhagen Music Society until his death. He married Emma, the daughter of composer Hartmann in 1852. He wrote eight symphonies of a Mendelssohnian stamp, and among his many other compositions none is more beautiful than the secular cantata *Elverskud* which so impresses Peer.

76. *LP* pp. 48–49.

77. Ibid. p. 57.

78. Ibid. p. 57.

79. Beethoven: 'From the Sketch-Books: Notes on the Pastoral Symphony', in *Beethoven Letters, Journals and Conversations*, edited, translated and introduced by Michael Hamburger. London: Thames & Hudson, 1951.

80. Robert Simpson, *Beethoven Symphonies*, London: BBC Music Guides, 1970, pp. 41–43.

81. *LP* p. 63.

82. Ibid. p. 71.

83. Ibid. p. 75.

84. Ibid. p. 76.

85. See Chapter 4, 'The Master Thinker of Bayreuth' of Part III, 'The Artistic Revolution', in Jacques Barzun, *Darwin, Marx, Wagner* (1941) New York Doubleday: Anchor Books, 1958, p. 273.

86. *LP* p. 76.

87. *Y by Y* 1855.

88. Andersen describes this visit in the supplement to his autobiography, *The Fairy-Tale of My Life* as commissioned by Horace E. Scudder for his American edition of 1871, new edition. New York: Cooper Square Press, 2000: 'Wagner impressed me fully as having a most genial nature, and it was a most happy hour, – such a one as I have never had since, p. 417.

89. *LP* p. 89.

90. Ibid. p. 90.

91. *D* p. 366.

92. 'The Jumpers' – from the year before 'The Shadow' – is one of Andersen's most delightful and subtle tales, one which leaves us pleasurably and thought-provokingly unsure how to take it. The flea, the grasshopper and the skipjack ('Springgaaset') hold a public competition as to who can jump the highest. The prize will be the king's daughter. Each competitor is sure he will be the winner. The flea jumps so high that he disappears, and watcher says he hasn't jumped at all; the grasshopper, who proudly claims descent from Ancient Egypt and now lives in a little toy house made of cards, jumps right into the king's face – which irritates him. But the skipjack – made of a goose's wishbone, two rubber bands, some sealing wax and a mahogany stick – jumps, after a pause, right into the lap of the princess herself. So how can he not be proclaimed victor? The flea, who knows that his jump was the highest, takes himself off to join a foreign army, among whom, it's said, he dies. But the grasshopper contemplates the whole episode and decides that in the world it's appearances that count. He then starts his own beautiful sad song, and the last sentence tells us that the author has heard the whole story from him. This story arose, Andersen tells us in his Notes, spontaneously to meet the request of some children.

93. *D* p. 367: 'Peter Koch thought Lucky Peer shouldn't have died but experienced adversity and yet remained Lucky Peer'.

94. *LP* p. 68.

95. As in *D* p. 367: 'our age has no use for weakness, but strength'.

96. Carl Nielsen (1865–1931). Denmark's greatest and most famous composer, was born, like Andersen, in Fyn, to a poor peasant family living south of Odense, where there is now a museum to him next to Andersen's own. Nielsen's six symphonies – of which the admirable first two are clearly post-Brahmsian compositions – are original, deeply thought works, each an independent artefact following its own organic laws. Carl Nielsen was much concerned with progressive tonality, reflecting the idea that his works should externalise, argue out and resolve inner conflicts while remaining 'pure' music, like the symphonies of his contemporary fellow Nordic, Sibelius. Nielsen's journey from obscurity to world fame is as remarkable as Andersen's. At 14 he was playing bugle and alto trombone for the army's 16th Battalion at Odense, and then went to Copenhagen to study at the Royal Academy in 1884. In 1891 he married Anne Marie Brodersen, a sculptor who became very famous in her own right. It was a difficult marriage, Brodersen devoting herself to her work at the expense of her family, Nielsen having a number of affairs, including one with his children's nanny, which brought about a marital hiatus of eight years. His popular opera *Maskerade* (Masquerade), with a libretto based on Holberg, was first performed at Andersen's beloved Kongelige Teater, Copenhagen on 11 November 1906. He wrote – partly in emulation of Andersen – a delightful, though not always accurate, memoir of his childhood, *Min Fynske Barndom* (*My Childhood on Fyn* 1927). He wrote incidental music to Oehlenschläger's *Aladdin* (1919), and one of his most enchanting works is his secular cantata, *Fynsk Forår* (*Springtime in Fyn*, 1922). See Daniel M. Grimley *Carl Nielsen and the Idea of Modernism*. Woodbridge: The Boydell Press, 2010.

97. See Elias Bredsdorff *HCA* p. 274. Entry for 22 May 1875: 'Now Jonas came, helped me to put on warm, dry clothes; I lay back in bed very feeble. Jonas spent the night here, staying in the front room.'

98. Letter of 5 September 1870: see *Y by Y* 1870.

99. The Franco-Prussian War. See Alistair Horne, *The Fall of Paris: The Siege and the Commune 1870–1871*. London: Penguin Books, 2007; Geoffrey Wahro, *The Franco-Prussian War: The German Conquest of France in 1870–1871*. Cambridge: Cambridge University Press, 2003; Michael Howard, *The Franco-Prussian War: The German Invasion of France 1870–1871*. London: Rupert Hart Davis, 1961.

100. In *Eventyr og Historier. Ny Samling*. (*Fairy-Tales and Stories. New Collection*). For detailed presentation of its many features see *Tatar AA* pp. 298–305 (as 'The Most Astonishing Thing').

101. *E og H Vol V* p. 175.

102. Ibid. p. 177.

103. Ibid. p. 177.

104. Ibid. p. 177.

105. Ibid. p. 179.

106. Ibid. p. 180.

107. Ibid. p. 182.

108. The Melchiors and the Henriques were two extremely rich and exceptionally cultured and refined Jewish families with whom Andersen became friendly – and of whom indeed he was a frequent house-guest – in the mid-1860s. Moritz Melchior (1816–84), a merchant in tea, coffee and sugar, had married Dorothea (1823–85) the sister of Martin Henriques (1825–1912), husband of Therese (1833–82), a talented musician. In addition to grand Copenhagen residences, the two families had fine villas outside the city – the Melchiors at Rolinghed ('Tranquillity'), with lovely gardens going down to the sea and fine views over the Øresund of Sweden, and the Henriques not far off at Petershøi. Hospitable over the years to a whole range of interesting international writers, composers, artists – Bournonville, Gade, Ibsen, Edmund Gosse among others – they were extremely sympathetic to Andersen's temperament and needs, and he was devoted to both families, being particularly close to the two wives. Jackie Wullschlager, who writes exceptionally well about them – and their relationship to and with Andersen – says, surely truly, 'Like him, the Melchiors and the Henriques stood at the heart of Copenhagen society and yet felt themselves to be outsiders. Their Jewishness set them apart; swarthy, dark-haired and dark-eyed, the two families looked different from most Danes ...' Jackie Wullschlager *HCA* p. 391 – and we have seen throughout this study the strong, deep-rooted affinity Andersen consistently felt with Jewish people.

109. *Y by Y* 1872.

110. For example, at the very outset of his German travels of 1831, while preparing for his first important book, he was writing in his diary for 18 May: 'My teeth are monstrously painful. The nerves are in fact delicate tangents that imperceptible movements of air play upon, and that's why those teeth are playing the devil with me – first piano, then crescendo, all the melodies of pain at every shift in the weather.' *D* p. 25.

111. Elias Bredsdorff *HCA* p. 265. The beauty of this translation couldn't be surpassed.

112. *E og H Vol V* p. 288.

113. Ibid. p. 298.

114. Ibid. p. 303.

115. 'Nattergalen', 'The Nightingale' appeared in *Nye Eventyr. Første Bind. Første Samling* (*New Fairy-Tales. First Volume. First Collection*) on 11 November 1843.

116. 'Hun duede ikke', 'She Was No Good' first appeared in December 1852 in the Danish Folk Calendar for 1853.

Index